The Business of Tourism

We work with leading authors to develop the
strongest educational materials in business
studies and geography, bringing cutting-edge
thinking and best learning practice to a global market.

Under a range of well-known imprints, including
Prentice Hall, we craft high quality print and
electronic publications which help readers to understand
and apply their content, whether studying or at work.

To find out more about the complete range of our
publishing, please visit us on the World Wide Web at:
www.pearsoneduc.com

The Business of Tourism

Sixth edition

J Christopher Holloway

An imprint of **Pearson Education**

Harlow, England · London · New York · Reading, Massachusetts · San Francisco · Toronto · Don Mills, Ontario · Sydney
Tokyo · Singapore · Hong Kong · Seoul · Taipei · Cape Town · Madrid · Mexico City · Amsterdam · Munich · Paris · Milan

Pearson Education Limited
Edinburgh Gate
Harlow
Essex CM20 2JE

and Associated Companies throughout the world

Visit us on the World Wide Web at:
www.pearsoneduc.com

First published 1983
Second edition 1985
Third edition 1989
Fourth edition 1994
Fifth edition 1998
Sixth edition 2002

ISBN 0 273 65563 9

British Library Cataloguing-in-Publication Data
A catalogue record for this book is available from the British Library

Library of Congress Cataloging-in-Publication Data

Holloway, J. Christopher.
   The business of tourism/J. Christopher Holloway.-6th ed.
     p. cm.
   Includes bibliographical references (p.).
   ISBN 0-273-65563-9 (pbk.)
   1. Tourism. 2. Tourism-Economic Aspects. I. Title.

G155.A1 H657 2001
338.4'791-dc21

                                                          2001036038

10 9 8 7 6 5 4 3 2 1
05 04 03 02 01

Typeset by 3 in Giovanni Book
Printed and bound in China
SWTC

Contents

Preface to the sixth edition

In my preface to the fifth edition, published in 1998, I wrote that the pace of change in tourism was intensifying. Little could I have guessed at the acceleration of that change which would occur over the following three years. My earlier intention with this new edition was to do some modest updating – a new table and illustration here, some corrections to text there, perhaps some minor expansion in the contents where readers felt that the basics had been covered too briefly. In the event, I find that I have once again ended up preparing what is essentially a complete rewrite, even though the format remains virtually unchanged.

The points that concerned me in preparing the earlier edition – the rapid obsolescence of material, the process of merger and takeover in the various sectors of the industry which made a mockery of any attempt at contemporary expertise – have become magnified. The challenge of preparing a text which continues to provide the underlying principles and some contemporary examples drawn from the industry is undermined by the distinct possibility that some of the examples will no longer exist by the time the text gets into print! The only possible solution to this problem, which is unlikely to abate over the next few years, is to produce a web site with regular updatings so that tutors using the text as a teaching tool and students of tourism looking for an introductory overview of the industry are not totally out of touch with what is going on in this fascinating business. The possibilities of this will be explored in the near future.

It also seems to me that research information in the public domain is decreasing, even as the need for it increases. This is undoubtedly in part a direct result of the hard-nosed commercialism that dominates in the public sector, as funding is reduced. Information now must be sought using the latest technology, too, so web sites and CD-ROMs replace hard text and telephone calls (too difficult to find a human being on the other end of the line). Is it just my imagination, or does this process take much longer, and cost far more, than traditional searches through the covers of books and journals?

Inevitably, the text gets a little longer with each edition. This reflects my efforts to cater for all those tutors who offer their positive and supportive comments as to how the text might be further improved – but never suggest what might be dropped! I have tried to meet these requests, by expanding a little on business travel, the significance of sustainable tourism, and internationalization, especially the integration of the industry within the European countries. I have, of course, included copious references to the impact of information technology in the industry, especially in areas such as distribution policy, and I have tried to draw some conclusions about where the industry is going over the next decade.

What has also intrigued me is the widening of what tourism embraces as a concept, and in this edition, for example, I have included some discussion about 'dark tourism' – the increasing interest shown by certain groups of tourists in visiting sites of gloom and despondency, from cemeteries to sites of recent warfare (Vietnam), from places of climatic catastrophe (Mount St Helens, sites of recent earthquakes) to sites of the very darkest tragedy (concentration camps, Anne Frank's house in Amsterdam). This is a far cry from the original concept of getting away from one's troubles and unwinding, and the evidence so far suggests that this trend is a positive thing, one which reveals the tourist as someone searching for truth, for understanding, for moral improvement. At the same time, the mass tourist movement has never been more criticized, and the image of the tourist becomes ever more negative as the media fill their pages with stories of air rage on board aircraft, and of beer-swilling louts and noisy rave parties in every popular beach destination from Ibiza to Pattaya Beach. Notwithstanding the movement for sustainable tourism, the wholesale destruction of formerly attractive beach and rural areas continues apace, as numbers increase around the world and the relative cost of going on holiday abroad falls.

The acceleration in the number of textbooks coming on-stream also continues, as will be evident in the bibliography at the end of this text (and this is only a selection of those available!) These are now being published in such numbers that very few, if any, market gaps remain, and very few sectors remain unexplored in depth. Most, however, appear to be written to meet the needs of academics rather than practitioners – a point often raised by those practitioners when reviewing them. In a sense, this brings me full circle: my original intention was to produce a text which would provide a respectable overview of the industry and how it operates, both for new students of tourism and for practitioners who had not had the opportunity to benefit from any formal education in tourism but who sought to learn more about its operation, simply and conveniently. I hope this text still meets this need.

My thanks, as ever, to those who have helped in the preparation of the text, especially Neil Taylor, Managing Director of Regent Holidays, who has been helpful over many editions with his practical contributions of hard-nosed facts.

Whilst every effort has been made to trace the owners of copyright material, in a few cases this has proved impossible and we take this opportunity to offer our apologies to any copyright holders whose rights we may have unwittingly infringed.

List of Abbreviations

AA	Automobile Association
ABTA	Association of British Travel Agents
ABTAC	Association of British Travel Agents' Certificate
ACD	Automatic Call Distribution
ACE	Association of Conference Executives
AIC	Airbus Integrated Company
AIEST	Alliance Internationale d'Experts Scientifiques de Tourisme
AIT	Air Inclusive Tour
AITO	Association of Independent Tour Operators
APEX	Advance Purchase Excursion Fare
ARTAC	Association of Retail Travel Agents' Consortia
ASTA	American Society of Travel Agents
ATB	Automated Ticketing and Boarding Pass
ATC	Air Traffic Control
ATOC	Association of Train Operating Companies
ATOL	Air Travel Organisers' Licence
ATTF	Air Travel Trust Fund
ATTT	Association of Tourism Teachers and Trainers (formerly ATT Association of Teachers of Tourism)
AUC	Air Transport Users' Council
AVE	*Alta Velocidad Espagnola* (Spanish high-speed train)
b2c	business to consumer
BA	British Airways
BAA	Organization operating airports, now privatized, formerly publicly owned British Airports Authority
BABA	Book a bed ahead
B&B	Bed and breakfast

BEA   British European Airways, later merged with BOAC to form British Airways
BHA   British Hospitality Association
BH&HPA   British Holiday and Home Parks Association
BHTS   British Home Tourism Survey
BITOA   British Incoming Tour Operators' Association
BITS   Bureau International de Tourisme Sociale
BNTS   British National Travel Survey
BOAC   British Overseas Airways Corporation, later merged with BEA to form British Airways
BRA   British Resorts Association
BTA   British Tourist Authority
BTI   Business Travel International
BWB   British Waterways Board

CAA   Civil Aviation Authority
CAB   Civil Aeronautics Board (USA)
CBI   Confederation of British Industry
CECTA   Central European Countries Travel Association
CGLI   City and Guilds of London Institute
CIM   Chartered Institute of Marketing
CIMTIG   Chartered Institute of Marketing Travel Industry Group
CIT   Chartered Institute of Transport
CLIA   Cruise Lines Industry of America
COTAC   Certificate of Travel Agency Competence
COTAM   Certificate of Travel Agency Management
COTICC   Certificate of Tourist Information Centre Competence
COTOP   Certificate of Tour Operating Practice
CPT   Confederation of Passenger Transport
CRN   Countryside Recreation Network
CRS   Computer Reservations System
CTC   Certified Travel Counsellor
CTT   Council for Travel and Tourism

DCMS   Department for Culture, Media and Sport
DTI   Department of Trade and Industry

EADS   European Aeronautic Defence and Space Company
EC   European Commission
ETB   English Tourist Board (now the English Tourism Council)
ETC   English Tourism Council (also European Travel Commission)
EU   European Union

FTO   Federation of Tour Operators

GBTA	Guild of Business Travel Agents
GDP	Gross Domestic Product
GDS	Global Distribution System
GISC	General Insurance Standards Council
GIT	Group Inclusive Tour-basing fare
HCIMA	Hotel and Catering International Management Association
Htf	Hospitality Training Foundation
IAE	International Aero Engines
IATA	International Air Transport Association
IBTA	International Business Travel Association
ICAO	International Civil Aviation Organisation
IFAPA	International Foundation of Airline Passenger Associations
IFTO	International Federation of Tour Operators
II	Interval International
IIT	Independent Inclusive Tour
ILG	International Leisure Group
IPS	International Passenger Survey
IT	Inclusive Tour, also Information Technology
ITM	Institute of Travel Management
ITS	International Tourist Services
ITT	Institute of Travel and Tourism
ITX	Inclusive tour-basing excursion fare
IUOTO	International Union of Official Tourist Organisations (now WTO)
LTT	Lufttransport-Unternehmen Touristik
LTU	Lufttransport-Unternehmen
MIA	Meetings Industry Association
MOMA	Museum of Modern Art, New York
MMC	Monopolies and Mergers Commission (now Competition Commission)
MTAA	Multiple Travel Agents' Association
MTOW	Maximum take-off weight
NAITA	National Association of Independent Travel Agents (now Advantage)
NBC	National Bus Company
NCVQ	National Council for Vocational Qualifications
NPTA	National Passenger Traffic Association
NTB	National Tourist Board. Also the former National Training Board of ABTA
NUR	Neckermann und Reisen
NVQ	National Vocational Qualifications
OECD	Organisation for Economic Cooperation and Development

PATA	Pacific Area Travel Association
P&O	Peninsular and Oriental Steam Navigation Company
PSA	Passenger Shipping Association
RAC	Royal Automobile Club
RCI	Resort Condominiums International
RDAs	Regional Development Agencies
RTB	Regional Tourist Board
SAS	Scandinavian Airlines System
SNAT	Societé Nouvelle d'Armement Transmanche
SNCF	Societé National de Chemins de Fer
SOLAS	Safety of Life at Sea
SPR	Size to passenger ratio
SSSI	Site of Special Scientific Interest
STB	Scottish Tourist Board (now VisitScotland)
STOL	Short take-off and landing
TAC	Travel Agents' Council
TDAP	Tourism Development Action Plan
TGV	Train à Grande Vitesse
TIC	Tourist Information Centre
TIM	Tourism Income Multiplier
TIP	Tourist Information Point
TIQ	*Tourism Intelligence Quarterly*
TOC	Tour Operators' Council
TOMS	Tour Operators' Margin Scheme
TOP	Thomson Holidays' computer reservations system
TOSG	Tour Operators' Study Group (now FTO)
TRIPS	Tourism Resource Information Processing System
TSA	Tourism Satellite Account
TTC	The Travel Training Company
TTENTO	Travel, Tourism and Events National Training Organisation
TUI	Touristik Union International
UATP	Universal Air Travel Plan
UBR	Uniform Business Rate
UKTS	United Kingdom Tourism Survey
UN	United Nations
UNESCO	United Nations Educational, Scientific and Cultural Organisation
VAT	Value Added Tax
VFR	Visiting Friends and Relatives
VTOL	Vertical take-off and landing

WISE   Wing-in-surface effect
WPC   Wave-piercing catamaran
WTB   Wales Tourist Board
WTO   World Tourism Organisation
WTTC   World Travel and Tourism Council

Chapter 1   An introduction to tourism

OBJECTIVES

After studying this chapter, you should be able to:

- define what is meant by tourism, both conceptually and technically, and distinguish it from travel, leisure and recreation;
- identify the characteristics of the tourism product;
- list the various forms of tourist destination, identifying the attraction of each;
- explain why destinations are subject to changing fortunes.

Defining tourism

In a book dealing with tourism, it is sensible to begin by trying to define exactly what we mean by the term, before we go on to examine the different forms which tourism can take. In fact, the task of defining tourism is not nearly as easy as it may appear.

While it is relatively easy to agree on technical definitions of particular categories of tourism or tourist, the wider concept is ill defined. First, it is important to recognize that tourism is just one form of recreation, along with sports activities, hobbies and pastimes, and that all of these activities are discretionary uses of our leisure time. Tourism usually incurs some expenditure, although this is not *necessarily* the case: someone cycling or hiking in the countryside on a camping weekend in which they carry their own food may contribute nothing to the econ-

omy of the region. Many other examples could be cited in which tourism expenditure is minimal. We can say, then, that tourism is one aspect of leisure which usually, but not invariably, incurs some expenditure by the participant.

Tourism may be further defined as the movement of people away from their normal place of residence. Here we find our first problem. Should shoppers travelling from, say, Bristol to Bath, a distance of twelve miles, be considered tourists? And is it the *purpose* or the *distance* which is the determining factor? Just how far must people have to travel before they can be counted as tourists for the purpose of official records? Clearly, our definition must be specific. In the United States, the National Resources Review Commission established in 1973 that a domestic tourist would be 'one who travels at least fifty miles (one way)', and this was confirmed by the

1

US Census Bureau, which defined tourism eleven years later as a round trip of at least one hundred miles. However, the Canadian government defines it as a journey of at least twenty-five miles from the boundaries of the tourist's home community, while the English Tourism Council measures leisure away from the home as a distance of not less than twenty miles and three hours' journey time, so consistency has by no means yet been achieved.

One of the first attempts to define tourism was that of Professors Hunziker and Krapf of Berne University, in 1942. They held that tourism should be defined as 'the sum of the phenomena and relationships arising from the travel and stay of non-residents, in so far as they do not lead to permanent residence and are not connected to any earning activity'. This definition helps to distinguish tourism from migration, but it makes the assumption that both *travel* and *stay* are necessary for tourism, thus precluding day tours. It would also appear to exclude business travel, which is connected with earnings, even if that income is not earned in the destination country. Moreover, distinguishing between business and leisure tourism is extremely difficult, since most business trips will combine elements of leisure activity.

In 1937, the League of Nations recommended adopting the definition of a 'tourist' as one who travels for a period of at least twenty-four hours in a country other than that in which he usually resides. This was held to include persons travelling for pleasure, domestic reasons or health, persons travelling to meetings or otherwise on business, and persons visiting a country on a cruise vessel (even if for less than twenty-four hours). The principal weakness in this definition is that it ignores the movement of domestic tourists. Later, the United Nations Conference on International Travel and Tourism, held in 1963, considered recommendations put forward by the IUOTO (now the World Tourism Organisation), and agreed to use the term 'visitor' to describe 'any person visiting a country other than that in which he has his usual place of residence, for any reason other than following an occupation remunerated from within the country visited'. This definition was to cover two classes of visitor:

(a) tourists, who were classified as temporary visitors staying at least twenty-four hours, whose purpose could be categorized as leisure (whether for recreation, health, sport, holiday, study or religion), or business, family, mission or meeting;

(b) excursionists, who were classed as temporary visitors staying less than twenty-four hours, including cruise travellers but excluding travellers in transit.

Towards an agreed definition

Once again, these definitions fail to take into account the domestic tourist. The inclusion of 'study' in this definition is an interesting one, since it is often excluded in later definitions, as are longer courses of education.

A working party for the proposed Institute of Tourism in Britain (which later became the Tourism Society) attempted to clarify the issue, and reported in 1976:

> Tourism is the temporary short-term movement of people to destinations outside the places where they normally live and work, and activities during their stay at these destinations; it includes movement for all purposes, as well as day visits or excursions.

This broader definition was reformulated slightly, without losing any of its simplicity, at the International Conference on Leisure-Recreation-Tourism, organized by the AIEST and the Tourism Society in Cardiff in 1981:

> Tourism may be defined in terms of particular activities selected by choice and undertaken outside the home environment. Tourism may or may not involve overnight stay away from home.

Finally, the following definition devised by the WTO was endorsed by the UN Statistical Commission in

1993 following an International Government Conference held in Ottawa, Canada in 1991:

> Tourism comprises the activities of persons travelling to and staying in places outside their usual environment for not more than one consecutive year for leisure, business or other purposes.

The above definitions have been quoted at length because they reveal how broadly the concept of tourism must be defined in order to embrace all forms of the phenomenon. Indeed, the final definition could be criticized on the grounds that, unless the activities are more clearly specified, it could be applied equally to someone involved in burglary! With this definition, we are offered guidance on neither activities undertaken nor distance to be travelled. In fact, with the growth of second-home owners, who in some cases spend considerable periods of time away from their main homes, and time-share owners, it could be argued that a tourist is no longer necessarily 'outside the home environ-

ment'. It is also increasingly recognized that defining tourists in terms of the distances they have travelled from their homes is unhelpful; locals can be viewed as 'tourists' within their own territory if they are engaged in touristic activity, and certainly their economic contribution to the tourism industry in the area is as important as that of the more traditionally defined tourist.

Figure 1.1 illustrates the guidelines produced by the WTO to classify travellers for statistical purposes. Some loopholes in the definitions remain, however. Even attempts to classify tourists as those travelling for purposes unconnected with employment can be misleading if one looks at the social consequences of tourism. Ruth Pape has drawn attention to the case of nurses in the United States who, after qualifying, gravitate to California for their first jobs, since employment is easy to find and they can thus enjoy the benefits of the sunshine and leisure pursuits for which the state is famous. They may spend a year or more in this job before moving on, but the point

Figure 1.1 Defining a tourist. (*Courtesy The World Tourism Organisation*)

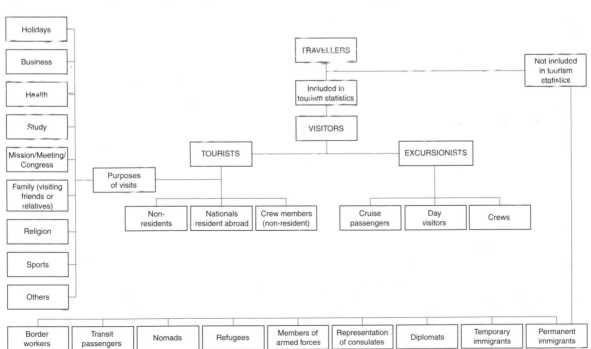

here is that they have been motivated to come to that area not because of the work itself, but because of the area's touristic attractions. Many other examples could be given of young people working their way around the world (a kind of twentieth-century Grand Tour?), or workers seeking summer jobs in seaside resorts.

Finally, we must consider the case of pensioners who choose to retire abroad in order to benefit from the lower costs of living in other countries. Many Britons have moved to southern Spain or the Canary Islands after retirement, while Americans similarly gravitate to Mexico; they may still retain their homes in their country of origin, but spend a large part of the year abroad. Canadians, known as 'snowbirds' because of their migrant behaviour, also come down in their mobile trailers to the sunshine states of the US southwest during the winter months, to escape the harsh winters of Canada. Once again, the motive of all of these people is not simply to lower their costs of living, but also to enjoy an improved climate and the facilities which attract tourists to the same destinations.

Conceptually, then, to define tourism precisely is an all but impossible task. To produce a technical definition for statistical reasons is less problematic. As long as it is clear what the data comprise, and one compares like with like, whether interregionally or internationally, we can leave the conceptual discussion to the academics. With the advent of contemporary mass tourism, perhaps the most accurate definition of a tourist is 'someone who travels to see something different, and then complains when he finds things are not the same'!

The tourist product

Having attempted a definition of the tourist, we can look at the tourist product itself. The first characteristic to note is that this is a service rather than a tangible good. The intangibility poses particular difficulties for those whose job it is to market tourism. A tourist product cannot, for example, be inspected by prospective purchasers before they buy, as can a washing machine, video recorder or other consumer durable. The purchase of a package tour is a speculative investment, involving a high degree of trust on the part of the purchaser, the more so since a holiday is often the most expensive purchase made each year (although with increasing affluence, many consumers are now able to purchase two or more such holidays annually).

It has often been said that 'selling holidays is like selling dreams', and this is to a great extent true. When tourists buy a package tour abroad, they are buying more than a simple collection of services, such as an airline seat, hotel room, three meals a day and the opportunity to sit on a sunny beach; they are also buying the temporary use of a strange environment, incorporating novel geographical features – old world towns, tropical landscapes – plus the culture and heritage of the region and other intangible benefits such as service, atmosphere and hospitality. The planning and anticipation of the holiday may be as much a part of its enjoyment as is the trip itself; recalling the experience later, and reviewing slides, videos or photos are further extensions of the experience. These are all part of the product, which is therefore a psychological as well as a physical experience.

The challenge for the marketer of tourism is to turn the dream into the reality. The difficulty of achieving this is that tourism is not a homogeneous product; that is, it tends to vary in standard and quality over time and under different circumstances, unlike, say, a television set. A package tour, or even a flight on an aircraft, cannot be consistently uniform; a bumpy flight, or a long technical flight delay, can change an enjoyable experience into a nightmare, and a holiday at the seaside will be ruined by a prolonged rainy spell. Because a tour comprises a compendium of different products, an added difficulty in maintaining standards is that each element of the product should be broadly similar in quality. A good room and fine service at a hotel may be spoilt by poor food, or the flight may mar an otherwise enjoyable hotel stay. An element of chance is always present in the purchase of any service, and where the

Figure 1.2 The World Travel Market, London. *(Photographed by the author)*

purchase must precede the actual consumption of the product, as with tourism, the risk for the consumer is increased.

Another characteristic of tourism is that it cannot be brought to the consumer; rather, the consumer must be brought to the product. In the short term, at least, the supply of this product is fixed; the number of hotel bedrooms available at a particular destination cannot be varied to meet the changing demands of holiday-makers during the season. The unsold hotel room or aircraft seat cannot be stored for later sale, as is the case with tangible products, but is lost forever. Hence the great efforts that must be made by those in the industry to fill empty seats or rooms by last-minute discounting or other techniques. If market demand changes, as it does frequently in the business of tourism, the supply will take time to adapt. A hotel is built to last for many years, and must remain profitable over that period. These are all problems unique to tourism, and call for considerable marketing ingenuity on the part of those in the business.

The nature of a tour

To analyse the topic of tourism systematically, it will be helpful at this point to examine more closely the characteristics of a tour under five broad categories.

The motivation for touring

Motivation identifies first the purposes of a visit. There are three broad categories of purpose:

1. holidays (including visits to friends and relatives, known as VFR travel);
2. business (including meetings, conferences etc.);
3. other (including study, religious pilgrimages, health etc.).

It is important to distinguish between the purposes of visits, because the characteristics of each category will differ. Business travel will differ from holiday travel, in that the business person has little discretion in choice of destination or the timing of the trip. Business trips frequently have to be arranged at short notice, and for specific and brief periods of time. Business travellers need the convenience of frequent, regular transport, efficient service and good facilities at the destination. Because the company will be paying for all the travel arrangements, the individual traveller will be less concerned about the cost of travel than if they were paying themselves. Higher prices are unlikely seriously to deter travel, nor will lower prices encourage more frequent travel. We can say, therefore, that business travel is relatively *price inelastic*. Holiday travel, however, is highly *price elastic*; lower prices will encourage an increase in the number of travellers generally, and will encourage others to switch their destinations. Leisure travellers will be prepared to delay their travel, or will book well in advance of their travel dates, if this means that they can substantially reduce their costs.

We therefore need to identify the reasons why a specific type of holiday or resort is chosen. Different people will look for different qualities in the same destination; a ski resort, for example, may be selected because of its excellent slopes and sporting facilities, because of its healthy mountain air, or because of the social life which it offers to skiers and non-skiers alike.

The characteristics of the tour

These define what kind of visit is made and to where. First, one can distinguish between *domestic* tourism and *international* tourism. The former refers to travel taken exclusively within the national boundaries of the traveller's country. The decision to take one's holidays within the borders of one's own country is an important one economically, since it will affect the balance of payments, and reduce the outflow of money from that country.

Next, what kind of destination is being chosen? Will travel be to a seaside resort, a mountain resort, a country town, a health spa or a major city? Is it to be a single-centre visit, a multicentre one (involving a stopover at two or more places) or a tour which will involve extensive travel with brief overnight stays along the route? Or will a cruise be taken, in which case statisticians have to decide whether to count this as international travel if the vessel visits foreign ports.

Next, what length of time is being spent on the trip? A visit that does not involve an overnight stay is known, as we saw earlier, as an excursion, or is frequently referred to as a 'day trip'. Expenditure by day-trippers is generally less than that of overnight visitors, and statistical data on these forms of tourism are often collected separately. A visitor who stops at least one night at a destination is termed a 'tourist', but can, of course, make day trips to other destinations; these could even involve an international trip. For instance, a visitor staying in Rhodes may take a trip for the day by boat to the Turkish mainland. For the purposes of Turkey's records, that visitor will be recorded as an excursionist.

Finally, for the purpose of accurate record keeping, some maximum length of time must be established, beyond which the visitor can no longer be looked upon as a tourist. There are different approaches here, some using a low figure of three months, others six months and in some cases a full year is viewed as the maximum period.

Mode of tour organization

This further refines the form which the travel takes. A tour may be *independent* or *packaged*. A package tour, for which the official term is 'inclusive tour', (IT), is an arrangement in which transport and accommodation are purchased by the tourist at an all-inclusive price. The price of the individual elements of the tour cannot normally be determined by the purchaser. The tour operator which puts together the package will buy transport and accommodation in advance, generally at a lower price because the products are being bought in bulk, and the tours are then sold individually to holiday-makers, either directly or through travel agents. Agents and operators can also package independent tours, or even tailor-made tours, by taking advantage of special net fares and building the package around the specific needs of a client.

The composition of the tour

This consists of the elements comprising the visit. All tourism involves travel away from one's usual place of abode, as we have seen, and in the case of 'tourists', as opposed to 'excursionists', it will include accommodation. So we must here identify the form of travel – air, sea, road or rail – that is to be used. If air transport is involved, will this be by charter aircraft or scheduled flight? If an overnight stay, will this be in a hotel, guesthouse, campsite or self-catering facility? How will the passenger travel between airport and hotel – by coach, private taxi or airport limousine? A package tour will normally comprise transport, accommodation and transfers, but in some cases additional services will be provided in the programme, such as car hire at the destination, excursions by coach or theatre entertainment.

The characteristics of the tourist

An analysis of tourism must also include an analysis of the tourist. We have already distinguished between the holiday-maker and the business traveller. Now we must identify the tourist in terms of nationality, social class, sex, age and lifestyle. What stage of their life cycle are they in? What type of personality do they have?

Such information is valuable not only for the purpose of record keeping; it will also help to shed light on the reasons why people travel and how patterns of travel differ between different groups of people. Research is now focusing much more intently on personality and lifestyle as characteristics which determine the choice of holidays, rather than looking simply at social class and occupation. The more that is known about such details, the more effectively can those in the industry produce the products that will meet the needs of their customers, and develop the appropriate strategies to bring the products to the attention of their customers.

The tourist destination

We can now examine the tourist destination itself. This is quite a complex topic, as a destination can be a particular resort or town, a region within a country, the whole of a country or even a larger area of the globe: for example, a package tour may embrace three separate countries of South America. In some cases the destination can be highly precise, as in the case of a resort hotel which provides a range of leisure facilities on site. In such cases, it may be the tourist's objective to visit the hotel purely and simply because of the facilities the hotel provides, and the entire stay will be taken up with enjoying these facilities alone. This is a characteristic which is commonly found among certain resort hotels in the USA.

However, all destinations share certain characteristics. Their success in attracting tourists will depend upon the quality of three essential benefits that they offer the tourist: attractions, amenities (or facilities), and accessibility (or ease of getting to the destination). These benefits will be discussed shortly. Here, we will first look in more detail at the nature of the destination itself.

Varieties of destination

Destinations are of two kinds: they may be either 'natural' or 'constructed'. Most are 'managed' to some extent, whether they are natural or constructed; national parks, for example, are left in their natural

Figure 1.3 Traditional tourism: sun, sea and sand – the beach at St Ives, Cornwall. (*Photographed by the author*)

state of beauty as far as possible, but nevertheless have to be managed, through the provision of access, parking facilities, limited accommodation, litter bins etc.

The type of tourist destination with which we are most familiar is the *seaside resort*. The attractiveness of the seaside is the combination of sun, sand and sea, which still appeals to the largest segment of the tourist market, either as a form of passive recreation – lying in a deckchair or on the sand and watching the sea – or a more active pastime, including swimming and other watersports, beach games, and the like. The most significant shift in the movement of tourists in the past thirty years has been that of the northern Europeans away from their own beaches to those of the Mediterranean, as prices for air transport fell and the tourists could be assured of sunshine – something that was always a gamble when holidaying in northern Europe. Similarly, lower fares have enabled the Americans to fly to their warmer beaches in Florida or California, or even further afield to Mexico and the Caribbean, abandoning the traditional northern beaches of resorts such as Atlantic City, New Jersey or the Long Island beaches of New York State.

Some seaside resorts that are not blessed with guaranteed sunshine have nevertheless managed to retain a substantial share of the remaining market for domestic holidays, with top resorts in Britain draw-

ing over a million visitors a year, particularly the more conservative tourists, who tend to be in the older age brackets. Resorts such as Blackpool, Torquay, Scarborough, Brighton, Newquay and Bournemouth have continued to attract tourists by a process of continual investment and updating of their attractions; for example, by providing more all-weather facilities, and conference centres to attract business visitors all year round. Some have also been successful by promoting the resort as a base from which to explore the surrounding countryside, rather than as a static holiday resort – important, when one realizes that most tourists arrive at the seaside in their own cars today.

A second category of destination is the *town* or *city*. Urban tourism has grown steadily in recent years, fuelled by a growing interest in cultural activities such as visits to theatres, museums and art galleries, as well as interest in historical architecture and in the opportunity to undertake shopping expeditions. Britain is well placed to attract large numbers of tourists, both domestic and overseas, to these destinations, as it has a plentiful stock of towns of both architectural and historic importance. Capital cities, including of course London, have long exercised a particular draw for the tourist, and the recent growth in short-break holidays of one to three nights has fully capitalized on opportunities to visit Europe's premier cities. Barcelona has become a leading city for short-break holidays, combining all the benefits a tourist seeks: good shops and restaurants, outstanding architecture by Antonio Gaudi, quality hotels, fine museums and substantial investment in the local infrastructure in the past few years. It also benefits from competitive prices compared with similar cities elsewhere in Europe.

As with all resorts, the urban resort with an established reputation and image attracts the tourist more readily than those towns which have no clear image. Cities like London, Paris, Rome, Venice and Amsterdam all have clearly recognized images – although it is interesting to note that in the 1990s the London Tourist Board expressed concern that Japanese tourists were diverting to Paris rather than

London; the reason was that among Japanese visitors female tourists are in the majority, and they perceived Paris as being gentler and more feminine than London. Such is the power of the image to influence tourist choice.

Cities as diverse as Glasgow and Barcelona have succeeded in creating an image of a destination with many unique attractions to offer the visitor. Some cities, however, suffer from a lack of a clearly defined centre to provide the focus for a visit. Los Angeles, Moscow and Tokyo all have this disadvantage, which reduces their appeal to the independent traveller.

Many cities benefit from having a waterfront, or watersite, often part of a defunct working harbour. Only recently has the tourist potential of these sites been recognized, and what was formerly a decaying port transformed into an area of recreation for residents and visitors alike. An outstanding example of this is the Inner Harbour of Baltimore, USA (see Figure 11.3), which, through a combination of private and public investment, has become a magnet for tourists due to the wide variety of attractions that have been developed along the harbourfront. In Australia, Sydney's Darling Harbour has similarly benefited from renewal as a leisure and marine site, while in the UK more than a dozen waterfronts have been renovated, while retaining the many attractive warehouses and other features of their former port status. London's Docklands, the Albert Dock area of Liverpool (the site of the Tate Gallery's first provincial art gallery), Southampton's Ocean Village development and Bristol's Historic Floating Harbour have all taken on a new lease of life as areas of leisure as well as commercial activity.

Third, the *countryside* offers a very wide range of attractions to the tourist. The natural beauty of the country is an attraction which was first recognized in the Romantic era of the nineteenth century, but the desire to get away from the congestion of big cities has led to renewed interest in the tranquillity of the natural landscape in more recent times.

Mountains have strong appeal to the tourist, and offer the benefits of year-round tourism; in summer for walks and simply to admire the beauty of the peaks, and in winter, for winter sports. The Alps and Dolomites in Europe and the Rocky Mountains in North America draw millions of tourists each year. Similarly, lakes, rivers and canals – the latter form of watersite coming into favour for leisure boating – all provide opportunities for relaxation and leisure activities in addition to their natural beauty.

The lakes of Sweden and Finland, and Britain's Lake District and Norfolk Broads regions, have all been well exploited for tourism. Some areas, such as the Norwegian fjords and Switzerland, are fortunate enough to benefit from a combination of lakes and mountains, offering visitors exceptional landscape appeal. Other natural draws include safari parks (especially in East and South Africa), wilderness

Figure 1.4 The appeal of mountains and water: Athabasca Falls, Banff National Park, Canada. (*Photographed by the author*)

Figure 1.5 Quintessential England: Robin Hood's Bay. (*Photographed by the author*)

Attractions, amenities and accessibility

Earlier, it was made clear that all these destinations require adequate attractions, amenities and accessibility if they are to appeal to large numbers of tourists. Let us look at these three characteristics in turn, and in greater detail, here.

The more attractions a destination can offer, the easier it becomes to market that destination to the tourist. Listing and analysing attractions is no easy matter, especially when one recognizes that what appeals to one tourist may actually deter another.

In the description of destinations given above, it will have become clear that many of the attractions of a destination will be the physical features of that destination; the beauty of mountains, the fresh air of a seaside resort and the qualities of a particular beach, the architecture and 'atmosphere' of a great city. To these can be added numerous purpose-built attractions to increase the pulling power of the destination. For example, Blackpool maintains its lead among the seaside resorts in Britain by investing in indoor entertainments, a conference centre and other features which will appeal to a cross-section of tourists; cities like Paris build new museum and exhibition complexes such as the Pompidou Centre and the Musée d'Orsay, or entertainment centres such as the new Opera House in the Bastille area; rural areas offer stately homes or castles as focal points for visits by day-trippers. Sometimes, the constructed attraction becomes a destination in its own right, as is the case with theme parks like Disneyland Paris. The success of many spa towns on the Continent rests on their ability to combine constructed attractions such as casinos with the assumed medical benefits of the natural springs, while the popular ski resort must provide adequate ski runs, ski lifts and après-ski entertainment to complement its combination of suitable weather and mountain slopes.

The operation of managed visitor attractions is dealt with in some detail in Chapter 11. At this point, it will be sufficient to draw the reader's attention to certain distinctions in the nature of attractions.

areas like the great national parks of North America, and the more tranquil, undulating scenery of the English countryside, which, with its combination of pleasantly winding country lanes and small, picturesque villages, is the ideal basis for a touring holiday by car or coach. Some regions of the world offer natural spectacles of immense significance for tourism, such as Niagara Falls, on the US–Canada border, or the Grand Canyon in America's west.

All of these destinations can suffer from overuse. The problems this raises, and the need for careful management of city centres, beaches and natural countryside, are subjects to which we shall return in Chapters 16 and 17.

Figure 1.6 French castles are major site attractions: (a) Chateau Azay-le-Rideau, (b) the gardens at Villandry Chateau. (*Photographed by the author*)

First, attractions may be either *site* or *event* attractions. Site attractions are permanent by nature, while event attractions are temporary, and are often mounted in order to increase the number of tourists to a particular destination. Some events have a short time scale, such as an air display by the famed Red Devils close-formation flyers; others may last for many days (e.g. the Edinburgh Festival) or even months (the ten-yearly Floriade Garden Festival in Holland). A destination which may have little to commend it to the tourist can nevertheless succeed in drawing tourists by mounting an unusual exhibition, while a site destination can extend its season by mounting an off-season festival of arts.

Second, destinations and their attractions can be either *nodal* or *linear* in character. A nodal destination is one in which the attractions of the area are closely grouped geographically. Seaside resorts and cities are examples of typical nodal attractions, making them ideal for packaging by tour operators. This has led to the concept of 'honeypot' tourism development, in which planners concentrate the development of tourism in a specific locality. Aviemore in Scotland (currently undergoing extensive upgrading of its facilities) is an example of a purpose-built nodal tourism resort, with its attractions and amenities closely integrated. Linear tourism, on the other hand, is that in which the attraction is spread over a wide geographical area, without any specific focus. Examples include the Shenandoah Valley region in the United States, the Highlands of Scotland or the Scandinavian lakes and countryside – all ideal for touring holidays, rather than just 'stay-put' holidays. Motels or bed-and-breakfast accommodation spring up to serve the needs of the transient tourist, who may stay only one or two nights at any one destination.

Readers are reminded that much of the attraction of a destination is intangible, and depends upon the image which the potential tourist has of it. India will be seen by one group of travellers as exotic and appealing, while others will reject the destination because of its poverty or its alien culture. Images of a destination, whether favourable or unfavourable, tend to be built up over a long period of time, and once established are difficult to change. Britain, for instance, is still seen by many as a fog-engulfed, rain-battered island with friendly but rather reserved inhabitants – an image frequently stereotyped in the media. Overcoming such stereotyping is an important task of the national tourist board of the country.

Amenities are those essential services catering for the needs of the tourist. These include accommodation and food, local transport, information centres and the necessary infrastructure to support tourism – roads, public utility services and parking facilities. Naturally, such amenities will vary according to the nature of the destination itself; it would clearly be unsuitable to provide an extensive infrastructure in an area of great scenic beauty such as a national park, and those planning to visit such a destination will recognize that the availability of hotels and restaurants must inevitably be limited. Such sites are likely to attract the camper and those seeking only limited amenities.

It should also be recognized that on occasion the amenity itself may be the attraction, as was discussed earlier in the case where a resort hotel offers a comprehensive range of *in situ* attractions. Similarly, a destination like France, which is famed for its regional foods, will encourage tourists whose motive in travelling may be largely to enjoy the food. In this case, the amenity is its own attraction (see Figure 15.12).

Finally, a destination must be accessible, if it is to facilitate visits from tourists. While the more intrepid travellers may be willing to put themselves to great inconvenience in order to see some of the more exotic places in the world, most tourists will not be attracted to a destination unless it is relatively easy to reach. This means, in the case of international travel, having a good airport nearby, regular and convenient air transport to the region at an affordable price, and good local connections to the destination itself. Cruise ships will be attracted by good deep-water ports with moorings available at reasonable cost to the shipping line, and situated at a convenient distance from major attractions in the area. Cities such as Helsinki, Stockholm and Tallinn have the great advantage of providing deep-water moorings close to the very heart of the capital. Other travellers will be drawn by good access roads or rail services, and coach links.

On the other hand, if access becomes too easy, this may result in over-demand and resultant congestion, making the destination less attractive to the tourist. The introduction of new motorways in Britain has opened up the Lake District and the West Country to millions of motorists, many of whom now find themselves within a two-hour drive of their destination. This has led to severe congestion from day-trippers during the peak summer months.

It should be noted that the *perception* of accessibility on the part of the traveller is often as important as a destination's actual accessibility. Many people in Britain perceive Corfu as being more accessible than Cornwall, in terms of travelling time. Such perceptions will undoubtedly affect decision making when tourists are making travel plans.

Now that we have looked at what motivates the tourist to visit certain destinations, let us look at some examples of these destinations to see how their benefits act as a magnet for large numbers of tourists.

The seaside resort

Bournemouth, England

Bournemouth is counted among the half-dozen top seaside resorts in Britain, with a reputation that goes back to the Victorian era. In fact, the town has built on its Victorian heritage as a central theme, highlighting the many fine buildings and splendid shopping malls of the late nineteenth century, and incorporating Victorian-style street furniture and lighting in the recently pedestrianized centre. The heritage theme is enhanced by two piers, one of which has been virtually rebuilt in recent years to bring it up to modern standards and ensure its long-term future.

The town has good transport links: close to a motorway from London, fast Intercity rail connections with London and other parts of the country, with an international airport and ferry services from the Continent at nearby Poole, Southampton and Portsmouth. It is well sited on Britain's warm south coast, in a sandy bay with gently shelving beaches (which are scrupulously cleaned each day). The beaches have gained Blue Flag awards, and although winter storms frequently deplete the sand, the council regularly augments the beach by adding freshly dredged sand.

The town benefits by not being entirely dependent upon tourism, with the result that shopping, from speciality shops to department stores, is on a par with the best in Britain. Good entertainment is available at all levels (Bournemouth has, for example, a symphony orchestra of international standing), and this is supplemented throughout the

Figure 1.7 The coast at Bournemouth. (*Photographed by the author*)

summer by special events such as the Bristol–Bournemouth vintage car rally, power-boat festivals and illuminations.

The town boasts mature central gardens, originally planted a century ago, and floral displays for which it has gained awards. As a base for touring it is among the best sites in the country. The older towns of Poole and Christchurch on each side offer historical and cultural interest, while the New Forest, the Isle of Purbeck and the Dorset countryside are all within easy reach of the motorist. Poole harbour, said to be the second-largest natural harbour in the world, offers a magnificent setting for the boating enthusiast. Bournemouth has also been successful in drawing the business visitor, who may be willing to come out of season, through the construction of the seafront International Centre, which provides facilities for the leisure and conference visitor alike. The success of the town can be judged by the wide range of accommodation available, from five-star hotels to bed and breakfasts; the town's guidebook lists over 650 places to stay.

Figure 1.8 Royal Crescent, Bath. (*Courtesy Bath Tourism Bureau*)

The historic town

Bath, England

This city firmly established its reputation as a spa over two hundred years ago, based on springs which were first valued for their medical benefits during the time of the Roman occupation. Its attraction initially lay in the supposed healing properties of these mineral springs, and it became fashionable to 'take the waters' for the sake of one's health at this and other contemporary spas in England. Patronage by royalty and other members of the establishment reinforced the success of the city as a social venue, and over a period of time the town gradually changed from being merely a fashionable resort to a fashionable place of residence. In the twentieth century, the town experienced a regeneration of tourism, as interest focused on the extensive remains of the Roman baths and the superb collection of Georgian buildings with which the city is endowed. The town has become a popular venue for both domestic and overseas tourists.

Mass tourism has been aided by its proximity to London – a convenient day trip for the foreign tourist – and by the fact that it is close to the M4 and M5 motorways. Bath is noted for the quality of its entertainment and shopping, and the city's success has been further boosted by a growing number of unique museums, and cultural events such as the annual Bath Festival. Complemented by a good stock of accommodation and eating places, the city is now a major tourist destination, although tourist officials are concerned that its geographical location close to London makes it difficult to encourage many overseas visitors to stay overnight.

The city comes full circle as a tourist resort with the restoration of its two lesser baths for medical treatment. These are expected to attract high-spending spa tourists and are under construction at the time of writing with a view to reopening around 2003.

The site/event destination

Oberammergau, Germany

This village resort in Bavaria manages to combine both site and event attractions. As a mountain resort in the Bavarian Alps, the village lies at the heart of Europe, accessible through Munich by air from all over the world, and with good road connections from elsewhere in Germany, and from Austria. It is both a winter and summer resort, offering summer guests peace and tranquillity, healthy mountain air, outstanding alpine scenery and opportunities for hiking and mountaineering. In winter, the resort offers winter sports opportunities and the usual appeal of a snow-clad landscape. The village is picturesque, with many of its wooden or rendered houses painted with murals in the local folk idiom. There are high-quality shops for the tourist, including wood-carving shops, while the established up-market shopping centres of Munich and Garmisch-Partenkirchen are less than an hour's drive away. The town boasts excellent leisure facilities, including a modern indoor–outdoor swimming pool complex, and a good stock of accommodation at all prices. However, the fame of the resort rests

Figure 1.9 The Passion Play at Oberammergau, Germany. (*Courtesy Verkehrs- und Reisebüro Gemeinde Oberammergau OGH*)

Figure 1.10 Event tourism: morris dancers outside Jorvik Museum, York. (*Photographed by the author*)

principally on its famous Passion Play, which has been performed once every ten years since the Middle Ages. This event is a draw for international tourists from all over the world, and overseas tour operators vie with one another to obtain an allocation of seats for the performances in order to package a programme. In other years, the theatre where the play is staged still draws countless day trippers.

The successful destination

Three important points should be highlighted in relation to tourist destinations. First, the chances of their long-term success will be significantly enhanced if the benefits they offer are unique. There is only one Oberammergau Passion Play, just as there is only one Eiffel Tower, Grand Canyon or Big Ben, and these attractions can provide the focus for a destination's marketing campaign. Because of the singular properties of 'heritage' tourism, these types of destination retain their attraction even if their prices may become less competitive with other destinations, providing the increase is not exorbitant by comparison.

However, it is true to say that the majority of the mass tourism movement is directed at sun, sea, sand destinations, which the Mediterranean and Caribbean countries provide so effectively. Such des-

tinations are seldom unique, nor do their customers require them to be so. The tourists will be satisfied as long as the amenities are adequate, the resort remains accessible and prices are competitive. Indeed, the similarities in attraction and amenity, as well as the way these destinations are marketed, gives rise to the concept of the 'Identikit' destination, which results from the evidence produced by market research studies designed to find common denominators among the various international markets in order to develop a product with guaranteed mass demand. These Identikit destinations have been developed through the activities of multinational tourism organizations. In the development of such destinations, the emphasis changes from an attempt to distinguish the product to one which concentrates on maintaining or improving its image, by offering good standards which reflect value for money and ensuring that the destination remains competitive with other, similar destinations. The characteristics of Identikit destinations are discussed in greater detail in Chapter 3.

The second point to stress is that the more benefits a destination can offer, the greater the attraction of the destination. Multiple attractions provide added value, and the concentration within a specific geographical area of a number of different products appealing to different markets (such as the City of Bath, and the region surrounding Bournemouth) will improve the chance of success.

Finally, it should be clear that resorts cannot rest on their laurels. Most destinations depend at least to some extent on the return visitor, and will need continually to update and augment their range of attractions to encourage repeat visits. This means constant investment. Destinations, like all products which depend upon consumer demand, have 'life cycles', in which they experience periods of growth, expansion and, eventually, decline. If we examine the history of any well-known resort we can see the truth of this. Along the French Riviera, Nice, Cannes, Antibes, Juan les Pins and St Tropez have all in turn enjoyed their periods as fashionable resorts, but ultimately, their visitors moved on to more fashionable resorts, often to be replaced by less fashion-conscious, less free-spending tourists.

A decline into decay, all too evident in many British seaside resorts today, can only be arrested through redevelopment and innovation. In some cases, resorts have been allowed to run down to an extent where the cost of renovation may be beyond the scope of the council, and decay becomes inevitable.

Questions and discussion points

1. What potential problems can you foresee in less developed countries turning to tourism in order to boost their economy?

2. Identify two tourism destinations known to you, one of which is attracting a growing number of tourists, the other facing a decrease in tourism. Account for the changing fortunes of each. Is either likely to experience a change in demand in the future? What would need to be done by the destination facing decline, if it were to increase its attractiveness?

3. Explain the differing requirements of business and leisure travellers for (a) air transport and (b) hotel accommodation. Do the growing numbers of businesswomen have needs distinct from businessmen that should be catered for by transport companies or hotels?

Assignment topics

1. You have recently taken up the position of Assistant Tourist Officer in a county of your choice. The county has only recently created a tourism department, and your immediate superior is preparing a new plan of action to increase the number of visitors during the next five years. She asks you to produce a brief report for her which:

    (a) looks at trends over the past decade in domestic and incoming tourism;

    (b) identifies significant trends and forecasts the future flow of tourism within Britain;

    (c) suggests relative advantages and disadvantages of the county in attracting more visitors.

    Your report should specifically indicate the shortcomings you find in the amount and quality of the statistical data you seek, and what further research you think may be needed to guide the department in its planning.

2. As an incoming ground handling agent serving the needs of the US market, you have been approached by a specialist tour operator, Ralph Quackenbusch of Quackenbusch Tours, Sacramento, California. He is interested in bringing groups to your area of the country, and has written to you to ask for your assessment of local towns which might be attractive to older Californian residents. Select one town you consider might be suitable, and subject this to an evaluation of its attractions, amenities and accessibility for this overseas market, bearing in mind that some groups will be wanting to spend some time in London, while others will prefer to come more directly to your part of the world.

    Write a short business letter spelling out the attractiveness of the destination as you see it.

Chapter 2   The history of tourism: from its origins to the age of steam

Objectives

After studying this chapter, you should be able to:

- explain the historical changes which have affected the growth and development of the tourism industry from its earliest days;
- understand why particular forms of travel and destinations were chosen by the early tourists;
- identify and distinguish between enabling conditions and motivating factors affecting tourism demand.

Introduction

A study of the history of tourism is a worthwhile occupation for any student of the tourism business, not only as a matter of academic interest, but because there are lessons to be learned which are as applicable today as in the past. One thing we learn from history is that the business of tourism three thousand years ago shared many of the characteristics of the business as we know it today. Many of the facilities and amenities demanded by modern tourists were provided – albeit in a more basic form – from the earliest days of travel, including accommodation, catering services, guides and souvenir shops.

The earliest forms of leisure tourism can be traced as far back as the Babylonian and Egyptian empires. A museum of 'historic antiquities' was open to the public in the sixth century BC in Babylon, while the Egyptians held many religious festivals attracting not only the devout, but many who came to see the famous buildings and works of art in the cities. To provide for these throngs during the festivals, services of all kinds sprang up: vendors of food and drink, guides, hawkers of souvenirs, touts and prostitutes. Some early tourists took to vandalizing buildings with graffiti to record their visit and Egyptian graffiti dating back to 2000 BC have been found.

From about the same date, and notably from the third century BC, Greek tourists travelled to visit the sites of healing gods. Because the independent city-states of ancient Greece had no central authority to order the construction of roads, most of these tourists travelled by water, and since most freight also travelled in this fashion, the seaports prospered.

Figure 2.1   The first Olympic Games, held in Greece.
(*Courtesy The Greek National Tourist Organisation*)

The Greeks, too, enjoyed their religious festivals, which in time became increasingly oriented to the pursuit of pleasure, and in particular, sport. Already by the fifth century BC Athens had become an important destination for travellers visiting the major sights such as the Parthenon, and inns – often adjuncts of the temples – were established in major towns and seaports to provide for the travellers' needs. Innkeepers of this period were known to be difficult and unfriendly, and the facilities they provided very basic: a palette to sleep on, but no heating, no windows and no toilet facilities. Courtesans 'trained in the art of music, dance, conversation and making love' were the principal entertainment offered.

Early guides and guidebooks

Much of what we know of travel during this early period is due to the writings of Herodotus, who lived between c. 484 and 424 BC, a noted historian and early traveller who can be accurately described as the world's first significant travel writer. He has recorded extensively, and with some cynicism, the tall stories recounted to him by the travel guides of the day. It appears that these guides varied greatly in the quality and accuracy of the information they provided. The role of guides was divided between those whose task was to shepherd the tourists around the sites (the *periegetai*) and those whose function it was to provide information for their charges (the *exegetai*). Liberties with the truth included the story that the great pyramids at Giza extended downwards into the earth to the same extent as their height, and that the perfection of the white marble used in the greatest statues was such that viewers risked damaging their eyesight unless they averted their gaze. The philosopher Plutarch wrote to complain, a century before the birth of Christ, that guides insisted on talking too much about the inscriptions and epitaphs found at the sites, choosing to ignore the entreaties of the visitors to cut this short.

Guidebooks, too, made their appearance as early as the fourth century BC, covering destinations such as Athens, Sparta and Troy. Pausanias, a Greek travel writer, produced a noted 'Description of Greece' between AD 160 and 180 which, in its critical evaluation of facilities and destinations, acted as a model for later writers. Advertisements, in the form of signs directing visitors to wayside inns, are also known from this period. However, it was under the Roman Empire that international travel first became important. With no foreign borders between England and Syria, and with the seas safe from piracy due to the Roman patrols, conditions favouring travel had at last arrived. Roman coinage was acceptable everywhere, and Latin was the common language of the day. Romans travelled to Sicily, Greece, Rhodes, Troy, Egypt – and, from the third century AD, to the Holy Land. The Romans, too, introduced their guidebooks (*itineraria*), listing hostels with symbols to identify quality in a manner reminiscent of the present-day Michelin Guides. The Roman poet Horace published an anti-travel ode following his travel experiences from Rome to Brindisi in 38–37 BC.

It is interesting to note, too, the growth of travel bureaucracy at this stage. An exit permit was required to leave by many seaports, and a charge was made for this service. Souvenirs acquired abroad were subject to an import duty, and a customs declaration had to be completed.

Rome, too, suffered its share of 'cowboy operators'. Among the souvenirs offered to Roman travellers were forgeries of Greek statues, especially works bearing the signature of Greece's most famous sculptor, Praxiteles. Roman writers of the day complained of Athens as a 'city of shysters', bent on swindling the foreign tourist.

Domestic tourism also flourished within the Roman Empire's heartland. Second homes were built by the wealthy within easy travelling distance of Rome, occupied particularly during the springtime social season. The most fashionable resorts were to be found around the Bay of Naples, and there is evidence of early market segmentation between these destinations. Naples itself attracted the retired and intellectuals, Cumae became the resort of high fashion, Puteoli attracted the more staid tourist, while Baiae, which was both a spa town and a seaside resort, attracted the down-market tourist, becoming noted for its rowdiness, drunkenness and all-night singing.

The distribution of administrators and the military during the days of the Roman Empire led to Romans making trips abroad to visit friends and relatives, setting a precedent for the VFR movements of the present day. The rapid improvement in communications which coincided with the Roman conquests aided the growth of travel; first-class roads, coupled with staging inns (precursors of the modern motels), led to comparatively safe, fast and convenient travel unsurpassed until modern times. There is even recent evidence of leisure cruises taken by super-rich Romans; a 150-foot cruise ship, designed to provide luxurious travel along the coastal waters of the Mediterranean, was discovered by divers off the Sicilian coast in 2000. The ship was fitted with bedroom suites and even passenger lounges for social interaction.

Travel in the Middle Ages

Following the collapse of the Roman Empire, and the onset of the so-called Dark Ages, travel became more dangerous, difficult and considerably less attractive, and more synonymous with *travail* (literally, a painful and laborious effort, and the origin of the word). The result was that most pleasure travel was undertaken close to home, though this is not to say that international travel was unknown. Adventurers sought fame and fortune through travel, merchants travelled extensively to seek new trade opportunities, strolling players and minstrels made their living by performing as they travelled (the most famous of these must be Blondel, a native of Picardy and friend of King Richard I, the 'Lion-Heart', whom he is reputed to have accompanied on the latter's Crusade). However, all these forms of travel would be identified either as business travel, or travel from a sense of obligation or duty. In order for people to travel for pleasure, the conditions favouring travel must be in place.

Nonetheless, closer to home, holidays played an important role in the life of the public. The word 'holiday' has its origin in 'holy days', and from earliest times religion provided the framework within which leisure time was spent. For most people, this implied a break from work, rather than a movement from one place to another. The village 'wakes' of the Middle Ages, held on the eve of patronal festivals, provide an example of such 'religious relaxation'. Such public holidays were, in fact, quite numerous, and far more so than today – up until as recently as 1830 there were as many as thirty-three Saint's days in the holiday calendar, dispelling the myth of peasants engaged almost constantly in hard manual labour. For the pious intent on fulfilling a religious duty, pilgrimages would be undertaken to places of worship, and Chaucer's tales of one pilgrimage to Canterbury provide evidence that there was a pleasurable side to this travel, too.

Developments in road transport in the seventeenth to early nineteenth centuries

Before the sixteenth century, those who sought to travel had three modes in which to do so: they could walk (many who were too poor to afford any form of transport had to do so, regardless of the distance involved), they could ride a horse, or they could be carried, either on a litter (carried by servants, and restricted largely to the aristocracy) or on a carrier's wagon. This horse-drawn vehicle was slow and appallingly uncomfortable, being without springs. The roads of the time were poorly surfaced, pot-holed and in winter deeply rutted by the wagon wheels which churned the road into a sea of mud, making the journey an endurance test for passengers. The journey was also unsafe: footpads and highway-men abounded on the major routes, posing an ever-present threat to wayfarers. Apart from royalty and the court circle, who were always well guarded, only a handful of wealthy citizens, such as those with 'country seats' (second homes in the country) travelled for pleasure until well into the eighteenth century.

The development of the sprung coach was a huge advance for those who were obliged to travel. The invention in its most primitive form is traced to the Hungarian town of Kocs in the fifteenth century, and by the mid-1600s coaches were operating regu-larly in Britain, with a daily service recorded between London and Oxford. The concept of the stagecoach, for which teams of horses would be used and changed at regular points along the route, greatly aided mobility. These appeared in England as early as the seventeenth century, and were in use widely throughout continental Europe by the middle of the eighteenth century (Austria, for example, introduced its first services in 1749). The construction of these coaches, in which the body of the coach was 'sprung' by being suspended from primitive leather straps, encouraged travel by offer-ing a greater measure of comfort. In the eighteenth century the introduction of turnpike roads, which provided improved surfaces for which tolls would be charged, enabled stage coaches carrying between eight and fourteen passengers to cover upwards of forty miles a day during the summer. However, this still meant that a journey to Bath from London would take some three days, while the four hundred miles to Edinburgh took fully ten days. The later introduction of metal, leaf-spring suspension also added to comfort. Stagecoaches also greatly aided the development of the North American colonies, with a service between Boston and New York intro-duced in 1772, and other routes serving Providence (Rhode Island), Philadelphia and Baltimore. However, mail coaches, which were to provide additional passenger accommodation, were not to make an appearance until the 1780s in Europe and the USA.

Travel of some distance requires accommodation. At this time, such accommodation was basic. Inns sprang up to serve the needs of overnight guests and to provide fresh horses, while lodgings or 'chambers' were available for rent to visitors when they arrived at their destinations.

Around 1815, the discovery of tarmacadam revo-lutionized the road systems of Europe. For the first time, a hard surface less subject to pitting and ruts enabled rapid increases to be made in the average speed of coach services. Charabancs, public coaches with rows of transverse seats facing forward, have been identified as far back as 1832; the term was later applied to the first motor-coaches used for leisure travel in the early twentieth century. By the 1820s, the horse-drawn omnibus was a common sight in London and Paris, greatly improving local city trans-port. Mail coaches were now covering the distance between London and Bath in twelve and a half hours, and the London–Brighton run was reduced to a little over five hours.

The Grand Tour

From the early seventeenth century, a new form of

tourism developed, as a direct outcome of the freedom and quest for learning heralded by the Renaissance. Under the reign of Elizabeth I, young men seeking positions at court were encouraged to travel to the Continent to finish their education. This practice was soon adopted by others high in the social circle, and it eventually became customary for the education of a gentleman to be completed by a 'Grand Tour' (a term in use as early as 1670) of the major cultural centres of Europe, accompanied by a tutor and often lasting three years or more. Travel for reasons of education was encouraged by the fact that under Elizabeth I a special licence had to be obtained from the Crown in order to travel abroad, though universities had the privilege of granting licences themselves for the purpose of scholarship. The publication in 1749 of a guidebook by Dr Thomas Nugent entitled *The Grand Tour* gave a further boost to the educational tour, and some intrepid travellers ventured as far afield as Egypt. While ostensibly educational, as with the spas the appeal soon became social, and pleasure-seeking young men of leisure travelled, predominantly to France and Italy, to enjoy the rival cultures and social life of cities such as Paris, Venice and Florence. By the end of the eighteenth century, the custom had become institutionalized for the gentry.

As a result, European centres were opened up to the British traveller. Aix-en-Provence, Montpellier and Avignon became notable bases, especially for those using the Provence region as a staging post for travel to Italy. When pleasure travel followed in the nineteenth century, eventually to displace educational tours as the motive for Continental visits, this was to lead to the development of the Riviera as a principal destination for British tourists, aided by the introduction of regular steamboat services across the Channel from 1821 onwards. However, the advent of the Napoleonic wars early in the nineteenth century inhibited travel within Europe for some thirty years. By the time of Napoleon's defeat, the British had taken a greater interest in touring their own country.

Political hindrance to travel

Travel outside the boundaries of one's country had always been subject to restrictions, as we have seen from some of the constraints imposed by the state under the Roman Empire. Few people travelled any great distance, and those who did so were generally involved with affairs of state. Monarchs were suspicious of intrigues and alliances with foreign states, and vetted such travel carefully, issuing letters of authority to members of court, ostensibly to facilitate travel but equally to ensure that they were familiar with the movements of their subjects.

Passports have their origin in the medieval *testimoniale*, a letter from an ecclesiastical superior given to a pilgrim to avoid the latter's possible arrest on charges of vagrancy. Later, papers of authority to travel were more widely issued by the state, particularly during periods of warfare with neighbouring European countries. However, when Belgium sought to require visitors to present passports for inspection in 1882, there was widespread indignation in the British press. The introduction of compulsory passports as a permanent requirement in Britain is of relatively recent origin, dating only from 1916, as a result of controls introduced during World War I. The institution of a formal immigration service in the UK is also a twentieth-century phenomenon, being established under the Aliens Act 1905.

We should also not underestimate the importance of a common currency, and the difficulties and expense incurred when changing currencies while travelling abroad. As we have seen, under the Roman Empire the universal acceptance of Roman coinage proved to be a great facilitator for travel, in contrast to the wealth of currencies even within individual countries in the Middle Ages. Fynes Moryson, an academic who travelled extensively on the Continent, was to write in 1589 of finding over twenty different coinages in Germany, five in the Low Countries and as many as eight in Switzerland. Moneychangers cheated the visitor and were sometimes difficult to find. With the forthcoming adoption of the euro as a common currency throughout several countries within the European Union – the first such common currency since the days of the Roman Empire – it is interesting to speculate upon the boost that this move will give to tourism in the opening years of the twenty-first century.

Political hindrance in the form of taxation should also not be underestimated, even in very early periods of tourism history. Taxes on travelling have a long history – indeed, the first spa tax is known to have been introduced in Bad Pyrmont, Saxony, as early as 1413. Governments have traditionally seen the imposition of taxes on tourists as a convenient way of raising revenue, and equally history reveals how tourists resist high taxation by selecting alternative destinations or attractions that are less highly taxed or untaxed.

The development of the spas

Spas were already well established during the time of the Roman Empire, but their popularity, based on the supposed medical benefits of the waters, had lapsed in subsequent centuries. They were never entirely out of favour, however; the sick continued to visit Bath throughout the Middle Ages. Renewed interest in the therapeutic qualities of mineral waters can be traced to the influence of the Renaissance in Britain and other European centres.

In 1562, Dr William Turner published a book drawing attention to the curative powers of the waters at Bath and on the Continent. Bath itself, along with the spa at Buxton, had been showing a return to popularity among those 'seeking the cure', and the effect of Dr Turner's book was to establish the credibility of the resorts' claims. In 1626, Elizabeth Farrow drew attention to the qualities of the mineral springs at Chalybeate in Scarborough, which became the first of a number of new spa resorts. In the same year, Dr Edmund Deane wrote his *Spadacrene Anglica* which drew attention to what he claimed were 'the strongest sulphur springs in Great Britain' at Harrogate. This rapidly led to the popularity of the town as a spa resort, a role it con-

Figure 2.2 The Roman baths at Bath. (*Courtesy Bath Tourism Bureau*)

tinues to enjoy today. Soon, an astonishing number of spa resorts sprang up, sometimes in unlikely places; Streatham in south London, for instance, became briefly fashionable following the discovery of mineral springs there in 1659.

Taking the cure rapidly developed social status, and the resorts changed in character as pleasure rather than health became the motivation for visits. Bath in particular became a major centre of social life for high society during the eighteenth and early nineteenth centuries, aided by visits from the monarchs of the day. Under the guidance of Beau Nash at the beginning of the eighteenth century, it soon became a centre of high fashion, deliberately setting out to create a select and exclusive image. The commercial possibilities opened up by the concentration of these wealthy visitors were not overlooked; facilities to entertain or otherwise cater for these visitors prolif-

Figure 2.3 The Continental spa: the hot spring at Karlovy Vary (Karlsbad), Czech Republic. (*Photographed by the author*)

There are interesting parallels between the decline of the English spas and that of the English seaside resorts one hundred and fifty years or so later. The spa towns were seen as attractive places in which to live, and residents gradually supplanted visitors. These residents tended to be older, and their demand for more passive and traditional entertainment, with a preference for entertaining at home rather than seeking commercial entertainment, hastened the spas' economic decline. However, it was the rise of the seaside resorts which did much to undermine the success of the inland spas, just as later it would be the rise of the Mediterranean resorts which would lead to the decline of the British seaside resort.

The rise of the seaside resort

Until the Renaissance, bathing in the sea found little favour in Britain. Although not entirely unknown before then, such bathing as occurred was undertaken unclothed, and this behaviour conflicted with the mores of the day. Only when the sea became associated with certain health benefits did bathing gain popularity. The association of seawater with health did not find acceptance until the early years of the eighteenth century, and initially the objective was to drink it rather than bathe in it. It is perhaps to be expected that health theorists would eventually recognize that the minerals to be found in spa waters were also present in abundance in seawater. By the early eighteenth century, small fishing resorts around the English coast were beginning to attract visitors seeking 'the cure', both by drinking seawater and by immersing themselves in it. Not surprisingly, Scarborough, as the only spa bordering the sea, was one of the first to exploit this facility for the medical benefits it was believed to offer, and both this town and Brighton were attracting regular visitors by the 1730s. But it was Dr Richard Russell's noted medical treatise *A Dissertation on the Use of Sea Water in the Diseases of the Glands, particularly the Scurvy, Jaundice, King's Evil, Leprosy, and the Glandular Consumption*, published in 1752 (and two years earlier in Latin),

erated, changing the spas into what we would today term holiday resorts rather than watering places. The building of a Pump Room as a focal point within Bath was a key development leading to the town's success as a resort, while Harrogate similarly benefited by the construction of its own Pump Room in 1841–42.

Eventually, in the early nineteenth century, the common characteristic of resorts to go 'down-market' through their life cycle led to a changing clientele, with the landed gentry replaced by wealthy merchants and the professional class. By the end of the eighteenth century, the heyday of the English spas was already over, although they were to have a far longer life cycle on the Continent (see Figure 2.3).

which is credited with popularizing the custom of sea bathing more widely. Soon Blackpool, Southend and other English seaside resorts were wooing bathers to their shores. Blackpool, in fact, had attracted some categories of sea bather well before its growth as a resort; workers in the area are known to have travelled there by cart in order to wash off the accumulation of dirt resulting from their jobs. The heyday of these 'Padjamers', as they were known, was in the century between 1750 and 1850.

The growing popularity of taking the cure, which resulted from the wealth generated by the expansion of trade and industry in Britain at the time, meant that the inland spas could no longer cater satisfactorily for the influx of visitors they were attracting. By contrast, the new seaside resorts offered almost boundless opportunities for expansion. Moral doubts about exposing one's body in the sea were overcome by the invention of the bathing machine, and the resorts prospered.

Undoubtedly, the demand for seaside cures could have been even greater in the early years if fast, cheap transport had been developed to cater for this need. But in the mid-eighteenth century, it still took two days to travel from London to Brighton, and the cost was well beyond the reach of the average worker, at the equivalent of six weeks' wages. Accommodation provision, too, grew only slowly, outpaced by demand. But all this was to change in the early nineteenth century.

First, the introduction of steamboat services reduced the cost and time of travel from London to the resorts near the Thames Estuary. In 1815, a service began operating between London and Gravesend, and five years later, to Margate. The popularity of these services was such that other pleasure boat services were quickly introduced to more distant resorts. This development required the construction of piers to provide landing stages for the vessels; the functional purpose of the seaside pier was soon overtaken by its attraction as a social meeting-point and a place to take the sea air.

However, it was also the introduction of steamboat services linking Britain and Continental Europe which posed the first threat to the British seaside resorts. Brighton established a ferry link with Dieppe as early as 1761, and later, this was followed by links from Shoreham and Newhaven to France. It has been estimated that by the 1820s some 150,000 visitors a year were travelling from Britain to mainland Europe, many for the purposes of visiting coastal resorts. At first, from about 1780 onwards, travel was concentrated along the Riviera, between the mouth of the Var and the Gulf of Spezia. The Italian resorts benefited from direct steamer services from London and Liverpool to Genoa. Soon, French resorts were attracting British visitors along the north coast between Boulogne and Cherbourg. The British visitors insisted on facilities which met their particular needs, including churches of favourite denominations and British shops, chemists, physicians and newspapers; the more successful French resorts quickly provided these. From 1880 onwards, the Train Bleu offered wealthy British visitors elegant sleeping accommodation from Paris to the Riviera, popularizing not only summer but also winter holidays to escape the cold of the British climate.

The conditions favouring the expansion of travel in the nineteenth century

From this brief history of travel from earliest times to the nineteenth century, we can see that a number of factors have been at work to encourage travel. We can divide these into two categories: factors that make travel possible (*enabling* factors), and factors that persuade people to travel (*motivating* factors).

In order for travel to be possible at all, people must have adequate time and money to undertake it. However, throughout most of history, and until very recently, both of these have been the prerogative of a very few members of society. Leisure time for the masses was very limited; workers laboured from morning to night, six days a week, and were encouraged to treat Sundays (and the not infrequent Saint's days) as days of rest and worship. Wages were barely adequate to sustain a family and pay for the basic necessities of life. The idea of paid holidays was not even considered until the twentieth century.

Equally important, the development of pleasure travel depends upon the provision of suitable travel facilities. The growth of travel and of transport are interdependent; travellers require transport that is priced within their budget and that is fast, safe, comfortable and convenient. As we have seen, none of these criteria began to be met until the latter half of the eighteenth century, but from the early nineteenth century onwards rapid improvements in technology led to transport that was both fast and moderately priced.

The development of transport during the nineteenth century will be examined in greater detail shortly. But good transport must be complemented by adequate accommodation at the traveller's destination. The traditional hospices for travellers in the Middle Ages were the monasteries, but these were dissolved during the reign of Henry VIII and the resulting hiatus acted as a further deterrent to travel for everyone apart from those planning to stay with friends or relatives. The gradual improvement in lodgings that accompanied the introduction of the mail coaches and stagecoaches went some way to correcting this shortcoming. However, the general inadequacy of facilities away from the major centres of population meant that towns such as London, Exeter and York, with their abundant social life and entertainment as a magnet, were to become the first centres to attract large numbers of visitors for leisure purposes.

Other constraints awaited those prepared to ignore these drawbacks to travel. In cities, public health standards were low, and travellers risked disease, a risk compounded in the case of foreign travel. Exchange facilities for foreign travel were unreliable, rates of exchange were inconsistent and travellers risked being cheated, so they tended to carry large amounts of money with them, making them prey to highwaymen. Foreign currencies were, in any event, chaotic, as we have noted earlier – in the sixteenth century, for instance, Germany, with its multiplicity of small states, had no fewer than twenty coinages as well as the Reich's Dollar, while there were similar multiple coinages in other European countries. Before unification, Italy, a popular venue for the cultural tourist, boasted sixteen different coinages. As we have also seen, travel documents of some kind were generally necessary, and at times not easy to come by; political suspicion frequently meant long delays in obtaining permission to travel.

Removing such constraints will encourage growth in travel. However, the real motivation for travel must be intrinsic, a wish to travel for its own sake, to get away from one's everyday surroundings and become acquainted with other places, cultures and people. It was the rapid urbanization of the population in Great Britain which provided the impetus for travel in the nineteenth century. The industrial revolution had led to massive migration of the population away from the villages and countryside and into the industrial cities, where work was plentiful and better paid. This migration was to have two important side effects on the workers themselves. First, workers became conscious of the beauty and attractions of their former rural surroundings for the first time. Cities were dark, polluted and treeless. Formerly, workers had little appreciation of their environment – living in the midst of the natural beauty of the countryside, they accepted it without question. Now, they longed to escape from the cities in what little free time they had – a characteristic still evident among twenty-first-century city dwellers. Second, the type of work available in the cities was both physically and psychologically stressful. The comparatively leisurely pace of life in the countryside was replaced by monotonous factory work from which any change of routine and pace was welcome.

The expansion of the British economy which took place as a result of the increased productivity created by the industrial revolution led to growth in real purchasing power for every worker, while worldwide demand for British goods created a huge business travel market. Increased wealth stimulated rapid growth in the population at this time, too.

In short, Britain at the beginning of the nineteenth century stood poised on the threshold of a considerable escalation in the demand for travel. The introduction of modern transport systems at this point in history was to translate this demand into reality.

The age of steam

The railways

Two technological developments in the early part of the nineteenth century were to have a profound effect on transport and the growth in travel generally. The first of these was the advent of the railway.

The first railway was built in England, between Stockton and Darlington, in 1825. It was to herald a major programme of railway construction throughout the world, and a major shift in the facility to travel. We have noted the problems of travelling by road up to that point; and, although travel by canal had been possible by 1760, it was too slow a mode to attract travellers, being used essentially for the carriage of freight. As a means of transport for all purposes, it was to suffer a rapid decline after 1825, when railways made travel at 13 mph possible for the first time – at least three miles an hour faster than the fastest mail coaches. In the decade following the introduction of a rail link between Liverpool and Manchester in 1830, trunk routes sprang up between the major centres of population and industry in Britain, on mainland Europe and throughout the world; in the USA, for example, passenger services on the east coast were being built from the 1820s, and by 1869 a transcontinental link was in place. One of the last great rail routes, the Trans-Siberian, opened in 1903, connecting Moscow with Vladivostok and Port Arthur.

In the UK, after their initial function to serve the needs of commerce, new routes emerged linking these centres to the popular coastal resorts such as Brighton, bringing these within reach of the mass of pleasure travellers for the first time. On the whole, however, the railway companies appeared to be slow to recognize the opportunities for pleasure travel offered by the development of rail services, concentrating instead on providing for the needs of business travellers. Certainly, in the 1840s, the growth of regular passenger traffic was enough to occupy them; between 1842 and 1847, the annual number of passengers travelling by train rose from 23 million to 51 million. Competition between the railway companies was initially based on service rather than price, although from the earliest days of the railways a new market developed for short day trips. Before long, however, entrepreneurs began to stimulate rail travel by organizing excursions for the public at special fares. In some cases, these took place on regular train services, but in others, special trains were chartered in order to take travellers to their destination, setting a precedent for the charter services by air which were to become so significant a feature of tour operating a century later. As an indication of the speed with which these opportunities were put into place, within twelve days of the rail line to Scarborough being opened in 1845, an excursion train from Wakefield was laid on to carry a thousand passengers to the seaside.

Thomas Cook, contrary to popular opinion, was not, in fact, the first entrepreneur to organize tours for the public. Sir Rowland Hill, who became chairman of the Brighton Railway Company, is sometimes credited with this innovation (others have suggested that the first package tour can in fact be traced to a group of tourists taken from Wadebridge to Bodmin to witness a public hanging!), and there were certainly excursion trains in operation by 1840. However, Cook was to have by far the greatest impact on the early travel industry. In 1841, as secretary of the South Midland Temperance Association, he organized an excursion for his members from Leicester to Loughborough, at a fare of one shilling (the equivalent of five pence) return. The success of this venture – 570 took part – encouraged him to arrange similar excursions using chartered trains, and by 1845 he was organizing these trips on a fully commercial basis.

The result of these and similar ventures by other entrepreneurs led to a substantial movement of pleasure-bound travellers to the seaside. In 1844, it is recorded that almost 15,000 passengers travelled from London to Brighton on the three Easter holidays alone, while hundreds of thousands travelled to other resorts to escape the smoke and grime of the cities. The enormous growth in this type of traffic can be appreciated when it is revealed that by 1862 Brighton received 132,000 visitors on Easter Monday alone.

Supported by a more sympathetic attitude to pleasure travel by public authorities such as the Board of Trade, the railway companies themselves were actively promoting these excursions by the 1850s, while at the same time introducing a range of discounted fares for day trips, weekend trips and longer journeys. By 1855, Cook had extended his field of operations to mainland Europe, organizing the first 'inclusive tours' to the Paris Exhibition of that year. This followed the success of his excursions to the Great Exhibition in London in 1851, which in all had welcomed a total of three million visitors.

Cook was a man of vision in the world of travel. The success of his operations was due to the care he took in organizing his programmes to minimize problems; he had close contacts with hotels, shipping companies and railways throughout the world, ensuring that he obtained the best possible service as well as cheap prices for the services he provided. By escorting his clients throughout their journeys abroad he took the worry out of travel for the first-time traveller. He also made the administration of travel easier by introducing the hotel voucher in 1867, which allowed tourists to prepay their hotel accommodation and to produce evidence to the hotels that this had been done. In 1873 he introduced the 'circular note', the precursor to today's traveller's cheque, which helped to overcome the problems caused by the many different coinages in Europe. The latter was not a totally new concept; a certain Robert Herries set up the London Banking Exchange Company in 1772 in order to issue similar documents, but it was Cook (and later in North America, American Express) who popularized these ideas, which made travel far more tolerable for the Victorian traveller.

The coincidental invention of photography in the mid-nineteenth century further stimulated overseas travel for reasons of prestige. For the first time, visitors abroad could be photographed against a background of the great historical sites of Europe, to the envy of their friends.

The expansion of the railways was accompanied by a simultaneous decline in the stagecoaches. Some survived by providing feeder services to the nearest railway stations, but overall road traffic shrank, and with it the demand for the staging inns. Those situated in the resorts were quick to adapt to meet the needs of the new railway travellers, but the supply of accommodation in centres served by the railways was totally inadequate to meet the burgeoning demand of this new market. A period of hotel construction began, in which the railway companies themselves were leaders, establishing the great railway terminus hotels which came to play such a significant role in the hotel industry over the next hundred years. The high capital investment called for by this development led to the formation of the first hotel chains and corporations.

Social changes in the Victorian era all encouraged travel. The new-found interest in sea bathing meant that the expanding rail network favoured the developing resorts, accelerating their growth. At the same time, Victorian society placed great emphasis on the role of the family as a social unit, leading to the type of family holidays for which the seaside was so well suited. The foundations of traditional seaside entertainment were soon laid – German bands, 'nigger minstrels' and pierrots, Punch and Judy shows, barrel organs, donkey rides and the seaside pier all became essential components of the seaside holiday. Resorts began to develop different social images, partly as a result of their geographical location: those nearer London or other major centres of population developed a substantial market of day-trippers, while others deliberately aimed for a more exclusive clientele. These latter generally tended to be situated further afield, but in some cases their exclusivity arose from the desire of prominent residents to resist the encroachment of the railways for as long as possible.

Bournemouth, for example, held out against the extension of the railway from Poole until 1870. Some areas of early promise as holiday resorts were quickly destroyed by the growth of industry – Swansea and Hartlepool, for example, and Southampton, where beaches gave way to the development of docks.

Health continued to play a role in the choice of holiday destinations, but the emphasis gradually switched from the benefits of sea bathing to those of sea air. Climate became a feature of the resorts' promotion. Sunshine hours were emphasized, or the bracing qualities of the Scarborough air, while the pines at Bournemouth were reputed to help those suffering from lung complaints. Seaside resorts on the Continent also gained in popularity and began to develop their own social images – Scheveningen near the Hague, Ostend, Biarritz and Deauville offered the same magic for British holiday-makers as the Mediterranean resorts were to provide a century later. Some overseas resorts flourished in reaction to middle-class morality in Victorian England; Monte Carlo, with its notorious gambling casino, was a case in point. This desire to escape from one's everyday environment was as symptomatic of nineteenth-century life as it was to become in the middle of the twentieth century. Of course, these destinations on the Continent were to attract only the relatively well off, and the railways produced the service to cater for these high-spend tourists. Trains such as the Blue Train, which entered service between Paris and the Côte d'Azure and Rome in 1883, and the Orient Express of the same year, operating from Paris to the Black Sea, provided unsurpassed levels of luxury for rail travellers on the Continent. Long-distance rail services became possible with the introduction of sleeping cars, invented in the USA by George Pullman in 1864 and introduced into Europe by the French Wagon-Lits company in 1869.

Other forms of holiday-making, opened up by the advent of the railways on the Continent, arose from the impact of the Romantic Movement of mid-Victorian England. The Rhine and the French Riviera benefited from their new-found romantic appeal, while the invigorating mountain air of Switzerland, combining the promise of better health with opportunities for strenuous outdoor activities, was already drawing tourists from Britain by the 1840s. Mountaineering became a popular pastime for the British in the 1860s, and was later spurred on by the introduction into Switzerland of skiing. The origins of skiing are lost in antiquity, but using skis as a sport is credited to a certain Bjorland Blom, Sheriff of Telemark in Norway, in the 1660s. By the beginning of the 1890s a number of individual British visitors to that country had transported the sport to Switzerland, while Mathias Zdardsky similarly brought skis to his native Austria in 1890. Sir Henry Lunn, the British travel entrepreneur, is credited with the commercialization of winter ski holidays in Switzerland, having organized packages to Chamonix before the end of the nineteenth century. The railways made their own contributions to these developments, but above all they encouraged the desire to travel by removing the hazards of foreign travel that had formerly existed for travellers journeying by road.

Steamships

Just as the technological developments of the early nineteenth century led to the development of railways on land, so was steam harnessed at sea to drive new generations of ships. Here, necessity was the mother of invention. Increasing trade worldwide, especially with North America, required Britain to develop faster, more reliable forms of communication by sea with the rest of the world. Although, as we have seen, ferry services were operating as early as 1761 between Brighton and Dieppe, the first regular commercial cross-Channel steamship service was introduced in 1821, on the Dover–Calais route. The railway companies were quick to recognize the importance of their links with these cross-Channel ferry operators, and by 1862 they had gained the right to own and operate steamships themselves. Soon after, control over the ferry companies was in

Figure 2.4 *Hindostan*, built in 1842, opened P&O's service between Suez and Calcutta in 1843. (*Courtesy P&O (The Peninsular and Oriental Steam Navigation Company)*)

220 days at a cost of some £200 – more than the average annual salary at the time.

The Suez Canal, opened in 1869, stimulated demand for P&O's services to India and beyond, as Britain's Empire looked eastwards. The global growth of shipping led, in the latter part of the century, to the formation of shipping conferences, which developed cartel-like agreements on fares and conditions applicable to the carriage of traffic. The aim of these agreements was to ensure year-round profitability in an unstable and seasonal market, but the result was to stifle competition by price, and eventually led to excess profits which were to be enjoyed by the shipping companies until the advent of airline competition in the mid-twentieth century.

the hands of the railways, which rapidly expanded the cross-Channel services.

Deep-sea services were introduced on routes to North America and the Far East; the Peninsular and Oriental Steam Navigation Company (later P&O) is credited with the first regular long-distance steamship service, beginning operations to India and the Far East in 1838. This company was soon followed by the Cunard Steamship Company which, with a lucrative mail contract, began regular services to the American continent in 1840. Britain, by being the first to establish regular deep-sea services of this kind, came to dominate the world's shipping in the second half of the century, although it was soon to be challenged by other leading industrial nations on the popular North American route. This prestigious and highly profitable route prospered not only from mail contracts but also due to the huge demand from passengers and freight as trade with the American continent expanded. Later, the passenger trade would be boosted by the flow of emigrants from Europe (especially Ireland) and a smaller but significant number of American visitors to Europe. Thomas Cook played his part in stimulating the package tour market to North America, taking the first group of tourists in 1866. In 1872, he went on to organize the first round-the-world tour, taking twelve clients for

Other late-nineteenth-century developments

As the Victorian era drew to a close, other social changes came into play. Continued enthusiasm for the healthy outdoor life coincided with the invention of the bicycle, and cycling holidays, aided by promotion from the Cyclists' Touring Club, which was founded in 1878, enjoyed immense popularity. This movement not only paved the way for later interest in outdoor activities on holiday, but may well have stimulated the appeal of the suntan as a status symbol of health and wealth, in marked contrast to the earlier association in Victorian minds of a fair complexion with gentility and breeding. The bicycle offered for the first time the opportunity for mobile rather than centred holidays, and gave a foretaste of the popularity of motoring holidays in the early years of the following century.

As tourism grew in the later years of the century, so the organizers of travel became established institutionally. Thomas Cook and Sir Henry Lunn (whose name is retained in the company Lunn Poly) are two of the best-known names of the period, but many other well-known companies became established at this time. Dean and Dawson appeared in 1871, the Polytechnic Touring Association (the other half of the Lunn Poly name) in the following year, and Frames Tours in 1881. In the United States, American Express (founded by, among others, Henry Wells and William Fargo of Wells Fargo fame) initiated money orders and traveller's cheques, although the company did not become involved in making holiday arrangements until early in the twentieth century.

Mention has already been made of the impact of photography on nineteenth-century travel. As the century drew to a close, the vogue for photography was accompanied by the cult of the guidebook. No British tourist venturing abroad would neglect to take a guidebook, and a huge variety of these soon became available on the market. Many were superficial and inaccurate, but the most popular and enduring of those published were those of John Murray, whose Hand-books appeared from 1837 onwards, and Karl Baedeker, who introduced his first guidebook (of the Rhine) in 1839. By the end of the century Baedeker had become firmly established as the leading publisher of guidebooks in Europe.

In this chapter we have seen how social and, in particular, technological change had begun to make mass travel feasible. In Chapter 3 we will see how contemporary mass tourism developed, with further advances in technology and, above all, improved standards of living throughout the developed world.

Questions and discussion points

1. What factors inhibited travel in the Middle Ages? Are there any similarities you can detect with factors that still inhibit travel at the beginning of the twenty-first century?

2. How successful do you think the reopening of the Bath spa will be? Will it enjoy the same benefits as spas on mainland Europe? Could other spas be similarly rejuvenated in Britain? What form of support should government, local authorities or other bodies offer which would help to regenerate the use of spas? Explain why spas in Britain have fallen into disuse, while those on the Continent remain popular.

3. What differences and similarities can you find between modern tourism and travels of the earlier Greeks and Romans? Are there lessons for twenty-first-century tourists that can be learned from these early travellers?

4. History reveals many examples of adaptation by entrepreneurs to changing tourist needs and circumstances. Discuss what changes will be necessary to allow entrepreneurs to meet the needs of present-day tourists.

Assignment topics

1. Prepare a set of notes, and deliver a talk, on either the Grand Tour or the spas in Britain. The research for these notes should have a complete and properly constructed bibliography (use the bibliography at the back of this book as a guide for the correct presentation of a bibliography). Draw on some verbatim comments from the research material to enliven your talk.

2. Write a short article (about 800 words) for your local newspaper which argues that travel in earlier times was more exciting and rewarding than travel today.

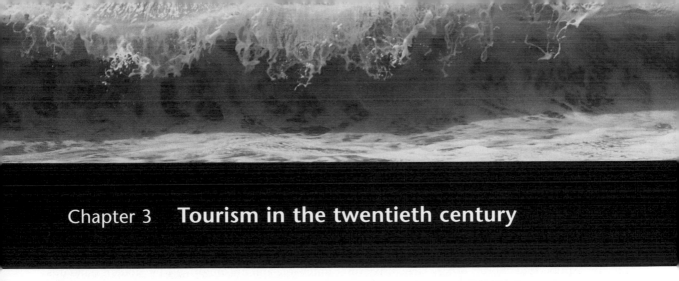

Chapter 3   Tourism in the twentieth century

Objectives

After studying this chapter, you should be able to:

- describe the growth of the mass tourism movement;
- explain the origins and development of the package holiday;
- analyse the factors influencing travel in the twentieth century and up to the present day.

The first fifty years

The origins of mass tourism

In the opening years of the twentieth century, travel continued to expand, encouraged by the increasing wealth, curiosity and outgoing attitudes of the post-Victorian population, and by the steady improvement in transport. Travellers had become safer from disease and physical attack, mainland Europe was relatively stable politically, and documentation for British travellers uncomplicated – since 1860, passports had generally not been required for travel to any European country. The popularity of French Riviera resorts as places for wealthier British visitors to spend the winter is evidenced by the fact that immediately before World War I some 50,000 UK tourists are estimated to have been wintering on the coast.

Disastrous though it was, the Great War proved to be only a brief hiatus in the expansion of travel, although it led to the widespread introduction of passports for nationals of many countries. The prosperity which soon returned to Europe in the 1920s, coupled with large-scale migration, meant unsurpassed demand for travel across the Atlantic, as well as within Europe. The first-hand experience of foreign countries by combatants during the war aroused a sense of curiosity about foreign travel generally among less well-off sectors of the community for the first time. These sectors were also influenced by the new forms of mass communication which developed after the war – the cinema, radio and ultimately television, all of which educated the population and encouraged an interest in seeing more of the world.

Forms of travel also began to change radically after the war. The railways went into a period of steady decline, following the introduction of the motor car. Motorized public road transport and improved roads led to the era of the charabanc – at first, adapted from army surplus lorries and equipped with benches to provide a rudimentary form of coach. These vehicles achieved immense popularity in the 1920s for outings to the seaside, but their poor safety record soon resulted in licensing regulations governing road transport. For those who could afford superior public transportation, more luxurious coaches also made an appearance. Coach company Motorways offered Pullman coaches, generally accommodating fifteen people in comfortable armchairs with tables, buffet bars and toilets. These coaches operated to many parts of Europe and North Africa, were used on safaris in East and Central Africa, and even provided a twice weekly service between London and Nice, taking a relaxing five to six days for the trip.

However, it was the freedom of independent travel offered by the private motor car which contributed most to the decline of the railways' monopoly on holiday transport. The extensive use of the motor car for holidaying has its origins in the United States, where, in 1908, Henry Ford introduced his popular Model T at a price which brought the motor car within reach of the masses. By the 1920s, private motoring was a popular pastime for the middle classes in Britain, and the threat to domestic rail services was clear, although Continental rail services survived and prospered until challenged by the coming of the airlines. In an effort to stem the decline, domestic rail services in Britain were first rationalized in 1921 into four major companies – the London, Midland and Scottish Railway (LMS), the London and North Eastern Railway (LNER), the Great Western Railway (GWR) and the Southern Railway (SR) – and later nationalized following World War II, remaining under public control until again privatized in the mid-1990s.

The arrival of the airline industry signalled the beginning of the end, not only for long-distance rail services but, more decisively, for the great steamship companies. British shipping lines had been under increasing threat from foreign competition throughout the 1920s, with French, German and US liners challenging British supremacy on the North Atlantic routes particularly. The first commercial air routes were initiated as early as 1919 within Europe. The infant air services were expensive (nearly £16 between London and Paris, equivalent to several weeks' average earnings) and uncertain (passengers were warned that forced landings and delays could occur). It was therefore many years before air services achieved the reliability and low price which would make them competitive with world shipping routes. Pan American Airways introduced transatlantic air services in the 1930s (initially using flying boats), but in addition to their expense the aircraft proved unreliable and uncomfortable by modern standards, and long-distance journeys necessitated frequent stopovers. In the early years, commercial aviation was more important for its mail-carrying potential than for the carriage of passengers. Only with the technological breakthroughs in aircraft design achieved during and after World War II did air services prove a viable alternative to shipping for intercontinental travel.

The arrival of the holiday camp

Among the major tourism developments of the 1930s, the creation of the holiday camp deserves a special mention. Aimed at the growing low-income market for holidays, the camps set new standards of comfort, offering 24-hour entertainment at an all-inclusive price, were efficient in operation and included child-minding services – a huge bonus for young couples on holiday with their children. This was in marked contrast to the lack of planned activities and the often surly service offered by the traditional seaside boarding houses of the day.

The origin of these camps goes back to early experiments by organizations such as the Co-operative Holidays Association, the Workers' Travel Association and the Holiday Fellowship (although summer camps for boys such as that run by Joseph Cunningham on the Isle of Man have been dated as early as 1887). However, their popularity and widespread acceptance by the public have commonly been ascribed to the efforts and promotional flair of Billy (later Sir Billy) Butlin. Supposedly Butlin, who

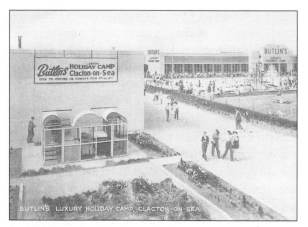

Figure 3.1 The early days of the holiday camp: Butlin's luxury holiday camp at Clacton-on-Sea, 1940s. (*Courtesy Butlins*)

The popular movement to the seaside

In spite of the rising appeal of holidays abroad, mass tourism between the wars and in the early post-World War II era remained largely domestic. This period saw the seaside holiday become firmly established as the traditional annual holiday destination for the mass of the British public. Suntans were for the first time seen as a status symbol, allied to health and time for leisure. Blackpool, Scarborough, Southend and Brighton consolidated their positions as leading resorts, while numerous newer resorts – Bournemouth, Broadstairs, Clacton, Skegness, Colwyn Bay – grew rapidly in terms of both visitors and residential population. Until the Great Depression of the 1930s, hotels and guesthouses proliferated in these resorts. The tradition of the family holiday, taken annually over two weeks in the summer, became firmly established in Britain at this time.

built his first camp at Skegness in 1936, met a group of disconsolate holiday-makers huddled in a bus shelter to avoid the rain on a wet summer afternoon. It is thought he was also influenced by a visit to Trusville Holiday Village in Mablethorpe, Lincolnshire, which had been opened and operated successfully by Albert Henshaw since 1924. Butlin determined to build a camp with all-weather facilities, for an all-in price. The instant success of the concept led to a spate of similar camps built by Butlin and other entrepreneurs such as Harry Warner and Fred Pontin in the pre-war and early post-war years. On the Continent, pre-war Germany had introduced the concept of the highly organized and often militaristic health and recreation camp which enabled many to enjoy holidays who would otherwise have been unable to afford them.

In France, the *villages de vacance* arose from similar political and social influences. The success of this concept of all-in entertainment was later to be copied by hotels, and the hotel with its leisure complex became a popular development in the United States even before the war.

Interest in outdoor holidays and healthy recreation was also stimulated by the Youth Hostels Association in 1929 (the French equivalent opened in the same year), which provided budget accommodation for young people away from home.

The growing threat of competition from the European mainland was already apparent, for those who chose to take note of it. From the 1920s onwards, the Mediterranean Riviera had begun to attract a summer, as well as a winter, market from the UK, while the resorts of northern France were seen as cheaper and began to offer competition for the popular south coast resorts of Brighton, Hove, Folkestone and Eastbourne. These nearby French resorts, however, were seen primarily as places for short summer holidays, rather than the longer winter stays which had been popular with wealthy British clientele in the nineteenth century.

The growth of government involvement

It was in this period that Britain experienced the first stirrings of government interest in the tourism business. Britain was well behind other European countries in this respect; Switzerland, for example, had long recognized the importance of its inbound tourism and was actively involved in both tourism promotion overseas and gathering statistics on its visitors.

The British Travel and Holidays Association was established by the government in 1929, but with the theme 'travel for peace', its role was seen as essentially promotional, and its impact on the industry relatively light, until a change in status some forty years later. By the outbreak of World War II in 1939, the British government had at least recognized the potential contribution tourism could make to the country's balance of payments; equally, it had recognized the importance of holidays to the health and efficiency of the nation's workforce. The French government had already introduced holidays with pay in 1936; publication of the Amulree Report in 1938 led to the first Holidays with Pay Act for Britain in the same year. This encouraged voluntary agreements on paid holidays and generated the idea of a two-week paid holiday for all workers. Although this ambition was not fulfilled until several years after the end of World War II, by the outbreak of war some 11 million of the 19 million workforce were entitled to paid holidays – a key factor in generating mass travel.

Tourism since World War II

The aviation industry and the post-war desire for travel

As had occurred after World War I, World War II also led to an increased interest in overseas travel, arising from a desire to see the sites of such battles as those fought on the Normandy beaches and at St Nazaire. The extensive theatre of war had introduced combatants not only to new countries but to new continents, generating new friendships and an interest in diverse cultures. Another outcome of the war, which was radically to change the travel business, was the advance in aircraft technology which was soon to lead to a viable commercial aviation industry for the first time. With the ending of the war in 1945, the first land-based commercial transatlantic flight took place between New York and Bournemouth, calling at Boston, Gander and Shannon. This flight, oper-

ated by American Overseas Airlines using a Douglas DC4, served to point the way ahead, although cost and the time involved, necessitated by the frequent stops, ensured that long-haul flights would not become popular for some time.

The surplus of aircraft in the immediate post-war years, a benevolent political attitude towards the growth of private sector airlines, and the appearance on the scene of air travel entrepreneurs like Harold Bamberg (of Eagle Airways) and Freddie Laker aided the rapid expansion of air travel after the war. But more significantly for the potential market, aircraft had become more comfortable, safer, faster and, in spite of relatively high prices in the early 1950s, steadily cheaper by comparison with other forms of transport. Commercial jet services began with the ill-fated Comet aircraft in the early 1950s, but already by that time advances in piston-engine technology had ensured that air travel prices would fall substantially. With the introduction of the commercially successful Boeing 707 jet in 1958, the age of air travel for the masses had arrived, hastening the demise of the great ocean liners. The number of passengers crossing the Atlantic by air exceeded those by sea for the first time in 1957, and although the liners continued to operate across the Atlantic for a further decade, their increasingly uncompetitive costs and the length of the journey time resulted in declining load factors from one year to the next. The new jets, with average speeds of 800–1,000 kph, compared with older propeller-driven aircraft travelling at a mere 400 kph, meant that an air traveller could reach a far more distant destination within a given time. This was particularly valuable for business journeys where time was crucial.

The early 1970s saw the arrival of the first supersonic passenger aircraft, the Anglo-French Concorde. Never truly a commercial success (the government wrote off the huge development costs), it nevertheless proved popular with business travellers and the wealthy. Travelling from London or Paris to New York in three and a half hours, it allowed business people for the first time to complete their business on the other side of the Atlantic and return home without a hotel stopover. The limited range and carrying capacity (100 passengers) of the aircraft, and restrictions against sonic booms over land, acted as severe constraints on operable routes, and the fatal crash near Paris of a chartered Concorde in 2000 led to the withdrawal of the aircraft for an undetermined (at the time of writing) period. It is unlikely that any further supersonic aircraft development will take place for at least twenty years.

The development of the package tour

The package tour depends upon the ability of tour operators to charter aircraft for their clientele, in order to drive down prices. The purchase of new jets by the large airlines left a large supply of good, second-hand propeller-driven aircraft, which were often purchased cheaply by smaller companies to undertake charter operations. These were able for the first time to transport holiday tourists to Mediterranean destinations both faster than, and almost as cheaply as, trains and coaches. These new charter services soon proved highly profitable. Initially, government policy ensured that charters were restricted to troop movements, but as official policy became more lenient, the private operators sought new forms of charter traffic. The package holiday business resulted from cooperation between these carriers and entrepreneurs in the travel business. Although there are instances of charter flights as early as the 1920s (Thomas Cook, for example, had organized an escorted charter, believed to be the first, to take fans from New York to Chicago in 1927 to see the Dempsey–Tunney heavyweight title fight), and the National Union of Students is known to have been organizing charter flights for its members as early as 1949, Vladimir Raitz is generally credited with establishing the mass charter air movement as we know it today. In 1950, under the Horizon Holidays banner, he organized an experimental package holiday trip using a charter flight to Corsica. By chartering the aircraft and filling every seat instead of committing himself to a block of seats on sched-

uled air services, he was able to reduce significantly the unit cost of his air transport and hence the overall price to his customers. He carried only 300 passengers in the first year, but repeated the experiment the following year and was soon operating profitably. His idea was copied by other budding tour operators, and by the early 1960s the package holiday to the Mediterranean had become an established product for the mass holiday market. While the Spanish coastline and the Balearic islands received the greatest proportion of these tourists, Italy, Greece and other Mediterranean coastal regions all benefited by the 'rush to the sun'. Other northern European countries were also soon setting up their own package holiday arrangements to the Mediterranean, and began to compete with Britain for accommodation along the Mediterranean coast. In Denmark, Pastor Eilif Krogager conducted a group of package tourists by coach to Spain in 1950, using the name of his village, Tjaereborg, as the company name. In 1962, Tjaereborg Travel moved into the air charter market with the formation of Sterling Airways, which was to become western Europe's largest privately owned charter airline.

In Britain, difficulties in the economy forced the government to impose ever stricter control over the purchase of foreign currency. By the late 1960s the foreign travel allowance had been cut to only £50 per person. There was, however, a silver lining to this particular cloud: it encouraged people to take package holidays rather than travel independently, and the industry continued to flourish. The limits were relaxed from 1970 onwards, and with further liberalization of air transport regulations, and longer paid holidays, which encouraged a growing number of tourists to take a second holiday abroad each year, a new winter holiday market emerged in the 1970s. Through the more even spread of package holidays throughout the year, operators found that they were able to reduce their unit costs still further, and package holiday prices continued to fall, boosting off-season demand. It should be recognized, however, that Britain was not alone within Europe in imposing currency restrictions during these years; indeed,

Figure 3.2 A wide-bodied jumbo jet. (*Permission of British Airways and Adrian Meredith Aviation Photography*)

exchange controls were not totally abolished in France until as recently as 1990.

A further technological breakthrough in air transport occurred in 1970, when the first wide-bodied jets (Boeing 747s), capable of carrying over 400 passengers, appeared in service. The unit cost per seat fell sharply, and the result was an increased supply of seats at potentially cheaper fares. This innovation meant that once again the aviation industry had to unload cheaply a number of obsolescent, although completely airworthy, smaller aircraft, and these were quickly pressed into service for charter operations.

The movement to the sun

By the 1960s, it was clear that the future of mass market leisure travel was to be a north–south movement, from the cool and variable climates of North America and northern Europe, where the mass of relatively well-off people lived, to the sunshine and warmth of the temperate to tropical lands in the southern part of the northern hemisphere (see Figure 3.3). These southern countries were also for the most part less developed economically, and offered low-cost opportunities for the formation of a tourism industry. The new breed of tourism entrepreneurs involved with packaging tours recognized this trend

very early on. Major hotel corporations, too, were quick to seize the opportunities for growth in these countries, and chains such as Sheraton and Hyatt in the USA quickly expanded into Mexico and the Caribbean, as well as into Florida and Hawaii, the states offering the most attractive climates for tourism development. In Europe, British and German tour operators such as Thomson and TUI developed bulk inclusive tours to the Mediterranean and North Africa, and with increasing volume were able to charter jumbo jets for the first time, bringing prices still lower. As transport costs fell, operators were able to attract a mass market for long-haul travel on chartered jumbo jets. Florida, boosted particularly by the attractions of Disney World and Miami Beach, has become almost as popular a destination for Europeans as the major Mediterranean destinations.

The expert packaging of these tours has been extended to many other types of destinations in the past twenty years. Tours to cultural and heritage sites, to capital cities such as London, Paris, Rome or Brussels, and river cruises on the Rhine or Danube have all been efficiently packaged and sold to the northern European market. The result was that by the end of the 1960s, some 2.5 million Britons were taking packaged holidays abroad each year. By the end of the 1980s, this had grown to over 11 million, with over 70 per cent of the British population having been abroad on holiday at least once in their lives.

Other trends in the flow of international tourism are also evident. There is, for example, a strong north–south movement in the flow of Japanese tourists to Australia. While the expansion of Japanese tourism generally is noteworthy, and most European countries have benefited from this, travel time to Australia is shorter and, equally important, because the travel is largely within the same longitude there is no time change or jet lag to face. With typically only eight days of holiday, avoidance of jet lag becomes an attractive bonus for the market, and makes Australia doubly attractive to the Japanese. Absence of jet lag also promises to accelerate tourism to South Africa from the European nations, provid-

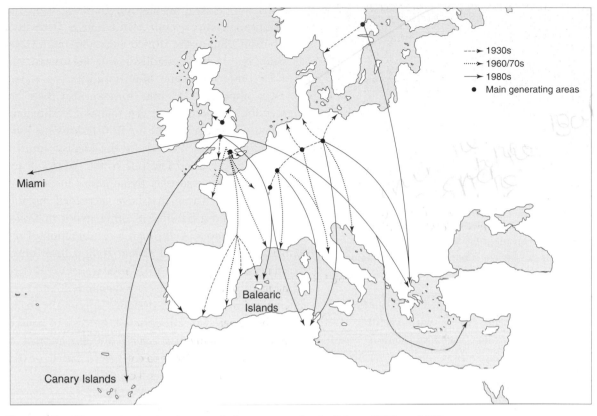

Figure 3.3 Changes in destination trends for mass-market holidays, 1930s to 1980s

ing that the twin threats of growing crime and political disturbance can be overcome.

Destinations in the Pacific are beginning to attract Europeans in significant numbers, and have long attracted the Japanese and Australian markets. However, a large proportion of these visitors use the Pacific islands as stopover points for a night or two, rather than as a holiday base. The impact of technology can be seen when for the first time aircraft became capable of flying direct between the USA and Sydney, with the introduction of the Boeing 747-400SP aircraft. Tahiti, slightly off the direct route between these continents and long established as an attractive stop-over point but expensive for longer holidays, immediately suffered a sharp decline in visitors as the airlines concentrated their promotion on direct services between Los Angeles and Sydney or Auckland.

Identikit destinations

The net result of these developments in tourism for the mass markets has been the establishment of destinations for particular market segments which, in all but their location, are very often remarkably similar. A convention centre, for example, may contain a conference building which may be usable for other purposes, with committee/lecture rooms, modern single or twin bedded hotel rooms with private facilities, restaurants with banqueting rooms, bars, exhibition space, indoor and outdoor sports facilities and good scheduled transport links. The location may be Portsmouth, Basel or Rio – once inside their hotel or conference centre, delegates may not even notice where they are.

The larger the mass market, the less distinctive destinations are likely to be, especially if the destination

Figure 3.4 An Identikit destination: the Mediterranean beach. (*Courtesy Thomson Holidays*)

is small and recently developed. One can find newly built 'marina' type resorts with yachting basins, hotel/apartment/villa accommodation, similar restaurants, cafes and shops, and golf, tennis, watersports, folk singers and barbecue nights in any one of a dozen countries around the Mediterranean, the Caribbean, North Africa and the South Pacific. These 'Identikit' destinations are the result of comprehensive market research among various generating markets to find products with guaranteed mass demand. They may be compared with the piecemeal development of resorts two or three generations ago which may have had purely local or domestic attractions.

Not all destinations are similar, of course. While many may be 'down-market' in their attraction – that is, they may offer cheap tourism to a large number of people, with the image of great popularity – others may offer an up-market Identikit image, allegedly offering higher quality and thus more expensive services to fewer people. So in the former category we may think of Benidorm, Magaluf, Benitses in the Mediterranean, Miami Beach in Florida, or Seefeld in Austria, while in the latter category we may think of Tahiti, Fiji, Malindi in Kenya, or Barbados. Many Identikit destinations have been developed through the activities of multinational tour companies such

as the all-inclusive resorts run by Sandals in the Caribbean, France's Club Méditerranée, Germany's Robinson Club or the United States' Sheraton Hotel chain. Within their establishments the tourist will find a comforting degree of uniformity.

It is important to note, however, that there are exceptions to the rule of the Identikit destination, particularly in the field of the British domestic holiday resort. Recent research by the English Tourism Council has revealed that one of the failings of the English seaside resorts is their failure to project a unique image. Those that have succeeded, notably Blackpool and a handful of other major or minor resorts, have done so through a combination of significant investment and differentiation from other, often similar, resorts.

Mass tourism has therefore demanded, and been supplied with, products designed specifically for its needs as revealed through the process of market research, i.e. products which are *user-oriented* as opposed to *resource-oriented* (that is, based on the resources available at a destination).

Private motoring and holidays

After a slow post-war recovery, standards of living rose steadily in the 1950s and after. Many people could consider buying a motor car for the first time, even if it were second-hand. For the first time, the holiday masses had the freedom to take to the roads as a family in their own private car, and the popular routes between London and the resorts on the south coast were soon clogged, in these pre-motorway days, with weekend traffic.

The flexibility which the car offered could not be matched by public transport services, and both bus and rail lost the holiday traveller. In 1950 some two out of every three holiday-makers took the train for their holidays in Britain. This fell to one in seven by 1970. In this period, private car ownership in Britain rose from 2 million to over 11 million vehicles, while by the end of the 1980s it had risen to some 20 million.

This trend led in turn to a growth in camping and caravanning holidays. Ownership of private caravans stood at nearly 800,000 by the end of the 1980s (excluding static caravans in parks), while 13 million holiday-makers in the UK took their holidays in a caravan. This development has been a cause for some concern, however; the benefits to a region of private caravan tourism are considerably less than most other forms of tourism (owners can bring most of their own food with them, and do not require accommodation), while caravans tend to clog the holiday routes in summer. Both mobile caravans and static caravans on site are something of an eyesore, too.

The switch to private transport led to new forms of accommodation to cater for this form of travel. Britain saw the development of its first motels, modelled on the American pattern, the contemporary version of the staging inn catering for transit passengers. The construction of a new network of motorways, and other road improvements, brought the more distant resorts closer to centres of population, in some cases changing both the nature of the market served and the image of the resort itself. The ever resourceful tour operators met the private car threat to package holidays by devising more flexible packages such as fly-drive programmes. Hotels, too, spurred on by the need to fill their rooms off-peak, devised their own programmes of short-stay holidays tailored to the needs of the private motorist. Demand for hire cars abroad rose, as the overseas holiday-maker was emboldened to move away from the hotel ghettos, and the car rental business benefited accordingly.

The shipping business in the post-war period

In the passenger shipping business, hit by rising prices and competition from the airlines, shipping companies were gradually forced to abandon their traditional liner routes in the 1960s. Some companies attempted to adapt their vessels for cruising, though not entirely successfully; vessels pur-pose-built for long-distance fast deep-sea voyages are not ideally suited for cruising, either economically or from the standpoint of customer demand. Many were incapable of anchoring alongside docks in the shallow waters of popular cruise destinations such as the Caribbean. Companies that failed to embark on a programme of new construction, either due to lack of resources or lack of foresight, soon ceased trading. Others, such as the Cunard Line, were taken over by conglomerates outside the travel or transport industries. However, many new purpose-built cruise liners, of Greek, Norwegian and later Russian registry soon appeared on the market to fill the gaps left by the declining maritime powers. These vessels, in spite of their registry, were to be based primarily in the Caribbean or Mediterranean waters. British shipping was not entirely without innovations at this time, however; Cunard initiated the fly-cruise concept in the 1960s, with vessels based at Gibraltar and Naples, where passengers flew out to join their cruise in chartered aircraft.

If the rapid escalation of fuel and other costs during the 1970s threatened the whole future of deep-sea shipping, the ferry services by contrast achieved quite exceptional levels of growth from the 1950s onward. This largely resulted from the increased demand from private motorists taking their cars abroad, influencing particularly routes between Scandinavian countries and Germany, and between Britain and Continental Europe. Growth in demand was also better spread across the seasons, enabling vessels to be in service throughout the year with respectable load factors (although freight demand substantially boosted weak passenger revenue in the winter period). Regular sailings, with fast turnarounds in port, encouraged bookings, and costs were kept down by offering much more restricted levels of service than would be expected on long-distance routes. Hovercraft and jetfoil services were introduced across the Channel, although their success was limited by technical problems and their withdrawal in rough weather.

Government policy in the mass market era

In Britain, the end of the 1960s was marked by a new direction in government policy towards tourism, with the introduction of the 1969 Development of Tourism Act. This Act, the first in the country specifically and uniquely devoted to tourism, established a new framework for public sector tourism, which took into account the industry's growing importance to the British economy. For the first time, also, conservation became an issue, as the number of foreign visitors to Britain leapt. The former laissez-faire attitude of successive governments gave way to recognition of the need for adequate planning and control in order to balance supply and demand, to maintain the quality of the tourist product, and to safeguard consumers' rights. Thus, tour operators became licensed by the government for the first time in the 1970s, and government incentives were introduced for the construction of hotels and other tourist facilities. The first serious efforts were made to categorize and register the accommodation sector, although resistance by hoteliers eventually led to a voluntary form of registration only. The failures of public sector planning and control in other countries (notably Spain) where exceptionally high growth rates in visitors were recorded, added fuel to the government's concern.

By the 1980s, however, the Conservative government's attitude to tourism had shifted to passive encouragement rather than active financial support. Grants provided under the terms of the 1969 Act were discontinued in England, and policy became one of encouraging partnerships between the private and public sectors. This policy has been continued under the Labour government which took office in 1997. Responsibility for tourism was in turn transferred, first from the Department of Trade and Industry to the Department of Employment, and then in 1992 to the newly created Department of National Heritage. In 1997, following the Labour victory in the elections, this department's name was changed to the Department for Culture, Media and Sport, within which a Minister for Film and Tourism reports to the Secretary of State. Some efforts were made to coordinate the various government departments' interests in tourism through the establishment of committees such as the Inter-Departmental Tourism Coordinating Committee. On the whole, however, the government adopted a 'market forces' and hands-off approach to tourism development, and increasingly by the end of the 1980s people were looking towards the European Union (EU) for legislation governing the industry. The EU responded through the introduction of a number of measures designed to liberalize air and road transport, to harmonize hotel classification, to ease frontier controls and to harmonize sales tax and duty-free regulations throughout the EU. Most importantly, from the standpoint of the consumer, however, were measures aimed at providing greater protection for the traveller buying package holidays. These measures will be discussed at greater length in Chapter 15.

The growing importance of business travel

The growth in world trade in these decades saw a steady expansion in business travel, individually and in the conference and incentive travel fields, although the recession of the late 1980s and early 1990s caused cutbacks in business travel as sharp as those in leisure travel. As economic power shifted between countries, so emerging nations provided new patterns of tourism generation: in the 1970s, Japan and the oil-rich nations of the Middle East led the growth, while in the 1980s, countries such as Korea and Malaysia expanded both inbound and outbound business tourism dramatically.

Today, business travel of all kinds is of immense importance to the tourism industry, not least because the per capita revenue from the business traveller greatly exceeds that of the leisure traveller. Motivational factors involving business travel are discussed in Chapter 5, but here it must be stressed that business travel often complements leisure travel, to spread the effects of tourism more evenly in the economy. A major factor is that business travellers are not generally travelling to areas that are favoured by leisure travellers; business people have to go to locations where they are to conduct business, and this generally means city centres, often in cities that have little to attract the leisure tourist. Travel also takes place all year round, with little peaking, and hotel demand occurs between Mondays and Fridays, encouraging the more attractively situated hotels to target the leisure market on weekends. Often, spouses will travel to accompany the business traveller, and their leisure needs will have to be taken into consideration; thus, in practice it is very hard to distinguish between business and leisure tourism, especially in terms of spend.

Although business travel is more price inelastic than leisure travel, efforts to cut costs in the world of business today are ensuring that the business traveller no longer spends as freely as formerly. Fewer business travellers now travel first class or business class on airlines, less expensive hotels are booked and there is even a trend to travel on weekends to reduce prices. Companies are buying many more tourism products, particularly air tickets, through the Internet, where they can shop around for the cheapest tickets, and budget carriers are attracting a growing proportion of their business from these travellers. These changes are not seen as short-term trends, and in future any distinction between the two major tourist markets is likely to become less apparent.

The conference and incentive travel business

Conferences and formal meetings have become very important to the tourism industry, both nationally and internationally, with rapid growth each year since the 1960s. The British conference market alone is responsible for the organization of some 700,000 individual conferences each year, the very large majority lasting just one or two days, and as most of these are held in hotels this market is vital to the accommodation sector. Major conferences, such as that of the American Bar Association, which accounts

for up to 25,000 delegates each year travelling all over the world (the 2000 conference was held in London), have a huge impact on all sectors of the industry, from hotels to the destination itself, which will benefit from expenditure in shops, theatres, nightclubs and other centres of amusement. To serve the needs of the largest conferences, international conference centres seating up to 5,000 or more delegates have been built in major cities such as London and Berlin, but the number of conferences of this size is inevitably limited, and the competition to attract them intense. The logistics of organizing these and other major events are generally in the hands of professional events organizers, most of which in Britain will belong to the Association of Conference Executives (ACE). As international conferences generally have English as the common language (although simultaneous translations are always available where necessary), countries like Britain and the USA greatly benefit from this market.

Exhibitions also account for another form of business travel. Major international exhibitions can be traced at least as far back as the Great Exhibition, held at Crystal Palace in London in 1851, and World Fairs have become common events in major cities around the globe as a means of attracting visitors and publicizing a nation's culture and products. Many national events are now organized on an annual basis, some requiring little more than a field and marquees or other temporary structures – the Royal Bath & West agricultural show being one example of a major outdoor attraction, held annually in the UK's West Country. As these events have grown and become more professionally organized, so have they, too, become an important element in the business of tourism.

The all-inclusive holiday

Mention has already been made of the trend to *all-inclusive* holidays. As the term indicates, this holiday includes everything – food, alcoholic drinks, watersports and other entertainment at the hotel. The attractions of this form of tourism are obvious – it is seen by tourists as offering better value, because they can pay up front for the holiday, know what their budget will be well in advance, and be unconcerned about changes in the value of foreign currency, or the need to take large sums of money abroad. For the more timid foreign traveller, or those who are concerned about being badgered by local souvenir sellers and 'beach salesmen', there is the added reassurance that they do not even have to leave the hotel complex to enjoy their holidays. However, there are clearly serious implications for the local economy, as local bars, shopkeepers and others no longer stand to benefit from the influx of tourists, while greater profits flow back to the operators in generating countries who control the leisure site. This form of tourism may be judged far removed from the concept of sustainable tourism, although operators themselves would argue that by keeping tourists in 'ghettos' they are in fact helping to reduce the negative impact of tourism on locals.

This form of tourism originated in the Caribbean, and up-market tour operators such as Sandals have promoted these programmes very successfully to the US and European markets. However, the concept later moved down-market and became popular in the more traditional European resorts such as those of the Balearic Islands. Further expansion is seen as a direct threat to the livelihood of many in the traditional coastal resorts.

Factors influencing changes in tourism demand

It is fitting to complete this chapter by recognizing that patterns of demand in tourism are affected by two distinct sets of factors. First, we have factors which cannot be predetermined or forecast, but which influence changes sometimes with very little advance warning. The second set of factors will include cultural, social and technological changes going on in society, many of which can be forecast and for which there is time to adapt tourism products to meet new needs and expectations.

In the first category we must include changes influenced by economic or political circumstances, climate and natural or artificial disasters. Some of these we have touched on earlier in this text, and economic influences will be examined more thoroughly in the following chapter. It will be salutary to look at just some of the factors which have produced swings in demand for foreign tourism in recent years.

In 1997, Hong Kong ceased to be a British colony, and was handed over to the Chinese administration. Uncertainty about the effect of this change led to a sharp slump in sales to that destination. Kenya suffered in the same year from short-term fears of disturbances in the run-up to an election, while in the longer term the emergence of a more virulent and vaccine-resistant form of malaria was discouraging tourists. The Asian financial crisis that summer reduced travel from the Far East, but actually encouraged some westerners to travel to the region to benefit from better exchange rates. At the same time, forest fires in the region, particularly in Indonesia, caused widespread smog throughout the Far East and dissuaded other westerners from travelling. A strong pound within Europe increased demand for short-haul travel from Britain to Spain and Greece, but travel to the United States fell by 4 per cent as the dollar strengthened against the pound. Volcanic eruption in Montserrat in 1997/98 virtually terminated the market for tourism to that country for the next three years. Also in the Caribbean, an outbreak of food poisoning and other health and hygiene fears in the Dominican Republic saw the burgeoning tourism market to that island collapse. Bad weather throughout the summer in Britain in 1998 boosted foreign bookings not only for that year, but also for the following year – a common 'lead-lag indicator', as people expect similar weather at home in the following year.

Of these factors, only the handover of Hong Kong was predictable in advance, and even in that case the consequences for tourism could not be known. The lesson for the industry is to be prepared for change, often at very short notice, and to build up an organization and products which are flexible and adaptable to new circumstances.

Changes in society are easier to predict, as are long-term trends in travel patterns. All too often, however, the industry has been slow to respond to these indicators. We know, for example, that only one family in four in the UK now conforms to the stereotypical family of two parents and two children, and that increasing numbers of people are living alone or bringing up children as single parents, yet demand for single accommodation is often difficult to meet and the 'untypical' composition of families is not welcomed by operators whose pricing structure may weigh unfairly against such tourists. Travellers of all kinds are more sophisticated and demanding, often being more familiar with world travel destinations and attractions than those selling the products. This produces a new kind of challenge for professional service which the industry is still a long way from meeting. Children particularly are exercising much more influence in travel decisions, and are tending to travel more with friends than in the traditional family group. Other changes come about through changes in individual behaviour of tourists, and these will also be examined in the closing paragraphs of this chapter.

There are many other clear trends in the industry in the opening years of the twenty-first century for which suppliers and agents must learn to cater. Greater choice in consumer purchasing of all kinds is leading to demand for more flexible packages of differing durations; many will require tailor-made approaches to packaging, and companies are establishing divisions specifically for this purpose. This, however, is more labour intensive, and requires greater product knowledge.

The mass demand for passive beach holidays is giving way to demand for more active holidays of all kinds, even from those in the upper age brackets among tourists. Special interest holidays now cater for the widening range of interests of a leisure-oriented society. Young people are seeking greater thrills from their adventure holidays, and hang-gliding, power-gliding, bungee jumping and sundry other thrill holidays are becoming commonplace. Adventure holidays, both domestic and foreign, are now widely packaged by operators and appeal to a wide range of markets.

In the latter years of the last century tour operators attempted to gain market share by cutting prices and making budget offers which often fell below the quality levels anticipated by consumers. Selling on price rather than quality became the keynote for the industry. Consumers were encouraged to buy on price and seek out the cheapest. Inevitably the rising toll of complaints forced companies to reconsider value for money and quality assurance, although deep discounting remains the bugbear of the industry, both for traditional package tours and for the cruise market.

In the format of package tours, we find demand

Figure 3.5 The linear tour: an example of the 'milk run' around Britain

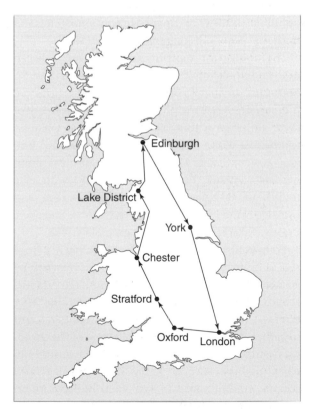

moving in two distinct directions. On the one hand, self-catering has become increasingly popular, partly as a cost-saving exercise but equally as a means of overcoming the constraints imposed by package holidays in general and the accommodation sector in particular. Set meals at set times gave way to 'eat what you please, where you please, when you please'. In reply, the package tour industry provided the product to meet this need: the French *gîte* holidays became popular and across southern Europe self-catering villas and apartments flourished, while in the UK demand moved from resort hotels and guesthouses to self-catering flats. Hundreds of thousands of Britons invested in time-share property in order to own their own 'place in the sun', or increasingly found their own accommodation abroad, while the operators provided 'seat-only' packages on charter aircraft to cater for their transport needs.

The other side of the coin is reflected in the growth in demand for all-inclusive holidays, which we looked at earlier in this chapter. This particular type of holiday is likely to experience continuing demand both for short- and long-haul destinations.

The market for short-break holidays of between one and three nights has also expanded rapidly, becoming frequently an addition to the principal holiday. The UK industry has benefited, as many of these are taken within the UK, helping to make up for the loss of the traditional two-week summer holiday at the seaside. The choice in short-break destinations abroad has also widened, with the traditional destinations of Paris, Amsterdam and Brussels being joined by Barcelona, Rome, Budapest, Prague, Cracow, Reykjavik and even New York.

Long-haul traffic in particular has shown a huge rise as growing disposable incomes are matched by ever-reducing air fares, especially across the Atlantic. Holidays to Florida and other parts of the USA boomed, and in spite of the hygiene worries referred to earlier, the Dominican Republic, one of the cheapest destinations in the Caribbean, also continues to enjoy popular success. Many holiday-makers still seeking a traditional sun, sea, sand holiday are no longer content merely to lie on the beaches of the Mediterranean, but are travelling as far afield as Pattaya Beach and Phuket in Thailand, Goa in India and Mombasa in Kenya.

The importance of the 'grey panther' market is finally being recognized by the industry, as the growing market of over-50s spend increasing sums on international travel. In Britain, this group now represent a third of the British population, and holds 80 per cent of the national wealth and 60 per cent of the savings. In addition, they receive £6 billion in inheritance every year, a windfall seen as very attractive to the tourism industry. Many over-50s are retiring earlier to indulge in travel, especially long-haul and cruising.

The traditional 'law of tourism harmony', in which every aspect of the tour would be broadly of similar standard and quality, has given way to a 'pick and mix' approach, in which savings may be effected in one area in order to indulge oneself in another. Tourists may decide, for example, to choose cheap B&B accommodation while eating out in expensive restaurants. The term 'Hilton Hippies' has been used to describe those who may want to engage in rough activities such as mountain biking by day, but who look for luxury in their overnight accommodation. This is another example of the more flexible approach to packages which the travel industry is learning to cater for.

Those charged with the task of marketing to tourists must be fully familiar with patterns of tourist behaviour, and any trends which might suggest these are changing. Some of these changes will be generated by tourists themselves, others will come about as a result of changes taking place in the business environment. Many can be readily forecast, simply by projecting existing trends; for example, statistics provided by the government will identify changes in the make-up of the population, and we know that as the 1990s progress into the twenty-first century, older people will form a greater proportion of the population. What we must also take into account is other complementary changes. Older people are much fitter, and more adventurous, than they were a few years ago, and will be looking for more activity holidays. They will also enjoy a higher income than in the past; far from retiring on a modest pension, many will have inherited homes which they will translate into disposable cash, to invest or to spend on long-haul holidays. This, coupled with the fact that an increasing number are likely to opt for early retirement, allowing them to travel extensively, makes the older market a particularly attractive one for tourist businesses.

In most developed countries, those in work are likely to enjoy increased disposable incomes and a higher propensity to travel abroad. On the other hand, there will continue to be a relatively high number of unemployed in the population, most of whom will be unable to take holidays of any kind. In the past, those with spouses who have not wished to travel abroad have tended not to do so themselves, but lifestyle changes could mean that an increasing number of happily married couples will choose to holiday separately, each 'doing their own thing'.

The pace of change in the tourism world is speeding up all the time, and just as the generating countries are having to learn to adjust to rapidly fluctuating economic swings, so must entrepreneurs who have to cater for these changes learn to identify them as they occur, and for whatever reason, whether economic, social, political or technological, and to react quickly by providing the products their clients seek. Today, however, there is a new factor in the equation, the need to ensure that any new initiatives are in line with the need for sustainable development.

Questions and discussion points

1. The holiday camp business has changed rapidly in recent years. What accounted for these changes, and how has the industry responded? What further changes are likely, and does the traditional holiday centre in Britain have a future?

2. Cunard Line is building a new *Queen Mary 2* to redevelop the traditional line voyage between England and New York. Can this form of travel be successfully resuscitated? How is it likely to differ from the earlier line voyages which terminated in the 1960s?

3. Is there an inevitable clash between the concept of sustainable tourism and the demand for all-inclusive holidays?

Assignment topics

1. As a research officer in the Planning and Development Department of Sunny Tours, you have been asked by your Head of Department, Lucia Lamamoor, to provide her with a report on the relationship between sunbathing and skin cancers. She is interested in knowing whether this is a factor that might influence the development of the company's tours over the next few years.

   Trace any references you can find to the subject, and identify the main issues discussed in the articles. Design and undertake a pilot survey which will help you to know whether the public are aware of the problem and if they are taking action of any kind. Write a short report to your Head of Department, giving the main findings and suggesting what further research should be undertaken.

2. As an assistant in the Marketing Department of New Wave Tours, a medium-sized tour operator, you have been asked to give your Marketing Manager, Jimmy Murphy, your views on the growth destinations for the next few years. The company has largely dealt with the traditional sun, sea and sand tours to the Mediterranean, but is thinking of going further afield. Examine trends, particularly in long-haul tours, and summarize these in a report to Murphy, supported by figures where possible.

   Murphy is also concerned about a possible drop-off in the sale of package tours generally, in favour of independent travel. Within your report, give your views, and suggest what action the company should take.

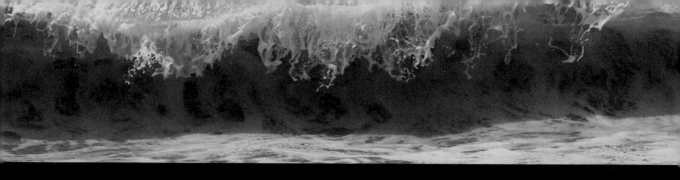

Chapter 4   The economics of tourism

Objectives

After studying this chapter, you should be able to:

- identify the economic benefits of tourism for a nation, both nationally and regionally;
- be aware of the principal trends in tourism, as they affect Britain specifically, and the world generally;
- understand how tourism is measured statistically;
- recognize the limitations of statistical measurement.

Introduction

Tourism is a human activity which arises in part from the economic circumstances of the consumer. It also has an economic impact upon nations and regions. For both these reasons, we need to study and understand the economic nature of tourism. This is a topic which is complex, and can only be touched on in this text; readers who wish to examine the subject in depth are referred to texts designed for this purpose, such as Bull (1995). The aim of this chapter will be primarily to explore the economic impact of tourism resulting from national and international tourist flows, and the ways in which this is measured and recorded. In later chapters, the economics of the firm, the industry and its various sectors will be examined.

First, however, we will look at the movement of tourists internationally, and some of the economic factors influencing these flows.

The international tourist market

Travel and tourism is probably the single most important industry in the world. It currently accounts for at least 6 per cent of the world's gross domestic product (GDP), and employs 127 million people around the world, one job in every fifteen. According to the most recent estimate by the World Tourism Organisation, some 663 million international trips were taken in 1999, with worldwide tourism receipts (excluding the cost of international fares) reaching $456 billion. These figures do not include the vast number of people taking trips within their own country; probably six times this number will take a trip lasting at least four nights. (see Table 4.1).

Table 4.1 A profile of international tourism, 1950–99

Year	Arrivals (m)	Receipts ($bn)
1950	25.3	2.1
1960	69.3	6.9
1970	159.7	17.9
1980	284.8	102.4
1990 (R)	458.2	268.9
1995 (R)	568.0	403.0
1996 (R)	600.0	438.0
1997 (R)	620.0	438.0
1998 (R)	637.0	441.3
1999 (P)	663.0	456.0

Note: excludes international fares.
(R) revised; (P) provisional.
Source: The World Tourism Organisation.

The rapid increase in international travel during the early post-war years, exceeding 10 per cent per annum from 1950 to 1960, could not be permanently sustained, of course, and it reflected the pent-up demand which the war years, and the slow economic recovery after the war, had constrained. However, it is worth noting that between 1970 and 1998 annual growth averaged 4.9 per cent, even remaining above 4 per cent in the early 1990s when there was a global recession. The good news for the tourism industry is that world tourism shows no sign of abating; the WTO estimates that by 2020 1.6 billion tourists will be travelling abroad each year, spending $2 trillion, while domestic tourism is expected to account for 16 billion tourists spending $8 trillion. Long-haul travel is expected to account for 24 per cent of all international travel by that date. In spite of this increase, the WTO estimates that, even after taking into account those unable to travel due to factors such as poverty, infirmity or age, this number will represent only some 7 per cent of the potential world market for tourism (World Tourism Organisation, 1999).

International tourism is generated for the most part within the nations of Europe, North America and Japan, the result of low prices, frequent flights, and large, relatively wealthy populations (see Table 4.2). Japan in particular has been growing strongly as

a tourist-generating country in recent years, due to its wealth and a growing willingness on the part of its population to take holidays. Traditionally, the Japanese work ethic militated against their taking all the holidays to which they are entitled, but with government encouragement and changes in attitude to work and loyalty to their firms, the Japanese have taken to travelling abroad in greater numbers and for longer periods of time. As a result, Japan is now among the top five generating countries which together are responsible for well over half the total expenditure on foreign travel.

It is interesting to note the changes occurring over time among the generating countries. While the

Table 4.2 Leading tourism-generating countries, 1997 (based on tourism expenditure)

Country	Expenditure ($bn)
1. USA	51.2
2. Germany	46.2
3. Japan	33.0
4. UK	27.7
5. Italy	16.6
6. France	16.6
7. Canada	11.3
8. Austria	11.0
9. Netherlands	10.2
10. China	10.2

Source: The World Tourism Organisation.

Table 4.3 Leading tourism-receiving countries, 1998 (based on provisional receipts)

Country	Receipts ($m)
1. USA	71,116
2. France	29,900
3. Italy	29,800
4. Spain	29,700
5. UK	21,034
6. Germany	16,429
7. China	12,602
8. Austria	11,184
9. Canada	9,400
10. Turkey	7,800

Source: The World Tourism Organisation.

Figure 4.1 Line-up of superferries at Tallinn, Estonia (*Photographed by the author*)

leading half-dozen countries change little from one year to another, China has joined the top ten as the country enjoys relatively more freedom of movement, while the Russian Federation has moved into eleventh place as a generating country, with Poland and other former eastern bloc countries all showing strong growth. The so-called tiger economies of the Pacific region, including Taiwan, Korea, Thailand and Malaysia, have also experienced a major upsurge in foreign travel, only briefly interrupted when the Thai baht collapsed in the summer of 1997. The United States has overtaken Germany to become the leading generating country, but its huge outflow of funds resulting from this is offset by its role as the leading destination country, while Germany gains much less benefit.

Countries such as China, the Russian Federation and South Africa have great potential for growth as destination countries, although the political picture is clouded. Russia still requires visas from western countries, a major drawback in attracting tourists in view of their expense, while Estonia, by contrast, requires none. Its capital, Tallinn, has also benefited from its seaboard location an hour and forty minutes by fast ferry from Finland's capital, Helsinki (see Figure 4.1), resulting in a huge flood of tourists travelling between these cities.

Simply looking at receipts will not give a sound picture of the value of tourism to an economy. The countries with the highest per capita receipts are those where prices are highest, including Sweden, Denmark and Japan, with the UK well down the list. The highest spend per capita by tourists coming to Britain tends to be among the Scandinavians, especially Icelandic visitors, while those from Eastern Europe spend least. In economic terms, the financial value of tourism to a country is more important than the number of tourists it receives, so it is important

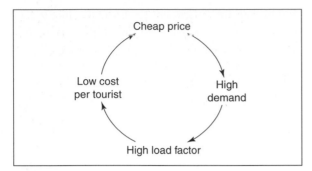

Figure 4.2 The relationship between cost, price and demand

to assess the average daily spend of tourists from different countries, and the average length of time tourists from a particular country spend when visiting a country. One must also always take account of factors likely to lead to the growth or decline of tourism from each country. The potential for further growth remains high for those living in former Soviet bloc countries, although their per capita expenditure will in many cases be small. On the other hand, a growing elite in these countries are high-spend tourists whom destination countries are keen to attract. The potential from Japan remains high also, as fewer than 10 per cent of the population have travelled abroad, and their spend per capita is high. This is partly accounted for by their high spend on shopping and souvenirs for friends and relatives. Australians are also high spenders, together with tourists from Thailand, Taiwan and Singapore. In spite of the high revenues received from Americans travelling abroad, only 11 per cent of the population actually possess a passport; most American tourists tend to travel to adjacent countries which do not require them to carry passports, and because of the size and diversity of their own landscape, many are content to take their holidays within their own country, so the *propensity* to take holidays abroad is another important characteristic to take into account.

We should also recognize that, while tourism expenditure in aggregate will be highest from wealthy countries having large populations, the high disposable income among the populations of smaller nations with a significant proportion of wealthy residents, such as Switzerland or Luxembourg, will tend to lead to higher levels of participation in international tourism – and where international borders are so close to places of residence, as is the case with these two countries, this will significantly increase the propensity to travel abroad.

While (as we shall see in the next chapter) there are many factors which motivate people to travel abroad, the major factor will be the relative cost, compared with their income. Since greater demand also leads to lower prices, with transport and accommodation costs falling for each additional person booked, there is a direct relationship between cost, price and demand (see Figure 4.2).

This helps to explain the vicious price wars in the travel industry, designed to capture market share and increase numbers, which have been so much a feature of competition in the travel industry over the past twenty years.

Other factors to take into account include attitudes to the use of leisure time. In the USA, some 30 per cent of the workforce take less than half the holiday time to which they are entitled. The Japanese, as we have seen, seldom take their full entitlement; with average holiday lengths of 17 days, they typically take only 9.5 days. Even in the UK, 25 per cent of the working population fails to take its full entitlement.

Britain's place in world tourism

Britain has enjoyed comparable growth, both in its outbound and inbound markets, with other western nations. At the beginning of the 1950s, Britons were only taking some 5.5 per cent of their holidays abroad; but by 1999 this had risen to 46 per cent. In 1999, British residents took 54 million trips abroad, and 27 per cent went abroad at least twice that year. UK visitors to France, at 11.7 million, slightly exceed those to Spain at 10.5 million, but the proportion of those on package tours is far greater in the case of the latter destination. France's appeal, because of its proximity to England and the nature of its tourist attractions, is for self-drive holidays in particular, and the Eurotunnel services between Folkestone and Calais, as well as improvements to cross-Channel ferry services, have facilitated this movement. The growth in long-haul holidays has also been marked, particularly to the United States, which received over 4 million visitors from Britain in 1999.

The propensity of the British to take a holiday – that is, the ratio of those taking holidays out of the total population – is high. Around 60 per cent of Britons take a holiday of four nights or more, and this figure has remained relatively unchanged for many years, having peaked in 1980 at 62 per cent. However, this is not as high as many other European countries. Over 80 per cent of Switzerland's population, and a similar number from Sweden, take a holiday every year. This northern participation rate is almost certainly due to the inhospitable climate and long winter nights, followed by the desire of many in the population to take a holiday in the sun.

In most respects, future trends for British travel appear healthy. The British have now firmly adopted the habit of taking an annual holiday. Not only are disposable incomes growing; inherited wealth is also having an impact on holiday spending, as those in

middle age inherit properties from the first generation of parents to own their own homes on a wide scale. Many older people enjoy good health and leisure time, having retired early. On the other hand, pensions are now worth less as they are no longer linked to increases in average earnings, and the government is moving towards upping the retirement

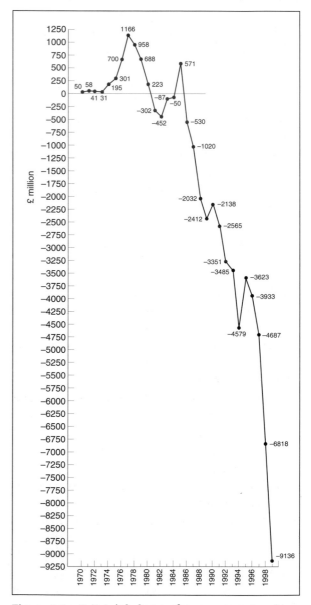

Figure 4.3 Britain's balance of payments on tourism account, 1970–99

Table 4.4 Trends in British holiday taking: foreign holidays and inclusive tours, 1990–99

Year	Holidays (000s)	Inclusive tours (000s)
1990	21,255	11,391
1991	20,630	10,646
1992	23,100	12,600
1993	25,133	13,600
1994	27,337	15,164
1995	27,808	15,166
1996	26,765	13,901
1997	29,138	15,394
1998	32,306	17,437
1999	34,283	18,597

Source: Business Monitor MQ6. © Crown copyright.

age. Workers are encouraged to invest a greater proportion of their income into saving for pensions. Savings have to be increased, or insurance taken out, to pay for possible nursing home care in older years. These factors, common throughout the developed world, have persuaded forecasters that while holidays will become more frequent, they will be of shorter duration, and spread more evenly throughout the year.

Britain received nearly 25½ million visitors in 1999, spending over $12.6 billion. Of these, a little under 10 million were tourists on holiday. The number of British tourists travelling abroad on holiday is therefore more than three times greater than the number of foreign holiday-makers visiting Britain. The WTO has forecast that the inbound numbers will double by 2020. However, the gap between expenditure by British residents abroad and expenditure in Britain by tourists from abroad continues to widen, with the result that there is an expanding balance of payments deficit on tourism account over the past decade (see Figure 4.3). However, Britain does benefit substantially from incoming and domestic tourism; nearly 1.8 million people are estimated to be working in tourism or a related activity, and tourism accounts for some 4.5 per cent of all export earnings (and nearly a quarter of all services exports). This compares with over 20 per cent in Spain, which, in view of the volatile nature of the business, might appear to many observers to be an over-dependence upon tourism in the economy. However, some economists have argued that these figures grossly underestimate the actual value of tourism to Britain; the World Travel and Tourism Council has put Britain's annual earnings in excess of £105 billion for travel and tourism and related businesses, more than 12 per cent of GDP, and has forecast that this could rise to £174 billion by 2010.

The value of economic data

Gathering data on tourists is a vital task for the government of a country, both for use by its own national tourist office and for the benefit of the providers of tourism services. Governments need to know the contribution which tourism makes to the economy in terms of income, employment, investment and the balance of payments. Concern with regional development requires that these statistics be sufficiently refined to allow them to be broken down by region. Governments will also wish to compare their tourism performance with that of other countries, as well as to establish their performance in attracting tourists to the country over a period of time.

Tourism organizations, whether in the public or the private sector, need such data to enable them to forecast what will happen in the future. This means identifying trends in the market, patterns of growth and changing demand for destinations, facilities or types of holiday.

On the basis of this knowledge, future planning can be undertaken. The public sector will make recommendations and decisions regarding the *infrastructure* and *superstructure* needed to support growth. Infrastructure will include, for example, the building of new airports or the expansion of existing ones, the provision of new or improved roads to the growth destinations, and the improvement of other services such as public utilities including water and electricity, which will be needed to cope with the expected expansion of tourism. Some of these plans may take many years to implement. The discussions surrounding the building of a fifth terminal at London's Heathrow airport have taken a decade to date and may take another decade before the terminal becomes operational, assuming the go-ahead is given. In the meantime, congestion in the air forces carriers to switch air traffic to alternative airports, including airports such as Schiphol in the Netherlands. Similarly, the new fast rail track for Eurotunnel's service from London to the Channel Tunnel took many years before approval was granted, and will not be fully operational before 2007. This will encourage a greater flow of tourists between London, Brussels and Paris and beyond, as well as diverting air traffic to rail.

Superstructure is comprised of the tourist facilities needed – hotels, restaurants, shops and other services the tourist takes for granted. It cannot necessarily be assumed that these services will be provided by developers in the private sector. If a new destination is being developed, there will be a degree of risk involved while the destination becomes established, and developers may be reluctant to invest in such projects as hotels until there is proven demand for the destination. Governments or local authorities can themselves undertake the construction of hotels, as often occurs in developing countries, or they can encourage hotel construction by underwriting costs or providing subsidies of some kind until the destination becomes established. Similarly, private companies can use the statistics which demonstrate growth or market change by extending or adapting their products to meet the changing needs of the marketplace.

To show how this information can be used, let us take the example of a destination such as London, which attracts a high volume of overseas visitors. The flow of these visitors will be affected by a great many different factors: if tourists can purchase more pounds sterling for their own currency, or if air fares have fallen to the destination, or if a major event such as an international exhibition is being organized, this will encourage tourism to the city. If London is being hit by a spate of terrorist bomb attacks, as occurred in late 1992, this may dissuade people from travelling, especially if they are travelling from generating countries such as North America, where there is particular sensitivity to the threat of terrorism. Negative first impressions, such as air pollution in the city, extensive littering, a decaying and overcrowded public transport system, even large numbers of homeless people on the streets, can affect tourism adversely, and tourists may decide to go elsewhere, or recommend to their friends that they do so.

Recessions may be hitting countries to a different extent, so that in one year the forecast might be for a reduced number of tourists from the USA, but a growth in the number from Japan. In the third quarter of 2000 the pound fell sharply against the dollar, while remaining relatively strong against European currencies. This would have encouraged Americans to travel to Britain, and the British to visit the Continent, while tourists from countries like Germany and France would have been dissuaded from coming to Britain and fewer British would have visited the USA. Indeed, in the run-up to the introduction of the euro, the pound sterling see-sawed in value against the euro, and the consequent uncertainty tended to destabilize the travel industry's forward planning. This adds another element of risk to product pricing, which can be offset to some extent by the forward purchasing of foreign currencies. If Britain does eventually join the euro, one benefit will be help in stabilizing the travel business, and it will also allow British travellers to share with their colleagues in other EU countries the benefits of using a single currency across several countries, leading to a substantial saving on foreign exchange, when calculating the costs of a holiday abroad. Such savings are less likely to be welcomed by those in the industry who provide foreign exchange facilities, however!

Companies and tourist offices will have to take all of these factors into account when drawing up their promotional campaigns – and may need to consider employing staff with the appropriate languages to deal with any new incoming markets. On the basis of the forecasts made, organizations must decide where they will advertise, to whom, and with what theme. To give just one example, it has been revealed that in recent years the Japanese market has been tempted to Paris rather than London, as Paris is seen by the many female Japanese visitors as being more 'feminine' a destination, and therefore less challenging. This might require the London Tourist Board, as part of its marketing campaign in that country, to set itself the task of generating a softer image for the city.

It will be seen from this last example that international tourism depends on more than merely economic behaviour of tourists. It will also be influenced by motivation arising from the tourists' efforts to meet their psychological or sociological needs. These latter motivations will be examined in the following chapter.

The economic impact of tourism

It is the concern of this chapter to examine the economic effects of tourism, and how these are measured. As in other industries, tourism affects the economy of those areas – whether regions, countries or continents – where it takes place. These are known as tourist *destinations*, or *receiving areas*, and many become dependent upon an inflow of tourism to sustain their economy. This is especially true of developing countries, some of which are largely or almost totally dependent upon tourism. The areas from which the tourists come to visit these destinations are known as *generating areas*, and, of course, as the tourists are taking their money with them to spend in other places, this represents a net loss of revenue to the generating area, and a gain to the receiving area. We can say that incoming tourist spend is an *export*, while outgoing tourist spend is an *import*.

The flow of tourists between generating and receiving areas can be measured in four distinct ways. We must examine the effect on *income*, on *employment*, on the area's *balance of payments* and on *investment and development*. Let us look at each of these in turn.

Income

Income is generated from wages and salaries, interest, rent and profits. In a labour-intensive industry such as tourism, the greatest proportion is likely to be derived from wages and salaries paid to those working in jobs either directly serving the needs of tourists or benefiting indirectly from the tourists' expenditure. Income will be greater in those areas which generate large numbers of tourists, where visitors tend to stay for longer periods, where the destination attracts an up-market or more free-spending clientele, and where there are many opportunities to spend. A destination such as the Côte d'Azure, for example, satisfies most of these criteria, attracting not only many overseas visitors for a fairly long season (even through the winter some tourists will be attracted to the milder climate) but also bringing in many domestic tourists from other areas of France. A number of up-market resorts such as Nice, Cannes, Antibes, St Tropez and Juan les Pins provide a good range of relatively expensive hotels; there are also expensive shops and restaurants, casinos, night-clubs and discos where the high-spend tourists can be relieved of their money. There are opportunities for water-based activities such as yachting or fishing, with marinas to attract the wealthy motor yacht owners, and there are numerous attractions nearby which bring in the day excursionists by coach or private car. Finally, the area is also well served with conference and exhibition halls, which attract high-spend business tourists.

It is important to recognize that while income may be greatest where wage levels are high, and there is relatively little unemployment in the area, tourism may in fact be of greater value in those areas where there are few other opportunities for employment. In Britain, to take one example, tourism is of prime importance in areas where there is little industry, such as in the Scottish Highlands, western Wales and Cornwall. The tourism industry is often criticized for providing only low-wage, seasonal employment, but this is in fact a gross exaggeration, and many posts associated with the tourism business are neither seasonal nor temporary. As to low-wage jobs, one must take into account that without tourism, many workers would be unemployed or forced to move away from the area, given that there are few alternatives.

Income is also generated from interest, rent and profits on tourism businesses. This could include, for example, the interest paid on loans to an airline in order to buy aircraft, or rent paid to a landowner for a car park or campsite near the sea. We must also count taxation on tourism activities, such as sales tax on hotel bills, duty and taxation on petrol used by tourists, and the direct taxation which many countries levy on tourists to raise additional public income. In Austria, to give one example, there is a *Kurtaxe* imposed on accommodation to raise money for the local authority. Many countries, including the

Table 4.5 Percentage of national income represented by tourism in selected countries

Country	Percentage
Antigua and Barbuda	87
Maldives	82
Balearics	81
St Lucia	46
Barbados	33
Bermuda	29

Source: Spiegel Special, 'Urlaub Total' No. 2 1997.

UK, levy a *departure tax* on all international passengers travelling by air, while in the USA airline taxes are levied on both departing and arriving travellers.

The sum of all incomes in a country is called the national income, and the importance of tourism to a country's economy can be measured by looking at the proportion of national income created by tourism. In Britain this is estimated to be about 3.6 per cent (about 5.7 per cent of all consumer spending), including income from accommodation, tourist transport and all kinds of extras for which tourists pay. This may seem a small percentage, but even engineering, the country's largest industry, only contributes about 8 per cent to the national income. By contrast, some regions of the world, particularly the Caribbean countries, are heavily dependent upon the income from tourism, as Table 4.5 demonstrates. Some might see this as an unhealthy overdependence upon one rather volatile industry.

Attempts to measure the impact of tourism are always difficult, because it is difficult to distinguish the spend by tourists and the spend by others in restaurants or shops, for example. In resorts, even such businesses as laundromats – which we would not normally associate with the tourism industry – might be highly dependent upon the tourist spend where, for instance, a large number of visitors are camping, caravanning or in self-catering facilities. Furthermore, tourism's contribution to the income of an area is enhanced by a phenomenon known as the *tourism income multiplier* (TIM). This arises because money spent by tourists in the area will be re-spent by recipients, augmenting the total. The multiplier is the factor by which tourist spend is increased in this process. This is easiest to demonstrate by way of the following example.

Example

A number of tourists visit Highjinks on Sea, spending £1,000 in hotels and other facilities there. This amount is received as income by the hoteliers and owners of the facilities, who, after paying their taxes and saving some of the income, spend the rest. Some of what they spend goes to buy items imported into the area, but the rest goes to shopkeepers, suppliers and other producers inside the area. These people in turn pay their taxes, save some money and spend the rest.

Let us assume that the average rate of taxation is 20p in the pound and that people are saving on average 10p in the pound of their gross income, and are therefore left to spend 70p in the pound on goods and services. Let us further assume that of this 70p in the pound spend, 20p is spent on goods and services imported from other areas, while the remaining 50p is retained within the local community. The original £1,000 spent by the tourists will then circulate in the local community as shown in Figure 4.4, in the category 'first circulation'.

Of the 50p spent within the community, some will go to local suppliers of such items as food. The shopkeepers or restaurateurs then pay their employees, who in turn shop in other shops locally, although some of what they purchase will have been brought into the region from outside. This second circulation will be further spent by the recipients, and so the cycle goes on, with a declining expenditure at each level of circulation. These cycles are illustrated in Figure 4.4, under the categories of second circulation, third circulation, and so on.

Each time the money is circulated in this way, some will be lost to the area. Taxes paid are transmitted outside the area, some of the savings may be similarly removed from the area, and some of the spend has gone to pay for goods imported into the

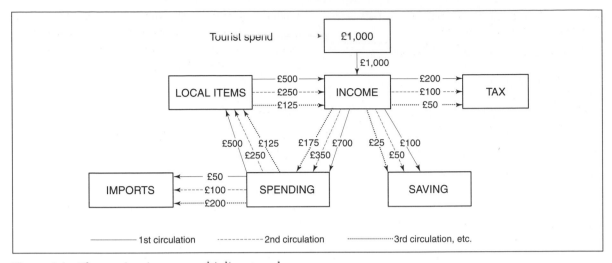

Figure 4.4   The tourism income multiplier at work

area from other regions of the country or even from abroad. Expenditures in which the money is lost to other areas are known as *leakages* from the system. Leakages in this sense can therefore be regional or national, the latter being a loss of revenue to the country as a whole.

So far, how much income has been created? From Figure 4.4 we can see that it is £1,000 + £500 + £250 + £125 + ... A progression is developing, and by adding up all the figures or by using the appropriate mathematical formula, we will find that the total sum is £2,000. The original injection of £1,000 by tourists visiting the area has multiplied by a factor of 2 to produce income of £2,000.

It is possible to forecast the value of the multiplier if one knows the proportion of leakages in the local economy. In the example above, tax was 20/100ths of original income, savings were 10/100ths of income and imports were 20/100ths of income. Total leakages therefore amount to 50/100ths, or half the original income. The multiplier can be found by applying the formula:

$$\text{Multiplier} = \frac{1}{\text{Proportion of leakages}}$$

In the example given, the multiplier was 1/0.5, or 2.

So in an economy with a high proportion of leakages, such as high tax rates (although we must remember that the government may choose to reinvest this tax money in the local economy, so much of it may not be lost for all time), or where many of the goods demanded by consumers are imported, TIM may be quite low, and the economy will not benefit greatly from tourism. Local hotels may also be foreign-owned, so that profits achieved are then transmitted to the hotel chain's head office and so lost to the area. This might be true of other tourist facilities in the area, and even local ground handling agents or coach operators may be owned by companies based elsewhere, leading to further losses in the multiplier effect. On the other hand, where many firms are in the hands of locals, and leakages are minimized in this way, the TIM may be quite high, and tourism will contribute far more than the amount originally spent by the tourists themselves. The principal reasons for leakages include:

- cost of imported goods, especially food and drink;
- foreign exchange costs of imports for the development of tourist facilities;
- remittance of profits abroad;
- remittance of wages by expatriates;
- management fees or royalties for franchises;
- payments to overseas carriers and travel companies;
- costs of overseas promotion;

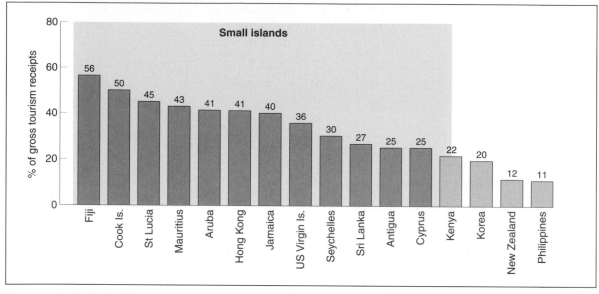

Figure 4.5 Leakage of foreign exchange earnings: sixteen countries. (*Courtesy The World Tourism Organisation*)

- additional expenditure on imports resulting from the earnings of those benefiting from tourism.

Many studies have been undertaken of the TIM in different areas, ranging from individual resorts such as Eastbourne and Edinburgh to entire countries such as Barbados and Fiji. In most cases, the multiplier has varied between 1 and 2.5 (estimates have put it at about 1.7 for Britain as a whole, and around 1.2–1.5 for individual towns and regions in the UK), although in the case of some destinations in the developing world which depend heavily on outside investment and must import much of the food and other commodities demanded by tourists, the figure may be well below 1. Barbados, for instance, has been estimated at 0.60. Leakages in western developed nations are generally estimated at around 10 per cent of tourism income, while in developing economies with strong tourism dependency such as Fiji, the Cook Islands, Mauritius and the Virgin Islands, estimates suggest that imports consume between 36 and 56 per cent of gross tourism receipts.

Employment

Tourism is also important to an economy because it generates employment. In some tourism-dependent economies, such as the Caribbean, as many as 25 per cent of all jobs are associated with the tourism industry. Jobs will be created in travel agencies, tour operators and other intermediaries who supply tourist services in both the generating and destination areas. Transport companies such as airlines will also employ staff to serve tourists in both areas. But the bulk of employment will be in the destination country, with jobs ranging from hotel managers to deckchair attendants, from excursion booking clerks to cleaners employed in the stately homes that are open to the public, or maintenance staff who maintain the rides at leisure centres or theme parks in the resort.

Many of these jobs are seasonal or part-time, so that tourism's contribution to full-time employment is considerably less than its contribution to 'job-hours'. While this is a criticism of the industry in economic terms, and one that has resulted in large sums of money being spent in an effort to lengthen the tourist season in many resorts, one must be reminded that these jobs are often being created in areas where there is little alternative employment. It is also worth making the point that many of the jobs attract those who wish to work seasonally, such as students seeking jobs as resort representatives during the summer, or householders who wish to open their house for summer periods only as bed and breakfast establishments.

Earlier, it was pointed out that Britain has more than 1.7 million workers involved in 'tourism or an associated activity'. This represents some 6.5 per cent of the British labour force. About 120,000 new tourist jobs were created between 1994 and 1999, making tourism a major growth area for employment. However, there is a problem about measuring the so-called 'related activities'. How is one to determine what is to be included in the tourism employment statistics? A high proportion of jobs will be in hotels and catering, by no means all of which are concerned with tourists. Estimates of those actually employed in the more narrowly defined 'travel and tourism industry' in Britain are thought to be much lower. In 1991, ABTA's National Training Board undertook a study of the travel services sector, embracing tour operating, retail travel and business travel, which concluded that around 80,000 were directly employed in these fields, of which perhaps 12,000 were in management posts (*An Occupational Mapping of the Travel Services Industry*, 1991). This figure is estimated to have risen to approximately 122,600 by the end of the last century.

Clearly, for countries which are major receiving destinations or which enjoy a strong domestic demand for tourism, employment figures will be far higher. On balance, tourism as a form of employment is economically beneficial, although efforts must be made to create more full-time jobs in the industry. The extent to which tourism benefits employment can be seen when it is appreciated that roughly one job in fifteen in the world is directly ascribed to tourism. The World Travel and Tourism Council goes further, having estimated that world employment may be as high as 255 million people,

with tourists generating over 10 per cent of worldwide GDP – a measure of the total value of goods and services produced by the world's economy. Tourism is considered by many to be the largest industry in the world, and it is certainly the fastest growing. If global tourism expands as forecast, by the year 2006 worldwide employment will be as high as 385 million, with annual expenditure of $7.1 trillion. This would represent 11.5 per cent of GDP.

Just as tourism is globally important, so it is important for regions within an economy. The multiplier which affects income in a region affects employment in the same way. If tourists stay at a destination, jobs are directly created in the tourism industry there. These workers and their families resident in the neighbourhood must also buy goods and services locally, their families require education and need medical care. This in turn gives rise to jobs in shops, schools and hospitals to serve these needs. The value of the employment multiplier is likely to be broadly similar to that of the TIM, assuming that jobs with average wage rates are created.

However, recent developments in technology are threatening labour opportunities in tourism. For example, computer reservations systems (CRS) are rapidly replacing manual reservations systems, and as a result many booking clerk jobs in large companies such as airlines, tour operators and hotel chains are disappearing. Similarly, the trend towards online bookings via the Internet threatens jobs in travel agencies and suppliers. Fortunately for the future of the industry, at the 'sharp end', where the tourist seeks a high level of personal service at the destination, the nature of the tourist experience will ensure that technology cannot replace many jobs. However, the success of tourism in a country will be in part dependent upon an adequate supply of skilled labour, with the right motivation towards employment in the industry and appropriate training. Here, Britain has some way to go. Turnover of labour is high (attributable to relatively poor salaries and working conditions compared with many other fields of business), training, while having improved considerably over recent years, still lags behind that of many other countries, and attitudes towards working in a 'service industry', where many people in Britain still equate service with servility, make recruitment of good staff difficult.

Balance of payments

In a national context, tourism may have a major influence on a country's balance of payments. International tourists are buying tourist services in another country, and these payments are noted in a country's accounts as 'invisibles'. A British resident going on holiday to Spain will be making an invisible payment to that country which is a debit on Britain's balance of payments account and a credit to Spain's balance of payment. The money spent by an American visitor to Britain is credited to Britain's balance of payments, becoming an invisible receipt for Britain, while it is debited as a payment against the American balance of payments. It is important to remind readers at this point that the outflow of British money being spent abroad by British residents counts as an *import*, while the inflow of foreign holiday-makers' money spent in Britain counts as an *export*.

The total value of receipts minus the total payments made during the year represents a country's *balance of payments on the tourism account*. This is part of the country's entire invisible balance, which will include other services such as banking, insurance and transport. This latter item is of course also important for tourism. If an American visitor to Britain decides to travel on a British airline, then a contribution is made to Britain's invisible receipts, while if a Briton going on holiday to Spain does so on Iberia Airlines, that fare is credited to Spain, and represents a payment on the British balance of payments account.

Throughout the 1970s, Britain enjoyed a surplus on its tourism balance, reaching a peak during 1977, the year of the Queen's Silver Jubilee. Since then, however, spending by British tourists travelling abroad has increased faster than receipts the country has gained from overseas tourists, with the result that there has been a net, and steadily increasing, deficit since 1986, and this deficit is now approaching £10 billion a year (see Figure 4.3).

For a country like Britain, which has experienced a steady decline in the terms of trade (amount of our goods sold abroad, compared with the amount of goods we import) it is important to try to redress the balance by a better showing on our invisible exports. As can be seen, however, tourism is not producing a net gain for Britain either – a matter about which we should be concerned. The government will attempt to resolve this deficit by encouraging more visitors to visit Britain, through the marketing efforts of the national tourist boards, or encouraging more Britons to stay at home and enjoy their holidays in their own country. However, the lure of the sun is a strong magnet for British tourists, and the tourist boards may find it easier to attract the overseas tourist to Britain. Some countries, particularly developing countries, could not afford this kind of drain on their financial resources, and would be forced to impose restrictions either on the movement of their own residents, or on the amount of money which they may take abroad with them. Other countries suffer severe deficiencies in their tourism balance of payments, but can offset this with manufacturing exports. Germany and Japan are examples of countries heavily in deficit on the tourism balance of payments, but which nevertheless enjoy a surplus overall through the sale of goods overseas. By contrast, Spain and Italy both enjoy a strong surplus on their tourism balance of payments as they are popular receiving countries with fewer residents going abroad for their own holidays.

Investment and development

One factor helping to determine the success or otherwise of tourism in a region is the level of investment, whether private or public, in the industry. Unfortunately, tourism, and leisure generally, are seen by private investors as high-risk investments. Banks are reluctant to lend money for tourism projects, and developers are less willing to take investment risks. This will often mean that tourism cannot take off until the public sector is prepared to 'kick-start' the economy; that is, to invest risk capital in order to encourage tourism development. This might take the form of grants or low-interest loans to private developers, or in some more centrally planned economies it may mean that government itself builds and operates facilities such as hotels for tourists.

A good example of this 'partnership' between the public and private sectors is the development of the Disneyland site near Paris, involving investment of many hundreds of millions of dollars. The French government, in order to ensure that the Disney Corporation built in France rather than in competitive European countries, provided subsidies to attract the company to the site near Paris which was eventually selected.

Investment is something of a 'chicken and egg' situation. There may be an unwillingness to invest until a flow of tourists to the area can be demonstrated, while the area will in turn attract few tourists until they can see evidence of sufficient facilities to attract them. However, once tourism is shown to be successful, private developers or government agencies are often willing to invest even further in the area – in short, success breeds success. Economists refer to this as the *accelerator* concept. Areas which have benefited from this phenomenon include Spain in the 1960s, Hawaii, Tunisia and the Languedoc-Roussillon region of France in the 1970s, and Turkey and Greece in the 1980s and 1990s. Naturally, the attraction of these regions to tourists will also attract other industries, which will recognize the benefits to be gained from a large inflow of consumers, and the attraction of a pleasant working environment for staff. Resorts such as Bournemouth and Brighton in Britain, or the fast-expanding resorts of Florida in the USA and the Gold Coast in Queensland, Australia, have all benefited from this process.

Unfortunately, the relationship between tourism growth and economic development is uneven, due to other complicating factors such as the rate of inflation, the ability of an area to diversify and attitudes to work among the local labour force. Consequently,

risk in investment remains high, as it does in many other areas of the economy.

Statistical measurement of tourism

Gathering data on tourism is a vital task for the government of a country. Governments need to know the contribution which tourism makes to the economy in terms of income, employment, balance of payments and investment. Figures must be available in sufficient detail to know how they have affected regional as well as national economies. Governments will wish to examine trends over time, not only within the country, but in comparison with the performance of other, competing countries. National tourist offices will use this information to forecast growth, to plan for tourism in their areas, and as a guide to their promotional campaigns.

Information must be both quantitative and qualitative in nature; that is, data should be provided not only about the numbers and composition of tourists but also about their nature and purpose. For example, British statistics should include:

1. the number of visitors to Britain;
2. how these are distributed over the months of the year;
3. the countries generating these tourists, and the number of tourists they generate as a proportion of the whole;
4. the growth, year on year, of these tourists;
5. their spend in Britain, in absolute terms and how they distribute the spend between accommodation, transport, shopping, catering etc.;
6. their mode of travel, i.e. what form of transport they use, whether they are travelling independently or on an inclusive tour;
7. the type of accommodation they use;
8. the purpose of their visit, whether leisure, business, VFR, etc.;
9. demographic profiles: age, group composition, social class;
10. sociographic profiles: personality, lifestyle, interests and activities;

11. what these tourists seek, and the extent to which they are satisfied with what they find.

This is a great deal of information, and when one remembers that it must also be collected for British residents travelling abroad and for British residents taking their holidays within Britain, the task of collecting the data is daunting. However, it is vital that governments undertake this collection of data, and that, as far as is possible, the data that are collected are based on commonly defined criteria, so that meaningful comparisons can be made between countries. If the collection of data allows the nation to know what trends are developing over time, what patterns of growth are taking place, and how tastes and preferences are changing over time, this information will enable governments to determine where to site roads and airports, where to plan for expansion in local government plans, and in what countries to increase or decrease the spend on advertising (as well as how to redirect the theme of advertisements, when it is found that new types of tourist are being reached). The private sector will benefit from this information in deciding whether and where to invest in hotels or tourist attractions, and the form these facilities should take. Similarly, those in the industry require an understanding of the propensity to take holidays – that is, the proportion of the population choosing to take a holiday each year, and in particular a holiday abroad, or to take more than one holiday a year – and how this propensity is affected by a growth in disposable income. Public sector planners must be aware of the multiplier effect, which will call for sophisticated research techniques if measurement is to be accurate.

We will examine the most commonly used measurements of tourism here, under two categories: international surveys and national surveys.

International surveys

Statistics of intra-European and transatlantic tourist flows were collected even before World War II. However, the systematic collection of tourism data on a global scale can be dated to the early post-war years, and methods of measurement have been gradually refined and improved in recent years, particularly in those developed countries which have seen tourism expand rapidly.

Global tourism statistics, covering traffic flows, expenditure and trends over time, are produced and collated annually by the WTO and the Organisation for Economic Cooperation and Development (OECD). Figures are published in the WTO's *World Tourism Statistics Annual Report* and *Tourism Compendium*, and in the OECD's annual *Tourism Policy and International Tourism*. These statistics, however, are not always strictly comparable, as data gathering methods vary and differences in definition of terms remain.

In Britain, information on travel into and out of the country is obtained in a variety of ways. Until the early 1960s, most basic data on incoming tourism were obtained from Home Office immigration statistics, but as the purpose of gathering such data was to control immigration rather than to measure tourism, the data had major weaknesses, including failure to distinguish the purpose of travel – obviously a key statistic in surveying tourists. The government therefore decided to introduce a regular survey of visitors entering and leaving the country. The *International Passenger Survey* (IPS) has enabled data to be collected on tourists since 1964, and the survey, which is undertaken by the Office of National Statistics for the Department for Culture, Media and Sport and the national tourist boards, interviews a representative sample (256,000 people in 1999, or 0.2 per cent) of all international travellers, recording the number of visitors, the purpose of their visit, the geographical region visited, their expenditure, mode of travel, transport used and duration of stay. Information is based on country of residence; so, for example, the large number of British visitors living in America and travelling to visit friends and relatives in Britain each year would be counted as American visitors. This information is published quarterly, and compounded annually, in the government's *Business Monitor* series (MQ6, *Overseas Travel and Tourism*).

Numerous other surveys, both public and private, are undertaken, and these provide additional data on tourism volume and expenditure. Reduced resources have led to cutbacks in the collection of data by the public sector bodies, but commercial research organizations such as STATS MR carry out substantial research on overseas tourism and make the results available on subscription to businesses.

National surveys

In Britain, as in other countries in Europe, surveys are regularly carried out on tourism flows within the country. The most important of these is the *UK Tourism Survey* (UKTS). This survey is carried out on a monthly basis by NOP Consumer Market Research on behalf of the English Tourism Council and the Scottish, Wales and Northern Ireland Tourist Boards. Residents of the UK over the age of 15 are interviewed in their homes, and information is collected on the volume and value of all trips involving at least one overnight stay. This is now the only national survey carried out on a regular basis since the *British National Travel Survey* (BNTS), which researched holidays only, was dropped in 1998.

Information on day visitors is less complete. A UK Day Visits Survey is carried out on an ad hoc basis, the last of which was in 1998. Individual members of the Countryside Recreation Network, particularly the Countryside Agency, also conduct occasional day visit surveys, but none has been undertaken since 1998.

A Holiday Intentions Survey, to determine how people in Britain intended to spend their forthcoming summer holidays, used to be carried out in the spring each year by the English Tourist Board and the European Travel Commission, but is now undertaken only on an ad hoc basis, the most recent being in 1999. Finally, the UK Occupancy Survey, which surveys hotel occupancy in Britain, is still conducted annually, under the auspices of the four boards.

Techniques and problems of tourism measurement

From the descriptions of the methods of gathering UK tourist statistics outlined above, it can be seen that most research employs quantitative methods, in order to provide descriptive information about issues such as when and where tourists travel, where they come from, how long they stay and how much they spend. In some cases, this information is available in considerable detail; for instance, expenditure can be broken down into sector (shopping, food, accommodation etc.) and data on visits can be identified by tourism region within the country. Although the data collected are not above criticism, by and large there is a sufficient body of information on which to make decisions.

However, research dealing with why people travel is far more limited. This is beginning to change, as organizations become more concerned with understanding the behaviour of tourists: how they choose their destinations, what they do when they arrive and why, what satisfies them, their purchasing patterns (preference to book directly rather than through an agent, or to book early rather than close to departure time). None of these questions is easily answered by use of the structured questionnaire, and a more qualitative approach to research is needed. This can involve lengthy interviews in the home, or in 'panels' or groups of up to eight consumers who will talk about their behaviour under the guidance of a skilled interviewer. Some information is best obtained by observation rather than questioning; for example, by watching how customers visiting a travel agency choose their brochures from the racks. All these types of research are expensive, and time consuming to administer. What is more, unlike quantitative methods, they cannot be subjected to tests of statistical probability in order to 'prove' the accuracy of the findings, no matter how carefully and scientifically the information is collected. Many organizations are therefore reluctant to commission research involving qualitative methods, although a growing number of research experts now recognize that they may produce richer and more complete data than the more common survey. After all, the information provided by the use of questionnaires will only be as accurate as the honesty of the answers, and it is particularly difficult to know if respondents are answering questionnaires honestly or with sufficient thought about the questions. This problem is compounded where mailed questionnaires are used.

Asking questions of arriving passengers at a destination is in reality an 'intention survey' rather than an accurate picture of what those passengers will actually engage in while in the country, while surveys carried out on departing travellers will require recall – at best, guesswork, especially where the aim is to assess the expenditure which the tourist has incurred.

Even if common definitions are used, direct comparisons may be misleading. An international journey may require an American resident to make a trip of several hundred kilometres, or to cross a stretch of water, which will usually mean forward planning, while a resident of Continental Europe may live within a couple of kilometres of an international border and think nothing of crossing it regularly for shopping or a meal out. In some cases, it is difficult to think of border crossings as international; no border control has existed for some years, for instance, between the Netherlands, Belgium and Luxembourg, and new agreements between other countries within the European Union have led to open borders and no statistical monitoring of visitor flows. Some countries still use hotel records to estimate the number of visitors – a system known to be notoriously inadequate, because visitors travelling from one hotel to another are double counted, while those visiting friends and relatives will be omitted entirely from the count.

While international standards for methods of data collection and definition of terms have become widely accepted, particularly among the developed countries, small variations continue to make genuine comparison difficult, not only between countries but within a country over a period of time. Above all, if specific types of tourist activity are being examined, as part of a larger sample of general tourists, limits of confidence may fall sharply. Certain British Tourist Authority (BTA) survey material will produce results that are accurate only to within 20 per cent either way, due to the small number of respondents in the particular category being examined.

Accurate measures of tourist expenditure are equally difficult to make. Shopping surveys have problems distinguishing between residents and tourists, and tourists themselves frequently under- or over-estimate their expenditure. Above all, much of the real tourist expenditure is lost to statistical collection, especially in developing countries, because it is not taken into account. This includes secondary spend by recipients of tourist moneys, and even direct spend by tourists in shops and other outlets.

In an effort to provide more accurate assessment, the WTO has introduced the concept of the *tourism satellite account* (TSA). This technique attempts to include all these indirect expenditures and their resultant contribution to GDP, employment and capital investment. The technique was approved as an international standard by the United Nations Statistical Commission in 2000. However, its implementation is fraught with difficulties; it is not only expensive and time consuming to employ, but accepts all tourism expenditure as beneficial, disregarding the question of sustainability. Neither can the results revealed in one country or region necessarily be transposed to another. Each situation is unique, and there is no magic formula which will allow estimates of statistical measure to be obtained without full-scale research within the area.

The issue of sustainability is a critical one here. It can be argued that we are far too concerned with measuring the economic impact of tourism on a region at the expense of the social or environmental impact. The industry's sole concern with growth in annual trends may conceal the very real danger that the number of tourists visiting a region will eventually exceed the number which the region can comfortably contain. Statistics on the ratio of tourists to residents, for example, or the number of tourists per square kilometre would provide some guidance on the degree of congestion experienced by the region.

However, the social impact of tourism is also the outcome of many other variables, and statistical measurement is still a comparatively recent art which will require continual refinement in the future for the purposes of both economic and social planning.

Questions and discussion points

1. What are the main purposes behind the collection of tourism statistics? What other information could be obtained at the time passengers are interviewed for the IPS which would be helpful for tourism executives?

2. How serious for the British economy is the deficit on the balance of payments on the tourism account? What steps could be taken to improve the position?

3. Examine the link between tourism leakages and sustainable tourism, with particular reference to the employment of locals versus nationals from other regions or foreign workers. Some areas with severe labour shortages, such as the Channel Islands, have long-term agreements to import labour during the tourist season (in the case of the Channel Islands, from Portugal). Is this the ideal solution, and how acceptable is this practice from the standpoint of sustainable tourism?

Assignment topics

1. You have recently taken up the position of Assistant Tourist Officer in a county of your choice. The county has only recently created a tourism department, and your immediate supervisor is preparing a plan of action to increase the number of visitors over the next five years. He has asked you to provide him with a brief report which:

   a) looks at trends in domestic and incoming tourism over the past decade;

   b) identifies significant trends and forecasts for the future flow of tourism within Britain;

   c) suggests the relative advantages and disadvantages the county has to offer in attracting more visitors.

   Your report should specifically indicate the shortcomings you find in the amount and quality of the statistical data you seek, and what further research you think will be needed to guide the department in its activities.

2. You are shortly to attend an interview for a post in the national tourist office of a less developed country which is a popular tourism destination. At the interview, you will be asked to make a five-minute presentation about the economic advantages of tourism for the country, identifying some of the key statistics which will support your evidence.

   Prepare for your talk, and write it up in the form of a set of notes, with supporting data. You may choose the country concerned. Your report should also include sustainable tourism issues.

Chapter 5   Tourist motivation and behaviour

Objectives

After studying this chapter, you should be able to:

- distinguish between motivating and facilitating factors;
- understand the nature of the psychological and sociological demand for tourism;
- recognize how the product influences consumer demand;
- be aware of some of the main theories of consumer behaviour, such as decision making and risk avoidance.

Introduction

An understanding of why people buy the holidays or business trips they take, how they go about selecting their holidays, why they choose one particular company over another, and why they choose to travel when they do is vital to those who work in the tourism industry. Yet curiously, we know relatively little about tourist motivation, and although we gather numerous statistics which reveal a great deal about who goes where, the reasons for these choices are little understood. This is not entirely the result of a lack of research, because many large companies do commission research into the behaviour of their clients, but as this is 'in-house' research, the information it reveals is confidential to the company concerned, and seldom becomes public knowledge.

Motivation and purpose are closely related, and earlier in this book the principal purposes for which tourists travel were identified. These are categorized into three broad categories: business travel, leisure travel and miscellaneous travel, which would include, *inter alia*, travel to visit friends and relatives, travel for one's health and religious travel. However, simply labelling tourists in this way only helps us to understand their general motivation for travelling; it tells us little about their specific motivation, nor about their needs and wants, which are a reflection of that travel, and how these needs and wants are met and satisfied. It will be the purpose of this chapter to explain these terms, and the complex interrelationship of factors which go to make up the choice of trips taken by tourists of all kinds.

The tourist's needs and wants

If we ask the prospective tourist why they want to

travel to a particular destination, they will offer a variety of reasons, such as 'it's somewhere I've always wanted to visit', or 'some friends recommended it very highly', or 'it's always good weather at that time of the year, and the beaches are wonderful; we've been going there regularly for the past few years'. Interesting as these views may be, they actually throw very little light on the real motivation of the tourists, because they have not helped to identify the tourists' *needs* and *wants*.

People often talk about their 'needing' a holiday, just as they might say they need a new three-piece suite for the lounge, a new dress or a better lawnmower. Are they in fact expressing a need, or a want? 'Need' suggests that the products we are asking for are necessities for our daily life, but this is clearly not the case with these products. We are merely expressing a desire for more goods and services, a symptom of the consumer-oriented society in which we live. So let us start by examining what it is we mean by a need.

People have certain physiological needs, which are essential for their survival: they need to eat, to drink, to sleep, to keep warm and to reproduce – all needs which are essential to the survival of the human race. Beyond these needs, we also have psychological needs which are important for our well-being, such as the need to love and be loved, the need for friendship, and the need to value ourselves as human beings and to have others value and respect us. Many people believe we also have inherently within us the need to master our environment, and to understand the nature of the society in which we live. Abraham Maslow conveniently grouped these needs into a hierarchy (see Figure 5.1), suggesting that the more fundamental needs have to be satisfied before we seek to satisfy the higher level needs.

The difficulty in exploring these needs is that many people may actually be quite unaware of their needs, or how to go about satisfying them. Others will be reluctant to reveal their real needs; for example, few people would be willing openly to admit that they travel to a particular destination to impress their neighbours, although their desire for status within the neighbourhood may well be a factor in their choice of holiday and destination.

Some of our needs are *innate*, that is, they are based on factors inherited by us at birth. These include biological and instinctive needs such as eating and drinking. However, we also inherit genetic traits from our parents which are reflected in certain needs and wants. Other needs and wants arise out of the environment in which we are raised, and are therefore *learned*, or socially engineered. The early death of parents, or their lack of overt affection towards us, may cause us to have stronger needs for bonding and friendship with others, for example. As we come to know more about genomes, following the discovery of the human genetic code early in the twenty-first century, so we are coming to appreciate that our genetic differences are in fact very slight, indicating that most of our needs and wants are conditioned by our environment.

Travel may be one of several means of satisfying a need, and although needs are felt by us, we do not necessarily express them, and we may not recognize how travel actually satisfies our particular needs. Consequently, if we re-examine the answers given

Figure 5.1 Maslow's hierarchy of needs. (*Source: From Motivation and Personality by A. Maslow (1987). Reprinted by permission of Pearson Education, Inc., Upper Saddle River, NJ 07458*)

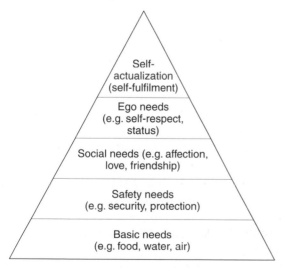

Self-actualization (self-fulfilment)

Ego needs (e.g. self-respect, status)

Social needs (e.g. affection, love, friendship)

Safety needs (e.g. security, protection)

Basic needs (e.g. food, water, air)

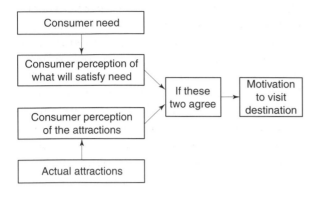

Figure 5.2   The motivation process

earlier to questions asking why we travel, it may be that in the case where respondents are confirming the desire to return to the same destination year after year, they are actually expressing the desire to satisfy a need for safety and security, by returning to the tried and tested. The means by which this is achieved, namely a holiday in a resort well known to them, reflects the respondents' 'want', rather than their need.

The process of translating a need into the motivation to visit a specific destination or to undertake a specific activity is quite complex, and can best be demonstrated by a diagram (see Figure 5.2)

A potential consumer must not only recognize that they have a need, but also understand how a particular product will satisfy it. Every consumer is different, and what one consumer sees as the ideal solution to the need, another will reject. A holiday in Benidorm, which Mr A thinks will be something akin to paradise would be for Mr B an endurance test; he might prefer a walk in the Pennines for a week, which Mr A would find the nearest thing to purgatory. It is important that we all recognize that each person's perception of a holiday, like any other product, is affected by their experiences and attitudes. Only if the perception of the need and of the attraction match will a consumer be motivated to buy the product. The job of the skilled salesperson behind a travel agent's desk is to subtly question clients in order to learn about their interests and desires, and find the products to match.

General and specific motivation

We have established that motivation arises out of the felt wants or needs of the individual. We can now go on to explain that motivation is expressed in two distinct forms, known as *specific motivation* and *general motivation*.

General motivation is aimed at achieving a broad objective, for example that of getting away from the routine and stress of the workplace in order to enjoy different surroundings, and a healthy environment. Here, health and relief of stress are the broad motives reflecting the needs discussed above. If the tourist decides to take their holiday in the Swiss Alps, where they will be able to take walks in fresh mountain air and enjoy varied scenery, good food and total relaxation, these are all specific objectives, reflecting the means by which their needs will be met. Marketing managers sometimes refer to these two forms of motivation as 'push' factors and 'pull' factors; the tourist is being pushed into a holiday by the need to get away from their everyday environment, but other factors may be at work to pull, or encourage, them to travel to a specific destination. For this reason, marketing staff realize that they will have to undertake their promotion at two distinct levels, persuading the consumer of the need to take a holiday, and also to show those consumers that the particular holiday or destination the organization is promoting will best satisfy that need.

If we look at the varied forms of leisure tourism which have become a part of our lives in the past few years, we will quickly see that certain types of holiday have become popular because they best meet common, and basic, needs. The 'sun, sea and sand' holiday, which caters to the mass market, is essentially a passive form of leisure which entails nothing more stressful than a relaxing time on the beach, enjoyment of the perceived healthy benefits of sunshine and saltwater bathing, good food and reasonably priced alcohol (another relaxant). The tendency among certain groups of tourists abroad to drink too much, and to misbehave generally, is again a reflection of need, even if the result is one which we have come to deplore because of its impact on others. Such tourists seek to escape from the constraints of their usual environment, and to enjoy an opportunity to 'let their hair down', perhaps in a more tolerant environment than they would find in their own home country. Those travelling on their own might also seek opportunities to meet other people, or even find romance (thus meeting the need to belong and other social needs). In the case of families, parents can simultaneously satisfy their own needs while also providing a healthy and enjoyable time for their children on the beach; parents may also be given the chance to get away and be on their own while their children are being cared for by skilled childminders. What is provided is therefore a 'bundle of benefits', and the more a particular package holiday, or a particular destination, can be shown to provide the range of benefits sought, the more attractive will that holiday appear to the tourist compared with other holidays on offer. In this case, the bundle will be made up of benefits which are designed to cater to both general and specific needs and wants.

Today, there is a growing demand for holidays which offer more strenuous activities than are to be found in the traditional 'three S' holidays, such as trekking, mountaineering or yachting. These appeal because they attract those whose basic needs for relaxation have already been satisfied (and their desk-bound jobs may involve mental, rather than physical, strain); they are now seeking something more challenging. Strenuous activities provide opportunities for people to test their physical abilities, and while this may involve no more than a search for health by other means, there may also be a search for competence, another need identified by Maslow. Because these holidays are also purchased by like-minded people, and are often provided in small groups, they can also help to meet other ego and social needs.

It must also be recognized that many tourists are constantly seeking novelty and different experiences. However satisfied they might be with the former holiday, they will be unlikely to return to the same destination, but are forever seeking something more

challenging, more exciting, more remote. This is in part an explanation for the growing demand for long-haul holidays. For other people, these increasingly exotic tourist trips satisfy the search for status.

The need for self-actualization can be met in a number of ways. At its simplest, the desire to 'commune with nature' is a common trait among many tourists, and can be achieved through scenic trips by coach, by fly-drive packages in which routes are identified and stopping-off points recommended for their scenic beauty, by cycling tours, or by hiking holidays. Alternatively, the quest for knowledge can be met by tours such as those offered to cultural centres in Europe, accompanied by experts in particular fields such as archaeology. Self actualization can be aided through packages offering painting or other artistic 'do-it-yourself' holidays. Some tourists seek more meaningful experiences through contact with foreign residents, where they can come to understand the local cultures. This process can be facilitated through careful packaging of programmes arranged by organizers, who build up suitable contacts among local residents at the destination. Local guides, too, can act as 'culture-brokers' in overcoming language barriers or helping to explain local culture to inquisitive tourists.

As people come to travel more, and as they become more sophisticated, or better educated, so will their higher-level needs predominate in their motivation for a particular holiday. Companies in the business of tourism must always recognize this and take it into account when planning new programmes or new attractions for the tourist.

Motivators and facilitators

We have dealt up to now with the factors that motivate tourists to take holidays. However, in order to take a holiday, the tourist requires both time and money. These factors do not motivate in themselves, but they make it possible for prospective tourists to indulge in their desires. They are known for this reason as facilitators.

Facilitators play a major role in relation to the specific objectives of the tourist. The availability of more money, for instance, means that the choice of destination is wider for the tourist. Better accessibility to a destination, or more favourable exchange rates against the local currency, easier entry without political barriers, and friendly locals speaking the language of the tourist will all facilitate the choice of destination.

If all consumers responded in the same way to given stimuli, the life of marketing managers would become a great deal easier. Unfortunately, consumer behaviour is by no means an exact science, and individual influences on motivation which help to explain the behaviour of tourists as they become aware of, search out and choose their holiday destinations are extremely complex. Nevertheless, we can identify the major factors behind these influences and they are either psychological or sociological in nature.

Psychological and sociological factors influencing motivation

Buying behaviour and decision making

Before anyone can choose to undertake a holiday, they must become aware of the destinations from which they can choose, and obtain information about these destinations. They then have to develop a favourable stance towards particular destinations, and finally become sufficiently committed to one over other choices to buy a particular holiday. Marketing theorists have developed a number of models to explain this process of buying behaviour, some of them extremely complex, as they try to integrate more and more factors into the model. Perhaps the best known, as well as the simplest model, is known as AIDA (see Figure 5.3).

Marketing aims to move the consumer from a stage of unawareness, either of the product (such as a specific destination or resort) or the particular brand (such as an individual package tour company,

- Awareness
- Interest
- Desire
- Action

Figure 5.3 The AIDA model

or a hotel), through each of these stages to a point where the consumer is persuaded to buy a particular product and brand.

The first step in this process is to move the consumer from unawareness to awareness. This entails an understanding about the way in which the consumer learns about new products.

If you, the reader, think for a moment about how you came to learn about a particular destination you have visited, you will quickly recognize how difficult it is to pinpoint all the influences – many of which you may not be consciously aware of. Every day, consumers are faced with hundreds of new pieces of knowledge, including information about new products. If we are to retain any of this information, the first task of marketing is to ensure that we perceive it, i.e. become conscious of it.

Perception is an important part of the process by which we learn. It involves the selection and interpretation of the information which is presented to us. As we cannot possibly absorb all the messages with which we are faced each day, many are consciously or unconsciously 'screened out' from our memories. If we are favourably predisposed towards a particular product or message, there is clearly a greater likelihood that we will absorb it. So, for example, if our best friend has just returned from a holiday in the Cayman Islands, and has enthusiastically talked to us about the trip, if we then spot a feature on the Cayman Islands on television this may arouse our interest, even if, up to the point our friend mentioned the place, we had never even heard of it. If what we see on the television programme reinforces the image of the destination which we gained from our friend, we might be encouraged to seek further information on the destination, perhaps by contacting the tourist office representing the destination. At any point in this process, we might be put off by what we find – for instance, if we perceive the destination as being too far away, too expensive, or too inaccessible for the length of time we are contemplating a trip, we may search no further. If, on the other hand, the search process leads us to form a positive image of the destination, we may start mentally comparing the destination with others towards which we were favourably disposed. The process of choice involves constant comparison, weighing up one destination against others, estimating the benefits and the drawbacks of each as a potential holiday destination. As this process goes on, three things are happening.

The tourism 'image'

First, we are developing an image of the destination in question. This image may be a totally inaccurate one, if the information sources we use are uninformed, or deliberately seek to distort the information they provide. We may then find that we become confused about the image itself. For example, in 1993 the media carried many reports of muggings carried out against tourists in the Miami area, while the destination itself continued to try to disseminate a positive image of the resort, and brochures of the tour operators likewise concentrated on selling the positive benefits with little reference to the potential dangers faced by tourists.

Images are built around the unique attributes which the destination can claim. The more these help to distinguish the destination from other similar destinations, the greater the attraction of the destination to the tourist. Those destinations which offer truly unique products, such as the Grand Canyon in the USA, the Great Wall of China near Beijing, or the Pyramids at Giza, Egypt, have an in-built advantage – although in time the attraction of such destinations may be such that it becomes necessary to 'demarket' the site to avoid over-popularity. In the early 1990s the Egyptian Tourist Office in particular faced the problem of negative publicity associated with attacks against tourists by fundamen-

talists in other parts of the country, closely following on over popularity of the area as a destination for international tourists. Much of the promotion undertaken by tourist offices has the long-term objective of generating a positive image of a destination, so that when it is being considered by the tourist, the favourable image generated will give the destination an edge over its competitors.

By contrast with the above examples, many typical seaside resorts suffer from having very little to distinguish them from their competitors. Simply offering good beaches, pleasant hotels and well-cooked food is not enough in itself; in some way, an image must be *induced* by the tourist office to distance the resort from other similar resorts, so that, for example, if changes in exchange rates or inflation rates work against the destination, it may still be seen as having 'added value', and will retain a loyal market.

Attitudes to the product

So much for image. Next, we find we are developing an attitude towards the destination. This attitude, which is a mix of our emotional feelings about the destination and our rational evaluation of its merits, will help to determine whether we would consider it a possible venue for a holiday. It should be stressed at this point, however, that we may have a negative image of the destination, but still retain a positive attitude towards travel there, because we have an interest in seeing the destination. This was often the case with travel to the communist bloc countries before the collapse of their political systems at the end of the 1980s. The troubles in Northern Ireland throughout the 1990s also led to an interest in viewing the sites which were the subject of so much negative press publicity.

Risk as a factor in tourism choice

Finally, in this process of consumer choice, we will also be weighing up the perceived risk we run in travelling to the destination. All holidays involve risk in some way – risk of illness, of bad weather, of being unable to get what we want if we delay booking, of being uncertain about the product until we see it at first hand, about its representing value for money. We will be asking ourselves what risks we are running, whether there is a high likelihood of their occurrence, whether the risks are avoidable, and how significant would be the consequences. Some tourists, of course, will relish a degree of risk, as this gives an edge of excitement to the holiday, so the presence of risk is not in itself a barrier to tourism. Others, however, are 'risk averters' and will studiously avoid risk wherever possible. Clearly, the significance of the risk will be a key factor; there will be much less concern with the risk of poor weather than with the risk of crime. Risk averters will book early; they may choose to return to the same resort they have visited in the past, knowing its reliability; they will book a package tour, rather than travel independently. The American Hilton and Holiday Inn chain hotels have been eminently successful throughout the world by offering some certainty about standards, in countries where Americans could feel at risk from 'foreign' food, poor plumbing or other inadequacies of a tour which can become preventable by good forward planning. Travel businesses such as cruise lines, which offer a product with a reassuring lack of risk, can make this an important theme in their promotional campaign.

Risk is also a factor in the methods chosen by customers to book their holidays. There is evidence that much of the continuing reluctance shown by tourists to seek information and make bookings through Internet providers can be attributed in part to the lack of face-to-face contact with a trusted – and, hopefully, expert – travel agent, and in part to the suspicion that information received through the Internet will be biased in favour of the information provider.

Some theories of decision making

The process of sorting through the various holidays on offer and determining which is the best to choose is inevitably complex, and individual personality traits will determine how the eventual decision is arrived at. Some people undertake a process of *extensive problem solving*, in which information is sought about a wide range of products, each of which is evaluated and compared with similar products. Other consumers will not have the patience to explore a wide variety of choices, and will deliberately restrict choice, with the aim of 'satisficing' rather than being certain of getting the best possible product. This is known as *limited problem solving*, and will provide the benefit of saving time. Many consumers engage in *routinized response behaviour*, in which choice changes relatively little over time. This is a common pattern among brand-loyal consumers, for example, and some holiday-makers who have been content with a particular company or destination in the past may opt for the same again. Finally, some consumers will buy on *impulse*. While this is more typical of products costing little, it is not unknown among holiday purchasers, and is a pattern of behaviour that can be stimulated and serviced by late availability offers particularly.

Pressures from society

We are all members of society, we are influenced by others in society and we react to the norms and values reflected in society. We all like to feel that we are making our own decisions about the products we choose, without always realizing how other people's taste influences our own, and what pressures there are on us to conform.

When we claim that we are buying to 'please ourselves', what exactly is this 'self' that we are pleasing? We are, in fact, composed of many 'selves'. There is the self that we see ourselves as, often highly subjectively; the Ideal self, representing how we would like to be; there is our self as we believe others see us, and the self as we are actually seen by others; and there is – perhaps – a real self, the unknown self that we are objectively. Whether that real self actually exists is questionable. Readers will be aware that they put on different 'fronts' and act out different roles according to the company in which they find themselves, whether family, best friend, lover, employer. Do any of these relationships truly reflect our real self?

The importance attached to this theory of self, from the point of view of this text, is the way in which it affects those things we buy and with which we surround ourselves. This means that in the case of holidays we will not always buy the kind of holiday we think we would most enjoy, or even the one we feel we could best afford, but instead we might buy the holiday which we feel will give us status with our friends and neighbours, or will reflect the kind of holiday we feel that 'persons in our position' should take. Advertisers will frequently use this knowledge to promote a destination as being suited to a particular kind of tourist, and will perhaps go further, using as a model in their advertisements some well-known star of TV or films, who will reflect the 'typical tourist at the destination' with whom we can then mentally associate ourselves.

In the same way, status becomes an important feature of business travel, as business travellers are aware that they are representing their company to business associates and must therefore create an impression. Since the company also accepts this view and is paying their bills, it can be seen why business travel generates more income per capita than does leisure travel!

Fashion and taste

Many tourism businesses, including destinations, suffer from the effect of changing consumer taste, as fashion changes and as 'opinion leaders' find new resorts to champion. It is difficult to define exactly what it is which causes a particular resort to lose popularity with its public – although clearly, if the resources it offers are allowed to deteriorate, the market will soon drift away to seek better value for money elsewhere.

Sometimes, however, it is no more than a change in fashion which causes tourism to fall off. This is likely to be the case where the site was a 'fashionable' attraction in the first place. This happened to Bath after its outstanding success as a resort in the eigh-

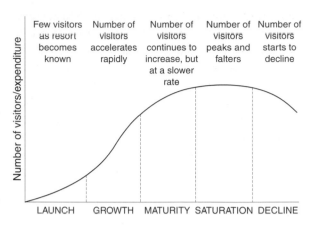

Figure 5.4   The life cycle of a resort

teenth century, and can be seen again in the case of several seaside resorts in the late twentieth century, such as St Tropez (fashionable in the 1960s and 1970s after film star Brigitte Bardot chose to reside there). It is the case, however, that all products, including tourism, will experience a life cycle of growth, maturity, saturation and eventual decline if no action is taken to arrest it (see Figure 5.4). Generally, this will entail some form of innovation or other investment helping to revitalize the product.

In Chapter 3 we looked at some of the changes which come about as a result of behavioural change. Fashion, of course, is an element of this. There is a swing towards better health and well-being which may well impact on tourism. Physical fitness is already playing a larger role in our lives, and holidays will need to cater for this increased demand. Activity and outdoor holidays, in particular, stand to benefit from these developments. Greater concern about what we eat must lead to better food, better preparation, better hygiene and a cuisine which caters for increasingly segmented tastes, from veganism and vegetarianism to gluten-free and fat-free diets. An interest in personal development and creativity, and a growing desire to lead a full, rich life promises well for those planning special-interest and activity holidays of all kinds, especially the arts.

Better health, of course, includes greater concern about the dangers of skin cancer resulting from exposure to the sun. These dangers are already well documented; in 1998, 1,640 people died of malignant melanoma in Britain. Melanoma results from sudden and intensive exposure to the sun, typically as a result of sunbathing. There were a further 44,000 cases of carcinoma, a cancer which develops through more gradual exposure over a much longer period of time, such as occurs as a result of working outdoors (many jobs in tourism contribute to this problem, including work as a lifeguard, ski instructor or coach driver). In Australia, where love of the sun is inbuilt in the culture, 270,000 new cases of skin cancer are diagnosed each year, of which 1,000 prove fatal. As the depletion of the ozone layer heightens risk, so tourists will be forced to reconsider the attraction of the beach holiday – at least, in the format in which it has been offered up to the present. The fashion for suntans may well disappear; this was, after all, a twentieth-century phenomenon, as until the early part of this century tans were disparaged by the middle class as indicative of those working outside, i.e. 'the labouring classes'. However, in spite of widespread media coverage on this subject, it is proving difficult to change long-standing attitudes, and it is recognized that few younger readers are likely to absorb this lesson!

Lifestyle and marketing

Marketers are paying much more attention now to people's lifestyle, which may better reflect the kind of products they will purchase than many other factors more traditionally associated with purchasing patterns, such as socio-economic class (based on occupation and education) or age. Lifestyle is a more complex concept, and is therefore more difficult to measure, but several theorists suggest it can best be measured by looking at the activities (or attitudes), interests and opinions of the individual – hence this measure of lifestyle has come to be known as the 'A–I–O Model'. An awareness of the benefits sought from a particular product will also reveal something of the lifestyle of an individual, and will then allow the marketer to segment markets by the benefits

sought – a more accurate targeting of the market than a judgement based on socio-demographic variables alone.

Personality traits

Several researchers have attempted to measure the impact of personality on choice. Perhaps the best known, in the field of tourism research, is Stanley Plog (see Figure 5.5).

Plog developed a theory which classified the United States population by the extent to which they are either *allocentrics*, meaning those seeking variety, self-confident, outgoing and experimental, or *psychocentrics*, meaning those who tend to be more concerned with themselves and the small problems of life, are often anxious, and inclined to seek security. Psychocentrics would therefore be more likely to return to resorts which are familiar to them, to stay closer to home and to use a package holiday for their travel arrangements, while allocentrics would be disposed to seek new experiences, in a more exotic destination, travelling independently. Of course, these are extreme examples, and in practice most holidaymakers are likely to fall somewhere between the extremes, as *mid-centrics*. Those tending towards the psychocentric were found by Plog to be more commonly from lower income groups, but it is equally these groups who are more constrained financially as to the kind of holiday they can afford to take. Whether Plog's findings are similarly applicable to European markets is by no means certain.

Plog recognized that personalities change over time and that, given time the psychocentric may become an allocentric in their choice of holiday destination and activity, as they gain experience of travel. It has long been accepted that many tourists actually seek novelty from a base of security and familiarity. This would enable the psychocentric to enjoy more exotic forms of tourism and can be achieved, for instance, by tourists travelling through unfamiliar territories by coach in their own 'environmental bubble'. The provision of a familiar background to come home to after touring, such as is

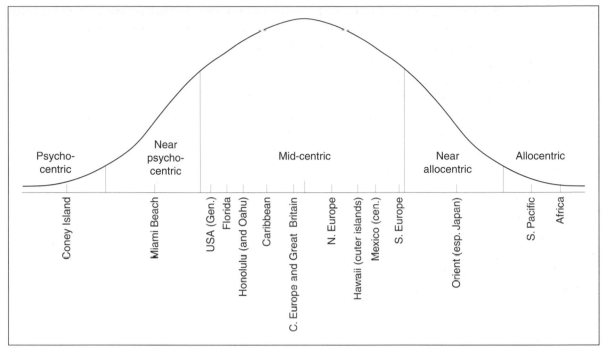

Figure 5.5 Personality and travel destination choice: the allocentric–psychocentric scale. (*Source: S. Plog, 'Why destination areas rise and fall in popularity', paper presented to the Southern California Chapter of the Travel Research Association, 1972*)

offered to Americans at Hilton Hotels or Holiday Inns (referred to earlier in this chapter) is a further means of reassuring the nervous while in unfamiliar territory.

It is a point worth stressing that extreme psychocentrics (or indeed, those unable to travel through disabilities) may benefit from experiences of virtual travel, as increasingly sophisticated computers can replicate the experience of travel to exotic locations with none of the risk or difficulties associated with such travel. Already, armchair travellers can benefit from the experience second-hand of travel abroad through the now numerous holiday programmes and travelogues available via the television screen.

Socio-demographic factors

By far the most common means of segmenting markets, and assessing the likely appeal of different products to different types of tourist, is by examining the socio-demographic distinctions between travellers. These include differences of age, gender and occupation, and are the easiest form of information to obtain about tourists. They are therefore a popular set of data to be collected in all tourist market research.

Market differentiation by occupation is one of the most common ways of categorizing consumers. Occupation is the principal criterion for identifying social class, and six categories have been established (see Figure 5.6). These particular categories are employed by the National Readership Survey and the Institute of Practitioners in Advertising. In 1997, 17 per cent of the UK adult population fell into the AB category, 28 per cent in the C1 category, 22 per cent in the C2 and 33 per cent in the DE. The proportion of those travelling on holiday each year is, as one would expect, far higher among the higher brackets than the lower. Categorizing demand for a company's products by social class can be a useful

- A Higher managerial, administrative or professional
- B Middle managerial, administrative or professional
- C1 Supervisory or clerical, junior managerial
- C2 Skilled manual workers
- D Semi- and unskilled manual workers
- E Those at lowest levels of subsistence

Figure 5.6   Socio-demographic segmentation by occupation

exercise for determining advertising spend and media to be employed. Similarly, breaking down demand by age group is also helpful, and even vital if the aim is, say, to develop holidays with particular appeal to young people. As we have seen, however, it is often not enough in itself to explain the variation in choice between different tourist products, and we must look to consumer psychographics for a fuller explanation of motivation and behaviour.

The motivation of business travellers

What we have examined in this chapter applies mainly to the leisure traveller. Those travelling on business may well have different criteria to be considered.

We noted earlier that business travellers are less price sensitive and more concerned with status. They are motivated principally by the need to complete their travel and business dealings as efficiently and effectively as possible within a given time frame – this reflects their company's motivation for their trip. They will, however, also have personal agendas to take into account. Through the eyes of their company, then, they will be giving consideration to issues such as speed of transport and convenience in getting to their destination, the punctuality and reliability of the carrier, and the frequency of flights so that they can leave at a time to suit their appointments and return as soon as their business is completed. Decisions about their travel are often taken at

very short notice, so arrangements may have to be made at any time of the day or night. Travel needs to be arranged on weekdays rather than weekends – most business people like to spend their weekends with their families. Personal motivation enters the scene when the business traveller is taking a spouse or partner with them, and when leisure activities are to be included as an adjunct to the business trip. A business person may also be interested in travelling with a specific carrier in order to take advantage of frequent flyer schemes which allow them to take a leisure trip with the airline when they have accumulated sufficient miles. This may entail travelling on what is not the cheapest or most direct route.

Factors such as these can cause friction between the traveller and their company, since the decision about whether to travel, and how and when, may not rest with the traveller themselves, but rather with a senior member of the company, whose concern may have more to do with ensuring the company receives value for money than any considerations of comfort or status.

Questions and discussion points

1. What 'image' does the town in which you live or work have? Pool the opinions of about 20 people (if possible, find a few who are not originally from the town, and obtain their views on how they felt about it before coming there). How would you use the information if you were planning to encourage tourism to the town?

2. What makes a resort 'fashionable'? Compare and contrast one currently unfashionable and one fashionable resort. What is it that distinguishes the successful one? Can 'fashion' in a tourist resort be manipulated?

3. In a group, discuss your own personal preferences for a holiday destination and activity. How far do these reflect your own personality? Would you sometimes choose a holiday that appears an allocentric choice, and sometimes one that appears more like a psychocentric choice? What might account for this?

Assignment topics

1. You are working in the Sales and Development section of a large tour operator, which plans to launch a new programme of long-haul tours next year to some of the smaller Caribbean islands.

   (a) Compile information about the long-haul market in general, and find out as much as you can about the market profile to the Caribbean or similar holidays;

   (b) You will be expected to arrange for an educational study trip for some key 'opinion leaders' (not including travel agents) to the destination. Draw up a list of 15 people (by job, if not by name) whom you would plan to invite for the trip, and plan a four-day itinerary for them.

   Produce a short report with your findings on both of the above tasks for your Head of Department.

2. You are interested in the relationship between the sun and skin cancer, and want to know what young people know about the issue and their feelings. Is it affecting their behaviour on holiday? If so, how?

   Draw up a questionnaire to find out as much information as you can about the issue, and carry out a survey on 30 young people. Analyse the responses and present the results in a brief presentation.

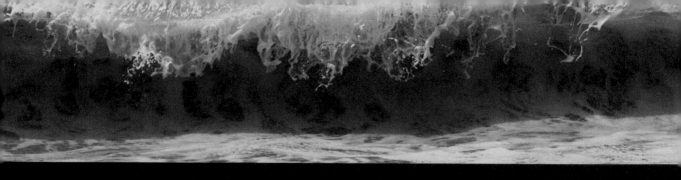

Chapter 6   The structure and organization of the travel and tourism industry

Objectives

After studying this chapter, you should be able to:

- identify the integral and associated sectors of the tourism industry;
- understand the chain of distribution and how this is applied within the tourism industry;
- distinguish between the different forms of integration within the industry, and identify the reasons for this integration.

The tourism chain of distribution

The demand for tourism is met by the concentrated marketing efforts of a wide variety of tourist services. Together, these services form the world's largest and fastest-growing industry. Because some of these services are crucial to the generation and satisfaction of tourists' needs, while others play only a peripheral or supportive role, defining what is meant by a 'tourism industry' is fraught with difficulties. Several services, such as catering and transport, obviously serve the needs of other consumers apart from tourists. Other services, such as banks, retail shops and taxis – or laundrettes in a resort where a significant number of tourists are in self-catering facilities – may only serve tourist needs incidentally to local residents' needs, although at certain times of the year their revenue may be heavily dependent upon the visitors. Inevitably, what one decides to include under a defi-

nition of the tourism industry must be to some extent arbitrary, but Figure 6.1 provides a framework for analysis based on those sectors commonly seen as forming the core of the industry. An examination of these sectors will form the basis for the bulk of this book.

Figure 6.1 is also an illustration of the *chain of distribution* in the travel and tourism business. This term is used to describe the system by which a product or service is distributed from its manufacturing source to the eventual consumers; the alternative term *marketing channel* is also used to describe this system. Traditionally, products are distributed through the intercession of a number of intermediaries who link producers, or manufacturers, with consumers. These intermediaries are either wholesalers, who buy in large quantities from suppliers and sell in smaller quantities to others further down the chain, or they are retailers, who form the final link in the chain and

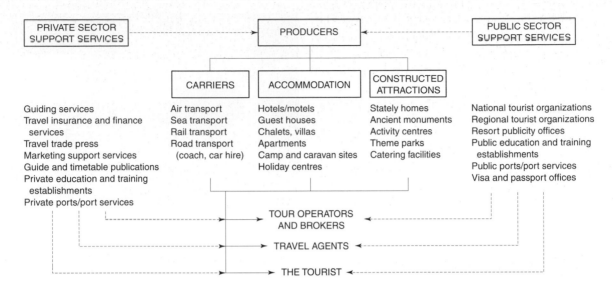

Figure 6.1 The network of sectors in the tourism industry

sell products individually to the consumer. The structure of the chain of distribution is shown in Figure 6.2.

Producers, of course, are not obliged to sell their products through the chain. They may choose to sell direct to consumers, or direct to retailers, thus avoiding some or all of the intermediaries. Wholesalers in turn sometimes sell products direct to the consumer (a common example being 'cash and carry' companies), avoiding the retailer. All these alternatives can be found in Figure 6.1, and all are common forms of distribution within the tourism industry.

As we have seen earlier, the tourism product consists essentially of transport, accommodation and attractions, both constructed and natural. The producers, or 'manufacturers', of these services include air, sea, road and rail carriers, hotels or other forms of tourist accommodation, and the various forms of constructed facilities designed to attract the tourist, such as stately homes or heritage sites, amusement parks and purpose-built activity centres such as skiing resorts. These services can be sold to the tourist in a number of ways, either direct, through travel agents (the retailers of the tourism industry) or through tour operators or brokers, who can be described as wholesalers of tourism.

Tour operators can be accurately viewed as wholesalers because they buy a range of different tourist products, such as airline seats, hotel rooms or coach transfer facilities, in bulk, 'packaging' these for subsequent sale to travel agents or to the tourist direct. By buying a number of individual services in this way and packaging them into a single product – the 'package holiday' – they are seen by some theorists as *producers* of a new product rather than wholesalers of an existing product. This is a debatable point, but in the author's view they are best viewed as intermediaries, in the sense that their fundamental role is

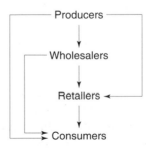

Figure 6.2 Marketing channels, or the chain of distribution

to bulk-purchase, and then sell individually. This view is reinforced by the trend for tour operators increasingly to sell seat-only aircraft flights rather than a total package. In this sense, they are coming closer to the role of the *broker*.

Brokers are most actively involved in the distribution system in the air transport sector, although they may also be involved with bulk purchase of hotel rooms or certain other services. As with tour operators, by purchasing aircraft seats in bulk they are able to negotiate much lower prices, which can be sold on to tour operators or travel agents either individually or in quantity, at net prices, allowing the other intermediaries to determine their own profit level and selling price for the seats. One of the most common forms of brokering in the travel industry is found in the role of the *consolidator*. These are specialists working in airline brokerage who bulk-purchase unsold charter aircraft seats for sale through intermediaries, thereby helping airlines to clear unsold 'stock'.

Travel agents form the retail sector of the distribution chain, buying travel services on request by their clients. They carry no stock, simply acting as an intermediary between the consumer and the supplier, or *principal*, and their main role is to provide a convenient network of sales outlets for the travelling public. Agents do not normally charge for their services, receiving their remuneration in the form of a commission on each sale they negotiate.

A wide variety of support services interact with this central distribution system of producers, wholesalers and retailers. For convenience, these can be divided between public sector organizations (those directly controlled or organized by central or local governments) and those privately owned. The former include national tourism organizations such as tourist offices, government-operated airports or seaports, passport and visa services, and other ancillary services such as public education and training institutions offering courses in tourism. The private sector includes services offered by freelance guides, travel insurance and financial services (including foreign exchange and credit card facilities), privately

Figure 6.3   Card and travel services provided by American Express. (*Courtesy American Express*)

operated airports or seaports, travel trade newspapers and journals, publishers of travel brochures, guides and timetables, and a number of specialist marketing services such as travel consultants or brochure design agencies.

The success of the tourism industry is dependent upon a close working partnership between the private and public sectors. Many tourist attractions, such as heritage sites, are publicly owned, either by the state or by local authorities, while public authorities are also frequently responsible for the promotion and distribution of information about tourism (through, for instance, their tourist information centres). This interrelationship between the private and public sectors, which is an important aspect of the dynamics of the tourism industry, will be explored in later chapters.

Common-interest organizations

A feature of the tourism industry is the extent of association, voluntary or otherwise, that has taken place between businesses and/or public sector bodies that share similar interests or complement one another's interests in some way. Such associations can take a number of forms, but typically three can be identified:

1. *sectoral organizations*, based on the interests of a particular sector of industry (or link in the chain of distribution);
2. *destination organizations*, concerned with a specific tourist destination, whether resort or region;
3. *tourism organizations*, based on a concern with tourism activity as a whole.

These can in turn be subdivided between trade organizations and professional organizations. The latter are normally composed of individuals whose common interest is likely to be based on objectives which include establishing educational or training qualifications for the industry or the sector, devising codes of conduct to guide members' behaviour, and limiting or controlling entry to the industry or sector. Membership of such bodies is often associated with a personal drive to enhance status and prestige. Trade bodies, by contrast, are groupings of independent firms whose common purpose will include such aims as the opportunity to exchange views, cooperation (especially in the functions of marketing), representation and negotiation with other organizations, and the provision of identifiable services to their members. At times, such organizations will become involved in activities more generally associated with professional bodies, such as entry to the industry or sector, or the provision of appropriate education and training.

It should be noted that the structure of these bodies may vary considerably. In some cases, particularly in the case of the larger organizations, there may be a paid administrative staff to carry out the functions of the organization, while in the case of smaller bodies (such as local marketing consortia) there may be no full-time staff, and the administration of the organization is often carried out by volunteer staff seconded from member companies. An important characteristic of trade bodies, however, is that their membership is made up of autonomous companies or other organizations subscribing to the common purpose of the body concerned.

Sectoral organizations

Probably the most numerous organizations are those which reflect sectoral interests. As we have seen, there is a wide range of sectors making up the tourism industry, and each of these can be expected to have at least one common-interest association. Professional bodies catering for sectoral interests include the Chartered Institute of Transport (CIT) and the Hotel, Catering and International Management Association (HCIMA). The Chartered Institute of Marketing (CIM) has a section devoted to travel industry members, known as the Chartered Institute of Marketing Travel Industry Group (CIMTIG), while tourism educationalists and consultants each have their own professional body – the Association of Tourism Teachers and Trainers and the Tourism Society Consultants' Group (both autonomous divisions of the Tourism Society). Some bodies provide their own training for the industry (e.g. CIT), while others rely on training organizations set up separately for this purpose (e.g. the Hospitality Training Foundation, HtF).

Sectoral trade bodies may be national or international in scope. One of the most influential among international bodies is the International Air Transport Association (IATA), which is global in scale, while the International Federation of Tour Operators (IFTO) draws its members from European national tour operating bodies. Examples of British national bodies include the Association of British Travel Agents (ABTA), which represents both tour operators and travel agents, the Federation of Tour Operators (FTO), an influential consultative body made up of around twenty leading British tour operating companies, the Meetings Industry Association (MIA) and the British Resorts Association (BRA). Similar bodies are to be found in all countries with a developed tourism industry. The American Society of Travel Agents (ASTA), for example, fulfils a similar role in the USA as does ABTA in the UK, but also draws on members from other sectors of industry, as well as overseas members, due to the importance and influence of the USA as a tourist-generating country.

The Role of ABTA

ABTA has in the past played a key role as a sectoral trade body in the British travel industry, and for this reason it will be useful to examine this organization's role here, and to consider its relationship with other sectors of industry. Its role with respect to its own members, whether tour operators or travel agents, will be dealt with in forthcoming chapters. However, as a result of legislation within the European Union which has had the effect of reducing the monopoly position enjoyed by ABTA in the past, its influence waned to some extent in the latter half of the 1990s, and other organizations are springing up to meet the needs of tour operator and travel agency groupings.

ABTA was founded in 1950, initially to represent the interests of travel agents, and later, as operating developed discretely from the retail sector, those of tour operators. It acts as a mouthpiece for these two sectors of industry and is consulted by government and by other bodies on issues of national concern and on legislation affecting the industry. It is gov-

Figure 6.4 The ABTA logo (*Permission of ABTA*)

erned by a Board of Directors, to which a Council of Regions (comprising the eleven regional chairs) reports. Two separate councils, the Tour Operators' Council (TOC) and Travel Agents' Council (TAC), serve the interests of each sector, and day-to-day operations are in the hands of standing committees covering regulatory, trade and functional activities. These include relationships with other sectors such as aviation and transport, technology and code of conduct committees and a joint tour operator/travel agents committee to consider issues concerning the relationship between the two sectors. Ad hoc committees will also be formed to deal with special matters as they arise. ABTA also works closely with the Travel Training Company (TTC), which is responsible for approving vocational qualifications for the industry. This body in turn works closely with the City and Guilds of London Institute (CGLI), the educational validating body.

From 1965 until 1992, ABTA was legally permitted to operate a 'closed shop', whereby tour operating members were required to sell their products exclusively through ABTA member travel agents, who in turn could only sell packages organized by tour operating members. This process, known as 'Operation Stabiliser', was overturned by an EU Directive which, in common with broader EU policy, required tourism products to be available to consumers without restraint on channels of distribution. As a result, ABTA has had to fundamentally rethink its role as a trade body, as membership is no longer an essential to trade for tour operators and retailers. Many felt that such a re-evaluation of its role was long overdue, given that the interests of ABTA members have often been in conflict. The interests of tour operators, for example, will inevitably conflict with those of travel agents, and it becomes difficult for the trade body to represent both these sectors' interests equally. Conflicts also emerged between the larger tour operators and the smaller independents, as well as between the retail agency chains, which are responsible for about half of all the bookings in the UK, and the smaller independent travel agencies. In the case of tour operating, this led to the establishment

COMMON-INTEREST ORGANIZATIONS

of a separate body to represent the interests of independent operators, the Association of Independent Tour Operators (AITO), while in the case of retailing, the widening gap in interests between the so-called multiples (travel agency chains such as Lunn Poly, Going Places, First Choice, Thomas Cook and Travelcare, which operate hundreds of branches) and the independent agents made a reassessment of the ABTA role inevitable. Since the demise of Operation Stabiliser, a number of consortia of independent retailers have been established, including ARTAC WorldChoice, Advantage Travel Centres, Midconsort and the Global Travel Group.

ABTA also claims to serve the interests of travel consumers, although this must inevitably clash at times with its principal role in serving the needs of its members. However, in one respect, ABTA has served the travelling public exceptionally well. Apart from ABTA's Stabiliser role, it has undertaken the responsibility of protecting the consumer through a system of bonding, so that consumers booked through ABTA members have had their holidays protected, in the event of the collapse of either the agent or the operator concerned before or during the holiday. This insurance, which has worked so effectively in the British package tour market, was extended by the government, as part of the requirements contained in the European Union's Package Holiday Directive, to other forms of travel, and now embraces non-ABTA bookings too, but ABTA continues to offer its bonding scheme to members, and remains a force, albeit a reduced one, within the British travel scene. Additionally, ABTA operates an arbitration system for any consumers who are dissatisfied with the way in which complaints has been handled by their tour operator or travel agent. In 1998, 1,371 cases were dealt with by ABTA under this system, with 716 awards being made in favour of the customer. ABTA's role is discussed further in Chapters 12 and 13.

Destination organizations

A destination organization is one drawing its membership from public or private sector tourism bodies sharing a common interest in the development or marketing of a specific tourism destination. That destination may be a resort, a state or region, a country or even an area of the globe. Membership of such bodies is open to firms or public sector organizations rather than individuals. These bodies generally share two common objectives:

1. to foster cooperation and coordination between the various bodies that provide, or are responsible for, the facilities or amenities making up the tourism product;
2. to act in concert to promote the destination to the travel trade and to tourists.

Consequently, these organizations are trade, rather than professional, bodies. Examples range from such globally important regional marketing bodies as the Pacific Area Travel Association (PATA) and the European Travel Commission (ETC), to local marketing consortia made up of groups of hotels or tourist attractions within a particular region or resort. A marketing consortium currently comprising public sector tourism interests in Germany, Austria, Hungary, the Czech Republic, Slovakia and Poland was formed in 1999 as the Central European Countries Travel Association (CECTA) in order to market more effectively this large European region, and to stress its geographically central, rather than eastern European, roots. At the other end of the scale, the Bournemouth Hotels and Restaurants Association, the Devon Association of Tourist Attractions, and the Association of Bath and District Leisure Enterprises are all typical examples in Britain of limited-area groupings within a single country.

Tourism organizations

The activities of some bodies transcend the sectoral boundaries within the industry. These organizations may have as their aim the compilation of national or international statistics on tourism, or the furtherance of research into the tourism phenomenon.

The World Tourism Organisation (WTO) is undoubtedly the most significant global body concerned with the collection and collation of statistical information on international tourism. This organization represents public sector tourism bodies from most countries in the world, and the publication of its data enables comparisons of the flow and growth of tourism on a global scale.

Similarly, the Organisation for Economic Cooperation and Development (OECD) also has a tourism committee composed of tourism officials drawn from its member countries, which provides regular reports comprising comparative data on tourism developments to and within these countries. Other, privately sponsored, bodies have been set up to produce supporting statistics, such as the World Travel and Tourism Council (WTTC), whose members are drawn from over 30 leading airlines and tourist organizations. This body also regularly commissions and publishes research data. An equivalent body exists within the UK, known as the Council for Travel and Tourism (CTT).

Many countries with a strongly developed tourism industry will establish professional bodies composed of individual members drawn from several or all sectors of the industry. The purpose of these bodies is to promote the cause of the tourism industry generally, while simultaneously encouraging the spread of knowledge and understanding of the industry among members. In Britain, there are two professional bodies devoted to the tourism industry generally, although they tend to draw their membership from different sectors of industry. The Institute of Travel and Tourism (ITT) originated as an institute designed to serve the needs of travel agents and tours operators, and still draws its membership largely from these sectors, while the Tourism Society, a more recently formed professional body, attracts its membership particularly from the public sector, tourist attractions and the incoming tourism industry. As has been pointed out earlier, this body also draws significantly for its membership on tourism consultants and educationalists.

Occasionally, organizations are established outside the tourism industry, if tourism comes within their provenance. Such a body is the Confederation of British Industry's Tourism Action Group, established in 1993 to help advance the interests of tourism as one area of business. This body has concerned itself principally with improving tourism career appeal and the quality of training on offer to new recruits to the industry, improving the marketing of tourism overseas to the UK, ensuring tourist attractions come up to expectations in their quality, and improving accessibility for tourism through an integrated transport system within the UK. In this work, the CBI complements many of the concerns of sectoral organizations within tourism.

Integration in the tourism industry

A notable feature of the industry over recent years has been the steady process of integration that has taken place between sectors of the tourism industry. If we refer to our earlier model of the chain of distribution (Figure 6.2) we can identify this integration as being either *horizontal* or *vertical* in character. Horizontal integration is that taking place at any one level in the chain, while vertical integration describes the process of linking together organizations at different levels of the chain.

All business is highly competitive, and the tourism industry is no exception to this rule. Such competition, often encouraged by government policy, has been evident within the British tourism industry ever since the development of the mass market in travel, which began in the 1960s. The process accelerated in the 1980s, following policies of deregulation in the transport sector, which affected both airlines and coach companies. Competition forces companies to seek ways of becoming more efficient in order to cut costs. Integration makes this possible, by enabling companies to benefit from economies of scale: by producing and selling more of a product, the supplier reduces the unit cost of each product, since the fixed costs incurred are spread over a larger number of units, whether these are hotel bedrooms, aircraft seats or package tours. At the same time, buyers of these products, such as tour operators, can obtain lower net prices if they buy in larger quantities, just as airlines can negotiate lower prices if they order more aircraft from the manufacturers. The savings achieved through both these economies of scale can be passed on to clients in the form of lower prices, making the product more attractive to the consumer.

The benefits of size

Large companies offer other benefits to both the supplier and the tourist. Suppliers, knowing the reputation of the major companies in the field, are anxious to do business with them, secure in the belief that such corporations are least likely to collapse in the face of competition (a belief that is not always well founded, as shown by the collapse of the International Leisure Group at the beginning of the 1990s). The tour operator's operational risks are minimized, because suppliers, faced with an overbooking situation, will be less likely to turn away the clients of their best supporting companies. Similarly, hotels uniting into larger groups will be able to negotiate better deals through their own suppliers for the bulk purchase of such items as food and drink, while airlines will bring greater bargaining strength to the negotiating table in their dealings with foreign governments for landing rights or new routes.

Most companies, asked to identify their organizational goals, would cite market expansion as a major objective. Growth in a competitive environment is a means of survival, and history testifies to the fact that few companies survive by standing still. Integration is a means of growth, enabling a company to increase its market share and simultaneously reduce the level of competition it faces, by forcing less efficient companies out of business.

Greater sales mean more revenue, and therefore potentially more funds to reinvest in the company to assist expansion. This in turn enables the company to employ or expand its specialist personnel. Nowhere is this more true than in those companies whose branches are individually quite small. A small chain of travel agents, for instance, or of hotels, may for the first time become able to employ specialist sales or marketing staff, or recruit its own legal or financial advisers. Higher revenue also releases more money for the marketing effort – a programme of national advertising in the mass media may become a real possibility for the first time. Few readers will have missed the frequent – and highly effective – post-Christmas TV advertising campaigns of the multiple travel agents, which have enabled the market leaders to extend still further their share of the travel market at the expense of the independents.

In addition to these broad benefits offered by integration generally, there are other advantages specific to horizontal or vertical integration, and these will be examined in turn.

Horizontal integration

Horizontal integration can take several forms. One form is the integration between two companies offering competing products. Two hotels may merge, for example, or two airlines competing on similar routes may unite. Such mergers may result from the takeover of one company by another, or they may simply result from a voluntary agreement between the two to merge and obtain the benefits, identified above, of a much larger organization. Voluntary unions, however, can be established which allow the companies concerned to maintain their autonomy while still obtaining the benefits of an integrated organization. This is the case of a consortium – an affiliation of independent companies working together to achieve a common aim or benefit. One example of this affiliation is the marketing consortium, which allows independent companies to gain economies of scale in, for example, mass advertising or the publication of a joint brochure. Alternatively, the consortium may have its prime benefit in the purchase of supplies at bulk prices for its members – a feature of certain hotel consortia, and of groupings of independent travel agents like Advantage Travel, which in this way can negotiate higher commission levels from tour operators and other principals.

A second form of integration occurs between companies offering complementary rather than competing products. Tourism, as we have seen, is defined as the travel and stay of people. Close links therefore form between the accommodation and transport sectors, which are interdependent for their customers. Without hotel bedrooms available at their destinations, airline passengers may be unwilling to book seats, and vice versa. Recognition of this dual need has led many airlines to buy into or form their own hotel divisions, especially in regions of high tourist demand, where bed shortages are common. This trend was given impetus when the era of the jumbo jet arrived at the beginning of the 1970s, and airlines woke up to the consequences of operating aircraft with 350 or more passengers aboard, each requiring accommodation over which the airline had little or no control. This led to the integration of several major airlines and hotel chains. However, the intense competition between airlines during the 1970s and 1980s, which led to huge losses, coupled with the need to invest massively in new aircraft, obliged many of these airlines to sell their hotel investments to raise capital, in order to survive. Since those days, the more common relationship has been through closely linked computer reservations systems (CRSs), which allow the airlines a measure of control over hotel bedrooms without major capital investment in the accommodation sector.

Airlines which are not directly competing may also seek benefits of merging in order to feed one another's routes. British Airways' attempts during the latter part of the 1990s to buy into domestic airline businesses in the United States (which resulted first in the purchase of a minority interest in US Air and later the attempted integration between BA and American Airlines services, which failed to receive EU approval) provides a good example of one airline's recognition of the importance of complementary routes to its survival. Their transatlantic routes provide 'feeder' opportunities into the US network of domestic routes, yet cabotage rules do not allow foreign companies to operate domestic routes within the USA, and the share of foreign ownership in any US airline is limited to 25 per cent. This placed British Airways at a disadvantage against its American competitors crossing the Atlantic.

The changing nature of tourism demand may also cause companies to diversify their interests horizontally. A few years ago, shipping companies woke up to the realization that the future of long-haul travel lay with the airlines, and started to invest in the airline business as a means of survival. In most cases, however, the recognition came too late to save the companies, while the huge investments necessary to establish an airline were difficult to achieve at a time when the shipping companies' profits were dwindling or non-existent.

At the retailing level, integration is also common, but because the traditional development of travel agencies has led in many cases to regional strengths, integration has tended to be regionally based, leading to the development of so-called 'miniples' – agencies with a significant number of branches within one region of the country only, which may well, within that region, outperform the multiple agents. Although the last few years have seen a huge growth in the number of branches of the big multiples, the miniples have been able to expand and strengthen their performance within their regions at the same time. In some cases, this has led to travel companies taking over a miniple as a means of building or strengthening their profile in a particular region.

Tour operating has also experienced growth through integration in the past decade, first between large companies in Britain, and later internationally. The most prominent takeover was the acquisition of Horizon Holidays by Thomson Holidays in 1988, while the 1990s saw a spate of takeovers, including the takeover by Airtours of Aspro Holidays in 1993. This pattern is continuing into the twenty-first century, although takeovers are becoming more multinational in character. Thomas Cook took over Sunworld in 1996, but was itself taken over by German tourist interests. Subsequently Preussag, owner of the leading German operator, first purchased a majority share in Thomas Cook and then, in 2000, and in the biggest takeover to date, bought Thomson Holidays, with the proviso that Thomas Cook would then be resold. First Choice and

Airtours have both been active in the international field, purchasing leading tour operators in Canada during the early 1990s. Such integration in the principal travel sectors is likely to continue, with the emphasis remaining on international mergers, both within Europe, as competition within the European Union is facilitated in the process of post-1992 'harmonization', and on a global scale, particularly where airlines and hotels are concerned. Aspects of this internationalization process are discussed at the end of this chapter.

Vertical integration

Vertical integration is said to take place when an organization at one level in the chain of distribution unites with one at another level. This integration can be forward (or downward in the direction of the chain), such as in the case where a tour operator buys its own chain of travel agents, or it can be backward (or upward against the direction of the chain), such as in the case where the tour operator buys its own airline. Forward integration is obviously found more commonly, since organizations are more likely to have the necessary capital to buy businesses further down the chain of distribution, which require less capital investment. For example, even the largest travel agency chain would be unlikely to have the capital needed to form its own airline. Generally speaking, the higher in the chain of distribution, the greater the investment required.

As with horizontal integration, organizations can achieve significant economies of scale by expanding vertically. Where total profits in individual sectors may be slight, an overall level of profit may still be made by a parent organization controlling all levels in the chain. The package tour industry may be suffering in a year of intense competition, but those companies which control both airlines and retail sales outlets may nevertheless end up with an overall profit within the corporation as a whole.

As with the linking of complementary services in horizontal integration, many companies are con-

cerned to ensure the continuation of their supplies. A tour operator, which depends upon a continuous supply of aircraft seats and hotel beds, and which may be facing international competition for such supplies, can best ensure adequate and regular supplies by directly controlling them, i.e. by 'buying backwards' into the airline and hotel businesses as has Thomson Holidays. It should be borne in mind, however, that Thomson Holidays is now itself a part of a much larger international organization, the German company Preussag.

Large multinational corporations are well equipped financially to diversify their interests into new products when they see opportunities arise. Many large tour operators have followed just this process of vertical integration, either by integrating backwards or starting their own airline. Thus we find all the leading British tour operators today control their own airlines, with Cosmos Holidays, itself part of a large Swiss parent company, operating charter carrier Monarch Airlines, while Airtours and First Choice operate charter airlines Airtours International and Air 2000, respectively. These vertical links between airlines and tour operators are examined more fully in Chapter 12.

Integration leads to control

In the same way, many large tour operators have in recent years sought to own and operate their own hotels in key resorts abroad, to ensure the availability of rooms at a reasonable price. This can be achieved either by direct purchase, or by setting up joint venture companies with partners in the hotel industry, or other sectors of the industry. Such integration offers the added advantage of improved control over the quality of the product. This is frequently difficult to achieve in the case of foreign hotels, and, indeed, ensuring that standards are uniform, consistent and of the required quality is no easy matter in the case of a business composed of such diverse and disparate services. Although operators do own hotels, this has up to now been on a limited scale only, with many preferring to exercise control through a franchising scheme or branding, which allows control of standards while management remains in the hands of the hotel company.

Equally, the production sector will attempt to exercise control over the merchandising of its products. Airlines, shipping services and hotels are all multi-million pound investments, yet curiously they must each rely to a considerable extent on a fragmented, independent and frequently inexpert retailing sector for the sale of their products. Travel agents carry no stock, and therefore have little brand loyalty to a particular travel company. It is logical for the manufacturers to seek to influence the retail level by buying into retail agencies (British Airways has its own retail shops, for instance, as do many domestic US airlines, whose retail services compete with agents for the consumers' flight tickets). All the major British tour operators now have a strong chain of retail agencies through which they push their own products; Thomson Holidays owns one of Britain's largest chain of travel agents, Lunn Poly, while Airtours and First Choice operate their own chains, Going Places and Travel Choice.

In Britain, and within the European Union, vertical integration has drawn far less criticism from bodies such as the Competition Commission than has horizontal integration. The Monopolies and Mergers Commission, as it then was, investigated the horizontal takeover by Thomson Holidays of Horizon Holidays but ruled it was not against the public interest. However, the Commission did decide to investigate the growing control of travel agency chains by tour operators in the UK, and ruled that the links between operators and agents must be spelled out clearly at the point of sale (the travel agent). There are, however, some curious anomalies regarding the Commission's ruling, which exempts certain large operators and has failed to rule on sales via the Internet. Tourism organizations committed to growth and seeking to grow their operations are expected to continue this expansion across several sectors of the industry, both domestically and overseas, providing they are confident this will not open them to investigation by the monopolies bodies.

Vertical integration clearly poses a threat to independents in the retailing sector. Airlines or tour operators opening their own retail outlets are likely to attract the market away from the traditional agencies by competitive pricing or other marketing tactics. Some travel agents, as we have seen, are combating this threat by forming consortia which allow them to negotiate better returns from their principals. This may in time lead to the creation of 'own brand' labels for tour operating, if this is seen as the best means of competing with the multiples.

Conglomerates and international integration

No discussion about the changing structure of ownership within the tourism industry would be complete without examining the growing role of the conglomerates. These are organizations whose interests extend across a variety of different industries in order to spread the risks incurred by operating within a specific industry such as tourism. Although tourism has the reputation of being a highly volatile industry, the long-term growth prospects for leisure generally have attracted many businesses from outside the tourism industry itself. Breweries, for example, have expanded into hotels and holiday centres, while abroad the trend is well established, with most of Germany's travel and tourism businesses owned, through department stores, by the big banks.

Paralleling this diversification, as we have seen, the travel industry is also experiencing rapid internationalization of ownership. This is a process which has been hastened within Europe by the harmonization among member countries. Travel businesses are actively expanding their interests in each other's countries. While it is tempting to offer some examples of the current spate in such expansion, the pace of change is now so fast that any examples are likely to date very quickly. Readers are encouraged to keep in touch with the trade press in order to update their knowledge of this process. Suffice it to say that, increasingly, British travel companies must look beyond their own borders to understand the nature of the competition they face.

Questions and discussion points

1. With the greater freedom of operation in the travel business, are consumers better off than they were when tighter controls were exercised over mergers and takeovers? Did the Competition Commission's ruling on the links between tour operators and travel agents in Britain go far enough to ensure the protection of the customer?

2. Increasingly, tour operations in Britain are under the control of other European countries, especially German-owned companies. How will this affect the British consumer? Does it matter if travel companies are no longer British owned? What company might be next in Britain to be the target for a foreign takeover?

3. Large companies claim benefits of economies of scale in the size of their organizations. Are there also 'diseconomies of scale' which may inhibit their performance and productivity? Give examples, where possible, of tourism firms whose massive growth has led to problems for the organization.

Assignment topics

1. As a student attending a full-time travel and tourism course, you are undertaking a short period of industrial work experience in the office of a local travel agent, a branch of a major multiple.

   It is clear from the manager's attitude that she feels you are gaining no advantage in spending a long period studying tourism, declaring, 'I've usually found it preferable to take staff on direct from school and train them up in the way we operate here. My staff learn more in a week here than you will learn in a year at your college.'

   Write a set of notes setting out how you would answer this, identifying the benefits of formal education in tourism. Make clear in your answer how you would distinguish between training and education.

2. As a retail agent and member of the Advantage Travel consortium, you have been approached by that organization for help in drafting a letter designed to encourage more companies to join.

   Prepare a draft of your letter, which will be sent to the proprietors of small agencies, citing the advantages they might achieve by joining. You should take account of topical circumstances which might influence the arguments you set out in your letter.

   (Note: it may be helpful to discuss the benefits of Advantage membership with a present member of that organization before tackling this assignment.)

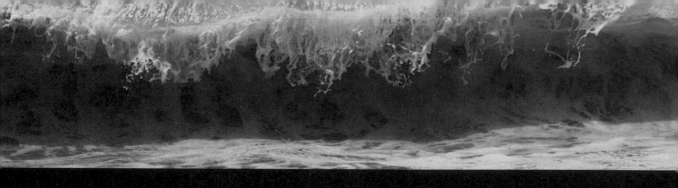

Chapter 7 Passenger transport: the aviation business

Objectives

After studying this chapter, you should be able to:

- understand the role that airlines and airports play in the development of tourism;
- explain how air transport is organized, and distinguish between different categories of airline operation;
- understand the reasons for air regulation, and the systems of regulation in force, both in the UK and internationally;
- explain how an air broker operates, and the importance of this role to the industry.

Introduction

Tourism is the outcome of the travel and stay of people, and, as we have seen, the development of transport, both private and public, has had a major impact on the growth and direction of tourism development. The provision of adequate, safe, comfortable, fast, convenient and cheap public transport is a prerequisite for mass market tourism. A tourist resort's accessibility is the outcome of, above all else, two factors: price (in absolute terms, as well as in comparison with competitive resorts), and time (the actual or perceived time taken to travel from one's originating point to one's destination). Air travel, in particular, over the past thirty years has made medium- and long-range destinations accessible on both these counts, to an extent not previously imag-

inable. In doing so, it has substantially contributed to the phenomenon of mass-market international tourism, with its consequent benefits and, increasingly as numbers multiply, drawbacks for the receiving nations.

Public transport, while an integral sector of the tourism industry, must also provide services which are not dependent upon tourist demand. Road, rail and air services all owe their origins to government mail contracts, and the carriage of freight, whether separate from or together with passengers, makes a significant (and sometimes crucial) contribution to a carrier's revenue. It should also be recognized that many carriers provide a commercial or social service which owes little to demand by tourists. Road and rail carriers, for example, provide essential commuter services for workers travelling between their places of residence and work. These carriers (and sometimes airlines, as in remoter districts of Scotland) provide an essential social and economic service by linking outlying rural areas with centres of industry and commerce, thus ensuring a communications lifeline for residents. The extent to which carriers can or should be commercially oriented while simultaneously being required to provide a network of unprofitable social routes is a constantly recurring issue in government transport policy.

Most forms of transport are highly capital-intensive. The cost of building and maintaining track in the case of railways, and of regularly re-equipping airlines with new aircraft embodying the latest technical advances requires massive investments of capital, which are likely to be available only to the largest corporations, and financial subsidies from the public sector may be essential. At the same time, transport offers great opportunities for economies of scale, whereby unit prices can be dramatically reduced. There is a high element of fixed costs, for example, for an airline operating out of a particular airport, whether that airline operates flights four times a day or once a week. If these overheads can be distributed over a greater number of flights, the costs of an individual seat on a flight will fall.

The question of economies of scale is one for caution, however. There comes a point where the growth of organizations can result in diseconomies of scale, which can well offset any benefits of size. The inability of some major airlines to compete with leaner, more efficient airlines is a case in point. Major airlines, for reasons of prestige, tend to opt for expensively furnished high-rent city centre offices, imposing added burdens on overheads.

The airline business

In Chapter 3 we explored the way in which the development of air transport in the second half of the twentieth century contributed to the growth of tourism, whether for business or pleasure. Travel by air has become safe, comfortable, rapid and, above all, cheap, for two reasons.

The first reason is the enormous growth of aviation technology, especially since the development of the jet airliner after World War II. The first commercial jet (the De Havilland Comet, operated by BOAC) came into service on the London–Johannesburg route in 1952. Problems with metal fatigue resulted in the early withdrawal from service of this aircraft, but the introduction of the hugely successful Boeing 707, in service first with Pan American Airways in 1958, and later the first jumbo jet, the Boeing 747, which went into service in 1970, led to rapid falls in seat cost per passenger kilometre (a common measure of revenue yield). These costs fell both in absolute terms and relative to costs of other forms of transport, particularly shipping, which up to the mid-1950s had dominated the long-haul travel business. Both engines and aircraft design have since been continuously refined and improved; wings, fuselage and engines have been designed to reduce drag, and engines have become more efficient and less fuel-hungry. Increases in carrying capacity for passengers and freight have steadily reduced average seat costs, with jumbo jets accommodating up to 500 passengers. The planned introduction of the Airbus 'superjumbo' A380, a double-decker aircraft seating between 550 and 800 passengers, expected to come into service around 2005, will offer new economies of scale. However, prices to passengers can only fall if a high proportion of these seats are filled; in the past, sudden jumps in capacity have posed problems for airlines on some routes until seat demand caught up with supply. Of course, the introduction of these huge new aircraft will pose additional problems, in their need for longer runways and new methods of ground handling. The prospect of loading and unloading up to 1,600 passengers for one aircraft within a short space of time is daunting, and will require extensively redesigned terminals – but there are precedents in the loading and unloading of cruise ships, which are now being designed to take up to 3,500 passengers, all of whom have to be disgorged in a short space of time for excursions at ports-of-call. Airlines, however, are motivated to introduce such large aircraft not only for reasons of efficiency but also as a means of overcoming the problem of growing congestion at airports throughout the world, particularly the leading hub airports where there are acute shortages of take-off and landing slots.

The only aircraft whose design runs counter to this drive for economies of scale is the supersonic Concorde, introduced into service in 1976. Concorde carries 100 passengers at speeds in excess of 1,400 miles per hour, but its appeal for airlines is limited owing to its high cost of operation, restriction in numbers carried, comparatively short range and excessive noise, which limits its use largely to routes over oceans rather than over land. The aircraft's high development costs had to be written off to make its operation commercially viable, and only thirteen were in service with British Airways and Air France on transatlantic services, up to the point where the crash of a chartered Concorde in France in 2000 led to the grounding of all these aircraft. At the time of writing both airlines have plans to reintroduce this service after modifications to the aircraft, subject to approval from the aviation authorities. There are no plans as yet for the construction of a second generation of supersonic aircraft of this size, although a number of companies are looking at the feasibility of building supersonic executive aircraft with strictly limited passenger capacity.

Periodically, crises occur in world oil supplies, such as that experienced in 1973–74. Although these have proved to be generally of short duration, oil is a finite fuel, and demand is expected to outstrip supplies within twenty to forty years. Moreover, oil prices are unstable and have been fluctuating rapidly in early 2001. Consequently, the aircraft industry is constantly searching for new means of powering aircraft, and, in the shorter term, new ways of improving fuel economy. In the past, this has been achieved through a combination of improved engine efficiency and reduced weight (some airlines went as far as reducing the number of pages in their in-flight magazines to trim weight!). Airlines facing low profits from competition have to weigh up the advantages of introducing the latest fuel-efficient aircraft against the high capital costs of buying them – a problem which will be discussed later in this chapter.

Many experts believe that the jet engine has now reached a stage of evolutionary sophistication which will make it increasingly difficult to produce further economies, and cost-cutting exercises have replaced technological innovation as a means of reducing prices to the public. However, the search for more economy goes on; there are promising developments in recent research which suggest that the problems of carrying liquefied hydrogen rather than kerosene as fuel have been largely overcome. This would provide three times the energy per unit, and allow aircraft to increase their range substantially.

During the 1980s, the technological focus changed to the development of quieter aircraft, and aircraft capable of taking off from, and landing on, shorter runways. The emphasis on quieter engines originated in the United States, where controls on noise pollution forced airlines to re-equip their fleets, or to fit expensive modifications to existing aircraft. In turn, the airlines have pressed governments to relax controls over night flying, which would enable them to operate around the clock, easing congestion and increasing their productivity. The British government has shown itself reluctant to permit more than a token increase in night flying, especially from the congested London airports.

Short take-off and landing (STOL) aircraft built by companies such as Fokker, Short and Saab for commuter services, seating 30–50 passengers, and slightly larger aircraft built for regional services, and typically carrying 70–110 passengers, such as BAe Systems' RJX, Fairchild Dornier's 728 and 928JET and the Bombardier and Embraer CRJ and ERJ families, have all helped to revolutionize business travel, allowing the siting of airports much closer to city centres. London City Airport, situated in the Docklands area (see Figure 7.1), is an example of such a development which has been partly dependent upon STOL technology for success. Although the airport was hampered by the lack of good connections to central London, it now operates profitably.

Figure 7.1 RJ-85. (*Permission of London City Airport Ltd*)

Another factor in the development of mass travel by air was the enterprise and creativity demonstrated by both air transport management and other entrepreneurs in the tourism industry. The introduction of net inclusive tour basing fares for tour operators, variable pricing techniques such as Advance Purchase Excursion (APEX) tickets and stand-by fares, and more recently frequent flyer programmes, in which passengers collect additional free miles based on the mileage they accumulate with a carrier, have all helped to stimulate demand and fill aircraft seats. A major development in recent years has been the growth of low-cost, no-frills airlines like easyJet and Ryanair. Not all of these have been successful (Debonair failed dramatically in 1999) but the leading contenders have made serious incursions into the profitability of major airlines, forcing these to develop their own low-cost divisions. British Airways introduced budget airline Go in 1998, although retrenchment resulted in its sale to a conglomerate in 2001; the Dutch airline KLM followed in 2000 with Buzz.

An equally important development for the scheduled carriers in the past three decades has been the chartering of aircraft to tour operators. In the 1960s, this was largely on an ad hoc basis for weekly departures, but later this became a time series basis (in which the aircraft is placed at the disposal of the operator throughout the season, or even for the entire year). Chartering aircraft in this way, to operators who could achieve very high load factors on each aircraft, helped to reduce unit costs to a point where low-cost package tours, especially to such destinations as the Spanish east coast and Majorca, brought foreign holidays within reach of millions in the UK and western Europe.

The organization of air transport

It is convenient to think of the civil aviation business as composed of a number of elements, made up as follows:

1. equipment manufacturers
2. airports
3. air navigation and traffic control services
4. airlines.

As was mentioned earlier, however, each of these is not dependent only on tourists for its livelihood. Apart from other forms of civilian passenger, they also serve the needs of the military, as well as those of freight and mail clientele. However, tourists represent for each a significant element of the markets served, and therefore they must be counted as components of the tourism industry.

Equipment manufacturers

Equipment manufacturers are made up of companies manufacturing commercial airframes and engines. The demand for airframes (fuselages and wings) can be conveniently divided between those for large jet aircraft, typically carrying between 130 and 500 passengers, which provide the bulk of passenger services throughout the world, and those for smaller aircraft seating as few as eighteen passengers, which are employed chiefly on business routes or provide feeder services from rural airports. Separately classified are those companies manufacturing private jets such as the Learjet, typically seating four to nine passengers. These also have a role to play in business tourism, with air taxi services.

Within the first category, the world market is dominated by just two manufacturers: the US-owned Boeing Aircraft Company, which is responsible for the major proportion of aircraft manufacture and which swallowed the second largest airframe manufacturer, McDonnell Douglas, in 1996, and Airbus Integrated Company (AIC), the consortium responsible for building the European Airbus, 80 per cent of which is built in mainland Europe and 20 per cent (the wings) by BAe Systems in the UK. The majority share in the Airbus consortium is held by the European Aeronautic Defence and Space Company (EADS), which comprises French-owned Aerospatiale Matra, German-owned DaimlerChrysler Aerospace AG (DASA) and Spanish-owned Construcciones Aeronáuticas (CASA). Virtually the entire production of passenger aircraft is now in the hands of these two large organizations, reflecting the enormous costs and high levels of competition entailed in building passenger aircraft today. BAe also cooperates with other companies in the construction of smaller aircraft, to compete more effectively in the global market.

Aircraft engines are manufactured quite separately, and three companies also dominate this market: GE Aircraft Engines (USA), Pratt & Whitney (USA) and Rolls-Royce (UK). The latter two have formed a consortium known as International Aero Engines (IAE), which also includes MTU (Daimler-Chrysler) and Aero Engines Corporation of Japan, a move once again designed to compete more effectively for world orders. Pratt & Whitney and GE Aircraft Engines are also cooperating in the USA on the production of aero engines for the new superjumbo, in competition with Rolls-Royce. As with airframes, we can see that this market, too, is effectively controlled by an oligopoly, and that the cost of aircraft development and production is now so high that international cooperation between leading companies is essential.

The world's commercial fleets consist of a total of around 12,000 western-built aircraft, and a forecast by Boeing in 2000 suggests that demand for new aircraft over the next twenty years will exceed 22,300, at a current cost of some $1.5 trillion. A cumulative rise of about 5 per cent per annum in passenger numbers is expected over this period, with average seat capacity also rising sharply as economies of scale encourage the purchase of larger aircraft. When it is revealed that a single Boeing 747-400 currently costs up to $197 million, and the new generation of A380 aircraft will cost well in excess of $200 million each, it can clearly be seen that the manufacture of aircraft is one of the world's largest businesses which can play a vital role in the economy of aircraft manufacturing nations. Small wonder that other fast-developing countries are also seeking to enter this lucrative market, often with the backing of western aircraft companies: the world's fourth-largest airframe manufacturer, Brazilian company Embraer, for example, is partly owned by French airframe interests.

A major question mark hangs over the development of the new superjumbo – specifically, whether the future of the airline business will be in high-frequency, low-volume routes, or low-frequency, high-volume routes. Airbus Industrie is convinced that there is a market for these giant aircraft, because the decreasing availability of take-off and landing slots at major airports and the growth of international air traffic favours large jets. It believes that by 2005 some 35–40 city pairs will have reached saturation point, and expansion could only be achieved then by an increase in passenger capacity. It is forecasting demand for the A380 over the twenty years from launch date (2005) as 1,200 (plus a further 300 for freight operations), while Boeing is convinced that future demand is for fewer trunk routes and more point-to-point services requiring small to medium-sized jets. Its own forecast is for fewer than 500 aircraft, and it claims only some 15 routes could support these giants. If proved correct, Airbus will be unlikely to break even on the huge investment necessary to build these aircraft. Boeing is putting its faith in the new 777 twin-engined wide-body aircraft, although there are rumours that the company has a fall-back position to construct a superjumbo if the Airbus venture goes ahead – Boeing cannot afford to be left out of this contest. Boeing is known to be examining the feasibility of building a blended-wing body delta-shaped aircraft with an 800-seat capacity which would require a fuel load less than three-quarters that of a traditional jumbo, and be far quieter in operation.

The manufacture of smaller aircraft is more splintered. Leading competitors in the market include the Swedish Saab Aircraft, which niche-markets the 37-seat Saab 340 and 58-seat Saab 2000, both turboprops, DaimlerChrysler's Dornier division, which produces a high-cost, high-quality aircraft now deemed too expensive for the marketplace, the Canadian Bombardier, which swallowed up Short Brothers of Belfast and produces the 50-seat Canadair SE and the 36-seat Dash 8 turboprop, and the consortium of Aero International (Regional), comprising British Aerospace, Aerospatiale of France and Alenia of Italy, which currently offers the Avro RJ 80–100 seat jet, the turboprop ATR 42 and 72 (50 and 74 seats) and the Jetstream 41, a turboprop with 29 seats. These manufacturers face challenges from manufacturers in the developing world with lower cost bases, such as Brazil's Embraer, which offers the ERJ 145, 170 and 190 regional jets, and Indonesia's IPTN, which formed an alliance with CASA of Spain to produce a 50-seat turboprop.

The smaller of these aircraft are mainly twin turboprops, while the larger aircraft, seating up to 50 or more, tend to be pure jets. After the advent of deregulation in the USA, the demand for smaller aircraft rapidly increased to fill the need for feeder services from rural airports into hub airports, where connections would be made for long-haul or intercontinental flights. Later, the trend to regional city-to-city services calling for somewhat larger aircraft, and the stabilization of the US airline business after initial expansion, has led to overcapacity among the regional aircraft makers.

A number of aircraft companies, among them American, French and Russian, are looking into the feasibility of building a supersonic business jet (SSBJ), for which it is believed there is a ready market available, either for charter or for fractional ownership (a form of time share which gives corporations access to a certain number of flight hours each year).

If technical problems, particularly in engine development, can be overcome, these might arrive on the market as early as 2010.

Airports

Airports ownership varies from country to country. Sometimes they are publicly owned (often by local authorities) but elsewhere they may be in private ownership, and sometimes ownership is split between the public and private sectors. In many German airports, for example, local and state governments may share the responsibility for running the airport, while in Milan control is exercised by a combination of local government and private enterprise. In Britain, many regional airports are in local authority hands, including Leeds-Bradford, Norwich and Teesside, while others, such as Manchester, Belfast, Cardiff, Glasgow, Edinburgh and the London airports, are privately operated. Bristol International, which was operated as a public–private partnership for some years, is now in private hands after a local authority sell-off. Seven of the major international UK airports are owned and operated by BAA, a private corporation formed by the denationalization of the former state-run British Airports Authority, under the terms of the Airports Bill (1985). BAA also owns and operates airports overseas as diverse as Pittsburgh and Indianapolis, Naples and Melbourne.

The significance of ownership is that where airports are under the control of the public sector, it may be possible for some of the overheads and direct costs to be concealed, so that the airport's performance figures are improved, while under private ownership it becomes easier to raise money for expansion or new ventures. The leading six airports in Britain, based on passenger throughput in 1998, were:

London Heathrow	60,360,000
London Gatwick	29,033,000
Manchester	17,206,000
Stansted London	6,830,000
Birmingham	6,608,000
Glasgow	6,481,000

Heathrow is the busiest airport in the world, in terms of international passengers; however, Atlanta, Georgia in the USA takes the lead when domestic air passengers are included, with over 72 million passengers a year.

Airports require a good balance of passengers and freight to be profitable, although they may also earn a substantial proportion of their revenue and profits through other commercial activities, such as the sale of duty-free goods (where international flights are involved), catering services or franchises for local car rental companies. Their earnings from the airlines are based on a complex set of landing charges, which are designed to cover parking charges, landing fees and a per capita fee for passengers carried – thus a jumbo aircraft will be charged a considerably higher landing fee than a small aircraft. In cases where civil aviation authorities pass on the cost of air traffic control to the airports, or where the airport itself is responsible for this (as at Jersey Airport), a share of these costs will also be charged to landing aircraft.

The abolition of duty-free sales within the European Union in 1999 impacted on airline and airport profitability, but in the latter case was offset as the leading airports directed their marketing effort into expanding shopping facilities generally, including duty paid. BAA took over the largest company in the USA dealing with duty-free goods, to protect profit margins. Evidence suggests that many travellers are willing to spend time and money on the purchase of goods at airports; one 1997 study found that airport profits rise by 20 per cent for every ten minutes passengers are kept waiting by delayed aircraft – so it is not in an airport's interest to reduce congestion! In the mid-1990s, average 'dwell' time at European airports was 94 minutes.

The congestion problem at major international airports is becoming so intense that efforts are being taken to develop technology which will help to improve ground handling. This will become even more urgent as the new generation of superjumbos is phased in. Increased automation is helping to speed up the throughput of passengers, and two forms of ticketing are being introduced, albeit gradually. One is the Automated Ticketing and Boarding Pass (ATB), a ticket printed on card which allows check-ins as short as 20 minutes; while 'E-Tickets' are virtual tickets which can be issued at airports by swiping credit cards or E-Ticket Access cards, avoiding the need to check-in in the normal method. However, these systems only allow passengers to bypass check-in counters when they have no hold baggage and are on a domestic trip (passports still have to be checked for international movements), and British Airways was forced to reverse its decision to work only with electronic tickets when these proved unpopular with a large proportion of agents and passengers. BA has also initiated online bookings, which provide seat choice and advance check-in facilities for business class passengers, which speeds up ground handling. In the USA most flights are domestic, and the introduction of so-called 'ticketless travel' has been received favourably; almost half of all journeys in 1999 were ticketless.

In spite of these developments, there are finite limits to the number of passengers for which an airport can cater, and those such as Heathrow are already close to their capacity. The addition of a further runway (Heathrow plans a fifth terminal within the next few years, on which an announcement is pending; this will allow the airport to accommodate an additional 20 million passengers) may postpone the inevitable point where capacity is reached, but air corridors are already overcrowded in Europe, and increasingly aircraft are forced to 'stack' at busy periods, wasting fuel; this creates a knock-on effect delaying later take-offs, and the combined effects of poor weather, lightning air traffic control strikes and the need for increased security in checking baggage at times of terrorist activity have all led to serious problems of congestion at busy airports all over the world.

In Britain, the pressures on London airports have encouraged the government to seek to disperse traffic to regional airports. However, the importance of major hubs for interline passengers making connections means that the failure of Heathrow to expand would severely affect London's economy. Schiphol

Airport in Amsterdam has already sought to benefit from London's congestion by picking up British regional passengers, particularly those bound for intercontinental connections, and is planning to expand to seven runways by 2020, effectively doubling flight capacity. Paris Charles de Gaulle similarly is seeking to become the major European hub, with an expansion to seven terminals with capacity for 80 million passengers.

The regional airports have shown their enthusiasm for expansion, but have not always had the support promised by the British government, which has shown itself reluctant, for example, to give approval to American carriers wishing to expand into regional airports. Some also face difficulty due to local authorities' unwillingness to expand facilities in the face of opposition from local residents.

Airlines have great difficulties at the congested airports in gaining take-off and landing slots for new services they plan to operate. Slots are awarded to airlines through processes of negotiation, which usually take place in November each year, to cover flights in the following year. Scheduled services receive priority over charter, and the so-called 'grandfather' rights of existing carriers (a concept challenged by the European Union) tend to take precedence over new carriers – so much so that at airports such as Heathrow, a new airline which seeks to gain slots may find it necessary to take over an existing airline in order to do so. This can give even financially troubled airlines high paper value if they control a large number of slots at significant airports.

Navigation and air traffic control

The technical services which are provided on the ground to assist and control aircraft while in the air and in landing and taking off are not normally seen as part of the tourism industry. However, their role is a key one in the operation of aviation services. Air traffic control (ATC) has the function of guiding aircraft into and out of airports, giving pilots (usually in the form of continually updated automatic recordings) detailed information on ground conditions, wind-speed, cloud conditions, runways in use, and the state of navigation aids. ATC will instruct pilots on what height and direction to take, and will be responsible for all flights within a geographically defined area.

ATC systems are being updated throughout Continental Europe to allow many more aircraft movements to take place within a given period, as a means of overcoming congestion. In Britain alone, it is estimated that at any one time during daylight hours there are some 200 aircraft in the skies; aircraft movements (take-offs and landings) in Britain are expected to rise from around 2 million annually in 2001 to some 3 million by 2016. Key air corridors such as those between London, Paris and Frankfurt will be the first to gain the benefits of improved ATC systems, although computer failure has severely delayed the introduction of the new system in Britain. The control centre at West Drayton will be largely phased out when the new centre at Swanwick comes into service, six years late, in 2002. A further centre is planned at Prestwick. The planned privatization of ATC services in Britain, following privatization in the USA, is not universally popular and will introduce a further challenge for the service.

Additional help to ease congestion has been given by the improvement in altimeters on board aircraft; those flying transatlantic and fitted with the latest equipment are permitted to halve the vertical distance between aircraft, from 2,000- to 1,000-foot intervals. It is planned to adopt similar guidelines within Europe to ease congestion, although concern has been expressed widely over safety factors in this measure. The present horizontal distance apart which aircraft must maintain, nose to tail, is ten minutes' flying time (at a height of 29,000 to 41,000 feet), with aircraft held at least 60 miles apart laterally. If these lateral gaps could also be halved, this would permit an eight-fold increase in the number of flights operating, although the problems of congestion at the airports themselves would remain to be solved. Landing intervals stand at 45 seconds, and London's two major airports, Heathrow and Gatwick, are experimenting with cuts to allow intervals of 37 seconds – again, not without controversy.

Airline services

The services provided by airlines can be divided into three distinct categories: scheduled services, non-scheduled or charter services (in US parlance, supplementals), and air taxi services.

Scheduled services

Scheduled services are provided by some 650 airlines worldwide, of which just over 250 are members of IATA. They operate on defined routes, domestic or international, for which licences have been granted by the government or governments concerned. The airlines are required to operate on the basis of their published timetables, regardless of passenger load factors (although flights and routes which are not commercially viable throughout the year may be operated during periods of high demand only). These services may be publicly or privately owned, although there is now a global movement among the developed nations towards private ownership of airlines. Where fully state-owned airlines continue to operate, as in the case of Greece's Olympic Airways and those of many developing countries, the public airline is recognized as the national *flag-carrier*, or predominant (and generally publicly owned) airline. In the case of some European airlines, such as Alitalia in Italy (53 per cent government owned) and SAS in Scandinavia (50 per cent), governments have reduced their stakeholding but still retain control, while the Dutch government retains only a nominal holding in KLM Royal Dutch Airlines, and the French government plans to reduce its holding in Air France to 53 per cent. In the UK, since British Airways was privatized in 1987 all airlines are now in the private sector.

Airlines operating on major routes between hub airports within a country are known as *trunk route* airlines, while those operating from smaller, often rural airports into these hubs are referred to as *regional* or *feeder* airlines. In the case of the USA and certain other regions, these may also be termed *commuter* airlines, as their prime purpose is to serve the needs of commuting business people, many of whom regu-larly use these routes. The growing development of 'hub and spoke' routes will be discussed later in the chapter.

Charter services

Charter services, by contrast with scheduled services, do not operate according to published timetables, nor are they advertised or promoted by the airlines themselves. Instead, the aircraft are chartered to intermediaries (often tour operators) for a fixed charge, and these intermediaries then become responsible for selling the aircraft's seats, leaving the airlines only with the responsibility for operating the aircraft. The intermediaries can change flight departures, or even cancel flights, transferring passengers to other flights.

With the liberalization of air service regulations within Europe – a key element in European Union policy for air transport – the distinction between scheduled and charter services is becoming less clear-cut. Efforts have been made by some charter companies to operate scheduled services – although with mixed success, as they have neither the market-ing experience nor the organizational structure to support selling directly to the public. However, the growth of seat-only sales on charter aircraft (esti-mated at up to 20 per cent of the total inclusive tour market from the UK into European destinations) is a clear indication of the direction in which the market is moving. Many scheduled carriers have their own charter subsidiaries; for example, Lufthansa operates a charter subsidiary known as Condor.

Air taxi services

Air taxis are privately chartered aircraft accommodat-ing between four and eighteen people, and used particularly by business travellers. They offer the ad-vantages of convenience and flexibility; routings can be tailor-made for passengers (for example, a feasible itinerary for a business day using an air taxi might be London–Paris–Brussels–Amsterdam–London, a near-impossible programme for a scheduled service),

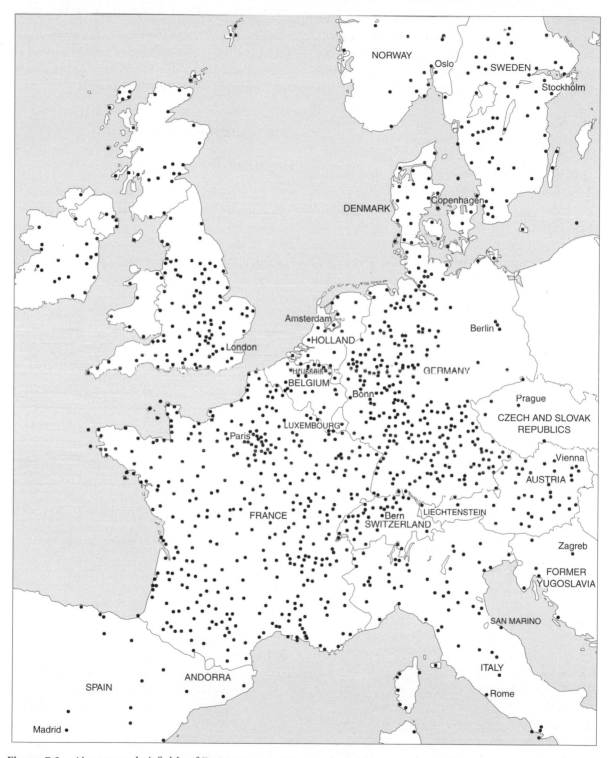

Figure 7.2 Airports and airfields of Europe

and small airfields close to a company's office or factory can be used. There are some 350 airfields suitable for air taxis in Britain alone, and a further 1,300 in western Europe (see Figure 7.2), compared with only about 200 airports receiving scheduled services. Flights can be arranged, or routings amended, at short notice, and with a full flight the cost for chartering can be commensurate with the combined business class fares for the number of staff travelling.

Aircraft in use range from helicopters like the Bell Jet Ranger, or the piston-engined Piper twin Comanche (each seating three or four people, with a range between 350 and 900 miles), up to aircraft such as Embraer's Bandeirantes, which are capable of carrying 18 passengers up to 300 miles, and to top-of-the-market Gulfstream V aircraft costing over $40 million. Larger aircraft can also be chartered as needed. Most air taxi journeys are in the range of 500–600 miles, and therefore these aircraft are ideal for many business trips within Europe. In the UK alone, some 150 air taxi companies are available to meet the needs of the market.

Some corporations which formerly ran their own fleet of executive aircraft have switched to using air taxis, as purchase is difficult to justify unless the aircraft concerned have a very high usage.

Air transport regulation

The need for regulation

With the growth of the airline industry, regulation on both national and international routes has become necessary for a number of reasons. First and foremost there is the question of passenger safety, which requires that airlines be licensed and supervised. For reasons of public concern, other regulations are needed in such areas as noise and pollution control.

Since air transport has a profound impact on the economy of a region or country, governments will take steps to encourage the development of routes which appear to offer prospects of economic ben-

Figure 7.3   Air taxi: Gates Learjet 35A, seating eight passengers. (*Courtesy Northern Executive Aviation Ltd, Manchester, UK*)

efits, and to discourage those which appear to be suffering over-capacity. While the policy of one government may be to encourage competition, or to intervene where a route monopoly is forcing prices up, another government's policy may be directed to rationalizing excessive competition in order to avoid energy waste, or even to protecting the profitability of the national flag-carrier. Some governments are tempted to provide subsidies in order to support their inefficient flag-carriers; private airlines in Europe have long complained of this unfair protection against competition. Although forbidden by the Treaty of Rome within the EU, this ruling was often ignored by those member countries where the state retained a financial interest in its air carriers.

Another characteristic of such protection is the *pooling* arrangements made between airlines operating on certain international routes, whereby all revenue accruing on that route is apportioned equally between the carriers serving the route. This may appear to circumvent competition on a route, but is also one means of safeguarding the viability of the national carrier operating in a strong competitive environment. In developing countries, where governments are anxious to earn hard currency, the support of the national carrier as an earner of hard currency, through arrangements such as this, may be justifiable. Pooling arrangements are often entered into, where the airlines are not of comparable size, in order to safeguard the smaller carrier's capacity and revenue. By rationalizing schedules, pressure is reduced on peak time take-off slots, and costs are reduced. Financial arrangements between the pooled carriers usually limit to a fixed maximum the amount of revenue transferred from one carrier to the other, to reduce what may be seen as unfair government support for an inefficient carrier. Increasingly, such pooling arrangements are no longer acceptable, and may indeed by illegal, as is the case in the USA.

In some areas, air transport is an essential public utility which, even where commercially non-viable, is socially desirable in order to provide communications with a region where geographical terrain may make other forms of transport difficult or impossible (as is the case with areas such as New Guinea, Alaska or the Hebrides in Scotland). In some cases, a government may subsidize one or more of its airlines in order to ensure a service is maintained.

Systems of regulation

Broadly speaking, air transport operations are regulated in three ways:

1. Internationally, scheduled routes are assigned on the basis of agreements between governments of the countries concerned.
2. Internationally, scheduled air fares are now subject to less and less control, as in both North America and Europe airlines are free to set their own fares. However, governments can still intercede where predatory pricing is involved, and in practice, within Europe, fares are permitted to fluctuate between acceptable maxima and minima. In developing areas, however, the extent of regulation is often far greater, with airlines agreeing fares which may then be mediated through the traffic conferences of the International Air Transport Association. Agreed tariffs arrived at in this way are then subject to ratification by the governments of the countries concerned. Generally, less direct control is exercised over domestic fares.
3. National governments approve and license the carriers which are to operate on scheduled routes, whether domestically or internationally. In the UK, the Civil Aviation Authority (CAA) has this responsibility and is also responsible for the licensing of charter airlines and of tour operators organizing package holidays abroad.

The worldwide trend is to allow market forces to determine the shape and direction of the airline business, and regulation is today less concerned with routes, frequency, capacity and fares, and more concerned with aspects of safety. However, disagreements between governments over the regulation of routes or airlines can at times lead to major conflict, as is the case with the long-standing dispute between the British and US governments regarding traffic rights across the Atlantic, which is discussed below.

Air transport regulations are the result of a number of international agreements between countries dating back over many years. The Warsaw Convention of 1929 first established common agreement on the extent of liability of the airlines in the event of death or injury of passengers, or loss of passenger baggage, with a limit of $10,000 on loss of life, and similar derisory sums for loss of baggage (compensation is payable on weight rather than value, and at the time of writing is limited to around £14 per kilogram). Inflation soon further reduced the value of claims, and liability was reassessed by a number of participating airlines, first at the Hague Protocol in 1955, where the figure was increased to $20,000, and again at the Montreal Agreement in 1966, at which time the United States imposed a $75,000 ceiling on flights to and from the USA, and it was agreed that the maximum liability would be periodically reviewed. In 1992, Japan waived all limits for Japanese carriers, and in the following year, the UK government unilaterally required British carriers to increase liability to a limit of 100,000 SDRs (Special Drawing Rights, a reserve currency operated by the International Monetary Fund, and equivalent to about $140,000). Finally, in 1995 IATA negotiated an *Intercarrier Agreement on Passenger Liability* which was designed to enforce a blanket coverage for all member airlines, whereby any damages would be determined according to the laws of the country of the airline affected. However, not all airlines agreed to implement this.

The five freedoms of the air

Further legislation concerning passenger aviation resulted from the Chicago Convention on Civil Aviation held in 1944, at which eighty governments were represented in discussions designed to promote world air services and to reach agreement on standard operating procedures for air services between countries. There were two outcomes of this meeting: the founding of the International Civil Aviation

Organisation (ICAO), now a specialized agency of the United Nations, and the establishment of the so-called *five freedoms of the air*. These comprise the privileges of:

1. flying across a country without landing;
2. landing in a country for purposes other than the carriage of passengers or freight, e.g. in order to refuel;
3. off-loading passengers, mail or freight from an airline of the country from which those passengers, mail or freight originated;
4. loading passengers, mail or freight on an airline of the country to which those passengers, mail or freight are destined;
5. loading passengers, mail or freight on an airline not belonging to the country to which those passengers, mail or freight are destined, and off-loading passengers, mail or freight from an airline not of the country from which these originated.

These privileges were designed to provide the framework for bilateral agreements between countries and to ensure that carriage of passengers, mail and freight between any two countries would normally be restricted to the carriers of those countries.

The move to greater freedom of the skies

Other freedoms not discussed by the Convention, but equally pertinent to the question of rights of operation, have been termed the 'sixth and seventh freedoms'. These would cover:

6. carrying passengers, mail or freight between any two countries on an airline which is of neither country, but is operating via the airline's own country;
7. carrying passengers, mail or freight directly between two countries on an airline associated with neither of the two countries.

These various freedoms can best be illustrated using examples (see Figure 7.4).

While a handful of countries expressed a prefer-

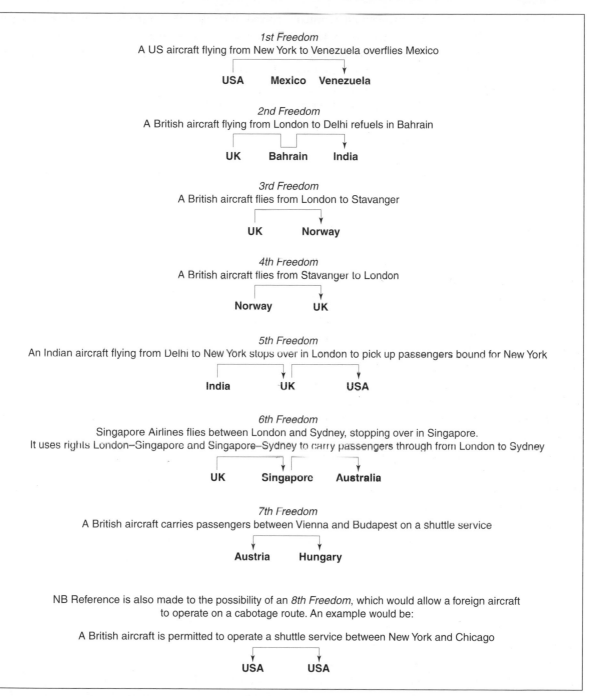

Figure 7.4   Some examples of the freedoms of the air

ence for an 'open skies' policy on regulation, most demanded controls. An International Air Services Agreement, to which more than ninety countries became signatories, provided for the mutual exchange of the first two freedoms of the air, while it was left to individual bilateral negotiations between countries to resolve other issues. The Convention agreed not to regulate charter services, allowing countries to impose whatever individual regulations they wished. Few countries, in fact, were willing to allow a total open skies policy for charters.

The Anglo-American agreement which took place in Bermuda in 1946, following the Convention, set the pattern for many of the bilateral agreements which followed. This so-called *Bermuda Agreement*, while restricting air carriage between the two countries to national carriers, did not impose restrictions on capacity for airlines concerned, although this was modified at a second Bermuda Agreement reached in 1977 (and ratified in 1980), in line with the tendency of many countries in the intervening years to opt for an agreement which would ensure that a percentage of total traffic on a route was guaranteed for the national carriers of the countries concerned. It was Britain's intention, in this renegotiated agreement, to avoid over-capacity on the route by restricting it to two British and two American carriers. A further agreement in 1986 extended the agreed capacities across the Atlantic, following a three-year moratorium on new services by the British and American governments. However, in line with the policy of deregulation which both the North American and European nations have introduced, the tight control over capacity has been relaxed and new routes have been agreed. The concept of *reciprocity* remains important, however, with the British government only willing to concede new routes for American carriers if reciprocal routes are granted to British carriers. These carriers are also concerned that the US restricts foreign ownership of American airlines to 25 per cent, thus effectively restricting operational control to US ownership. At the time of writing, the long-standing conflict between American and British air interests across the Atlantic is unre-

solved, with the US government unwilling to allow the carriage of passengers by foreign carriers between US domestic airports, and the British government unwilling to provide US carriers with more landing and take-off slots at London's Heathrow Airport. To exert pressure on the British government, the US Department of Transportation held up the then-planned merger between British Airways and American Airlines, hindering the growth of an important global strategic alliance. Meanwhile, US carriers have operating rights between European cities, giving them an advantage over European carriers, which are restricted by cabotage rules from operating similar services in the USA.

Carriage on routes within the national territory of a country (the so-called *cabotage* routes) is not subject to international agreement, and is normally restricted to the national carriers of the country concerned. In some cases, however, this provides opportunities for a country's national carriers to operate exclusively on international routes, in cases where these countries have overseas possessions. This is the case, for example, on routes out of the UK to destinations such as Gibraltar, or on services between France and Réunion Island, or the islands of Guadaloupe and Martinique in the Caribbean. Under the EU's programme of liberalization of the air within member countries, the cabotage regulation, the final barrier to total freedom of operation, was dropped in 1997. Any airline of any member country can now file to operate services between cities within another member's borders, so that, for example, British Airways can now choose to operate between Paris and Milan, or between Milan and Rome, while Alitalia or Air France can provide a service between Manchester and Aberdeen. While this liberalization should, in theory, have opened up competition and encouraged a wealth of new services throughout the EU, in practice the difficulty of getting slots at congested airports, as well as delaying tactics by some governments attempting to support their own national carriers, have meant that few new services have been introduced in the immediate aftermath of the Act, and virtually none at hub airports.

The role of IATA

For many years, effective control over air fares on international routes was exercised by the International Air Transport Association, a trade body comprising some 80 per cent of the world's airlines which operate on international routes. The aims of this organization, which was restructured in its present form in 1945, have been to promote safe, regular and economic air transport, to provide the means for collaboration between the air carriers themselves, and to cooperate with the ICAO and other international bodies for the promotion of safety and effective communications. However, it was IATA's fare-fixing role which aroused most controversy, since the association has in the past acted as a legalized cartel. Fares were established at the annual fare-fixing Traffic Conferences by a process of common agreement between the participating airlines, subject to ratification by the airlines' governments. In practice, this ratification became largely automatic.

Critics of IATA argued that, as a result, fares became unnecessarily high on many routes, and competition was stifled. Often, the agreed fares were the outcome of political considerations in which the less efficient national flag-carriers pushed for prices unrelated to competitive costs. IATA also controlled many other aspects of airline operation, such as the pitch of passengers' seats, which dictated the amount of leg-room they could enjoy, and even the kind of meals that could be served on board. As a result, the airlines were forced to concentrate their marketing effort on such ephemeral aspects of the product as service, punctuality or even the design of cabin crew uniforms, rather than providing a genuine measure of competition.

It was widely felt that this had led to inertia among the participating carriers, with agreements resulting from a desire to avoid controversy among fellow members. Nor had the cartel ensured profitability for its members, since they faced open competition from non IATA carriers which successfully competed both on price and added value.

Led by the United States, and soon followed by other countries, airlines chose to withdraw from this price-fixing mechanism, and as a result IATA restructured its organization in 1979 to provide a two-tier organization: a tariff section to deal with fare-fixing, for those nations which wished to continue doing so, and a trade section to provide the benefits which an international airline body could offer. IATA's role in price-fixing has become steadily less important, and airlines have been left also to determine their own service and catering arrangements. The principal benefit offered by IATA today is the central clearing house system, which makes possible financial settlements between members, in the same manner as the British clearing banks. Tickets and other documents are standardized and interchangeable between IATA members, compatibility is established between members in air fare constructions and currency exchange rates, and other procedures, such as the appointment, through licensing agreements, of IATA-recognized travel agents, are standardized throughout the world. The computerized Bank Settlement Plan, introduced in the UK in 1984, permits the monthly settlement of accounts with appointed agents through a single centre rather than with each individual airline, and has enabled financial transactions to keep pace with the enormous growth in airline travel.

British regulation of air transport

In the UK, the Civil Aviation Act of 1971 led to the establishment of the Civil Aviation Authority, which has five regulatory functions:

1. responsibility for regulating air navigation services (jointly with the Ministry of Defence), through Britain's Air Traffic Control services;
2. responsibility for the regulation of all British civil aviation, including air transport licensing, the award of licences (ATOLs) to air travel organizers, and approval of air fares;

3. responsibility for the airworthiness and operational safety of British carriers, including certification of airlines, airports, flight crew and engineers;
4. acting as adviser to the government in matters concerning domestic and international civil aviation;
5. a number of subsidiary functions, including the research and publication of statistics, and the ownership and management of eight airports in the Highlands and Islands of Scotland.

Prior to the Civil Aviation Act, no clear long-term government policy had been discernible in respect to aviation in the UK. As governments changed, so attitudes to the public or private ownership of carriers changed. With the aim of providing some longer-term direction and stability a committee of enquiry into civil air transport, under the chairmanship of Sir Ronald Edwards, was established. The report, *British Air Transport in the Seventies*, appeared in 1969. The Edwards Report, as it became known, recommended that the government should periodically promulgate civil aviation policy and objectives, that the long-term aim should be to satisfy air travellers at the lowest economically desirable price, and that a suitable mix should be agreed between public and private sector airlines. The state corporations (BOAC and BEA) were confirmed in their role as flag-carriers but were recommended to merge and to start charter and inclusive tour operations. The idea of a major second-force airline in the private sector, to complement and compete with the new public airline, was proposed, as was the suggestion that a more liberal policy be adopted towards the licensing of other private airlines. Finally, the report proposed that the economic, safety and regulatory functions carried out by the previous Air Transport Licensing Board, the Board of Trade and the Air Registration Board should thereafter come under the control of a single Civil Aviation Authority.

The Civil Aviation Act, which followed publication of this report in 1971, accepted most of these proposals. BOAC and BEA were merged into a single cor-poration, British Airways, while British Caledonian was confirmed as the new second-force airline, following the merger of Caledonian Airways and British United Airways, and the new Civil Aviation Authority was formed.

The CAA is financed by the users of its services, which are mainly the airlines themselves. Any excess profits are expected to be returned to the users through lower charges for its services. A subsidiary of the CAA is the Air Transport Users' Council (AUC), which acts as a watchdog for air transport customers. There is also an international body serving this purpose, known as the International Foundation of Airline Passenger Associations (IFAPA), which has its headquarters in Geneva.

UK government policy after 1971

In its proposal to introduce a second-force airline in Britain, the Edwards Report clearly saw this as a mechanism to compete with the publicly owned flag-carrier across the North Atlantic routes. After the formation of British Caledonian, the government granted the carrier North Atlantic routes in 1973. Within two years, however, government policy had changed to 'spheres of influence', with the second-force airline licensed for complementary rather than directly competitive routes. Ignoring British Caledonian's claim that two British carriers on the North Atlantic routes would increase the British share of the total market by taking away business from American carriers, the CAA redistributed routes, giving British Caledonian South American routes, and restricting the North Atlantic largely to British Airways. A White Paper in 1976, *Future Civil Aviation Policy*, indicated the prevailing policy to end dual designation – a policy later overturned by the Conservative government during the 1980s as support for a totally deregulated air transport system gathered momentum. An open skies policy being favoured by both the US and British governments in the 1980s led to effective deregulation of fares and capacity across the Atlantic, as well as on domestic routes in both countries. British Airways was privatized in 1987, and the subsequent redistribution and licensing of routes for smaller British carriers set the scene for liberalization throughout Europe.

Deregulation of air transport

Deregulation, or 'liberalization' as it has come to be known in Europe, is the deliberate policy of reducing state control over airline operations and allowing market forces to shape the airline industry. The US led the way with the Airline Deregulation Act of 1978, which abolished collusion in air pricing. The US regulatory body, the Civil Aeronautics Board (CAB), progressively relinquished control over route allocation and fares, and was itself disbanded at the end of 1984. Market forces were then to take over, the government expecting that inefficient large carriers would be undercut by smaller airlines with lower overheads and higher productivity.

In fact, the actual outcome was very different, and has caused advocates of deregulation in Europe to reconsider the case for total freedom of the air. The opening years of deregulation saw a rapid expansion of airline operations, with a three-fold increase in new airlines. Among the established airlines, those that expanded prudently, such as Delta, prospered, while others, such as Braniff, became over-ambitious and committed themselves to a programme of expansion which, as fares became more competitive, they could not support financially. While a few routes saw substantial early rises in fares, especially on long-haul domestic flights, on the whole fares fell sharply, attracting a big increase in passengers. This growth was achieved at the expense of profitability, forcing airlines to cut costs in order to survive. New conditions of work and lower wage agreements were negotiated, with some airlines abandoning union recognition altogether. Some airlines reverted to propeller aircraft on short-haul routes to cut costs, and worries began to emerge about safety and airlines cutting corners to save on maintenance. Indeed, air safety violations doubled between 1984 and 1987.

Within a decade of deregulation, more than a hundred airlines (including two out of three of the newly launched airlines) had been forced out of business or absorbed, as profits changed to losses. Poor morale among airline crew, due to uncertainty about their future job security, led to indifferent service.

Supplementals, as the charter operators are known in the USA, were particularly badly hit, as scheduled services dropped their fares. They had neither the public recognition nor the marketing skills to embark on an expansion in their operations, and many simply ceased to operate. In the longer term, what has occurred has been the survival and growth of the 'mega-carriers' – some ten major airlines, of which the 'big three' – Delta, American and United hold the lion's share of the air travel market. Far from expanding opportunity, deregulation led to smaller airlines being squeezed out, or restricted to less important routes, by the marketing power of the big carriers. This process of concentration continues: in 2001 American Airlines took over TWA, which had been operating under Chapter 11 bankruptcy rules, while United Airlines narrowly failed in its efforts to take over US Air's routes. American Airlines now controls 25 per cent of the US market.

The second major characteristic of deregulation was the development of a 'hub and spoke' system of operation, in which feeder air services from smaller 'spoke' airports provide links to connect with long-haul flights of the mega-carriers out of the hubs. This pattern has enabled the airlines to keep prices down. Airports such as New York, Chicago, Atlanta, Fort Worth/Dallas and St Louis became major hubs for domestic and international flights, some dominated by a single carrier.

Developments in the period 1990–2000

In the early 1990s, the struggle to survive became more acute. Famous names such as Pan American disappeared, and many US domestic carriers were forced to operate under America's Chapter 11 bankruptcy regulations, which permit an airline to continue to operate although officially bankrupt, while restructuring its finances. The huge losses sustained by even the biggest airlines led to cancellations of new aircraft orders, the sale of assets, and finally to the formation of alliances with major international carriers, a trend which has become of major importance in the early years of the twenty-first century. Airline retrenchment led in turn to great difficulties for manufacturers of aircraft, which experienced widespread cancellations of orders in favour of leasing, or the purchase of second-hand equipment, while the traditional leasing market in turn dried up.

Hub and spoke development, after its initial success in the United States, was challenged by new, low-cost regional carriers operating city-to-city on less significant routes. Some of these have been particularly successful, notably Southwest Airlines, a low-cost airline offering 'no frills' flying at budget fares, and operating medium-size aircraft spoke to spoke in direct competition with the dominant hub and spoke operators.

By the end of the century stability had returned, with a pattern emerging of powerful US mega-carriers on key domestic and international routes seeking alliances with leading foreign airlines in order to offer truly global air services. This phenomenon is examined in more detail at the end of this chapter. Smaller airlines have opted to concentrate on niche marketing, but the growth of budget airlines has been limited, partly by effective marketing by the leading carriers, and partly by public concern over safety on the new budget airlines (the fatal 1996 crash of budget carrier Valujet did nothing to reduce this concern). The big carriers have established their own low-cost operations (Delta created Delta Express, American Airlines opened its Eagle division), while the much-criticized practice of 'bracketing', in which larger carriers lay on cut-price flights shortly before and after those of rival cheap carriers, has threatened the survival of many new airlines. Only where the airline has sufficient resources to pack a route with flights (as was the case with Southwest Airlines) has this tactic proved impractical.

European liberalization

Elsewhere in the developed countries, governments have also supported the steady erosion of state regulatory powers. In Australia, liberalized air policy has led to the establishment of new airlines, and for the first time a competitively priced domestic air service. Europe's airlines have also moved slowly towards a 'market forces' policy, although in those countries where the state retained a financial investment in its airlines the liberalization policy of the European Commission was accepted only slowly; Iberia and Air France continued to receive public subsidies long after these became technically contrary to EU regulations. The EU eased the transition towards liberalization by phasing this in over three stages between 1987 and 1997, after which all EU carriers have become free to fly anywhere within the EU, including cabotage routes, at any fare. However, the lack of availability of slots at major airports has severely hindered the expansion of airline competition.

In Britain, airline deregulation occurred much earlier, following a number of individual bilateral agreements with fellow EU members, notably Ireland and the Netherlands. This policy led to a substantial growth in the number of domestic carriers, as well as the numbers of passengers travelling. Britain has also experienced the development of new low-fare airlines during the 1990s, although shortages of slots at the major airports forced these to operate out of less popular airports, especially Luton and Stansted. High start-up costs for operators joining dense routes, high marketing costs to establish a new name in the public eye, and the success of frequent flyer programmes among the large carriers further constrained small carriers, while their low prices made levels of commission unattractive to agents, making distribution difficult – several opted to sell direct rather than through travel agents. Nevertheless, in spite of the prominent failure of one of these carriers – Debonair collapsed in 1999 – others have been more successful, notably easyJet and Irish carrier Ryanair, which has successfully competed head-on with Aer Lingus. As we saw earlier, some large carriers retaliated by launching their own low-cost carriers – Go in the case of British Airways (later hived off), Buzz by KLM. Claims that some large carriers are using predatory pricing are yet to be substantiated – US investigations by the Justice Department found cost structures difficult to ascertain.

One side effect of liberalization has been the virtual demise of the 'bucket shops' – non-appointed travel agents who sold off illegally discounted airline tickets dumped on the market at short notice by airlines with spare capacity. Their place has been taken by brokers, who may legally contract with the airlines for spare capacity and sell this cheaply through travel agents (who were formerly forbidden to deal with the bucket shop operators). Increasingly, however, airlines are selling off unsold seats cheaply through the World Wide Web network, and the growth of Internet companies with programmes designed to handle these products is one of the leading characteristics of the airline business at the beginning of the new century. This will be examined later in the chapter.

The potential explosion of passenger traffic resulting from liberalization is, as we have seen, severely curtailed by problems of congestion. Europe is rapidly approaching saturation. There are limits to the number of aircraft movements that can be handled at an airport within a given time, and runways and terminals are already stretched to the maximum at peak times. Air corridors are also overcrowded in Europe, and the 'stacking' of aircraft above airports prior to landing is costing airlines huge sums of money in wasted fuel. As we have seen, progress has been made in increasing the efficiency of air corridors by reducing height intervals between aircraft on some routes, and it may be possible to reduce nose to tail intervals as technology improves; air traffic control systems in Europe are becoming coordinated and improved to handle greater numbers of flights. The easing of restrictions on night flights would be a further aid to growth (as would approval for a fifth terminal at London's Heathrow Airport) but local resistance, organized into powerful lobbies, has to be overcome

first. Building larger aircraft may prove to be a solution in the short term, although as we have seen earlier in this chapter Boeing is not convinced that there is a market for superjumbos, pointing to the trend to smaller aircraft to maximize yield. Such aircraft are likely to be introduced only on the most heavily travelled routes, such as those across the North Atlantic, or between London and Singapore or Tokyo. However, the problems of having to enplane and deplane up to 800 passengers, as well as cleaning and refuelling, in a short space of time will have to be overcome. While the development of new, fast rail services between the European capitals may offer some help by reducing demand for air travel on routes of up to about 500 miles, the overall growth in demand for air services poses severe problems for the industry in the long run.

One further worry about the results of liberalization should receive a mention: the issue of air safety. Cost competition is driving some airlines to use older aircraft, or aircraft registered outside the UK. While the CAA has imposed restrictions on British scheduled airlines using foreign aircraft, there are no restrictions on UK tour operators chartering such aircraft to operate into and out of the UK, nor is any firm control exercised over the use of foreign aircraft registered in other EU countries. There are legitimate worries that some operators are contracting for old, even obsolete, aircraft from developing, and especially former communist bloc, countries in order to keep down costs.

The economics of airline operation

The development of an airline route is something of a Catch-22 situation. Airlines require some reassurance about traffic demand before they are willing to commit their aircraft to a new route, while air travellers in turn look for regular and frequent flights to a destination in order to patronize a route. There is usually an element of risk involved in initiating a new route, especially since seat prices are likely to be high to compensate for low load factors (the number of seats sold as a percentage of total seats available) and high overheads (for both operating and marketing) before traffic builds up. When a route has proved its popularity, however, the pioneer airline is faced with increasing competition, as other airlines are attracted to the build-up of traffic – unless governments decide to control market entry. In an open market economy, the original airline faces lower load factors, as the market is split between a number of carriers, requiring it to either increase fares or reduce profit margins; yet it may well have kept prices artificially low initially, in order to build the market and recoup launch costs later. Key routes such as those across the North Atlantic attract levels of competition which can make it difficult to operate any services profitably, and many airlines operating on these routes have suffered losses and low load factors on these routes for a number of years.

The development of 'hub and spoke' systems

Major airlines in the United States recognized that attempting to serve all airports with maximum frequency city-to-city flights was uneconomic, and developed the concept of the *hub and spoke* system. The hub airports provide transcontinental and intercontinental services, while the spokes are designed to offer connections from regional airports to meet these long-haul services. The latter services can be provided in aircraft that are smaller and cheaper to operate (often turboprops) by low-cost carriers, often working in strategic alliances with the major carriers. Flights are then banked into complexes, and in theory greater efficiency is achieved; a hub with 55 spokes can create 1,500 'city pairs' in this way. Larger aircraft can be used between hubs, and higher load factors and better utilization of aircraft are achieved. Some 40 hubs have since been established in the US alone, serving 25 of America's largest cities. The popularity of this new development is revealed in that by 1995, three-quarters of all passengers at Atlanta airport were transferring to other flights, while half of those at Chicago, Denver and Dallas/Fort Worth were on hub and spoke flights. Similarly, in Europe the hub and spoke system has been developed by a number of airlines. One good example is KLM which, with Schiphol Airport as its hub, has built up some ten waves of spoke flights a day to feed into its European and long-haul services. In this way, the airline has been able to attract traffic from UK regional airports to connect with its major routes, in direct competition with long-haul flights from London's airports. Sabena and Air France have similarly developed hub and spoke systems based on Brussels and Paris.

Such systems are generally better suited to feed long-haul flights, as the additional stopover time called for by joining via a spoke is only a small proportion of the total journey. However, it later became apparent that there are also diseconomies in operating these systems. The organization of hub and spoke flights requires the establishment of frequent waves of closely spaced banks of arrivals and departures, resulting in peaks and troughs at the hub airports, which puts further pressure on congested air and terminal space, and leads to delays. It also requires larger numbers of ground handling staff during peaks, and involves further peaking expenses. Obviously, on-time performance becomes even more significant under these circumstances, and if airlines are forced to delay departures while waiting for delayed inbound flights, costs also rise. Some airports are clearly better suited than others to this problem; Schiphol has benefited by hub and spoke flights being based in the same terminal, so that delays in connection are less catastrophic than at Brussels airport, where connections have to be made between terminals by airport bus.

There is now growing evidence that in some circumstances, airlines remaining outside the hub and spoke system can be more profitable, by charging a higher fare for non-stop services, so that smaller demand may still be equally profitable. This applies particularly to business flights, where non-stop services are seen as critical. We have noted elsewhere the success of Southwest Airlines, particularly, in gaining market share by flying city-to-city within the USA.

However, there are clear limits to the extent to which city-to-city services can be viable, based on the distances to be travelled.

The growth of strategic alliances

As the problems arising from open competition are obviously going to be long term, a huge global restructuring exercise is now taking place, as airlines jockey to be among the survivors in a war of attrition. As we have seen, observers expect perhaps as few as a dozen mega-carriers, of which only three or four will be European, to survive beyond the early years of the twenty-first century.

European airlines had seen, and taken account of, developments in the North American market; they recognized that size, providing economies of scale and economies of scope, would be crucial to survival in the future. They also noted that US domestic carriers were expanding into transatlantic routes, some benefiting from fifth freedom rights in Europe, posing further threats to market share. The way forward for the European carriers was seen as either mergers and takeovers, or the development of strategic alliances with US carriers.

Alliances were easier to establish, but experience showed that they could prove less durable. Political differences and differences of management style frequently hindered effectiveness. The short-lived relationships between British Airways and United Airlines, and between Lufthansa and Air France were cases in point, while the much-vaunted attempt in 1993 to form an alliance between Swissair, Austrian Airlines, SAS and KLM, known as Alcazar, also foundered before being implemented, due to failure to agree on a US partner. The movement of airlines between the various alliances to gain competitive edges also demonstrates the highly fluid nature of these alliances.

Evidence now points to the success of strategic alliances as being dependent upon expansion in three stages. First, there is a need to secure a dominant share in the home market. British Airways undertook expansion especially through franchising,

absorbing 100 per cent of Brymon Airways and soon holding six franchises in the UK, as well as a further four overseas. Air France absorbed Air Inter, TAT and UTA (although it was forced to unload TAT to secure UTA, France's second largest carrier). KLM absorbed Netherlines, and a share in Transavia. The second step is to gain a strong foothold in the main European countries, especially the UK, France and Germany. This was achieved, for example, by SAS, which controlled 40 per cent of British Midland by the early 1990s, and by KLM Royal Dutch Airlines, which purchased Air UK. BA meanwhile established a German carrier, Deutsche BA, with a 49 per cent interest by 1992, and also bought minority interests in GB Airways and the French carrier TAT. The final stage is the globalization of the carrier, especially by investments in North America and the Asia/Pacific region. Again, BA became a leader in this strategy, taking a minority investment in Australian carrier Qantas in 1992, and seeking similar investments in US carriers (where foreign ownership is limited to 25 per cent). These latter enterprises, however, have proved less successful; a short venture into links with US Air proved abortive, but there are on-going efforts to form a close alliance with American Airlines, subject to approval by both US and EU authorities.

What is now seen as the way forward is through the new global alliances which are emerging. These embrace key airlines in Europe, North America and the Asia/Pacific region. While the specific membership of each of these appears to change frequently, the picture at mid-2000 was as follows:

1. *One World* (formed 1998) with current members British Airways, American Airlines, Qantas, Cathay Pacific, Iberia, Finnair, Aer Lingus, Lan Chile, Malev and Aerolineas Argentinas;
2. *Qualiflyer* (1998) with Swissair, Sabena, Crossair, AOM (a French carrier partly owned by Swissair), Air Littoral, Air Europe, TAP Air Portugal, LOT Polish Airlines, Turkish Airlines, PGA and Volare;
3. *Star Alliance* (1997) with Lufthansa, SAS, United Airlines, bmi British Midland, Thai Air, Air Canada, Varig, Air New Zealand, Ansett Australia,

Austrian Airlines, Lauda Air, Tyrolean Airways, All-Nippon Airways, Singapore Airlines (linked to Virgin Atlantic) and Mexicana;

4. *Wings* (1989) with KLM/Northwest, Continental Airlines, Alitalia, Braathens, Kenya Airways and Malaysian Airlines;

5. *Skyteam* (2000) with Air France, Delta, Aeromexico and Korean Airlines. Swissair, Sabena and American Airlines have code-sharing agreements.

This drive for globalization is an inevitable consequence of the growth of the international aviation business. A strategic alliance offers opportunities for growth, and for marketing benefits that cannot be achieved as an individual airline. For example, it allows domestic spokes to be tacked on to international routes, as the alliance between the US carrier Northwest and Dutch carrier KLM has demonstrated; it increases the viability of marginal routes, and it allows carriers to compete on routes where separately they do not hold rights. Alliances enable companies to reduce costs by using larger aircraft to meet overall demand, and by sharing operational costs such as counter space at airports and baggage handling. Marketing costs such as advertising may also be shared.

Alliances may range from the marginal, such as having an interline agreement to accept one another's documentation and transfer of passengers, to marketing agreements such as joint frequent flyer programmes and operational agreements such as blocking space on one another's aircraft to sell their seats. However, the most common advantage to be gained is that of code-sharing.

Code-sharing

Domestic code-sharing was in practice within the United States as long ago as 1967, but was first introduced internationally in 1985, when American Airlines and Qantas agreed to share codes on routes across the Pacific. Under a code-sharing agreement, two airlines agree to share codes on through routes, for example between New York and San Francisco

and from San Francisco to Sydney. This has the marketing advantage of appearing to be a single through flight, but there are also very concrete advantages for passengers, in that flight timings are coordinated, transfer times between stopovers may be reduced (and carriers will often hold connecting flights for up to 20 minutes for passengers connecting from flights which are code-shared), and baggage can be checked through to final destination, reducing baggage loss. Carriers can sell each other's flights as if they were their own, and will frequently block off space to do so. A further advantage is that code-shared flights are featured on computer reservations systems before other connections, as these offer the passenger 'best choice'. They may also benefit from multiple listing on the CRS, since they will be listed under both carriers' services.

By the mid-1990s, over 400 code-sharing alliances were in operation worldwide, and it is clear that these offer airlines a major marketing and operating advantage.

The establishment of code-sharing across the Atlantic has been crucial to the successful marketing of long-haul travel, and has been extensively used by European carriers to gain access to US domestic destinations. European airlines recognize that US airlines will continue to dominate the global market-place, partly due, of course, to the huge demand for both domestic and international travel by American travellers. Success for the European carriers will depend upon establishing closer links with at least one of the major US carriers.

Airline costs

The selection of suitable aircraft for a route is the outcome of the assessment of relative costs involved (of which there are two kinds) and the characteristics of the aircraft themselves.

Capital costs

When supply outstrips demand, as is the case where there are many second-hand aircraft on the market, and intense competition for sales exists between the remaining aircraft manufacturers, airlines can drive very hard bargains when purchasing new equipment. It must be remembered that costs for new aircraft are usually a package embracing not only the sale of the aircraft itself, but also the subsequent provision of spares.

According to the ICAO, the global growth in demand for passenger services between 1997 and 2016 will exceed 5 per cent annually, while in the Asia/Pacific region it will reach 7 per cent. Expected investment in aircraft over the next two decades is well in excess of $1 trillion. Attractive loan terms are likely to be a key factor in closing sales, and some manufacturers are willing to offer very favourable trade-ins on old aircraft in order to sell their new models. Increasingly, however, airlines are cutting back on orders for new aircraft, and leasing instead of purchasing their aircraft (or even selling their existing aircraft and leasing them back, in order to release capital). A crucial decision, as was discussed earlier in this chapter, is to determine which type and size of aircraft to buy. The new superjumbo A380 to be produced by the Airbus consortium, for example, has been estimated to cost up to £132 million each (a price likely to rise by the time it goes into production). Getting the figures right will be crucial for management in the future of the aviation industry.

Operating costs

Mile for mile, short-haul routes (up to 1,500 miles) are more expensive to operate than are long-haul, due to two factors. First, short-haul travel requires a greater frequency of take-offs and landings, and in taking off, an aircraft consumes substantially more fuel than it does once it attains its operational ceiling during the flight. Aircraft are charged by airports for landing and parking, so naturally they will have to absorb more landing charges, also. Second, short-haul aircraft spend a proportionately greater time on the ground. Aircraft are only earning money while they are in the air, and depreciation of their capital cost can only be written off against their actual flying

time. For this reason it is important that they are scheduled for the maximum number of flying hours each day. According to the efficiency of the airline, and of the airports into which the airline operates, productivity can be increased without impairing the (legally determined) minimum service and maintenance time required (Boeing 747 servicing entails 35–60 work-hours, with a complete overhaul involving 10,000 work-hours, after 6,000 hours of flying). Here, the American carriers appear to be more successful than the European, with the big three US carriers flying at least ten hours per day on short- and medium-haul flights, against a European average of only seven hours (although there are marked differences between the productivity of the various airlines within Europe). In the USA, aircraft turnarounds (time spent on the ground between landing and take-off) can be as low as 30 minutes, while in Europe a minimum of 45 minutes is the norm.

Long-haul aircraft normally operate at a ceiling of 30,000–40,000 feet (supersonics at 50,000–60,00 feet), while short- and medium-haul aircraft will operate at lower ceilings. While the cost of getting the long-haul aircraft to its ceiling will be higher, once at these heights there is little wind resistance and the rate of fuel burn falls considerably.

Costs can be subdivided between the direct costs of operating and indirect costs. The former will include flight expenses (salaries of flight crew, fuel, in-flight catering), plus maintenance, depreciation, aircraft insurance, and airport and navigation charges. Airport charges will include landing fees, parking charges, navigation charges (where these are passed on to the airline by the airport) and a per capita cost according to the number of passengers carried. Navigation charges vary according to the weight of the aircraft and the distance flown over a particular territory.

After 1998, the notional weight of passengers was increased, adding to costs. The previous 75 kg for males and 65 kg for females was replaced by a notional weight of 84 kg per capita (already adopted by US and some other carriers), in recognition of the trend to increased body weight internationally.

Japanese airlines operate on a notional body weight of 73 kg (regardless of the nationality of those carried), which enables Japanese carriers to gain advantage over others by providing more seats.

Depreciation is the cost of writing off the original purchase price of the aircraft against the number of hours it flies each year (which may be as high as 4,000 hours per year). Total depreciation periods vary; in the case of smaller, relatively inexpensive aircraft it may be as short as eight to ten years, while wide-bodied jets may be depreciated over periods as long as fourteen to sixteen years. A residual value of typically 10 per cent of the original purchase price is normally allowed for. In some cases, it might be considered prudent to write off aircraft more quickly, because obsolescence can overtake the operating life, and airlines must keep up with their competitors by re-equipping at regular intervals. However, with falling profits, few airlines find it easy to re-equip, and the tendency is to extend depreciation time. On top of this, insurance costs will range around 3 per cent per annum of the aircraft's purchase price.

Indirect costs include all non-flight expenses, such as marketing, reservations, ground handling, administration and other insurances such as passenger liability. These costs will vary very little however many flights are flown, and large airlines will clearly benefit from economies of scale here.

Fuel costs globally are quoted in US dollars, and will therefore vary not only according to changing oil prices but also according to changing currency exchange rates. Airlines can contract to buy fuel in advance if they fear rising costs; again, larger airlines with bigger financial reserves are better placed to do so.

All airlines are seeking new means of trimming their costs to stay competitive. Typical techniques noted in the 1990s include reducing the labour force, while renegotiating wage levels and conditions of service (while BA has been notably successful in achieving this, it has been at the expense of good staff–management relations). International carriers have moved some activities to low-wage countries – for example, Swissair, based in a high-wage economy, moved its accounts to India and some of its main-tenance to Ireland, while contracting out its cleaning services. KLM contracted out its catering services, while American Airlines has moved its accounts department to Barbados. Smaller airlines are contracting out their maintenance to foreign countries. Savings can also be achieved by forming low-cost subsidiaries, a move which BA and other similarly high-cost European carriers have exploited.

Aircraft characteristics

These will include the aircraft's cruising speed and 'block speed' (its average overall speed on a trip), its range and field length requirements, its carrying capacity and its customer appeal. In terms of passenger capacities, airline development tends to occur in leaps; thus, with the introduction of jumbo jets, the number of seats on an aircraft tripled, and with the new generation of superjumbos there will be a further sharp increase in capacity. While average seat costs fall sharply as seat numbers are increased, this can only be reflected in lower prices to passengers if sufficient seats are filled.

Carrying capacity is also influenced by the *payload* which the aircraft is to carry, i.e. the balance between fuel, passengers and freight. An aircraft is authorized to 'take off at MTOW (maximum take-off weight)',

Figure 7.5 Small planes, such as this Islander, are used for short flights from the British mainland to surrounding islands. (*Permission of British Airways and Adrian Meredith Aviation Photography*).

which is its empty operating weight plus fuel and payload. At maximum payload, the aircraft will be limited to a certain range, but can increase this range by sacrificing part of the payload – i.e. by carrying fewer passengers. Sacrificing both fuel and some passenger capacity may allow some aircraft to operate from smaller regional airports with short runways.

Cost savings can be made in a number of ways when using larger aircraft. It is a curious fact that the relative cost of pushing a large aircraft through the air is less, per unit of weight, than a small one (incidentally, this principle also holds true in shipping operations, in that large ships are relatively cheaper per unit of weight to push through the water). Larger aircraft experience proportionately lower drag per unit of weight; they are more aerodynamic. They can also use larger, more powerful engines. Equally, maintenance and cleaning costs per seat are lower.

The marketing of air services

Aside from economic considerations, the customer appeal of an aircraft depends upon such factors as seat comfort and pitch, engine quietness and the interior design of cabins. In a product where, generally speaking, there is a great deal of homogeneity, minor differences such as these can greatly affect the marketing of the aircraft to the airlines, and in turn the appeal the airline can make to its prospective passengers.

It is for the marketing division of an airline to determine the destinations to be served, although these decisions are often influenced by government policy and regulation. Marketing personnel must also determine levels of demand for a particular service, the markets to be served and the nature of the competition the airline will face. Routes are, of course, dependent upon freight, as well as customer considerations, and a decision will have to be reached on the appropriate mix between freight and passengers, as well as the mix of passengers to be served – business, holiday, VFR etc. An airline can be easily panicked into changing routes unless it recognizes that circumstances can provide opportunities as well as threats. A good example is seen in the collapse of the so-called tiger economies in Asia at the end of the 1990s. In spite of the economic depression experienced by many of these countries, air traffic to the region actually rose, as western travellers took advantage of currency collapses to increase their leisure travel to the area.

Flight frequencies and timings will be subject to government controls. For example, it is common to find that governments will limit the number of flights they will allow to operate at night. Where long-haul flights, and hence changing time zones, are involved, this can seriously curtail the number of flights an airline can operate. Traffic congestion will have an additional 'rationing' effect.

It is particularly important for business travellers to be able to make satisfactory connections with other flights. To gain a strategic marketing advantage over competitors, an airline will want to coordinate its flights with complementary carriers, with which it must have interline agreements (allowing the free interchange of documents and reservations). In planning long-haul flights, the airline must also weigh up whether to operate non-stop flights, or to provide stopovers to cater for passengers wanting to travel between different legs of the journey (known as 'stage' traffic). Stopovers will permit the airline to cater for, or organize, stopover holiday traffic – which might be particularly attractive for passengers across the Pacific, for instance, allowing additional duty-free shopping. However, it may dissuade business passengers from booking, if their prime interest is to reach their destination as quickly as possible, and an alternative non-stop flight exists. Tahiti experienced a sharp downfall in visitors when the stretched 747-400 was introduced on the transpacific route, and it first became possible to fly non-stop between Australia and North America.

Yield management

Following the planning stage, the airline must determine its pricing policy. Fixing the price of a seat is a complex process, involving consideration of:

1. the size and type of aircraft operating;
2. the route traffic density and level of competition;
3. the regularity of demand flow, and the extent to which this demand is balanced in both directions on the route.
4. the type of demand for air service on the route, taking into account demand for first or business class, economy class, inclusive tour basing fares and other discounted ticket sales;
5. the estimated break-even load factor (the number of seats which must be sold to recover all costs). Typically, this will fall at between 50 and 60 per cent of the aircraft's capacity on scheduled routes. The airline must aim to achieve this level of seat occupancy on average throughout the year.

The last two points are critical to the success of the airline's marketing. The marketing department is above all concerned with *yield management*, the overall revenue which is to be attained on each route. Yield can be defined as the *air transport revenue achieved per unit of traffic carried*, or the total passenger revenue per revenue-passenger mile. It is measured by comparing both the cost and revenue achieved per available seat mile (ASM). Balancing the proportion of discounted seats and those where full fares can be charged, whether in economy of business class, is a highly skilled undertaking, since there is a need to ensure that any reduction in full fare will lead to an overall increase in revenue. This is achieved through a combination of pricing and the imposition of conditions governing the fares.

Business class, for example, will achieve much higher levels of profit than economy or discounted tickets; an airline with 10 per cent of its seats given over to business class may achieve 40 per cent of its income from the sale of these seats. However, expected demand for seats on a particular route will call for fine judgement. Discounted tickets must attract a new market, not draw higher paying passengers to save money, so they must be hedged with conditions making them unattractive to prospective business class passengers.

Airlines have determined that in many cases they can increase yield by downsizing their aircraft, and often at the same time increasing flight frequency. This increased frequency can also build new passenger traffic, leading to still greater yield, especially where business traffic is concerned – as epitomized by the shuttle services operating on the Boston–New York–Washington corridor, where carriers can offer half-hour flight intervals. BA has recently changed its marketing strategy by focusing on its premium-priced seats at the expense of economy, and shrinking capacity by replacing 747s by smaller aircraft operating more frequent services. Studies revealed yield increases of 28 per cent by introducing smaller aircraft with a smaller economy section, while the increased cost penalty incurred in operating a smaller aircraft was only 11 per cent. However, this advantage must be contrasted with the probable additional capital cost of purchasing new, smaller aircraft for the route.

Boosting yield through frequent flyer programmes

In order to boost overall yield, many airlines introduced the concept of frequent flyer programmes, by which passengers purchasing airline tickets were entitled to extra free travel, according to the mileage covered. This marketing campaign has been hugely successful; it has been estimated that by the mid-1990s there were over 80 frequent flyer programmes in operation around the world, with some 120 million members benefiting. American Airlines' AAdvantage scheme, the first introduced (in 1981) now boasts over 30 million members. The Air Miles programme allows miles to be accumulated on the value of products purchased at other outlets, including shops, hotels and petrol stations, as well as air travel. The global alliances which recognize the Air Miles accumulated through all participating carriers gain a huge marketing boost. Air Miles was recently separated from its parent British Airways and is now an independent organization, while BA has set up its own BA Miles programme, which will largely benefit its long-haul passengers. The popularity of these schemes has led to so many free seats being offered that airlines are now imposing limitations on their use (United Airlines at one point found that virtually all passengers on its Hawaii-bound flights were frequent flyers, virtually eradicating yield on this route). Seven schemes now dominate this market:

AA AAdvantage
United Airlines Mileage Plus
BA Executive Club
Qualiflyer
KLM Flying Dutchman
Lufthansa Miles & More
Northwest WorldPerks

In a marketing tie-in, the AAdvantage scheme also allows passengers from Swissair, Sabena, Crossair and Turkish Airlines to benefit, building loyalty for these carriers.

Deep discounting

All scheduled services operate on the basis of an advance reservations system, with lowest (APEX) fares being available on routes where the booking can be confirmed some time in advance of departure. This allows the airline to judge its expected load factors with greater accuracy. To fill up the odd seats that are not pre-booked, the airline offers stand-by fares, available to those passengers without reservations who are prepared to take their chance and turn up in the expectation of a seat being free. On many routes, particularly business routes, the chances of seats being available are good, because business passengers frequently book more than one flight, to ensure they can get back as quickly as possible after the completion of their meeting. Airlines will overbook to allow for the high number of no-shows (up to 30 per cent on some routes), but must exercise caution in case they end up with more passengers than they can accommodate. If this occurs, they can upgrade to a better class, or compensate the overbooked passengers financially, while providing seats on another flight, but this may not be sufficient to satisfy the irate business passenger.

An alternative system, employed on high-density routes, is the shuttle, for which no advance reservations are needed, and on which all passengers are guaranteed a seat. If need be, an extra flight is added to cope with surplus demand. Such a service can only be commercially viable on those routes experiencing a high level of regular (typically business) demand in both directions, such as Los Angeles–San Francisco or Boston–New York–Washington in the USA, or London–Glasgow in Britain.

The airline distribution system

Air tickets are sold and distributed through the traditional outlets of travel agents as well as direct to passengers through airline offices or, increasingly, through rapidly expanding alternative systems employing the latest, rapidly changing technology. The distribution system consists of two elements, the reservation (or booking), and the issue and delivery of the ticket. The protection of agents in the issue of air tickets has been a major issue in recent years, with airlines seeking to reduce their marketing costs by selling direct while avoiding antagonizing their agents, who will still be responsible for the majority of bookings made. In particular, electronic ticketing (commonly referred to as 'e-ticketing') and so-called ticketless travel are making real inroads into cost. A study in the USA in 1999 found that issuing tickets through travel agents cost airlines between $6 and $8, while e-tickets purchased through the Internet reduced this cost to around $1. This encourages the airlines to push direct sales. The result has been a worrying (for travel agents) fall in the number of airline tickets booked through intermediaries; in the United States, between 1996 and 1998 the percentage of tickets sold thus fell from 80 per cent to 52 per cent. Simultaneously, airlines in North America and Europe have cut back commission rates, or have drawn up agreements to pay flat-rate fees for the issue of tickets, varying only between short-haul and long-haul flights. This is challenging agency profitability and forcing agents to examine the introduction of fee charging. Such a move, however, may further deter customers from booking through agents. In the USA, airlines are also moving to corporate self-booking for key business travellers, with carriers installing the necessary equipment in larger companies to allow customers to book direct via the Internet.

There is little doubt that the challenge represented by these moves (which will be echoed increasingly by other travel suppliers in the future) will require agents to reconsider their whole rationale and means of operation. Already, new directions in seat sales are developing, with American Express arranging to bulk-buy airline tickets from Virgin Atlantic and Continental Airlines at 30 per cent discount to sell to their clients.

The first step in the introduction of high technology in the airline distribution system was the computerized reservations system (CRS), which provided agents and their clients with a fast and accurate indication of flight availability and booking service, together with rapid fare quotations so that the best prices for a given route combination could be secured. The next step was the introduction of the global distribution system (GDS), in which leading airlines held major shareholdings. These rapidly spread to embrace worldwide hotel, car rental and other reservations facilities, and the leading GDSs battled for market leadership among travel agents worldwide. The US systems, notably SABRE, APOLLO and Worldspan, either competed against or integrated with the two leading European systems, GALILEO and AMADEUS.

The importance of dominance in this field lies in the way in which agents make use of the information displayed. Access is made through the system to a large number of major world airlines, and 75–80 per cent of all bookings are made from the first page of information. Although bias in the way information is displayed is illegal under US and EU law, it is still technically possible to present some information in a manner that favours particular carriers. Airlines are now seeking to expand the information providers in order to give agents access to tour operators' and other travel services' booking systems. Ultimately, it is anticipated that a single system will dominate the industry.

However, the GDSs are in turn having to face the challenge of the Internet, which further lowers distribution costs, and provides carriers with a direct line to their customers without high charges. The early 2000s saw a huge growth in companies (the so-called 'e-tailers', or electronic retailers) providing online Internet airline booking services, particularly for late availability – although the viability of some of these must be questioned as the GDSs themselves begin to establish online agencies to encourage direct bookings. The GDS companies argue that the establishment of web sites by intermediaries is unnecessary, given that they themselves are coming to utilize the World Wide Web to provide the same range of travel products. It remains to be seen whether the intermediaries can compete successfully with these well-established and proven systems.

At the same time, airlines are also setting up their own web sites for interactive reservations and information. This process is proceeding rapidly as this book goes to press. Five US airlines – American, Delta, United, Northwest and Continental – launched Orbitz in 2000, while BA has launched Online Travel Portal Limited with nine other carriers, including Air France, Lufthansa, KLM and Swissair. These web sites provide a further challenge for independent Internet flight booking companies like ebookers.com, Expedia and Travelocity in their efforts to sell seats direct to the public, although these airline distribution channels raise questions about monopolistic trading which could eventually lead to investigation by antitrust bodies in the USA or Europe.

The extent to which online bookings are replacing traditional channels of distribution may be judged when it is revealed that Ryanair sold 65 per cent of its seats through its direct online reservations system in the opening weeks of 2001, while easyJet claimed by the same date that 86 per cent of tickets were being sold in this manner. Low-cost carriers in particular are keen to expand sales through the Internet to keep down costs.

Future developments in the technological revolution are likely to involve the expansion of digital television in the home, which will provide channels for consumers in their own home to communicate with the airlines direct, and book their airline tickets. This must inevitably lead to a further shrinking of sales through the more traditional distribution outlets.

The role of the air broker

One comparatively little known role in the airline business is that of the air brokers. These are the people who act as intermediaries between aircraft owners and their customers. They provide a level of expertise to business clients, travel agents or tour operators who may not have the time or the knowledge to involve themselves in long negotiations for the best deals in chartering aircraft seats. They maintain close contact with both airlines and the charter market, and can frequently offer better prices for charters than tour operators could themselves obtain. They play an important role in securing aircraft seats in times of shortage, and in disposing of spare capacity at times of oversupply. The broker takes charge of the entire operation, booking the aircraft and taking care of any technical requirements, including organizing the contract and arranging any special facilities. In their role as so-called *consolidators*, they assist in consolidating tour operators' flights to ensure maximum load factors are achieved (see Chapter 12). The body representing their interests in the UK is the Air Brokers' Association.

Once again, this role is one which may be challenged by the new direct booking systems coming into play using the web.

Questions and discussion points

1. Is the growth of direct selling via the Internet or other new technological means inevitably going to mean the decline of the traditional travel agency as an outlet for the purchase of air tickets? Will direct purchase be as attractive for leisure passengers as for business travellers? How might the traditional agent survive in the face of these threats?

2. European countries have looked at the possibility of redistributing slots at airports in order to allow new carriers to gain access. What are the arguments for and against this practice? Would doing so improve air services for passengers?

3. An increase in flight delays at peak times in Europe seems inevitable, given the congestion on key routes. Will this encourage more people to use land transport, e.g. the Channel Tunnel? Why has the take-up for the Eurostar service between London and Brussels been comparatively weak?

4. Argue the case for or against high-frequency low-volume flight operations, and make a judgement about whether Boeing or Airbus is right about the future direction of air transport.

Assignment topics

1. As a member of staff with responsibility for route planning at Gemini Airways, a new scheduled airline planning to start up in Britain shortly, you have been asked to assess the impact of deregulation in the United States, and to consider how far patterns established there are being repeated following liberalization in Europe. Produce a report for your Director, Route Planning and Development, which:

   (a) examines the short- and long-term effects of deregulation in North America;

   (b) analyses the airline business environment in Europe, and the policies of the EU and Britain in particular.

Your Director is particularly keen to know whether you believe 'hub and spoke' development is the way forward in Europe as it was in North America.

2. As a member of Gemini's team, you have been asked by the Director of Operations to stand in for him at a visiting lecture to be given to a mixed group of students of tourism and transport studying at a nearby educational institution. The theme of the talk is 'Problems of managing yield in scheduled airline operations'. Prepare a set of notes for your talk, which is intended to last about 20 minutes.

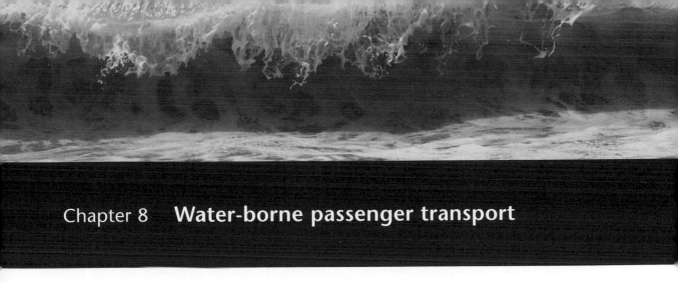

Chapter 8   Water-borne passenger transport

Objectives

After studying this chapter, you should be able to:

- identify each category of water-borne transport, and the role they play in the tourism industry;
- understand the economics of cruise and ferry operations;
- be aware of principal world cruise routes;
- be familiar with other forms of leisure transport by boat, and their appeal to tourists.

Introduction

Although air services today play the leading role in providing transport for tourism, transport by water-borne vessels of all kinds continues to play an important role in the industry. While air transport offers the advantage of speed, which is often a critical factor in the choice of long-haul travel, travel by water still offers many unique advantages. Cruising, in particular, is enjoying a popularity boom that has not been seen since the heyday of the inter-war period; it offers the advantage of total relaxation and an all-inclusive price which allows the passenger to be carried from one destination to another in comfort and safety, without the need constantly to pack and unpack. Short-sea (ferry) vessels have achieved new levels of comfort and speed on many routes, to a point where they will now attract tourists not just

in order to travel from one point to another, but to enjoy a 'mini-cruise' which provides food and entertainment that a few years ago could only be found on a luxury cruise liner. Technological developments have helped to reduce high operating costs, while new forms of water-borne transport have been developed, such as the hovercraft, jetfoil and the twin-hulled catamaran ferry. These have provided rapid communication over short sea routes and sometimes, as in the case of the hovercraft, across difficult terrain.

The pleasure that people find in simply being afloat has spawned many recent tourist developments, from yacht marinas and self-drive motor craft to dinghy sailing in the Mediterranean and canal barge holidays in Britain and on the European mainland. The continuing fascination with steam engines has led to the renovation and operation of lake steamers in England and paddle steamers in the USA. Increasingly, we find that the division between transport and entertainment is becoming blurred, as the journey, or even the vessel, becomes an end in itself, rather than merely a means of arriving at one's destination.

In this chapter, we will investigate the appeal and operation of a variety of water-borne forms of transport, ranging from seagoing vessels to river, canal and lake craft. We can divide these into five distinct categories: 'line voyage' liners, cruise liners, short-sea, or ferry vessels, inland waterways and other excursion vessels, and privately chartered or owned pleasure craft. These will be examined in turn.

The ocean liners

Line voyage services are those offering passenger transport on a port-to-port basis. This form of transport has declined to a point where very few such services exist any longer, and those that do tend to be seasonally operated. The reasons for this decline are not hard to identify.

From the 1950s onward, advances in air transport enabled fares to be reduced, especially on popular routes across the Atlantic, to a point where it became cheaper to travel by air than by ship. The shipping lines, which until the advent of aircraft had no competition from alternative forms of transport, could not compete: they faced rapidly rising costs for fuel and labour in a labour-intensive industry. The gradual decline in passengers, as these switched to the airlines, led to losses in revenue for the shipping companies which made it impossible to consider renovating ageing fleets or replacing them with new vessels. By 1957, more passengers were crossing the Atlantic by air than by sea, and the demise of the worldwide passenger shipping industry was imminent. Leading routes, such as Cunard Line's transatlantic services, P&O's services to the Far East and Australia, and Union-Castle and British India Lines' services to South and East Africa, were either withdrawn or reduced to a skeleton service. The resulting

shake-up in management led to attempts to regenerate traffic, mainly by extending cruising, but vessels built for fast line-voyage services are not ideally suited to alternative uses, and the appeal of cruising was also entering a period of decline. A small but loyal demand for sea transport remained among those, usually older, passengers who suffered fear of flying, or who enjoyed sea voyages and had time to spend to reach their destinations, and a few lines were able to continue to operate to serve these markets. The *Queen Elizabeth 2* of Cunard Line (see Figure 8.1) continues to provide a regular summer service between Southampton and New York, cruising for the balance of the year, while the *St Helena*

Figure 8.1 (a) The Queen Elizabeth 2, flag ship of the Cunard Line. (*Permission of Cunard Line Ltd*)

(b) The chart room in the Queen Elizabeth 2. (*Permission of Cunard Line Ltd*)

(built with a British government subsidy to provide a connection between the UK and the island dependencies of St Helena and Ascension) operates a regular passenger–cargo service between South Wales and South Africa, via the island colonies. The latter ship, however, is as important for its freight capacity as its passenger. A handful of other passenger-cum-freighter services exist around the world, such as the Mauritius Shipping Corporation's services between Mauritius, Reunion Island and South Africa; services from Tahiti carrying up to 60 passengers to the Marquesas islands and Tuamoto atolls in the South Pacific, and vessels, some carrying nearly 1,200 passengers, operated and subsidized by the Indian government, which connect the mainland to the Andaman and Nicobar Islands.

Most of the remaining passenger-carrying vessels operating around the world are built essentially to carry cargo. A maximum of 12 passengers is carried on such vessels (the limitation is due to the requirement of the International Maritime Organisation that the crew include a doctor if more than twelve passengers are carried), while some vessels are fitted only with an owner's suite, carrying two passengers, but they are all clearly designed for lovers of sea travel for its own sake. Freight demand means that neither departure dates nor ports of call can be guaranteed, nor can it be certain that passengers will be allowed to disembark to visit the destinations en route. Entertainment is limited on board, and passengers dine with the ships' officers. However, these ships do attract an enthusiastic market, and often bookings have to be made a year or more in advance.

With hindsight, it is easy to pinpoint the inevitability of shipping's decline. Certainly, enterprise was restricted by the so-called 'conferences', such as the Transatlantic and Transpacific Passenger Conferences, which governed the operation of fleets worldwide and restricted open competition. However, it must also be recognized that shipping management bears much of the blame for failing to adapt the product to changing needs. Ships built for operating in the 1950s failed to meet the needs of the post-war market; insufficient cabins with en-suite

facilities were available to meet the needs of the American market in particular, and the vessels' specifications and size made them inflexible and unsuitable for routes other than those for which they were built. Because shipping companies did not recognize early enough the threat that the airlines posed for the future of their companies, they were slow to move into that sector themselves, and those that eventually attempted to do so found the capital investment required was beyond them.

In the 1970s, the traffic conferences were finally swept away, and shipping associations became more concerned with promotion than with regulation. In Britain, the Passenger Shipping Association, which represents all shipping interests, concerns itself principally with marketing and training on behalf of its members.

Whether the long-term decline of line voyages can be reversed is debatable, but at least on one route there is promise of a new golden age. Cunard is currently building the world's largest ocean liner, *Queen Mary 2*, due to be launched in 2003. It is planned that this ship, more than twice the size of the *Queen Elizabeth 2*, at around 150,000 gross registered tons, will re-establish the twin-liner service across the Atlantic after an absence of more than thirty years.

Cruising

After the 1950s, the passenger shipping industry shifted its emphasis from line voyages to cruising. Initially, this transformation proved difficult; vessels in service at the time were for the most part too large, too old and too expensive to operate for cruising purposes. Their size was a limiting factor in the number of ports they could visit, and they were built for speed rather than leisurely cruising. Fuel bills can be cut by operating vessels at slower speeds, but ideally cruise ships should be purpose-built to achieve their maximum operational efficiency. During the 1960s and 1970s, this meant ships of 18,000–22,000 tons, carrying some 650–850 passengers. However, changes in demand and advances in marine technology have enabled recent cruise ships to be purpose-built in a variety of sizes. Providing there is sufficient demand, optimum profits can be achieved by employing larger vessels, and the trend since the 1980s has been to build ships of steadily increasing tonnage, first in the range of 50,000–70,000 tons, and later in excess of 100,000 tons, and capable of carrying up to 3,800 passengers.

There are more than 250 cruise ships operating worldwide, more than half of which operate out of US ports. Some 5.9 million Americans took a cruise in 1999, a figure which represents over 60 per cent of all cruise passengers in the world. In Europe as a whole, cruises are taken by approximately 1.9 million – or just over 1 million when UK cruises are excluded. A further 750,000 cruise from countries in Asia. The UK holds about 5 per cent of the share of world cruise ships – a marked decline over earlier years, although in 2000 the British government announced plans to lower the taxation rate on British shipping to help reverse this decline in tonnage. In terms of passenger demand, Britain takes second place after the USA, with about 7 per cent of the world cruise market, followed by Germany, Italy and France. All the developed countries are experiencing a marked increase in demand for cruising, after a long period of decline, and growth in this market has averaged between 9 and 15 per cent per annum since the early 1990s. Even more encouraging, extrapolations by the Cruise Lines Industry of America (CLIA) forecast continued increases to 13 million by 2005 and a potential long-term market for cruising of around 35 million passengers, stimulating the shipbuilding boom that began during the 1990s.

At the time of writing, some 60 cruise ships were on order for delivery before the end of 2005, with a total value in excess of £14 billion. The majority of these will be built by just four West European yards – Fincantieri, Kvaerner Masa-yards, Chantiers d'Atlantique and Meyer Werft – passenger shipbuilding in Britain having gone into terminal decline by the 1970s. Most of these vessels will be larger than 60,000 tons, and some will carry close to 4,000 pas-

sengers. At least 330,000 beds will be available at the end of this period, even after allowing for the withdrawal of older vessels.

The largest ship afloat at the time of writing is Royal Caribbean Line's *Voyager of the Seas*. At 142,000 tons and carrying a maximum of 3,840 passengers, her operating costs will still be only marginally greater than conventional ships, while the addition of 500 cabins with consequent increases in on-board spend will boost overall profitability. With building costs that can go as high as $500 million, these ships represent an enormous investment for their owners, and something of a gamble, given the escalation in fuel prices experienced in 2000. Plans for a 250,000 ton giant, to be called *America World City* and carrying up to 6,200 passengers, are on hold at the time of writing, as efforts to raise the capital necessary have faltered. Allowing for the anticipated withdrawal of older ships, the net increase in supply is still expected to exceed the growth in demand for cruising, posing questions over the future profitability of shipping companies. Trends evident in the early twenty-first century anticipate further programmes of rationalization and integration among the largest companies.

The whole concept of a cruise holiday has changed from its traditional image; cruise ships are coming to be seen as floating holiday resorts which conveniently move from one destination to another, offering new scenery every day and non-stop entertainment on board. The very large tonnage allows not only a vast range of public rooms, which, on the newest ships includes facilities for climbing walls and ice rinks, but also ensures that passengers have the widest conceivable choice of acquaintances to meet and make friends with on board.

At the other end of the scale, a market has been revealed for vessels of typically 3,000–10,000 tons, carrying around 100–200 passengers. The smaller of these provide a 'yacht-like' form of cruising for those who are prepared to pay the higher prices these vessels are obliged to charge. Such ships are able to enter harbours far smaller than would be possible for the traditional cruise ships, opening up new ports of call for cruising, such as Cadiz or the further reaches

Figure 8.2 Royal Viking line cruise liner off Waterford Harbour, Ireland. (*Photographed by the author*)

of the Amazon River. Small ships can also negotiate constricted canals, such as the Corinth Canal in Greece and the Panama Canal, which is no longer navigable by the largest cruise vessels.

There is an important issue relating to the size of cruise vessels, and that is the question of their *sustainability*. It is debatable whether building ever larger cruise ships is an appropriate strategy for the tourism business, whether or not these could be

profitable. The effect on small island economies of vessels disgorging up to 4,500 passengers simultaneously at any one port, and within a strictly limited time period, must be judged against any possible benefits of visitor spend. However, the logistics and viability of putting such large numbers of people ashore and organizing shore excursions for them is another factor that will have to be weighed carefully; passengers are reluctant to queue up for two hours or more in order to go ashore or return to their vessels.

Cruise routes

Broadly, the world's major cruise routes are located in seven regions of the globe (see Figure 8.3). These are:

- the Caribbean, Bermuda and the Bahamas, including the coast of Central and South America;
- the west Coast of North America, Mexico, the USA (including Alaska) and Canada, plus Panama Canal transit routes;
- the Mediterranean, divided between the western and eastern sectors;

Figure 8.3 Major cruise routes of the world

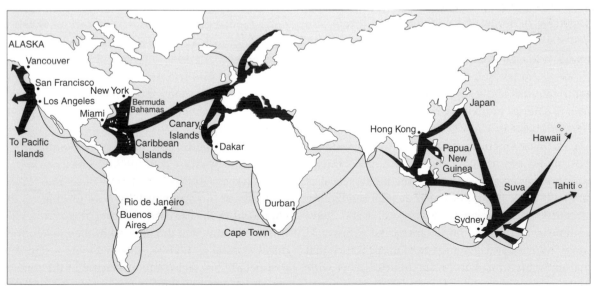

- the Pacific islands and Far East;
- the Baltic Sea, northern European capitals and the North Cape;
- West Africa and the Atlantic islands of the Canaries, Madeira and, increasingly, the Azores;
- round the world.

There is also growing interest in round-Britain cruising, allowing calls at the Shetland, Orkney, Hebridean and Faroe Islands, and including visits to such remote outposts as St Kilda, which no longer has a permanent population.

Most cruising, however, takes place in either the Mediterranean or the Caribbean. These two regions account for over 60 per cent of all cruises, with the Scandinavian and Baltic regions accounting for a further 10 per cent. Most of these routes are seasonal, and this will mean that shipping companies may be obliged to move their vessels from one region of the globe to another to take advantage of peak periods of cruising demand. Movements for this purpose are termed *positioning voyages*, and provide lines with the opportunity to sell these sailings as long cruises, or even line voyages, where transatlantic sailings are involved. The Baltic and North Cape cruises, for example, are operated during the northern hemisphere's high summer, with the North Cape cruise in particular operating in July to offer passengers the advantage of seeing the midnight sun. This is also true of Alaskan cruises, which benefited from the perceived political instability of some Mediterranean cruise itineraries; American cruise passengers are generally cautious about foreign travel, and give preference to sailings in their own waters, or those nearby. The Caribbean also benefits from the proximity of the islands to the American mainland, as well as a climate that allows year-round cruising, although winter's more temperate climate attracts the highest level of demand. Ports in Florida, such as Fort Lauderdale, Miami/Port Everglades and Port Canaveral, have become by far the most important bases for the world cruise industry, and demand from Europe is such that charter flights from Europe are attracted to provide connections with vessels departing from these ports.

Competition is encouraging operators to seek new routes. Recent growth is found in Canada and New England, the East Coast of Africa, to include Madagascar, the Seychelles and Mauritius, and the Indonesian 'spice islands'. New bases where costs are low are also sought; Carnival's Windstar division, for example, switched its *Wind Song* from Tahiti to Costa Rica in 1997 to reduce operating costs.

Over the past forty years fly-cruising has made a significant contribution to the growth of cruising. Passengers are carried by the cruise company on chartered aircraft to a warm-water base port from which they can cruise directly. This overcomes the problem of poor weather and rough seas (the Bay of Biscay, off northern Spain, can be a notoriously unpleasant stretch of water to cross at any time of the year), and ensures that passengers can be enjoying the sunshine and calm seas of the Mediterranean or Caribbean from day one of their cruise holiday. Although the traditional, often older, cruise passengers at first resisted this move, it soon proved popular among an increasingly younger cruise market. However, recent years have shown a continuing demand for ex-UK cruises, and companies such as Cunard, Fred Olsen and the UK tour operators are increasing their cruising from UK ports.

The search for new destinations and more adventurous cruising has led to new routes being opened up. Emulating American adventure cruises, companies such as Noble Caledonia and Jules Verne have pioneered Pacific inter-island cruises and voyages in the Arctic and Antarctic regions, often using smaller, purpose-built vessels. Russian vessels with specially strengthened hulls are chartered to operate in polar regions.

Long-haul routes have also become popularized through the fly-cruise concept, and Singapore in particular has sought to expand as a cruise base for the world cruise market which is now turning to the attractions of the Far East. However, these cruises are still largely aimed at the top end of the market, with prices starting as high as £500 or more a day. The past decade has seen a rapid increase in the total of British passengers taking a cruise (around 860,000

Table 8.1 The largest markets for cruising, 1999

USA	5,894,000
Britain	859,631
Germany	327,000
Italy	225,000
France	223,810
Spain	60,000
(Other European	148,000)

Source: Passenger Shipping Association Annual Cruise Statistics.

Table 8.2 Major destinations of the British cruise market, 1999

Mediterranean	279,115
Caribbean	143,401
Short cruises (ex-Cyprus)	91,383
Atlantic islands	67,142
Scandinavia/Baltic	55,191
Alaska	15,107
Far East	13,652
Other ocean cruises	81,252
River cruises	113,388

Source: Passenger Shipping Association Annual Cruise Statistics.

were estimated to have travelled in 1999, a 12.5 per cent jump over the previous year).

Around 80 per cent of cruises sold to the British are fly-cruises, although interest in sailing directly from UK ports has risen in recent years. Two very strong growth areas are in river cruising, up by 48 per cent over the previous year, and in the new short cruises out of Cyprus to the Holy Land, sold mainly to holiday-makers on the island of Cyprus, which increased by 45 per cent in 1999. The demand for river cruising will be looked at a little later in this chapter.

The nature of the cruise market

In talking about 'the cruise market' one is in danger of drawing on the traditional images of cruise ships: on the one hand, ships filled with conservative and rather elderly passengers who choose to spend their days at sea playing bridge and drinking cups of bouillon, and on the other hand, ships with the image of floating holiday camps, peopled by hyperactive, middle-aged passengers looking for non-stop entertainment and five-times-a-day opportunities to eat. While undoubtedly such stereotypes exist, the image conveyed is far too simplistic.

While the key factors which determine cruise demand can be identified as price, length of cruise and destination, there are a number of other factors to take into account, not least the efforts made by the shipping companies to appeal to niche markets through their activities or destinations. The interest in cruising has expanded massively in recent years, and several distinct forms of cruise company have emerged. First, there are the long-established lines, such as Hapag-Lloyd and P&O, which are strongly dependent upon their home markets and which attract significant numbers of repeat purchasers who tend to be brand-loyal to specific companies, and often to individual vessels. Second, there are the major international cruise companies which draw on global markets and are tending to dominate the industry. These include Carnival, the largest cruise company, Royal Caribbean Cruise Line and Princess Cruises, formerly a division of P&O and demerged in 2001. Third, there are smaller companies with narrower focuses, which may offer more adventurous destinations or activities designed to appeal to particular markets. Examples include Swan Hellenic, also a division of P&O, which offers cultural cruises, generally in the Mediterranean, accompanied by experienced guides and lecturers, and Viking River Cruises, whose small vessels are well suited to Baltic itineraries, and are designed to appeal to an up-market cultural audience (see itinerary and map, Figure 8.4). Expedition cruising, offering more adventurous destinations such as the Chilean fjords and Antarctica, in which landings are made by zodiac tenders, call for a more energetic (although not necessarily younger) market. These ships are often chartered to specialist tour operators that search out and organize ever more adventurous holiday destinations.

Cruising appeals on a number of levels. The all-inclusive nature of a cruise, in which unlimited – and

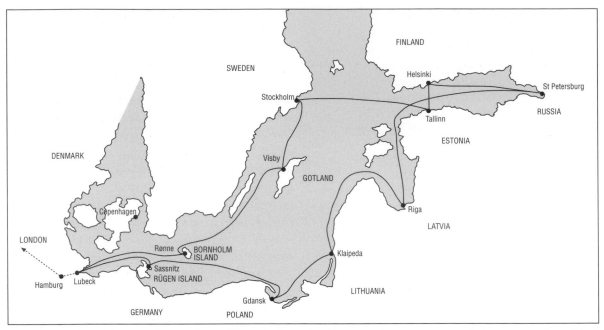

Figure 8.4 Scandinavia and the Baltic 'milk run'. The Baltic itinerary given as an example in this map is an ideal niche-marketing programme. The Swiss/French-owned ship operating the programme is only 3,000 tons, carrying 180 passengers. The two-week itinerary allows the ship to call at nine different countries, with only one day at sea without a port of call. The trip is sold as a fourteen-day round-voyage, or as a week-long cruise with connecting flights out of and into St Petersburg. The market is predominantly British, Swiss and German.

often excellent – food is on offer, the general ambience on board, the high levels of security that isolation on a ship can provide, the attraction of travelling with 'like-minded people' with whom it is easy to make friends, being thrown together within a confined space, the absence of constraint on the amount of baggage carried, all offer significant benefits. Indeed, for those with a fear of flying, cruising provides the only means of travelling abroad.

While the concept of a floating hotel has become of importance in selling cruises, most passengers still expect ships to look like ships. A great deal of care goes into the design of a modern cruise liner, to provide the illusion of greater space, as well as maximum revenue-earning opportunities for the shipping company in the form of shops, hairdressing facilities, casinos and bars. Design also takes account of the nationality of those travelling; cruise ships aimed predominantly at the US market tend to make greater use of plastics, gilt stairways, mir-

rors, neon lights and bright colours, while the more traditional European, and particularly British, market will expect greater use of wood (although safety standards at sea encourage the use of more fire-retardant materials today) and quieter, more refined decoration.

Cruising is still seen as an older person's holiday, but this image is beginning to fade, as new cruise companies such as Carnival encroach on the traditional cruise market and reach a younger group of holiday-makers. Indeed, Carnival claims an average age on board in the mid-twenties for its 'disco' ships operating short cruises in the Caribbean. Such cruises are sold in the US as package holidays, comparable to the all-inclusive resort on land; the result is that cruising represents about 6 per cent of all US package holiday business, compared to less than 3 per cent in the UK.

In Britain, according to the Passenger Shipping Association (PSA), the average age of cruise passengers is 54, and a quarter of all UK passengers now fall between the ages of 45 and 54. Airtours claimed an average of only 48 years on its 1999 cruises, down five years from sailings only two years earlier. Undoubtedly, the new generation of family ships, such as those operated by the Walt Disney Company, and the budget cruises offered by UK mass-market tour operators are having an impact on the traditional British cruise market.

Shipping companies have recognized the difficulty of appealing to varied markets, and varied nationalities, on the same vessel, however appealing this might be economically. Multinational passenger mixes call for multilingual announcements, as well as entertainment, on board, which will not be an attractive selling point, and passengers from different countries, have widely varying habits and preferences in on-board entertainment. Passengers from Latin countries, for instance, prefer to take dinner later than those from the UK or USA. One result of these differences is that cruise companies are tending to *niche market*, whether by price, by brand, or by type of cruise offered. Carnival Cruise Lines, the world's largest cruise company, now offers no fewer than eight distinct brands, while Britain's P&O Line operates under that name with four vessels, but operates in the primarily American market with the brand name Princess Cruises. The up-market small liner *Minerva* is operated under the Swan Hellenic banner, while P&O bought into the continental European market in 2000, taking over Festival Cruises and a controlling interest in the German cruise liner *Aida* in partnership with Arkona Touristik. The Disney Corporation caters to the family market with its two new ships, while Saga Holidays, the UK company catering to the over-50s, operates its *Saga Rose* exclusively for older customers.

Shipping companies are laying emphasis on product differentiation, while continuing to introduce new on-board facilities to meet the expectations of an increasingly sophisticated cruise market. One noted trend is to wider variety in catering on board. P&O's *Oriana*, to take one example, has introduced a pizzeria on board, while Crystal Cruises offers a choice of Italian, Japanese and Chinese restaurants on its vessels.

The economics of cruising

In spite of the rise in popularity of cruising, it remains a highly volatile market, and is quickly affected by adverse events, as was witnessed during the Libyan crisis and the hijacking of the *Achille Lauro* by terrorists in the Mediterranean in 1985, which resulted in the collapse of the Mediterranean cruise market. The area was only just recovering when the 1991 Gulf War, and consequent threat of Iraqi terrorism strikes, again frightened away the Mediterranean cruise bookings, particularly those from the US market. Americans are cautious travellers, and seek security abroad; the perception of danger in the Mediterranean caused many to switch bookings to safer waters in the Caribbean and Alaska, both of which experienced something of a boom in those years. Cruise companies were forced to reposition their vessels to the Caribbean, which already suffered from over-capacity, so that in spite of rising demand, the acute competition led to deep discounting in the region, and profits suffered.

Cruising is both capital-intensive and labour-intensive. A modern cruise liner can easily exceed $250 million to build, with some costing as much as $500 million (costs for the projected 250,000 ton vessel are likely to exceed 1 billion dollars), although the life expectancy of a cruise ship is far greater than an aircraft, and, allowing for rebuilding and complete renovation, a fifty-year productive life would not be unusual. Vessels also need a substantial number of crew – a four- or five-star cruise liner would carry as many as one member of crew for every two passengers carried. With such labour costs, it is not difficult to see why luxury cruises are selling at up to a thousand dollars a day. However, once again economies of scale can pare costs, and companies operating large fleets, such as Carnival Cruise Lines in the USA, can reduce the cost per unit of marketing and administration. It is also more economical to operate large ships rather than small ones, and the trend, as we have seen, is to build bigger and bigger vessels, to take advantage of this. However, some in the industry feel that there are dis-economies of scale in operating ships over 110,000 tons, and it is likely that the current spate of new ships in the region of 100,000–150,000 tons will be the largest in general use for cruising. Five-star operators such as Silversea Cruises face a different problem, however. While overall profitability is hard to achieve for these vessels with low capacity, if capacity is significantly increased the line faces difficulties in delivering the same level of quality service. Optimum viability is believed to be achieved, therefore, with vessels of around 25,000 tons carrying a maximum of 400 passengers.

Large companies also benefit by receiving greater support from travel agents, who prefer to deal with companies having a greater number of ships, and therefore a larger choice of both sailings and destinations.

Large ships are able to pare costs by reducing the ratio of crew to passengers, and by providing smaller cabins, with larger areas given over to public use. This provides space for shopping and other sales opportunities. Dining rooms accommodate large numbers within relatively confined spaces either by having two sittings for meals, or by providing only large tables; tables for two are rare on board ships. However, some companies have capitalized by designing their ships to permit all passengers to be accommodated in the restaurant at a single sitting – an attractive marketing advantage.

A useful rule of thumb in judging the relative luxuriousness and spaciousness on board ship is to ascertain the size to passenger ratio (SPR), sometimes referred to as the passenger-space ratio (PSR). This is based on the vessel's gross registered tonnage divided by the number of passengers carried. If this amounts to 20 or less, the ship is likely to appear crowded, while a figure approaching 60 would be considered luxurious, and command high daily rates.

Further economies are obtained by calling at a greater number of ports on any itinerary, and spending more time in port, both of which help to reduce

fuel burn while at the same time increasing the passengers' satisfaction. A reduction in speed also saves on fuel, but if vessels are to travel slowly and also call at numerous ports, it is essential that these ports are grouped closely together. For this reason, the Caribbean, with its many islands of differing nationality, makes an ideal cruise destination.

One example of effective cost reduction in the shipping business is demonstrated by Cunard, which in 1996 took the decision to extend the journey time for its *Queen Elizabeth 2* between the UK and New York from five to six days. While this achieved significant savings on fuel burn, reducing average speed from 28.5 knots to 23 knots, it also offered other marketing advantages; higher on-board spend was encouraged, while the passengers themselves saw an additional day's cruising as an added benefit; it also allowed the ship to arrive at a more convenient time of day for those with onward travel arrangements.

Further economies can be achieved by putting passengers ashore by tender (ship's launches), rather than tying up alongside. This may be a practical alternative when islands are forcing up mooring costs; however, it does delay disembarkation, and will be a less attractive selling point.

Cruising will be severely damaged by any rapid rise in fuel prices, as occurred during the oil crisis of 1973–4. The escalation of oil prices in summer 2000 also led to higher prices and weakened demand. Demand will also be affected by increased labour costs, and the decline in the fleets of the established maritime nations such as Britain can be partly accounted for by their uncompetitive operating costs compared with their cheaper competitors. Lower-cost nations such as Greece and Russia have in turn built up their own fleets, while the more expensive nations have been forced to cut costs by registering their fleets in developing countries such as Panama or Liberia, and by recruiting crews from low labour cost countries such as the Philippines or India, often to the chagrin of the trade unions representing maritime crews in the developed nations.

Finally, cruise lines have to ensure that their ships are used for the maximum amount of time during the year (just as airlines do) – although this does not necessarily mean their use for cruising only. Some companies charter cruise ships to tour operators, while others have successfully chartered ships for use as floating hotels when accommodation pressures force tourist destinations to find alternative accommodation for special events; Cunard was even successful in chartering its largest vessel, the *Queen Elizabeth 2*, for a period for Japan to use as a hotel; this represented a substantial saving to the company on operating costs, as it required no use of fuel for transport.

The cruising business

Although demand rose strongly during the 1990s, it was outpaced by the growth in supply, not only in the number of vessels but also their overall size and capacity. This has led to fierce competition in the industry and deep discounting. Profits slimmed, and, as has been the case with so many other sectors of the tourism industry, this has led to greater market concentration. Three companies are now coming to dominate the cruise market, together controlling about half the global market share: Carnival Cruise Line, Royal Caribbean International and P&O Line. The trends are for these companies to get still larger; Royal Caribbean took over Celebrity Cruises in 1997, while Carnival took over Costa Cruises in the same year and in 2000, with Star Cruise Line as partner, purchased 92.6 per cent of Norwegian Caribbean Line, the world's fourth largest cruise company. As mentioned earlier, P&O has also expanded by the purchase of Festival Cruises and other European cruise interests.

Carnival Cruise Line deserves special mention because of the way in which it has changed the face of cruising since the mid-1970s. The company was formed in 1972, and at the time of writing owned and operated 30 ships, sailing under four major brand names: Carnival Cruises, a budget-priced mass-market operation, Holland America Line, a middle-priced company, Seabourn Cruise Line, the up-market end of the company's cruise business, and

Cunard Line, perhaps the world's best-known brand name in cruising although now offering only two vessels, the *Queen Elizabeth 2* and *Caronia*. Carnival also controls Windstar Cruises, a specialist company offering luxury sail-assisted ships, and, as previously mentioned, Costa Cruises.

Carnival has in particular been able to attract a much younger than average market for its major division, which offers relatively cheap cruises of short duration, using large vessels of typically 70,000–100,000 tons or more. Its most recent vessels accommodate typically between 2,000 and 3,000 passengers. The fanciful names of the ships (e.g. *Paradise*, *Ecstasy*, *Sensation* and *Imagination*) are pointers to the expectation of their passengers as to the kind of experiences these cruise ships promise. They are sold as 'fun cruises' offering a wide range of on-board facilities, including shops and casinos (Carnival has claimed that some 14 per cent of its total revenue is on-board spend). It attracts young, relatively high-spend passengers (the company claims that the average age of its passengers is 48, while 30 per cent of its cheaper market is under 35). This may be compared with Cunard's market, whose average age is over 60.

Carnival has also taken care to market to recognized niches. Its Fiesta Marina division of Hispanic-oriented tours was developed to tap into Spanish- and Portuguese-speaking markets in the US and Latin America, based on a home port of San Juan, Puerto Rico, a US dependency. Food, wine and entertainment on board have been designed for Hispanic tastes, and dining hours are later than usual, in accordance with Hispanic preferences.

Over-tonnage in American waters has forced cruise companies to turn to the European markets to fill ships. Many carriers now offer free flights to the Caribbean to join cruise ships based there, as an incentive to attract this market.

Health and safety

The dominance of the Americans in the world cruise market, and American concern with both safety and hygiene, have resulted in strict standards being imposed on all foreign flag-carriers operating out of, or calling at, US ports. All such ships are subject to unannounced inspections from the US Vessel Sanitation Program. Vessels are rated for the quality of their water, food preparation, cleanliness, storage and repairs. An acceptable rating is 86 points out of 100, but it is not uncommon for even leading cruise ships of the world to be given grades considerably lower than this. Owners are then required to raise their standards. Adverse publicity in the press is a further incentive not to fail these tests. Owners are also required to be bonded against financial collapse. More recently constructed vessels incorporating higher standards of safety can attract lower insurance premiums. These vessels are also more technically advanced, and have lower operating costs, with the result that older ships find it difficult to compete. In this respect, the shipping and airline businesses are experiencing similar problems. Medium-sized operators are likely to be absorbed over the next few years by the three or four largest companies, leaving only the niche market cruise operators to remain as independents in the field.

Tour operator cruising

While cruises are sold as package holidays in the United States, and tour operators there have also played a part as intermediaries in bringing the product to the notice of the travelling public, British tour operators have been slower to move into the cruise market. During the 1970s, some operators, including Thomson Holidays, did charter or part-charter cruise ships which they incorporated into their programme of inclusive tours, but these attempts ran into a number of problems. Efforts to bring down the overall prices of cruising led to dissatisfaction with standards of service and operation. More recently, Airtours, one of Britain's leading operators, decided to take advantage of the trend to cruising in the UK, and in 1995 introduced its own ship, *Carousel*. Selling Mediterranean cruises at lead-in prices of £399, and marketing them as merely alternatives to

the traditional package holiday but with all meals and entertainment thrown in, for little more than the price of a package holiday, Airtours brought Carnival-style low-budget cruising holidays to the British holiday public. This proved to be an enormously popular service, carrying over 100,000 passengers in its first year of operation. This encouraged the company to enlarge its fleet, while Britain's two other major operators, Thomson Holidays and First Choice, soon followed into cruising. In 2000, Royal Caribbean International bought a 20 per cent stake in First Choice, aiming to form a joint cruise company and with the clear intention of using the operator's retail outlets to push cruise sales in the UK.

The entrance of tour operators into the mass-market cruise business has changed the face of British cruising. Airtours has not only reduced the average age of cruise passengers, but has introduced a whole new market to cruising; 80 per cent of its passengers are first time cruisers. Tour operators also helped to popularize the short cruise in the British mass market, which brought down cruise prices; today, the seven-day cruise has greatly enhanced the appeal of this form of holiday for both European and American passengers. Substantial growth is in the short cruises in the Mediterranean, particularly those sold as an add-on to Cyprus holiday-makers, while similarly in the North American market short cruises to the Bahamas, Bermuda and the Caribbean have boosted the market for cruising.

It is still likely, however, that most cruising will retain an up-market image in the UK. While British operators and their cruise partners can be expected to exploit fully the low-budget cruise holiday market to the Mediterranean and Caribbean, the bulk of sales is likely to remain centred on middle price cruising, sold direct or through a limited number of specializing travel agents. Indeed, it is in the middle-priced accommodation that cruise demand is expanding fastest. The market for this form of cruising is very loyal – both P&O and Cunard have claimed 60–70 per cent of their market to be repeat bookings. One difficulty in disseminating sales more widely through agents is the specialized knowledge required of the cruise product; fewer than one in ten British travel agents is productive in booking cruises, and counter staff lack the expertise and experience to sell them. In recent years, the PSA, the marketing arm of the passenger shipping business in the UK, has attempted to overcome this problem by mounting a special campaign to train agents, and has successfully trained staff in some 1,000 branches to provide a professional cruise sales service to their clients.

The future of the cruise industry looks healthy, in terms of the growth in numbers booking, if less so in terms of profitability. Less than 0.4 per cent of Europeans have cruised, compared with some 2 per cent of the US population, which suggests considerable scope for growth. If Europeans cruised at the same level as Americans, this would inject another 5 million cruise passengers into the market. Greater efforts are now being made to differentiate products, rather than depending upon discounting to sell unsold cabins. Certainly Carnival, with its niche-marketing among the younger holiday-makers in the US, has led the way in this direction, while other companies have focused on theme cruising to survive (cruise lines now offer a huge variety of special-interest cruises, ranging from botanical cruises to 'classical civilizations' cruising in the Mediterranean accompanied by specialist, often well-known, guest lecturers, and from classical music cruises to jazz cruises, with on-board orchestras). Some cruise companies, including the Disney Corporation with its two 85,000 ton liners *Disney Magic* and *Disney Wonder*, are targeting the family market, while other shipping operators have experimented with new types of vessel. Radisson has introduced twin-hull catamaran vessels, and both Windstar Cruises and Club Méditerranée offer a new generation of luxury sail-assisted ships to attract a new market. Companies such as Society Expedition Cruises offer small, luxury cruising for around a hundred passengers to exotic destinations such as the Amazon and Antarctic, while Seabourn's Sea Goddess ships offer a retractable platform at the stern from which passengers may swim, snorkel or sail while the ship lies at anchor.

One of the more exciting developments is Cunard's plan to reintroduce its two-ship fast transatlantic service between Southampton and New York, after a break of more than 30 years. As mentioned earlier in this chapter, a new ship, *Queen Mary 2*, is to join the *Queen Elizabeth 2* for this purpose. Whether this heralds a new life for line voyages in general remains to be seen.

The longer-term future of the shipping industry may be boosted by new marine technology now under development, such as the SES-200 Surface Effect Ship, which rides above the surface of the sea, or superconducting electromagnetic propulsion vessels which have been tested in Japan and offer potential speeds above 100 knots. Waterjet propulsion is also under test for a new breed of container ship; the proposed 'Fastship', using a semi-planing monohull, is expected to be capable of speeds exceeding 40 knots, and may be adaptable later for cruise vessels. Such developments could further encourage the reintroduction of line voyages between major ports in the world, although this is unlikely to occur in the near future.

While the expansion of the cruise business is to be welcomed for the benefits it can bring to holiday-makers and companies alike, there are downsides which have to be taken into account, too. The emphasis on on-board spend and the creation of ships which are virtually leisure complexes in their own right, with all the amenities provided at an 'all-inclusive resort', means that destination countries suffer from the same drawbacks experienced from the growth of such resorts. On-board spend simply means less spend ashore, less money going into local shops, bars and transport companies. Some companies have purchased their own, usually deserted, islands on which they can land their passengers for barbecues and lazy 'beach days', ensuring once again that no expenditure goes into the local economy. At the same time the growth in size, as we have seen, threatens massive congestion at small island ports. Leisure transport generally is also beginning to draw criticism for its pollution effects. Large cruise vessels are fuel-hungry (if not to the same extent as thirty years ago), and one estimate has suggested that marine engines in total account for about 8 per cent of all the world's nitrous oxide emissions – admittedly a large proportion of this would be accounted for by the enormous growth in private ownership of luxury motor yachts, but cruise vessels must bear their share of responsibility for increasing atmospheric pollution, as must passenger aircraft.

Ferry services

The term 'ferry' is one which embraces a variety of forms of short-distance water-borne transport. This includes urban transport, in cities such as Stockholm, where outlying suburbs and surrounding towns are reached by water from the city centre. Ferries of this type also attract tourists, either as a convenient form of local transport or as an original way to view the city. Some ferries, such as the Staten Island ferry, which links Manhattan with the borough of Staten Island in New York, and Hong Kong's Star Ferry, have become world famous and a 'must' for visiting tourists. Other notable ferry rides include the Bosporus ferries linking Europe and Asia in Istanbul, the Manly ferry between Sydney and Manly in Australia, the Niteroi ferry in Rio de Janeiro, the Mersey ferry in Liverpool (immortalized in pop music), the Bainbridge Island ferry in Seattle, the Oakland ferry in San Francisco, the Devonport and Waiheke inland ferries in Auckland, New Zealand and the Cacilhas ferry in Lisbon. Most of these, of course, are designed to provide an essential service for local commuters, but inevitably they also provide important attractions for tourists either wishing to get a different view of the city or planning to visit more remote areas of a country, and where convenient links by air may not be possible; examples of the latter include the Greek islands, or the Hebrides off the west coast of Scotland, the Isle of Wight off the south coast of England, and crossing the Strait of Messina, between Italy and Sicily.

However, the key ferry routes for tourists are those major links between countries separated by water, such as across the English Channel, or between the Scandinavian countries, or across the Adriatic between Italy and Greece. These routes may be vital for those wishing to take their car on holiday, and also provide an attractive alternative to flying for those with time to spare. Additionally, there are many places in the world where transport is dependent upon good national ferry services, due either to the number of islands belonging to the territory or the difficulty of reaching coastal destinations by air or sea. A notable example is the west coast of Norway, where small towns cut off from land routes and air connections depend upon the *Hurtigruten*, or fast route, where daily ferries call at dozens of ports between Bergen and the North Cape. This itinerary has become so popular with tourists that full-size cruise vessels now ply the route. Other popular routes include the west coast of Canada and Alaska and the Hebridean islands off mainland Scotland's western coast.

The significance of the short-sea ferry market can be appreciated when it is learned that by the mid-1990s some 2,150 ro-ro (roll on-roll off) ferries were estimated to be in operation worldwide; in the UK alone some 50 million passengers travel by ferry each year, more than half of these crossing to the Continent, while services out of British Columbia in Canada carry some 24 million passengers a year. Of course, not all these will be counted as tourists, and this is an important point to remember; typically, ferry services provide a communication network for local populations, while taking advantage of visitors to boost numbers and become profitable.

The growth of short-sea voyages within Europe during the past two decades can be hailed as a major success story. The rise in demand for ferries during the 1980s and 1990s can be partly attributed to the general growth of tourism and trade in this region, especially of trade between European Union countries, but growth of private car ownership also played a significant part in raising demand. France in particular has always been a destination with a strong attraction for independent British holiday-makers travelling with their cars, and the strengthening of the pound against the franc, in both 1997 and 2000, played a major role in attracting UK holiday-makers back to France in large numbers. There has also been a large rise in coach transport between Britain and the Continent, as coach companies introduced long-distance coach routes linking London with the capitals of Europe.

In spite of the challenge offered by the Channel Tunnel linking Britain and France since 1994, Dover remains by far the most important of the ports serving the Continent, and with the formation of P&O Stena Line, uniting the services of P&O and Stena to offer a no-booking, 'turn up and go' joint service with frequent sailings round the clock, the ferry companies have been able to show that they can remain a viable form of cross-Channel transport.

Good marketing by the ferry companies has played a part in stimulating traffic over the years. New routes have been developed to tap regional markets and to provide greater choice, so that passengers have been able to choose to travel to the Continent from Portsmouth to Caen, or from Plymouth to Roscoff or St Malo, as well as on the longer established routes out of Harwich, Dover, Folkestone and Newhaven (see Figure 8.5). Not all of these routes have proved viable, as price slashing attracts tourists to the most popular, even if not the most convenient, routes.

From Britain, routes can be conveniently grouped into four geographical regions:

• English Channel (short-sea crossing) routes,

Figure 8.5 Major passenger/car ferry services from ports in the British Isles. (*Permission of Travel Weekly*)

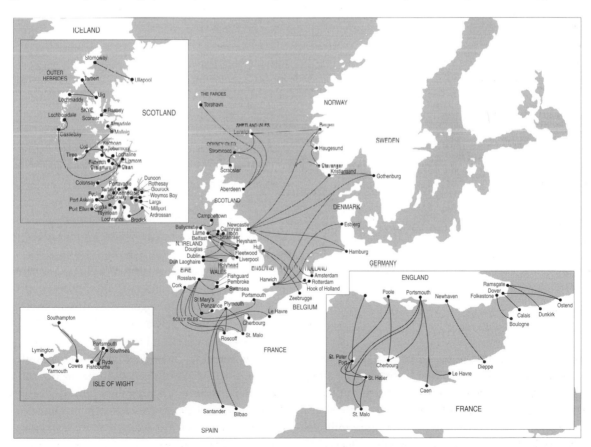

including services from ports such as Ramsgate, Dover, Folkestone and Newhaven;

- Western Channel routes, including services from Portsmouth, Southampton, Poole, Weymouth and Plymouth;
- North Sea routes, including services from North Shields, Hull, Felixstowe, Harwich and Sheerness;
- Irish Sea routes, including services from Swansea, Pembroke, Fishguard, Holyhead, Liverpool, Stranraer, Cairnryan and the Isle of Man.

It should be stressed that while these have been identified as key ports, services operating out of these ports do vary from time to time, as competition forces out some companies and others attempt to operate new routes in their place. The expectation that a route, once announced, will continue to operate for many years is no longer true; the period 1995–97 saw many failures, including the Brighton–Fécamp route, Eurolink's Sheerness–Vlissingen service, Sally Ferries' Ramsgate–Dunkirk service and Brittany's Poole–St Malo route. Stena Line also withdrew its Southampton–Cherbourg service during this time, replacing it with a service between Portsmouth and Cherbourg in the following year. Traditional ferries were even withdrawn in 1999 from the traditional Newhaven–Dieppe route, whose history of service stretched back to 1825.

In addition to these major routes, there are a number of important smaller ferry services operating in the UK, such as those linking the Hebridean islands of Scotland and the Orkney and Shetland islands; shorter services operate to the Isle of Wight, the Isle of Man, the Scilly Isles and Lundy Island in the Severn Channel.

The economics of ferry operating

As with cruising, operating short-sea ferry routes is expensive in both capital investment and in direct operating cost. Modern ferries on many routes are now nearly as large and sumptuous as cruise ships, and building costs can run into hundreds of millions of pounds. Within the European Union, ferries are expected to be written off over a 27-year timespan, although Greece has traditionally operated its ferries for as long as 35 years.

Profitability is achieved through a combination of maximum usage of equipment, plus on-board sales. The termination in 1999 of duty-free sales within the European Union had a significant impact on cross-Channel revenue (which had accounted for up to 50 per cent of ferry companies' turnover), forcing ticket prices up. Rapid turnarounds in port at the end of each journey are essential, as are round-the-clock sailings, with ideally an even volume of business all year round and a balanced flow of demand in both directions. In practice, this is, of course, difficult to achieve, and in winter, when much of the pure holiday traffic dries up, the ferry services become very dependent upon freight to contribute to their costs.

The shorter sailings to France, Belgium and Holland attract much better market demand than do the longer routes to Scandinavia, Germany and northern Spain, although the ferry companies on the latter routes have achieved considerable success in marketing the longer (24 hours or more) sailings as mini-cruises. Their success is modelled on the enormously popular service between Stockholm, Sweden and either Turku or Helsinki, Finland, which, in addition to providing one of the most scenic routes anywhere in Europe for a ferry service, also attracts customers through the sale of relatively cheap on-board drinks, in a region where alcohol is prohibitively expensive. As a result, the ferry market between these two countries has grown to a point where the two major carriers, Silja Line and Viking Line, can support a string of super-ferries, the largest of which, at 60,000 tons, is capable of carrying in excess of 3,000 passengers (see Figure 8.6). By including a stop at the Finnish-owned Åland Islands, which have special status within the European Community, and by diverting other ships to make a call at Tallinn, Estonia, duty-free goods can continue to be sold on board these vessels, retaining their popularity for the short-break market. Nevertheless, the ending of duty-free sales forced Silja to withdraw some services as no longer profitable.

Figure 8.6 The new superferries: Silja Line's *Silja Symphony* at Helsinki. (*Photographed by the author*)

Off-peak sailings on the shorter routes can be boosted by low fares, with a wide range of discounted prices aimed at differing market segments. Quick round-trips on the same vessel, or short stopovers of one to three nights have expanded, particularly, for the British market, those offering shopping expeditions to the French hypermarkets before Christmas. While the termination of duty-free goods on these routes cut the market for short trips to France initially, the removal of customs barriers on duty-paid goods within the European Union, and the relatively low cost of duty-paid alcoholic drinks in France compared with Britain, later helped to boost sales on cross-Channel vessels.

At extreme off-peak periods, and for night sailings which attract fewer bookings, it may be the ferry companies' intention only to price the product to make a contribution to fixed costs, rather than to ensure profitability on every crossing. Low fares may nonetheless stimulate on-board spend which will make a useful contribution to total revenue. The ferry companies have increased their general shopping facilities in their newer ships in order to boost duty-paid sales. While this has not fully made up for the loss of duty-free revenue, it has helped to reduce the impact of the withdrawal of this facility.

Both the leading British carriers have made strenuous efforts to cut their operating costs in recent years, particularly their labour costs. First P&O, and later Stena, introduced new labour practices into their companies, which have increased the efficiency of crewing, but only after serious confrontations with the seamen's union. Against this, however, the SOLAS (Safety of Life at Sea) regulations which came into effect following the Stockholm Agreement, signed in 1997 between Great Britain and six northern European countries, have substantially added to building costs. The objective of these regulations was to increase the safety and stability of ro-ro ferries, following the disastrous *Herald of Free Enterprise* sinking at Zeebrugge in 1987, but the shipping companies won a compromise from the government on the timing of its introduction, which meant that regulations would be introduced in stages, with the final implementation delayed until December 2004. In the meantime, concern over ferry safety remains an important factor. The subsequent sinking of the ferry *Estonia* in the Baltic in 1994 with the loss of around 1,000 lives revealed that there was still good reason for concern. The Stockholm Agreement requires vessels operating into and out of ports in the seven countries to be capable of remaining upright in waves up to 4 metres high and with 50 centimetres of floodwater on the car deck. It will require the fitting of all vessels with transverse bulkheads which will improve stability in rough seas, but the ferry companies are having to face major bills (around £1 million per vessel) and the further worry that the obligatory modifications will both reduce car capacity and slow down the loading and unloading of vessels, delaying turnrounds.

The Channel Tunnel and the ferry services

The Channel Tunnel, perhaps the greatest threat to cross-Channel ferries since their inception, was opened to passenger traffic at the end of 1994, although the build-up to its full operation was slow. The background to this is described more fully in Chapter 9, but here we should examine the impact upon ferry services of the land link.

Eurotunnel, operators of the Channel Tunnel,

suffered a number of setbacks in building and operating the Tunnel, including repeated delays in opening, delays in obtaining equipment to run through the Tunnel, and a disastrous and costly fire in a freight wagon at the end of 1996 which caused a great deal of damage to the interior of the Tunnel and led to reduced services over a number of months. Eurotunnel's original estimates for passenger carryings proved wildly optimistic, but nonetheless the company achieved a 51 per cent share of the Dover Straits traffic (Dover/Folkestone to Calais/Boulogne) by 1999, with P&O Stena Line gaining a further 30 per cent. Eurostar, which offers rail connections between London, Paris and Brussels, has also succeeded in diverting a substantial number of air travellers back to rail on the London to Paris route.

The ferries were forced to retaliate. P&O and Stena invested heavily in their short-sea operations, and merged their services on the short-sea route between Dover and Calais, following investigation by the Monopolies and Mergers Commission (now the Competition Commission). Improvements in passenger handling facilities at Dover were introduced, which allow passengers to check in just 20 minutes before sailing. New, faster ferries were introduced, with the crossing between Dover and Calais reduced from 90 minutes to 75 minutes. Marketing emphasis has been shifted to selling the crossing as part of a holiday, with time to relax and unwind on board. The opposition is disparaged as offering no more than 'a toilet and a light-bulb'. Larger, more luxurious ships on the route are reinforcing the concept of a mini-cruise, with the result that the short-sea routes have held up reasonably well, although other less competitive routes have suffered badly from the fiercer competition. On the medium-distance crossings, a new generation of fast ships and catamarans is being introduced; this has resulted in crossing time from Portsmouth to Cherbourg, for example, being reduced from five hours to two hours forty-five minutes.

Both Eurotunnel and the ferry services engaged in a destructive price war at the end of the 1990s. With stability returning after the turn of the century and following the P&O–Stena merger, prices rose sharply, with the leading ferry operators dropping brochure pricing in 2000 to allow for more flexible pricing structures designed to achieve better overall yields.

The worry for the market leaders out of Dover must be whether they can attract sufficient trade during the winter months, when the Tunnel is coming to be seen by many passengers as a preferable choice to a rough sea crossing, even if only 75 minutes long.

New modes of crossing

In spite of the introduction of the new fast ferries, alternative and still faster forms of water transport are becoming popular on many short- and medium-range routes. In turn, hovercraft, hydrofoils and catamarans have come into service to offer the benefits of speed and a certain degree of novelty. Hovercraft were used to initiate the first fast ferry crossings across the Channel in 1968. They offered several advantages over the traditional ferries: riding on a cushion of air just above the surface of the water, and able to travel over land as well as water, they avoided the usual capital costs associated with dock facilities, as the craft could simply be beached on any convenient and obstacle-free foreshore. Unfortunately, they also offered their passengers a somewhat bouncy and

Figure 8.7 P&O's new fast catamaran ferry. (*Courtesy David Neale*)

noisy ride by comparison with the more traditional ferries, and could not operate in seas greater than 2.5 metres. The vessels also suffered many technical problems in their development and throughout the years of their operation, and were finally withdrawn from service in 2000, to be replaced by catamarans. The hydrofoil offers better prospects for future development, even though it, too, suffered from technological teething problems (it was withdrawn from the Brighton–Fécamp route because of the high number of enforced cancellations on technical grounds). This vessel operates with a conventional hull design, but when travelling at speed the hull is raised above the surface of the water on blades, or 'foils'. This enables the vessel to travel at speeds of up to 60 knots. Recent models have been powered by jet engines (jetfoils) but their unreliability on open waters and inability to contend with high waves have hindered their adoption in British waters.

The most promising recent development in ferry operations appears to be the high-speed wave-piercing catamaran (WPC). These have been operating on cross-Channel services since 1991, and have now replaced the hovercraft. They are mainly twin-hulled vessels large enough to accommodate cars, travelling at speeds up to 40 knots. Although suffering from technical difficulties when first introduced, this type of vessel has been refined, and now operates successfully from Britain to Ireland and the Continent, and has been introduced on such key routes as the Dover–Calais and Harwich–Hook of Holland routes. Catamarans have also proved popular on routes across the Baltic Sea and other key European routes. The popular Seacats (twin-hull) and Superseacats (monohull) offer a valuable service for passengers wanting the fastest possible crossing to the Continent but who might find the Channel Tunnel claustrophobic. The latest HSS (highspeed sea service) twin-hull ferries introduced by Stena have further stretched capacity, carrying up to 1,500 passengers and 375 cars. The downside, however, is the higher fuel burn of all these craft, and constraints still remain on their operation in rough weather – waves above 4 metres (3.5 metres on earlier Seacats)

lead to cancellations, a serious constraint in winter months. What is becoming clear, however, is that for a great many holiday-makers the trend is to choose faster surface vessels which can compete with the Tunnel on time.

Another interesting development is that of the Solar Sailor, a 100-passenger catamaran ferry which went into service in Sydney Harbour in 2000. This vessel operates with solar and wind power, with a backup electric motor running from batteries which store the energy the craft collects while running on alternative energy sources. It is silent, smooth, creates no pollution whatever, and its photocells are boosted by 20 per cent by the sun's reflection in the water. Further development of this form of vessel may well encourage its operation across the Channel.

Work on still more advanced vessels is under way; in France, a 40 knot quadrimaran, operating on four hulls which offer a much smoother ride, has been under development since the early 1990s. Although this vessel is seen primarily as a freight carrier, it offers potential ultimately for development as a passenger carrier. Foil-catamarans, a hybrid of the jetfoil and hovercraft, have also been tested to prototype stage. Capable of speeds of 30–40 knots, their low resistance in the water leads to 30 per cent greater fuel efficiency, and they would therefore make a very useful contribution in the competitive UK ferry market. Another type of fast ferry, the Hoverplane, combines elements of catamaran, hovercraft and wing-in-surface-effect (WISE) in its design. WISE operates on the principle that a stable cushion of air is generated by a wing flying close to ground or water; by travelling on this dense layer of air, the craft benefits from reduced drag and increased lift, thus achieving high fuel economy. Speeds of up to 100 mph are anticipated, at one-fifth of the normal fuel cost of a ferry, which should enable prices to be much lower than at present. Craft should be capable of carrying between 80 and 150 passengers over distances of up to 250 miles. An added advantage of such a vessel is that it requires neither runway nor port in the accepted sense of the words.

Other European ferry operations

While this text has focused primarily on connections between the UK and its Continental neighbours, the continuing importance of other routes, especially within Europe, must be recognized. In the Mediterranean, ferries provide not only vital connections to travellers on a port-to-port basis, but also the opportunity to package these routes as mini-cruises calling at a variety of different countries. By way of example, services are available in the eastern Mediterranean between Venice, Dubrovnik, Piraeus, Iraklion and Alexandria, or between Istanbul, Piraeus, Larnaca, Lattakia (Syria) and Alexandria. Since the political disruptions in the Balkans, the new and modern ferry service between Patras (Greece) and Ascona (Italy) has become of much greater importance, and a new fast ferry service has also been introduced between Nice and Corsica. Tourists who traditionally think only of travel by air to Majorca may be unaware of the alternatives of travel from Barcelona by catamaran with Trans-mediterranea.

The Greek economy is heavily dependent upon its shipping interests, with some 10 million passengers using ferries within the country each year. The significance of this area of the economy to Greece, both in the cruise and ferry markets, is such that the country received temporary dispensation from the lifting of cabotage restrictions which opened up competition elsewhere within the European Union. Cruises operating out of and back to Greek ports were protected for Greek companies until 1999, and coastal shipping such as ferry services were to receive additional protection until 2004. However, following the disastrous sinking of the poorly maintained and elderly ferry *Express Samina* in 2000, the Greek government interceded to withdraw the licences of some older vessels and agreed to bring forward cabotage deregulation to 2002. This will open up Greek ferries to competition from other European ferry companies, and is encouraging the Greek owners to invest heavily in new equipment.

Despite EU opposition, some member countries

Figure 8.8 The popular Stockholm–Tallinn service. (*Photographed by the author*)

Figure 8.9 The world's fastest ferry: Silja Line's *Finnjet*. (*Photographed by the author*)

have continued to subsidize their shipping interests. Brittany Ferries received a £40 million subsidy from the French government in 1996 despite protests from UK companies.

Ferry operations in the Baltic call for special mention. Services here connect the Scandinavian countries, and in turn provide vital connections for travellers between these countries and Germany. Independence for the three Baltic states of Latvia, Estonia and Lithuania, the rebuilding of the historical port of Gdansk (formerly Danzig) in Poland and the reunification of Germany have all renewed interest in these destinations for tourists, and both cruise ships and ferry crossings have achieved considerable growth in this area. The benefit of having St

Petersburg in Russia as a major port in the Baltic has further stimulated interest in the region. The Helsinki (Finland)–Tallinn (Estonia) route, only an hour and forty minutes by fast ferry, offers the tourist the opportunity for an attractive mini-cruise coupled with bargain priced shopping, but, as reported earlier, the major draw in this area remains the overnight Stockholm–Helsinki route, now operating with 60,000 ton superferries carrying up to 2,800 passengers at a time. The obvious success in this region in selling what were originally merely transport connections as luxury mini-cruises has established a trend which the British ferry operators are keen to emulate.

Coastal and inland waterways tourism

The attraction of water offers many other opportunities for tourist activity, both independently and in forms which have been commoditized and packaged for the tourist. Inland waterways in particular – lakes, rivers and canals – provide exceptional opportunities for recreation and tourism, and in Britain the renovation of former canals, derelict locks and similar watersites has added in recent years to the many opportunities for river and lake recreational travel.

The major waterways of the world have long attracted the tourist. The Nile River, in Egypt, has provided inland waterway cruising for many decades, and in recent years the popularity of this stretch of waterway led to an enormous expansion in the number and size of cruise ships operating as package holiday products up to the early years of the 1990s. However, the volatility of the tourism business is well illustrated by the collapse of the Egyptian inland cruise market in the mid-1990s when the country was hit first by terrorism in which tourists were targeted explicitly, and then by drought, which caused navigational difficulties in the upper Nile region. In 2000 the Nile returned to popularity as the major river cruise destination. Other popular river cruises are those provided along the Danube (between

Table 8.3 Most popular rivers for cruising

1. Nile
2. Rhine
3. Danube
4. Volga and Neva
5. Rhone and Seine
6. Others including Po, Elbe, Yangtze, Mississippi, Murray, Douro

Source: Passenger Shipping Association Annual Cruise Statistics.

Passau in Germany and Constanta in Rumania), the Rhine between Holland and Germany, and the French rivers Seine and Rhone (see Table 8.3). Other rivers with strong tourist appeal include the Mississippi in the USA (where traditional paddle wheelers offer a nostalgic cruise experience) and the Yangtze and Li Rivers in China, while the Russian rivers, the Italian river Po, the Portuguese river Douro and the German Elbe are all gaining tourists. In South America, the Amazon River is sufficiently large to allow ocean-going ships to navigate as far inland as Iquitos in Peru. All of these services are packaged as tours and sold to tourists throughout the world.

Public craft also play an important role in tourism on inland waterways as well as along coasts. Excursion boats such as the paddle steamer *Waverley* (Figure 8.10) and the traditional steamer *Balmoral* carry tourists on coastal trips in Britain during the

Figure 8.10 The *Waverley* sails on a coastal excursion from Bristol. (*Photographed by the author*)

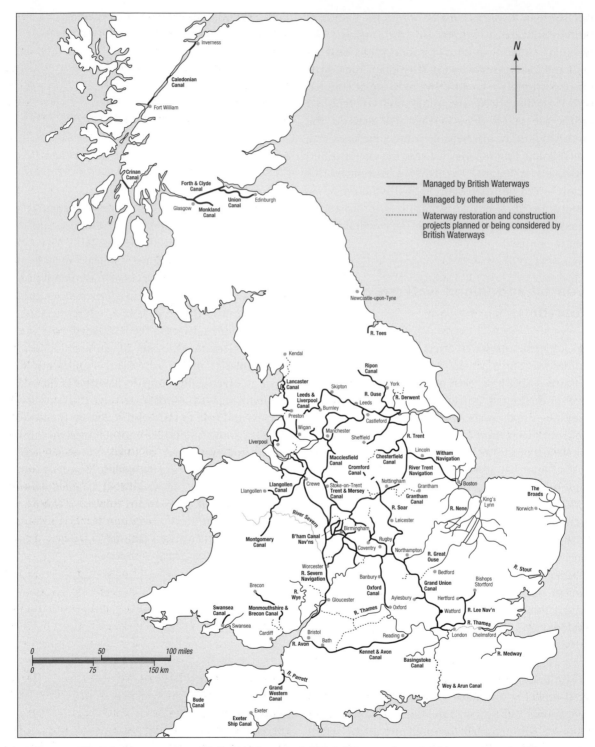

Figure 8.11 The inland waterways of Britain. (*Courtesy British Waterways (www.britishwaterways.co.uk)*)

summer from ports in Scotland, South Wales and the West Country. The lakes steamer remains a familiar sight in many parts of the world, providing an important tourist attraction in the US and Canadian Great Lakes, the Swiss and south German lakes, the islands of southern Sweden around Stockholm and the Scottish lochs and English Lake District in Britain. However, it is the growing attraction of rivers and canals for the independent boating enthusiast which perhaps holds the greatest potential for development over the next few years. The networks of rivers and canals in countries such as Britain, Holland and France have been redeveloped and exploited for tourism in recent years, and canals such as the Burgundy canals and the Canal du Midi in the South of France, and the Gota Canal in Sweden are being discovered by British tourists in growing numbers.

Britain itself is particularly well endowed with canals and rivers suitable for navigation (see Figure 8.11). In the mid-1800s, the nation could boast of some 4,250 miles of navigable inland waterways, many of which had been developed for the movement of freight. As these became redundant with the advent of the railways, they fell into disrepair, and many stretches became no longer navigable. However, in recent years the British Waterways Board (BWB) has encouraged the development and use of these waterways for pleasure purposes and, in partnership with private enterprise, and aided by voluntary bodies, it has helped to restore and reopen many formerly derelict canals. Today, some 2,000 miles of navigable British waterways are maintained by the BWB, catering for a wide range of tourist interests, and attracting a total of 10 million visitors a year. This figure includes 200,000 holiday hire boaters, 900,000 private boaters and 1.3 million pleasure trip boaters.

The British have a long-standing tradition for enjoying holidays afloat, and the popularity of areas such as the Norfolk Broads for water-based tourism dates back to the early twentieth century. The reopening of many formerly derelict waterways has made it possible for boat hire companies to organize packages which allow enthusiasts to follow a circular route during a one- or two-week holiday, without the need to travel the same stretch of water twice.

Apart from those stretches of water maintained by the BWB, a further 1,250 miles of navigable waterway are preserved by other bodies. Over 300 miles of formerly derelict canals have either already been returned to use, or are under development. The Waterways Trust, focusing on those inland waterways not controlled by British Waterways, is developing the first new canal in England for over a hundred years; the Millennium Ribble Link, linking Lancaster canal to the River Ribble and scheduled to open in 2001, will form the first stage of an inland waterways route from London to the English Lake District. Now foreign as well as British tourists are becoming attracted to the tourism potential these waterways offer.

This form of tourism does suffer from the fact that the market has become highly competitive and the season is relatively short. Most pleasure boat companies are small, family-run concerns, achieving low returns on capital invested and generally low profits. Effective marketing, especially to the overseas tourist, is a problem where companies' budgets for promotion are small and the destination being sold is linear (the Kennet and Avon Canal, for instance, runs through different regional tourist board areas, making unified marketing difficult). In such circumstances, cooperative promotion between the small boat companies themselves, working with other private sector interests, may be the best solution.

Sustainability is an important factor in inland waterways, too. Apart from the dangers of pollution from fuel and oil leaks in sensitive freshwater areas, the erosion of river banks and sheer congestion on popular stretches of waterway create further problems. One interesting development has been the introduction of a solar powered boat on the Norfolk Broads in 2000. With no fuel emissions, this environmentally friendly 12-seater boat operating in one of England's most sensitive regions is an important initiative, as well as one which significantly reduces costs for its operator.

Watersite development

In a similar fashion, the closure and subsequent dereliction of many of Britain's major docklands offered another opportunity for redevelopment of these sites for recreation and tourism. Although primarily a consequence of urban redevelopment policy, the restoration of waterfront property in sites such as Bristol's Historic Floating Harbour, Salford Quays, Liverpool's Albert Docks, Southampton's Ocean Village and, of course, the London Docklands, has in turn generated tourism to these sites, following the construction of marinas and the subsequent introduction of waterbuses and ferries, scenic cruises, floating restaurants and other leisure attractions. Lottery and millennium funding in Britain has spurred on the development of watersite attractions, notably the architecturally innovative Lowry Centre in Salford with its adjoining pedestrian footbridge designed by Antonio Calatrava, the Millennium Square development on Bristol's Harbourside, the Walsall Art Gallery adjacent to the canal network and the redevelopment of Birmingham's city centre canal network around Brindley Place. Similar developments have also taken place abroad, especially within the USA and Canada. The astonishing success of Baltimore's Inner Harbor development sparked off similar schemes in New York, San Francisco, Boston and Toronto, all of which now attract tourists in large numbers. In Europe, Stockholm and Oslo have both restored their decaying harbour sites, and in Australia, Sydney's Darling Harbour has likewise been the subject of extensive renovation, making these cities more attractive for visiting tourists. While most of these sites are of course planned for multiple use, including shops, offices and residential communities, the leisure use of the sites will inevitably attract the tourist and generate new forms of income for the cities concerned.

Seagoing pleasure craft

This chapter would not be complete without some mention of the growing demand for holidays aboard seagoing pleasure craft, a demand which is now being met by the travel industry. It has been estimated that there are more than 400,000 boat owners in Britain, and some 2 million people sail for pleasure. This is naturally leading to demand for institutionalized boating holidays. Small private companies are increasingly offering package holidays aboard small sailing ships or steamboats, with facilities ranging from the luxurious, where the passengers are guests, to the more basic, where passengers play an active part in crewing the boat. On the other hand, tour operating companies are catering to the mass demand for boating holidays by offering flotilla cruising holidays, especially in areas where there are many small islands which provide a sheltered anchorage and good weather conditions. The Greek islands and certain Caribbean islands, such as the Windward and Leeward

Figure 8.12 Flotilla sailing in Turkey. (*Courtesy Pat Collinge (photographer) and Sunsail Worldwide Sailing Holidays*)

groups, offer ideal conditions for these types of package holiday, in which individually hired yachts sail together in flotilla formation from island to island. In this manner, the tourist has the benefits of independent use of the yacht while enjoying the social life of the group when together at anchor (see Figure 8.12).

Questions and discussion points

1. Explain why cruising enjoys a higher level of demand in North America than in Britain, and suggest what more needs to be done by British shipping companies to increase the cruise market.

2. Cunard Line will shortly launch a new superliner on the North Atlantic which will allow the company to reintroduce its traditional twin-liner line voyages between New York and Southampton. Assess the likelihood of success of this venture, and what markets the company will aim to attract. Given the time scale for the crossing (six days), can the business traveller be attracted?

3. Compare and contrast the two ferry routes,
   (a) Harwich to Esbjerg, Denmark;
   (b) Stockholm, Sweden to Helsinki, Finland.

Both involve one night on board, but appeal to different markets and motivations. Identify both, and explore the nature of these distinctions between the two routes. What conclusions can be drawn about the nature of ferry services in general from your observations?

Assignment topics

1. You are employed in the Cruise Planning Department of a major British shipping company. Your manager has asked you to prepare a study to investigate the possibility of launching a new series of one-week themed cruises which will provide the maximum number of ports of call. The ship to be used is new to the company – a small (5,500 ton) vessel carrying 260 passengers, built in 1978 and recently renovated. Her cruising speed is 18 knots. The ship is to be used for a series of cruises over a period of twelve weeks during the summer.

   Determine a base port (allowing a fly-cruise programme), route and ports of call. Suggest a minimum selling price for the programme after comparing competitors' prices and itineraries. What is distinctive about the programme you have proposed, and which markets will it set out to attract? Describe a programme of shore excursions which will prove attractive to these markets.

2. As a result of the closer ties which have developed between Britain and the rest of the EU, a German leisure corporation, Gesellschaft für Internationalen Reiseverkehr, is examining opportunities to expand into the British market. They already have interests in inland waterways cruising on the Continent, and have asked you, as a research officer with a firm of consultants retained by the company, to carry out a study of the opportunities in Britain. They are contemplating setting up, or purchasing, a company operating a hire fleet of narrow boats based on a section of Britain's inland waterways network, which would enable holidaymakers to hire vessels for circular trips, avoiding the necessity of retracing their journey over the same route.

   In the first instance, you are asked to provide a brief report to the company identifying one or more suitable locations. You should also present evidence of factors favouring growth of this particular form of leisure activity. Your report should be suitably illustrated with maps and graphs.

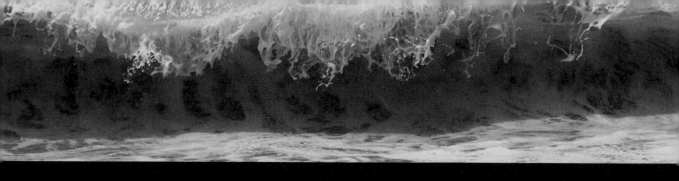

Chapter 9 Other modes of tourist travel

Objectives

After studying this chapter, you should be able to:

- understand the role and scope of public and private railways in the UK, in terms of their importance to tourism;
- be aware of the role and significance of the coach industry in tourism;
- recognize the importance of the private car for tourism;
- understand the role of car hire in tourism, both at home and abroad;
- be aware of the increasing significance of tourist travel by cycle and on foot.

The role of the railways in tourism

Considering their long lead over other carriers in providing public service transport, it may be thought surprising that the railways in Britain took so long to adapt to the needs of mass-market tourism in the late twentieth century. Certainly the railways played a major role in the provision of tourist transport throughout the first half of the last century, but as ownership of private cars grew, so tourist traffic on the railways fell. The process had already become noticeable before World War II, and accelerated after 1947, when the railways were nationalized in Britain. The switch to travel by private car, coupled with the rapid expansion of freight transport by road, led to severe difficulties for the railways in Britain and other developed nations during the 1950s and 1960s, which they attempted to solve by substantial reductions in their routes. This resulted in their focusing on the main intercity routes, and cutting back unprofitable branch lines. Many smaller resorts and other destinations that could have attracted tourists dependent upon public transport became inaccessible by rail. The alternative of coach links connecting with rail termini makes tourist travel inconvenient and time-consuming, and this, coupled with continuing fare increases, soon made the railways an unattractive choice for many destinations. The difficulties following privatization of the railways in Britain in the late twentieth century, coupled with long-term lack of investment, particularly in track and signalling, when in public hands, have resulted in rail travel becoming a poor alternative for tourist movements. Nevertheless, railways in Britain still play an important role in bringing domestic tourists from the major conurbations to key English resorts such as Brighton, Bournemouth and Torquay, and the long-term potential for railways remains significant. In Continental Europe, especially in France, this potential is already being developed.

In the 1970s and 1980s, public rail transport in Britain became more marketing-oriented, and, helped by the escalation in fuel prices following the oil crisis of 1973, succeeded in winning back some of the domestic tourists from private car travel. Packages using rail transport were introduced on a larger scale than for many years. The packages proved to be popular for the short-break market, particularly to London. By the mid-1980s, however, tourists were reverting to car trips, and the sale of rail packages declined, leading to British Rail selling off its loss-making holidays division to the private sector. However, efforts to entice the rail travel enthusiast proved more successful, even though these were limited in scale. Nostalgic day trips and excursions using famous old steam trains proved popular, as did short breaks using Intercity trains, and packages aimed at the over-55s. Recognizing that unsold off-peak seats represent substantial lost revenue, the railway used variable pricing policies and promotions, sometimes in cooperation with well-known retail stores, to attract the tourist and excursionist back to the railways.

Unlimited travel tickets were also made available, in Britain and in mainland Europe, for inbound tourists buying tickets before departure from their own countries. The Britrail pass allowed overseas tourists to travel freely over the rail network within Britain, while Eurailpass offered similar benefits for travel within Continental Europe. A railpass in Scandinavia allowed unlimited travel by rail within the region and a 50 per cent reduction on interconnecting ferry services. Such schemes proved highly popular with independent tourists visiting Europe, especially the young backpacker market.

The privatization of rail transport

Towards the end of the twentieth century it became clear that action would have to be taken to improve the railway systems, both in Europe and North America. Heavily subsidized, and lacking adequate investment over many years, railways were in a parlous state. Two alternatives presented themselves; either for the state to move railways out of public ownership, or to agree to a programme of massive state investment to increase the appeal of the railways as a form of public transport. In Britain, the Conservative government then in power took the decision to denationalize the railways. Private companies were to be allowed to bid for individual routes within the British Rail system, while Railtrack, the state-run body responsible for the maintenance and operation of all track, signalling and stations, was to be sold off as a separate company. The government's belief was that a privatized railway system would be more efficient, would end the drain on government funds through subsidies and would compete effectively against other forms of transport by new private investment which would attract travellers back on to the railways. By early 1997 twenty-five train operating units in the UK had replaced the former monolithic rail system, and a further three companies were formed to control rolling stock.

While passenger traffic did increase on most services, partly as a result of better marketing, passengers became confused about the range of choice facing them, and journeys involving the services of more than one rail company became more complex. Competition between the rail companies led to passengers not being fully informed about the range of services available or the cheapest fares for their itineraries. Concern rose over the lack of promised investment by the rail companies and the impact of cost-cutting by some companies in order to boost profits, which in some instances led to safety violations, and even accidents. Some disastrous mishaps arising from broken rails forced Railtrack into expensive investment in updating track and signals, severely disrupting mainline services. Distribution systems for rail tickets also suffered. Travel agents were already abandoning the sale of rail tickets as unprofitable before the advent of privatization; this has been hastened by the additional complexities of dealing with a score of different rail companies.

The rail companies have been less innovative in seeking improvements in their distribution systems. A computerized reservations system, ELGAR, was introduced, initially to handle bookings for the Channel Tunnel's Eurostar service and later extended to all members of the Association of Train Operating Companies (ATOC). The system offers agents a combined reservations, ticketing and back office facility, but has been fraught with teething problems. Eurostar's marketing and distribution has been strongly criticized; onward bookings beyond Paris and Brussels can no longer be made to any European destination, but are limited to the major railway stations. Systems to sell tickets to the public via the Internet on all British rail services are under consideration.

In other respects, the ambition to meet the needs of the tourist market remains strong. The Special Trains division of British Rail is now in private hands, and continues to provide a limited number of special steam and electric excursions which had proved popular with domestic and foreign tourists alike in the past. A handful of domestic tour operators also continue to specialize in offering domestic and continental rail travel, but although the potential exists for a greatly expanded market for rail travel within the European Union, this is not really being tapped in Britain as yet. As we have seen, the Eurostar rail service has yet to exploit its potential connections with the new high-speed train services on mainland Europe, which could appeal strongly to international tourists.

The Channel Tunnel and the railways

In Chapter 8 we examined the impact of the Channel Tunnel on ferry operations from the UK. Here, we must examine its impact on rail and road services in Britain and in mainland Europe.

The Channel Tunnel is one of the great engineering feats of the twentieth century – although, contrary to popular belief, not the longest underwater rail tunnel in the world: Japan's Selkan Tunnel, 32.5 miles long, has been carrying rail traffic for a number of years. The first direct rail link between Britain and France was completed and opened to traffic in 1994, after frequent delays. It offers passengers the choice of two forms of transport: passenger travel on Eurostar from London to either Paris or Brussels, calling at Ashford in Kent and Lille in northern France (with opportunities to transfer to high-speed trains for onward travel in Europe), and Eurotunnel's vehicle-carrying rail service operating between Cheriton (near Folkestone) and les Coquelles (near Calais), a distance of some 50 kilometres, of which 37 kilometres is under the Channel itself. Cars are driven on to double-deck carriages (higher cars, those with trailers, and coaches are accommodated in single-deck carriages). These are then transported across the Channel and can be driven off to connect directly with the French motorway in a little over thirty minutes after leaving England.

At the insistence of the Conservative government, the Tunnel was privately financed without any contribution from the state. Its construction involved leading-edge technology, and the project ran into delays and huge cost over-runs, leaving the parent company, Eurotunnel, with massive debts of some £9 billion.

Overambitious estimates of traffic and revenue were not realized, but this is not to say that the Tunnel has not been a success. Within two years of operation, it had made sufficient inroads into the share of the short-sea market to badly worry the ferry companies, which were obliged to slash prices to compete. A severe fire in the Tunnel during November 1996 disrupted traffic for six months, but Eurostar still carried some 5 million passengers during 1996, and by the turn of the century was carrying 60 per cent of all passenger traffic between London and Paris and 50 per cent of the London–Brussels passenger market. By the same date Eurotunnel could claim 54 per cent of the cross-

Channel car market and 61 per cent of Dover–Calais car traffic. In 1998, Eurostar's passenger rail services were taken over by a consortium of rail, road and air transport businesses, with National Express coaches holding 40 per cent of the company.

The rail route from London has been particularly attractive for the business traveller, for whom a first-class service is available, and who can travel city centre to city centre in around three hours, compared with closer to four hours by air, allowing for check-in time and the inevitable delayed departure. A journey time of two hours from London Waterloo to Lille enables the tourist to connect with the French TGV (*Train à Grande Vitesse*) high-speed trains for onward travel to southern France or contiguous European countries; Lille–Bordeaux is a five-hour trip, while Calais to Marseille is of similar duration, with the opening of the final section of line beyond Valence in 2001. This brings Marseille within seven hours of London, making the journey competitive with air travel (typically five hours including connections to local airports).

The contrast between investment in the public railways in France and the lack of investment in Britain's private railways is marked. SNCF, the publicly operated rail service, and RFF, France's equivalent of Railtrack, which is responsible for building and maintaining tracks, are investing millions of francs of government money which is not expected to be recovered for at least fifty years. Britain's privately operated services, meanwhile, are cutting investment in order to concentrate on vital safety maintenance. Railtrack may be unable to fund the second stage of the high-speed line between London and Folkestone, already delayed for at least ten years, while Eurostar is delaying introduction of services planned to operate from London to Amsterdam, and from UK regional cities to Paris, citing insufficient demand.

The failure to complete the 68-mile high-speed rail link through Kent, which would reduce journey times by a further half-hour, is a severe blow to attempts to attract tourists away from air transport. With the high-speed line in place on the Continent,

Figure 9.1 Two high-speed train services: (a) Japan's *Shinkansen* (Bullet Train). (*Permission of the Japan Information and Cultural Centre (JICC)*). (b) France's *Train à Grande Vitesse* (TGV). (*Courtesy SNCF. CAV photo Bruno Vignal*)

services between London and Brussels are reduced to two hours forty minutes travel time. Estimates in France have shown, for example, that for journeys of up to two hours, rail will capture some 90 per cent of all traffic, while for journeys of up to three hours, rail will still capture 75 per cent. The research also revealed that 25 per cent of the passenger traffic carried by the first TGV service was newly generated traffic.

Nonetheless, the advent of the Tunnel has still led to a substantial increase in the numbers of people travelling between Britain (particularly London and the southeast) and the Continent. Popular tourist destinations such as Canterbury, which are now brought into reach for day excursions and short-break visitors, are under pressure from the huge increase in tourism, leading to considerable difficulties for the local authorities in managing congestion and catering for increasing numbers of cars on these roads.

Eurotunnel's debt creates obvious difficulties in attempting to compete on price with the ferries. The company reached agreement with its major creditors to reschedule its debts, and is now trading at a profit on its operating revenue, although crippling interest payments inhibit competition with the ferries, and prices were pushed up in 2000 and 2001 to more realistic levels after cut-throat competition for several years. Nevertheless, if independent estimates for the increase of passengers over the next twenty years prove to be correct, the Tunnel's long-term future looks promising. The novelty factor undoubtedly boosted carryings in the initial years of operation, and fears expressed about market resistance to long journeys under water seem to have been laid to rest. Moreover, those using the Tunnel have generally expressed satisfaction and willingness to use this service regularly in the future. Ultimately, when the massive capital costs of the Tunnel have been repaid, its low operating costs contrasted with the capital and labour-intensive ferry services would suggest high prospects for success. Indeed, long-term forecasts by Eurotunnel indicate that capacity in the present tunnel will be reached by 2025, and plans have been submitted for a second tunnel. This could be a road tunnel with the option of an additional rail link, but the question of how funding could be raised for this massive new investment, for which work would need to begin by 2010, remains unanswered.

Figure 9.2 The Eurotunnel train. (*Permission of QA Photos Limited (www.qaphotos.com)*)

Investment in the European rail network

Britain's Continental partners have taken a different approach to rail investment. Recognizing the importance of an effective rail network as an element in an integrated public transport policy, they have taken the decision to invest heavily to achieve this, aided by European Union support. In 1990, the EU approved the formation of a Trans-European Network (TENS) of high-speed road and rail links, the bulk of which were to be completed by 2005. Estimates have suggested that rail would account for more than 23 per cent of all passenger kilometres travelled in western Europe by 2010, alleviating the pressure on air and road services. Since then, France has invested more than £22 billion to build its 300 kph TGV service, much of which is now in place, while Germany found £54 billion to build its own network of 280 kph ICE (Intercity Express) trains. Italy has introduced its *Pendolino* 250 kph tilt-body train on the Milan to Rome route, while Spain's AVE (*Alta Velocidad Espagnola*) offers a high-speed, two hours and fifteen minutes service between Madrid and Seville which within six years was carrying 80 per cent of all passenger traffic on this route. As a result, three further lines in Spain are under construction or planned. Thalys, a consortium of Belgian, French and Dutch rail interests, has been developing similar high-speed links between its member countries and Germany, with the popular Paris–Brussels route coming down to a mere one hour and twenty-five minutes. Sweden's hugely successful X2000 high-speed train, which reduced the journey between Stockholm and Gothenburg to less than three hours, increased rail's share of this market from 30 per cent to 52 per cent, encouraging the extension of the service to Oslo, Norway, as well as to other Swedish cities. Norway's *Signatur* tilting train was introduced between Oslo and Kristiansand in 1999, its immediate popularity encouraging the introduction of other routes throughout Norway.

The French TGV network in particular has proved very attractive to the tourist market, with British tourists able to connect at Lille for Belgium, Holland, Germany and southern routes; the 1,216 km route between London and Nice can now be covered in a little over ten hours, and Lyons is now just a three-hour journey from Paris. Once the new high-speed link from London to the Channel Tunnel is in place, fast through-trains are likely to come into service, offering the prospect, for example, of overnight ski-trains between London and the Alps. However, planning delays mean that the British link will not be fully open until at least 2007, and may be still further delayed.

Further improvements are well advanced. Spain plans to operate still faster trains on its Madrid–Barcelona service, to open by 2004, with speeds of up to 350 kph, while Germany's ICE3 330 kph train will halve the journey time between Cologne and Frankfurt. RENFE, the Spanish railway system, has introduced popular hotel trains for overnight journeys between Madrid and other European capitals, and SNCF French Railways is cooperating with the Italian railways to provide new overnight sleeper trains between the two countries.

Improved equipment and service, rapid connections between major cities, and the avoidance of delays in congested airports are making European rail services appear increasingly attractive to the tourist market, and there is little doubt that rail services will figure prominently in the future of European tourism. As in Britain, train enthusiasts are being catered for by the introduction of services which provide a nostalgic and luxurious journey by rail for the tourist trade. A leading example of this is the Al Andalus Express, a vintage luxury train composed of twelve carriages built in the 1920s and 1930s, operating between major tourist centres in southern Spain such as Seville, Jerez and Granada during spring and autumn. This itinerary is featured in upmarket programmes of European tour operators. Hungary has introduced the *Imperial Explorer*, employing carriages built originally for the use of high-level party members under the communist regime, as a feature to attract tourists to destinations outside Budapest.

Bridge building is making its own contribution to the rail networks of Europe, especially in Scandinavia. In Denmark, bridges across the Great Belt and across the Sound between Denmark and Sweden have now opened up the prospect of continuous rail travel between London and Stockholm or Copenhagen, promising a huge increase in international tourism for the Malmö district of southern Sweden.

Luxury rail journeys around the world

Although routes and standards of service have declined in many other countries, railways still have a useful role to play in the carriage of both passengers and freight, and for the many tourists who are enthusiasts railways continue to exercise a fascination. Countries in which steam trains still operate, such as India and China (although sadly the former are now being phased out), attract both independent travellers and the package tour operator, and luxury rail travel on restored or recreated early twentieth-century rolling-stock drawn by steam trains, much romanticized on television, continues to attract tourists to destinations such as India, which offers 'The Palace on Wheels', while Rovos Rail's 'Pride of Africa', a train with 1930s' carriages, is chartered out to tour operators to provide an equally luxurious service between East and South Africa, via Victoria Falls. The Orient Express offers luxury train journeys between Malaysia and Singapore. Australia has extensively promoted its famous trains, the 'Indian Pacific' (a three-day service across the country between Perth and Melbourne) and 'The Gan' (across the red centre to Alice Springs), and Orient Express has introduced another luxury tourist train, the Great South Pacific Express, which operates between Cairns and Sydney. Long intercontinental rail journeys reminiscent of an earlier age of travel, such as the trans-Siberian route, have been exploited by specialist tour operators to provide unusual packages for the rail aficionados.

In North America, rail travel in the 1960s and 1970s declined in the face of lower air fares and poor marketing by the railway companies themselves, which chose to concentrate on freight revenue at the expense of the passenger services. The continuing losses suffered by most US rail companies, and the importance of the rail network in social communications, led the government to integrate rail services in the country into a centrally funded public corporation known as AMTRAK. This organization has achieved some success in reversing the decline of passenger traffic, although many of the great names of the past, such as the Santa Fé Superchief and the 20th Century Ltd, have gone for ever, and with them some of the mystique of North American rail travel. Nonetheless, North American railways still pass through some of the finest scenery in the world, such as the Canadian Rockies and the western states, providing a base for future regeneration of interest in rail trips for the European tourist and tour operator alike. Rail journeys to the Rockies already form an important element in excursions for those booking cruises out of west coast North American ports. New Talgo tilting express trains offer fast and comfortable transport out of Seattle down the west coast, while on the eastern seaboard, a new high-speed rail link between Boston, New York and Washington opened in 2000; the *Acela* train cuts the journey between Boston and New York from five hours to just over three, with the introduction of a 150 mph express service. This service is also likely to have strong appeal to foreign tourists.

In Japan, the *Shinkansen* (popularly known as the Bullet train; see Figure 9.1(a)) has changed the face of high-speed transport, and its reliability and high levels of service have proved immensely popular with tourists. The journey between Tokyo and Osaka, for example, takes three hours city centre to city centre by train, compared with an hour's flying time between airports, and 80 per cent of all passengers now use the train for this journey.

The future of high-speed trains is promising for tourism. Both Germany and Japan are developing magnetic levitation (MAGLEV) trains, and in 1997 Japan's MLX-01 broke the world speed record for a train, travelling at 280.3 mph. Germany had hoped

Figure 9.3 The private railways and railway transport museums of Britain and Ireland. Over fifty private railways offer tourists pleasure trips of between one and twenty miles. (*Courtesy Heritage Railway Association and Ian Allen Ltd.*)

to be the first country to introduce this system, between Berlin and Hamburg, but the high cost of building it (estimated at over 6 billion euros) and a saving of only twenty minutes on the journey time now make this project look unviable. In the US, rail authorities have tested the Cybertran, a cross between a high-speed train and a light railway system, which is designed to provide fast, non-stop service at speeds of up to 150 mph between US cities. Russia and America have held talks to discuss the construction of a 50-mile tunnel under the Bering Strait and a 4,600 mile rail track to provide a surface transport link between the two countries. While designed primarily as a means of competing with shipping across the Pacific for the carriage of freight, it would also enable the rail enthusiast to travel by rail between London and New York in 14 days. However, the costs of all these developments are substantial (the US–Russian project is estimated at £27 billion alone), and they are unlikely to materialize until well into the twenty-first century. Some of these initiatives will provide strong competition for short-haul air services, particularly on major business routes. In view of the existing congestion in air routes, which can only get worse as the integration of Europe progresses, the development of alternative high-speed land routes is vital if trade – and tourism – are to prosper.

The 'little railways' as tourist attractions

With the electrification of the railways in Britain, nostalgia for the steam trains of the pre-war period has led to the re-emergence of many small private railways. Using obsolete track and former British Rail rolling-stock, enthusiasts have painstakingly restored a number of branch lines to provide an alternative system of transport for commuters and travellers as well as another attraction for domestic and overseas tourists. In Britain alone, there are over 250 railway preservation societies, and some 40 private lines are in operation (see Figure 9.3), with a further 400 other projects either in hand or under consideration.

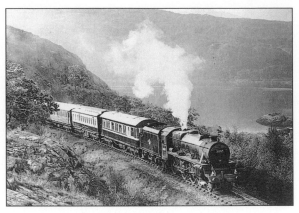

Figure 9.4 The 'Royal Scotsman'. (*Courtesy Abercrombie & Kent Ltd, London*)

Some of these depend largely upon tourist patronage, while others principally serve the needs of the local community; their profitability, however, is often dependent upon a great deal of voluntary labour, especially in the restoration of track, stations and rolling-stock to serviceable condition. Since these services are generally routed through some of the most scenic areas of Britain, they attract both railway buffs and tourists of all kinds, and undoubtedly enhance the attractiveness of a region for tourism generally.

Britain, too, has taken advantage of tourists' nostalgia for luxurious steam trains and antique carriages, most notably with the resurrection of the former Venice–Simplon–Orient Express, extensively renovated and providing a level of luxury and service seldom seen since the heyday of the railways in the period between the wars. Although now operating only as far as Venice, the train has been successfully marketed to the US and British markets. Carriages used on the London–Folkestone leg of the journey have also been successfully employed for nostalgic day trips to other British resorts like Bath. In Scotland, a second successful venture has been the introduction of the 'Royal Scotsman' (see Figure 9.4). Although without benefit of a genuine pedigree, the 1920s'-style train has been packaged with success in the American market, offering a very up-market tour of the Scottish Highlands. These enterprises demonstrate that market niches exist for unusual rail programmes, which can undoubtedly be emulated in other tourist regions.

Coach travel

Coach operators today offer a wide range of tourist services to the public, both directly and through other sectors of the industry. These services can be categorized under the following headings:

1. express coach routes, both domestic and international;
2. private hire services;
3. tour and excursion operations;
4. transfer services.

Long-distance coach services provide a cheap alternative to rail or air travel, and the extension of these services both within the UK and from the UK to points in Europe and beyond has drawn an increasing number of tourists at the cheaper end of the market, particularly among the younger age groups. Younger passengers have also been attracted to adventurous transcontinental coach packages which have provided, for a low all-in price, both transport and minimal food and lodging en route (often under canvas). These services have been severely curtailed in recent years, however, due to political problems in transit countries such as Iran and Iraq. An alternative is the sleeper-coach, an innovation scarcely known in Britain, although on the Continent, particularly in the German market, this is a popular form of budget long-distance coach holiday. In this form of transport, the coach pulls a sleeper trailer which at night can accommodate all the passengers in sleeping bunks (see Figure 10.9c).

However, for the most part coach travel remains the mode of transport of the older traveller, and the highest proportion of coach holidays are taken by those aged between 55 and 64; two-thirds of all coaching holidays are taken by the over 45s. This is in spite of efforts by the coach operators themselves to attract a younger market. This is perhaps unsur

Figure 9.5   Continental touring by coach.

prising, given the advantages which coach services offer to the older market – not just low prices (reflecting low operating costs vis-à-vis other forms of transport) but the convenience of door-to-door travel when touring, overcoming baggage and transfer problems, courier assistance, especially in overseas travel, where the elderly avoid problems of language and handling documentation, and now, arrangements are often made to pick up passengers at points convenient for their homes. One result of this is that coach companies traditionally benefit from high levels of repeat business. Coach companies are now taking the view that their marketing efforts are best spent on raising the frequency of sales to the older market, rather than trying to attract a new younger market; the former market is expanding rapidly, as people retire earlier in increasing numbers. The most popular holiday destinations for British clients are Germany's Rhineland and Bavarian regions, the Austrian Tyrol and the Swiss Alps. While the long-distance coaching market on the Continent is holding up reasonably well, the trend is to short-break holidays by coach, in keeping with the growth of short-break holidays in general.

The operation of coach tours is a highly seasonal one, however, and companies are often forced to lay off drivers and staff out of season, unless they can obtain sufficient ad hoc charters or contract work (such as school bussing). Most coach companies specialize in certain spheres of activity. While some operate and market their tours nationally, others may concentrate on serving the needs of incoming tourists and tour operators, by providing excursion programmes, transfers between airports and hotels, or complete coach tours for overseas visitors. These coach companies must build up close relations and work closely with tour operators and other intermediaries abroad or in the home country.

Legislation in the coach business

Under the terms of the Transport Act 1980, in order to set up or operate a coach service, an operator must apply for a coach operator's licence. This is granted by the Traffic Commissioners, with conditions which limit the operation to a specified number of vehicles. Licences normally run for five years, although under some conditions the term can be shorter. Before granting a licence, the Traffic Commissioners must be satisfied that the applicant has a good financial record and adequate resources to operate the number of coaches for which the licence has been requested. At least one responsible member of the company must hold an individual transport operator's licence, which is essentially a certificate of professional competence based on management experience and appropriate educational qualifications (for example, membership of the Chartered Institute of Transport). The Commissioners must also satisfy themselves that the operator will provide satisfactory maintenance facilities (or in lieu, a contract with a supplier of such facilities), and the operating centre where the vehicles are to be garaged must be specified.

Coach operating conditions now fall into line with EU Directives, which are designed to ensure adequate safety provisions for passengers. The concern with safety has been highlighted by recent incidents in the coaching industry, most notably a series of serious accidents on the Continent involving holiday coaches. The EU regulation governing drivers' hours (No. 543/69) dictates the maximum number of hours' driving permitted for each driver per day.

These regulations apply automatically to all express journeys by coach with stages over 50 kilometres. The controversial tachograph, introduced in the EU in 1970 and adopted by Britain in 1981 following the Passenger and Goods Vehicles Recording Equipment Regulations 1979, provides recorded evidence of hours of operation and vehicle speeds by individual drivers. While there can be little doubt that implementation of these regulations has led to higher safety standards in the industry, the effect has also been to increase the cost of long-haul coaching operations, making it more difficult to compete with rail or air services. To permit through journeys without expensive stopovers, two drivers must be carried, or, more commonly, since rest periods must be taken off the coach, drivers are exchanged at various stages of the journey. With the constraint of a limited number of seats on each coach, this has the effect of pushing up costs per seat by a significant amount.

The financial security of coaching operations has been increased through the Confederation of Passenger Transport UK, requiring that members be bonded for 10 per cent of their touring turnover, as insurance against the financial collapse of a member.

Deregulation and its aftermath

Substantial changes occurred in the UK coach industry following the 1980 Transport Act, which ended the licensing regulations affecting express coach services on routes of more than 30 miles.

Prior to this, the licensing system favoured the development of national and regional oligopolies; the trunk routes were effectively controlled by three major carriers, the National Bus Company, Wallace Arnold and Ellerman Bee Line. National, however, dominated the market. Apart from these three, some 220 licensed coach companies shared the regional routes, the result of historical developments within the coaching industry. Companies wishing to compete with the established carriers had to apply for a licence to the Traffic Commissioners, who were generally prepared to consider granting one only where a new service was envisaged, or a new market tapped.

Applications could be refused on the strength of existing operators' complaints that their business would suffer. This obviously inhibited competition, and there was little incentive for creative marketing. Similar restrictions applied to all coach tour operations (with the sole exception of tours operated by coach companies on behalf of overseas tour operators on which all passengers had been pre-booked abroad).

With the ending of regulation, a spate of new coach services of all types was introduced in 1981. A number of important regional coach companies came together to form British Coachways, a consortium designed to compete with the National Bus Company on the express routes. National responded to the challenge by expanding into the formerly restricted regional territories to compete with the monopolies there. The then state-owned British Rail became the immediate target of the coach operators, who introduced new, low-priced express services between major city centres, initially attracting a considerable amount of traffic away from British Rail, until that organization responded with its own highly competitive discounted fares.

The chief beneficiary of deregulation appears to have been the National Bus Company, whose dominant size allowed it to gain at the expense of its rivals by offering greater frequency of service and flexibility. With its huge fleet of coaches and a national network of routes, at short notice it was able to replace a defective vehicle with little inconvenience to its passengers, an advantage denied to its smaller rivals. However, smaller companies operating newer or unusual vehicles (such as luxurious foreign-built coaches costing up to £250,000 apiece) provided the larger companies with some competition, although in time most companies found that, given the prices they were forced to charge to recover their investments, they simply could not generate adequate demand for the luxury coaches, and many suffered large losses due to these investments.

The British Coachways consortium also was unable to maintain its challenge to the National Bus Company's operation, and went into liquidation in 1982. Fears were expressed that the cut-throat competition the coaches were being forced into would lead to falling standards of maintenance and safety. Few small companies had the resources to engage in a major price war.

Before deregulation, the market for coach services had been virtually static. The deregulation of the industry stimulated demand, but also led to an even greater supply of new coach seats on the market, with the result that load factors for most operators actually fell. While National was able to strengthen its market share of coaching operations, the Monopolies and Mergers Commission felt disinclined to investigate coach operations, taking the view that the coach operators' principal competitor was British Rail, and that competition between rail and coach was driving down fares.

A general concern about coach standards and quality control led in 1985 to the formation of the Guild of British Coach Operators, a commercial body whose aim was to promote high standards of service, safety and maintenance, and to reassure the travelling public of the continuing benefits of travel by coach.

Subsequently, the 1985 Transport Act set the scene for almost total deregulation of Britain's bus industry in the following year, opening to competition all local bus routes outside London (provision for later deregulation in London was made in the Act). Passenger Transport Executives and District Councils were required to transfer their bus companies to private companies covered by the Companies Act. The Transport Act had two important implications for the tourist industry. First, it required the break-up and privatization of the 60 subsidiaries of the National Bus Company, providing small bus operators with greater scope to compete with the former NBC empire. This process, which was completed in 1988, led to the establishment of seventy-two separate companies, more than half of which were sold to their own management. Second, the resulting competition on the short bus routes led to an overall growth in the number of vehicles, for which operators tried to find alternative uses outside of peak travel periods. Equally, of course, the long-distance coach operators became free to operate their equipment on bus routes.

While the Act led to random fluctuations in fares, as bus companies competed on the lucrative city commuter routes, no systematic change in pricing policy became evident. The major result of the Act was the reinforcement of an oligopolistic market among the national carriers which bears comparison with the deregulation of the US airlines a decade earlier.

There were three major beneficiaries of deregulation. The first of these was National Express, the company formed out of the erstwhile National Bus Company, which not only retained its identity in the long-distance route market, but went on to establish Eurolines as a division of its Continental services, at the same time buying out rival Euroways from Wallace Arnold in 1988. The second beneficiary was Stagecoach, a small private company which through aggressive acquisitions became one of Britain's leading bus and coach companies. Finally, another powerful company appeared on the scene, First Bus (later renamed FirstGroup), which through acquisitions of prominent local companies, such as Badger Line in the southwest, was to form the third major force in this triumvirate, controlling a quarter of the UK bus market by the turn of the century.

The expansion of activities by these three companies into other spheres of travel has been a notable phenomenon. National Express bought five of the new rail franchises and an interest in the Eurostar service from London to mainland Europe. It has expanded abroad by buying bus services in the USA, Australia and New Zealand, as well as a New York airport. Stagecoach bought another of the rail franchises, together with one of the three rolling-stock leasing companies (ROSCOs), and invested in Italian rail services, bus services in the USA, Hong Kong, New Zealand, Portugal and the largest bus company in Sweden. FirstGroup took ownership of one rail franchise and a holding in another (Great Western Trains), together with bus services in the USA and Hong Kong, and a controlling share of Bristol International Airport (which it subsequently sold). Two other companies, Arriva and Go-Ahead Group, also made significant inroads into the coaching business. Arriva invested in transport in the Netherlands, Denmark, Sweden and Spain, and Go-Ahead controls Thames Trains, a major passenger rail service. There is some question about the long-term viability of these companies in the face of competition from the 'big three', however. The experiences in privatization of British bus and coach operations have been watched with interest by companies on the Continent, and the future of bus transport looks to be in the private sector, both in Europe and further afield.

As with the bus companies, coaching companies specializing in the inclusive tour markets have also tended to concentrate since deregulation. In the initial years, Wallace Arnold took over the Bee Line operation and formed a powerful competitor to Shearings, the other market leader. Shearings itself attempted to take over Wallace Arnold in 1997, a bid that proved unsuccessful.

In common with the US airline industry a decade earlier, deregulation of the bus and coach industry appears to have had the opposite effect to that intended, with the growth of a handful of powerful oligopolistic carriers.

Figure 9.6 A line-up of coaches from seven countries at Oslo's famous Vigeland Sculpture Park. (*Photographed by the author*)

On the transnational scene, one interesting development has been the growth of shuttle services between Britain and the Continent. Led by National Express's Eurolines service, these international stage journeys, travelling as far afield as Poland, Hungary, Greece, Finland and Turkey, expanded after the early 1980s, although their success varied according to the relative strength of sterling against other European currencies, and the differential between air and coach fares.

Also on the international scene, mention should be made of the importance of coach operations in North America. Two powerful coach companies, Greyhound Lines and Continental Trailways, dominated the domestic coach market in North America, and their low fares enabled them to compete successfully against both the huge network of domestic air services and the private car. However, in 1982, road passenger transport was also deregulated in the USA, leading to a flood of small, low-priced coach companies, against which neither of the two giants could compete. Trailways cut services in an effort to remain profitable, but ultimately merged under new management with the Greyhound Corporation in 1987. After further restructuring and the introduction of new vehicles, including minibuses, Greyhound rose once again to dominate the market until challenged by a newcomer, US Bus, launched in 1998 with smaller, more comfortable vehicles. Greyhound's future, at the time of writing, appears uncertain, the company having been rescued from financial collapse once already in 2000.

Finally, mention should be made at this point of the Gray Line organization, an American franchise offering coach excursions and tours not only within the USA and Canada, but also in numerous other countries. Franchising globally on this scale is a comparative rarity in the tourism business, but offers a pointer to the possible direction which the industry will take in the future, as large companies go multinational.

The private car

Undoubtedly, the increase in private car ownership has done more to change travel habits than any other factor in tourism. It provided families in particular with a new freedom of movement, with increased opportunities to take day excursions as well as longer trips. From the 1950s onwards, the costs of motoring fell in relative terms, and car owners also tended to take into account only the direct costs of a motoring trip, rather than the full cost, which would include depreciation and wear and tear. Thus, car transport was favoured over public transport.

The effect of this preference on the travel industry has been considerable. The hotel and catering industry responded by creating motels, roadside cafes and restaurants, while formerly remote hotels and restaurants suddenly benefited from their new accessibility to the tourist. Car ferry services all over Europe flourished, and countries linked by such services experienced a visitor boom (France remains, for the British, the leading holiday destination, being seen primarily as a destination for the independent and mobile tourist). Camping and caravan holidays also boomed, and tour operators reacted by creating flexible self-drive car packages, including packaged camping and *gîte*-style holidays in France. Fly-drive and rail-drive packages were introduced. In the USA, a market developed for motor-homes or motorized caravans, which have become widely known in that country as RVs (recreational vehicles). These originated with the invention of the Curtiss Aerocar in the 1930s, but have grown in popularity to a point where today some 25 million Americans make use of them each year. The industry responded by providing new and more luxurious camping facilities, with the franchise company Kampgrounds of America ensuring water and electricity were available on all sites. The railways, too, adapted to meet the needs of the motoring tourist, introducing motorail services which allowed tourists to take their cars by rail with them on longer journeys, such as to the south of France.

In the twenty-first century, the desire for greater flexibility, coupled with the introduction of the Channel Tunnel, suggests that the demand for motoring holidays is unlikely to fall, providing energy costs do not increase dramatically (and at the time of writing, these costs are rising sharply, forcing up petrol prices in Britain). However, this growth is by no means entirely beneficial for tourism. The need for new roads to cater for the explosion in car ownership has meant that many bypasses have been built around towns and villages. Apart from the environmental damage sustained by the countryside, this also has the effect of discouraging the impulse visitor from stopping and spending money in the towns. At the same time, the expansion of motoring and private car ownership in a small country such as Britain is leading to enormous problems of pollution and congestion. In 1998 (the latest figures available at the time of writing), car ownership in Britain stood at 23.1 million. Forecasts indicate that this will have risen to at least 31 million by 2025. It was estimated in 1996 that Britain possessed sixty-seven vehicles for every kilometre of road in the country, far higher than the EU average. Small resorts and scenic attractions cannot expand sufficiently to meet the demand for access and parking facilities without damaging the environment which the motorist has come to see. The growing interest in our society for ecologically friendly tourism will inevitably discourage motorists from taking their cars to such destinations. Greater control can be expected in the future through developments such as 'park and ride' schemes, already provided at congested resorts like Bath, Oxford and St Ives in Cornwall, which require visitors to park their cars outside the resort and use public transport to travel into the centre. Rationing by high prices for car parking (as has been introduced in Oxford) or by limiting access or denying facilities for car parking (as occurs at the more popular US National Parks and is now finding favour in some of the British National Parks) will inevitably become a characteristic of future tourism destinations when demand rises to a point where there is insufficient physical space to accommodate all who wish to arrive in their private cars.

The car rental business

It has been estimated that there are over 1,000 car hire companies operating in Britain, with more than 130,000 cars available for hire (many being fleet cars on hire to private companies). The car rental business owes a substantial proportion of its revenue (and in many resorts, virtually all its revenue) to the tourist. While in total only 30–40 per cent of car hire is associated with leisure, small companies and local car hire operators get a disproportionate share of this, while the large corporations have the lion's share of the business travel market.

Car rental companies can be divided into two categories:

1. the large international companies, or franchise operators;
2. small, generally locally based, independent hire companies.

Most of the larger companies charge broadly similar prices, but offer a choice of cars, hiring locations and flexibility (for example, the ability to pick up a car at one location and drop it at another). This flexibility and convenience makes them more attractive to business travellers, who are less sensitive to price, but who insist on speed of service, reliability and a more luxurious standard of car.

On the other hand, there are literally hundreds of small local hirers, who generally offer limited choice but low price and the convenience of a local pick-up – although perhaps from only one or two locations. Because of their reliance on the leisure market, these operators work in a highly seasonal business, where they may be unable to maximize their opportunities for business in summer because they have insufficient vehicles. In addition, there are a handful of specialist car hire operators who provide very luxurious vehicles, high-powered sports cars or even classic vehicles, for a small up-market leisure or business clientele.

The competitive nature of the industry has once again resulted in good marketing playing a key role in the success of individual car rental companies. The expansion of outlets has been greatly aided by the introduction of franchising – Budget was the first car hire company to franchise in Britain, as long ago as the 1960s, but all the large corporations now do so. Three other factors have been critical:

1. Contracts with airports and railways. This allows the car rental company to maintain a desk at the airport or terminal. Opportunities for business which are provided by desk space in these locations make contracts very lucrative, and they are fought for between the major corporations, occasionally changing as competitors offer higher bids at the termination of a contract agreement.
2. Links with airlines and hotels. This establishes good relations with, and hence referrals from, hotel chains and larger airlines, generates huge volumes of business, and is critical for maximizing sales opportunities for business travel bookings. Large hotel chains may also offer desk space for the car rental company in their reception area.
3. Computer reservations systems (CRS). The development of a good CRS (and increasingly global distribution systems; GDSs), together with accessibility to these systems via major airline GDSs such as SABRE or GALILEO, plays an increasingly important role in the success of the larger car rental companies, which cannot afford not to be linked to major systems. Some car rental systems are now starting to take live bookings on the Internet. This form of reservation, which will be extended to the general public also, will play an increasingly important role in car rental sales in the future, and will have an impact on travel agency sales.

Car rental companies also court the travel agents, who can provide a good proportion of advance sales for business and leisure travel. Attractive rates of commission of 15 per cent or more are offered to gain agency support. However, a comparatively small proportion of bookings for car rental are made through the trade in the UK, when compared with the USA. The growing seat-only airline reservations market has helped to expand the demand for car hire overseas, as has the increasing confidence shown by British package tourists abroad in hiring cars at their destination.

Trading conditions for the car hire companies remain difficult in the face of continuing high levels of competition in the trade.

Cycling and tourism

Since the end of the last century, holiday-makers have shown much greater interest in cycling holidays, which are seen as ecologically friendly. The Cyclists' Touring Club boasts some 70,000 members in Britain, and several specialist holiday firms have been established in recent years to cater for those seeking organized cycling holidays in Britain and on the Continent. These include both leisure and sporting activity (off-road) pursuits, reflecting the growth in ownership of hi-tech equipment such as mountain bikes. Tour operators like Cycling for Softies, which specializes in cycling holidays in France, provide vehicles for the transfer of cyclists' baggage between accommodation stops, leaving their clients to travel light; this form of touring has proved very popular.

There are fears that the rise in car numbers on rural roads, resulting from drivers seeking relief from the growing congestion on trunk roads in Britain, will make cycling far more dangerous on roads where there is no dedicated cycle path, and this discourages the individual cycling holiday. Britain is now following the lead of other European countries like the Netherlands and Denmark, in providing dedicated paths for cyclists in and around towns, and new traffic-free long-distance cycle routes are also being established. Nevertheless, cycling still accounts for less than 2 per cent of all trips in Britain, compared with 18 per cent in Denmark and 11 per cent in Germany. Efforts are being made to increase cycle use, both for local and tourism use. Millennium Commission lottery funding of more than £43 million was made available to the charity Sustrans to begin work on a National Cycle Network which by 2005 will provide a total of 10,000 miles of

Figure 9.7 The UK National Cycle Network (*Courtesy Sustrans*)

Tourists on foot

In examining the role of transport, it is important not to forget the significant role played by tourists who travel mainly on foot. Walking holidays in the mountains have a long tradition, and hiking and trekking have both grown in popularity in recent years. Ramblers' associations represent the interest of these long-distance walkers, taking steps to ensure that rights of way are protected over both public and private land in Britain. The European Ramblers Association was established in 1969, and since that time eleven European long-distance paths – the longest, from Norway to Turkey, stretching some 4,500 miles – have been established, often refurbished from long-existing routes. Some of these, such as the E2 Grande Traversée des Alpes or the five pathways through the Austrian Alps, are well maintained and extensively used; others, such as those in southern Italy, Romania, the Ukraine and Turkey, have yet to be opened officially, although they are in use. Two of these European footpaths extend into England and Scotland, the route E2-GB stretching from Stranraer to Dover and eventually connecting with the Grande Traversée des Alpes. Such routes are particularly popular with German and Dutch hikers, and are expecting to attract growing numbers of British tourists.

Questions and discussion points

1. How successful have the newly privatized railways been in tapping into the potential tourist market in the UK? What major changes affecting tourists have there been as a result of the changeover to privatization? Could the railways do more to tap this market?

2. In the early years of the Channel Tunnel, a great deal of criticism was expressed about the marketing of the Eurostar and Eurotunnel (then called 'le Shuttle') services. What problems did customers of the Tunnel experience, and have they yet been resolved?

3. Given the forecast increases in private cars on

dedicated cycleway in Britain, carrying in excess of 100 million journeys every year and linking up with similar cycle routes across Europe. The full UK network is shown in Figure 9.7.

In the interests of improving the environment, steps are being taken to improve opportunities for cyclists in Britain to take their cycles on trains, which would encourage rural tourism by bike. While all train services in Britain offer this facility, rules governing their carriage differ with each of the twenty-five railway companies and on every route, discouraging this practice. Integrated transport planning should include and facilitate this opportunity, too.

British roads by early this century, how will the country cope with this increase? What action has been taken to implement an integrated transport system since the election of the Labour government in 1997? Evaluate the likely success in particular of (a) road pricing and (b) motorway tolls as means of improving the transport system. How would the introduction of such systems affect tourists visiting Britain?

Assignment topics

1. As a member of the planning team of Universe Tours, a company specializing in coaching holidays on the Continent, you have been asked by your boss to investigate the possibility of running a new series of tours to the former eastern bloc countries of Poland, Hungary and the Czech and Slovak Republics. Undertake research to identify the main attractions for the British market in these countries, and plan at least three different tours, with a maximum length of 14 days, to one or more of the countries. You should also discover any possible pitfalls of arranging tours to these areas, and bring these to the attention of your manager in the report.

2. Universe tours is considering whether to move its clients between Britain and the Continent by Eurotunnel or by ferry. Investigate the relative advantages and disadvantages of each, together with prices, and prepare a short report for your manager outlining your recommendations, with justification.

3. You are employed with a small incoming tour company based in London, dealing mainly with the American market. Your boss has asked you to draft a sales letter which will be sent to leading American tour companies with which your organization works, explaining that you are starting to provide, from next year, a new programme of tours by rail in Britain, using chartered trains and carriages. Write the letter, concentrating on the appeal of a rail journey, the benefits it could offer and why the American tourist could be expected to enjoy it. The letter should close with a sales pitch which will ensure that the operator comes back to you for more information – the principal aim of your message.

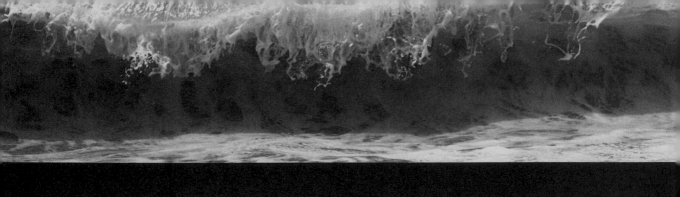

Chapter 10 The hospitality sector: accommodation and catering services

Objectives

After studying this chapter, you should be able to:

- explain the structure and nature of the hospitality sector, distinguishing between the various categories of tourist accommodation and catering services;
- describe how accommodation is classified and the problems involved in classification;
- understand the nature of demand for accommodation, and how the sector has responded to changing patterns of demand over time;
- be aware of the relationship between the hospitality sector and other sectors of the tourism industry.

Introduction

In this chapter, we are principally concerned with examining the commercial accommodation and catering sector. It must not be forgotten, however, that this sector must compete with a large non-commercial hospitality supply which is equally important to tourism; the VFR (visiting friends and relations) market is substantial, and in addition there is a wide variety of other forms of accommodation used by tourists, including the tourists' own camping and caravanning equipment, privately owned boats and even second homes, of which there are more than 70,000 in the UK alone. There is also a growing market for home exchanges, and the swapping of time-share accommodation, which the industry has encouraged through the establishment of time-share exchange companies.

It is, in fact, difficult to distinguish between the strictly commercial and non-commercial aspects of the hospitality business. Youth hostels and YMCAs, for example, are not necessarily attempting to make a profit, but merely to recover their operating costs, while it is increasingly common to find educational institutions such as universities and schools hiring out their student accommodation to tourists outside the academic terms, in order to make some contribution to the running costs of the institutions.

Other forms of tourism which by their nature embrace accommodation would include privately hired yachts, or bookings on a cruise; and, as we saw in the previous chapter, there are certain forms of long-distance coach operation which include sleeping berths, while in many countries it is possible to take a holiday on a specially chartered train which also serves as the tourists' hotel throughout the trip. To what extent should all these services be counted as elements of the commercial accommodation available to tourists? Certainly, any study of tourism must take account of these forms of overnighting. Tourists staying in private accommodation away from their homes are nonetheless engaging in tourism, and may also be making a contribution to the tourism spend of the region, through their spend on local travel and entertainment. They must therefore be counted in the tourism statistics for the region. Apart from this, they may also be commercially exploited. Tour operators, for instance, provide flight-only sales to meet the needs of those who own villas and apartments abroad, while airlines, recognizing that home exchanges can represent a healthy source of flight revenue, have developed and commercialized the home-exchange business by establishing directories to assist people in arranging exchanges. Some national or regional tourist offices keep directories of home owners who are prepared to make exchanges, and others maintain lists of local householders willing to invite guests from overseas into their homes for a meal (a particular feature of US hospitality).

The structure of the accommodation sector

The accommodation sector comprises widely differing forms of sleeping and hospitality facilities which can be conveniently categorized as either serviced (in which catering is provided) or self-catering. These are not watertight categories, as some forms of accommodation, such as holiday camps or educational institutions, may offer serviced, self-service or self-catering facilities, but they will help in drawing distinctions between the characteristics of the two

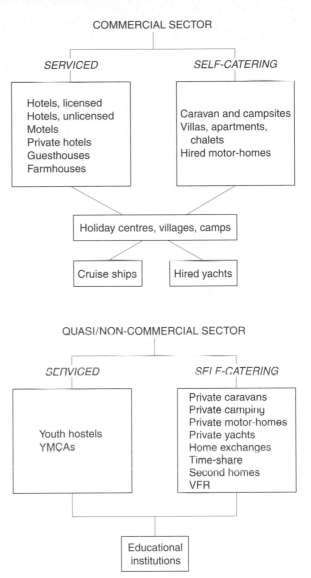

Figure 10.1   The structure of tourist accommodation

categories. Figure 10.1 provides an at-a-glance guide to the range of accommodation which a tourist might occupy.

Hotels are the most significant and widely recognized form of overnight accommodation. They also form one of the key elements of most package holidays. However, what constitutes a hotel and distinguishes it from other forms of accommodation is not always clear. The English Hotel Occupancy Survey defines it as an establishment having five or more bedrooms, not identified as a guesthouse or boarding house and not listed as providing bed and breakfast accommodation only.

A feature of the industry is that, as mass tourism has developed, so have the large chains and corporations in the accommodation sector. The hotel and motel business has reached a stage of maturity in which a few major companies have come to dominate the international market. In Britain, about a third of hotels with eleven or more rooms are now part of big chains, mainly British owned, and similar patterns can be detected in other developed countries. This expansion has been achieved not only through direct ownership, but also through the process of franchising, whereby hotels and motels are operated by individual franchisees paying royalties to the parent company for the privilege of operating under a brand name. This form of expansion has been used with great success around the world by companies such as Holiday Inns, while the Friendly Hotel group holds European franchises for such well-established brand names as Quality Hotels, Comfort Hotels and Sleep Inns. Since these chains market their products more aggressively, advertising extensively, working closely with large tour operating organizations globally and providing an effective distribution network using computer reservations systems linked to the airline CRSs, they tend to play an even more significant role in the industry than their market share might suggest (in total bed terms, their accommodation is still minimal by comparison with the many small independently owned facilities, which have less ready access to the other sectors of the tourism industry).

Ownership and styles of hotel accommodation

Leading chains around the world have tended to diversify their brands to appeal to a wide variety of markets. American, British and French chains in particular retain a strong hold on the global accommo-

dation market, featuring such notable corporations as Six Continents Hotels, formerly Bass (which operates nearly half a million rooms, and owns such brands as Crowne Plaza, Holiday Inn and Inter-Continental), Marriott International (with nearly three hundred thousand rooms in Marriott, Courtyard and Travel Inn lodgings) and two rapidly growing French groups, Accor and Groupe Envergure, which are now European leaders in the accommodation market. Such hotels aim to create an international and uniform marketing image to assist their sales around the world. In the past, leading chains were often in British hands, but in recent years this tendency has declined, with, for example, the former Forte brands now dispersed (and prestige brand le Meridien now in Japanese hands).

The expansion internationally of the two French groups is particularly interesting, given that the French have not had a strong showing to date in other sectors of the global market. Again, their intention has been to satisfy a variety of market niches through brands. Accor offers accommodation from luxury to budget, and includes ten brand names, among them the international chains Sofitel Demeure, Novotel, Suitehotel, Mercure, Coralia, Etap, Ibis and Formule 1, while the Envergure group owns the two-star Campanile Hotels along with Hotel 1, Bleu Marine and Clarine chains. Both companies have sought in recent years to penetrate

Figure 10.2 The international brand: Holiday Inn Express (*Photographed by the author*)

Figure 10.3 The new budget chains in France: a B&B Hotel at Joue le Tours, France. (*Photographed by the author*)

the UK market. Further afield, other notable chains have been established; the Mandarin group concentrates on the Pacific Rim area, while Oberoi Hotels, founded in India, has also expanded into Egypt, the Far East and Australia, with its Oberoi, Trident and Rajvilas brands. As with other sectors of the tourism industry, there is a growing belief that a handful of mega chains such as these will come to dominate the world tourist market within a few years, while independents will seek to exploit niche-marketing opportunities.

A recent trend within the large chains has been concentration on the development of budget-price properties, long left to the independent sector. In Britain, well-established leisure corporations such as Granada or catering subsidiaries of the big brewers were leaders in the development of what they now prefer to term 'limited service' hotels, to distinguish them from the type of accommodation sought by the backpacker market. The ETC estimated that there were over 40,000 limited service rooms in Britain in 2000. Brands new to Britain, such as Days Inn and Sleep Inn, are joining more familiar brands like Travelodge and Travel Inns to capture this fast-growing market, especially in city-centre properties which attract growing numbers of short-break tourists.

In mainland Europe, Accor Hotels has exploited the deficiency in this sector by introducing the super-budget chains Formule 1 and Etap, while others in France have popularized low-budget brands such as B&B Hotels, Mister Bed, Villages Hotels, Unhotel and Fimotel. These very low priced hotels have managed to reduce costs by developing a unitary design and automating many of the services provided; reception desks are only manned for short periods of the day, and at other times entry is by the insertion of credit cards into a machine on the external wall. Similarly, breakfasts are self-service and highly automated. The introduction of this style of hotel into the UK has not been simple; land costs push up prices in Britain, while furnishings and service appeared too basic for the British market: for example, carpet soon replaced the linoleum which French hotel guests had seemed more willing to accept.

In Britain, the breweries have long been associated with the lodging industry, whose origins are to be found in historical inn-keeping. The Vaux brewery sold its Swallow Hotel chain to the Whitbread brewery in 1999, which owns the Marriott chain in the UK. Bass sold its brewery division and renamed its hotels division Six Continents. One of the largest chains in the world, it controls some of the best-known brands in Britain and developing franchise relationships with other brands such as Queens Moat Hotels. Bass owns over 1,100 Express by Holiday Inns, while Whitbread has rapidly expanded its Travel Inn chain and Scottish & Newcastle operates the Premier Lodge chain.

Figure 10.4 The new budget hotels in Britain: the City Inn, Bristol (*Photographed by the author*)

Figure 10.5   (a) The designer hotel: Hotel du Vin & Bistro, Bristol. (b) Courtyard, Hotel du Vin & Bistro. (*Photographed by the author*)

The competition between luxury hotels has led to new forms of market segmentation. Country house hotels or town house hotels place emphasis on more personal service, while boutique hotels and designer hotels, especially those taking advantage of the fashion for minimalism, have attracted widespread publicity in London and New York. Other brands offer all-suite hotels, while hotels which have been converted from buildings formerly used for other purposes have deliberately retained the original character, and have therefore appealed strongly to a market jaded by standardization and uniformity. A good example is the small private chain Hotel du Vin & Bistro, with four properties in Britain and highly praised restaurants. Such developments reveal the way forward for hotel design; the days of the monolithic concrete block, favoured in the development of new resorts in the Mediterranean and elsewhere in order to permit rapid construction and cheap operation, are ending, as the sophisticated travel market seeks better service and more character in its lodgings.

Hotels that can offer attributes that are unique to the country visited are enjoying much greater popularity. The *Paradores* in Spain, or the *Pousadas* of Portugal, national chains of state-operated inns located in historic properties, are proving highly successful in spite of their premium prices, while traditional *haciendas* in Mexico and the *ryokans* of Japan, which offer an authentic flavour of the country's culture, greatly appeal to the independent travel market. In Britain, individual character properties owned by the National Trust, the Landmark Trust and similar organizations are greatly in demand: one of the National Trust's most popular properties is Peel Bothy, a tiny former shepherd's home at Steel Rigg, Northumberland offering only very basic facilities – but seen as full of character.

In an effort to counteract the influence of the large chains, a number of independent hotels have banded together to form marketing consortia which will allow them to obtain some of the economies of scale achieved by the large chains, such as benefits of mass purchasing or mass marketing. Some of these consortia, such as Best Western Hotels and Inter Hotels, now operate on a global scale, while other national brands, such as Flag Hotels of Australia, have established a strong national image in their overseas marketing. Similarly, some of the leading privately owned hotels in Britain have banded together to create consortia in order to market themselves more effectively at home and abroad. This is a highly appropriate strategy when developing a niche approach; for example, 'Small Luxury Hotels of the World' has focused on building an image of high-standard but personal hotels around the UK, while Grand Heritage Hotels, an American-owned consortium which is now drawing membership from high-graded UK hotels, emphasizes luxury and status.

Figure 10.6 The stately house as accommodation: the Lord of the Manor Hotel, Upper Slaughter, Gloucestershire. (*Photographed by the author*)

For the leisure traveller, the switch away from faceless concrete hotels of the 1950s and 1960s coincides with a rising interest in the 'country cottage' style of accommodation, which is now being exploited by major tour operators. This may be a direct outcome of the interest in French *gîtes* accommodation in the 1980s. Another grouping, 'Mansions and Manors', consists of around 200 manor house owners who will offer bed and breakfast accommodation on a selective basis to the 'right kind of clients' but do not wish to commercialize their product or advertise it directly to the public. This product is therefore marketed directly through tour operators in the USA.

Classifying and grading accommodation

It is no simple matter to differentiate between accommodation units of differing types and standards. The process of classification in the hotel and catering industry, either for purposes of legislation or for the systematic examination of business activity, has been attempted on several occasions in Britain in the past (for example, under the Standard Industrial Classification System). However, these attempts were mainly designed to distinguish hotels and other residential establishments from sundry catering activities. Statistics seldom distinguish, for example,

between guests staying at hotels and motels. Within the small independent sector, the problem is even greater. There is a broad spectrum of private accommodation which ranges from the 'private hotel', through boarding house and guesthouse accommodation to bed and breakfast establishments, and in Britain, under law there is no clear distinction between the private hotel and the boarding house. The only distinction between these two and the guesthouse is that the latter will have not more than four bedrooms, or accommodation for a maximum of eight guests. This distinction is important for legislative purposes, but need not concern us further here. However, tourists are interested not only in what different grades of hotel offer in the way of facilities, but also in the *quality* of the accommodation and catering they are being offered. To clarify these features, we need to distinguish between three terms: categorization, classification and grading. Although these terms are often used interchangeably, the following are their widely accepted definitions:

- *Categorization* refers to the separation of accommodation by type, that is, distinguishing between hotels, motels, boarding houses, guesthouses etc.
- *Classification* distinguishes accommodation on the basis of certain physical features, such as the number of rooms with private bath or shower etc.
- *Grading* identifies accommodation according to certain verifiable objective features of the service offered, such as the number of courses served at meals, whether 24-hour service is provided etc.

Readers will note, however, that none of these refers to the assessment of quality, which calls for subjective evaluation, and is therefore far more difficult – and more costly – to validate, especially when standards, particularly in catering, can change so rapidly over time.

Provision was made under the Development of Tourism Act 1969 for the compulsory classification and grading of hotel accommodation in Britain, but this was widely resisted by the industry itself, and the British Tourist Authority made no attempt to impose it, instead relying upon a system of voluntary registration first introduced in 1975. The separate National Tourist Boards of England, Scotland and Wales were left to devise their own individual schemes. However, urged on by the Scottish Tourist Board in particular, the three boards in 1987 agreed a common scheme which graded hotels into six categories: either 'listed', for the most basic property, or from one to five 'crowns', depending upon the facilities offered. The system remained a voluntary one, but hotels taking part received regular checks from inspectors, and could only display their blue and white signboard or advertise in Regional Tourist Board publications after they had been approved. The hotels are charged an annual fee. While the system was clearly an improvement on the previous form of classification, in which the hotels themselves were responsible for advising the tourist boards of the facilities they provided, because it remained voluntary only a very small proportion of the total accommodation sector in Britain became registered.

Two years later, the boards agreed a unified system of grading quality, additionally awarding the symbols 'Approved', 'Commended', 'Highly Commended' or 'Deluxe' in ascending order of quality. This was planned to take into account such subjective issues as hospitality, service, food and decor. These awards take no account of the facilities or status of the unit, which allows even a humble 'listed' unit to be rated as 'Deluxe', if it meets the quality criterion. Other types of accommodation subsequently received symbols, too; moons were awarded to lodges, keys to self-catering accommodation, and 'Qs' to holiday centres. Wales, however, chose to develop its own scheme separately from England and Scotland. The self-catering scheme was applied to a range of different units, including cottages, flats, bungalows, houseboats and chalets, and quality was assessed using the same form of assessment as was used for the hotels. Grading became based on such features as the appearance of the building, the decor and lighting, heating and furnishing, floor coverings, and the crockery and utensils provided.

This system also proved far from satisfactory, given that the private sector had devised its own schemes for grading hotels, some national, some international in scope, and these were often more widely recognized by members of the public than were the public sector designations. Of the private sector schemes, the best known in Britain were those offered by the two motoring associations, the AA and RAC, both of which provided a star rating. In addition to these schemes, there were a number of guides on the market which provided subjective assessment of catering in hotels and other establishments, the best known being the *Michelin Guide*, *Egon Ronay's Guide* and the *Good Food Guide*.

Over the years, further attempts were made to introduce legislation for a common grading scheme for hotels. The harmonization process within the EU gave an additional boost to these initiatives. Although some member countries do impose compulsory registration within their own borders, different grading schemes have been in use throughout the EU, each involving different criteria, so the problems of standardizing within Europe remain. Clearly, however, no attempt to standardize throughout the EU could be considered unless the UK could itself put forward an agreed standard within its own boundaries. Consequently, talks were held in 1996 between the tourist board representatives and the two motoring organizations in order to try to achieve a commonly recognized system throughout the UK. The outcome of these talks was only a partial success. The English Tourist Board and the two motoring organizations agreed to adopt a common scheme from the year 2000, based on hotel ratings of one to five stars; the Scottish Tourist Board rejected the scheme on the principle that they wished to lay greater emphasis on quality rather than facilities, and therefore adopted a parallel scheme in 1997, while Wales introduced its own scheme in 1999. In consequence, Britain remains without a commonly agreed scheme, nor will any attempt be made to register hotels compulsorily for the foreseeable future. However, agreement was reached between the three boards and the motoring organizations to adopt a common classification scheme for bed and breakfast establishments from the year 2000.

Consequently, under the newly adopted scheme approved by the English Tourism Council (as it is now referred to), the AA and the RAC awards between one and five *stars* to hotels based on their overall quality, standard of food and range of facilities available, while equivalent *diamonds* are awarded to guesthouses, inns, farmhouses and bed and breakfast institutions according to their levels of quality as determined by cleanliness, guest care, comfort, standard of food and facilities. At the same time, the former key ratings applied to self-catering have been amended to star ratings.

As far as common systems across Europe are concerned, the British Hospitality Association feels that comparisons between hotels of similar status in different countries are virtually impossible to make. There are further complications, for example in the fact that some countries impose higher rates of sales tax on their five-star properties, making it unattractive for hotels in those nations to upgrade their property, even if standards are comparable with a five star property in Britain. In the meantime, tour operators have devised their own systems for assessing those properties used on package tours abroad, to meet the needs of their own clients, leading to additional confusion among the travelling public. Thomson Holidays, for example, uses its 'T-rating', based in part on its own customers' assessment of the accommodation.

The nature of demand for accommodation facilities

The hotel product is made up of five characteristics: its location, its mix of facilities (which will include bedrooms, restaurants, other public rooms, functions rooms and leisure facilities), its image, the services it provides (including such indefinable features as the level of formality, personal attention, speed and efficiency of its staff), and the price which it is prepared to charge.

The location of a hotel will invariably be the first consideration when the tourist is selecting a hotel. Location implies both the destination (resort for the holiday-maker, convenient stopover point for the traveller, city for the business traveller) and the location within that destination. Thus, businesspeople will want to be accommodated in a city-centre site close to the company they are visiting, while the seaside holiday-maker will seek a hotel as close as possible to the beach, and transit travellers will want to be accommodated at a hotel convenient to the airport from which they are leaving. In economic terms, a trade-off will occur between location and price, as the leisure traveller looks for the hotel closest to the beach which still fits the budget, or the transit traveller opts for a more distant hotel which is prepared to offer a free transfer to the airport. Location is, of course, fixed for all time; if the resort itself loses its attraction for its visitors, the hotel will suffer an equivalent decline in its fortunes.

The fact that high fixed costs are incurred in both building and operating hotels compounds the risk of hotel operating. City-centre sites are extremely expensive to purchase and operate, requiring high room prices. The market may resist such prices, but is nevertheless reluctant to be based at any distance from the centres of activity, even when good transportation is available. This has been evidenced in the problems faced by incoming tour operators in accommodating American visitors in central London at prices competitive with other city centres. The reluctance of many overseas tour operators to base their clients in accommodation on the outskirts of the city has led to loss of business in favour of other European capital cities.

Again, the demand for central London hotels, leading to high capacity and profits, has caused those in the hotel business to maximize profits by upgrading their accommodation and appealing to the business client, rather than catering for the leisure tourist's demand for budget accommodation. The French Accor Group was among the first to identify this market gap and, as we have seen, set about catering for the lower price bracket with its Formule 1 and Etap brands.

Hotels will seek to maximize their revenue by offering a wide range of different tariffs to the different market segments they serve. By way of example, one city hotel provides, apart from the normal rack rate, at least nine other rates, including special concessions to corporate bookings, conference rates, air crew, weekender traffic and tour bookings. In the climate of recession experienced by hotels in recent years, it has also been possible for clients to negotiate substantial discounts if they book late in the day; the hotel management, recognizing that any sale is better than none, allows the desk clerks to come to an agreement against any realistic offer, which may be as much as 50 per cent lower than rack rate.

Hotel companies may be further constrained by the need to meet building codes present in the location where they are building. Increasingly, concern about the environment and widespread recognition of the damage done to the architectural styles of resorts swamped by high-rise hotel building have led local authorities to impose stringent regulations on new buildings. This may mean using local (often more expensive) materials in place of concrete, limiting the height of hotels to four or five floors (some tropical destinations restrict hotel building to the height of the local palm trees), or restricting the total size of the building to ensure it is in keeping with surrounding buildings (see Figure 10.7).

Some characteristics of the hotel product

The demand for hotel bedrooms will come from a widely distributed market, nationally or internationally, whereas the market for other facilities which the hotel offers will often be highly localized. In addition to providing food and drink for its own residents, the hotel will be marketing these services to other tourists or members of the local population at a short distance from the site. Clearly, a very different market segment will be involved, calling for different marketing techniques of advertising, promotion and distribution.

Another characteristic of the hotel product is that it is seldom uniformly in demand throughout the year. Tourist hotels suffer from seasonality, involving high demand during summer peaks and little or no demand during the winter troughs, while hotels catering chiefly to business people may find business dropping off during the summer. Business hotels also suffer from periodicity, in which demand is

Figure 10.7 International hotel chains designed to complement the vernacular architecture of their cities: (a) Ibis Hotel, Belgium; (b) Novotel Hotel, Belgium. (*Photographed by the author*)

focused on the Monday to Thursday nights, while there is little demand from Friday to Sunday night. The lack of flexibility in room supply, coupled with the perishable nature of the product (if rooms are unsold there is no opportunity to 'store' them and sell them later) mean that greater efforts must be made to unload unsold accommodation by attracting the off-peak customer or the leisure market to business hotels at weekends.

Even with creative marketing and high discounting, many tourist hotels in highly seasonal resorts will find their occupancy levels falling alarmingly in the winter, and must then face the decision whether it is better to stay open in the winter, in the hope of attracting enough customers to make some contribution to overheads, or to close completely for several months of the year. The problem with the latter course of action is that a number of hotel costs, such as rates, depreciation and salaries for management staff, will continue whether or not the hotel remains open. Temporary closure may also result in difficulties in recruiting good staff, if jobs are known to be only seasonal. In recent years, more hotels, especially the larger chain hotels, have opted to remain open, and to offer special packages for those willing to come off-season. The increase in second holidays and off-season short breaks in Britain has helped to make more hotels viable year-round, although room occupancy remains low out of season in many of the more traditional resorts. Here, the hotel sector is also heavily dependent on the extent to which the public sector is willing to invest in order to make the resort attractive out of season. Towns such as Bournemouth, through a process of continuous investment and a deliberate attempt to attract the conference and non-seasonal market, have been able to draw in a high number of winter tourists, making it possible for many more hotels to remain open year-round. This in turn stimulates further business, as local attractions and events are also encouraged to stay open throughout the year.

While we have talked chiefly in terms of the physical characteristics of the hotel, the psychological factors which attract the visitor are no less important. Service, 'atmosphere', even the other guests with whom the customer will come into contact, all play a role when the choice of hotel is made. Only about 22 per cent of British holiday-makers choose to stay at hotels or guesthouses when holidaying in the UK, compared with some 47 per cent who do so when abroad. This is obviously the result of the large VFR market in the UK, as well as the growing demand for camping, caravanning and self-catering holidays. According to the Overseas Visitors' Survey, 59 per cent of overseas visitors stay at hotels at some point when visiting the UK, although the pattern varies, and many will choose a variety of different forms of accommodation during their tour. Some 20 per cent choose to stay in bed and breakfast accommodation, with 14 per cent staying in unlicensed hotels or guesthouses. Factors such as class, age and lifestyle will also have a bearing on the choice of sleeping accommodation. In particular, the nature of, and consequent demand for, large hotels will be quite different from that of the small guesthouse or bed and breakfast unit. A large hotel may well provide attractions of its own, distinct from the location in which it is situated; indeed, in some cases the hotel may be a more significant influence on choice than the destination. This is often true of the large hotel/leisure complex providing a range of in-house entertainment as in the case of a number of North American and, increasingly, European hotels. Similarly, some hotels are so closely linked with the destination they serve that the combination of stay at hotel/destination becomes the established pattern. This is seen in Canada, where resorts such as Lake Louise and the Chateau Lake Louise Hotel are inextricably linked (see Figure 10.8). This type of hotel and resort combination is still a rarity in Britain, although Gleneagles Hotel in Perthshire, Scotland, with its golfing links, provides one example. It is, however, increasingly a characteristic of the package holiday hotels, and has been taken a stage further with the growth of the all-inclusive packaged hotel at which all food, drink and entertainment are included in the price. The Sandals Hotel chain based in the Bahamas and Caribbean was a major initiator in this development.

Figure 10.8 The hotel–resort complex: Chateau Lake Louise, Banff National Park, Canada. (*Photographed by the author*)

By way of contrast, a noticeable trend in recent years has been the fall-off among guests staying at non-licensed accommodation in the UK, although licensed hotels have been able to retain their overall share of the accommodation market.

The provision of a good range of attractions, as well as a drinks licence, can help to offset the disadvantages which result from the unavoidable impersonality of the large hotels. As the chains increase their hold on the total pool of hotel beds, an increase in the average number of rooms in each hotel follows, since larger hotels benefit from economies of scale. However, in Britain, hotels with more than a hundred rooms remain the exception, and British hoteliers still emphasize the personal nature of their service as a feature of their marketing. As we have already noted, the trend to smaller hotels, as the travel market becomes more sophisticated, is hurting those resorts which have concentrated on building the modern concrete block style of mass-market hotel; this is particularly noticeable in the former Soviet bloc countries, where small hotels of western standards are virtually unknown. Elsewhere, there has been greater sensitivity to changes in fashion. In Majorca, local authorities have introduced legislation requiring old hotels to be destroyed before new, higher quality buildings can be constructed,

and this has led to the removal of many 1960s concrete eyesores in ageing resorts like Magaluf, in favour of hotels with greater character. In the USA, where change and novelty is a feature of market demand, hotel companies have deliberately 'themed' their properties to distinguish them from others, either through the style of their architecture or their interior decoration. This, as was pointed out earlier in the chapter, is now becoming a common approach in expensive hotels around the world. Flamboyant architecture, often reminiscent of gothic fortresses, is springing up in the most unlikely places, from Sun City in southern Africa, where a purpose-built resort complex is designed to provide a simulacrum of 'African culture', to the recently built Royal Towers of Atlantis, on Paradise Island in the Bahamas, where the extravagant Bridge Suite is on offer at £15,000 a night – and is heavily in demand. The chain hotels also provide in their budget for regular changes of decor to keep up to date. Older hotels have responded by emphasizing their traditional values and style. With the current boom in nostalgia, older hotels which can retain the style of yesteryear while nevertheless offering the modern features such as good plumbing which western tourists demand, can find a ready market for their product. A good example here is the recently restored Raffles Hotel in Singapore, which reopened after an extensive facelift which successfully blended modern comforts with the traditional architecture of the colonial era.

Increasingly, the search for 'character' properties is leading consumers to seek something different in their sleeping arrangements, and this is being catered for, especially in the package holiday market. For example, long-haul travellers can book into an authentic and traditional native 'long house' in Malaysia (that at Skrang, Sarawak, has been adapted for tourist use since 1981), while tourists to Canada have the choice of staying in a North American Indian tepee in Manitoba or an Inuit igloo in the Hudson Bay area. At Oak Alley, Georgia, the former slave quarters have been refurbished to accommodate tourists, while Bandera, Texas, offers a wide range of dude ranches. European hoteliers, too, have

Figure 10.9 Contrasts in accommodation in India. (a) The Umaid Bhawan Palace, luxury hotel in Jodhpur and home of the Maharajah. (b) basic overnight accommodation at Sam Dunes, near Jaisalmer. (c) Rotel Tours of Germany offer 'sleeping buses' on Indian tours. (*Photographed by the author*)

created hotels of character out of often unprepossessing sites and materials. In Prague, the former secret police detention centre has become one of the most popular youth hostels in Europe, while Jukkasjärvi in Swedish Lappland provides visitors with an opportunity to sleep in a hotel carved entirely out of ice – it is rebuilt each year after the summer thaw!

British hoteliers, too, have not been slow to develop themes based on the properties their hotels occupy. Old magistrates courts, police and railway stations, even a former boatman's brothel, have all been converted into tourist accommodation and have retained many of their original characteristic features to offer unique appeal to their customers. The point which must be emphasized here is that accommodation is seen by the customer as much more than simply a 'room to sleep in'. Rather, it is a total leisure experience, comprising a range of different services and emotional experiences which together go to make up the holiday or business stay.

The domestic holiday hotel

The traditional British domestic holiday in a small seaside guesthouse or hotel has been under threat now for a number of years, and many of these types of accommodation unit have been forced out of business. First, there has been the steady trend to taking holidays abroad, where packages can often be no more expensive than in the UK, but provide much better value for money and, of course, guaranteed sunshine. As a result of their experience, British holiday-makers are now demanding the same facilities in their UK hotels as they found abroad, including better food, a better choice of entertainment, and a private bathroom. This has meant that hotel proprietors have faced a huge increase in capital investment in order to raise their standards; not all have been able to find the means to do so. The Section 4 grants available for hotel construction and improvement under the 1969 Development of Tourism Act were withdrawn in England in 1989 (and more recently in Scotland and Wales), and high interest rates made loans more difficult for hoteliers to consider. The introduction of the Uniform Business Rate (UBR) in 1990 had the effect of raising many hotels' rates at a time of recession when they could least afford such increases. The hoteliers' difficulties have been compounded by the trend for domestic holidays to be of shorter duration, even though short breaks have helped to extend the season. Shorter stays raise room costs, which cannot easily be recovered by higher prices, particularly in a recession where the market is extremely price sensitive.

Liberalization of the licensing laws in 1988, permitting alcoholic drinks to be served on weekday afternoons, has been one of the few rays of sunshine in an otherwise difficult period for the industry. This has also helped to boost sales in pubs and inns catering to the tourist, which can now compete more equally with their European neighbours. Traditional accommodation units also face the challenge of a shift to self-catering, both in Britain and abroad. This has come about partly in an effort to hold down holiday prices, but of at least equal importance is the demand from tourists for more flexible types of accommodation and catering than have been available in the small hotels and boarding houses. The once-popular fully inclusive holiday comprising three meals a day, taken at fixed times of the day in the hotel, no longer meets the requirements of the modern tourist, who may wish to tour the surrounding area by car during the day, and will therefore want to eat irregularly, or even forgo a midday meal. Self-catering accommodation meets these needs effectively, and its popularity abroad with British tourists has led to the rapid expansion of similar facilities in the UK, at the expense of the boarding houses. Many smaller hotels have adapted their premises to provide self-catering units in order to survive. Motels have also expanded in number to meet the need for flexibility in touring holidays, but these units are really better suited to larger countries, where they serve the needs of the long-distance motorist travelling on a motorway network.

The B&B unit

The increasing desire of many tourists, particularly overseas visitors to Britain, to 'meet the people' and enjoy a more intimate relationship with the culture of the country they are visiting has benefited the smallest forms of accommodation unit, such as the guesthouse or bed and breakfast establishment. These are generally family run, catering to business tourists in the towns and to leisure tourists in country towns, rural areas and the seaside. B&Bs in particular provide a very valuable service to the industry, in that they can offer the informality and friendliness sought by many tourists (many have no more than three bedrooms), cater for the impulse demand that results from holiday-makers touring by car or bicycle, and conveniently expand the supply of beds during peak periods of the year in areas which are highly seasonal, and where hotels would not be viable. There are estimated to be about 11,500 B&Bs in the UK, of which more than one-third have been certified under the tourist boards' grading systems. Most have six or fewer guests, since this obviates payment of business rates, and neither a fire certificate nor public liability insurance is required to operate.

This form of accommodation was virtually unknown in North America until relatively recently, but has boomed since the 1980s, as the Americans and Canadians brought back with them the experiences they had gained in Europe. However, in general these North American properties have moved upmarket to provide much more luxurious accommodation and facilities than would normally be found in their European equivalent.

Farmhouse holiday accommodation

Farmhouse holidays have also enjoyed considerable success in recent years, both in the UK and on the Continent. European countries with strong agricultural traditions, such as Britain and Denmark, have catered for tourists in farmhouse accommodation for many years, and as farmers have found greater difficulty in paying their way through farming alone, due

Figure 10.10 A farm holiday. (*Courtesy Irish Tourist Board*)

to the reduction in agricultural subsidies within the EU, they have turned increasingly to tourism as a means of boosting revenue, particularly in the off-season. A study of farm tourism carried out in 1991 revealed that 15 per cent of all farms in England (and 24 per cent in the West Country) have some form of tourism project on their land. The simultaneous trend to healthier lifestyles and the appeal of natural food and the outdoor life have also helped to make farm tourism popular. Within the Assisted Areas, and particularly in Wales, tourist boards have provided financial assistance and training for farmers interested in expanding their accommodation for tourism. Both Ireland and Denmark have been notably successful in packaging modestly priced farm holidays for the international market, in association with tour operators and the ferry companies. In the case of Denmark, this has been a logical development to attract tourists to what is generally recognized as an expensive country for holidays based on hotel accommodation.

The market for camping and caravanning holidays in the UK is substantial; 17 million holidays were taken at caravan, camping and holiday parks in 1998, and around 10 per cent of all holidays in Britain are taken in caravans alone. Bourne Leisure, one of the leading firms in the caravan park business, attracts about a million holiday-makers a year to its nineteen sites, which operate under the British Holidays banner. While many holidays are, of course, taken in private caravans (of which there are over 500,000 in Britain, down from a peak of 650,000 in the late 1970s), caravan parks remain popular, and have become an accepted part of the holiday scene; there are over 4,200 holiday parks on mainland Britain to cater for caravanners. Holiday parks entered the tourist boards' grading schemes in 1987, with the introduction of agreed codes of practice for operators, and a trade body, the British Holiday and Home Parks Association (BH&HPA) has been formed to represent the interests of operators.

Holiday centres

Holiday camps were very much a British innovation, introduced on a major scale in the 1930s by three noted entrepreneurs, Billy Butlin, Fred Pontin and Harry Warner. Their aim was to provide all-in entertainment at a low price in chalet-style accommodation which would be largely unaffected by inclement weather. The Butlin–Pontin–Warner style of holiday camp became enormously successful in the years prior to World War II and the early post-war era, but all three organizations have now been absorbed into large corporations. Market leader Butlins, with about 2 million guests a year and three sites at Skegness, Minehead and Bognor Regis, is now owned by Bourne Leisure, along with the Warner and Haven Leisure brands, while Pontins is part of Scottish & Newcastle breweries. While Butlins and Pontins focus on family entertainment, Warner holidays are marketed to adults only. Haven's 56 sites (with a further 47 in Europe) are divided into three categories, 'lively, all-action', 'leisurely' and 'relaxing', to reach different markets.

For the most part, the balance of the market is split between a large number of independent companies operating a small number of sites. The market for holiday centres remains highly seasonal, falling almost entirely between May and September. It had been customary for centres to close during the winter months, but improved marketing, including mini-breaks and themed events, has helped to extend sales into the 'shoulder' months of spring and autumn. As a percentage of the total accommodation used in domestic tourism, though, holiday centres remain relatively small.

Holiday centres have been affected as much as any other accommodation facilities by changes in public taste. Before the war, they attracted a largely lower-middle-class clientele, but in the post-war period their market became significantly more working class, and the canteen-style catering service and entertainment provided reflected the needs of this market segment. Bookings were made invariably from Saturday to Saturday, and most clients booked direct with the companies. Each company had a quite distinct image for its clientele, who were strongly brand-loyal and booked regularly with their favourite company.

More recently, these camps have attempted to move up-market, a process heralded by a change in their names from camps to holiday centres, villages or parks. The former working-class orientation has been modified to cater for wider social tastes. Large chalet blocks have given way to smaller units with self-catering facilities. A choice of catering styles has been introduced, ranging from fully serviced through self-service to self-catering, the latter enjoying the greatest rates of growth. Butlins in particular has invested huge sums of money to redevelop its remaining centres and give them a more up-market image. However, Butlins faces strong competition from the new wave of centres, the holiday villages.

The new holiday villages

Holiday villages offer a new concept in resort marketing. Spearheaded by Center Parcs, which now has fifteen sites in Europe, they offer a very different kind of holiday experience to the traditional holiday centre. Their former competition for this form of holiday is the Oasis Forest Holiday Village, launched in 1997 by the Rank Organisation and bought by Center Parcs in 2001.

The Center Parcs phenomenon represents one of the most interesting developments in the domestic holiday market. The first of these up-market holiday villages was introduced into Britain in 1987, since when two further properties have been built in the UK. The Dutch company responsible for bringing this innovation to Britain operated a number of sites on the Continent, but these were later sold, first to British, and later German, interests. Offering a wide choice of all-weather facilities (most notably a vast indoor pool designed to resemble a tropical beach), the villages had an extraordinary measure of success in their early years, with an average 96 per cent occupancy year-round. Later, competition from other large leisure companies like Rank reduced occupancy levels and there is now some danger of overbuilding in the field.

Billy Butlin's early attempts to introduce his holiday camp concept to the Continent were unsuccessful, but the more up-market holiday village has been highly successful. The market leader is Club Méditerranée, French-owned and with a worldwide spread of holiday villages, from France to Tahiti. The success of this organization, which started its package programmes in 1950, has been attributed to its unique approach to its clients, who are referred to as *gentils membres*. It has been the practice for beads to be used instead of hard currency to purchase drinks on site; this has heightened the feeling for the holiday-makers of being 'divorced from the commercial world' while on holiday. However, this organization also experienced a decline in profits after failing to keep pace with holiday centre development at the end of the 1990s, and was forced into an expensive programme of renovation to restore its position in the market.

Second-home and time-share ownership

Some word is also appropriate here about the growth of second-home ownership, which is influencing the tourism industry. In Britain, increasing disposable income, especially among those living in London and the southeast, has led to massive growth in

Figure 10.11 Second homes are also rented out as holiday accommodation at the Watermark Club, Cotswold Water Park. (*Photographed by the author*)

second-home ownership, both within Britain and in countries such as Spain, France and Greece. Demand for second homes in attractive rural areas of Britain such as the Lake District and the Cotswolds has encouraged local authorities to impose restrictions on their construction. In the Cotswolds, for example, planning permission for holiday homes in the Cotswold Water Park forbids the use of these properties as permanent homes. Many such homes serve a dual purpose, being rented out as holiday homes when not occupied by the owners (see Figure 10.11).

Where an outright purchase is beyond people's means, the concept of time-share offers an alternative means of taking a holiday in one's second home in the UK or abroad. Estimates place time-share ownership at around 1 million, with 37 per cent of properties located in the Canary Islands, 20 per cent elsewhere in Spain and 18 per cent in the UK. Together, this major new market has initiated substantial demand for seat-only sales on charter aircraft, and poses a new threat to the traditional accommodation sector – indeed, some hotels in Britain have responded to the challenge by converting some or all of their accommodation for time-share ownership.

Time-share is a scheme whereby an apartment or villa is sold to several co-owners, each of whom purchases the right to use the accommodation for a

given period of the year, which may range from one week to several weeks. The initial cost of the accommodation will vary not only according to the length of time for which it is purchased, but also depending on the period of the year, so that a week in July or August, for example, may be three or four times the cost of the same accommodation in winter.

The scheme is reported to have been initiated at a ski resort in the French Alps in 1965, although the Ring Hotel chain in Switzerland was developing along similar lines some years before this. By the early 1970s, time-share had been introduced in the USA, and the concept had also arrived in Britain by the mid-1970s. Since then it has enjoyed enormous success, boosted by schemes allowing owners to exchange their properties for others around the world during their period of ownership. A number of time-share exchange organizations have been established, of which the largest and best known are RCI (Resort Condominiums International) and II (Interval International). These companies keep a register of owners, and, for a fee, will facilitate home exchanges around the world, and organize flights.

There are well over 2,000 time-share resorts, with at least a hundred in the UK alone. Unfortunately, the sheer popularity of time-share has led to high-pressure sales techniques by less reputable organizations using 'street touts' to approach tourists visiting resorts abroad, and this has led to some poor publicity for the scheme in the press. The Timeshare Developers' Association was formed to give the industry credibility, and to draw up a code of conduct for members, and since 1991 a Timeshare Council has overseen the regulation of time-share within the UK. The Office of Fair Trading keeps a watching brief on development within the UK.

Time-share is not without its problems. It has been found to be difficult to resell property due to the amount of new time-share property on the market, and in some cases management and maintenance fees have been high. There can be a problem in getting widely dispersed owners together to take decisions on the management of the property. Notwithstanding these difficulties, time-share remains popular, and is likely to grow as a threat to the traditional package holiday.

Educational accommodation

The significance of the educational accommodation sector must also be recognized. Universities and other institutions of higher education, seeking to increase contributions to their revenue through the rental of student accommodation during the academic holidays, have marketed this accommodation for budget holidays to tour operators and others. Often situated in green-field sites near major tourist destinations, such as Stirling or York, the universities have experienced considerable success in this new venture, and have further expanded their involvement with the leisure market by providing other facilities such as activity centres and public rooms for themed holidays. More than 1.5 million holidays are now sold each year in the UK using the accommodation of educational institutions.

The distribution of accommodation

Large hotel chains enjoy substantial advantages in gaining access to their markets. Many international chains have close links, through ownership or financial interest, with the airlines, a situation dating back to the early 1970s when airlines, introducing their new jumbo jets, hastily set about establishing connections with hotels to accommodate their increasing passenger numbers. This relationship today gives the hotel chains access to the airlines' global distribution systems (GDS), computerized reservations networks which constitute a vital factor in selling rooms to the international market.

Large hotels depend upon group as well as individual business, so they must maintain contact with tour operators, conference organizers and others who bulk-buy hotel bedrooms. The tourist boards can play a part in helping such negotiations by organizing workshops abroad to which the buyers of accommodation and other facilities will be invited.

Virtually all of the larger hotel chains, and many smaller hotel companies, have today installed their own computer reservations systems to cope with worldwide demand for immediate confirmation on availability and reservations. Some chains maintain their own offices in key generating countries (and of course each hotel will recommend business and take reservations for others in the chain), while independent hotels reach the overseas markets through membership of marketing consortia or through representation by a hotel representative agency. These hotel representatives are not merely booking agents; they are on contract to the hotels they represent and will offer a complete marketing service. Some agencies, such as William R Galley Associates, R M Brooker and Utell International, generalize in the hotels they represent, while others specialize, either choosing to represent hotels within a specific geographic area such as the Caribbean (as does Windotel), or dealing with niche market hotels, such as smaller, 'character' hotels.

Sales made through hotel representatives are normally commissionable at 10 per cent to the representative. This does not prejudice the commission normally allowable to travel agents, so a hotel being represented abroad may well find that a high proportion of its sales are costing as much as 20 per cent of the room price to obtain. The smaller hotel with low margins must consider carefully whether it can afford to pay out such a large share of the room price to obtain the business – yet alternative ways of reaching a foreign market are not easy to find. However, the promise offered by the Internet is beginning to change this. Even small companies today can be information providers on the World Wide Web, and as computer software becomes increasingly interactive, allowing the public to book rooms directly through the computer, global marketing becomes a reality for the independent hotel as well as the large chains.

Travel agents will be thought of as the first means of reaching the market. However, few agents, apart from those dealing regularly with business travellers, are prepared to handle hotel bookings as a normal part of their activities. Domestic bookings are traditionally dealt with directly by the client, and agents are also unwilling to get involved as there is no common agreement on whether commission will automatically become payable on sales through an agent. Some hotels will pay a standard 10 per cent, but others will allow only a lower commission, or will restrict commissions to sales achieved outside their peak periods. Many agents are also unwilling to deal with overseas hotels without making a charge for the service (which will normally involve a fax or telephone call, resulting in a total handling cost which could well exceed the commission accruing on the sale). However, there is a growing tendency for hotels to package their product in the form of short breaks or longer holidays, which may be sold like any other package through the agent. Here, the agent is clear about the commission accruing, but may still be reluctant to stock the brochure due to the limited amount of rack space available to display such offers.

Clients for UK holiday centres have traditionally also booked direct, but this pattern is changing, as the centres themselves make greater efforts to produce packages which can be sold through agents. Companies like Butlins can now expect to sell at least 60 per cent of their product through travel agents.

Finally, mention should be made of the sale of accommodation through public sector tourism outlets. This is commonly found on the Continent – the Dutch tourist offices (VVVs) provide a reservation service for tourists, and have done so for many years – and today tourist information centres (TICs) in the UK also offer a booking service, as one reflection of their increasingly commercial role. The 'Book a bed ahead' (BABA) system allows visitors to book either hotel or farmhouse accommodation through local TICs, for which a fee is charged and for which the TIC receives a commission from the principal. Increasingly, such bookings can be undertaken using a local computer reservations system, which improves the service which the TICs can provide.

Environmental issues

All sectors of the tourism industry are becoming sensitized to the issue of eco-tourism, or ecologically sound tourism which can be sustained as tourist numbers continue to grow. Hotels are in a position to take a lead on this issue. They are also frequently the recipients of complaints by the eco-tourism lobby as a result of their practices; for example, hotels in Goa, in India, have been strongly criticized because of their profligate use of water for showers, swimming-pools etc. in an area where the local inhabitants suffer from water shortages due to drought.

Where there are shortages of water, as for example in the Channel Islands in Britain, many hotels will encourage their guests to use water sparingly – to shower rather than bath, to ensure taps are turned off and to take other measures which reduce waste. Hotel proprietors have recognized, for instance, that many guests would prefer not to have their towels and sheets replaced daily, and savings can be effected by offering guests the choice of fresh linen (which they may indicate by leaving towels on the floor in the morning) or reuse of their linen (indicated by hanging towels up). One example of an eco-friendly approach in the industry is the launch of the International Hotels Environment Initiative, in which a dozen major hotel corporations are collaborating. The initiative sets out to monitor environmental performance of the participating hotels, and to offer practical advice, especially to small independent hoteliers, on how they can manage their hotels in a more environmentally sensitive manner. This includes encouragement to reuse linen, the efficient use of energy in the hotel, consideration of methods of rubbish disposal and even the replacement of throw-away shampoo containers with shampoo dispensers in the bathroom. Such measures can provide substantial savings on costs for the hotels themselves, as well as helping to improve the environment as a whole and ensuring that as far as possible tourism in hotels is environmentally sustainable.

Questions and discussion points

1. Discuss the relative attractiveness of French *gîtes* to the British market and British B&Bs to foreign visitors. What are the particular features of each which appeal to the respective markets? To what extent has each country tried to copy the other's unique accommodation concept, and have such attempts been successful?

2. Argue the case for and against compulsory registration and grading of accommodation in Britain. Should this include some attempt to assess quality? How should the cost of any such scheme be covered?

3. Does the concept of time-share offer opportunities for the travel industry which it has not yet tapped? And what threats does its growth pose for the industry?

4. What can be done to correct an acute shortage of budget accommodation in major cities such as London? And how can cost, quality and value for money be reconciled?

Assignment topics

1. The Raymonde Hotel is a small county-town property which has recently benefited from the growing demand for rural tourism, especially short, out-of-season breaks. Following three successful seasons, the hotel has received planning permission for an extension which will bring the total number of rooms up to eighty-two.

   The result of this growth in capacity is that the General Manager, Jonathan Bromley, is keen to take advantage of sales opportunities wherever they can be found. Until now, little active marketing has taken place, beyond publication of the hotel's details in local tourist literature and ad hoc advertisements in the *London Evening Standard* (but no check has been kept on how much business these draw).

   Mr Bromley has asked you, as a member of his back office staff, to investigate new ways of increasing sales. He is interested in exploring the potential for direct sales via the World Wide Web, although some of his colleagues are sceptical about the value of such distribution methods for the immediate future. He wants you to assess this, and to consider other means of reaching the public via new technology – for example, through the escalating numbers of late availability reservations systems coming on-stream on the Web. Provide him with a report which examines both of these issues, and makes recommendations about specific web sites available.

2. Following the submission of your report, Mr Bromley has complimented you on the care and detail that went into it. One outcome is that you have been appointed to the position of the hotel's first sales representative, with a commensurate increase in salary.

   Mr Bromley has read in the trade press of the success enjoyed by some hotel proprietors, particularly abroad, who have 'themed' their properties, or introduced special events, to make them more attractive. He is particularly taken by the idea of the 'murder weekends' which a number of hotels in Britain have introduced. He asks you to look into the possibility of theming or developing special events, but wants to make the hotel distinctive rather than emulating what other hotels have done. His main aim is to increase the out-of-season trade, as the hotel is already getting very high occupancy rates between early June and late September.

   Provide him with a report which suggests a theme, how it should be introduced and the market it is expected to attract.

Chapter 11 Visitor attractions and visitor management

Objectives

After studying this chapter, you should be able to:

- understand the range of opportunities provided by differing types of tourist attraction;
- differentiate between linear and nodal tourism, and between constructed and natural attractions, and categorize them;
- appreciate the problem for attractions of changing taste and fashion, and propose solutions to overcome this;
- recognize the potential for new attractions.

Introduction

Any examination of the visitor attractions sector must start with a definition of what exactly is meant by this term. It is, after all, the attraction which prompts the tourist to travel in the first place; but the concept of an 'attraction' is a very broad one, encompassing a great many different sights – and sites. Often we use the term synonymously with 'destination'; the attraction of a holiday by the sea primarily consists of warm water, a good beach and a pleasant climate. The attraction of a trip by car through the countryside is the scenery, but this will be heightened for some by the occasional stop at a village for a walk around and a visit to a pub, while for others the pleasure of the trip may be a picnic stop, somewhere perhaps where facilities have been provided for this purpose by the local authority. At the other extreme, an attraction may be a very specific site: a stand-alone museum in the countryside such as the Blaenavon Big Pit in Wales, or the home of the composer Sir Edward Elgar near Worcester.

Some authorities suggest that the definition of an attraction should be that it has the primary purpose of admitting the public for entertainment, interest or education. This can hardly be the case for a seaside resort, however, which also serves the need of local residents, nor can it be the case for Buckingham Palace, where much of the building remains the private apartments of the reigning monarch. Perhaps it is easiest just to accept that any site that appeals to people sufficiently to encourage them to travel there in order to visit it can be judged a 'visitor attraction'.

It will be helpful, however, to make some effort to categorize attractions. We can identify at least three categories which will help in examining the nature of attractions:

1. Attractions may be *constructed* or *natural*. The former will include buildings of all types (or even whole towns), and attractions such as Hadrian's Wall or the Great Wall of China; the latter will include National Parks, waterfalls, lakes or other geographical phenomena. Natural attractions may also be subdivided according to whether they are in any sense 'managed', or are left entirely to nature to develop.

2. Attractions may be *nodal* or *linear* in character. Thus, the seaside resort or capital city will invite the tourist to focus the visit within a clearly designated and narrowly defined area, while linear tourism is concerned with the movement of tourists from one place to another. Examples of linear tourism include touring holidays by car or coach, and driving along a scenic coastal road such as Big Sur in California.

3. Attractions may be distinguished between *sites* and *events*. Some events are temporary; indeed, some are of very short duration. These are also either constructed or natural; the Changing of the Guard is a ceremony that attracts many overseas tourists visiting London, while the spring high tides which create the famous Severn Bore along the River Severn, the annual migration of wildebeest across the Serengeti Park in East Africa, and the regular eruptions of Old Faithful, the geyser in Yellowstone National Park in the USA, are all examples of natural events that attract the tourist. Many sites, of course, owe their attraction to an event happening in the past: Liverpool became a place of pilgrimage for many overseas youngsters not because of any inherent attraction but due to its links with the Beatles in the 1960s, while Lourdes, as a place of religious pilgrimage, owes its appeal entirely to an event occurring in 1858, when 14-year-old Bernadette Soubirous was said to have experienced a vision of the Virgin Mary.

The English Tourism Council, which regularly monitors visits to specific visitor attractions, rather than destinations, divides these broadly into the following categories:

- historic properties
- museums and art galleries
- wildlife parks
- gardens
- country parks
- workplaces
- steam railways
- leisure attractions
- other attractions.

In all, there are some 6,164 such attractions in the UK for which entrance figures are maintained, including over 1,500 historic properties and an equal number of museums. To this number must be added the numerous buildings open to the public for which no attendance records are kept. There are, for instance, nearly 3,000 Grade I listed churches in England alone. Even during the recession of the 1990s, many new attractions continued to open each year, while lottery funding at the end of the century gave a huge boost to the opening of new attractions. A few of these proved almost instant successes; Our Dynamic Earth in Edinburgh estimated, and budgeted for, 430,000 visitors a year, but actually received 500,000 in the first four months. Many others, however, were hopelessly over-optimistic in their estimates, in their efforts to get a share of the billions being made available from the special millennium funding and the National Lottery. The National Centre for Popular Music in Sheffield, opened in 1999, was effectively bankrupt within seven months, having estimated 400,000 visitors a year but achieving only a quarter of this figure, while the centrepiece of the new tourist attractions, the Millennium Dome, was forced to downscale anticipated attendance figures soon after opening, and on more than one occasion had to appeal to the government for additional funds in order to remain open in 2000. While the Dome became the major attraction in Britain, in terms of attendance figures,

Figure 11.1 Urban tourism: the New Millennium Square in Bristol with (left) the Imaginarium. (*Photographed by the author*)

in the first year of the century, the huge costs associated with its launch and operation ensured that it could never have become a commercial success. At the other end of the scale, some small attractions receive fewer than 10,000 visitors each year, but are not necessarily seen as failures, if business plans are carefully managed.

It is important to recognize that many destinations owe their appeal to the fact that they offer a cluster of attractions within the immediate locality. The attraction of the seaside is heightened – particularly in Britain, with its uncertain climate – by its being able to offer, either in the town itself or within a short drive, a number of sites which are not weather-dependent, such as museums, amusement arcades, retail shopping malls, theatres and industrial heritage sites.

Seaside resorts

Britain suffers from an uncertain summer climate, which ensured the decline of the seaside holiday as soon as British tourists could afford to travel abroad in large numbers. In spite of this development, which we have examined in earlier chapters, by the end of the twentieth century one in three British holiday-makers still spent their main holidays at the sea-

side in Britain. However, they stayed for shorter periods than in the past – holidays of eight nights or more decreased by some 14 per cent between 1990 and 1999. During this period, there was also a marked movement away from short breaks at the seaside to short stays in rural or urban areas of the country.

Some of the leading resorts recognized this trend and, through significant investment or pinpoint marketing, managed to retain and expand their markets. Blackpool, which continues to attract some 17 million visitors a year, retains its strong tourist market by promoting itself as the casino capital of England, and has augmented and upgraded its facilities to appeal to this type of visitor. The town's illuminations are unique, and internationally famous; first introduced as long ago as 1912, they represent an investment of nearly £2 million a year, and continue to attract many tourists who would not dream in the normal way of holidaying in the town. Bournemouth, too, has notably invested in new facilities to retain its tourist market, including an international conference and entertainment complex. It announced plans in 2000 to invest a further £500,000 to create an artificial reef which will provide waves of up to six feet for surfers. By attracting watersports enthusiasts and mounting international surfing competitions, Bournemouth expects to remain firmly on the map of leading resorts (a similar artificial reef has also been successfully created off-shore at Surfer's Paradise in Australia). The council claims that the reef will also enhance coastal protection, and therefore qualify as an environmentally sustainable tourism development. Similarly, Brighton attracts both British and Continental tourists, partly due to its proximity to London, but also due to the appeal of its premier (and recently restored) attraction, the Royal Pavilion, and its new (and costly) marina. The ETC, in a published report in 2001, recognized the success of these leading seaside resorts, but accepted that many others were no longer viable, and would need to seek alternative means of reviving their economies. What is apparent is that Identikit destinations will no longer suffice for the British seaside resorts; if they are to survive as tourist destinations, they must develop unique images.

This is particularly true of the many smaller resorts in Britain, some of which attract fewer than 2,000 visitors a week. All too often, in the face of the continuing flight of retired people to the seaside, this has meant converting former hotels and guesthouses into homes for the elderly, and the decline of many famous resorts is all too apparent to the present-day visitor. Even among these resorts, though, there are success stories. Padstow has boosted its tourism through the fortuitous television coverage of cookery programmes featuring Rick Stein, who owns a number of seafood restaurants in the town. Some resorts have been able to attract a new type of tourist, the overseas visitor who has come to learn English. By the early 1990s, over 600,000 foreign visitors were arriving in Britain each year with this intention, and many of the 1,000 schools of English are situated in resorts such as Eastbourne, Worthing and Bournemouth to offer additional appeal to the language market. The benefit of these visitors is also the length of stay, which averages thirty days, although average spend by most of these tourists (excluding, of course, business executives who come to improve their language skills) will inevitably be less per day than regular tourists on holiday.

By contrast, many resorts which have lost tourists in recent years have chosen, or been forced through lack of funds, to go down-market. Unfortunately, this end of the market suffered severely in the recessions of the late twentieth century, compounding the difficulties faced by the weaker resorts, which lost out to the competition of discounted accommodation at better resorts.

Three-quarters of all tourists visit the seaside in Britain by car, and improved accessibility via motorways and road upgrading to resorts in the southwest and North Wales has enabled many more tourists to consider day trips and short breaks to such destinations. These have helped to some extent to alleviate the impact of the decline in long domestic holidays.

The image of Britain's seaside resorts has also suffered from publicity about water and beach pollution levels. Britain has over 500 beaches that are regularly monitored under EU supervision. Of these, only half reach the recommended standards, and over 8 per cent failed even to reach minimum standards set. Blue Flags are awarded to those resorts reaching high standards of cleanliness, but only 57 awards were made to British beaches in 1999, placing British beaches only ninth in Europe. The Blue Flag scheme, which is operated by the Foundation for Environmental Education in Europe, is based on criteria such as litter, graffiti and car parking facilities as well as water quality standards. Blackpool's beaches consistently fail to reach acceptable standards, and while the council is taking steps to improve this record, they argue that the town's appeal rests not on swimming but on the entertainment provided on-shore. Their visitor numbers seem to support this premise.

The British pier

The idea of a pier is a particularly British phenomenon; very few are to be found abroad, while at one time Britain boasted more than a hundred. These soon proved to be an attraction in their own right at many of Britain's most popular seaside resorts. The first pier was constructed at Weymouth in 1812, soon followed by that at Ryde, Isle of Wight, in 1813. Their heyday, however, occurred between 1850 and the early 1900s. They were first constructed to serve as walkways to reach the numerous paddle steamers providing excursions by sea for the seaside holidaymakers, but were soon used for 'promenading', a popular Victorian pastime. There is a continuing nostalgia for them among the British public, and those that remain (some 43 in the UK in varying states of preservation) are currently enjoying something of a revival: 1996 was declared the Year of the Pier in Britain, to encourage awareness of the pier and its historic and cultural role in British tourism. The formation of a National Piers Society to further the interest and regeneration of the piers has led to five piers being restored, two new ones being built, and others planned for restoration, including the outstanding West Pier in Brighton, closed since 1975 and the only Grade 1 listed pier in the country.

The seaside resort abroad

Seaside resorts elsewhere in the world, and particularly on the Continent, have faced problems in the last few years that are familiar to the British. With the development of mass tourism, it is inevitable that resorts will wax and wane in popularity, and continual upgrading of facilities to attract the mass tourist market is essential. The Spanish resorts, many of which were first developed for mass tourism in the 1960s, suffered from a lack of investment due to the complacency of local authorities in these resorts, which saw numbers increasing each year. Inevitably, deterioration of the fabric of the often poorly constructed concrete hotel blocks of the 1960s, coupled with inflation which made the country less attractive by comparison with other Mediterranean destinations such as Greece, and later Turkey, led to a downturn in visitor numbers from the traditional generating countries. The country was fortunate in some respects to be able partially to offset this slump through the growth in tourism from Russia and other former eastern bloc countries, as tourists from these countries sought their first package holidays abroad. Nevertheless, the lower spend per capita of these markets made them less attractive to local tourist enterprises. Formerly popular resorts such as Benidorm on the east coast of Spain and Magaluf in Majorca became increasingly concerned that their traditional markets were drifting away in favour of more recently developed and better kept resorts in other countries of the Mediterranean. The Spanish resorts took steps, however, to recover their markets. Benidorm invested heavily (over £300 million) to effect improvements. Magaluf and Palma Nova, major resorts in Calvia, where tourism was responsible for over 80 per cent of all income, started a process of eliminating their older hotels and replacing them with better built (and higher graded) ones. Regulations were tightened up; four- and five-star

hotels were required to provide at least 60 square metres of land for each bedroom, compared to only 15 square metres in 1990. As a result, the slide downmarket was arrested at these two resorts.

The future of the seaside

The long-term future of seaside resorts is in question, given the alarming growth in skin cancer occurring as a result of exposure to the sun. This danger is increasing rapidly as the world's protective ozone layer is reduced by atmospheric pollution. The danger has now been recognized for some years, especially in Australia, where in Queensland as many as one in three of the population is affected, and the government has mounted a strong campaign to reduce exposure. The 'slip, slap, slop' campaign (slip on a T-shirt, slap on a hat, slop on suncream) has been effective in educating the public in a country of sun-lovers. In the United States, over a million new cases of skin cancer are reported each year, and the problem has also been well publicized in Britain, where around 42,000 cases of skin cancer yearly were reported by the end of the 1990s.

Skin cancer is of two varieties. Carcinoma occurs as a result of long-term exposure to the sun, common among people such as construction workers and farmers who spend long hours each day in the sun. Melanoma results from short but intensive exposure to the sun, such as is experienced by tourists on holiday. The danger of malignant melanoma is greatest for fair-complexioned tourists, especially those from Anglo-Saxon races such as Britons, Germans and Scandinavians, and young children are particularly at risk, although the effects of such exposure may take many years to develop into cancer. There are about 3,000 cases of malignant melanoma in Britain each year, and the figure is rising rapidly as a result of the growing number of Britons visiting hotter climates for their holidays since the 1960s. Many tourists either remain ignorant of the danger or choose to disregard it; the vogue for a 'healthy-looking' suntan remains a powerful motivator for sunbathing. Behaviour patterns, nonetheless, are expected to change gradually over the next few years, even if tourists do choose to continue to visit seaside resorts. Heliophobia, or fear of the sun, is in some cases persuading holiday-makers to take holidays away from the seaside, while others are encouraged to be more cautious by applying high-factor suncreams, or reducing their activities outdoors between eleven o'clock and three o'clock, when the sun is at its greatest intensity. The seaside resorts are coming to recognize that if they are to survive they must construct more indoor facilities and offer their visitors better protection from the sun while on the beach.

Spa tourism

Britain could boast of more than two hundred and fifty active spas in the seventeenth century. Some were surprisingly urban; Streatham Vale, now in the London suburbs, was a popular watering hole as early as 1659. By the end of the twentieth century barely a dozen of these remained, and only one spa, that at Droitwich, continued to offer medical treatment, with a private hospital offering an indoor brine bath. On the Continent, though, spa tourism remains popular, and occupies an important place in the tourism industry of several countries. In Germany and the Czech and Slovak Republics thermal treatment, in mud or mineral water baths, plays an important part in health care (although the high cost of providing such care resulted in Germany, in 1996, cutting back the amount of time its citizens were permitted to stay at spas when funding was provided by the state). Nevertheless, some 15 million Europeans daily immerse themselves in thermal waters in the belief that 'the cure' will alleviate their ailments, and the spas of Europe continue to benefit from this belief.

In Britain, which formerly attracted many domestic tourists to its spa towns, as we saw in Chapter 2, medical experts became more sceptical about the health benefits of spas in the twentieth century. Recent evidence concerning sufferers from osteoarthritis and osteoporosis, and a growing interest in alternative medicine generally, is causing some medical experts to re-evaluate their former views, and this is encouraging some former spas to reopen. Bath, with the aid of Lottery funding, plans to reopen two of its former spas early in the 2000s for private medical treatment, and National Lottery funding is also being made available at Buxton, Malvern, Leamington Spa, Harrogate and Tunbridge Wells. Others may choose to follow suit if demand is evident, although not all funding will necessarily go towards recreating the medical facilities of these famous spas.

The attractions of the former spa towns remain an important element in heritage tourism; Bath, Cheltenham, Harrogate and Buxton are still popular destinations for tourists due to the attraction of their infrastructure, which was originally built to serve the needs of health tourists.

In spite of the lack of medical facilities at British spas, a number of tour operators in the UK are featuring spa treatment abroad in their promotions, and over 300,000 British tourists continue to travel abroad for treatment each year.

Urban tourism

Visitors are increasingly attracted to towns and cities. Visits to urban destinations rose by two-thirds in the last decade of the twentieth century, and some 30 per cent of all trips of one to three nights are now urban, as the tourist attractions of these destinations become more widely recognized, both in the UK and elsewhere. Britain is fortunate in that most incoming visitors have as their motivation the desire to see the country's heritage, much of which is found in the urban areas. Apart from London and its myriad attractions, architecturally, historically and culturally, all the leading destinations in Britain are dependent upon their heritage to attract the overseas tourist. The university towns of Oxford and Cambridge, the Shakespeare connection with Stratford-upon-Avon, Windsor with its royal castle, the cities of Bath, York,

Figure 11.2 The glass pyramid, the Louvre, Paris. (*Photographed by the author*)

Edinburgh and Chester, all feature on the standard 'milk-run' tours sold to the package tour market abroad. Apart from their beauty, all these cities ben-efit from having a clear-cut image in the public eye, and strong associations which are easy to market as products composed of a complex of benefits.

On the Continent, cities such as Amsterdam and Paris, which enjoy their status as capitals, also benefit from their situation at the heart of Europe and their unique cultural attractions; Amsterdam offers the particular benefit of its canals and waterways, while Paris has enhanced its traditional attractions with a range of controversial but powerful modern build-ings in recent years. These number at least a dozen, including the Pompidou Centre, the glass pyramid and new extension at the Louvre, the complex of new twenty-first-century architecture at La Défense, the Musée d'Orsay, the science and technology complex at La Villette and the new Opera House at the Bastille. However, smaller towns have also been

Figure 11.3 Dockland redevelopment: the success of Baltimore's Inner Harbour, USA. (*Photographed by the author*)

successful in attracting large numbers of tourists through a combination of accessibility and urban attractions. Notable in this field are Barcelona, Dublin, Rome, Prague, Bruges, Venice and Vienna. Even Reykjavik, capital of Iceland, has become a popular short-break destination for Europeans due to its lively nightlife and the curiosity of its surrounding landscape, with a visit to a hot geyser an obligatory add-on.

While large cities like Paris and London have the capacity to absorb substantial numbers of tourists, smaller, very popular cities like Oxford suffer from severe congestion in summer, as thousands of foreign tourists visit by coach and car during the peak months, creating major problems in tourist management for the local authority. Marketing of these destinations has to focus on tight planning and control, coupled with efforts to extend the holiday season, so that tourists can be managed more easily.

Aided by government urban redevelopment funds, the inner-city regions of several British towns have enjoyed a renewal and are now attractive to tourists; former warehouses, woollen mills in the north of England, and other sites of industrial strength in the eighteenth and nineteenth centuries have been converted into museums or other buildings to attract tourism and leisure. Notable among the successes have been the cities of Bradford and Glasgow, both suffering the worst features of urban decay at the beginning of the 1980s, but offering splendid examples of Victorian architecture, which has now become fashionable again after a long period out of favour. Bradford benefits from its location close to the Yorkshire Moors and Haworth, home of the Brontës, and now forms an ideal base for touring, with good shopping and entertainment.

Derelict waterfront sites have similarly been rejuvenated, with the aid of grants, following the success of the redevelopment of the Inner Harbour at Baltimore, USA, and other American restoration schemes. Apart from the London Docklands, redevelopment work has taken place at Liverpool's Albert Dock, Bristol's Historic Harbour, Southampton's Docks, and at Salford, Manchester, Swansea, Cardiff,

Portsmouth, Plymouth, Newcastle, Gloucester, Glasgow and Dundee, all of which have expanded their tourist markets by adding dockland attractions. Many of these sites have a unique historical image to project, and using a combination of public and private funding, developers have introduced a range of amenities including shops, restaurants and entertainment to generate a new leisure market.

The illustrations here are drawn predominantly from British examples, but these are only symbolic of developments taking place in many countries where tourism is recognized as making, or capable of making, an important contribution to the local economy.

Rural tourism

The British climate, the bugbear of our seaside resorts, is also responsible for providing a major stimulus to tourism, in the beauty of the countryside. A temperate climate, with frequent precipitation, provides us with the richness of green fields and abundant woodland which, coupled with rolling hills and stretches of water, make up the idyll that is the quintessential rural scenery of the British Isles. In spite of its small land mass, Britain offers considerable diversity in its countryside, from the meadows and tightly hedged fields in the south and west of

Figure 11.4 The English landscape: rural Devon. (*Photographed by the author*)

Figure 11.5   Rural tourism: vernacular architecture in Jutland, Denmark. (*Photographed by the author*)

England to the dry-stone walls and bleak moors of the north, and from the flatlands and waterways of East Anglia and Lincolnshire to the lakes and mountains of Cumbria and the wild beauty of the Welsh mountains and the Highlands and Islands of Scotland.

As modern living forces more and more of us to live in built-up areas, so the attraction of the countryside grows, whether merely to take a day out on the weekend or to spend a longer holiday touring, or perhaps holidaying on a farm. England alone has 169,000 kilometres of rights of way, and the 1996 study of leisure day visits to the countryside reported that more than 1.3 billion trips were taken, averaging 16 miles round-trip, and constituting 26 per cent of all day visits. Rural tourism attracts international tourists, too, with a growing number of Continental visitors coming to tour Britain by car while in turn Britons take their cars to France or Germany to tour. The attraction of contrasts is important here; the Dutch, Danes and Swedes, whose countryside is limited to flatland and waterways, find great appeal in the undulating hills and mountains of their European neighbours.

To cater for this growing demand for rural recreation, Britain created a network of National Parks in England and Wales (see Figure 17.4). There are currently twelve parks with National Park or similar status, occupying 3.5 million acres and attracting over 100 million visitors a year; plans are under way to create a thirteenth for the South Downs in Sussex, while the first National Park in Scotland, Loch Lomond and the Trossachs, is also in the planning stage.

Hiking has become a popular pastime for tourists in recent years and Britain is fortunate to possess many country footpaths with public rights of way which the Ramblers' Association is anxious to protect, as pressures on the countryside grow. The National Parks and Access to the Countryside Act (1949) which established Britain's National Parks also created a network of long-distance footpaths which is enjoying growing popularity with hikers. These national trails are illustrated in Figure 11.6.

Figure 11.6   Major national trails in Great Britain

NATIONAL TRAILS

1 Speyside Way
2 West Highland Way
3 Southern Upland Way
4 Pennine Way
5 Cleveland Way
6 Wolds Way
7 Pembrokeshire Coast Path
8 Offa's Dyke Path
9 Peddars Way and Norfolk Coast Path
10 Thames Path
11 Ridgeway
12 North Downs Way
13 South West Coast Path
14 South Downs Way

Walking holidays are packaged for the inclusive tourist not just in Europe, but as far afield as the Himalayas and the wilderness areas of North America. Cycling, too, has experienced a regeneration of interest, as we saw in Chapter 9. This is a sport which is entirely dependent upon rural scenery (preferably flat land, although more active cyclists will also opt for hill touring). Both the independent traveller and the package tourist are attracted, with tour operators offering inclusive tours by bike to a growing number of countries. Both these forms of tourism are encouraged by the interest in 'green tourism', or environmentally friendly tourism, an issue which will be explored more fully in the final chapter of this book.

As we saw in Chapter 8, demand for leisure and recreation using boats has always been popular among the British, and the rural waterways of Britain provide ideal opportunities for water-based tourist activities, particularly at sites such as the Lake District and the Norfolk Broads, both of which enjoy National Park status. The canals and waterways of the Netherlands, France and Ireland, to name but three countries, all attract growing numbers of tourists seeking the pleasure of 'messing about in boats'. Waterfalls, too, exercise their own attraction, and major falls form unique settings for tourism. Those that are readily accessible, such as Niagara Falls on the Canadian/US border, and Victoria Falls on the Zambia/Zimbabwe border, enjoy considerable popularity, but more inaccessible falls, including the world's highest, Angel Falls in Venezuela, do not yet attract the number of tourists that could be anticipated at such a unique scenic attraction, were adequate transport and other infrastructure available.

Mountains attract both the passive and the active tourist. The Alps in central Europe have long been a focus of tourism, both as objects of awe and beauty to be admired passively or as scenic attractions on gentle walks, or more actively by climbers and mountaineers. The setting of Glencoe in Scotland, noted for its famous massacre of the Macdonald clan by the Campbells in 1692, provides historic appeal

in addition to its savage beauty. Activity holidays are one of the fastest growing fields in tourism, so that both mountaineering and winter sports provide great opportunities for growth. However, the enormous expansion in winter sports holidays has also put huge pressures on the Alps, which have a fragile environment easily damaged by overuse. The challenge of climbing major peaks in mountain ranges

Figure 11.7   English battle sites listed by English Heritage

LISTED SITES

English Heritage has listed 43 battle sites:

1 Maldon, Essex, 991; **2** Stamford Bridge, North Yorks, 1066; **3** Hastings, E. Sussex, 1066; **4** Northallerton, North Yorks, 1138; **5** Lewes, E. Sussex, 1264; **6** Evesham, Hereford & Worcester, 1265; **7** Myton, North Yorks, 1319; **8** Boroughbridge, North Yorks, 1322; **9** Halidon Hill, Northumberland, 1333; **10** Neville's Cross, Co. Durham, 1346; **11** Otterburn, Northumberland, 1388; **12** Homildon Hill, Northumberland, 1402; **13** Shrewsbury, Shropshire, 1403; **14** Blore Heath, Staffs, 1459; **15** Northampton, 1460; **16** Towton, North Yorks, 1461; **17** Barnet, N. London, 1471; **18** Tewkesbury, Glos, 1471; **19** Bosworth, Leics, 1485; **20** Stoke Field, Notts, 1487; **21** Flodden, Northumberland, 1513; **22** Solway Moss, Cumbria, 1542; **23** Newburn Ford, Tyne and Wear, 1640; **24** Edgehill, Warwicks, 1642; **25** Braddock Down, Cornwall, 1642; **26** Stratton, Cornwall, 1643; **27** Hopton Heath, Staffs, 1643; **28** Adwalton Moor, West Yorks, 1643; **29** Lansdown Hill, Avon, 1643; **30** Newbury, Berks, 1643; **31** Roundway Down, Wilts, 1643; **32** Winceby, Lincs, 1643; **33** Chalgrove, Oxon, 1643; **34** Cheriton, Hants, 1644; **35** Cropredy Bridge, Oxon, 1644; **36** Marston Moor, North Yorks, 1644; **37** Nantwich, Cheshire, 1644; **38** Naseby, Northants, 1645; **39** Langport, Somerset, 1645; **40** Rowton Heath, Cheshire, 1645; **41** Stow-on-the-Wold, Glos, 1646; **42** Worcester, 1651; **43** Sedgemoor, Somerset, 1685.

such as the Alps, Rockies and Himalayas has led to a number of specialist tour companies arranging special expeditions to destinations as far afield as Everest, where high levels of demand have now forced the Nepalese government to impose swinge-ing charges for climbing rights. Even packages costing in excess of £20,000 do not seem to stem the flow of demand.

Areas of woodland and dense foliage provide a different appeal for tourism. In Britain, there are over

Figure 11.8 National Parks in the USA and US territories

1 North Cascades	16 Bryce Canyon	31 Voyageurs	46 Glacier Bay
2 Olympic	17 Zion	32 Isle Royale	47 Haleakala
3 Mount Rainier	18 Rocky Mountain	33 Hot Springs	48 Hawaii Volcanoes
4 Crater Lake	19 Arches	34 Mammoth Cave	49 Virgin Islands
5 Glacier	20 Canyonlands	35 Great Smoky Mountains	50 Biscayne
6 Redwood	21 Mesa Verde	36 Shenendoah	51 Black Canyon of the Gunnison
7 Lassen Volcanic	22 Grand Canyon	37 Acadia	52 Death Valley
8 Yosemite	23 Petrified Forest	38 Everglades	53 Dry Tortugas
9 Kings Canyon	24 Theodore Roosevelt (north unit)	39 Kobuk Valley	54 Joshua Tree
10 Sequoia	25 Theodore Roosevelt (south unit)	40 Gates of the Arctic	55 Saguaro
11 Channel Islands	26 Wind Cave	41 Denali	
12 Great Basin	27 Badlands	42 Lake Clark	**Not shown**
13 Yellowstone	28 Carlsbad Caverns	43 Wrangell-St. Elias	56 National Park of American Samoa
14 Grand Teton	29 Guadalupe Mountains	44 Kenai Fjords	
15 Capitol Reef	30 Big Bend	45 Katmai	

fifty historic forests, and many further areas of wood-land that attract the day tripper or walking tourist. Burnham Beeches, near London, is noted for the superb foliage of its beech trees, while forests such as the New Forest (a royal forest, with its memorial commemorating the spot where King William Rufus met his death in a hunting accident) and Sherwood Forest, associated with Robin Hood, have close links with history, myth and literature. In the USA, New England states such as Vermont, New Hampshire and Maine attract large numbers of domestic and international tourists to witness the famous 'fall foliage' colours in the autumn. In South America, Africa and even northern Queensland in Australia, jungle and rainforests provide another form of attraction, and have been added to the list of exotic long-haul tourist destinations now offered by the inclusive tour industry.

Finally, mention should be made in this section of battlefields as tourist attractions, since most of these in Britain are located in rural areas. Many battlefield sites offer little for the tourist to see, the authorities feeling that the events taking place at the sites are best left to the visitors' imaginations. As a result, they are relatively undisturbed, but this also means that they are often under threat from development, or to provide access roads. English Heritage has listed forty-three sites in England as of historical import-ance (Figure 11.7). Battlefield tourism offers histori-cal interest in what are frequently rural sites, but also owes its popularity in part to the growth of 'thana-tourism', or tourism of the macabre, which will be discussed later in this chapter.

In North America, the National Park Service, established by Congress in 1916, has created fifty-five National Parks throughout the fifty states, as well as the US Virgin Islands and American Samoa (see Figure 11.8). The service is also responsible for over three hundred monuments and other cultural or his-torical sites, while each individual state also has its own state parks and monuments to attract tourists.

Agritourism

Rural tourism has long been popular with the inde-pendent traveller, and its importance to the economy of the countryside has been widely recognized in recent years. The concept of agritourism, which emphasizes sustainable tourism in largely agricul-tural areas, has become highly significant in tourism planning, led by the development of the *gîte* in France. French government grants were awarded in the post-war years to help convert crumbling farm buildings into rural cottages for tourist sojourns, and the gîte holiday became popular, particularly with the independent British tourist. The Portuguese *quin-tas*, or rural estates, also attracted a strong following from tourists eager to experience something a little different from the standard forms of holiday accom-modation. There is now a programme of strong financial support from the EU, with grants that are allowing rural tourism provision to become increas-ingly luxurious. Recent development also takes account of the interest in adventure sports, many of which are best enjoyed in the rural community, and outdoor sports such as ballooning, horse-riding and mountain biking are now catered for. Spain, Portugal, Cyprus and Italy have all invested heavily in agritourism. Notable developments include those in Epirus province in northwestern Greece and at Sierra Aracena, province of Seville.

Britain has also actively promoted its farming and rural holidays, which for farmers have become increasingly important as a source of revenue as tra-ditional farming revenues dry up. Tourist boards and local authorities have helped the private sector to develop new ideas in rural tourism. One example is that of the Heart of England Tourist Board, which has piloted short breaks involving culinary trails – a cider trail in Herefordshire, a pork pie trail at Melton Mowbray, famous for its pies – designed to link farmers, food producers and the tourism industry under the banner 'farms, food and peaceful sur-roundings'.

All rural sites need careful management to ensure that tourism does not ruin them. As increasing numbers of tourists visit such sites, whether in the developed world or the more primitive countryside of the less developed regions, greater control will need to be exercised to ensure that tourism is environmentally sustainable. This is also an issue to which we will turn our attention in the final chapter.

Purpose-built attractions

We now move away from the broader definition of a destination, to examine the role and functions of the purpose-built attraction. Attractions are not, of course, necessarily purpose-built for tourism; many, such as ancient monuments and historic buildings, served, or continue to serve, other purposes in their lives. Some – such as the great cathedrals – are open to tourists only as secondary users of their facilities; others, including some royal palaces, are not open to the public at all, but act as a magnet for tourists who merely seek to gaze at their exterior. Many, however, were constructed specifically to serve the needs of tourists, or at least to meet the recreational needs of locals, and these site will include museums and art galleries, theme and leisure parks, as well as a host of other purpose-built sites. Here, we will briefly examine in turn those that are the most significant for the tourism business.

Ancient monuments and historic buildings

Many historic buildings of course continue to serve their daily task with little thought to the interest or needs of the passing tourist. Towns and villages throughout the world contain buildings that are frequently old, or of architectural interest, and provide an attractive setting in which to sightsee, even though such buildings may now serve as homes, shops, offices or hotels (it is worth noting that over 2,500 hotels in Britain enjoy listed status as being of historic or architectural interest). Towns with an unusual number of such buildings, such as York,

Bath or Oxford in England, or Bruges, Prague or Florence on the Continent, will naturally attract the tourist, and inevitably some of the outstanding examples of these buildings may eventually lose their original purpose and will be adapted purely to serve the needs of the tourist. These are assessed as part of the 'national heritage'. Some may be identified by UNESCO as World Heritage Sites; there are nearly seven hundred such sites in the world now, in 105 countries. Recent listings include Salzburg's Old City and the Schonbrunn Castle in Vienna. In Britain, there are now approaching twenty sites which have been given this status by UNESCO (see Table 11.1).

Within Britain, buildings and sites are similarly listed on the grounds of their architectural or historical interest. In all, over 451,000 buildings have been singled out by the former Department of the Environment, Transport and the Regions, the main

Table 11.1 Britain's UNESCO World Heritage Sites

St Kilda archipelago, an uninhabited group of islands west of Scotland's Western Isles.
The Old and New Towns of Edinburgh in Scotland
Hadrian's Wall, the Roman wall built across northern England
Studley Royal Park and Fountains Abbey in North Yorkshire
Blenheim Palace, Oxfordshire
Ironbridge in the North Midlands
The City of Bath
Stonehenge, Avebury and the megalithic sites of Salisbury Plain, Wiltshire
Canterbury Cathedral, St Augustine's Abbey and St Martin's Church, Kent
The Tower of London
Palaces of Westminster, Westminster Abbey and St Margaret's Church, London
Giant's Causeway and the Causeway Coast, County Antrim
The Welsh castles and town walls of Edward I in Gwynedd
Durham Cathedral and Castle
Maritime Greenwich, London
Heart of neolithic Orkney
Blaenavon Big Pit, Wales

result of which is to ensure that they are not razed or changed without recourse to the Department. The definition of 'buildings' can include everything from a stately home to a telephone box, and all are graded into three categories in descending order according to their architectural or historical merit: grade I, II* or II. Only about 2 per cent achieve the highest listing, with a further 5 per cent listed as grade II*.

Heritage sites will include fortifications and castles, palaces, churches, stately homes and gardens. It is also important to appreciate that our heritage is not only composed of ancient buildings; many recent buildings of historical or architectural importance are now protected, and have become attractions in their own right. Recent history is exemplified by World War II sites, such as the Cabinet War Rooms in London, where Winston Churchill conducted affairs of state during aerial bombardments.

Modern architectural heritage includes the striking black glass Willis, Faber & Dumas Building in Ipswich, designed by Sir Norman Foster in 1975 and now a grade I listed building and the De La Warr Pavilion in Bexhill-on-Sea, designed by Mendelsohn and Chermayeff in the 1930s and now considered the outstanding modernist building of the twentieth century in this country. The explosion of new architecture around the turn of the century which resulted from generous National Lottery funding includes many buildings which have aroused the curiosity of tourists, both domestic and foreign. These include the Tate Modern museum in London, which received over 1 million visitors in its first six weeks of opening, the Lowry Centre at Salford Quays near Manchester and the Walsall Art Museum in the Midlands (see Figure 11.9). Such buildings attract not only art lovers; the more controversial the building, the more visitors can be expected. Nowhere is this more apparent than at the new Guggenheim Museum in Bilbao, Spain, which opened in October 1997 and attracted 1.36 million visitors in 1999, pumping an estimated $160 million into the Basque economy. This has encouraged the regional authorities to invest in tourism facilities, including a conference centre.

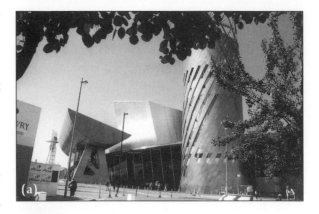

Figure 11.9 Modern architecture as tourist attraction. (a) The Lowry Centre, Salford Quays. (b) The Walsall Art Gallery, West Midlands. (*Photographed by the author*)

The fickleness of the British public towards its modern buildings is problematic, both in terms of whether such buildings deserve to be listed, and whether they are seen as worthy of a tourist visit. Listed buildings must have been built at least twenty years before they can obtain listed status, but experience would indicate that attitudes towards Britain's modern buildings, and whether they are seen as worth visiting, either on historical or aesthetic grounds, may take much longer to mature. Coventry Cathedral, severely damaged during World War II and rebuilt in unashamedly modern style after the war by the architect Basil Spence, was vilified for decades, but a poll conducted by English Heritage in 1999 now finds it to be the country's favourite twentieth-century building. Other formerly slated buildings now popular include Liverpool's Roman Catholic cathedral, the De la Warr Pavilion in Bexhill-on-Sea (mentioned earlier), the Royal Festival Hall in London and the Willis, Faber & Dumas Building.

Most English castles and other ancient monuments are now in the care of English Heritage, while those in Wales are cared for by the Welsh equivalent, Cadw, and those in Scotland by Historic Scotland, a branch of the Scottish Executive.

The Tower of London is by far the most visited heritage building, with well over 2 million visitors each year, due to its location in the heart of London and the added attraction of the Crown Jewels which are on display there.

Britain is also fortunate in having a large number of historic houses, many referred to as 'stately homes'. There are believed to be well over 6,000 such houses in Britain, of which over 800 are open to the public. A surprising number are still in private hands, and others are under the care of the National Trust (or National Trust for Scotland). These are prime tourist attractions for the excursion market, and are often sited in the heart of the countryside, attracting tourists to rural Britain. Some date from the period of the Norman conquest, while others, such as Winston Churchill's former home, Chartwell in Kent, are much more recent.

The first such property to open commercially in Britain was Longleat, the home of the Marquess of Bath, in 1949. In order to pay the massive costs of upkeep and death duties, Lord Bath realized that he would have to generate a substantial income for the estate, and later added other attractions, including a drive-through wildlife park. Other aristocrats soon followed suit, including Lord Montagu of Beaulieu, who added to the attraction of Beaulieu Palace a classic cars museum, a monorail and other forms of entertainment bordering on the funfair. Alton Towers, under the guidance of the entrepreneur John Broome, developed an entire theme park, and now entertains some 2.6 million visitors a year.

A growing interest in history has meant that the visiting public has gone beyond merely gazing in awe at the former wealth of Britain's aristocrats. Many quite humble homes which, through force of circumstance, have been little changed over the decades have now opened to the public. Beatle Paul McCartney's childhood home at 20 Forthlin Road, Allerton, Liverpool, is now in the hands of the National Trust and is a popular tourist attraction. One of the smallest homes open to the public is Toad Hall Cottage, an eel catcher's home in the Norfolk Broads, which opened its doors in the early 1990s and immediately attracted over 35,000 visitors a year. But perhaps the smallest 'enterable' constructed attraction in Britain is the gypsy caravan owned by the former radio entertainer and storyteller

Table 11.2 Top ten historic properties for paying visitors in England, 1999

Tower of London	2,422,181
Canterbury Cathedral	1,350,000
Windsor Castle	1,280,000
Westminster Abbey	1,268,215
St Paul's Cathedral, London	1,076,222
Roman Baths and Pump Room, Bath	918,867
Stonehenge, Wiltshire	838,880
Warwick Castle	793,000
Hampton Court Palace	699,218
Leeds Castle	569,505

Source: English Tourism Council.

'Romany' (George Bramwell Evens), which has been restored in its location at Wilmslow, Macclesfield.

A list of the most popular historic properties open to the public in England is given in Table 11.2. Similar lists are prepared by the Wales and Scotland bodies for historic properties in their regions.

It is also important to stress the significance of Britain's great churches for tourism. The numbers visiting sites such as Westminster Abbey (see Table 11.2) are now so great that there are serious problems of congestion, and the constant flow of tourists threatens the prime purpose of these buildings as places of worship. Some cathedrals, such as Salisbury and King's College Chapel in Cambridge, have attempted to introduce charges to help pay for the upkeep and added wear and tear arising from visitors, although those visiting to worship are exempted.

Britain is fortunate in having such a wealth of historic attractions, particularly as, for the most part, they are not weather dependent. Over half of all visitors to Britain participate in visits to heritage sites, while a quarter also attend performing arts events. Heritage was identified as one of the five original 'good causes' by the National Lottery, which contributed over £1.5 billion to some 5,000 heritage projects in the first five years of its operation.

Abroad, historic homes play no less a part in tourism. In Germany, Bavaria attracts by far the most foreign tourists, and this is certainly accounted for in part by the Disneyesque castles, with their wedding-cake architecture, erected in the nineteenth century by mad King Ludwig II. In Spain and Portugal many former stately homes, known as *paradores* in Spanish and *pousadas* in Portuguese, have been converted into luxury hotels to attract up-market touring visitors. Although history is much shorter in the new world, Americans take great pride in their heritage, and have carefully preserved many great buildings of the seventeenth and eighteenth centuries, including such historic homes as Monticello in Virginia, home of Thomas Jefferson, third president of the United States, a building now dedicated as a national shrine. Early colonial buildings at Williamsburg in Virginia have been restored with funds provided by the Rockefeller family, and the entire village has been preserved intact and is now a site of educational, as well as entertainment, value for tourists.

Gardens

Stately homes are frequently as noteworthy for their magnificent gardens as for their buildings. Great landscape architects of the eighteenth century like Capability Brown and Humphrey Repton built splendid parks to complement the buildings, and even in the twentieth century famous gardens were constructed, notably by the great landscape gardener Gertrude Jekyll, whose work was often used to complement that popular architect of great houses of the early part of the twentieth century, Sir Edwin Lutyens. Some famous estates, such as Stourhead in Wiltshire, are more renowned for their gardens than for the house itself. Other British gardens attracting large numbers of tourists are Kew Gardens, with well over a million visitors each year, the grounds of Hampton Court and Wisley Gardens. The proximity of all these to London helps to ensure their success, but the British are noted for their love of gardens and gardening, and will travel far afield to see unusual plants or beautiful settings. This has led to the development of specialist tours and cruises by the travel

Figure 11.10 Gardens as tourist attractions: Bodnant Gardens in North Wales, in care of the National Trust. (*Photographed by the author*)

industry to cater for this interest. Arboreta, which are essentially museums for living trees and shrubs, are particularly popular. Kew Gardens is the forerunner in this respect, but in Gloucestershire, Westonbirt Arboretum still manages to attract some 200,000 visitors every year. Many gardens popular with visitors are in the care of the National Trust, while the National Gardens Scheme ensures that many gardens attached to private homes not normally on view to the public are opened annually to raise money for charity. This scheme attracts thousands of visitors each year, by no means all restricted to domestic tourists. Following the success of the opening of the National Botanic Gardens in Carmarthenshire, Wales, is also actively promoting its gardens for tourist visits. France, too, benefits significantly from garden tourism, from their formal gardens attached to chateaux in the Loire valley to Monet's garden at Giverny, which has become a major international tourist attraction since its restoration.

Archaeological sites

Archaeology is the study of human antiquities, usually through excavation, and is generally thought to be concerned with pre- or early history – although

Figure 11.11 Archaeological tourism: the 5,000-year-old Skara Brae neolithic houses, Orkney Islands. (*Photographed by the author*)

recently the term has come to be used in reference to industrial archaeology, relating to study of the industrial relics of the eighteenth century. Areas where early civilizations arose, such as the countries of the Middle East, are rich in archaeological sites, and Egypt in particular attracts visitors from around the world to sites such as the Pyramids at Giza, the burial sites at the Valley of the Kings, and the temples of Luxor. Great Britain is also rich in early historical sites such as those at Chysauster prehistoric village in Cornwall, the Roman remains at Fishbourne in Sussex, with some of the richest mosaic flooring in the country, and the Skara Brae neolithic site in the Orkney Islands (see Figure 11.11). Myth and history are closely interwoven in our heritage, and the legend of King Arthur, which locates his castle of Camelot at Tintagel, or the association of this mythical king with the archaeological digs at Cadbury Camp in Wiltshire, exercise a fascination for young tourists in particular.

In the early 1990s, the world's largest collection of paleolithic art, embracing hundreds of ice-age drawings of animals, was discovered in a remote area of northern Portugal. A fierce battle then developed between those seeking to dam the area as a reservoir and others seeking to conserve the site for tourism. The latter won the day, and the Côa Valley Archaeological Park was opened to the public in 1996.

Industrial heritage

Britain was the seat of the industrial revolution in the eighteenth century, and over the past forty years interest has been awakened in the many redundant buildings and obsolete machinery dating back to this period. The fact that many of the early factories and warehouses were examples of splendid industrial architecture added zest to the drive to see these buildings preserved and enhanced for the purpose of tourism. Other European countries and the USA and Australia also quickly came to recognize the potential of redundant buildings. Lowell, in Massachusetts, where a number of early mills had survived intact, received massive federal government funding to be restored as an Urban Heritage Park, and since the conversion of its buildings into museums, offices and shops, it has enjoyed huge commercial success as an unusual tourist destination. A similar success has been recorded in Britain for Ironbridge, where the industrial revolution is claimed to have originated in 1709. Now a World Heritage site, it has enjoyed the benefit of substantial tourism investment on its seven sites spread over some six square miles.

The variety of industrial sites is astonishing. Early mining sites such as the coal and slate mines of South Wales or the copper mines of Cornwall have been converted into tourist attractions, as have former steam railways, docks and manufacturing sites. The textile mills of the north of England, driven out of existence by the import of cheap textiles from developing countries following World War II, have taken on new life as museums – or in some cases have been converted to attractive new homes. The open-air museums which are based on a combination of industrial archaeology and industrial heritage provide settings which, to be properly appreciated, will require many hours, if not days, of viewing, and have helped to turn former areas of urban decay into major tourist attractions. Apart from Ironbridge, other significant developments in Britain include Beamish open-air museum in the north of England, and the Black Country Museum near Dudley, in the Midlands. The Big Pit Mining Museum at Blaenavon in South Wales, and the Llechwedd Slate Caverns near Blaenau Ffestiniog in North Wales have both made important contributions to the local economy of their region, with tourism helping to replace the former dependency upon mining.

Early transport has provided another focus for tourist interest. In some cases, the equipment can be restored and used for entertainment; this is particularly notable with the many steam railways which are either in private hands or managed by trusts in Britain. Many of these railways run through very scenic countryside, especially those in Wales. We

Figure 11.12 The Vasa museum, Stockholm. (*Photographed by the author*)

have seen in Chapter 8 how older ships have been restored or maintained to offer trips, such as the *Delta Queen* on the Mississippi River in America, or the paddle steamer *Waverley* in Britain. In Bristol, the oldest surviving vessel built in Bristol's former shipping yards, the tug *Mayflower*, regularly provides trips through the floating harbour for visitors. Bristol is also the setting for Isambard Kingdom Brunel's *SS Great Britain*, the first iron-hulled screw-driven vessel, launched in 1843, brought back from the Falklands as a rusting wreck in 1970 and now being extensively restored with the aid of Lottery funding. Together with the city's famous suspension bridge, this early ship has now helped to create an image for the city to attract the tourist.

Earlier ships also provide unique attractions for their locations. Viking ships have been found in Scandinavia, and splendid museums created to display them – for example, that at Roskilde in Denmark. The only seventeenth century warship to survive is the Swedish *Vasa* which capsized and sank in Stockholm harbour soon after its launch in 1628. Raised in almost perfect condition, it is now a major museum attraction in Stockholm (see Figure 11.12). Still in Scandinavia, Oslo in Norway provides the setting for the *Fram*, the vessel in which Roald Amundsen sailed in 1910, on his way to become the first person to reach the South Pole. Similarly,

Captain Scott's vessel, the research ship *Discovery*, has now returned to Dundee where it was built in 1901, and serves as a museum.

The cost of preserving more recent vessels, due to their size, militates against their preservation. Perhaps the best known of all twentieth-century ships, the *RMS Queen Mary*, has been converted into a dry dock hotel near Long Beach, California, but persistently lost money for her developers after the ship was withdrawn from service and sold in the late 1960s. Britain, as a leading maritime nation, has sadly no examples of its great passenger vessels of the last century on display, although there are numerous examples of fighting vessels from that and earlier centuries preserved and open to the public. *HMS Belfast*, a World War II cruiser, is moored near Tower Bridge in London, and attracts some 200,000 visitors each year. Portsmouth is particularly lucky to have three great examples of our maritime history, including Nelson's flagship *HMS Victory*, the nineteenth-century *HMS Warrior* and the Tudor warship *Mary Rose*, raised from the sea in 1982 and still undergoing restoration. The combination of three vessels of historic value located close together in the same city acts as a powerful magnet for the day excursionist and helps to account for a high number of visitors.

Other forms of transport have also become museum attractions. There are numerous vintage car museums throughout Britain, although that at Beaulieu is probably the best known. Vintage aircraft are preserved at Yeovilton, among other sites, while elsewhere, museums have been devoted to early carriages, bicycles and canal-boats. As with other artefacts which are too large to house indoors, the costs of preservation are very high, adding to the difficulties faced by museums which wish to focus on such attractions. This was a factor in the collapse of the Exeter Maritime Museum in 1996.

Industrial tourism

Interest in our industrial heritage has now spread further to include an interest in modern industry. A number of companies have recognized the possibilities of achieving good public relations by opening their doors to the public, either to see work in progress in the factory, or to maintain a workshop or museum of some kind on site. Americans were the first to recognize the value of this from the point of public relations, and car companies in particular soon organized visits to manufacturing plants where prospective purchasers could watch cars being built. Today, this practice is widespread in the USA, and is particularly beneficial for tourism in the sense that most automobile plants are not sited in areas which would normally attract tourists. Among those currently open to the public are General Motors' Chevrolet Corvette factory in Bowling Green, Kentucky, which is one of that state's major tourist attractions, the Toyota Assembly Plant at Georgetown, Kentucky, GM's Saturn plant at Spring Hill, Tennessee, and the Nissan plant in the same state at Smyrna, BMW's plant at Spartanburg, South Carolina, and Ford's Lincoln plant at Wixom, Michigan, now the nearest such plant to Detroit, the traditional home of automobile manufacturing, which still remains open to the public. Some of these plants are booked months in advance, such is their popularity for visits.

There are other commercial benefits apart from public relations. Watching the production processes of, for example, modern china and glass will stimulate an interest in purchasing, and people can be encouraged to purchase direct at the factory shop. At Cadbury's, the chocolate confectioners located at Bourneville, England, chocolates have been made by hand and are sold to members of the public individually by members of staff in traditional costumes.

In 1980, the Sellafield nuclear fuel plant was opened to visitors to help counteract much negative publicity about nuclear energy appearing in the media. This quickly became a major, and quite unexpected, draw for tourists in the area, since when other nuclear processing plants have also opened their doors for guided tours of the site. The variety of factories and workplaces open to the public is now considerable, from leading companies such as the car manufacturers to small individual workshops like Langham Glass in Norfolk, which makes lead crystal glassware by hand and received an industrial award in 1993 for the numbers of tourists it was attracting. Another popular innovation has been access to the Scotch whisky distilleries in Scotland; of more than a hundred distilleries, over forty admit members of the public, and a distillery trail has been established for aficionados of single malt.

Many craftspeople depend upon tourists visiting their studios in order to sell their products, and as these studios are frequently set in the countryside, they will stimulate tourism to the area. For this reason, the Countryside Agency, formed in 1999 by the merger of the Rural Development Commission and the Countryside Commission, will sometimes provide financial aid to companies willing to open to the public, as they did in the case of Langham Glass.

Theme and amusement parks

Purpose-built theme and amusement parks are, not surprisingly, the major attractions for tourism, receiving the greatest number of visitors. The appetite for entertainment parks seems never-ending, and in Europe has a very long history: London's Vauxhall and Ranelagh Gardens date back to the seventeenth and eighteenth centuries respectively, while Denmark's famous Tivoli Gardens, first opened in 1843, have become one of the best-known centres of entertainment in the world, attracting over four million visitors annually. Bakken, near Copenhagen, lays claim to being the oldest amusement park in the world, having opened in 1583, while in North America Coney Island's Luna Park in Brooklyn, New York, was established at the end of the nineteenth century and in the summer was drawing 250,000 visitors a day by 1905. The heyday of the amusement park was the 1920s, after which parks experienced a general decline in attendance until the arrival of Walt Disney, who introduced the concept of the theme park. Today, amusement parks can be classified into three distinct categories:

1. local parks, catering largely to the day-tripper market;
2. flagship attractions, such as the Tivoli or Prater, Vienna, which draw on national markets and a significant number of foreign visitors;
3. icons, or destination parks, such as those of the Disney empire, which have become destinations in their own right and attract a worldwide market.

Among the latter, the four Disney parks in Florida, together with those near Tokyo and Paris, were attracting well over 80 million visitors by the end of the 1990s. Disney has since opened a further park adjacent to its Anaheim site in California, entitled California Adventure, to enhance the appeal of its first Disneyland complex. In Europe there are some 225 parks represented by Europarks, the European Federation of Amusement and Leisure Parks, which were together attracting around 160 million visitors by the end of the century. Again, these are dominated by a handful of major parks (see Figure 11.13).

The USA alone boasts over 750 amusement parks, attracting over 300 million visitors a year, but as will be apparent from a glance at Table 11.3, the Disney parks dominate the global picture. The clustering

Table 11.3 Top ten theme and amusement parks in the world, 1998

Tokyo Disneyland	16,686,000
Magic Kingdom, Walt Disney World, Florida	15,640,000
Disneyland, Anaheim, California	13,680,000
Disneyland Paris	12,500,000
Epcot Center, Walt Disney World, Florida	10,596,750
Disney-MGM Studios, Walt Disney World, Florida	9,473,750
Universal Studios, Orlando, Florida	8,900,000
Eventland, Kyonggi-Do, Republic of Korea	7,326,000
Blackpool Pleasure Beach, England	6,600,000
Disney Animal Kingdom, Walt Disney World, Florida	6,000,000

Source: *Swissair Gazette* Jul/Aug 1999.

Figure 11.13   Major theme parks in Europe

and scale of several of these attractions in one region of Florida, around Orlando, provides scope for the development of a major package holiday industry to be focused on this region; visitors tend to spend several days in visiting the parks, allowing the construction of a huge bedstock approaching 100,000 rooms.

The initial problems Disney faced in constructing its park near Paris provide an interesting case history in theme park management. Disney decided to build at a site accessible to the largest European market – some 17 million people reside within two hours'

drive of the site – rather than near Barcelona in Spain, partly due to subsidies promised by the French government. However, this decision ignored the inclement weather of northern Europe, which made it far more difficult to attract a market in the winter months. Disney also misjudged its market; the French resented the encroachment of American culture and initially proved more resistant to the attraction than the British and German markets, particularly as French tastes were not catered for (Disney failed to serve alcohol in its restaurants, in common with its practice in the USA, although the French traditionally enjoy a glass of wine with their meals). By adding more all-weather attractions and applying for licences to serve alcoholic beverages, Disney has now improved its appeal to the French, who now make up about half of all visitors, totalling around 12.5 million a year. Disney has now committed itself to building the delayed second phase of the development, to be called Disney Studio, which is expected to open in 2002; this is expected to boost visitor numbers to around 17 million a year.

This case history is interesting in the light of the failure of Britain's Millennium Dome to attract anticipated visitor numbers. This one-year attraction, built at a cost approaching £1 billion, was dogged by mismanagement and negative media coverage, but arguably its greatest weakness lay in the belief that the building itself held sufficient public appeal, rather than the attractions it contained, which appear to have been planned almost as an afterthought. It also lay on an inaccessible site to the east of London with poor public transport links and deliberately discouraged visitors from arriving by private car. Coupled with a relatively high entry charge and poor management of visitor flows which initially caused long queues to form for the major attraction, the relative lack of success of this one-year event was hardly unexpected. Nevertheless, the Dome still managed to achieve the status of most visited tourist attraction in Britain in 2000, and most visitors declared themselves satisfied with its displays.

Figure 11.13 identifies the major Continental sites and the larger UK sites. A number of the leading British theme parks attract over a million visitors every year, with Alton Towers in Staffordshire by far the biggest crowd-puller with over 2.6 million visitors. Other notable attractions include the Chessington World of Adventures, Flamingoland in North Yorkshire, American Adventure World near Ilkeston in Derbyshire, Lightwater Valley near Ripon, North Yorkshire, Frontierland in Morecambe, Lancashire, Thorpe Park in Surrey and Pleasurewood Hills, near Lowestoft in Suffolk. Entry numbers for

several of these exceed a million people each year, but it is questionable how many more such major attractions can be built and become viable; several big planned projects in recent years, including the massive Wonderland theme park planned as part of the redevelopment of the Corby steel mills site, have been abandoned or have not yet proceeded because of difficulty in raising capital. Britain also suffers from a poor winter for outside events, and many attractions do not attempt to remain open year-round.

The distinction between a theme park and a leisure park is not always a clear one, although the former is rather loosely based on some theme, whether geographical, historical or based on some other concept. The future is a popular theme, as it can allow the development to focus on advanced technology to attract the public. One of the most recent examples in Europe is that of Futuroscope, near Poitiers in France, where imaginative architecture of the future is combined with advanced technology; to cite one example, theatre seats are fitted with hydraulic jacks which move in sympathy with what is showing on the screen, so that sporting events such as white water rafting can be experienced as well as observed. The park attracted over a million visitors in its first year, 95 per cent of whom were French.

Many theme parks incorporate elements of the fun-fair, with parks vying with one another to construct the largest white-knuckle rides to attract the younger visitors. Blackpool boasts the 'Pepsi Max Big One', the highest and fastest roller-coaster in Britain, while Japan boasts the highest roller-coaster, the 'Fujiyama', at 259 feet, but the search for ever more gravity-defying rides has reached a point where the human body is now being subjected to dangerous levels of acceleration, and engineers believe nothing higher than 300 feet is feasible. However, these forms of entertainment can soon pall, and management must constantly up-date with new rides and other investment – perhaps at a level of some 5–10 per cent of the initial investment – to keep the attraction appearing 'new' to the public, and ensure repeat visits. Perhaps the ride to end all rides is that recently constructed at the Stratosphere hotel–casino complex in Las Vegas; known as the 'Big Shot' and built at a cost of $550 million, it offers brave (or foolhardy) tourists an inverse bungee jump, catapulting riders sixteen storeys to the roof in just 2.3 seconds, with four times the pull of gravity. The search goes on for the ultimate fun-fair experience without actually doing permanent damage to the participant!

Wildlife attractions

Wildlife is a growing attraction for tourists, and the industry has responded in different ways to meet this interest. At one time, the most common way for tourists to see wild animals would be in the numerous zoos which exist in most countries around the world. The keeping of collections of animals goes back at least two thousand years, but the present-day concept of a zoo dates back only to the eighteenth century. In Britain, although zoos are known to predate the turn of the nineteenth century, the founding of the Zoological Society in London by Sir Stamford Raffles at the beginning of that century led to the interest which Victorian England took in caged animals.

Today there are some nine hundred established zoos around the world, but attitudes to zoos have

Figure 11.14 Major wildlife parks in South and East Africa

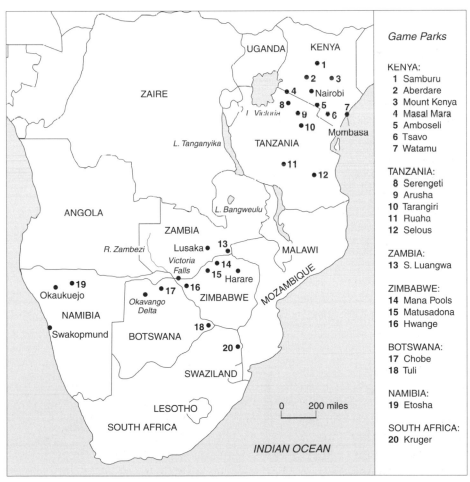

203

changed, as people in western countries have come to consider it cruel to keep animals in captivity. Nevertheless, zoos still enjoy high attendance figures, although not at the peaks to be found thirty years ago, and they are adapting to the new perspective by stressing their curatorial role in preserving rare species of wildlife, rather than the former emphasis on displaying animals for the purpose of entertainment. There was a fear at the end of the 1980s, as attendances fell, that London's famous zoo in Regent's Park might be forced to close. Although that fear receded with a massive private investment of capital, this sharpened awareness of zoos as a whole in Britain, renewing interest in visiting them, and encouraging the construction of better facilities to keep the animals in settings of less constraint.

With the growth of long-haul travel, more tourists are taking advantage of the opportunity to see these animals in the wild, usually in safari parks, of which the best known are situated in southern and East Africa (see Figure 11.14).

Some of these big-game parks have become world famous, including Kenya's Masai Mara, Tsavo, Amboseli and Samburu Parks, Tanzania's Serengeti National Park and South Africa's Kruger National Park. The attraction of these parks lies in the opportunity to see big game such as lion, elephant, leopard, buffalo and rhino, the so-called 'big five' (although poaching is rapidly diminishing the last of these). All of these parks feature in tour operators' long-haul programmes, although the political situation in both South Africa and Kenya, and the lack of

Figure 11.15   The World Federation of Great Towers. (*Courtesy World Federation of Great Towers*)

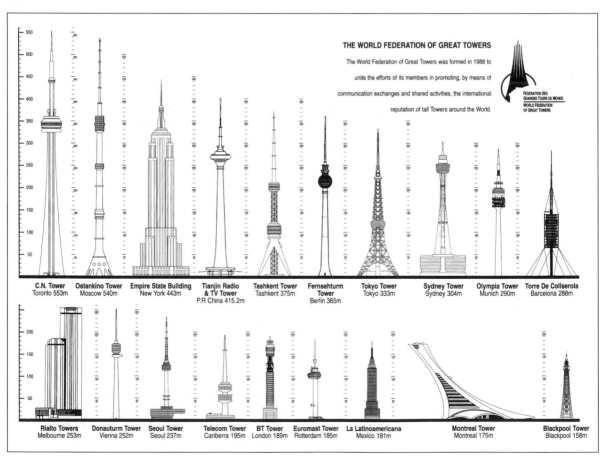

tourism investment in Tanzania, have prevented these countries maximizing their opportunities for tourism in recent years. This has been to the benefit of lesser-known parks in countries like Botswana.

With the decline in zoo attendance, there have been some efforts to introduce the atmosphere of the safari park in Britain, notably at the Marquess of Bath's property at Longleat in Wiltshire. Running costs for such projects are high, taking into account the need for maximum security to protect visitors; another safari park at Windsor was attracting close to a million visitors a year, but still proved a financial failure, closing in 1992.

Finally, mention must be made of wildfowl reserves and other miscellaneous centres where fauna are on display to the public. Ornithology is a popular pastime in Britain, and the Wildfowl Trust at Slimbridge in Gloucestershire has been a model for other sites around the country where birds can be viewed in their natural setting. Other attractions, for which tourism is a secondary consideration in some cases, include falconry centres and owl sanctuaries, while sanctuaries for other specific animals have been built in a number of places in Britain, an example being the seal sanctuary at Gweek in Cornwall. Sanctuaries, of course, exist to protect animals and to tend to wounded animals, but most are open to visitors, who make a useful contribution, through admission fees, to the running costs of the project.

Bird-watching in particular is attracting the specialist long-haul market, with tour operators such as Noble Caledonia offering cruises to the Arctic and Antarctic to study unusual bird life, frequently accompanied by well-known ornithological experts who will lecture to cruise passengers en route.

Other site attractions

The scope for providing new attractions to feed the insatiable appetite of the tourist is never-ending, and would be quite impossible to cover in a single chapter. In many cases, attractions are unique

Figure 11.16 The world's tallest tower: the CN Tower, Toronto, Canada. (*Photographed by the author*)

within their destination, but share commonalities with others in other areas or countries. This offers scope for joint marketing schemes or twinning. For example, a number of towns around the world are noted for their towers – always an attraction for tourists, especially if they are open to the public and offer distant views of the countryside or city (see Figure 11.15). The CN Tower in Toronto, at 553 m, is currently the world's tallest (see Figure 11.16), and for that reason alone will draw tourists, but others are known for their historical interest, especially those that have become symbols of their city such as Paris's Eiffel Tower (381 m) and the Rotterdam Euromast (185 m). Such towns can band together to share contacts, or market their towers jointly. Another recent example is the Walled Towns Friendship Circle, established as a marketing association in 1992 by a group of European towns which benefit from an encircling fortification wall.

Cultural tourism

Cultural tourism – however that is defined – is one of the fastest growing areas of tourism. In its widest definition, it encompasses both 'high' and 'low' culture: visits to museums and art galleries and to football matches; performances of music, both popular and classical; pilgrimages to literary sites ranging from the Brontës' Haworth and the bridge in Sussex identified as that from which 'Pooh-sticks' were played in A. A. Milne's Winnie-the-Pooh stories. The tourism industry has become adept at packaging and popularizing culture in all its forms. France, noted for its predominance in the fine art field, has packaged art trails covering Cézanne's sites at Aix-en-Provence, Monet's garden at Giverny, and areas associated with Gauguin, Manet, Renoir, Dégas, Pissaro and Sisley. Embracing wider tours, the 'circuit Pissaro-Cézanne' and 'circuit Toulouse-Lautrec' have proved popular for cultural tourists. Major exhibitions draw an international audience of mass tourists; 1.1 million visitors attended the Barnes Foundation's exhibition 'A Century of Impressionism' held at the Musée d'Orsay in Paris in 1993, while a later showing of the Barnes Foundation's collection in Germany drew such crowds that the museum exhibiting the collection stayed open all night. Britain's Royal Academy followed suit with 24-hour opening for its popular Monet exhibition in 1999, which helped to push visitor numbers to the Academy up to 1.4 million, making it the eighth most popular admission-charging visitor attraction in Britain that year.

Where a place is popularly identified with an author or artist, tourist interest follows automatically; where the link is less well established, it can still be built upon. Dylan Thomas's disparaging comments about the town and people of Laugharne have not stopped a steady flow of 25,000 visitors annually to the Boathouse where he lived between 1949 and 1953, in spite of the locals' preference to play down this link, while by contrast the town of Rochester in Kent, associated with Charles Dickens, has created a Dickens Festival and a Dickensian Christmas to attract tourism, and recently Crowborough in Sussex has endeavoured to promote itself as the home town of Sir Arthur Conan Doyle, establishing a Sherlock Holmes Festival in 1996.

The City of Culture concept

Cultural tourism has been given a boost in Europe by the EU's naming of a European City of Culture each year; the title was introduced in 1985, and exceptionally was awarded to no fewer than nine cities in the millennium year. The named cities qualify for EU funding, and, in jockeying for awards, contending cities make substantial investments in their cultural superstructure, further boosting tourism revenues. In Britain, there is the further incentive of National Lottery awards to named cities. In 2001, Rotterdam in the Netherlands and Oporto in Portugal were honoured with this title, while in 2002 Salamanca in Spain and Bruges in Belgium will be awarded the honour. In 2005, the title of the award changes to European Capital of Culture, and one country will then qualify each year to contest the title. Countries selected to date include:

2005 Ireland
2006 The Netherlands
2007 Luxembourg
2008 Great Britain
2009 Austria
2010 Germany

Britain was last awarded the EU title in 1990, when Glasgow celebrated its urban renewal and cultural growth. Some dozen British cities are potential contenders for the title in 2008, including front-runners Bradford and Milton Keynes.

Culture, the media and tourism

Britain has not been slow to develop the association between culture and tourism, supported by the popularizing of culture through the media, and most notably television and the cinema. Brontë country in Yorkshire offers its 'Great British Literary Tours', while the popularity of Jane Austen's books, following their filming in the mid-1990s, has been particularly noteworthy. Here, the attraction of top stars helps to boost appeal considerably; thus, Emma Thompson's and Anthony Hopkins' appearance in *Remains of the Day* was sufficient to boost attendance at Dyrham Park, Bath. In 1995, the BBC filmed *Pride and Prejudice* at Belton House, Lincolnshire, Sudbury Hall, Derbyshire and Lyme Park in Cheshire, the latter enjoying a ten-fold increase in visitors in its first week after the screening. A 'Darcy Walk' was quickly initiated to take advantage of this interest. In the following year, a Hollywood production of *Sense and Sensibility*, starring Emma Thompson and Hugh Grant, achieved similar success in promoting tourism for Saltram House in Devon. The TV series of George Elliot's *Middlemarch* drew tourists en masse to Stamford, in Lincolnshire, where the series was filmed (in preference to the original site in the book, Coventry, which wartime bombs and post-war redevelopment had rendered no longer suitable); 'Dr Lydgate's House' at Barn Hill was particularly sought out, and the town was not slow to take advantage; 'Middlemarch fudge' soon appeared for sale in the local sweet shops. The Alton Hotel in Birmingham, scene of the film *Four Weddings and a Funeral* starring Hugh Grant, has enjoyed virtually 100 per cent occupancy since the film was released. Osborne House on the Isle of Wight, the setting for the popular film *Mrs Brown* and featuring Dame Judi Dench as Queen Victoria, boosted its visitors by 39 per cent following the release of the film in 1996. The success of *Notting Hill*, starring Hugh Grant and Julia Roberts, particularly in the USA, was such that the BTA sent out maps to 250,000 travel agents around the world, identifying the locations of this film and of the co-contemporary *Shakespeare in Love* for London-bound

visitors. Local regions in Britain are now emulating this promotion with maps to attract the domestic tourist, with South West Tourism publishing a map covering 89 film and TV locations in six counties. Other RTBs are expected to follow suit.

The popularity of certain cult films will guarantee a steady audience of aficionados to the locations where the films were shot. Hundreds now visit the remote telephone box near Pennan, Morayshire, featured in the film *Local Hero*, while the enduring 1945 film *Brief Encounter*, shot at Carnforth Station in Lancashire, has enticed so many tourists (more than 100,000 annually), and from as far afield as Japan, that Railtrack is investigating the possibility of creating a theme park at the now deteriorating site. The long-standing popularity of the film *The Railway Children* (remade as a BBC-TV film in 2000), which featured the Keighley and Worth Valley Steam Railway in West Yorkshire, led to that company promoting its 'Railway Children' connections through leaflets, advertising and special events. In France, Provence tourist authorities have established a 'Marcel Pagnol route' to popularize the locations at which the French film *Manon des Sources* was filmed.

Popular television programmes set in attractive rural locations are a sure-fire draw for tourists. In Britain, the district around Hambleton in North Yorkshire is now promoted as 'Herriot Country', following the success of the TV series *All Creatures Great and Small*, featuring the veterinary stories of James Herriot, and a museum featuring 'The World of James Herriot' has opened. Goathland, in the North York Moors National Park and the setting for the popular TV series *Heartbeat*, was receiving 1.3 million tourists annually by 1997, against a modest 50,000 ten years earlier. Even negative publicity can attract the tourist; the Britannia Adelphi Hotel in Liverpool, subject of a critical 'fly-on-the-wall' documentary, ran a series of 'meet the cast' breaks to benefit from the popularity of the series.

The power of Hollywood is of course most noted in its own territory, and tourists both domestic and foreign flock to scenes filmed in the United States. To cite recent examples of areas that formerly drew few tourists and now, as a result of popular films, attract many: *Field of Dreams*, starring Kevin Costner, was filmed at Dyersville, Iowa (population 3,800) in 1988; 50,000 tourists a year are now attracted to view an empty cornfield with minimal tourist facilities. The popularity of Winterset (population 4,300) in the same state, and particularly the Northside Café which featured prominently in the film, was created by the film *The Bridges of Madison County* (1994), starring Clint Eastwood and Meryl Streep. These two remote sites are now the most visited destinations in Iowa.

Entire regions and countries can be similarly boosted by media exposure. Australia experienced a 20 per cent increase in visits from Americans as a result of the popularity of *Crocodile Dundee* in 1986. Scotland benefited from two feature films in 1995, *Rob Roy* starring Liam Neeson and *Braveheart* starring Mel Gibson, and has promoted the district in which the first film was based as 'Rob Roy Country'. Tunisia, where both *Star Wars* and *Raiders of the Lost Ark* were filmed, enjoyed enormous popularity following the filming of *The English Patient* at Sfax, Mahdia and an oasis at Tozeur; the Tunisian Tourist Office spent £20,000 in sponsoring the UK première of the film, and helped to develop an 'English Patient Route'. More recently, backpacker tourists have been attracted to India, based on the promotion of an alternative lifestyle in the film *Holy Smoke* (2000) starring Kate Winslet and Harvey Keitel.

While the mass media are the most influential in encouraging tourism, books must not be forgotten as an important influence, too. One of the fastest-growing destinations in Greece in the late twentieth century was Kefalonia, setting for the best-selling book by Louis de Bernières, *Captain Corelli's Mandolin*. The appeal of the destination was such that charter flights were laid on, with 65,000 arriving in 1998 from Britain, and an estimated 80,000 in 1999.

These are just a handful of examples to demonstrate the power of the media in influencing tourism, a factor that is, for the most part, fully taken into account and built upon by tourism authorities today, in their efforts to promote 'cultural tourism'. There

are worries, however, when these films are made in remote beauty spots which subsequently attract large numbers of tourists. Khao Phingkan in Thailand was the setting for the James Bond film *The Man with the Golden Gun*. This ideal setting was rapidly destroyed by unplanned tourism development. That the lesson has not been learned is evident in the example of Maya Bay on Phi Phi Lay Island, the setting for *The Beach*, released in 2000 and starring Leonardo di Caprio, where, in spite of good intentions on the part of the film crew, an invasion of backpacker tourists followed the film's success, destroying the very beauty the film had attempted to extol.

Museums and art galleries

Both museums and art galleries are visited by huge numbers of tourists each year. Many are established primarily to serve the needs of the local inhabitants, at least initially, while others have rapidly gained an international reputation. Examples of the latter include the British Museum, the Ashmolean Museum in Oxford, the Louvre in Paris, the Smithsonian Museum in Washington DC and the Museum of Modern Art (MOMA) in New York. The significance of these for tourism is that they can act as a catalyst for a destination, and in some cases become the major reason for a visit to the destination, especially in cases where outstanding exhibitions are on show.

Museums have a very long history, and in Britain date back to at least the seventeenth century, when some private collectors opened their exhibitions for a fee. John Tradescant's Cabinet of Curiosities provided the foundation for the Ashmolean Museum at Oxford University in 1683. The equally famous Fitzwilliam Museum art collection at Cambridge did not follow until 1816. In Britain now there are well over 3,000 museums, and of the 1,300 listed in the *Cambridge Guide to Museums*, there are 180 in London alone.

There are six categories of museum in Britain:

1. *National museums*, which are usually funded

directly by the Department for Culture, Media and Sport (DCMS) and include such famous museums as the British Museum, the National Gallery, the Tate Britain and Tate Modern art galleries, the Victoria and Albert Museum, the Imperial War Museum and the Royal Armouries, Leeds. Certain national museums are funded by the Ministry of Defence, such as the RAF Museum in Hendon, and the National Army Museum, both in London.

2 *Independent (charitable trust) museums*, financed by turnover; The National Motor Museum at Beaulieu is an example.

3. *Independent non-charity museums*, such as Flambards Museum in Helston, Cornwall. Some university collections are funded indirectly by the Department for Education and Employment.

4. *Regional museums*, which are funded publicly, or by a mix of public and private funding. The DCMS also funds museums such as the Geffrye and Horniman Museums in London and the Museum of Science and Industry in Manchester.

5. *Local authority museums*, such as the Cotswold Countryside Museum in Gloucester, or the Georgian House and Red Lodge Museums, owned by Bristol City Council.

6. *Small, private museums*, which depend entirely upon private funding.

Museums have experienced two boom periods in recent history, first during the period between 1970 and the mid-1980s, when many of them were able to take advantage of government grant aid, coupled with charitable status which avoided taxation, and later, in the lead up to the millennium celebrations, through Millennium Commission funding or Lottery grants. In the initial stage, a large number of redundant buildings, ideal for conversion into museums, became available, and the nostalgia boom and a generally positive view towards urban renewal and heritage all encouraged new museums to open. In the second stage, funding tended to favour larger projects.

The problem for those who manage museums is that the initial capital investment is not the only financial consideration. Indeed, many collections are donated, or gifts of money are made to establish a museum, but steadily rising operating costs are seldom met by increases in revenue, and after the first two or three years, during which time the museum has novelty value, attendance figures slump. As new museums are opened, so the available market to visit them is more thinly spread. Museums have also been badly hit in recent years by the consequences of the Education Reform Act, which has made the financing of educational visits – the core business for many museums – more difficult.

Many museum curators argue in favour of subsidies, on the grounds that their museums help to bring tourists into an area, where they can be encouraged to spend. Certainly, clusters of museums and other complementary attractions such as shops do give rise to greater tourism demand. The Castlefield site at Manchester is a good example of a 'critical mass' of attractions sited close together which make the destination an attractive day out. Conference and exhibition halls have long been underwritten by local authorities on just these grounds, but local authorities are today much more constrained financially, and in some cases have been forced to reduce the support they formerly provided to the museums in their territory. This has led to winter closures in some cases, or more restricted times of opening. Museums are having to become increasingly self-sufficient, and their curatorial role is now less significant than their marketing one. Even some of the major national museums have been obliged to introduce charges, or at very least 'suggested contributions'. One result was a very sharp drop in attendance at some of these leading museums, while those that did not introduce charges benefited. However, those that chose to charge have been able to spend money on refurbishing which, with government subsidies alone, would not have been possible.

Many of the millennium projects proved to be overly ambitious, especially in their projections of visitor numbers. Lottery funding was expected to be matched by other sources of funding, which in practice did not always prove possible. Projects that were not sited in traditional tourist destinations tended to struggle the most; the Earth Centre in Doncaster, built at a cost of some £100 million, was in trouble in its first year, and the National Centre for Popular Music in Sheffield, which achieved barely a quarter of its projected 400,000 visitors in its first year, became insolvent in 1999. The Arts Council, responsible for administering much of the lottery funding along with the Millennium Commission, now insists on business plans which give details of plans of action in the event that projections are not achieved.

It is interesting to compare the success of the Guggenheim Museum in Bilbao, discussed elsewhere in this text, with the picture in Britain. The Guggenheim received very strong government support and significant financial aid from the Guggenheim Foundation, and had the foresight to contract an outstanding architect, Frank Gehry, to design the unconventional building. The result was that tourists beat a path to its door, even though Bilbao was not a traditional tourist destination and had, at least at that point, little else to attract the tourist. Bilbao now enjoys success as a strong short-break destination.

New art galleries are being built in Britain as catalysts for urban regeneration. One of the more exciting projects has been the Lowry Centre at Salford Quays near Manchester (see Figure 11.9a). Over £100 million has been invested in this site, in the centre of an area of urban blight after the quays fell into disuse. Designed as a gallery for the display of the works of L. S. Lowry, it also features a large concert hall and entertainment centre. The architecture is as radical as that of the Bilbao Guggenheim, and on this ground alone the centre attracted a high number of visitors in its first year, well in excess of expectations. Similarly, the new art gallery at Walsall in the West Midlands (see Figure 11.9b) uses high quality design to promote further regeneration of a run-down canal network close to the city centre, and its construction has led to additional building in the area, including an unusually modern design bus station and The Wharf pub, situated on a newly created canal basin. Both these sites are located

within catchment areas with high populations, a factor favouring success.

To attract new audiences, and bring back former visitors, many museums are moving away from the concept of 'objects in glass cases' in favour of better interpretation and more active participation by the visitors. New techniques include guides dressed in period costume, audio-visual displays, self-guided trails using cassette tapes, reconstructions of the past, and interactive programmes which provide opportunities for hands-on experience. In the kitchen of the oldest house in Toronto, to take one example, the guide demonstrates the making of soap, provides souvenirs of the finished product to the visitors, and reveals that the soap can be eaten, too! Some museums are fully interactive, such as the new Explore at Bristol Museum, which is designed to explain science to the lay visitor by giving them the opportunity to become involved in practical experiments. At the Big Pit Mining Museum in Blaenavon, a former colliery transformed into a mining museum in 1980 and now a World Heritage Site, former miners act as guides, providing vividly illustrated tours which draw on their own former experiences in the mines. An example of a 'living history' museum can be found at Llancaiach Fawr Manor, a sixteenth-century fortified house in the South Wales valleys. Here, actor/interpreters (more correctly referred to on the Continent as 'animateurs') dressed in costumes of the period, guide visitors around the site, using the language and speech patterns of the time and authentically recreating the year 1645.

It is debatable what distinguishes a 'museum' from an 'attraction'. Many museums, for example, are the former homes of famous people, and the trustees have a curatorial and research role in safeguarding and investigating documents of the previous owner, as well as promoting tourist trade to the house for commercial reasons. A good example of this is Gracelands the former home of Elvis Presley in Memphis, Tennessee which, long after the star's death, continues to attract huge crowds of fans to see his house, his former possessions and his grave (see Figure 11.17). On the twentieth anniversary of the

Figure 11.17   Visitors attend the graveside of Elvis Presley at Graceland, Memphis, Tennessee. (*Photographed by the author*)

Table 11.4   Museum and art gallery admissions, 1999

British Museum	5,460,537
National Gallery	4,964,879
Tate Gallery, Millbank	1,822,428
Natural History Museum	1,739,591
Science Museum	1,480,000
Royal Academy	1,390,000
Kelvingrove Gallery, Glasgow	1,051,020
National Portrait Gallery	999,842
Victoria and Albert Museum	945,677
Royal Museum of Scotland	759,579

Source: *The Times*, 26 June 2000 © Times Newspapers Limited.

pop idol's death in 1997, thousands queued for hours to see the house and gravesite, with European tour operators organizing special air packages to the site. Graceland has become one of the major tourist attractions in the United States, and is listed in the National Register of Historic Places; with over 700,000 visitors annually, it is now second only to the White House itself in terms of annual visits.

Retail shopping

While shops are not considered in the normal way part of the tourism industry, there can be no doubt that they exercise a considerable attraction for tourists, and in many cases may be the sole attraction. The flood of visitors to London to take advantage of the January sales (particularly that held by Harrods, the best-known department store in the world, which will attract shoppers from all over the globe) is just one example of the power of shops to influence tourists. Internationally, one can cite examples such as the weekend shopping flights to capitals like Paris or Rome, or British shopping expeditions by ferry to the French supermarkets just before Christmas (the liberalization on duty-paid goods within the EU in 1993 resulted in a rise of some 18 per cent in passengers by ferry, as British shoppers flocked to the Continent to benefit). The great department stores such as Saks Fifth Avenue or Bloomingdales in New York, Kaufhaus des Westens (KaDeWe) in Berlin (claiming to be the largest store in the world) or even the humble Marks & Spencer in Oxford Street (which has laid claim to the highest turnover per square foot in the world) exercise considerable influence on visitor spend, and of course expenditure on shopping features in the tourism balance of payments.

Increasingly, shopping is being combined with other forms of leisure in the design of attractive shopping malls, which can attract huge numbers of visitors prepared to pass several hours enjoying themselves in an environment that encourages people to spend. Perhaps the outstanding example of this development is the Mall of America, built in 1992 at Bloomington, Minneapolis and claiming to be the second most visited site in the USA, with some 40 million visitors a year. At 4.2 million square feet, and offering 400 stores, 45 restaurants, 14 cinemas, a 7-acre amusement park and a miniature golf course, the site provides everything that the leisure shopper could hope for. It attracts a global market, and most notably brings in shoppers on direct flights from London, Amsterdam, Korea and Japan. North West Airlines has promoted flight packages between London and Minneapolis, as 'shopping breaks', with on-site hotel accommodation provided. Many of the

North American malls were developed underground as all-weather facilities where people could enjoy a leisurely shopping expedition even in winter, and they have since proved to be capable of attracting crowds from considerable distances away. In Britain, some towns have copied the American concept, and in recent instances have even gone as far as emulating the architecture of that continent, with 'New England'-style themes such as that found at the Bicester Village shopping centre near Oxford. Bicester, and similar malls in Swindon, Wiltshire, and Ellesmere Port, South Wirral, have focused on the concept of 'designer outlets' selling up-market products which bring up-market shoppers from some distances away. Others focus on size and choice, including such well-established new sites as the Lakeside Shopping Centre at Thurrock, Essex and Merry Hill Centre in Birmingham. 'Factory outlet' malls like those at Street in Somerset and Festival Park, Ebbw Vale in Wales offer direct sales to the public from manufacturers at discounts attractive enough to bring in tourists up to two hours or more driving distance away. The Gateshead Metro is the largest in the UK, but Covent Garden in London, which was developed out of the former fruit, flower and vegetable market, has been able to offer the equal attractions of a first-class set of nineteenth-century buildings tastefully restored as a shopping mall in the heart of London. With the added attraction of round-the-clock events such as buskers, this shopping facility has become an important addition to the visitor attractions of Britain's capital.

Events

Up to this point, we have dealt chiefly with fixed-site attractions. It is important to remember that tourists will also visit a place in order to participate in, or observe, an event. In some cases, these events occur regularly and with some frequency (for example, the Changing of the Guard in London); in others, the events are intermittent, perhaps annually or even less frequently (e.g. arts festivals such as the Venice Bienniale, held every two years, the four-yearly Olympic Games, or the Floriade flower festival which takes place in a different Dutch city every decade). In other cases, they may be one-off ad hoc arrangements to take advantage of a particular occasion. Such arrangements can last for as little as a few hours (e.g. a pageant to mark the reopening, after refurbishment, of Castle Park in Bristol in 1993), or as long as an entire year (the Millennium Dome exhibition in London to mark the year 2000).

Events are often mounted to increase the number of visitors to a destination, or to help spread tourism demand to the shoulder seasons. One interesting example of this is the costume events mounted by the Sealed Knot Society in England, a voluntary body with an interest in English history of the Civil War period, which, *inter alia*, recreates battle scenes on the original sites, drawing very large audiences. Other sites such as towns which in themselves may not be seen as having any particular merit for tourism may nevertheless mount a special event designed to bring the tourist there. Certain forms of event will be more likely to attract a market consisting of older or more wealthy people; these groups are more likely to have the freedom to choose the time of their travel and, indeed, may even wish to avoid the crowds that are common in the peak seasons. Some off-peak events have been so successful that the destination has managed to turn a low winter season into a peak attraction; the Quebec Winter Carnival is a case in point.

There is, of course, a direct relationship between the degree of attractiveness of the event and the distance visitors are willing to travel to visit it. The drawing power of the Olympic Games is so immense that huge crowds can be attracted from all over the world, and Atlanta's final contribution to secure the Games in 1996 amounted to over $2 billion. These costs were fully recovered in revenue achieved. However, in recent years the likelihood of overall losses appears high; Montreal notably lost over $2 billion in staging the Games in 1976, and is still paying off these debts. The success of Sydney in securing the

Games in the millennium year of 2000 was nevertheless seen as a major coup for Australia's tourism industry, and Athens is already investing substantial sums in infrastructure, including upgrading roadways and building a major new international airport, in preparation for the Games it will host in 2004. International Expo exhibitions such as that held at Seville in 1992, which are often used as a showcase to promote the country, will also attract a global audience willing to pay the high gate fees that are charged for entry. However, the success of such events can be jeopardized by local facilities such as hotels which may seek to hike their prices to an unacceptable level for that period. The failure of many millennium events over New Year's Eve 1999 has been ascribed to the exceptionally high prices charged by hotels, bars and other entertainment facilities – prices the providers claimed were justified by the need to pay staff substantial bonuses to retain their services for that night.

Smaller, but still significant, events capable of boosting the local economy are prominent features of many towns and villages around the world. Some have very long traditions. In Britain, ancient fairs continue to play a role in attracting visitors. Many trace their origins to the Middle Ages, often linked to the horse fairs organized by gypsies, and a strong element of Romany culture survives at these sites. Notable examples include the Ballymena Fair in

Figure 11.18 Event tourism: annual craft fair, New Hampshire, USA. (*Photographed by the author*)

Northern Ireland, the Appleby Fair in Cumbria, the Stow Fair in Gloucestershire and the Nottingham Goose Fair.

Arts festivals

Arts festivals, an important aspect of cultural tourism, have a long history in many countries, arising out of cultural and traditional festivals which often have local associations. In Britain alone, some 557 arts festivals have been identified, lasting from two days to several weeks in duration (key festivals appear in Table 11.5). More than half of these have been founded since 1980, and over 60 per cent are professionally managed. Most depend upon sponsorship and financial support from their local authority. The leading events in the UK, in terms of revenue achieved, include the Edinburgh Festival and Fringe Festival, and the BBC Promenade Concerts.

Several music festivals in Europe have achieved international recognition, and visitors make significant contributions to the economies of the cities

Table 11.5 Leading arts festivals in Britain, 2001

Brighton International Festival	5–27 May
Salisbury Festival	25 May – 10 June
Aldeburgh Festival of Music and the Arts	8–25 June
Ludlow Festival	24 June – 9 July
Chichester Festivities	1–17 July
York Early Music Festival	6–15 July
Harrogate International Festival	19 July – 4 August
Edinburgh International Festival	12 August – 1 September
Ross-on-Wye International Festival	16–27 August
Gloucester Three Choirs Festival	18–25 August
Norfolk and Norwich Festival, Norwich	3–14 October
Cheltenham Festival of Literature	12–21 October

Source: 'A calendar of culture', by Claudia Pritchard, *Observer*, 19 Nov 2000.

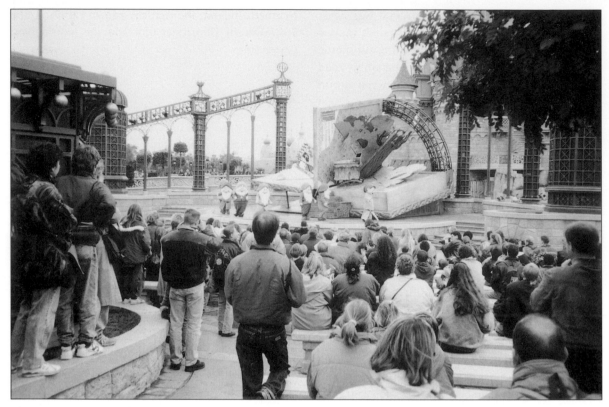

Figure 11.19 Site and event attraction: Snow White and the Seven Dwarfs parade at Disneyland, Paris. (*Photographed by the author*)

where they are held. In addition to these leading European music festivals there are countless smaller festivals in these countries, each of which makes an important contribution to local revenues through tourist visits. While the largest festivals tend to run during the tourist season, many smaller events are held outside the peak summer periods, especially in cases where sites are subject to heavy congestion during the season. Lengths of music festivals vary greatly, from two or three days up to, in the case of the Drottningholm (Sweden) summer season, more than three months.

Ad hoc events can always be built around a commemorative date; the year 2000, for example, was the two hundred and fiftieth anniversary of the death of Johann Sebastian Bach, and events were staged around the world, and especially in Germany, to commemorate this important date. Of course, if the

festivals are capable of drawing people from greater distances, and keeping them on site for longer periods of time, the average spend increases; visitors will need overnight accommodation and food, and will be tempted to spend money on other activities during their stay. Other festivals embrace the fine arts, crafts, drama, dance, literature or poetry. Some will commemorate historical occasions, and may be highlighted with parades, pageants and *son et lumière* events. Most provide an opportunity for hosts and guests to meet and get to know one another. As well as meeting a wide variety of tourist needs, they also fulfil an essential requirement of contemporary tourism, that of sustainable development.

Exhibitions of all kinds, cultural or otherwise, feature prominently in global tourism. The French, never slow to exploit their cultural tourism opportunities, mounted an unusual outdoor exhibition of controversial works by the Spanish sculptor Botero in 1992. What was unusual about this event was that the massive sculptures were arrayed along each side of the Champs Elysées, Paris's major arterial highway. So successful did this experiment prove, that four years later another sculptural display of fifty works by modern sculptors was similarly displayed along the same street, reinforcing Paris's reputation as *the* city of culture for the European visitor.

The growth and promotion of 'dark tourism'

The beauty of tourism is that the number of products that can be devised to interest the tourist is virtually unlimited. One reads regularly in the press of new ideas that have been promoted, of new – and frequently bizarre – reasons tourists advance for visiting a site. Perhaps our ideas of what is appropriate to view have changed a little since the nineteenth century, when in England people would travel considerable distances to view public hangings, while in the United States Coney Island amusement park displayed 300 dwarfs in 'Midget City' and publicly electrocuted Topsy, a performing elephant, as a tourist event. There remains, nonetheless, a fascination at times bordering on the macabre to observe scenes such as those exploiting sudden and violent death, sites which Chris Rojek [1] has termed 'black spots'. Rojek describes the flood of tourists to Scotland to see the scene of the Pan Am crash at Lockerbie in 1988. Similarly, following the earthquake which rocked the city of San Francisco at the end of 1989, visitors to the city were asking to be accommodated in hotels that 'overlooked the collapsed freeway'. The BBC reported in 1995 [2] that visitors to Blackpool were clamouring to 'ride the Alan Bradley Death Tram' after a character of this name was killed in front of the tram in the popular soap opera *Coronation Street*.

The term *thanatourism* [3], or 'dark tourism' has been used to describe the tourist fascination with death and the macabre. Motives for such tourism may be thought questionable, although travel to 'dark' sites cannot necessarily be ascribed to gratuitous pleasure – visits to World War II concentration camps are popular, for instance, but these, especially by Israeli parties, can often take the form of a pilgrimage, while for others the visit is tied in with historical interest. Major death sites associated with celebrities, however, do attract more than their fair share of curious observers; Jim Morison's tomb at Père-Lachaise cemetery in Paris is said to be the most visited grave in the cemetery; the outbuilding in Seattle where Kurt Cobain of pop group Nirvana fame committed suicide in 1994 was torn down, but the site is still visited by hundreds of admirers, just as hundreds still seek out the underground road tunnel in Paris where Diana, Princess of Wales, had her fatal car crash.

Whatever the merits of thanatourism, the quest for the bizarre features ever more prominently in tourist motivation. Sometimes this is a reflection of the desire for ever more dangerous activities, whether sporting or otherwise, particularly among the younger tourist. The *Sunday Times* [4] coined the term 'terror tourism' to describe the growing trend for tourists to plan visits to countries beset by political disturbances or even civil wars.

Let us take a look at one particular site with a dark history, little known even within its own country but with considerable potential for tourism visits. Moreover, this site houses a building with a strong claim to be both the largest building in the world and the historical centre for the origin of mass tourism. At Prora, on the island of Rügen in North Germany, lies the so-called Colossus of Prora, a huge holiday complex built on the authority of Adolf Hitler by the Kraft Durch Freude (KdF) movement in 1936, which within two years was organizing package holidays annually for more than 10 million Germans. It was Hitler's intention to build the grandest seaside resort in the world, one of five planned complexes, of which that at Prora was the only one completed before the outbreak of war. The original building was 4.4 km long, with 10,000 rooms designed to accommodate 20,000 holiday-makers. After the war, occupying Soviet troops attempted to

Figure 11.20 The KdF holiday complex at Prora, Rügen Island, Germany. (*Photographed by the author*)

blow the building up, but its size defeated them. The local authorities now are torn between destroying it and finding alternative uses, possibly as a spa. It currently houses a People's Army museum, the country's biggest youth hostel, a tram museum and accommodation for refugees, but receives virtually no promotion, even nationally, and appears on no maps. Most recently, a number of the buildings have been used for raves, with young Germans taking advantage of the site to go clubbing at minimum cost. The building's place in tourism history is assured, while its sheer bulk and ugliness typifying the architecture of its day (of which little remains today) make it a must for seekers of the bizarre.

The scope for innovative tourism

Some of the more curious tourist attractions in recent years, as well as efforts to develop tourist interest in the banal or bizarre, are listed below:

- Corpses displayed as tourist attractions. Perfectly preserved bodies retrieved from bogs in Denmark are on display in museums at Silkeborg and Moesgaard.

 The exhibition of corpses in this manner, however, raises serious ethical questions.
- At the Zhukovsky airbase south of Moscow, rides are available in MiG-25 Foxbat jet fighters. Heights of up to 83,000 feet are achieved, and costs can exceed £7,000 a ride. There is no shortage of takers.
- SATOUR, the South African Tourist Office, has introduced visits to Soweto Township, an impoverished suburb in which Nelson Mandela's former home is based. Visitors also glimpse Winnie Mandela's palatial house. Visits can also be made to Robben Island, the scene of Mandela's imprisonment, where his cell features prominently.
- China has opened the site of a hitherto secret armaments factory, to allow tourists to practise on the firing range with rocket launchers and anti-aircraft guns. The tour is particularly popular with Americans and Japanese.
- The world's first dung museum has opened at Machaba safari camp in Botswana. Necklaces of dried polished dung can be bought in the shop.
- In Sweden, moose droppings are sold as souvenirs to tourists visiting Lapland, and have been given as gifts to conference delegates. The reaction of the delegates was not recorded.
- Lignite pits near Hamburg attract tourists because of their resemblance to the lunar landscape.
- Two-hour guided tours are available around the municipal rubbish dump at Fresh Kills, Staten Island, New York. Visits to urban sewers have also proved popular in some cities.
- Plans have been drawn up in the Cayman Islands to sink a Russian destroyer off-shore. This will not only attract scuba divers, but will also offer protection to the coral reefs.
- Special tours and cruises are arranged for visitors to approach active or recently active volcanoes. These include sites in Ecuador, Sicily, Crete, Nicaragua, Iceland and the Azores.
- Walking tours across the arches of Sydney Harbour Bridge have proved immensely popular. A wetsuit and safety cable are obligatory accompaniments.
- Two hour guided tours are on offer in Berlin's red light district, with off-duty prostitutes acting as tour guides. They will answer clients' questions on all aspects of the city, including their own activities.

- At Bovington in Dorset, the army medical team put on realistic displays of amputations for visitors.
- A light bulb that has been burning continuously since 1901 in Livermore Fire Station, California, and is featured in the Guinness Book of Records, has become a minor tourist attraction. The station maintains a visitor book for comments.
- A public toilet has opened in Brisbane, Australia, at a cost of £1 million. Sited in a superb art deco building, it has viewing decks overlooking the sea.
- Tours of the Kennedy International Space Centre include observations of scheduled space shuttle launches.
- Omanis visit Salalah, on the southern tip of Oman, between June and September each year because of the unusual rainfall in the monsoon

season – this is the only area of the Arabian Gulf so affected. Perhaps the only example of rain attracting tourism?

Hoteliers are noted entrepreneurs, and many have introduced special events to attract out-of-season tourists, or fill rooms during the recent recession. 'Murder weekends' have been popular, while one hotel offered heavy discounts for people whose surname was Smith. Perhaps the prize for originality should be awarded to the group of hotels situated near the M25, London's notoriously crowded orbital motorway. These developed a series of 'M25 theme nights', with a 'motorway madness' banquet.

Other hotels attract tourists because of the bizarre form of their accommodation. In the USA, tourists can stay at an underwater hotel, Jules' Undersea

Figure 11.21 Recognition for a tourist attraction of the future. The Berlin Wall, photographed immediately prior to its destruction, bears a prophetic message. (*Photographed by the author*)

Lodge at John Pennecamp Coral Reef State Park in Key Largo, Florida; they can bed down in railway cabooses at the Featherbed Railroad Company in Nice, California; spend a night in the cellblock at the Jailhouse Inn in Preston, Minnesota; or sleep underground in the Honeycombs at the Inn at Honey Run, Millersburg, Ohio.

All of this only goes to show that in the tourism business, some far-out ideas can be made to work. No one believed that Bradford could be turned into a popular tourist destination in the 1980s, yet it went on to become one of the success stories of British tourism.

References

(1) Rojek, C. (1993) *Ways of Escape: Modern Transformation in Leisure and Travel*. Basingstoke, Macmillan.
(2) Technology Season, BBC2, 7 Nov 1995.
(3) See, for example, Foley, M. and Lennon, J. (2000) Dark tourism, *Continuum*. Also Seaton, A. V. (1996) Guided by the dark: from thanatopsis to thanatourism. *International Journal of Heritage Studies* 2: 234–44.
(4) *Sunday Times*, 16 March 1997.

Questions and discussion points

1. Blackpool now lays stress on its beachfront entertainment, rather than its attractions for swimmers and bathers. Is this the future marketing strength for the British seaside resort, and could other British resorts follow suit? Which seaside resorts are not largely dependent upon the attractiveness of their beaches?

2. Certain types of tourist attraction pose complex ethical problems for the industry. We have seen in this chapter how mummified corpses put on display have generated tourism, but not without criticism. Another example is the use of ecclesiastical buildings as tourist attractions, when their prime purpose remains that of a place to worship. Can the demands of tourists and worshippers be satisfactorily reconciled, and how? Can you think of other issues which raise ethical questions of this kind?

3. Identify any modern buildings in your area which could become the focus of tourist interest. How would you market these? Could visits to the interior be arranged, and what problems would be posed by efforts to organize this?

4. How might the buildings at Prora be redeveloped to cater for modern tourism, and how would they best be promoted? Prora is one of the few sites of the Nazi regime remaining; many others have been deliberately destroyed since the war, including Hitler's holiday home, the Eagle's Nest, at Berchtesgaden and Spandau Prison, where Nazi leaders were incarcerated after the war. Argue the case for and against retaining these buildings for tourism. (*Note*: at the time of writing, this argument continues over the retention of the former Hitler bunker in Berlin.)

Assignment topics

1. As an assistant in the local tourist office of your town, you have been asked to identify potential attractions in the town which have not yet received much promotional effort. Draw up a list for the Tourist Officer, which:

   (a) indicates priority in terms of the sites' relative importance for tourism;

   (b) makes clear what the particular features of the attractions are, and how they should be promoted;

   (c) identifies any problems and constraints in promoting them.

2. Pleased with your report, the Tourist Officer now asks you to become involved in two further projects. She wants to produce a brochure for the town which will offer two walking tours. The first is to be a 'tourist trail', which will suggest an itinerary around the town, taking in the key attractions, for those with only a limited time to spend. The second is to be a 'shopping trail', identifying unique shops that will be likely to appeal to tourists, for which an illustrated guide and map will be prepared. Detailed artwork is not required at this stage, but present the two guides in the form of plans or diagrams, with a suitable covering report justifying your choices.

   NB: For the purpose of this assignment, you may choose any town in the area, and the two trails do not have to be in the same town.

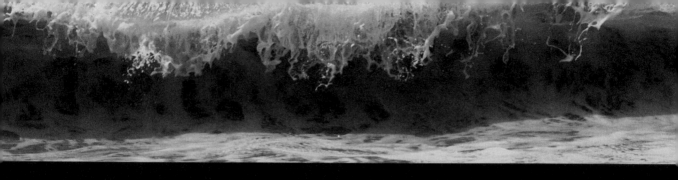

Chapter 12 Tour operating

Objectives

After studying this chapter, you should be able to:

- define the role of a tour operator, and distinguish between different types of operator;
- explain the functions of different types of operator;
- understand how operators interact with other sectors of industry;
- understand how the activities of operators are constrained;
- understand the basic principles behind the construction and marketing of a package tour;
- understand the appeal of the package tour to its various markets;
- evaluate alternative methods of tour distribution, and recognize the importance of new forms of electronic reservations and sales systems for operators and their clients.

The role of the tour operator

Tour operators perform a distinct function in the tourism industry; they purchase separate elements of transport, accommodation and other services, and combine them into a package which they then sell directly or indirectly to consumers. Their position in the market can be demonstrated by the diagram in Figure 12.1.

Tour operators are sometimes classed as wholesalers, in the sense that they purchase services, and *break bulk* (i.e. buy in large quantities in order to sell in smaller quantities). However, wholesalers do not normally change the product they buy before dis-

Figure 12.1 The place of the tour operator in the tourism system

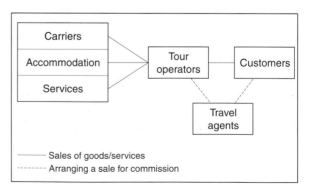

tributing it, and it is for this reason that some argue for an operator to be classed as a *principal*, or supplier, rather than a traditional 'middleman'. Their argument is based on the premise that by packaging a series of individual tourism products into a single whole new product, the *inclusive tour*, the operator is actually changing the nature of those products. In a sense, the operator becomes a 'light assembly' business, recognizing that the customers could well put together the same package themselves, but not necessarily at the same price, and less conveniently. The service which the tour operator provides is to buy in bulk, and thus secure considerable discounts from the suppliers which could not normally be matched by the customer buying direct. The operator is then able to assemble and present to the customer a package – the 'inclusive tour' – which is both convenient to purchase and competitively priced.

This service is also valuable to the principals in the travel and tourism industry. The travel industry operates in a business environment in which supply and demand are seldom in balance; nor can supply expand or contract quickly to take advantage of changes in demand. Both the airline and hotel businesses operate in circumstances which make it difficult to adjust their capacity in the short term. A scheduled flight, for example, *must* operate regardless of whether one passenger or a hundred are booked on it. A charter airline with a single type of aircraft – say a Boeing 757 with a maximum capacity of 239 passengers – cannot expand the number of seats to take advantage of peak opportunities, nor reduce capacity if demand falls slightly. We say that supply is 'lumpy'; that is, it cannot be expanded by a single seat, but must be expanded in blocks of seats, perhaps as many as 150 at a time in the case of aircraft. This is most clearly evidenced in the example of shuttle airline services, in which airlines have agreed to carry every passenger who turns up for a flight to a specific destination. If one too many passengers turns up for a flight, the airline must lay on another complete aircraft.

In these circumstances, carriers seek ways to adjust demand to fill available seats. This is important to keep down costs per passenger, and reduce waste of resources; the aircraft costs a certain amount of money to run, regardless of the number of passengers it carries, and this fixed cost is likely to be the major element in any transport costs. Tour operators have played a very useful role for the scheduled airlines, which can offer substantial discounts on seats that they know they themselves cannot fill. Here is one example to demonstrate this.

Example

Suppose that the fixed cost of flying a 140-seat plane from London to Athens and back is £27,000 (that includes capital costs, fuel, crew's wages etc.). Suppose also that the additional, or variable, cost per passenger is £26 (to cover administrative expenses such as writing the ticket, and providing in-flight refreshments, extra fuel, and so on). If the airline wants to budget for a small profit and estimates that at a price of £275 it can expect to sell 110 seats, then the cost and pricing looks like this:

Fixed cost	£27,000
110 passengers × £26	£2,860
Cost of return flight	£29,860
Sell 110 tickets at £275 each	£30,250
Profit	£390

Of course, if only 109 passengers show up, then sales drop by £275, costs by only £26, and the airline ends up losing £141. This is a very risky business!

This is where tour operators prove themselves so useful. By agreeing to purchase in bulk say, twenty-five seats, they can virtually ensure that the airline will fly at a profit. The question arises, what should the ticket price be? As far as the airline is concerned, anything above £26 a head will be profitable, as the fixed costs are already paid for. Tour operators will want the lowest price possible to ensure they can resell all twenty-five seats. Obviously, customers are unwilling to pay anything like the original £275 that was being asked, or they would have already booked with the airline itself. Let's say that after negotiating, the airline agrees to sell the seats to the tour operator at a net price of £150 each. The airline's budget now looks like this:

Fixed cost	£27,000
135 passengers × £26*	£3,510
Cost of return flight	£30,510
Sell 110 tickets at £275 each	£30,250
Sell 25 tickets at £150 each	£3,750
Revenue	£34,000
Profit	£3,490

*assumes all 25 seats are sold by tour operator.

The airline will now be very happy: it can afford to lose some of its standard fare-paying passengers and will still be in profit. What is more, it takes no responsibility for marketing the twenty-five seats which the operator must sell. The operator takes on this burden, which may involve it in heavy selling costs, but as long as it sets a sensible price which will still deliver a profit for the company after paying overhead costs, the customer will still be able to buy seats which represent good value. A figure of £199 might be considered reasonable under these circumstances.

To ensure that tour operators do not poach existing passengers, airlines usually impose various conditions on the resale of the tickets. The main condition is that the tour operator must build the trip into a package, or inclusive tour, and publish a number of brochures to prove it. However, the airlines themselves may also try to sell other seats to seat brokers, whose role is merely to buy seats in bulk and sell these off to any market it can find.

As the tour operators build their markets, so can they eventually decide that they will have enough customers to fill an aircraft, and can consider either part-chartering a plane with other operators, or even chartering a whole plane themselves. Eventually, they may be in a position to buy and operate their own airline to carry their customers, as do the leading British and other tour operators.

In exactly the same way, hoteliers attempt to use tour operators to fill their unsold bedrooms. They, too, have a high element of fixed costs in operating their properties, and are willing to provide substantial discounts to operators and others willing to commit themselves to buying rooms in bulk. As with airlines, once the fixed costs of the property have been covered by revenue, any price which more than pays for the variable cost will represent pure profit for the hotel. To this must be added the possibility that the operator, if the price is sufficiently attractive, may even be able to provide the hotel with guests during the winter period. This will mean that the hotel can retain staff year-round, possibly avoiding closing (closure means that no revenue is coming in at all, while the hotel will still attract costs for permanent staff, maintenance etc.). Hotels in the Mediterranean also find it difficult to reach the North European market direct, and so are delighted if their marketing is done for them by the tour operators in those countries. As a result, they have come to depend largely, and in some cases entirely, on tour operators to sell their rooms. In time, many larger operators started to run their own accommodation, but in practice this proved more difficult, and most operators eventually divested themselves of their overseas properties, preferring to sign contracts with overseas proprietors, often for the entire capacity of the hotel, and sometimes for several years in advance. The hoteliers' dependence upon these contracts and their inability to reach the marketplace in any other way has made them overly dependent upon tour operators, which in turn have used their dominant positions in the market to force down prices. The low profit levels achieved by the hoteliers meant cost cutting in the level of service they provided, with self-service menus offering clients limited choice. The number of complaints rose as a result. Unfortunately, at least as far as British clients are concerned, there is little apparent willingness to pay higher prices for better standards of service.

The specialized roles of tour operators

The domestic operator

Tour operators fulfil a number of roles, and are not only concerned with carrying traffic out of the country, although this is the role with which we most frequently associate them. Operators also exist to organize package holidays domestically, that is, to a destination within the country in which the tourists reside. These businesses form a much smaller element of the travel and tourism industry, because it is relatively simple for tourists to make their own arrangements within their own country. In the past, it was uncommon to find a tour operator which simultaneously organized both domestic and foreign package holidays, although of course the originator of the package tour, Thomas Cook, started as a domestic holiday organizer and later expanded into foreign holidays. However, as concentration in the industry develops and competition becomes fiercer, the larger operators are tending to expand into the domestic market. Thomson Holidays, one of the leading UK brands, briefly became a major player in the country cottage market. The longest established domestic programmes are coach tours, operated by such well-known companies as Shearings and Wallace Arnold. More recently, the larger hotel chains in Britain have also started their own package holiday programmes in order to help fill their rooms at weekends or in the off-peak seasons. The tourist boards in England, Wales and Scotland have strongly supported this development, and all three have helped to coordinate programmes of commissionable domestic inclusive tours in brochures available through retail travel outlets.

Fragmentation is evident in the sector organizing domestic programmes. Most companies are relatively small in this sector, and few are members of ABTA, or indeed of any travel organization. Most deal direct with the public, and are therefore not involved in retailing through the trade.

The incoming operator

Those countries such as Spain and Greece which are predominantly destination countries, rather than generating countries, will have an incoming travel sector that is as important as the outgoing. Organizations specializing in handling incoming foreign holiday-makers have a rather different role to that of outbound operators. Some are merely ground handling agents, and their role may be limited to organizing hotel accommodation on behalf of an overseas tour operator, or greeting incoming visitors and transferring them to their hotels. Other companies, however, will offer a comprehensive range of services, which may include negotiating with coach companies and hotels to secure the best quotations for contracts, organizing special-interest holidays or study tours, or providing dining or theatre arrangements. In some cases, companies specialize by the markets they serve, catering for the inbound Japanese or Israeli markets, for example.

In all, there are well over 300 tour companies in Britain which derive a major part of their revenue from handling incoming business. As with domestic operators, most of these are small companies, and more than a third are members of the British Incoming Tour Operators Association (BITOA), whose aim is to provide a forum for the exchange of information and ideas among members, to maintain standards of service and to act as a pressure group in dealing with other bodies in the UK who have a role to play in the country's tourism industry.

Incoming tour operators' services are marketed exclusively through the trade, and organizations work closely with public sector bodies in marketing their services.

Other specialization

Many operators recognize that their strengths can lie in specializing in some particular aspect of operating. Some outbound operators choose to specialize according to the *mode of transport* by which their clients will travel. Although our earlier example was based on air travel, other companies focus on coach transport, some (especially those involved in providing camping holidays abroad) organize package holidays for their clients which enable them to use their own private cars, and some have chosen to specialize in holidays using the railways. Ferry companies developed their own package tour programmes to promote sea travel using their services (although in recent years the British ferry operators have preferred to divest themselves of these activities in order to allow specialist operators to organize the programmes on their behalf). Naturally, the coach operators and railway companies have also sought to boost their carryings by building inclusive tours around their own forms of transport.

Finally, specialism among tour operators can be based on the markets they serve or the products they develop. The most common distinction is between on the one hand the *mass-market* operators, whose product – typically the 'sun, sea, sand' holiday – is designed to appeal to a very broad segment of the market, and, on the other hand, the *specialist* operator, which aims at a particular niche market. By trying to distinguish their product from those of their competitors, the niche market operators are not in such intense competition as are those in the mass market, and the product is less price sensitive as a result.

Specialists have a number of advantages over mass-market companies in the marketplace. Most carry small numbers of tourists, and can therefore use smaller accommodation units, such as the small, family-run hotels in Greece which are popular with many tourists, but are too small to interest the larger operators. As the specialist companies generally use scheduled carriers and do not have the level of commitment to a particular destination that their larger colleagues have, they can be more flexible, switching to other destinations if the market sours for any reason. Staff can generally be expected to have a better knowledge of the products, and as the market is less price sensitive, the intense price competition found in the mass marketplace is absent, allowing companies to make reasonable profits. However, if they are successful, there is always the danger that one of the larger operators will be attracted to their market and undercut them, as happened when Thomson Holidays decided to get into the Paris market and rapidly undercut the market leaders in that field.

Many companies seek to specialize by geographic destination. However, the danger of this particular specialism can be demonstrated in the collapse of the holiday market to Yugoslavia, following civil war in the 1990s. Yugotours, the leading specialist to the area, was forced not only to change its destination, but even its brand name, in order to build a new market, but still failed to re-establish itself, and the brand disappeared.

Specialism by market is common. Some companies choose to appeal to a particular age group, as do Saga Holidays, targeting the over-50s market, or Club 18–30, targeting the younger client. The singles market – fast growing, as social changes increase the proportion of divorced people in our society – is also served by specialists such as Solo Holidays. Obviously, there will be ample opportunity to specialize according to the specific interests, activities or hobbies of clients, and tour companies have been established to cater for such diverse needs as those of vegetarians, those with an interest in various cultural activities, golfing or angling enthusiasts,

Figure 12.2 Specialist holidays 'on safari'. (*Courtesy Abercrombie & Kent Ltd, London*)

or even such highly specialized activities as textile weaving. One company which has proved itself highly successful in specific targeting is Cycling for Softies, which caters for tourists interested in using bicycles as a mode of transport but still seeking comfortable and well-equipped overnight accommodation. This company's main focus is on travel in France, and it is therefore specializing both in destination and market served.

The role of air brokers

One other role should be examined here; that of those who specialize in providing seats in bulk to other tour operators. These specialists are known as *air brokers*, or where their business is principally concerned with consolidating flights on behalf of operators that have not achieved good load factors for their charters, they are termed *consolidators*. These must also now obtain Air Travel Organisers' Licences (ATOLs) from the CAA in order to operate.

Brokers negotiate directly with airlines, buying seats in bulk and arranging to sell these, either in smaller bulk blocks or even individually, to operators or travel agents. They provide the airlines, especially those companies which may find it difficult to obtain good load factors on some legs of their operations, with a good distribution service, and in return the airlines are willing to offer very low net rates to fill their remaining seats. The brokers put their own mark-up on the seats and take on the responsibility of marketing them for whatever price they can get. In doing so, they have largely replaced the former 'bucket shop' operators who performed a similar function but often infringed IATA regulations in 'dumping' tickets at discounted prices on the market. Deregulation on an international scale has now virtually eradicated the former illegal operations and made them 'respectable'. Many mark-ups are very low, the broker making money on the huge turnover of seats they achieve, and in short-term investments in the money market.

The structure of the outbound tour operating business

There are approximately 1,200 licensed tour operators in the UK, a figure which increased dramatically during the 1990s but has since stabilized. Of these, some 670 were members of ABTA at the beginning of 2000. However, the market is dominated by a small number of large operators, and the process of concentration into the hands of this small minority is ongoing. The four leading operators – Thomson Holidays, Airtours, Thomas Cook Group (JMC) and First Choice together held some 54 per cent of the market in 1999, based on applications for ATOL bonding. This trend to horizontal integration and concentration is also evident in other European countries. The second characteristic in the industry is an equivalent trend to vertical integration, with a growing number of the largest companies owning and/or controlling their own airlines and retail travel agencies. This trend has been less apparent on the Continent, at least as far as airline and tour operator links are concerned, but this picture is beginning to change with the development of a third characteristic, the very rapid process of internationalization of the industry throughout Europe, with concentration now taking place across borders in an effort to dominate the European marketplace.

The initial phases of concentration can be traced to the rapid expansion which took place in the tour operating business after the 1960s in Britain, but occurred slightly later in other parts of western Europe and North America. Leisure activities, and holidays in particular, were seen as substantial growth areas for the future by many industries in the 1960s, and encouraged many new companies to come into the business, while those already established expanded quickly to maintain their dominance in the field. This led to a cycle in which many companies collapsed, due to three main problems:

1. growing too fast, over-borrowing to finance the

expansion and in some cases lacking the management expertise to operate larger companies;

2. making insufficient profit to survive, in the face of intense competition which drove down prices;

3. being hit by external problems such as rises in the price of fuel, political unrest in some of the destination countries, and economic recession at home.

This has been a pattern for the industry throughout the past forty years. Even as far back as 1964, the industry's first major collapse – that of Fiesta Tours – led to tighter controls being imposed on members of ABTA. In 1974, the failure of the leading company of its day, Court Line and its subsidiary Clarksons Holidays, resulted in 50,000 passengers being stranded abroad at the height of the summer holiday season, as a direct outcome of the factors outlined

Table 12.1 Passengers authorized by CAA bonded tour licences,1999 (000s)

Thomson Holidays (a)	4,037
Airtours (b)	3,142
JMC (c)	2,825
First Choice Holidays (d)	1,967
Virgin	548
Cosmos	400
Kuoni	241
British Airways Holidays	228
Libra	192
Kosmar Villa	162
Manos (e)	155
Hotelplan/Inghams (Migros)	144
Saga Holidays	139
All other operators	5,983
Total bonded tours	22,183

(a) plus 294 under the Crystal brand.
(b) plus 318 under the Direct Holidays brand, 154 under the Cresta brand, 147 under the Panorama brand.
(c) plus 130 under the Thomas Cook brand and 127 under the Style brand.
(d) plus 850 under the Unijet brand.
(e) Manos was purchased the following year by Airtours.

Source: CAA figures.

above. In 1991, the International Leisure Group, owners of Britain's then second-largest tour operator Intasun, was brought down by a combination of recession at home, the weakness of the pound, cut-throat pricing against the leading operator Thomsons, and over-ambitious expansion, especially in the efforts of the company to develop scheduled services for its charter airline Air Europe. The collapse in 1995 of Best Travel, another company within the top seven, emphasized the continuing instability of the tour operating business, and encouraged further mergers and takeovers.

Most UK operators are very small companies, with perhaps only the top 40 being of any real significance in the market. Table 12.1 provides details of the largest companies, in terms of passenger numbers authorized by the CAA.

Although the picture of actual market shares changes rapidly throughout the year, on the basis of ATOL capacity, in 1999 Thomson Holidays would have held around 18 per cent of the UK market, Airtours 14 per cent, JMC (Thomas Cook Group) 13 per cent and First Choice 9 per cent. By the end of that year, however, the two leading companies were running much closer. Initial figures for all-inclusive tour carryings for the year ending September 2001 would indicate that Airtours may have overtaken its major rival, Thomson Holidays; at the time of writing, the contender held 5.33 million seats, giving it 17 per cent of the market, while Thomson, at 4.73 million, held 15 per cent.

With more than half of all package holidays sold through travel agents being organized by the four leading companies, there is obvious concern about an oligopolistic concentration. When the Monopolies and Mergers Commission, as it then was, investigated this concentration in the past (notably at the time of the takeover of Horizon Holidays by Thomson in 1988), it judged that this *horizontal* integration was not against the public interest, given that competition still ensured prices were kept down. Airtours, which has been primarily responsible for the fall in Thomson's market share, appears set on achieving the number one position, so the intense price cutting of recent years is likely to continue in the short term. In 2000, summer holidays for the following year were already being discounted by 30 per cent by the leading travel agents. What is perhaps more worrying is the trend to *directional selling*, in which those travel agencies owned by the leading operators are directing sales towards their parent companies at the expense of other competitors. One study, reported in *Travel Weekly*, of the peak (post-Christmas) holiday sales in 1999/2000 revealed 64 per cent of all sales at Going Places, owned by Airtours, were for that operator's products; 67 per cent of Lunn Poly sales were for parent Thomson Holidays and 62 per cent of Thomas Cook's sales favoured Sunworld, that company's leading operating brand.

Some companies have also been over-ambitious regarding the size of the potential market when forecasting their aircraft and accommodation needs for the coming year, and have contracted for too many seats and rooms, with the result that they are obliged to offload these at whatever price they can get during the season. This constant imbalance between supply and demand places severe pressures on profits in the industry, which have been meagre for the past two decades.

The leading operators believe that low-price strategies will eventually force out of the market the smaller and less efficient companies, leaving rich pickings to be shared among the remaining contenders. However, there is little evidence from past experience to support this view. As companies such as Horizon or Intasun have been absorbed or collapsed, so others have risen to take their place. The demise of ILG resulted in the formation of four new tour operating companies, each intent on picking up market share from their antecedent. While only two of these – Sunworld and Club 18–30 – were to survive the recession of the early 1990s, the growth of the former company in particular (now absorbed into the JMC brand), and subsequent rise in market share by others within the top ten, tend to suggest there is more scope for competition at the top than might have appeared to be the case. This does not refute the evidence that key market share tends to remain with the three or four leading players.

Efforts have been made in recent years by the smaller operators to regain the high ground, by impressing on the public their more personal levels of service and greater expertise, and to distance themselves from the mass-market operators. The Association of Independent Tour Operators (AITO), with a membership at the time of writing of some 150, works closely with the independent travel agents to sell distinctive products. The appearance of TIPTO (the Truly Independent Professional Travel Organisation) in 1999, launched to offset the directional selling by large agency chains of leading operators' products, reflects the concern felt among the smaller companies in the industry about the growing concentration of power in the hands of the leading companies. The new organization plans to deal exclusively with a selection of around 1,000 independent travel agents.

Profit squeezes have resulted in constant restructuring throughout the tour operating sector of the industry in recent years, leading to the collapse of some well-established names while others grew through mergers and takeovers. A short resumé of the most significant of these events during the years 1989 to mid-2000 will be helpful here:

1989
- Thomson Holidays takes over Horizon Holidays, Britain's third largest operator, obtaining 38 per cent of the market

1990
- Owners Abroad undertakes a staged purchase of the Redwing Holidays group from BA (until 1990–91)
- ILG buys Sol Holidays, and from Granada the Quest group of brand name holidays
- Airtours forms Eurosites camping division

1991
- ILG collapses

1992
- Novotours, formed after the ILG collapse, itself collapses

- Midland Bank sells Thomas Cook to German operator LTU (14 per cent) and German bank WestDeutsche Landesbank (WestLB) (86 per cent)
- Dan-Air collapses
- Airtours buys Pickfords retail chain

1993

- Riva Holidays, the second company founded following the collapse of ILG, also goes out of business
- Formation of Inspirations Holidays, which establishes a strategic alliance with Best Travel, forming Goldcrest Aviation. Inspirations develops joint venture with A T Mays chain to set up travel agencies
- Airtours attempts unsuccessfully to take over Owners Abroad, but acquires Aspro with its airline Inter European Airways and the Hogg Robinson retail chain, which it merges with Pickfords to form new agency Going Places
- Owners Abroad establishes a working relationship with Thomas Cook, which buys a 21 per cent share of the company

1994

- Thomson Holidays acquires its first domestic operation, Country Holidays, followed by purchase of Blakes Country Holidays and English Country Cottages
- Airtours acquires Scandinavian Leisure Group and Spanair from SAS
- Owners Abroad establishes International Travel Holdings in Canada, operating under the brand Signature. The company is renamed and re-launched as First Choice Holidays; old brands Tjaereborg, Martin Rooks and Sunfare are eliminated, and new direct-sell brand Eclipse launched
- Yugotours and Ultimate Holidays collapse

1995

- Best Travel, Britain's seventh largest operator, collapses, the biggest failure since ILG. Other collapses in the same year include Vilmar Travel, draining the Air Travel Trust Fund
- Inspirations buys the charter carrier Caledonian from British Airways

- Formation of Flying Colours Group, which purchases Club 18–30 and links this with its Sunset brand
- Airtours buys Canadian operator Sunquest Vacations
- Inspirations buys 28 branches of John Hilary Travel, giving it control over 88 A T Mays retail travel branches

1996

- Collapse of the Flight Company and Go-Air plunges the ATTF further into the red. Other collapses this year include All Jamaica, Sunstyle, Globespan and its airline Excalibur Airways
- Thomas Cook buys Sunworld (which also controls a Canadian operator) and Time Off
- Carnival Cruises, the leading US cruise company, buys 29.6 per cent of Airtours. Airtours buys Scandinavian company Spies

1997

- Monopolies and Mergers Commission gives green light for expansion of takeovers and mergers
- Flying Colours launches its own airline
- Suntours, specialist tour operator to Turkey, and domestic operator Rainbow Holidays collapse (the latter later rejuvenated by First Choice Holidays)
- Airtours buys Sun International, Belgium's largest operator and owner of British operators Cresta and Bridge Travel Group, and also Suntrips, Californian tour operator
- Thomson Holidays buys specialist operator Austravel, Crystal International Travel Group, Jetsave and Fritidsresor (Sweden's second largest operator)
- Carlson Group buys Inspirations Holidays

1998

- Thomson floats on stock exchange, buys Simply Travel, Magic Travel, domestic operator Blakes Holidays
- Airtours buys Panorama Holidays, Direct Holidays, and a minority stake in Germany's Frosch Touristik including airline and operator FTi (balance bought one year later)

- First Choice buys Hayes and Jarvis, Unijet, UK operator Rainbow, plus two regional travel agency chains Bakers Dolphin and Intatravel, with plans to build a nationwide chain under the brand Travel Choice
- Thomas Cook buys majority stake in Carlson's UK operations, including tour operator Inspirations, Caledonian Airways and Carlson WorldChoice retail chain. Cook's Sunworld Division buys Flying Colours Group, including brands Flying Colours, Sunset Holidays and Club 18–30
- Eurocamp buys rival camping operator Keycamp Holidays

1999
- Thomson buys Headwater Holidays, Spanish Harbour Holidays, Travel House (retailer and direct sell operator), and retail chains Sibbald and Callers Pegasus. Sets up no-frills operator Just. Fritidsresor buys leading Polish company Scan Holidays and Norway's Via Group (retail chain which includes operator Prisma Tours)
- Airtours launches hostile bid for First Choice, blocked by European Commission
- First Choice buys Sunsail Holidays and Meon Travel. Unsuccessful effort to merge with Kuoni
- Kuoni buys long-haul specialist Voyages Jules Verne
- Thomas Cook rebrands its main operating and airline divisions as JMC, drops brands Sunworld and Sunset, and integrates Inspirations into programme. Integrates Carlson WorldChoice into its retail operations under Thomas Cook banner. Establishes Thomas Cook Direct (direct-sell operation) and Thomas Cook Plus (hypermarket chain)
- Preussag, owners of Germany's leading operators, takes controlling interest in Thomas Cook
- Eurocamp rebrands as Holidaybreak

2000
- Preussag (owner of Germany's biggest operator, TUI Group) takes over Thomson Holidays, and prepares to sell its 51 per cent share in Thomas Cook to satisfy the European Commissioners

- Airtours acquires long-haul specialist Jetset, Manos Holidays (integrated with Panorama to form Panorama Manos), Sunway Travel (coach operator), and 50 per cent of Holetur Club (hotels)
- First Choice forms strategic alliance with Royal Caribbean Cruises, which takes 20 per cent of the company. First Choice also buys Ten Tours with operations in France, Germany, Austria, Belgium and Spain, and UK company Sunquest. Further purchases include Spanish company Barcelo Group's travel interests, with hotels in Spain and a stake in Air Europa, and Swiss company Taurus Tours
- Germany's second largest operator, C&N Touristik, owner of NUR brand, buys Thomas Cook from Carlson Corporation
- Holidaybreak buys Rainbow Holidays from First Choice, integrates and later drops the brand
- Germany's third largest operator, Rewe, acquires LTU and DER, integrating these into a single company holding 22 per cent of the German market
- Thomson Holidays sells its Holiday Cottages group to US-owned Cedant, the world's biggest accommodation franchiser.

2001 (to March)
- Thomas Cook and British Airways Holidays merge their long-haul scheduled tour operating interests, claiming 16 per cent of the market, close to that of market leader Kuoni
- First Choice buys Sun Holidays, chain of travel agencies in Canada
- Thomas Cook forms a marketing agreement with web site operator lastminute.com

Integration in the industry

Nothing spells out more clearly than this list the rapid changes taking place and the competitive environment within the industry. We are witnessing an escalation in mergers and takeovers, coupled with an increasingly international perspective in the tour

Table 12.2   Integration between the UK's leading operators, charter airlines and travel agents (mid-2000)

Airline	Tour operator	Travel agent
Britannia Airways	Thomson Travel	Lunn Poly
Airtours Aviation	Airtours	Going Places, Travel World
Air 2000	First Choice Holidays	TravelChoice, Bakers Dolphin, Holiday Hypermarket
JMC Air	JMC Holidays	Thomas Cook
Monarch Airlines	Cosmos Holidays/Avro	

operating business, as British and other European operators look abroad for opportunities to expand and dominate the market through purchasing power. The leading operators' purchases of North American companies is also partly explained by a desire to spread the seasonal flow of traffic, thus obtaining better year-round usage of aircraft. Risk is also reduced by ensuring a more even spread of revenue between markets in North America, the UK and mainland Europe.

After the Monopolies and Mergers Commission (now the Competition Commission) gave the industry the green light for further mergers in 1997, concentration in the hands of the big four operators rose sharply.

Along with this process of horizontal integration is that of vertical integration between tour operators, their suppliers and their retailers. In Britain (and to a lesser extent in other European countries) the operators have sought to maintain control over their transport supply in particular, usually through direct ownership of an airline. This helps them to control overall standards of the package, to increase overall profitability within the group, and at the same time to ensure the operator a supply of air seats and hotel rooms when demand is heavy, although operators often take the precaution of obtaining some of their seats through other airlines. This will enable them, when demand falls, to retain their own aircraft seats while 'dumping' other carriers' unwanted seats. There are further operational and marketing advantages in owning and controlling take-off and landing slots.

Operators need to be carrying around 400,000 passengers a year to secure the critical mass that will

make it economically viable to consider establishing their own airline. However, pressure on profits in recent years has caused a number of large operators to view leasing as a more attractive proposition to purchasing aircraft.

Because of this rapid escalation in integration, any description of the current structure of the industry in this text is bound to be no more than a snapshot at a given moment in time, and will no doubt be subject to modification even before this book gets into print. The picture at the time of writing is illustrated in Table 12.2.

Table 12.2 reveals that not only are the leading operators owners of the leading charter carriers in Britain, but that there are also close links between them and the major British travel agency chains. Table 12.3 also reveals the concentration in the market of the charter carriers owned by these operators.

The Competition Commission has shown little interest in investigating or controlling the process of horizontal integration in recent years, but did undertake an investigation into vertical integration in the industry. The then Monopolies and Mergers Commission was asked in 1996 to consider:

Table 12.3   Estimated market shares of the UK's leading charter airlines, 1999

Airline	Market share (%)
Britannia Airways	22
Monarch Airlines	18
Airtours Aviation	18
JMC	16
Air 2000	16
Others	10

1. whether agents under the control of tour operators sell those operators' programmes in preference to others, and whether they therefore offer the public biased advice on the purchase of inclusive tours;
2. whether vertically integrated companies control and fix prices of their programmes;
3. whether these agents fail to advise their customers of their links with tour operators;
4. the practice of agents of insisting that customers buy their own company's insurance policies, often at inflated prices, in order to benefit from the discounts offered on the holidays they sell;
5. whether agents are removing, or threatening to remove, from display brochures of independent agents if commissions payable are deemed insufficient.

The government was slow to act following the MMC report which recommended separation of insurance from discounting, the abolition of the status of 'most favoured customer' and the need to specify ownership of retail chains. In the event, by 1998 companies were being informed that they could not insist that customers buy the recommended insurances, but no further ruling was imposed until 2000, when the Department of Trade and Industry, under the Foreign Package Holidays Order 2000, ruled that agents owned by a tour operator and controlling more than 5 per cent of the package tour market would in future have to publicly identify their links with suppliers, both in promotional material and in their shop displays. At the time of writing, however, no ruling regarding the directional selling by agents of their own companies' products has been announced, in spite of the evidence that this is clearly taking place. Thomas Cook has not been obliged to follow this new ruling, on the grounds that the retailer is the parent company in this relationship – a curious logic. Neither are the links that have been formed between agency consortia and operators required to be made public. The Order makes no ruling about identifying links where selling involves call centres, web sites and teletext, even though these methods of distribution are growing rapidly. In these respects, the ruling goes no way towards satisfying the complaints of the independent operators and agents about unfair trading.

Tour operating within the European Union

The process of integration within the UK is paralleled to a large extent on the Continent, and other European companies have been actively purchasing holiday companies abroad, particularly within Britain. Investment in the tour operating business by foreign companies is nothing new (Cosmos has always been a Swiss-owned company) but inroads have markedly increased in recent years. The listing of developments given earlier will reveal that, with the exception of First Choice, all major British tour companies are now foreign-owned.

Germany is the leading country in Europe, both in terms of the number of package holiday-makers carried and the strength of the industry. Composition and ownership of the leading operators in the country are complicated, although ultimately a significant share of the industry is actually publicly owned through the states and the regional authorities, which control the savings banks. These in turn have invested heavily in tour operating businesses. Preussag, which owns TUI, the leading tour brand in Germany, sold some 13.5 million packages in 1999 and controls nearly 3,500 travel agencies, sixty aircraft and four ships. Operating control is in the hands of the Westdeutsche Landesbank (WestLB) whose major shareholder is the state of North Rhine-Westphalia. TUI Group controls about 15 different well-established tour brands. The second major operator is C&N Touristik, which was formed in 1998 as a joint venture between Lufthansa airline's charter wing Condor and the Karstadt/Quelle retailing organizations. This company controls Neckermann und Reisen (NUR), *inter alia*, a major player which has recently taken over a number of medium-sized German operators. Other major players include

Rewe, a leading supermarket chain which controls tour operator ITS and recently acquired LTU and its operating company LTT and DER Tours (formerly owned by the German railway) – these three are in the process of integration at the time of writing – and FTi (Frosch Touristik International), which the British operator Airtours now controls. In Germany, the control over travel agencies by the big players is squeezing out the independents and threatening those operators without significant retail outlets.

German operators also dominate the market in Belgium, the Netherlands and Luxembourg, while British companies such as Airtours and Thomson largely control operators in the Scandinavian countries. In France and Italy, there has been less foreign investment, and France's leading operator, Club Méditerranée, is regaining its position after a period of indecision. The Swiss operator Kuoni is not only the leading player in its own country, but has a strong presence in other European countries, making it Europe's fifth largest company.

As in Britain, all these operators have recognized the importance of building their numbers in order to buy at the lowest price and control the markets. Transnational mergers will become increasingly common, limited only by the anti-monopoly forces of the European Commission. Evidence of the strength of buying power among leading Continental operators can be seen in the comparative pricing structure between tour operators in Britain and on the Continent; where formerly it could pay for foreign residents to fly to Britain to begin their package holiday, there is a growing number of instances where the reverse is now the case, and standard packages can be bought at substantially cheaper prices by British customers if bought abroad.

Economic forces in tour operating

The expansion of leisure time and greater discretionary income during the latter part of the twentieth century led to a rapid rise in demand for overseas holidays in the early phases of this development, during both the winter and summer seasons, but the increase slowed in the later years, with a downturn in the final year of the century.

Tour operators, recognizing the strong growth potential in the overseas holiday market, sought to gain significant increases in market share while at the same time attempting to increase the total size of the market, by encouraging those who traditionally took domestic holidays to travel abroad. To achieve this, they slashed prices. Large companies used their purchasing muscle to drive down suppliers' prices (at some cost to quality in a number of cases); they introduced cheap, 'no frills' holidays through subsidiary companies such as Thomson's Skytours – and more recently, Just, a programme which offers no transfers, no in-flight meals and no resort representatives. Arguably, this new offering can barely be considered a package. However, the budget-conscious C2D market have been attracted by such packages, although dissatisfaction levels are likely to be higher. Finally, profit margins were trimmed. Thomsons and its leading competitors, each determined not to be

Table 12.4 Europe's dominant players (as at May, 2000)

Company	ITs (000s)	Travel agents	Planes	Ships	Hotels
Preussag	13,500	3,469	60	4	164
Airtours	9,000	940	47	11	26
Thomson	7,000	862	41	4	13
C&N	6,000	1,200	39	0	51
Kuoni	4,000	150	3	0	2

Source: 'Sun, sea and scaling up' © *Financial Times*, 16 May 2000.

Table 12.5 Package tours by air, 1990–99 (000s)

Year	Total AITs
1990	11.4
1991	10.6
1992	12.6
1993	13.3
1994	15.2
1995	15.3
1996	13.9
1997	15.4
1998	17.4
1999	15.0

Source: IPS.

undersold, engaged in the periodic repricing of their holiday programme during the selling season. Thomson, from 1983 onwards, introduced the strategy of brochure reissues with cheaper prices, and this became a regular feature of the tour operating price war. Holiday prices during the period remained relatively stationary as a result, while real buying power increased greatly.

While these moves certainly expanded the market, over-optimistic forecasts of traffic growth also led to surpluses in supply; capacity generally exceeded demand each year, and operators were then forced into offloading seats at bargain-basement prices. This factor has been a key one in the growth of late bookings. Traditionally, bookings for package holidays have occurred in the weeks immediately following Christmas, allowing operators more time to balance supply and demand, and aiding their cash flow – deposits paid by clients in January would be invested and earn interest for the company until its bills had to be paid, which in some cases could be as late as September or October. Holiday-makers soon came to realize, however, that if they refrained from booking holidays until much nearer their time of travel, they could snap up late booking bargains. The development of computerized reservations systems allowed operators to update their late availability opportunities quickly, putting cheap offers on the market at very short notice, which made late bookings convenient as well as attractively priced. The loss to the

operators themselves was considerable, with the opportunity to invest revenue and earn interest now falling from a period of months to only weeks. Uncertainty about the forward booking position also made tour operations management more difficult. Operators therefore set about reversing this trend, by a policy of *fluid pricing*. Introduced by Thomson Holidays in 1996 and soon copied by the other leading operators, this entailed offering holidays in the brochures at different prices, with high discounts for early booking and reduced discounts as the time of the holiday approached. Some operators even quoted prices above the highest brochure price, where demand was sufficiently strong, although the legality of this has been questioned. Not surprisingly, this led to a good deal of dissatisfaction among clients who had booked earlier at higher prices. In the latter years of the 1990s, operators also tended to launch their brochures for the following year at an ever earlier date, resulting at times in agents having to find room for brochures covering three different periods – summer and winter of the current year, and summer of the following year. *Travel Weekly* reported that while the summer 1996 brochures were launched by the major companies on 25 August of the previous year, subsequent years saw launch dates falling, to 4 July, 2 May, and in 1998 even as early as 30 April, until sense prevailed and a more rational approach adopted in recent years. There is evidence, however, that early launches did boost sales, and those operators for which the numbers carried meant everything clearly benefited.

The long-haul market

The tendency for all mass-market operators to focus on low price rather than quality or value for money led to this type of tour moving down-market. As it did so, tourists at the top end of the market, particularly those who had travelled frequently, began to travel independently more frequently, and to more distant destinations. The demand for long-haul packages throughout the period expanded much faster than the growth of short-haul tours, and has continued to expand throughout the recent period of recession. More than 20 per cent of all holidays are now taken to long-haul destinations annually, and this figure is expected to continue to increase at a faster pace than the more traditional package. The fastest growing destination has been the United States, with its particular appeal of Disney World Florida, New Zealand, Australia (especially during and following the 2000 Olympics) and Thailand, which has successfully sold the idea of long-haul sun, sea, sand holidays to destinations such as Pattaya Beach and Phuket.

The market leader for long-haul packages is Swiss-owned Kuoni Travel, with about a fifth of the market, with the newly-amalgamated companies of Thomas Cook and British Airways Holidays coming close to this figure, with substantial market shares held by the other three leading tour operators, Thomson, Airtours and First Choice.

Seat-only sales

The figures for inclusive tours by air given in Table 12.5 also contain seat-only sales, in which passengers, although ostensibly buying a package, are in fact only using the air-travel portion of the tour. This type of 'package' was originally introduced by operators to fill surplus charter seats; technically, to abide by international regulations, some form of basic accommodation had to be included in the package, although this was seldom used. After January 1993, EU legislation swept away the requirement to book accommodation within EU destinations. Seat-only sales have now become an important feature of the travel industry, as growing numbers of holiday-makers are either prepared to find their own accommodation abroad, or are seeking flights to carry them to their second homes, time-share apartments or friends' accommodation on the Continent. Even business travellers seeking to save money during the recession are known to have made use of this facility. Subsequently, seat-only packages also became available on block-booked seats on scheduled aircraft, offering the additional benefits for clients of no con-

solidations and daytime flights. Sales peaked at around 20 per cent of the total air IT market, and have now stabilized. Again, the top five tour operators control the overwhelming majority of the seat-only market, with Cosmos in this case gaining a better share of the market with its Avro product.

Recent developments

There is little let-up in the volatility of the tour operating business. Political circumstances in the destination country, such as was the case with the Kosovo conflict in the Balkans in 1999, which hit eastern Mediterranean resorts, and the activities of PKK terrorists in Turkey in the same year, affected operators which relied on those destinations. Fires in the Far East towards the end of the century led to cancellations to popular destinations for long-haul tourists, especially Indonesia and Malaysia.

Operators sought new locations to develop, where hotel capacity was cheap and readily available; first, the more remote areas of Greece, then Turkey became boom destinations for the British seeking sun at rock-bottom prices. The evidence suggests that the inclusive tour market for traditional 'sun, sea, sand' destinations has now probably peaked, with a little over 50 per cent of the population choosing a package when buying an overseas holiday, a proportion that is varying little from year to year. Around 70 per cent of the UK population has now had a foreign holiday at some point in their lives, a figure which shows little change over time. Thus, it is reasonable to assume that the first-time market has been captured, and the future growth of the IT market is likely to be concentrated on selling greater *frequency* of holidays, and with a focus on the variety of holidays offered.

The changing nature of our society is throwing up demand for new kinds of holiday, as we discussed in an earlier chapter. Growth areas include:

● Short breaks and city breaks, especially to more exotic destinations. Reykjavik, Barcelona and even New York have become popular destinations for short-stay tourism.

- Exotic long-haul, activity and adventure holidays. Elderly travellers are now far more active than formerly, and packages are being designed to meet their needs, too.
- All-inclusives are one of the fastest-growing forms of holiday. Introduced in 1976 by Sandals and Superclubs in the Caribbean, the concept has now expanded to short-haul destinations too. These are fully inclusive packages, even down to the inclusion of alcohol and all entertainment at the resort.

About 455,000 short-haul and 365,000 long-haul all-inclusive holiday packages were sold in 1998, with the big four operators selling over half the market. Although popular, their sustainability is questionable, given that customers do not need to go out of their complex to buy anything while they are on holiday, and local shops and services fail to obtain the same benefits from the tourists.

Operators are increasing their revenue through 'add-ons' especially when customers buy no-frills packages – and Thomson estimated that up to a third of their packages sold would be 'no-frills' in 2000. Operators are making additional charges for transfers, early check-in or late check-out of rooms, pre-bookable seats, transfers by taxi, use of prestigious airport lounges, and even charges to guarantee being seated next to a friend or relative. All such techniques are now being used to increase earnings.

Consumer complaints

One inevitable consequence of the process of 'trading down' was the increase in customer complaints. Studies revealed that some 40 per cent of complaints arose from the 'bargain basement' holidays, often based on late availability without guarantee of exactly what accommodation was to be provided. While operators were responding to consumer pressure for low-cost packages, consumers were unwilling to accept the very rational argument that they got what they paid for; minimum standards provided simply failed too often to meet consumer expectations. Even more worrying to operators was the fact that only 40 per cent of those dissatisfied were prepared to make an official complaint; others simply refrained from booking with the company again. The use by British operators of non-British-registered aircraft also led to concern over air safety. Older aircraft registered in central European countries such as Latvia are attractively priced for charter, but there may be less careful monitoring of maintenance and other safety factors such as crew hours, especially where these are chartered through other EU countries.

One source of customer irritation was the practice of operators applying surcharges to their final invoices. IT costs are affected by changes in the inflation rate, exchange rates or costs of supplies, particularly aviation fuel, which is priced in US dollars on the world market, and is therefore affected by either increased costs or changes in the relative values of the pound and dollar. Tour operators have to estimate their costs for all services up to a year ahead of time. They can anticipate higher costs by raising prices, which may make them uncompetitive, or they can take an optimistic approach and price low, in the expectation of stable or declining costs. Until 1988, the latter was more attractive, as moderate cost increases could be passed on to customers (within established limits) in the form of surcharges. Such surcharges, however, are resented by travellers, and are in any case not applied to scheduled fares (which can respond to market prices more quickly). It also became apparent that a handful of operators were misusing this facility and adding fuel surcharges in excess of cost increases, or even when actual fuel costs had not increased at all, as a means of raising profits sliced by open competition. The leading tour operators themselves helped to phase out surcharges by guaranteeing prices for the following year. Stability in price could be obtained by 'buying forward' the fuel required for the following year, but this is only practical for the largest operators with sufficient financial reserves. While there is no formal 'futures' market in aviation fuel, negotiation is possible on future purchases of fuel on an ad hoc basis, but clearly at a premium, and purchasing forward will further affect the operators' cash flow.

The introduction in 1996 by the government of an 'exit tax' for all flights out of the UK, amounting initially to £5 within the EU and £10 outside the EU (a rate that doubled at the end of 1997) resurrected the issue of hidden charges, with many tour operators not absorbing these taxes in their total price structures. Some claimed that to do so would make their prices unattractive against scheduled air rivals, most of whom never included the supplements.

While complaints to ABTA totalled over 17,000 in 1999, seen against a background of millions travelling this represents only a very small proportion of all holiday-makers buying a package tour. The previous year, 1,371 cases were dealt with under ABTA's arbitration scheme, and of these, 716 awards were in favour of the customer.

The nature of tour operating

Let us now turn to look at how inclusive tours are operated. An inclusive tour programme, as we have seen, is composed of a series of integrated travel services, each of which is purchased by the tour operator in bulk and resold as part of a package at an all-inclusive price. These integrated services usually consist of an aircraft seat, accommodation at the destination and transfers between the accommodation and the airport on arrival and departure. They may also include other services such as excursions or car hire. The inclusive tour is commonly referred to as a package tour, and most are single-destination, resort-based holidays. However, tours comprising two or more destinations are by no means uncommon, and long-haul operators frequently build in optional extensions to another destination in their programmes; a beach holiday in Kenya might offer an optional extension to one of the game parks, or a visit to the Chilean fjords, flying to Santiago, might offer the tourist the opportunity to extend the itinerary to Chilean-owned Easter Island. Linear tours, such as those offered by coach companies which carry people to different destinations or even through several countries, were at one time the most popular form of trip, and still retain a loyal following, mainly among older clients.

The success of the operator has usually depended on its ability to buy its individual products, put them together and sell them at an inclusive price lower than the customers could obtain themselves. Operators are in some cases booking several million beds for a season, and can thus obtain very low prices from the supplier. This must be seen by the customers as giving value for money. With the package holiday becoming more and more a standardized product, differing little between destinations, the destination or country has come to play a lesser part in customer choice; destinations will be readily substituted if the customer feels that the first choice is overpriced.

Tour operators keep prices low either by restraining profits, or by cutting costs. Cost savings are initially achieved by chartering whole aircraft instead of merely purchasing a block of seats on a scheduled flight. Further savings can be made by time-series chartering of the aircraft over a lengthy period of time, such as a whole season, rather than on an ad hoc basis. Ultimately, larger tour operators can further trim costs by running their own airlines, and this also allows them to exercise better control over their operations and the standards of their product. Owning your own aircraft ensures that when demand is there, you have the aircraft to meet it at a price you can afford. Emphasis then shifts to ensuring that the highest possible load factors – the percentage of seats sold to seats available – are achieved, and that the aircraft are kept flying for the maximum number of hours each day; aircraft are not earning revenue while stationary on the ground. This means careful planning to ensure turnarounds (time spent between arriving with one load of passengers and taking off with another) are as rapid as possible, commensurate with good standards of safety. Consequently, common flight plans involve establishing a 'W' flight pattern for the aircraft (see Figure 12.3), which produces the maximum usage of the equipment during a 24-hour period.

One problem arising from the tight scheduling of

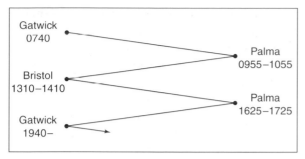

Figure 12.3 A typical 'W' flight pattern

W-pattern flights occurs when different operators contract for morning, afternoon and evening flights. If one operator decides to cancel, the airline concerned has to find alternative users for the aircraft, which may mean a longer flight commitment, causing delays, or a change of flights, to passengers already booked. The knock-on effect of delays can become very apparent if air traffic controllers go on strike or mount go-slows. Tight flight scheduling means that a delay in one flight could have repercussions on flights using the same aircraft for the next two or three days.

High load factors are achieved by setting the break-even (the number of seats to be sold on each flight to cover all operating, administrative and marketing costs associated with the flight) at a point as close as possible to capacity. This brings down the average seat cost to a level which will encourage people to travel. On many well-marketed charter flights, break-even is set as high as 90 per cent or higher, while actual average load factors may be as high as 96–98 per cent. The company makes its profits on the difference between these two figures, and since clearly every extra person carried is almost pure profit (virtually all costs having been covered), then substantial reductions can be made for last-minute bookings to fill these final seats. Of course, if break-even load factors have not been reached, the operator will not cover all costs, but it will still be better to attract as many people as possible for the flight, because they will at least make a contribution to the fixed costs of operating the flight, even if all

costs are not recovered. Passengers may also buy duty-free goods on board (if travelling outside the EU countries), which will make a further contribution to profit for the airline – or, taking a broader view, for the parent company of the jointly owned airline/tour operator.

Productivity in airline operations can be aided, as we have seen, by the procedure of *consolidating* flights. Charter flights with unacceptably low load factors can be cancelled, and their passengers transferred to other flights, or even departures from other airports. This helps to reduce the element of risk for the operator, otherwise break-evens would have to be set at a lower level of capacity, and fares would consequently be higher. Such consolidations are not available for groups carried on scheduled airline services, and are in any case subject to considerable restrictions, such as adequate advance notice being given to the client. Inevitably, they are unpopular with clients, and many companies now try to avoid their use.

The problem of seasonality

A problem facing all sectors of tourism is the highly seasonal nature of most tourist traffic. Nowhere is this more apparent than in the demand for package holidays in Europe. This market, however, is also highly price sensitive, and longer periods of holiday entitlement over the past twenty years have helped to encourage many people to take their second holiday abroad too – often outside of the peak periods of holiday demand. This meant that operators could spread their fixed costs more evenly over the entire year, rather than concentrating them into the summer periods, helping to reduce prices further. Most importantly, it allows the operator to contract for aircraft and hotels on a year-round basis. If only a summer season is programmed, the operator is left with a 'dead leg' twice in the year – an aircraft returning empty after the first flight of the season because it has no passengers to pick up, and an empty outbound flight at the end of the season to pick up the last clients returning home. The costs of these empty flights have to be built into the overall pricing structure of the programme, and if they can be avoided, by offering year-round programmes, clearly prices can be reduced.

Operators also use marginal costing techniques to attract their clients out of season. This means pricing the holidays to cover their variable costs and making some contribution to fixed costs. This recognizes that many costs, such as those encountered in operating hotels, continue whether the hotel is open or closed, and any guests that the hotel can attract will help to pay the bills. They will also enable the hotel to keep its staff year-round, thus making it easier to retain good staff. Some market segments – pensioners, for example – can be attracted to the idea of spending the entire winter abroad if prices are low enough, and hoteliers welcome these budget clients who can still be expected to spend some additional money in the hotel bars.

Operating scheduled programmes

Not all destinations allow charter flights to operate into their territory (often in order to protect bookings on the scheduled flights of the country's airline). Nor will there be sufficient demand to many destinations, such as those served by most long-haul programmes, to merit chartering an aircraft. For these forms of packaging, the net inclusive tour basing (ITX) or group inclusive tour (GIT) fares can be used by the operator, which may in this way either contract for individual seats based on client demand (around which a tailor-made holiday can be constructed), or contract for a block of seats on flights to satisfy the needs of a brochure programme.

Airlines will allow ITX fares to be applied subject to certain conditions attached to the programmes. A minimum number of brochures must be printed, and the programme must consist of a package of flight, accommodation and transfer or other feature. The tour programme can be organized using one or more carriers, but approval is usually sought through a particular carrier, which will validate the programme and provide a tour code number, which is

contained on each ticket issued. Tour operators making a forward commitment on seats must also obtain an Air Travel Organisers' Licence (ATOL) through the CAA.

Control over tour operating

Regulations restricting tour operators were very limiting when the mass tour market developed in the 1960s. In particular, the regulation known as Provision 1 made it impossible to price package tours lower than the cheapest regular return air fare to a destination. The sole exceptions to this rule were in the case of affinity groups, which involved charters arranged for associations whose existence was for a purpose other than that of obtaining cheap travel. Travellers were obliged to have been members of the organization for at least six months before they became eligible for low-cost flights. The rule was designed to protect scheduled carriers, and to ensure adequate profit for tour operators, but it severely hindered the expansion of the package tour business. It was also widely abused by club secretaries who back-dated membership, and many spurious clubs were formed in order to provide the benefits of cheap travel.

When the CAA was established in 1971, restrictions were lifted, initially only during the winter months (leading to a huge increase in off-season travel), but by 1973 this was extended to all seasons. However, at the same time the CAA tightened up control on tour operators themselves, introducing in 1972 the requirement to hold ATOLs for charters and block-booked scheduled seats, and at the same time introducing a system for vetting operators on their financial viability. Licences are not required, however, for domestic air tours, nor for travel abroad using sea or land transport.

Following the collapse of an important tour operator, Fiesta Tours, in 1964, which left some 5,000 tourists stranded abroad, the industry and its customers came to recognize the importance of introducing protection against financial failure. On the whole, in the UK successive governments have preferred to allow the industry to police itself rather than to impose additional controls, and this has been undertaken relatively effectively by ABTA on behalf of tour operators and travel agents in the UK. In 1965, ABTA set up a *Common Fund* for this purpose, anticipating legislation for the compulsory registration of tour operators. When this did not materialize, ABTA introduced its Stabiliser regulation, under which Common Fund provisions were to apply only to ABTA members' clients, and a reciprocal agreement was entered into whereby ABTA tour operators were restricted to selling their package holidays exclusively through ABTA travel agents. In turn, ABTA agents were restricted to selling tours operated by ABTA tour operators. Many agents, however, resented having to contribute to a fund to insure operators, and it also became clear that the provisions against collapse were inadequate. In 1967, the Tour Operators' Study Group (TOSG; later to become the Federation of Tour Operators, FTO), an informal group comprising approximately twenty of the leading tour operators, decided to establish its own bonding scheme. A bond is a guarantee given by a third party (usually a bank or insurance company) to pay a sum of money, up to a specified maximum, in the event that the company becomes insolvent. This money is then used to meet the immediate financial obligations arising from the collapse, such as repatriating tourists stranded at overseas resorts, and reimbursing clients booked to travel later with the company. TOSG's bonding scheme became a reality in 1970.

Later, ABTA itself introduced its own bonding scheme for all tour operating (and retail agency) members. The collapse in 1974, in the peak of summer, of the Court Line group brought down Clarksons Holidays, Britain's leading tour operator, and revealed once again that protection was inadequate. At this point the government stepped in to introduce an obligatory levy of 2 per cent of operators' turnover between 1975 and 1977. This levy, imposed by the Air Travel Reserve Fund Act of 1975, established the Air Travel Reserve Fund (later, this became the Air Travel Trust Fund). However, these reserves were severely depleted by collapses throughout the 1990s, particularly that of the International Leisure Group at the beginning of that decade, and the ATTF was obliged to call on the government for additional borrowing facilities when reserves ran dry.

The EU and legal issues in package holiday operations

In retrospect, Operation Stabiliser is seen to have worked effectively for its members. Its weakness lay in the fact that it failed to embrace operators outside the system, which was voluntary. With the collapse of several non-ABTA operators in the early 1990s, the weakness of the system was revealed.

Concern was shared by the European Commissioners, who were also looking at the problems of protecting consumers in other member countries. In 1991, the EC Directive on Package Travel was published, designed to extend responsibility to all sectors of the industry. The new regulations, which were to come into effect in 1993, covered non-air-based holidays also. The British Department of Trade and Industry (DTI) responded to the Directive with a Consultative Document to implement the Directive in the UK. The measures to be introduced included the following obligations:

1. all tours to be licensed;
2. a public protection fund to be set up, similar to that offered by the Air Travel Trust, covering other forms of package holiday;
3. tour operators to be required to observe certain minimum standards in brochure descriptions;
4. travel agents to become responsible, not only for the information contained in brochures they stocked, but for providing necessary advice to clients on booking (e.g. health requirements, passport and visa requirements, insurance needs etc.);
5. restrictions on surcharges and alterations to

bookings (although these were in effect weaker than those already imposed under ABTA regulations).

The imposition of these regulations brought considerable problems for operators and agents, not least because the interpretation of the regulations was unclear. In particular, it remained unclear about what exactly constituted a 'package holiday' – was this to include business trips and tailor-made holidays? Would all organizers of packages, such as clubs or schoolteachers organizing educational trips, be included? 'Occasional' organizers were to be excluded, but the interpretation of what constituted 'occasional' posed further problems. What was immediately apparent was that the long-standing Stabiliser regulation could no longer be enforced, as all operators and agents were now required to be bonded, and Stabilizer was discontinued in 1992.

The move to set up a Travel Protection Association to license surface operators was slowed by disagreements between the parties concerned about whether membership in the new body should be mandatory or voluntary. The FTO withdrew from discussions in order to implement its own scheme, and since then a number of alternative schemes have been introduced, in the form of either bonds or trustee accounts. Of these, the best known outside of the CAA and ABTA schemes are those of the FTO, the AITO (Association of Independent Tour Operators) Trust and the Association of Bonded Travel Organizers' Trust (ABTOT) for smaller operators. The Confederation of Passenger Transport (CPT), Passenger Shipping Association (PSA) and Yacht Charter Association operate their own schemes.

Initially, some believed that ABTA could no longer survive, but the significance of this body and the need to have a single body to represent the interests of tour operators and retailers as a whole has ensured that ABTA has survived, albeit in a much weakened version of its former self. Many operators have chosen not to remain members.

What does appear clear is that the additional burden of responsibility placed on tour operators led to some increases in cost for consumers, as operators attempted to cover themselves against any threat of legislation. The Package Travel, Package Holidays and Package Tours Regulations (1992) imposed much greater responsibility on operators; specifically, regulation 4 penalizes the dissemination of misleading information, and provides for compensation to be paid for any loss suffered by the consumer as a result of being misled, while regulation 15 makes the tour operator responsible if hotels or other suppliers fail to provide the accommodation or services contracted for.

As mentioned above, ABTA operates its own arbitration scheme to resolve complaints by customers about its members. This is at low cost to claimants, who are successful in about half of all cases brought. AITO provides a similar scheme. Alternatively, claims can be made through the courts under a new tracking system according to the level of claim; small track claims of up to £5,000 entail plaintiffs paying fees up to only £100 at the time of writing.

Planning, marketing and operating package tours

Planning for the introduction of a new tour programme or destination is likely to take place over a lengthy span of time, sometimes as long as two years. A typical time scale for a programme of summer tours is shown in Figure 12.4.

In planning deadlines for the programme, it is necessary to work backwards from the planned launch dates. One critical problem is when to determine prices. These have to be established at the last minute before material goes to printing, but inevitably this will be several months before the tour programme starts, and entails a good understanding (and some luck!) with regard to the movement of currency and the foreign exchange markets in the intervening period. This is a situation which could be considerably eased by Britain's entry into the European common currency, should that take place within the next few years.

RESEARCH/ PLANNING	YEAR 1	Summer	First stages of research. Look at economic factors influencing the future development of package tours. Identify likely selection of destinations.
		September/December	Second stages of research. In-depth comparison of alternative destinations.
	YEAR 2	January	Determine destinations, hotels and capacity, duration of tours, departure dates. Make policy decisions on size and design of brochure, number of brochures to print, date for completion of print.
NEGOTIATION		February/March	Tenders put out for design, production and printing of brochures. Negotiate with the airlines for charter flights. Negotiate with hotels, transfer services, optional excursion operators.
		April/May	Typesetting and printing space booked with printer, copy for text commissioned. Illustrations commissioned or borrowed. Early artwork and text under development at design studio, with layout suggestions. Contracts completed with hotels and airlines, transfer services etc.
		June	Production of brochure starts.
ADMINISTRATION		July	Determine exchange rates. Estimate selling prices based on inflation etc. Galley proofs from printer, corrections made. Any necessary reservations staff recruited and trained.
		August	Final tour prices to printer. Brochures printed and reservations system established.
MARKETING		September/October	Brochure on market, distribution to agents. Initial agency sales promotion, including launch. First public media advertising, and trade publicity through press etc.
	YEAR 3	January/March	Peak advertising and promotion to trade and public.
		February/April	Recruitment and training of resort representatives etc.
		May	First tour departures.

Figure 12.4 Typical time scale for planning a summer tour programme

Market research

In practice, the decision to exploit a destination or region for package tours is as much an act of faith as the outcome of carefully considered research. Forecasting future developments in tourism, which as a product is affected by changing circumstances to a greater extent than most other consumer products, has proved to be notably inaccurate. As we have seen, tourist patterns change over time, with a shift from one country to another and from one form of accommodation to another. With the emphasis on price, the mass tour operator's principal concern is to provide the basic sun, sea and sand package in countries that provide the best value for money. Transport costs will depend upon charter rights into the country, distance flown and ground handling costs. They will also be affected by the relative demand for, and supply of, aircraft in any given year. Accommodation and other costs to be met overseas will be the outcome of exchange rates against sterling, and operators must consider these vis-à-vis other competitive countries' currency values when considering how many clients they can anticipate travelling to any one destination. Operators also have to take into account such qualitative issues as the political stability of the destination, the support given to developing tourism to the destination by the carriers, or tourist office, of the country, and the relationship between the host and destination countries. Increasingly, the effect upon the environment of such new development must be considered, and how this can be effectively managed by the operators, the hotels they work with and the local authorities.

Once the tour operators have narrowed the choice to two or three potential destinations, they must produce a realistic appraisal of the likely demand to these destinations, based on factors such as the number of tourists the destinations presently attract, growth rates over recent years, and present shares held by competing companies. The mass-market operators are unlikely to be looking at a single year's programme – any commitment to a destination is likely to be for a substantial period of time, unlike the specialist operator, which may be more flexible in switching destinations according to changing demand. Mass-market operators will be considering long-term contracts with their hoteliers abroad, or even establishing their own hotels.

Availability of suitable aircraft for the routes must be ascertained. This will in part dictate capacities for the programme, since aircraft have different configurations, and on some routes where aircraft are operating at the limits of their range, some passenger seats may need to be sacrificed in order to take on board sufficient fuel to cover the distance. In some instances, provincial airport runways may be insufficient for larger, fully laden aircraft, and, again, fewer passengers may be carried to compensate.

All planning is, of course, also dependent upon the company having the necessary finance available to operate and market the programme.

The process of negotiating

Once the decisions have been made as to destinations to be served and numbers of passengers to be carried during the season, and dates of departure have been established, the serious negotiations can get under way with airlines, hotels and other principals, leading to formal contracts. These contracts will spell out the conditions for the release of unsold accommodation or (in the case of block bookings on scheduled services) aircraft seats, or the cancellation of chartered aircraft flights, with any penalties that the tour operator will incur. Normal terms for aircraft chartering are for a deposit to be paid upon signing the contract (generally 10 per cent of the total cost), with the balance becoming due on each flight after it takes place. In negotiating with charter services, the reputation of the tour operator is of paramount importance. If they have worked with that airline, or with similar charters, in previous years, this will be taken into account in determining the terms and price for the contract.

A well-established operator does not wish to be at the mercy of market forces in dealing with charter airlines. In any given year, the demand for suitable aircraft may exceed the supply, leading the larger tour operators to form or buy their own airline, just to ensure that capacity is available to them.

Part and parcel of the negotiations is the setting up of the tour operating flight plan, with decisions made on the dates and frequency of operations, the airports to be used and times of arrival and departure. All of this information will have to be consolidated into a form suitable for publication and easy comprehension in the tour brochure.

Hotel negotiations

Hotel negotiations, other than in the case of large tour operators which negotiate time contracts for an entire hotel, are generally far more informal than is the case in airline negotiating. Small and specialist tour operators selling independent inclusive tours (IITs) may have no more than a free-sale (or sell and report) agreement with hoteliers, by which the hotel agrees to guarantee accommodation for a specified maximum number of tourists (usually four) merely on receipt of the notification of booking from the tour operator, whether by phone, mail, telex or, more commonly now, fax or email. This arrangement may be quite suitable for small tour programmes, but it suffers from the disadvantage that at times hoteliers will retain the right to close out certain dates. As these are likely to be the most popular dates in the calendar, the operator stands to lose both potential business and goodwill. The alternative is for the operator to contract for an allocation of rooms in the hotel, with dates agreed for the release of those unsold, well in advance of the anticipated arrival dates.

Long-term contracts, either for a block of rooms or for the entire hotel, have the attraction of providing the operator with the lowest possible prices, but they carry a higher element of risk. Some contracts have been drawn up by operators for as long as five years, and while at first glance such long fixed-term price contracts may seem attractive, they are seldom realistic, and in an inflationary period may well have to be renegotiated to avoid bankrupting the hotelier. Such an event would obviously not be in the operator's interest.

In addition to the operator spelling out exact requirements in terms of rooms – required numbers of singles, doubles, twins, with or without private facilities, whether with balconies or seaviews, and with what catering provision, e.g. room only, with breakfast, half or full board – it must also clarify a number of other facts, including:

- reservations and registration procedures (including whether hotel vouchers are to be issued);
- accommodation requirements for any representatives or couriers (usually provided free);
- handling procedures and fees charged for porterage;
- special facilities available or needed, such as catering for handicapped customers, or special catering requirements such as kosher or vegetarian food;
- languages spoken by hotel staff;
- systems of payment by guests for drinks or other extras;
- reassurance on suitable fire and safety precautions;
- if appropriate, suitable space for a representative's desk and noticeboard.

It is also as well to check the availability of alternative hotel accommodation of a comparable standard in the event of overbooking. Of course, a hotel with a reputation for overbooking is to be avoided, but over the course of time some errors are bound to occur, and will require guests to transfer to other hotels. Tour operators must satisfy themselves that the arrangements made by the hotelier for taking care of clients in these circumstances are adequate. Any operator negotiating with a hotelier will be aware that they are likely to be sharing contracted space with other operators, not only within their own country but also from other countries. It is as well to be aware of one's own standing with the hotelier vis-à-vis other companies; for example, in Spain it is not uncommon to find that the German operators, which tend to pay higher prices for their rooms than do the British, will have their rooms protected in preference to British operators, when overbookings occur.

Independent companies are now finding themselves squeezed out of the market for European bed-stock, and even the mass-market operators are aware that greater concentration in the industry is leading to more difficulty in tying up contracts with popular hotels. For this reason, as demand rises for key Mediterranean destinations and also to ensure greater control over the major elements in the package, operators are showing renewed interest either in owning hotels at the destinations or at the very least having far more say in their management. First Choice announced in 2000 its intention to play a part in designing new hotels and influencing their layout, when long-term contracts are envisaged.

Ancillary services

Similar negotiations will take place with locally based incoming operators and coach companies to provide coach transfers between airport and hotels, and any optional excursions. Car hire companies may also be approached to negotiate commission rates on sales to the tour operator's clients.

The reliability and honesty of the local operator is an important issue here. Some smaller tour operators in the UK may not be in a position to employ their own resort representatives initially, hence their image will depend upon the level of service provided by the local operator's staff.

If the local company is also operating optional sightseeing excursions, procedures for booking these and handling the finances involved must be established, and it should be clarified whether qualified guides with a sound knowledge of the English language are to be employed on the excursions. If not, tour operators must reassure themselves that all driver-couriers will be sufficiently fluent in the English language to do their job effectively for the company.

The role of the resort representative

Tour operators carrying large numbers of package tourists to a destination are in a position to employ their own resort representatives. This has obvious advantages in that the company can count on the loyalty and total commitment of its own staff. A decision must be made as to whether to employ a national of the host country or of the generating country. The advantage of a man or woman from the local community is that they will be better acquainted with the local customs and geography, fluent in the language of the country and with good local contacts, which may make it easier to take care of problems (such as dealing with the police, local shopkeepers or hoteliers) more effectively. On the other hand, they are likely to be less familiar with the culture, customs or language of their clients, and this can act as a restraining influence on package tourists, especially for those on first visits abroad. Exceptional local representatives have been able to overcome this problem, and if they themselves have some common background with their clients, such as having lived for some years in the incoming tourists' country, they can often function as effectively as their counterparts from the generating country. However, some countries impose restrictions on the employment of foreign nationals at resorts, and this is a point which must be clarified before employing representatives.

The representative's role is far more demanding than is commonly thought. During the season, he or she can be expected to work a seven-day week and will need to be available on call for twenty-four hours each day to cope with any emergencies. Resort representatives are usually given a desk in the hotel lobby from which to work, but in cases where tour operators have their clients in two or more hotels in the resort, the representative may have to visit each hotel during some part of the day. Their principal functions include:

- handling general enquiries;
- advising on currency exchange, shopping etc.;

Figure 12.5 Overseas representative dealing with clients. (*Courtesy Thomson Holidays*)

- organizing and supervising social activities at the hotels;
- publicizing and booking optional excursions;
- handling special requirements and complaints, and acting as an intermediary for clients, interceding with the hotel proprietor, the police or other local authorities as necessary.

As operators necessarily become more commercial, so the importance attached to selling excursions has risen. Many representatives are given targets to achieve, and are rewarded financially for good performance in this function, which can make a major contribution to the operator's profits.

These routine functions will be supplemented by problems arising from lost baggage, ill health (needing to refer clients to local dentists or doctors), and even occasionally deaths, although serious problems such as these are often referred to area managers. The representatives must also relocate clients whose accommodation is for any reason inadequate, or when overbookings have occurred, and they may also have to rebook flights for their clients whose plans change as a result of emergencies.

The representatives' busiest days occur when groups are arriving or leaving the resort. They will accompany groups returning home, on the coach to the airport, ensuring that departure formalities at the hotel have been complied with, arrange to pay any airport or departure taxes due, and then wait to greet incoming clients and accompany them in turn to their hotels on the transfer coaches. In the not uncommon situation where flights are delayed, this can result in representatives having to spend very long hours at the airport, sometimes missing a night's sleep. On their return to the hotels, they must also ensure that check-in procedures operate smoothly, going over rooming lists with the hotel managers before the latter bill the company. Most operators also provide a welcome party for their clients on the first night of their holiday, and it is the representatives' task to organize and host this. This provides an important opportunity to initiate excursion sales.

Representatives can also expect to spend some time at their resort bases before the start of the season, not only to get to know the site but to report back to their companies on the standards of tourist facilities and to pinpoint any discrepancies between brochure descriptions and reality. This has become increasingly important under the new regulations imposed through the EU Directive on Package Holidays, and representatives are also expected to inform their companies if any changes occur during the season about which the clients must be notified at the time of booking. In an effort to reduce complaints and handle them at source, Thomson Holidays announced in 2000 its plans to introduce troubleshooters into key resorts who will be given greater authority than the representatives to dispense compensatory payments and settle complaints immediately without resorting to senior management.

The critical role played by representatives – frequently the only point of direct contact between the company and its customers – is recognized by operators, and today there are more opportunities for full-time positions, in which staff alternate between summer resorts and winter resorts, sometimes starting with positions as children's representatives, but with promotional opportunities to representative, senior representative, area supervisor and area manager.

Ultimately, progression must lie back in head office, where managers having overall responsibility for resort representatives recruit and train staff, organize holiday rosters, provide uniforms and handle the administration of the representatives' department. Nevertheless, many posts are still dependent upon seasonal staff (the largest companies will employ thousands of such staff each summer), and the drive to cut costs has affected these staff, too. Some operators have reduced staff by developing a 'service centre' accessible to clients by phone, avoiding the need for large numbers of peripatetic staff. However, this is a questionable practice if one accepts that the only clear distinction between one operator and another at a resort is in the quality of its representation.

Pricing the package tour

A key requirement for success in a tour operator's programme is to get the price right. The price must be right for the market, right compared with the price of competitors' package tours, and right by comparison with the price of other tours offered by the company.

Specialist operators which offer a unique product may have more flexibility and the freedom to determine their prices based on cost plus a mark-up that is sufficient to cover overheads and provide a satisfactory level of profit. The mass operators, however, must take greater account of their competitors' prices, since demand for package tours is, as we have

	£
Flight costs, based on 25 departures (back to back) on Boeing 737 148-seat aircraft at £14,750 per flight:	368,750
Plus one empty leg each way at beginning and end of the season:	
(a) out	7,375
(b) home	7,375
Total flight costs:	383,500
Cost per flight:	15,340
Cost per seat at 90% occupancy	
(133 seats), i.e. £15,340 ÷ 133	115.34
Plus air charges (air passenger duty,passenger service charges):	23.00
Net hotel cost per person, 14 nights half board:	225.80
Resort agent's handling fees and transfers, per person:	7.00
Gratuities, porterage:	1.00
Total cost per person:	372.14
Add mark-up of approx. 30% on cost price to cover agency commission, marketing costs (including brochure, ticket wallet, etc.), head office administrative costs and profit:	111.64
Selling price: say	485.00

seen, extremely price elastic, especially for programmes offered in the shoulder season or off-season. In the past in the UK there has been a tendency to follow the prices determined by the market leader, and economies of scale have been important in terms of reducing cost and undercutting rival prices. Below are two typical examples of cost-determined tour pricing.

Mass-market tour pricing

The first example (opposite page) is based on time-series charter travel and a two-week holiday to a destination such as Spain.

A small element of cost arises from VAT imposed on the relevant portion of the ground arrangements, and for operators whose company is not directly integrated with an airline, VAT must be added to the tour operator's margin under TOMS (the tour operators' margin scheme). Many companies would add a small fee, say £15, in order to build in a no-surcharge guarantee, especially in times of economic instability. Holidays which are cancelled are presently resold to the public, a source of considerable extra income, since refunds do not have to be made to the original customer (who recovers these costs from insurance, if there is a valid claim). However, the Office of Fair Trading is investigating this practice, and this bonanza is likely to be terminated in the near future. This may result in the operator being obliged to refund the initial customer.

In estimating the seat cost for aircraft, operators must not only calculate the load factor in which this cost is to be based but must also aim to achieve this load factor on average throughout the series of tours they will be operating. This must depend on their estimates of the market demand for each destination and the current supply of aircraft seats available to their competitors. Since high-season demand will frequently exceed the supply of seats to these destinations, there is scope to increase the above price, and hence profits, for the high-season months of the year, even if this results in the company being uncompetitive with other leading operators.

However, as operators have in the past tended to overestimate forecast demand, this is becoming a more risky procedure. In the off-season, meanwhile, supply is likely to exceed the demand for available packages, and the company may set its prices so low that only the variable costs are covered and a small contribution is made to the fixed costs (marketing, administration, etc.), in order to fill seats.

Each tour operator must carefully consider what proportion of its overheads are to be allocated to each tour and destination. As long as these expenses are recovered in full during the term of operation, the allocation of these costs can be made on the basis of market forces, and need not necessarily be apportioned equally to each programme and destination. In practice, most operators now recover overhead costs by determining a per capita contribution, based on anticipated head office costs for the year and the total number of passengers the company expects to carry. Under this system, of course, each tour carries the same burden of office costs regardless of destination or price. However, there is a case for a more marketing-oriented approach to pricing, based on consideration of market prices and the company's long-term objectives. In entering a new market, for instance, it may be that the principal objective is to penetrate and obtain a targeted share of that market in the first year of operating, and this may be achieved by reducing or even forgoing profits during the first year, and/or by reducing the per capita contribution to corporate costs. Indeed, to some destinations the operator may introduce loss-leader pricing policies, subsidizing the cost of this policy from other more profitable routes in order to get a footing in the market to the new destination.

Detailed consideration of value-added taxation has not been included here for the sake of simplicity. However, VAT is applicable on profit margins of the operators operating within the EU countries, and the operator will also be paying VAT incorporated into hoteliers' and other services' contractual prices. Most tour operators (but not all) have agreed to pay commission to agents on revenue which includes the VAT cost (which the operator can later recover).

Specialist tour pricing

This second example is of a specialist long-haul operator which uses the services of scheduled carriers to Hong Kong, with a group inclusive tour basing fare.

	£
Flight cost, based on net group air fares, per person:	370
Plus air charges;	40
Net hotel cost per person, 7 nights, twin room (HK$420 per room, = HK$210 per person; HK$1.40 = £2:	150
Transfers (£10 each way):	20
Sub-total:	580
Add agent's commission:	68
Total cost per person:	648
Selling prices:	
'Lead price' (offered on only one or two off-season flights):	679
Shoulder season price:	730
High season price (summer, Christmas and Easter holiday periods):	890

It will be noted that in the case of this specialist operator, prices reflect market demand at different periods of the year, and there is no equal distribution of office overheads; profits and most overheads are recoverable in the peak season prices charged to the market. The lead price gives very little profit for bookings made through the trade, but is strictly limited to one or two weeks of the year. On the other hand, high profits can be obtained over Christmas, Chinese New Year, during conferences and for other business committed to specific dates. There is a tendency to be more cautious about squeezing excess profits at periods of high demand; several Gulf States carriers are offering much lower prices to offset the need to change flights, so competition at all times of the year is quite high, and if charges are set too high operators may be left with availability during peak times – as operators selling air travel during the millennium found to their cost.

The pricing policy shown here is common among the smaller specialist operators, which tend to use less sophisticated pricing techniques when fixing target profits. Many specialists which operate in a climate where there is no exact competition for their product could be expected to charge a price which would give them an overall gross profit of 25 per cent or more, while most mass-market operators, and some specialists, will be forced by market conditions to settle for much lower margins.

In developing a pricing strategy for package tours, operators must take into account a number of other variables in addition to those shown above. Earlier, the point was made that price had to be right compared with all competing products on the market. For example, when setting a price for departure from a regional airport, the operator will look at how much more the client will be willing to pay to avoid a long trip to a major airport. In the example above of flights to Hong Kong, numerous competitors such as KLM, Swissair, Air France and SAS offer flights from regional airports with connections via their hubs which avoid passengers having to stay overnight at expensive London airport hotels, and the inconvenience of getting to Heathrow Airport on heavily congested motorways. Equally, if a flight is to leave at two o'clock in the morning, the price must be sufficiently attractive compared with others leaving during the day to make people willing to suffer this inconvenience. What special reductions are to be offered to children, or for group bookings? As seat and other costs will be unaffected, whatever reductions the company makes for these bookings will have to be recovered in profits achieved through sales to other customers.

As a general policy, members of the Federation of Tour Operators standardize the date each year in which rates of exchange are fixed against the pound sterling. This usually occurs at the end of June or beginning of July in the preceding year. This ensures that the public can make meaningful comparisons between the prices of tour programmes to similar destinations, and that the mass operators are competing 'on a level playing field'. However, operators can also *buy forward* the foreign currency they will require, to protect themselves against currency fluctuations. If they are involved in exchanging large sums of money, they can buy *futures* in the international money market. Needless to say, this involves speculation and an element of risk; if the operator guesses wrong, the company's prices may end up uncompetitive against those of other companies.

Discounting strategies

Discounts on published tour prices have become a widely accepted practice in the industry since retail price maintenance in the industry was curtailed in the 1980s. Originally applied to late bookings, in order to clear seats, the technique has more recently been used by the larger operators to persuade members of the public to book earlier, under a system of 'fluid pricing'. Other operators prefer to rely on guarantees to early bookers against any increases in price prior to their departure.

Since a legal challenge made in 1987 by one retailer, the Ilkeston Co-op's travel agency, against operators that forced agents to sell tours at prices determined by the operators themselves, retailers have been allowed to discount tours they sold by passing on to the clients a proportion of their commission. In practice, this has meant that the largest discounts can be allowed by the largest multiple travel agencies, which can negotiate target overriding commissions well above the 10 per cent norm, and in effect can pass on to their clients almost all the 10 per cent basic commission. As this percentage represents the total commission which most independent agents receive from operators, the independents cannot match this and therefore find it very difficult to compete. However, many try to offer alternative benefits, such as free insurance, to attract business. The heavy discounting policy of the two major chains, Lunn Poly and Going Places, in particular has been a major factor in boosting their share of the mass market. Until the Competition Commission ruled out the practice of tying sales of package tours

to compulsory insurance, on which high profits were available, this was common practice with the largest chains. There is little evidence of the industry moving away from deep discounting, however; Thomson Holidays and others were discounting tours by as much as 30 per cent at the launch of their summer 2000 programmes.

Costing the package

A tour operator, as we have noted, must purchase three main inputs which will comprise an inclusive tour: transport, accommodation and services. The latter will include transfers between terminals and the accommodation abroad, and the services provided by the company's resort representative at the site. The operator will also, of course, have to meet costs which arise within the company's headquarters; these will include administration, reservations, marketing and advertising etc. Finally, the operator will have to meet the cost of commission allowed to retailers, and of servicing those retailers. A typical inclusive tour from the UK might well have the kind of cost structure outlined in Table 12.6.

Since the profits achieved by most operators after allowing agency commissions are actually quite narrow – perhaps as little as 1–3 per cent of revenue, after covering all costs – the operator will seek to top up revenue in any other way possible. For the mass-market operator, the bulk of revenue – in excess of 50 per cent, normally – is achieved through the sales of

Table 12.6 Typical cost structure of an inclusive tour using charter air services

Costs	Percentage of overall costs
Charter air seat	45
Hotel accommodation	37
Other services at destination	3
Head office overheads	5
Travel agency commission	10
	100

summer holidays. Perhaps another 15–20 per cent will be achieved through a winter tour programme, and the balance of revenue is achieved through a mix of sales of excursions at the destination, the interest received on deposits and final payments invested, foreign currency speculation, and sale of insurance policies.

The normal booking season for summer holidays starts in the autumn of the preceding year, reaching its peak in the three months following Christmas, so a large proportion of deposits will have been paid by the end of March. Although the operators themselves will have had to make deposits for aircraft charters at the beginning of the season, and may also have had to make some advance to hoteliers to ensure their rooms are held, the balance of payment will not fall due until after the clients have completed their holiday. Operators will have the use of deposit payments for anything up to a year in advance, and will have final payments at least eight weeks before they themselves have to settle their accounts. This money is invested to earn interest, and in many cases this interest will actually exceed the profits made by tour operating itself. Clearly, one effect of the growing tendency of British holiday-makers to book their holidays later, and to pay by credit card, will be a fall in earnings by the operators, which may be forced to compensate by raising the price of their holidays.

Further profits are achieved through the sale of ancillary services, such as excursions, car hire and (if the airline used is part of the parent organization) the sale of duty-free goods to non-EU destinations on board flights. The withdrawal of duty-free sales within the EU hit some operator revenues quite severely, but it is not yet clear whether the pattern of tourist flows has changed as a result, with tourists switching to non-EU destinations to gain duty-free benefits. Countries such as Turkey or Malta could particularly benefit from any such development.

One further contribution to revenue is achieved by imposing cancellation charges. These charges will often substantially exceed any costs borne by the operator which result from the cancellation, and indeed the operator may well be able to sell the can-celled accommodation again, gaining double revenue. However, once again the EU Directive on Package Holidays now allows the substitution of names by the clients to replace cancelled bookings.

Finally, the issue of agents' commission is a key one, and will be discussed towards the end of the chapter. Given the pressure on operators to reduce their costs, the developments now taking place in seeking new means of remunerating agents have important implications for the future of the distribution network.

Perhaps the move to direct-sell operations, also discussed later in this chapter, is the most worrying trend of all for the independents, both agents and operators. The increasing ease of booking direct through the Internet (and bookings through digital TV are just coming on stream) is proving attractive to consumers now long familiar with computers, and if prices can drop significantly through the use of these systems, there can be little doubt that the repercussions within the industry will be immense.

Yield management

The high levels of competition for summer programme sales will require the operator to take a great deal of care to get the price of the company's packages right, so that sufficient demand is generated to fill available seats, while at the same time prices are not so cheap as to threaten profitability. This skill of *yield management* is frequently defeated by the excess capacity available on the market, forcing companies to 'dump' packages at whatever price they can realize which will, at least, help to make a contribution to the company's overheads. There is some evidence that companies are improving their skills at yield management by better forecasting or a willingness to reduce capacity in order to get a better balance between supply and demand. While such action has been taken largely through implicit agreements between the major operators, there is always the risk that the smaller operators will see this as an opportunity to steal some market share from the brand leaders, and increase their own capacity.

If prices are set too low initially, and late demand in the season results in a 'sell-out', the company will not have maximized its profit opportunity. At the same time, if the company finds itself involved in added expenditure in the course of the summer – for example, in providing accommodation and meals for clients delayed through air traffic control strikes or go-slows, which cannot be foreseen a year in advance but occur not infrequently in Europe (they were a notable feature of the summer 2000 trading period) – what might have been a slim but acceptable profit can soon be turned into an overall loss.

Another aspect of yield management is the decision taken on when to launch the new holiday programme. Companies launching ahead of their rivals will always hope to steal a larger proportion of the early booking market, and of course have revenue which can be invested over a longer period. While the pattern in the past is for a launch in September, as we saw earlier in this chapter the larger operators have been progressively launching earlier, with some summer holidays appearing on the market as early as April the previous year. The jury is still out as to whether the advantages of early sales achieved through this means are sufficient to offset the drawbacks, not least of confusing both agents and customers through the range of choice on offer at any given time.

The tour brochure

The tour operator's brochure is a vital marketing tool, being the main influence on the customer's decision to buy. Tourism is an intangible product which customers are obliged to purchase without having the opportunity to inspect it, and often from a base of very inadequate knowledge. In these circumstances, the brochure becomes the principal means of both informing customers about the product and persuading them to purchase it.

For this reason, very large sums are invested in the brochure itself, and in advertising to persuade the customers to enter the travel agent's and pick one up.

In particular, the production of the brochure will represent a very significant proportion of the total marketing budget for the year, with print runs, in the case of the largest operators, running into tens of millions, at a unit cost of well over £1 a copy. Accordingly, it is essential for the operator to ensure that this large expenditure achieves its intended results. In spite of this, however, there is considerable wastage. In one study undertaken by the environmental lobby Green Flag International, it was estimated that of 120 million British travel brochures printed in one year, 48 million were never used. This wastage rate, coupled with the high cost of each copy that is picked up and consulted free, was estimated to add approximately £20 to the price of the average package holiday.

Brochure design and format

Larger companies will either have their brochures designed and prepared in their own advertising department, or they will coordinate the production with a design studio, often associated with the advertising agency they use. The agency will help to negotiate with printers to obtain the best quotation for producing the brochure, and will ensure that print deadlines are met. Other operators will tackle the design of the brochure themselves, and this process is being increasingly aided by computer graphic packages which allow desktop publishing, by which means the operator is able to produce the entire contents of the brochure, including all illustrations, on an in-house computer. The computer will organize the layout, selecting the best location of text and illustrations to minimize use of space, thus helping to reduce cost. Naturally, the financial investment in the technology necessary to undertake this work is considerable.

Smaller operators which do tackle the design of the brochure themselves are best advised to use the help of an independent design studio, which can provide the professional expertise in layout, artwork and copy that are so important in the design of a professional piece of publicity material. Most printers

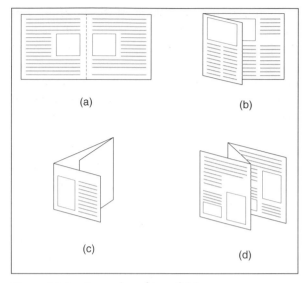

(a)

(b)

(c)

(d)

Figure 12.6   Examples of tour folders

have their own design departments which can undertake this work for their clients, but unless the company has had experience of the standards of work of their printer, they are probably better advised to approach an independent studio for this work.

The purposes the brochure serves will dictate its design and format. A single ad hoc programme, for example to a foreign trade exhibition, may be printed as nothing more than a leaflet, or if a limited programme of tours is contemplated these may be laid out in the form of a simple folder.

Folders can take a number of different forms, ranging from a *centrefold* to more complicated folds (see Figure 12.6). Larger brochures (or in printing parlance, *booklets*) consist of eight or more pages, printed in multiples of four sheets which require binding together in some manner. Smaller brochures are usually machine-bound by *saddle-stitching* (stapling through the spine), while larger brochures may be *side-stitched* with a glue-on cover, or bound as a book. It is not the aim here to discuss printing methods in detail, and the reader is referred for further reading in the subject to the many excellent books on print publicity.

Package tour brochures can be described as falling into three categories: *shell folders, umbrella* brochures and *regular* tour brochures. The use of a shell folder

is a convenient way to reduce printing costs, and is particularly suited for limited-capacity tour programmes or ad hoc specialist tours. Shells are blank folders interspersed with preprinted photographs, and are provided at low cost by airlines or national tourist offices to encourage smaller tour operators to run programmes using their services or destinations. The operators can overprint a suitable text describing their tour programme; since only the text needs to be added, a one-colour print run at low cost will meet the requirements of scheduled airlines for inclusive tour basing fares approval.

An umbrella brochure can be produced in order to allow a travel agent to become, effectively, a package holiday organizer. The brochure only covers the basic essentials to satisfy IATA airlines' requirements for independent inclusive tour operating, but this will allow the agent to build a tailor-made package around net tour basing fares. However, these brochures have largely fallen into disuse, as agents have the means of obtaining cheap airline tickets from a multitude of sources which may undercut regular inclusive tour basing fares.

The rest of the tour brochures are purpose-designed for regular package holiday series. They usually comprise all of an operator's summer or winter tours in a single brochure. However, many larger operators have diversified into a great many different types of holiday – long-haul and short-haul, coach tours as well as air holidays, lakes and mountain resorts as well as seaside resorts – and if all these were to be combined into a single brochure, it would run to hundreds of pages and be both clumsy to handle and very expensive to produce. There would also be high wastage, as clients who know the type of holiday they want will have to pick up the entire brochure to get their particular product. Operators have therefore produced individual brochures, even in some cases separate brochures by destination. One example of the range produced by a single operator is shown in Table 12.7.

As well as overcoming the problems identified earlier, this will have the added advantage of filling more of the agents' rack space, leaving less available

Table 12.7 Thomas Cook range of holiday brochures, 2000

JMC Summer Sun	JMC Turkey
JMC Essentials	JMC Greece
JMC Family World	JMC Cyprus
JMC All-inclusives	JMC Florida
JMC Select	JMC Tunisia
Tropical Shores	JMC Goa, Sri Lanka and the Maldives
JMC Winter Sun	JMC Portugal
JMC Beach Villas	JMC Airfares
JMC Lakes and Mountains	JMC Golden Circle

Thomas Cook Holidays (long-haul)
Club 18–30
Neilson
Style

space for competitors. If the leading half-dozen operators produce as many as 70–80 different brochures – all top sellers for agents – this will require the agents to devote as much as half their rack space to these brands.

The first task of a brochure is to attract attention. Operators have therefore developed a 'house style' for the covers of their brochures which is quickly recognized by customers, when placed on the agents' racks. These are usually images of attractive models in beachwear combined with an eye-catching symbol and house name across the top of the brochure. While some might contend that there is a disappointing sameness among the leading operators' brochures today, taken individually the quality and professionalism of their brochure design is outstanding. As brochures today must also reinforce an image of quality and reliability, the text and images contained in brochures must not only be attractive but also truthful, accurate and easily comprehended. Good layout, high-quality photography and suitable paper are all essential if the brochure is to do its job effectively.

Obligations affecting tour brochures

As was stated earlier, the brochure must both inform and persuade the potential tourist. Tour operators are selling dreams, and their brochures must allow consumers to fantasize a little about their holidays. But it is also vitally important that consumers are not misled about any aspect of their holiday. Care must be taken not to infringe the Trades Description Act 1968, section 14 of which deals with the offence of making false statements concerning the provision of services.

In the past, operators have invoked the law of agency in claiming that within their booking conditions they act as agents only in representing hotels, transport companies or other principals. However, the provisions of the Unfair Contract Terms Act 1977 went some way towards placing the burden of responsibility on operators themselves for the services they represent, and this was enhanced by the EU Directive on Package Travel. This simplifies proceedings for the tourist, who can sue the operator for offences for which their suppliers abroad are responsible, requiring the operator in turn to sue the supplier in the destination country.

The Consumer Protection Act 1988 makes it illegal to give a misleading indication of the price of goods and services. Operators must therefore ensure that the price panels in their brochures provide full details of the tour costs. ABTA's Tour Operators' Code of Conduct also imposes specific obligations upon operators to provide honest and accurate information, an obligation which EU law strengthened.

Information required in the brochure

To satisfy not only the ITX conditions but also the clients' need for information on regular charter programmes, the operator should include the following information in the brochure:

- the name of the firm responsible for the IT;
- the means of transport used, including, in the case of air transport, the name of the carrier(s), type and class of aircraft used and whether scheduled or charter aircraft are operated;
- full details of destinations, itinerary and times of travel;

- the duration of each tour (number of days/nights' stay);
- full description of the location and type of accommodation provided, including any meals;
- whether services of a representative are available abroad;
- a clear indication of the price for each tour, including any taxes;
- exact details of special arrangements, e.g. if there is a games room in the hotel, whether this is available at all times and whether any charges are made for the use of this equipment;
- full conditions of booking, including details of cancellation conditions;
- details of any insurance coverage (clients should have the right to choose their own insurance, providing this offers equivalent coverage);
- details of documentation required for travel to the destinations featured, and any health hazards or inoculations recommended.

A booking form is usually printed within the brochure for completing a reservation. The terms and conditions of the booking should appear in full in the brochure, but should not be printed on the back of the booking form, as they need to be retained by the customer.

Negotiating with the printer

Printers will not expect their clients necessarily to be experts in printing methods, but those involved with the processing and production of a brochure should be reasonably familiar with current techniques in printing and common terms used. Printers will need to know:

- The number of brochures required.
- The number of colours used in the printing. Full colour work normally involves four colours, but some cost savings should be possible if colour photography is not to be included.
- The paper to be used: size, format, quality and weight. The choice of paper will be influenced by several factors, including the printing process

used. Size may be dictated by the industry's requirements; for example, a tour operating brochure needs to fit a standard travel agency rack. Paper quality varies according to the material from which it is made. It may be glossy or matt, but will be selected for its whiteness and opacity. Inevitably, this requires some compromise, as very white paper tends to be less opaque, and one must avoid print showing through to the other side of the sheet. The weight of paper will of course depend upon its effect on the overall weight of the brochure, if this is to be mailed in quantity.

- The number and positions of illustrations (photos, artwork, maps etc.) used.
- Typesetting needs. There are over 6,000 typefaces from which to choose, and the style of type chosen should reflect the theme of the brochure, its subject and the image of the company.
- Completion and delivery dates.

When obtaining prices from the printer, operators should approach several companies, as quotes can vary substantially between printers. Many operators choose to have their brochures printed abroad. Good quality work can be produced at very competitive prices for long print runs, but obviously the operator will want to compare whether British printers can match prices quoted abroad, since use of a domestic printer will reduce transport costs. Most importantly, operators must avoid cutting corners to save money, as an inferior print job can threaten the whole success of the tour programme. The progress of the printing must be supervised throughout, either by the operator itself or its advertising agency. Proofs should be submitted at each stage of production to check on accuracy and a final corrected proof should be seen before the actual print run to ensure there are no outstanding errors.

The printer should be asked to quote not only for the actual number of brochures that are expected to be required, but for the run-on price for additional copies. Once a brochure is set up for printing, the cost of running off a few extra thousand is very small compared to the overall price, and it may be better to do this rather than having to reorder at a later date.

At the time of writing, there is some discussion on the possibility of dropping price panels from brochures altogether, to allow greater use of the fluid pricing mechanism. This has the obvious advantage of allowing the operator to change prices at will according to demand, but fear of consumer resistance has meant that no decision has yet been taken on this issue.

Brochure distribution and control

Tour operators must make the decision either to use all of the retail agencies available to them, or to select those whom they feel will be most productive for the company. Whatever decision is made, operators must also establish a policy for their brochure distribution to these agents. If equal supplies of brochures are distributed to every agent, many copies will be wasted.

Wastage can be reduced by establishing standards against which to monitor the performance of travel agents. A key ratio is that of brochures given out to bookings received. 'Average' figures appear to vary considerably among different operators; while one will expect to gain a booking for every three or four brochures given out (which may still mean that every booking carries the burden of some £6–7 in brochure production costs), specialist operators may have to give out as many as 25–30 brochures to obtain a single booking. The position is slightly improved when one remembers that each booking will involve typically between 2.5 and 3 persons. If figures consistently poorer than this are achieved by any of its agents, the operator should look for an explanation. The problem could be accounted for by the agent's lack of control over their own brochure distribution: do they merely stock their display racks and leave clients to pick up whatever numbers they wish, or do they make a serious attempt to sell to 'browsers'? Some agents go even further than this, and retain all stocks of brochures except a display copy, so that customers have to ask for copies of the brochures they require. This is instrumental in cutting down waste, as well as increasing sales opportunities.

It is now the practice of most operators to categorize their agents in some way, in terms of their productivity. This could typically take the following form:

	Bookings per year
Category A: top producing agents, multiples	100+
Category B: good agents	50–99
Category C: fair agents	20–49
Category D: below average agents	6–19
Category E: poor agents, producing little	0–5

Of course, for a specialist operator, the sales categories might be considerably smaller; a good agent may be producing as few as 10 bookings a year. However, the principle remains the same; the operator will determine, on the strengths of these categories, what level of support to give the agent. At the top of the scale, agents can expect to receive as many brochures as they ask for, while at the other end, perhaps the operator will be willing to provide only a file copy, or two to three brochures to work with. Many new or independent agents are finding it increasingly difficult to obtain any supplies of brochures from the major operators, which are increasingly narrowing the focus of their distribution policy.

The reservations system

In order to put a package tour programme into operation, a reservations system must be developed and implemented. The design of the system will depend upon whether reservations are to be handled manually (an increasingly rare system, given the current availability of low-cost computer programs to handle bookings) or by computer, and on whether the operator plans to sell through agents or direct to the public.

Most tour operators sell their tours principally through the high street travel agents, which still generate 80–90 per cent of all bookings made. This being the case, the operator must provide the best and fastest reservations system possible for the agent's use.

Manual systems have several disadvantages. A travel agent needs to contact the operator quickly when serving a client at the counter. If telephone lines are engaged, or not answered for long periods of time, the agent may become frustrated and decide to deal with a competitor who is easier to contact. Installing an automatic call distribution (ACD) system, by which calls are automatically queued until a line becomes free, will not prove entirely satisfactory, as agents face mounting phone bills while holding on until the line clears. This has led most operators to opt for a computer-operated reservations system.

All of the bigger tour operators (those carrying 50,000 or more clients) and virtually all smaller operators today have computerized reservations systems (CRSs); with advances in technology and declining costs for computer systems, reliance on a manual system even among operators carrying as few as 5,000 clients is becoming the exception rather than the rule.

Initially, the CRS operated only 'in-house', i.e. within the operator's own premises. Agents seeking to make a booking would telephone the operator, who tapped into the company's computer to check availability. It was but a short step from this to link the agent directly into the CRS, using a visual display unit (VDU) in the agent's office. Thomson, the market leader, was the first operator to decide that all bookings through agents should be handled in this fashion, forcing agents to invest in the appropriate hardware. Most other large companies rapidly followed suit.

These connections originally depended upon the use of telephone wires to link the agent's VDU to the operator's CRS. This posed problems of cost and time wasting for the agent, if lines were busy and there was difficulty in accessing a CRS. Subsequently,

agents were 'hard-wired' directly into the operators' CRSs, reducing time and allowing the agent to switch directly from one CRS to another without redialling.

Implementing a reservation

The computer will allow the agent to see whether the particular tour required is available, or if it is not, will automatically display the dates or destinations nearest to the client's needs. Once the agent has established that a package is acceptable to the client, a booking is made (sometimes an option can be taken for 24 hours, but operators are now tending to accept only firm bookings). Any late changes to the programme which are not in the brochure can be drawn to the attention of the client and agent on the screen at this time. The agent is provided with a code number to identify the booking, and obtains a completed booking form from the client, together with a deposit.

The computer booking is sufficient to hold the reservation, and booking forms are now held in the agent's files rather than, as formerly, sent to the operator with the deposit. The operator will issue an interim invoice to confirm the booking, upon receipt of the deposit, and a final invoice will be issued normally about ten weeks before the client is due to leave, requesting full payment eight weeks before departure. Changes to the programme cannot be made once the final invoice has been issued. After receipt of the final payment, the operator will issue all tickets, itineraries and, where necessary, vouchers, and despatch these to the agent, who forwards them to the client.

Prior to each departure, a flight manifest is prepared for the airline, with names of all those booked, and a rooming list is sent to the hotels concerned and to resort representatives where appropriate. The latter should go over the rooming list with the hotelier to ensure that all is in order prior to the clients' arrival.

Larger tour operators will have a customer relations department whose function is to monitor and handle passenger and agency complaints and ensure quality control in the operation of the tour programme.

Late bookings

Tour operators are anxious to fill every seat in their tour programme. The ability to react quickly to deal with last-minute demand for bookings plays a key role in fulfilling this objective. Around 40 per cent of summer holiday bookings are now booked after 1 April, and a similar booking pattern has emerged for winter holidays. Coupled with the offer of last-minute discounts, many operators have introduced procedures designed to pick up these late bookings, including the rapid updating of availability on computer reservations systems, and a booking procedure which allows tickets to be collected at the airport on departure. The new dot.com companies provide an excellent new medium for selling off unsold flights and accommodation at short notice.

The distribution network

The selection of retailers

Basically, the tour operator has to choose between two alternative methods of selling its tour programmes – either through retail travel agents, or direct to the public. Larger operators whose product is of universal appeal and whose market is national in scope will expect to sell the bulk of their holidays through the retail trade, but will be glad to receive occasional bookings direct also, as we have seen. Companies with a policy of selling direct to the public will be examined at the end of this chapter.

Few operators deal indiscriminately with all retail agents. As with most products sold, some 80 per cent of package holidays are actually sold through 20 per cent of the retail agents, while a large number of agents will make very few sales (the so-called 'Pareto principle'). The cost of servicing the less productive agents is often greater than the revenue they produce – they must not only be provided with expensive free brochures, but also receive regular mailings to update their information, and are supported by sales material and even, in some cases, visits from sales representatives of the operator. The operators must therefore decide whether to vary the support they offer to different agents, or even to dispense with the services of some agents altogether. We have already seen how brochure supplies will be varied according to the productivity of the agent. It has been the practice of operators to support their best agents by offering them an overriding commission of between 1 per cent and 5 per cent, in addition to the basic 10 per cent, for achieving target sales figures. The large multiples, due to the strength of their position in the retail trade, can negotiate the highest overrides, giving them the ability to discount substantially in order to attract yet more business.

Thomson Holidays has taken numerous changes of direction regarding its agents' remuneration in recent years, and this is illustrative of the efforts being made by the large operators to cut costs and increase productivity. Agency commission is a substantial element of cost, and there is now a move away from the traditional basic plus bonus payments schemes of the largest companies described above. In 1998, Thomson signified that agents' basic commission would be cut to 7 per cent under a three-tier structure, with new and tougher terms of agreement for those agents wishing to receive higher commissions of 10–12 per cent. Such agents were expected to devote more effort to selling Thomson products, and, most controversially, were to be asked to provide the operator with a list of the names and addresses of their Thomson clients. In return, Thomson agreed to provide greater sales support for its most favoured agents. Airtours, meanwhile, established a controversial link with the independent agents' consortium Advantage, a move which was interpreted by many in the trade as threatening the independence and objectivity of these agents. Such moves, coupled with increasing efforts to sell products direct to the public through direct-sell divisions and the World Wide Web, are an indication of the new directions in thinking demonstrated by the largest British operators, and represent a worrying trend for the independent agent.

There remains scope for some of the independent agents to increase their efforts to sell specialist or smaller tour companies' products. Some are focusing on the sale of holidays offered by the Association of Independent Tour Operators, whose products are niche marketed to avoid competing directly with the mass-market holiday destinations. Leading operators which do not have the benefit of direct support from a multiple would also find themselves at a disadvantage. Since First Choice identified this key weakness and took steps to establish its own chain at the end of the 1990s, only Cosmos among the leading five is without a dedicated chain.

The smaller operators, those whose market strengths lie in certain geographic regions, or those catering for specific niche markets often involving quite a small number of customers in total, are obviously not in a position to support a national network of retailers. Most will choose to sell direct to their customers, although a handful may try to concentrate sales through a limited number of supportive agents.

Relationships with travel agents

It is customary for tour operators to draw up a formal agreement with the travel agents they appoint to sell their services. These agreements specify the terms and conditions of trading, including such issues as the normal rates of commission paid, and whether credit will be extended to the agent or settlement of accounts must be made in cash.

An ill-defined area in these agreements is that of the application of the law of agency. A contract is between the principal and the client, and this raises the question of whether a travel agent is acting as agent of the principal or agent of the client. Some agreements will suggest that the agent is the agent of the principal, but since the collapse of Clarksons Holidays in 1974, when a large amount of money had been paid by customers to agents but had not yet reached the operator, it has generally been held that

this 'pipeline' money is rightfully the clients'; some agreements go so far as to specify this.

Under the terms of these agreements, the agent agrees to support and promote the sale of their principals' services. In return, the operator agrees to provide the support and cooperation necessary for the successful merchandising of the company's products, i.e. provision of adequate supplies of brochures, sales promotion material and sometimes finance for cooperative regional advertising or promotion campaigns. Operators will also try to ensure that their retailers are knowledgeable about the products they sell. This will be achieved through the circulation of sales letters or mail shots, by invitations to workshops or other presentations, and by inviting selected agents on educational study trips.

The educational study trip

The educational trip (or 'familiarization trip', as it is known in North America) is a study trip organized by principals (whether tour operators, carriers or tourist offices of the regions involved). Such trips are organized for a variety of purposes; for example, members of the media, or travel writers, will be taken to tourist destinations in order for the principals to gain free – and hopefully, positive – media coverage. Travel agents are also offered opportunities to undertake trips in order to improve their knowledge of the destinations, or to encourage them to sell the region or product. Visits to a destination are known to be one of the most effective means of encouraging agents to sell a particular package, and these organized trips also have a social function, enabling the operators to get to know their agents better and to obtain feedback from them. However, the cost of mounting educational trips is high, even if a proportion of the costs is met by the hotels in the destination, or the national tourist offices and carriers helping to organize the programme, and principals will try to do everything they can to ensure that the educational trip gives them value for money. This was not always the case in the past, where educational visits abroad were often treated as 'jollies', attractive as a social perk rather than an educational experience. The effectiveness of these educationals has been improved by more careful selection of candidates, by providing a more balanced mix of visits, working sessions and social activities, and by imposing a small charge for attendance, so that travel agency managers will take care to ensure that the expense is justified in terms of increased productivity and expertise among their staff.

Careful selection of candidates will ensure that all those attending share common objectives, and that, for example, senior agency managers and young counter clerks do not find themselves together on the same educational, to the discomfort of both. Monitoring performance, by soliciting reports from those attending and by checking the sales performance of staff from those agencies invited to participate, will help to ensure that the operators' money has been well spent.

The sales representative

Tour operators, like most larger travel principals, employ sales representatives to maintain and develop their business through travel agents, and to solicit new sources of business. The functions of the sales representatives are to call on present and potential contacts, advise agents and others of the services they offer, and support their agents with suitable merchandising material.

These representatives act as one point of contact between the agent and operator, when problems or complaints are raised, and the often close relationship that develops between representatives and their contacts is valuable in helping to build brand loyalty for the company. The personal contact enables them to receive direct feedback from the marketplace about client and agency attitudes towards the company and its products. Representatives are also likely to play a valuable role in categorizing agents in terms of their potential, and selecting sales staff for educational trips. However, making sales calls in person is expensive, and most companies have now switched to telephone sales calls to keep in touch

with all but their most productive agents. As with the resort representatives abroad, however, the sales representative is another means by which the company can be distinguished from its competitors, and the appropriateness of a trend to less personal contact is questionable. It is true that many agents have mixed feelings about the merits of sales representatives, who are seen by some as time-wasting socializers. It goes without saying that if the representatives are to do their job effectively, they must be well trained; those who are not sufficiently knowledgeable about their companies' or their competitors' products will relay a poor image of the company to the agent.

Direct sell operators

Apart from those operators who will inevitably sell direct to their clients, for the reasons outlined above, a handful of larger tour operators have chosen deliberately to market their products direct to the public. This movement was spearheaded by the Danish company Tjaereborg, which entered the British market in the late 1970s with a promotional strategy that asserted that directly booked holidays, by cutting out the agents' commission, would represent a saving to the customers. However, while isolated bargains were certainly on offer, many holidays were no cheaper, and sometimes more expensive than similar packages booked through an agent. The reasons for this are not hard to understand; while travel agency commissions were saved, huge budgets were required to inform and promote to the mass public. The company had to invest millions in heavy advertising in the media, and similar high costs were incurred by the need to have a large reservations staff and multiple telephone lines to answer enquiries from the public. These costs are, of course, fixed, while commissions are only paid to agents when the latter achieve a sale. Tjaereborg soon found, after initial success which was probably the outcome of curiosity, that it was unable to achieve greater market penetration, especially as Thomson Holidays had rapidly joined the competition with a direct sell division, Portland Holidays. Tjaereborg, after turning in an indifferent performance for several years, was sold to First Choice (then called Owners Abroad), which eventually replaced the brand with another direct sell operation, Eclipse.

The evidence suggests that traditional buying patterns die hard among British holiday-makers, with many customers still seeking the assurance of face-to-face contact with an agent, even if the product knowledge of that agent may be limited. However, there are some interesting variations in the pattern of agency sales; for example, those in the London area demonstrate a higher propensity to buy their holidays direct than do other Britons, and certain types of package tour, such as ski holidays and coach tours, also experience a higher proportion of direct bookings. The advent of interactive booking of travel arrangements using the Internet is expected to change this pattern dramatically over the next few years, as we shall see in the last section of this chapter.

The IT revolution and its impact on tour operating

No business is being transformed by information technology faster or more radically than the business of travel, and tour operating is arguably the most affected of all sectors of the business by developments occurring in this field. Of course, the advent of modern technology is no longer a recent phenomenon – after all, computers were widely introduced into the trade during the 1960s, hastening the demise of the traditional manual booking system. However, it is the scale and pace of recent development which is proving so disruptive for the industry, as new forms of booking and information facility become available to both the trade and the customer. Even the humble telephone has become a tool for providing new techniques to book holidays, with the growth of call centres and the recent development of WAP (Wireless Application Protocol), which allows customers to download material from various information sources into their mobile phones.

The key question is not whether these new techniques will replace the traditional methods of booking holidays, but rather how quickly this transition will occur, and what kind of future then remains for the traditional agency channels. At the time of writing, only a limited number of holiday sales are actually made online through the World Wide Web; by the end of 2000, it was estimated that only some dozen companies had fully integrated systems that permitted all bookings to be made from the same stock, either through viewdata or the WWW. Some others had systems that allowed software to bridge these alternatives, but operators had to load their stock separately into web sites. Most analysts believe that viewdata will have given way to Internet Protocol services by 2004.

Various explanations are advanced for the slow take-up of new systems by travel consumers. These range from the inherent conservatism of British consumers, to inadequate knowledge and skills in the use of IT, uncertainty about reliability of the many new dot.com companies, fear that revealing credit card details over the telephone may lead to fraudulent use, and concern about the impartiality of the information received through these channels. Undoubtedly, all of these have some validity in discouraging sales through new channels, and it must be recognized that the industry, too, has been conservative in applying new technology. However, the evidence favours the long-term growth of the high-tech booking system at the expense of traditional channels. Let us review these new systems briefly.

High-technology systems can be broadly defined as:

- information and reservations systems offered by the suppliers of travel products and available to travel agents or other retailers;
- similar systems offered by intermediaries on behalf of travel suppliers;
- similar systems offered by either suppliers, or through intermediaries, direct to the consumer.

The principal means of delivering these new systems include Internet services on the World Wide Web via the personal computer, interactive television channels and the increasingly sophisticated use of mobile telephones.

A feature of the rapid escalation of Internet online providers in the twenty-first century has been the subsequent and equally rapid collapse of many of these same companies, largely those acting as intermediaries for the travel suppliers. Inevitably, as suppliers set up their own communication networks to service agents or the public, this has threatened to undermine the intermediaries, which depend upon the commissions received from their suppliers. The trend is apparent in taking one example; Airtours bought a major US electronic distribution company in 2000. However, the intermediaries' role is assured as long as they can continue to offer a wide range of competitive products and are judged by the public to be impartial in providing these services. Whether major suppliers will be willing to continue offering their products through intermediaries if they can satisfactorily sell a sufficient majority of these direct to the public will determine the future success of the latter. Equally, directional selling by suppliers through their own online facilities will tend to undermine many sales through agents, and although this is unlikely ever to lead to the total demise of the travel agent – many consumers will still want to deal with retailers face to face – it will provide agents with a new challenge. Only those who can demonstrate that they are providing *added value*, through superior service, knowledge or some other aspect of the retailing function, are likely to survive. This may lead to agents imposing service charges in lieu of the traditional commissions which are currently their main source of income. The present intense competition among the intermediaries, and the establishment of new companies almost on a daily basis, reflects belief in the long-term future of this form of retailing, but is also likely to conclude with just a handful of companies surviving to serve truly global markets. In the meantime, rapid development of alternative channels is hindered by two further factors. Operators have been slow to realize the potential of the new technology – some are still frightened of it – and in general marketing costs remain high for suppliers attempting to sell direct to the public. Nonetheless, more and more operators are becoming aware that selling in this way will eventually allow suppliers to trim, and possibly even eradicate, their two major sources of expenditure, commission and brochures. Already much information on destinations and facilities is available for public viewing on the Internet, and before long all holiday information currently provided by operators through the medium of brochures will become accessible in this way.

Airlines, especially the budget air carriers, with a simpler product to sell, have successfully developed direct sell through web sites – Ryanair, for instance, now takes the majority of its bookings online. The more complex and expensive operation of booking a holiday online is also becoming more common. Web sites are already widely in use for cheap and late availability holidays, and inevitably the Internet will become a major force in retailing. Initially, this will come about as consumers gain increasing access to suppliers' sites. As this facility becomes more widely available to the public, so will sales through agents fall. At the same time, the growth of call centres, set up to take bookings over the phone, is providing a convenient choice of outlets, offering very competitive prices, for holiday customers. Fluid pricing strategies introduced by operators allow holidays to be more readily retailed through these call centres than through traditional channels. As a result, call centres are already impacting on the traditional multi-agency chains of the leading tour operators; early in 2001, Airtours announced the closure of 120 Going Places shops, following the discovery that one in four of its customers was now using either the telephone or web site to book their holidays.

In the longer term, interactive television promises to have an equally significant impact on the industry. In Britain, terrestrial TV is to be replaced by multi-channel digital television by 2010. Already, shopping channels and travel channels are available through cable and satellite TV, attracting the public into searching for, and booking, their holidays in this convenient manner. Asynchronous digital subscriber line technology allows viewers to choose what they watch, to pause and to rewind material they wish to study more closely. Although commercial agreements with the channel owners currently prohibit direct bookings on the TV screen, this is bound to be the next stage of development in retailing travel.

The speed of development of technology in this field is too rapid to allow a thorough treatment of the subject in a textbook. Students of tour operating must keep abreast of such developments through the trade press or other media. Suffice to add that in addition to reservations systems, computers are now used widely to provide accounts and management information quickly and accurately to both operators and agents, while larger operators have also introduced accounting systems which allow direct transfer of agency payments from the agents' bank account to that of the operator.

Questions and discussion points

1. The DTI ruled in 2000 that from October travel agents must publicly reveal their links with parent operators which control more than 5 per cent of the market. Is this sufficient to satisfy the complaints of the independent agents? And in what ways, if any, will the travelling public be affected by the ruling?

2. Explain the difference between incoming and outbound operators. Why is the former sector of the industry usually smaller and more fragmented? Why do the large outbound operators not get involved with incoming tours too?

3. How will German ownership affect the fortunes of Thomson Holidays? What benefits or disadvantages can you see for the holiday-maker by this development? Since publication of this text, what other changes in ownership have occurred among leading operators in Britain? Explain the reasons behind such changes.

4. What are the implications for the future of the industry and its customers in (a) the use of fluid pricing, and (b) the expansion in demand for all-inclusive holidays abroad?

Assignment topics

1. Industrial Holdings plc is a conglomerate with a rising investment in leisure. The company has retained Marketsearch Ltd, a group of consultants with whom you are employed, to weigh up the merits of entering the outbound tour operating business, either by taking over an established small to medium-sized company, or by setting up a new company. The company has ample financial resources to invest, but has reservations about investing in a field where profit margins are generally thin and competition high.

   You have been asked to provide an input into the preliminary report that Marketsearch is preparing for the company. Your employer has asked you to examine the profitability of the sector over the past five years, and to evaluate the current market and trends over the next five years. Using company annual reports where possible, research the state of the market and prepare a report in draft, with statistics that you plan to incorporate into the eventual final report.

2. As a former student of tourism, now employed by a seat broker, you have been invited back to your old college to talk to students on the subject of 'The seat-only market; where it's been, where it's going'. Prepare a set of notes for your talk, which will be expected to last about 30 minutes. As your talk will also make use of the overhead projector, you should prepare transparencies which you will use to illustrate your talk.

   (Note: the trade press from time to time has special articles on seat-only sales, which will help you in gathering up-to-date material.)

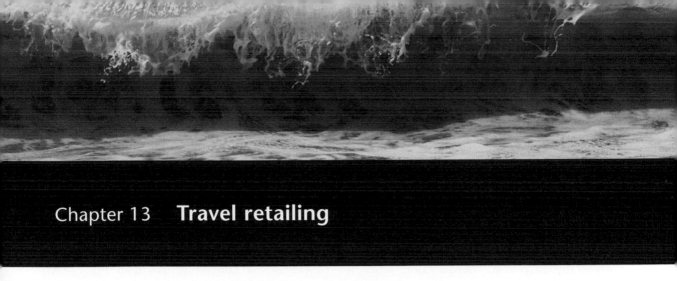

Chapter 13   Travel retailing

Objectives

After studying this chapter, you should be able to:

- explain the role of travel agents as a component of the tourism industry and their relationship with other sectors;
- identify the functions performed by an agent;
- be aware of the qualities necessary for effective agency management and service;
- understand the considerations and the requirements for establishing and running a travel agency;
- be aware of the constraints and threats under which agents operate, and evaluate alternative solutions for their survival.

Introduction

Most travel principals sell their products to consumers through the medium of travel agents. Such agents have been in existence for more than a hundred years; indeed, the oldest, now the tour operator Cox and Kings, traces its origins back to the eighteenth century. The Polytechnic Touring Association was set up at Regent Street Polytechnic, London, in 1888, originally as an agency for student travel, and was acquired by Sir Henry Lunn of Lunn's Travel in the 1960s. This company became Lunn Poly, one of Britain's leading chains, when taken over by Thomson Holidays in 1972.

The agents' main role in earlier times was to sell shipping and rail services, but with the coming of air transport and the development of the package tour business after World War II, travel retailers took on a new role.

Before the war, the shipping companies had been able to provide a good reservations and ticketing service direct to the public, with sales outlets in their city offices and at leading ports. Railways and coach operators had similarly established city centre terminals, from which they could dispense tickets direct to the public. However, when the airlines arrived on the scene, their airport terminals were situated well away from centres of population, and as a convenient network of travel agents was by that time in place, they decided against setting up their own chain of direct sales offices in favour of appointing agents to handle their sales. In turn, the agents expanded their distribution outlets to handle the new demand for air tickets. Only in the case of North America, where the volume of domestic travel by air is so substantial, did individual airlines establish city centre offices to deal direct with the public, and these continue to vie with agents for sales. British Airways has, in Britain, established a number of outlets in the leading city centres, but is still dependent upon travel agents for the bulk of its sales.

Historically, of course, Thomas Cook, which is today best known as a retailer, originated as a tour operator, only expanding later to retail travel services. In more recent times, it was the travel agents themselves who developed the first air package tours, as we have seen in Chapter 12. A handful of retail entrepreneurs had the vision to see that if they could buy air seats in bulk and reduce the cost of air fares, a huge mass market for foreign tours would develop. The packages they developed were, in turn, sold through other agents, and eventually became the retailers' largest source of revenue. Today, the vast majority of airline tickets, and eight out of ten package holidays, are purchased by consumers through retail agencies.

At the beginning of 2000 there were about 1,890 travel agents, controlling well over 7,000 agency branches in Britain which were affiliated to the Association of British Travel Agents (ABTA), the leading trade body representing both tour operators and travel agents. Although this number has remained fairly stable over the past twenty years, the composition of these agents has changed dramatically, with a fall in independent agencies as the major travel agency chains expanded.

Apart from these ABTA agents, there is also a growing number of independent agencies operating outside the ABTA framework. Because of the regulations which formerly constrained non-ABTA agents, these were limited in earlier years to selling fringe services such as coach trips, or operated as so-called 'bucket shops'. The latter term refers to outlets used by airlines to dump unsold tickets on the market at short notice and at heavily discounted prices. However, as the airline industry deregulated and consolidators were established to wholesale air tickets, discounted tickets became more widely available through ABTA/IATA appointed agencies, and the role of bucket shops declined sharply. Some continue to offer a technically illegal service in 'cross-border ticketing', a scheme whereby the agent issues a ticket for a two-leg or multi-leg journey in which the through cost is lower than the price for a single leg, and the first coupon of the ticket is discarded by the passenger. Thus, for example, if the fare between Athens and New York via London is less than the normal London–New York fare, a customer in London might be issued a through ticket with the section Athens–London discarded. This is contrary to IATA regulations, and is technically a legal offence.

Following the removal of Stabiliser regulations in 1992, agents became free to trade with all ABTA and non-ABTA tour operators, and are now subject only to legal requirements to carry satisfactory bonds against financial collapse. In the event, this has not led to the wholesale withdrawal of members from ABTA; the need for a powerful association to represent the interests of tour operators and retailers remains, and most retailers have chosen to retain their membership.

The role of travel agents

The travel agent's role is dissimilar to that of most other retailers, in that agents do not purchase a product for resale to their customers. Only when a customer has decided on a travel purchase do agents approach their principal on their customer's behalf to make a purchase. The travel agent does not, therefore, carry 'stock' of travel products. This has two important implications for the business of travel distribution. First, the cost of setting up in business is relatively small compared to that of other retail businesses, and second, agents are not seeking to dispose of products they have already purchased, so will therefore display less brand loyalty towards a particular product or company. However, in the past few years negotiations between principals and agents have led to higher commissions being paid to agents that achieve target sales, and this has resulted in agents becoming more commercial in their approach. This is particularly true of the multiples, or travel agency chains, which are owned by tour operators and push their parent companies' products, a process known as *directional selling*. Rather than the objective advice which customers could anticipate from an agency, it is now more common for them to be faced with a limited range of products which offer the agent the best return on sales. Some independents have tried to reverse this trend by claiming to offer objective advice, promoting the smaller, independent tour operators' products. The best-known organization devoted to this policy is the Campaign for Real Travel Agents (CARTA), with some 300 members at the time of writing. There has also been a tendency for independent agents to tie into consortia as a means of competing with the multiples, a process which will be examined later in this chapter. An international consortium has also been formed, the Worldwide Independent Travel Agents' Network (WIN), with membership in thirteen countries.

Arguably, the main role of the travel agent is to provide a convenient location for the purchase of travel. At these locations they act as booking agents for holidays and travel, as well as a source of information and advice on travel services. Their customers look to them for expert product knowledge and objectivity in the advice they offer, but, as we have seen, they may be disappointed, as agents choose to deal with an increasingly limited range of products on which they can maximize their revenue. In one sense, this is inevitable; the competitive nature of retail travel is such that margins are extremely thin, and agents must find whatever means they can of surviving. Nor is it realistic to imagine that sales staff – who are often young, generally inexperienced in travel themselves and poorly paid by comparison with other areas of retailing – can have a thorough knowledge of every product in the industry, with a product range of package tours alone drawn from well over 600 ATOL-holding bonded tour operators.

The range of products that an agent will choose to offer will vary, not only on the basis of the commission each earns but also depending upon the demand within the catchment area, the degree of specialization of the agency and the preferences and marketing policies of the proprietor. An agency that is attempting to provide a full range of services to the public would sell air tickets, cruise and ferry tickets, rail and coach transport, car hire, hotel accommodation and package tours (a growing number of which might be domestic). Ancillary services such as travel insurance, traveller's cheques and foreign exchange may also be offered, and some agents will also undertake to arrange travel documentation (such as procuring visas) for their clients. Some will even deal with theatre tickets.

However, these all-round agents are rapidly disappearing in the face of commercial pressure. Due to the small amount of revenue achieved on the sale of coach or rail tickets, many agents are now forgoing the sale of these types of transport, although some agents still believe it to be better to offer a full range of services even if some are loss making, on the grounds that the customer may return to buy other travel arrangements later. Nonetheless, research by Coopers and Lybrand in 1997 (Benchmarking Survey), which found that agents dealing with more than 200 operators generally had lower profit margins that those focusing on 20 preferred operators, tends to suggest that it makes financial sense to specialize.

Agents may specialize not only in the selection of products they offer, but in the markets they serve. The clearest distinction is between those that focus on business travel (serving the travel needs of the local, and in some cases national, business community) and those that concentrate on leisure travel. Focusing on the business community requires additional skills and knowledge, and while some agents do attempt to serve both markets, by establishing a separate business division within the company, they find it difficult to compete against the expertise, and buying power, that the specialist business agents can bring to bear. These large business travel specialists have come to dominate the market, led by organizations like American Express, Hogg Robinson and Carlson Wagonlit.

Setting up and running a travel agency

Travel agents are located in major city centres, in the suburbs of large towns, and less frequently in smaller towns. To be successful, they need to be sited close to the centre of the shopping district. They compete against other agents within a catchment area which, in the case of a large city, may extend only to the surrounding streets, while in the case of an important market town the catchment may draw on residents living within a radius of thirty or forty miles. Those agents whose location is close to city centres, or other centres of business and industry such as an industrial estate, will usually try to capture the business travellers within this field, and where a multi-million pound account is involved, they may go to the extent of providing an implant (or in-plant) office, based in the business client's premises but staffed by the agency, in order to handle the company's travel needs exclusively. To do this, the company must be certain of a substantial amount of ongoing revenue, as the cost of setting up another branch is not inconsiderable. Commissions earned may well have to be shared with the client, through discounting to the company. Increasingly, commission payments are being replaced by management fees, with the agent receiving bonus payments if it achieves agreed levels of saving for the client. If this is coupled with a credit agreement whereby the company only pays for its tickets after thirty days (or even longer), the agency may well find that the cost of servicing the business is too high.

It is also worth noting that agents in city centres will draw their clients not only from residents in the area but also from workers employed in the area, who may find it more convenient to make their travel arrangements close to their place of work, rather than nearer to their homes. On the other hand, the agency is also faced with the likelihood that a number of workers in the area will choose to pick up their brochures from the city branch, and make their reservations at an agency near their homes, where bookings can be arranged together with their spouses. This may mean a high turnover of brochures with little return for the city agency, a problem particularly common in London.

Setting up a travel agency in Britain requires little capital, for reasons already noted, nor are formal qualifications a prerequisite (unlike other European Union members). Consequently, the business appears extremely attractive to outsiders, who see it as a glamorous occupation with wonderful opportunities for cheap travel.

Anyone contemplating opening a travel agency will have to consider the merits of buying an existing agency, or forming a new one. There are considerable advantages in taking over an existing agency. To begin with, trading figures for recent years can be examined, and the viability of the agency evaluated, in relation to the asking price. A going concern can be expected to retain its loyal clientele, if service remains comparable, but against this, if there is a strong and loyal market already, the asking price for the agency may be high, to include the goodwill. 'Goodwill' embraces the reputation of the business and the expectation that existing customers will continue to buy there. In recent years, prices of independent agencies were pushed up by the eagerness of the chains to expand quickly by taking over independent local agencies. As this process has slowed, and there is now greater awareness of the difficulties of trading at a profit as an independent, so the value of agencies has dropped. Another advantage of buying an existing agency is that licences and appointments, once granted by principals, are generally retained under the new management. Staff, too, can be retained; even in the recession, good qualified and experienced staff were not easy to find, especially for those seeking to set up a new agency.

The attraction of starting from scratch is mainly a financial one; capital cost will be limited to office furnishings, fixtures, computers, phones, and perhaps a new external fascia. However, persuading principals to provide you with brochures, to offer you an appointment and to pay a commission on sales may prove difficult, especially if the area concerned is already well served by existing agents.

A travel agent once declared, 'there are only three important things in setting up an agency: location, location and location'. He was driving home the fundamental point that, to the customer, the convenience of the location is the main criterion in their choice of a travel agent. Any agent choosing a little-used side street away from the main shopping area, merely because rents or rates are lower, can be at a major trading disadvantage. Equally, it can be a mistake to scrimp on floor space and decor. Clients are attracted to roomy shops with plenty of rack space and a bright, cheerful, inviting atmosphere to tempt them in. Increasingly, windows are designed not as settings to display brochures or destination publicity, but as living advertisements for the shop interior. Good lighting, warm colours, comfortable chairs, desks rather than impersonal counters, all affect the client's perception of the agency and their motivation to enter the shop. Once inside, the good agent takes advantage of the opportunity to make a sale; but enticing the client through the door is the first step in selling. Needless to say, a street-level shop is

imperative; only an agency with a well-established clientele and not dependent upon the impulse purchaser (for example, agencies dealing largely with business or group travel) could risk moving to an upper floor.

Sites need to be researched carefully. Existing pedestrian flows should be noted (usually, one side of a major shopping street – often the sunny side – always appears to attract more people than the other) as should barriers, whether physical or psychological. For instance, shops on traffic 'islands' which force pedestrians to use subways to cross the road will find it more difficult to attract the passing trade. Parking is often difficult in town centres, but if there are too many restrictions and no nearby car parks, this can be a further important disincentive to the shopper. The local planning office should be consulted to examine any plans for redevelopment in the area. Residential redevelopment in the immediate area could be an important plus for the site, while commercial redevelopment nearby may pose a threat; another travel agency could well open in competition with you when the site is opened, and if attractive and more accessible, could poach much of your business. It may be better, under such circumstances, to consider delaying your own decision to open until you can rent in the new shopping plaza.

In law, a travel agency is an office, rather than a shop. This is important beyond mere semantics, since in the case of *Ilkeston Co-operative Travel* v. *Erewash Borough Council* (1988), it was determined that travel agents were exempt from the legal restrictions on Sunday trading applicable to retail shops, and could therefore open to trade. Sunday trading has become much more common in recent years, although often restricted to key booking periods of the year such as the post-Christmas booking season. Longer opening hours are necessary now to compete with bookings made on the Internet at any time of the day or night.

Traditionally, agents have earned their revenue in the form of commission on sales. Levels of commission have varied over time and according to the

Figure 13.1 Interior of a multiple travel agency. (*Courtesy Lunn Poly*)

travel product sold, but typically have been highest for package tour sales (between 10 and 15 per cent), with airlines paying slightly lower rates and other services even less. This pattern is likely to change in the future, however, as principals move to paying lower commissions or in some cases scrapping commissions in favour of fees. As we have seen in Chapter 12, Thomson led the way in reducing basic rates of commission paid to their agents, and introducing a complex reward system for greater sales effort, including directional selling. Later, the airlines similarly changed their payment structures to agents, led by British Airways, which has introduced lower fixed payments and encouraged the introduction of service charges by retailers. Airlines have faced heavy competition and reduced profits in recent years, and have actively sought ways in which their costs, including distribution costs, could be lowered. Some have reduced commission rates – in Germany, for example, Lufthansa reduced the rate of commission to agents from 9 per cent to 7.5 per cent, and Ryanair made a similar reduction for agents in the UK. In the USA, agents receive a basic 5 per cent only, and a cap of $100 for international tickets. Agents have resisted the termination of the commission structure, arguing that their customers would not only be angered by attempts to charge a transaction fee, but would be more likely to book direct with the airlines. The introduction of ticketless travel by some airlines, which not only saves airlines the cost of issuing tickets, but also encourages bookings direct, may further whittle away agency revenue.

Indeed, evidence from the USA tends to support the agents in their view that service charges are difficult to impose. Commissions were capped by the airlines there in the mid-1990s, but the public resisted attempts to impose service fees and turned to booking on the Internet. The number of agencies has dropped significantly each year since, largely, it is believed, due to this development, while many surviving agents switched to dependence upon sales of package holidays and cruises.

For most agents, package tour sales represent by far the largest proportion of their sales, although an increasing proportion of these involve some tailor-made elements. Typically, overseas holidays account for 60 per cent of sales, air tickets another 25 per cent, and ferry tickets some 4 per cent. Domestic holidays, a growing area of potential sales, have been estimated to take up to 4 per cent, while the remainder is divided between cruises, rail and coach bookings and miscellaneous services.

Value added tax (VAT) is payable by travel agencies on the 'added value' of package tours, i.e. on the commission earned by the agent. Payment to Customs and Excise is usually undertaken on behalf of the agents by the tour operators, but agents devising their own packages will make their own returns to Customs and Excise. For example:

Tour price		£200.00
Agent deducts:		
commission	£20.00	
VAT due	£3.50	
		£23.50
Agent remits to tour operator		£176.50
Agent remits to C&E		£3.50

Most principals today will offer higher rates of commission to agents that are members of consortia banding together to achieve agreed sales targets, in order to compete with the multiples. This can add 2.5 per cent or more to the earnings of the agent, particularly for the sale of package tours. However, it is still rare to find an agent averaging more than 10–11 per cent on the total of the revenue achieved during the year. Since it became legal to discount the price of travel products at the point of sale, the independent agents have been under particular pressure from discounting by the multiples. These large chains, because of their substantial buying power, can negotiate higher overriding commissions with the major tour operators – it was reported in 1999 that Going Places, acting on behalf of its own shops, those of its sister chain TravelWorld and some 350 Advantage agents, was negotiating a commission rate of 18 per

Table 13.1   Multiple agents' branches, 1999

Lunn Poly	900
Going Places	825
Thomas Cook	775
Travel Choice	229 (174 high street, 55 'Express')

cent (up from 15 per cent). Since the company also made no payments to its suppliers until eight weeks before its clients' departure, this example clearly demonstrates the power of the big distributors in the trade. It also allows the agent to pass 10 per cent or more back to its clients in the form of a discount,

Figure 13.2   Operational costs of an independent travel agency: a monthly profit and loss account to show typical expenditure

Sales		1,378,708	
Gross profit (commission at average 9.4%)		129,599	
Expenditure			
Personnel			
Salaries, NHI, pensions	57,768		
Staff travel, training, subscriptions	2,700		
		60,468	(50.49%)
Establishment			
Rent, rates, water	20,580		
Light and heat	2,640		
Insurance	1,875		
Cleaning	1,080		
		26,175	(21.86%)
Administation			
Computers, telephone	9,510		
Postage	2,040		
Printing & stationery	1,320		
Hire of equipment	4,020		
Advertising and publicity	2,400		
Publications, timetables	1,992		
		21,282	(17.77%)
Financial and legal			
Credit cards	3,288		
Bank charges	1,272		
Auditing and accounting	2,166		
Legal fees	324		
Bad debts	400		
		7,450	(6.22%)
Depreciation and amortization		4,386	(3.66%)
Total operational costs		119,761	(100.00%)
Net profit before tax		9,838	
Note: 0.71 as % of sales			

offering a price that few independents could hope to meet. Examples like this account for the phenomenal success of the leading chains like Going Places and Lunn Poly (see Table 13.1).

Out of an average gross profit of between 9 and 10 per cent, travel agents must pay all the running expenses of their agencies, including their own salary (see Figure 13.2). Only after these expenses have been met can they judge whether they have made a net profit or a loss for the year. One measure of the profitability, and particularly the productivity, of agents is to examine their turnover per employee. The Coopers and Lybrand Benchmarking Survey referred to earlier found that multiples were generally more profitable than independents, achieving a turnover of £253,000 per employee in 1997. However, if we take average commission to be just 10 per cent of turnover (a slightly conservative figure for the multiples), we are left with earnings of only some £25,000 per employee, before all costs, including salaries, are met. The 2000 Benchmarking Survey carried out by PricewaterhouseCoopers was scarcely more encouraging, giving an overall turnover of £271,000 per employee, and a net profit per employee of £3,574 – actually lower than three years earlier.

Of increasing importance to the profitability of agents is their status as 'cash' or 'credit' agents. Agents that have credit arrangements with their principals have the advantage of simpler recording procedures and improved cash flow, since they will hold clients' payments for longer before transmitting funds to the principals.

Travel agency skills and competences

It follows that, owing to the extremely competitive nature of the retail travel business, two factors become paramount if the agency is to succeed: good management and good service. Good management will ensure that costs are kept under control, that staff are motivated, and that the agency goes out actively to seek business rather than wait for it to come through the door. Good service will ensure satisfied clients, help to build a regular clientele and encourage word of mouth recommendation, which will increase the local share of the market for the agent.

Despite the expansion of the large chains in recent years, many travel agents are still small, family-run businesses in which the owner acts as manager, and employs two or three members of staff. In such an agency there is little specialization in terms of the usual division of labour, and staff will be expected to cope with all the activities normally associated with the booking of travel, which will include:

- advising potential travellers on resorts, carriers, travel companies and travel facilities worldwide;
- making reservations for all travel requirements;
- planning itineraries of all kinds, including complex multi-stopover independent tours;
- accurately computing airline and other fares;
- issuing travel tickets and vouchers;
- communicating by telephone and letter with travel principals and customers;
- maintaining accurate files on reservations;
- maintaining and displaying stocks of travel brochures;
- interceding with principals in the event of customer complaints.

In addition to product knowledge, therefore, the main skills that counter staff require will include the ability to read timetables and other data sources, to construct airline fares, to write tickets and to have sufficient knowledge of their customers to be able to match customer needs with the products available. All staff today are also required to be competent in operating computers and accessing computer reservations systems (CRSs).

The correct construction of airline fares and issue of airline tickets is a far more complex subject than might be apparent to the uninitiated, and entails a lengthy period of training coupled with continuous exercise of these skills. A number of internationally recognized courses are available to provide these skills, including in Britain those offered by British

Airways, which meet IATA requirements and can be taken up to the BA Fares and Ticketing Part II level, indicating full competence to meet any requirement for fare construction and ticketing.

For many air fares, however, agents are increasingly becoming dependent upon quotations given by carriers, either via the telephone or CRSs. Fares are now changed frequently, and agents must be in possession of the most up-to-date fares, as well as the lowest fares available for their clients. The ticketing function is also largely undertaken via computers, and arguably fare quotations and ticketing skills are becoming less important for most agency staff, apart from those dealing with business travel. An understanding of the principles underlying the construction of fares, however, can be helpful – for example, in explaining complex fares to customers – and of course there will be a continuing need for fares experts in the industry. The large travel agency chains have in some cases centralized this role, so that a handful of experts can quickly determine the lowest fares for a particular journey by air on request from a member of their counter staff at any of the company's branches.

In addition to counter staff functions, agency managers (who frequently spend time at the counter themselves) are required to fulfil a number of administrative functions. On the financial side, these will include:

- maintenance and control of the company's accounts;
- invoicing clients;
- effecting bank reconciliations;
- preparing and controlling budgets;
- providing an estimate of the cash flow in the company on a month by month basis;
- controlling expenditure.

The application of VAT to travel has added to their workload. Sales records must be kept, and sales returns completed regularly for travel principals. All these 'back office' jobs can today be computerized, even in the case of the smaller independent agency. Managers also have the task of safeguarding their stock of tickets and other negotiable documents, and

in addition have the usual tasks of recruiting, training and supervising office staff, and promoting their business in-shop and externally.

Customer contact skills

The way in which staff communicate with clients is, together with the essential product knowledge they display, a key ingredient in the agency's success. These communication skills can be divided into three distinct categories:

1. language skills
2. personal and social skills
3. sales skills.

There is widespread concern about the lack of basic language skills demonstrated by many British workers, and this applies not merely to a lack of foreign languages, but to a lack of competence in the way we use our own native tongue. Written communication to a client which demonstrates poor sentence construction, grammar or spelling reflects not just on the employee, but on the company itself. When such correspondence goes out under the signature of a senior member of staff, the image of the company suffers a still more serious blow.

Personal and social skills are even more important, but fortunately it lies within our own power, to a large extent, to exercise these skills. There is still a tendency in Britain to look down upon jobs which involve serving the public, which is all too often confused with servility. We are gradually learning as a nation that if we are to compete with our European colleagues, we must be prepared to offer the same level of 'service' in our service industries as they do. The acceptance of the credo 'the customer is always right' is the first move towards creating the right atmosphere for serving behind a counter, in a travel agency as in any other shop. Customers expect to be received warmly, and with a genuine smile of greeting; staff are expected to be unfailingly cheerful whatever stress they may be experiencing during their workday. These qualities need to become second nature to counter staff.

First impressions weigh heavily, and staff will be judged, too, by their dress and appearance. Tourism employees must be prepared to adjust to the constraints that the job imposes, if they wish to succeed in the industry. Employers will insist on neat hairstyles, suitably discreet make-up for female staff, and overall good grooming and appearance – often to the extent that counter staff in the agency chains will be required to wear a uniform – and personal hygiene is essential.

Deportment, too, is important. The way employees sit, stand or walk says a great deal about them and their attitude towards their customers. Staff who are exposed to the clients' view will be expected to look alert and interested when addressing their clients, to avoid slouching when they walk, and to sit upright rather than slumped in their chairs. These non-verbal signals all say a lot about the attitude of the company to its customers. The scene of employees filing their nails or talking to their friends on the telephone, while customers try to attract their attention, is a common one in training videos, and one that encourages us to think about how we present ourselves in public. A warm, welcoming smile and friendly manner when greeting a customer approaching the counter will convey a positive view of the company, and make the customer feel at home and in a buying frame of mind. Attentiveness to the customer is not only polite; it ensures that vital client needs are recognized, enabling the employee to match needs with products. When talking to customers and greeting them, the employee should maintain eye contact and a manner which will breed confidence in the agency and its staff's product knowledge. Even handshakes are important cues to confidence; they should be firm and offered willingly. Use of the client's name enhances the relationship.

Even the way in which staff answer the telephone can help to generate the right image of the company. Telephones should be answered quickly and competently. As there are no dress and appearance 'cues' from which the client can make a judgement, the voice becomes the sole basis of judgement. Trainers emphasize the need to smile, even over the telephone, as an impression of friendliness can still be conveyed in the voice. If clients are asked to hold on, they should be given the reason, and regularly checked to ensure they are still holding. If the person they are trying to reach is busy, an offer should be made to call them back and there should be a follow-up to ensure that they have been called back. Similarly, if the employee cannot give an answer immediately to a problem, they should offer to call the client back with the answer in a short while, and do so. A failure to call back is one of the most common sources of frustration to clients, and one that can easily lead to a loss of business to a competitor.

The sales sequence

Travel agencies are no longer order takers; to compete, they must go out and get the business. Good social skills build the atmosphere which encourages buying, but closing a sale requires an understanding of technique. Effective selling is the outcome of four stages in the selling process, which together make up the sales sequence:

1. establishing *rapport* with clients;
2. *investigating* clients' needs;
3. *presenting* the product to the clients;
4. getting clients to take action, by *committing* themselves to the purchase.

Below, each of these stages is examined in more detail.

Rapport

To sell products successfully, one must first match them to the customers' needs. If the clients buy a product they do not really want, or which does not provide the satisfaction they were looking for, they simply do not come back again. As no travel agency can survive without a high level of repeat business, achieving a one-time sale is clearly not enough; the customer must be satisfied in the longer term. To achieve this, the first step is to build a rapport, by engaging the client in conversation, gaining their trust and learning about their needs. This process allows the salesperson to judge how receptive the client is to new ideas, and how willing to have products sold to them. Some customers prefer to self-select, and should not be badgered into a sale, while others need and seek advice more openly.

To generate a two-way conversation, the opening phrase 'Can I help you?' has to be avoided – it simply invites the reply, 'No thanks, I'm just looking'. A more useful way of opening a conversation would be to use a phrase such as, 'Do you have a particular type of holiday in mind?', or, to a customer who has just picked up a brochure, 'That's a very good programme this year. Were you just looking for sun, sea, sand holidays, or had you something more adventurous in mind?' This forces a reply, and encourages the client to open a conversation.

Investigation

Once you have gained the client's trust, the next step is to investigate their needs more thoroughly. Once again, it is necessary to ask open questions, which elicit full answers. The sort of information needed to draw out the client will include:

- who is travelling, and the number in the group;
- when they wish to travel, and for how long;
- their preferred mode of travel;
- their choice of destination;
- what they expect to pay.

It must be recognized at the outset that the client will not necessarily have the answers to these questions. They may have only the vaguest idea about where they want to go, and what they want to do. Needs must never be assumed, even from a clear statement of intent: clients saying they do not want to take a package holiday may merely be revealing a deep-seated prejudice that such holidays are 'down-market', while on the other hand they may have had a bad experience of earlier such holidays. The salesperson's task is to tease out the real reason so that the appropriate product can be offered – for example, an IIT (independent inclusive tour) may suit, where the client would not be one of a crowd. In particular, one should never take for granted that the price the customer states they are willing to pay is the maximum; the industry has encouraged holiday-makers to believe that holidays are invariably cheap, but one is doing the client a disservice not to point out that cheapness is not necessarily value for money, and that by paying a little more one might have a better guarantee of satisfaction.

Presentation

Once the salesperson is satisfied that they know exactly what the client needs, they may go on to the next stage, that of presenting the products that they feel will suit the client. The aim will be to present not only the features of the holiday being offered, but also the benefits:

> Travelling in the early spring, you have the advantage of lower prices, yet this can be the nicest time of the year in the Austrian valleys, with the blossom out and before the mass of tourists arrive in the height of the season.

Product knowledge is, of course, critical for success in gaining the clients' confidence to a point where they are willing to accept one's recommendations. Even if the salesperson feels that what they are offering is exactly suitable for their client, it is always a good idea to offer an alternative, so that the client has the opportunity to choose. If the salesperson then demonstrates just how one holiday is a better buy than the other, this will make it easier for the client to decide on the choice being recommended.

At this stage in the sales sequence, the salesperson will often have to handle objections. Sometimes objections are voiced only because the client needs reassurance, or because they have not yet fully understood the benefits being offered to them. At other times objections occur because not all the client's needs have yet been met, and here a process of patient questioning may be needed once again to draw out the possibly hidden motives for the objections.

Commitment

This final stage is the process leading to closing the sale. This means getting the client to take action – ideally to buy, but of course some clients will need more time to consider the offer. The aim of the counter clerk is to get the best possible outcome from the sales sequence – taking an option, getting the clients to call back later, or getting them to agree that the salesperson may call them later to follow up the sale. The good salesperson is always looking for the buying signals that herald that the client is ready to buy: 'Would you like me to see if I can get you a reservation for that date?' can prompt the client who is dithering to take action. Care must be taken, however, never to push the client into a sale before they are ready to buy, or they may be lost for ever.

Finally, having received the deposit for a firm booking, the salesperson must remember that the sales job has not been finished. They must continue to show interest and concern for the client, helping to reinforce the sale and their commitment to return for later travel arrangements. Many agents now send a 'welcome home' card to their clients after their return from holiday, to invite them to come into the shop and talk about their experiences, and to ensure they will remember the agency in the future.

A good selling technique grows with experience, but it takes effort; effort to find out what the client really needs – effort to appear constantly friendly and interested, and effort to find the right product to match the needs.

The product portfolio

It is ironic that the travel product requires perhaps greater knowledge on the part of retail staff than does virtually any other product, while travel agents' salaries still lag behind those of other people in the distributive trade. This makes it particularly hard for agency managers to attract and retain qualified staff. Agents argue that competition and discounted prices make it impossible to pay higher salaries. Principals have come to accept that their retailers cannot be expected to have detailed product knowledge of every company's offerings, and concentrate instead on providing agents with easier access to information through CRSs and more informative brochures.

While the apparently unbiased service provided by the independent travel agent appears to be a marketing advantage, it is questionable whether clients themselves actually deal through an agent to gain this benefit, since the proportion of sales through travel agents is highest for the standard package holidays, which could arguably be booked direct with equal simplicity. This supports the view of many that travel agents only represent a convenient outlet for buying a holiday, rather than an advisory service.

Figure 13.3 Scotland's tourist board brochure offering commissionable domestic holidays. (*Courtesy VisitScotland*)

The low proportion of bookings achieved by travel agents for domestic holidays owes much to the traditional pattern of booking holidays in the UK. Domestic holiday-makers have tended in the past to contact principals direct to make their holiday bookings, often by writing to resort tourist offices for brochures and details of hotels. Holidays in Britain were neither conveniently packaged, nor seen by travel agents as sufficiently remunerative to justify devoting precious rack space to brochures or training staff in domestic product knowledge. However, two factors have tended to increase sales through agencies. First, UK holidays have risen in price vis-à-vis foreign holidays, so that sales of a holiday at home can equal or exceed the 'bargain basement' prices now offered overseas. Second, UK holidays are now better packaged by the tour operators, with the larger companies now involving themselves with home-grown products. These efforts are supported by VisitScotland which produces an annual brochure carrying products such as accommodation and attractions, all of which are commissionable to agents (see Figure 13.3).

Business travel

Agents have made strong efforts in recent years to tap the lucrative business house travel market – bookings for company employees travelling on business. The growth in the economy and in exporting has led to a parallel growth in corporate travel, often seen as highly profitable for the travel agent because capital spend is high and the market relatively price insensitive. Nearly 5 million business visits are made abroad every year from Britain, and this clearly constitutes a very attractive market to tap. However, increasing competitiveness among agents soliciting business travel, coupled with the drive for greater cost-efficiency in industry, has made this sector of the market more price sensitive. Business houses now seek, and usually can obtain, 'deals' with travel agents in exchange for agreements to place all their corporate business through the one agency. Agencies in turn attract business houses either by providing a standard rate of discount on all travel arrangements, or, more commonly today among the larger business agents, charging a management fee for their services. There are a number of options in drawing up a fee-based contract, the most common being:

1. a flat fee, usually payable per month;
2. rebate of the agency commission and a fixed amount charged per transaction;
3. a simple fee-per-ticket basis;
4. variable fees charged according to the complexity of the transaction;
5. a minimum fee charged per transaction with the guarantee of a minimum number of transactions per month.

It is also common to find contracts drawn up based on fees which depend upon the agency achieving a certain level of cost savings for the company. Agreements may also include the agency offering its client extended credit terms, whereby accounts do not have to be settled until ten to twelve weeks after the receipt of tickets. One drawback of a system in which commission is fully rebated to the client is that the supplier, such as a hotel, gains no sales benefit from increasing its commission rates to its distributors, and must look for other strategies to gain the agency's support.

Businesses are extremely demanding customers. The level of service which an agent must offer to retain their patronage is considerable. Companies often require reservations at very short notice, and will need service outside the normal office hours of the travel agent. They will expect documents to be delivered to their offices, and may also require the agent to obtain visas or offer other help with documentation. Therefore the additional costs of handling these arrangements must be considered by the agent, particularly where credit is offered to the business house. It is not unusual for companies to delay payments until well beyond the dates due, while the agent is still obliged to make payments to principals within the agreed times; thus the agent is helping to fund the company's cash flow at its own expense.

However, the attraction of large accounts, in many cases exceeding a million pounds a year, will be sufficient to ensure that agents compete for the business by offering extra levels of service, implants, fares expertise to guarantee lowest prices, and financial incentives.

Since the highest discounts can be offered by agents negotiating the best deals with their principals, this has once again led to the multiple branch agencies dominating the business house market; the Guild of Business Travel Agents (GBTA), with just forty members, is the professional body representing the leading business travel agents, and accounts for some 75–80 per cent of all airline tickets sold in the UK. The bulk of these sales are in the hands of a few key players, such as American Express, Hogg Robinson, Carlson Wagonlit, The Travel Company, Portman and Britannic. The role of the GBTA is to represent the interests of business agents and their clients, and to improve the standards and quality of travel for their members, through negotiation with suppliers such as airlines, airports and hotel chains. Some business travel agents are also members of international consortia, which offer them greater influence and purchasing power with principals. Hogg Robinson, for example, is linked in an international consortium of business travel agents known as Business Travel International (BTI), whose members include the largest French travel chain, Havas, the German chain Hapag Lloyd, and the US agency IVI, as well as Holland International of the Netherlands, Bennett Travel of Scandinavia and National Australia Travel. With the global buying power of this group, airline and other tickets can be purchased at the lowest possible price for business house clients. Hogg Robinson also strengthened its power in the global business travel market through the purchase in 1997 of Kuoni's business travel division on the Continent.

Large companies often employ specialist travel managers, who act as buyers of travel products for the employees, and therefore intermediaries between the employee and travel agency. Purchases arranged centrally in this way allow the company to benefit from increased know-how and better prices. These managers have their own professional body in the UK, the Institute of Travel Management (ITM), which seeks to use its influence to obtain better deals for its members, and acts as a mouthpiece and watchdog for this section of the industry. There is an equivalent organization in the USA, the National Passenger Traffic Association (NPTA), which has actually set up its own travel agency to make further cost savings for its members. Both the ITM and NPTA are represented in the International Business Travel Association (IBTA), which includes a number of Continental European organizations among its members.

The largest corporations in the UK have also recognized that they have the buying power to organize their own travel arrangements without the intercession of a travel agent, and increasingly negotiate direct with airlines for their tickets and discount agreements.

Travel agency appointments

Membership of trade bodies

In the UK there are no legal requirements to setting up as a travel agent, but in some countries, including most of those within the European Union, governments do exercise licensing control over agencies. However, most principals license the sale of their services through a process of agency agreements, or 'appointments', which are in effect a licence to trade and to receive commission for sales achieved. Some principals dispense with this formality – hotels, for example, will normally allow commission on any sales made through a reputable travel agency, without any formal agreement.

Up to 1993, any travel agent wishing to sell the products of an ABTA tour operator had itself to be a member of ABTA, while in turn ABTA tour operators could only sell their services through ABTA retailers. This reciprocal agreement, known as Stabiliser, and allowing ABTA to operate effectively as a closed shop, is technically a constraint on trade, and as such was challenged by the Office of Fair Trading. However, the Restrictive Practices Court upheld the agreement in 1982 after appeal by ABTA, on the grounds that it was in the public interest, and certainly, ABTA's in-house scheme of protection for consumers against the collapse of a member company was recognized as one of the best in the world. A Common Fund, provided out of membership subscriptions, was held by ABTA and drawn on to allow clients of a travel agency to continue with their holidays even if the travel agency they had booked with went into liquidation before the tour operator received payment for the tour. This complemented the protection offered by ABTA against the collapse of a tour operator, details of which have been outlined in Chapter 12.

New members of ABTA were required to take up a bond to cover a percentage of their revenue in the event of their collapse. The same conditions were not imposed on long-standing members, though, and this created difficulties in the case of one or two spectacular collapses such as that of Exchange Travel, in which ABTA had to meet the costs of lost revenue without adequate bonding. This imposed a drain on the reserve fund.

Thus, membership of ABTA provided many advantages, but it also imposed obligations on its members. Premises were open to inspection, and agents were obliged to abide by a strict Code of Conduct complementing that of the tour operator. However, many earlier conditions imposed on members by ABTA, such as a prohibition on discounting, and on the sale of non-travel products ('mixed selling'), were overturned by the Restrictive Practices Court. There has, in fact, been a considerable increase in the sale of non-travel products since restrictions were relaxed, particularly in the sale of complementary products such as luggage and electrical goods.

ABTA will investigate the travel agent's financial standing and qualifications for entry prior to admitting the company to membership. This period can take between six and twelve weeks. ABTA also requires members to have at least one member of their counter staff with at least two years of experience, although this period is reduced by six months for staff holding formal qualifications.

Formal training qualifications for the industry are both diverse and confusing. Not all the plethora of courses that have been introduced are universally welcomed or understood by the industry. After numerous changes to qualifications, both professional and academic, over the past few years, training provision is now overseen by Travel, Tourism and Events National Training Organisation (TTENTO), which monitors vocational courses but is not a training provider. The ABTA Certificate (ABTAC) is among the most recently introduced programmes, and is generally supported by the trade. It is offered by the trade's training body, TTC Training, which has close links with ABTA. National Vocational Qualifications (NVQs) are also offered, under the supervision of the City and Guilds which, along with Edexcel, are awarding bodies for travel services NVQs. Students in full-time education can follow General National Vocational Qualifications (GNVQs) or A levels in Travel and Tourism, while a raft of programmes for business travel staff has been introduced by the GBTA. ABTA itself has supported professional recognition for formal qualifications through the award of Certified Travel Consultant status (two years' experience plus ABTAC Primary or NVQ level 2 in Travel Services) and Certified Senior Travel Consultant status (four years' experience plus NVQ level 4, and a degree in travel and tourism or the GBTA Management Certificate). There is widespread uncertainty within the industry of the relative values of these numerous qualifications which are, at the time of writing, undergoing the test of time to ascertain their worth in practice.

As we have seen earlier, since the EU Directive on Package Travel was introduced in 1993, ABTA has not retained the same measure of control in the industry which it enjoyed formerly; to take one example, the organization no longer enjoys the exclusive rights to bond its members. Nonetheless it remains paramount among the travel associations, continuing to represent the interests of both tour operators and travel agents. Given the controversial conflict of interests between these two, and similar areas of conflict that can arise between the multiples and independent agencies, support for ABTA within the trade may seem surprising, but the importance of having a strong body to represent trade interests in consultations with government and other industry bodies, and the organization's role as a mouthpiece for the industry, have ensured ABTA's survival. Other bodies have been created to serve the narrower interests of segments of this industry, such as the Multiple Travel Agents' Association (MTAA), which concerns itself with the chains' special interests. The independent agents have increasingly formed themselves into consortia to represent their interests, mainly in negotiating with suppliers, and this feature will be examined a little later in the chapter.

As agents also sell travel insurance, steps are being taken to control this side of their operations also. The General Insurance Standards Council (GISC) was set up in 2000 by the insurance industry to improve standards through self-regulation, in the wake of government moves to regulate the industry. Membership, initially voluntary, became compulsory for all agencies selling insurance in 2001, in spite of independent agents' concern about the additional burden of costs this imposes.

Bonding

New ABTA agents, during their first year of trading, and agents judged by ABTA, after inspection of their accounts, to be at risk financially, have been required to post a bond which indemnifies them to clients and customers against the risk of their failure. Certain principals may also require the posting of a bond, even if an ABTA bond is held – for example, if the agent plans to hold a principal's ticket stock. A significantly higher bond would normally be asked of agents without limited liability (i.e. trading as sole traders or partnerships). Additionally, a retail agent which operates tours, whether in the UK or overseas, will also be required to put up a tour operating bond.

Bonding may be undertaken in one of three ways:

1. A sum of money equal to the value of the bond can be placed in a trust account. The agent can benefit from the interest accruing on the account, but cannot touch the capital itself. Since this could involve putting up a substantial amount of money, it is rarely chosen except by the largest corporations.
2. The agent can obtain an insurance policy for the amount required, paying an annual premium.
3. The agent's bank puts up the bond, against either company assets or, more commonly, the personal guarantees of the directors. A fee is charged which is substantially less than the premium paid for an insurance policy, but the directors become personally liable for the amount of the bond in the event of the company's failure.

As a safeguard, ABTA also has its own annual indemnity insurance policy which can provide additional funds if the bonds posted by an individual member are insufficient to cover the claims against the company in the event of its collapse.

Following the introduction of the EU Directive which made bonding compulsory for any tour operator or agent, agents now have the alternative of trading outside of ABTA, and making their own bonding arrangements through banks or other organizations. Many have chosen to do so, following a very substantial hike in the cost of bonding through ABTA itself. One example of a successful alternative is that of the Travel Trust Association, which enables member agents to use a trust account to protect their clients' funds, rather than purchasing a bond through insurance companies or banks. The association monitors its members to ensure compliance with the trust fund regulations.

Dealing with principals

Most contracts with principals are non-exclusive; that is to say, they do not prevent the agent from dealing with the principal's competitors. Occasionally, however, a contract may offer the agency the exclusive right to sell the product, and may further restrict the agent's ability to deal with other directly competing companies.

Unless expressly stated in the contract, agents do not have the automatic right to deduct their commission from the moneys due to the principal. If bonus commissions are paid for targets achieved, it is generally the case that these additional sums of money are paid to the agent at the end of the season, rather than immediately following the achievement of the target. These facts must be borne in mind by the agent in estimating cash flow.

A licence is required if commission is to be paid on the sale of services of members of IATA (apart from sales of purely domestic tickets). Since IATA travel makes up a substantial proportion of a typical travel agent's turnover, it is important for travel agents that wish to offer a full range of services (and doubly so for those dealing in business house travel) either to hold the necessary IATA appointment, or to have an arrangement with another agency that does so, whereby that agent will issue tickets on their behalf. New agents are permitted to sell air tickets and earn income by sharing commission with an established IATA agent.

Around 2,000 agency branches hold IATA appointments in the UK. IATA's Agency Distribution Office deals with applications for a licence, a process which can take up to forty-five days. A representative from IATA's Agency Investigation Panel visits the agent to judge whether the site is easily identified as a travel centre and suitable for the sale of tickets (while proof of turnover is no longer required of agents, IATA wishes to satisfy itself that the agency has the scope to generate business). The number and competence of staff will be judged; at least one member of staff will be expected to have two years' agency experience, and preferably hold a Certificate of Travel Agency Competence, ABTAC and/or an equivalent qualification in fares and ticketing (ABTAC allows six months remission in the experience required). The representative must also be satisfied that the agency premises are secure and ticket stock can be safeguarded.

If approved, a bond is taken out to cover the agency's anticipated monthly IATA turnover. An entrance fee is payable, and a small annual subscription. This approval enables the agent to sell the services of all IATA members. Separate plates are available for every IATA airline, and agents may hold stock of as many as 60 plates if they plan to draw tickets on each airline.

Approval is also required to make commissionable sales on the services of railways, National Coaches, domestic airline services and other principals such as shipping and car hire firms. Obtaining approval for most of these has been largely a formality for agents holding ABTA and IATA appointments. However, appointments to sell travel insurance will involve closer scrutiny, since the agent will be acting as a broker for the insurance service concerned; as noted above, insurance companies have tightened up on standards for their brokers, including retailers in the travel industry.

Profitability of travel agents

There are surprisingly few studies of travel agency productivity and profitability in Britain, although ABTA undertakes occasional studies of profitability among its members. Unfortunately, the sample responding to research surveys has often been quite small, throwing into doubt the results. Studies in the past have found that on average, ABTA members retained less than 1 per cent of their total turnover after expenses. That report did not make clear that success in creating high turnover may be as much a factor of location as of efficiency, nor that fast turnover is not commensurate with a professional standard of advice and sales assistance. A better pointer to profitability can be found in the trading results of the leading chains such as Lunn Poly, whose negotiating power with the major principals has enabled it to offer substantial discounts on package tours, so that in spite of one of the highest spends on advertising in the industry, it has still been able to push profits well above the industry average, while simultaneously retaining or increasing market share. The Coopers and Lybrand Benchmarking Survey published in 1997 produced some useful statistics revealing the generally larger profits achieved by the multiples and companies that chose to specialize in a limited number of suppliers' products, while subsequent Benchmarking Surveys by PricewaterhouseCoopers, sponsored by ABTA, have been the sole regular analyses of travel agents' finances available publicly.

It is becoming clear that the retail sector of the industry is now moving in two, or even three, distinct directions: towards specialist business travel; or towards the fast turnover 'leisure sales shop', a feature of the multiples' approach, which is essentially a booking service offering rock-bottom prices; or towards a more specialized advisory service for complex or expensive travel arrangements, without necessarily discounting. The latter move has its precedent in the US, where for a number of years travel experts holding the Certified Travel Counsellor (CTC) qualification have dealt with the more lucrative end of the package tour business, often based in independent agencies. It is these agencies which seem most likely to benefit if and when suppliers move to contracts which provide for lower commissions or fee-only payments, as customers who are seeking tailor-made services will be more disposed to pay fees for the services they are rendered. Meanwhile, the traditional travel agent, attempting to provide a wide range of services with little discounting, faces a future that is increasingly uncertain as other forms of distribution arrive on the scene, and opportunities are presented for the first time for members of the public to book direct with the suppliers using the Internet.

Evidence that many sectors of travel involve greater costs to the agency than the commissions they can achieve on sales has led a number of agents to move away from selling non-profitable products. At the same time, the proliferation of brochures, and the policy of leading tour operators to produce a range of different branded products each in their own brochure, has forced agents to re-evaluate their racking policies. With the typical travel agency only having rack space for around 145 brochures, of which up to 20 per cent may be filled with the products of the leading operators, there is little oppor-

tunity for the smaller and specialist operators to get their brochures racked. So far, only a handful of independent agents have attempted to redress the balance by niche-marketing, and those that have done so have tended to focus on the narrow long-haul and cruise markets. Some believe this may be the only way in which the independents will be able to compete with the multiples in the long run, although membership in a large consortium may offer a solution.

The move to fast turnover booking centres, typical of the large chains, is in part a recognition that salaries cannot be offered to provide the level of service demanded of a traditional travel agency. A number of developments are taking place at the beginning of the twenty-first century. Holiday Hypermarket, a chain of over fifty stores owned by tour operator First Choice, has been successful in increasing profits through a supermarket approach to sales, which inflates revenues – the company claimed the turnover of these stores could average over £25 million, compared with £1–1.5 million in the average high street store. This approach is being copied by others, notably by Thomas Cook, whose Thomas Cook Plus stores have been the most recent to borrow the concept. Thomas Cook has also introduced Thomas Cook Direct, a new direct sell operation for its tour operating products. Lunn Poly, meanwhile, is revamping many of its stores by introducing five specialist zones within the shop, each catering to a different market segment – long-haul, short breaks, summer sun, families and late bookings. The company also plans a string of superstores, and at the time of writing planned to cut up to a hundred traditional high street branches due to the pressure from e-commerce web sites.

The march of the multiples

The growth of the multiple travel agencies has been the key characteristic in this sector in recent years. Although the pattern is changing constantly and rapidly, the leading three agencies were estimated to hold 65 per cent of the market in mid-1999, with

Figure 13.4 The success of travel agents depends upon easy recognition: the facia and corporate design of Lunn Poly, a leading multiple agent. (*Photographed by the author*)

Lunn Poly taking 25 per cent and Going Places and Thomas Cook taking 20 per cent each (see Table 13.1).

First Choice, among Britain's four largest tour operators, was at a disadvantage in owning fewer retail outlets until 1999, when it announced plans to build its own chain of 1,200 shops, under the brand name of Travel Choice, into which it integrated its recently purchased chain of thirty-two IntaTravel agencies. It has also established a chain of express shops under the Holiday Hypermarket brand, and has purchased the sixty-branch West Country chain Bakers Dolphin, retaining the name which had marketing strengths in the region (see below).

As revealed in Chapter 12, directional selling is now ensuring that the majority of sales of the larger tour operators' products is achieved through their own agencies. The fear among the independents is that, as the power of these multiples grows, the parent companies will choose to retain the exclusive sale of their products through their own retail chains, reducing the independents to selling products of the smaller companies. This fear has not been assuaged by the announcement of the government's Foreign Package Holidays Order (2000) that the relationship between the three largest operators and their agents must be made clear to the public on agency windows and promotional material. The ruling is further undermined by the exclusion of Thomas Cook and its JMC operations, simply on the grounds that it is the retailer which owns the operator, rather than vice versa. The link between retail consortia and operators, such as that which exists between the Global Travel Group and Airtours or between WorldChoice and Thomas Cook, is also excluded from this ruling, as is any distribution by call centres, web sites or teletext – all becoming significant systems of retailing travel.

Competing with the multiples

Although the large number of branches owned by the leading chains appears to give them an insuperable advantage over the independents, this is not always the case. Within the regions, medium-sized regional chains can provide strong competition for bookings. These chains, commonly known as *miniples*, typically control between forty and a hundred shops. Their ability to remain independent must be questioned, however, given the purchase in the late 1990s of two of the largest of these; the sixty-branch West Country chain Bakers Dolphin was sold to leading operator First Choice Holidays and a scheduled seat wholesaler with a small tour operation, Gold Medal Travel, took over the one-hundred-branch North of England miniple Travelworld.

The independents have recognized that on their own they face an almost impossible task in competing with the multiples for the sale of mass-market holidays. As we have seen, the multiples are in a position to discount and undercut the holiday products, and the market has become sensitized to price bargains through the marketing campaigns of the big companies, to the exclusion of other possible benefits available through the smaller agency. The chains can also invest substantially in high technology computer systems to improve their performance, and in national advertising campaigns to draw in customers.

Independent travel agents have done what they could to cut costs or to increase turnover in order to compete, and many have realized that only through close collaboration with others will they be able to compete on price; this would allow them to negotiate for higher commissions based on greatly increased buying power. As a result, there has been massive growth in consortia. A consortium not only allows agents to compete with the multiples by negotiating with the mass tour operators for higher commissions on bulk sales, but it may also lead in time to the organization establishing its own tour operation, or even airline (although tentative efforts to cost the latter have so far dissuaded consortia of the viability of such a project).

Several major consortia have now appeared on the British market. Advantage Travel Centres, a chain which was formed in 1978 under the name National Association of Independent Travel Agents (NAITA) after breaking away from ABTA, has preferential rates with over a hundred travel suppliers. Agents may retain their independent names, but about 350 of the 850 members have chosen to emphasize their Advantage brand in the name. ARTAC Worldchoice, formed out of the Association of Retail Travel Agents' Consortia, founded in 1976, has some 800 outlets, of which over 600 have opted for the brand name in their facias. In 2001, the organization announced its intention of establishing its own chain of city-centre shops, under the Worldchoice brand, to compete with the multiples. Other consortia include the Global Travel Group and Midconsort, while the American organization TravelSavers, which counts over 2,500 agency members in the United States, is seeking at the time of writing to enter the British market to build a consortium of 500–600 agents. The potential buying power of these groupings of independent agencies provides them with a very real chance to compete with the large UK chains in reducing their costs, as well as ensuring that the smaller tour operating companies are represented in the high street.

Franchising has been less successful as a strategy to compete with the multiples. The first chain in Britain to attempt to franchise on a wide scale, Exchange Travel, went into liquidation in 1990, and the Canadian-based Uniglobe chain has similarly found it difficult to establish itself in the UK, in spite of a chain of offices exceeding 1,400 worldwide. The future of franchising remains uncertain. Arguably, a franchise, if it is to succeed, must offer a unique product of some kind which is not available through other distributive outlets; something which a travel franchise signally fails to deliver.

Distribution policy

As we have seen, the policy of mass-market tour operators in recent years has been directed towards selective distribution, the operator favouring a smaller number of productive agents rather than attempting to provide stock for all ABTA members. This policy has also been favoured by the multiple agents themselves, in choosing to stock the products of a few key operators which are responsible for perhaps 80 per cent of the total revenue in the mass market. Multiple agents also engage in directional selling, with Lunn Poly and Travel House favouring sales of their parent, Thomson Holidays, and discriminating against their leading competitors, Airtours and First Choice. In turn, Going Places and Travelworld, both owned by Airtours, favour their parent, while Travel Choice and Bakers Dolphin will favour parent First Choice. The Foreign Package Holidays Order (2000) requires these links to be made clear to customers, and as a result the companies affected are considering, at the time of writing, the value of changing their agency names to include the parental tour operator's name. Making clear the linkages between the large operators and their agents will not necessarily work to the advantage of the independent agents, however, as it may encourage the public to believe that Thomson holidays or Airtours holidays can only be purchased from the retail branches of those operators.

Thomas Cook has introduced a policy of racking only four hundred companies, of which thirty are identified as 'premium selection', while other companies have become even more selective, with the Holiday Hypermarket organization emulating warehouse retailing practice by stocking just the leading twenty operators' products. If this tendency becomes widespread over the next few years, smaller operators will have to find other means of reaching their customers.

The decision on what products to stock is taken not only because of what is thought will sell quickest or easiest. The introduction of tighter EU legislation over quality has forced many agents to reconsider the companies with which they deal, and while bonus commissions undoubtedly play a role in the decision, equally the service provided to the agent by the operator will be taken into consideration. Agents that encounter difficulty in getting through to operators on the telephone, or who find their complaints are not answered quickly, will feel less inclined to stock that operator's products. The personal relationship between travel agency staff and the principal is vital in this decision, and the role of a sales representative can be of immense importance in cultivating goodwill in the distributive trade. Here one must question the decision taken by so many principals to cut back their field representation as a cost-cutting measure. One can surmise that this is partly to fund a higher budget for selling direct.

New means of distribution

A number of notable developments in strategic marketing by retailers have taken place in the past few years, in addition to those significant developments already described above. One such change has been in the field of home selling, which has expanded rapidly. Personal travel counsellors and online travel counsellors who work on a freelance basis sell on behalf of an agency and earn commission from that agency. Lunn Poly merchandisers have been recruited to hand out leaflets at key resorts in Spain to holiday-makers (not necessarily their clients), offering discounts to those booking their holidays with Lunn Poly for the following year. Thomas Cook is the first travel chain to introduce its own credit card to build customer loyalty, with vouchers given away with the purchase of every travel product. As competition becomes fiercer, there can be little doubt that we will see an increase in these new forms of retailing and promotion.

The threat always remains of organizations outside the travel industry taking an interest in diversifying into travel retailing, especially where this is seen as a logical expansion of existing activities and the organization concerned has the ideal retailing operation to take on extra services. This has also been a threat in the past, but those who braved the market have tended to withdraw when the slim margins became evident. Both W H Smith, the newsagent and bookseller, and the Automobile Association have abandoned their sale of travel products in recent years. The complexity of selling travel has to be acknowledged, and this may well be a factor in the decision of so many other retail organizations to avoid the travel business, yet in the Netherlands, the sale of holidays through banks is long established, and in Germany large department stores have played a major role in travel retailing for many years.

Nonetheless, innovatory retailing appears constantly. The Post Office has been selling insurance and foreign exchange for several years, and has experimentally entered the market to sell air tickets. Both Tesco and Boots now retail travel insurance which undercuts that offered through travel agents, and Tesco announced its intention in 1999 to sell European flights direct to its Clubcard holders. In 2000, Tesco went on to introduce sales of foreign currency and traveller's cheques. The giant American discount supermarket chain Wal-Mart, which took over Britain's Asda chain in 2000, already operates a web site for booking cheap flights and hotels. Direct sell to readers of national and local newspapers and cooperative marketing promotions with other products have also helped to undermine travel agents' sales opportunities.

All these moves are being watched closely by the remaining independents, who see their margins squeezed ever tighter and are desperately seeking ways of rebuilding their businesses.

Direct sell

Can travel principals sell their products direct to the public at lower cost without losing sales? This is a vital question for both carriers and tour operators. Travel firms which have traditionally sold their products direct, such as some of the railways, and others such as small tour operators whose total carryings are too small to consider using agents to distribute their product, do not have to take into consideration the possible retaliation of the retail trade against companies which choose to ignore them, or cut them out. However, even these direct-sell companies usually recognize that to antagonize the retail trade may jeopardize marginal bookings, and they will not deliberately ignore agent support.

There is an obvious attraction to the mass operator in selling their product direct to the public. Selling direct cuts out the high cost of servicing intermediaries and of paying commission on each sale. On the other hand, it involves considerable capital expense in setting up sales offices, and direct marketing costs can be high, especially if a national advertising campaign is to be mounted. There will be a need for a large reservations department to deal with enquiries direct from the public, and a huge telephone system to cope with enquiries and bookings.

If principals which presently deal through travel agents decide to sell direct for the first time, or to increase the proportion of direct sales they currently achieve, they risk antagonizing their present distributors. Therefore any effort to increase sales in this way must be handled with extreme discretion, in order to avoid any loss of sales through ill will. British Airways was forced to abandon its own efforts to expand implants in the headquarters of leading corporations in the face of strong reaction from ABTA members, which threatened to switch their sales to rival airlines. The airline, however, continued to expand its network of city centre sales offices, in order to maintain control over sales, as much as to save on payment of commissions. BA has now introduced a scheme to end the traditional commission system and replace it with a range of payments which will more closely reflect the work involved in making a booking. This may lead to agents charging their customers a fee – but if customers can buy the same product without a fee direct from the airline, or

through the web, what incentive is there to book through an agent (apart perhaps from some slight added convenience)?

When the Channel Tunnel first opened, the management of Eurotunnel services largely ignored the strength of the trade, assuming that most clients would prefer to book their crossing direct, thus simultaneously antagonizing the trade and reducing their own sales opportunities. Later, the company realized its mistake and placed greater emphasis on the role of the agent in providing tickets for the cross-Channel tourism market.

The larger tour operators still depend upon travel agents for the sale of up to 80 per cent of their products. Smaller companies, generally those offering a few thousand holidays each year, cannot afford to distribute their products through agents, nor would most agents be willing to stock brochures of these companies, in view of the small number of potential sales they would achieve. Consequently, these operators may adopt one of two distributive strategies: either to find a selection of key agents (likely to be independents rather than chains) which would be willing to stock the product, or to sell all their holidays direct to the public. The growth of the web site has made this latter policy a great deal easier for the smaller company, as we shall see later in this chapter.

In addition to these, the mass-market tour operators have created products which they distribute direct to the public through specialist direct-sell divisions. These include Portland Direct, a division of the Thomson Travel Group, Eclipse, a division of First Choice, and Direct Holidays, an Airtours product. Additionally, Saga Holidays, the largest company specializing in holidays for the elderly, sells direct to its members through direct mail and its members' magazine.

Direct Holidays is an interesting recent development, since it is owned by Airtours but operates in direct competition with them. The Direct Holidays shops, so far about a dozen in number scattered around the UK, sell this product uniquely, offering no other holiday programmes, not even those of Airtours (see Figure 13.5).

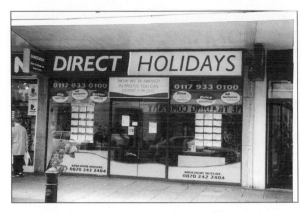

Figure 13.5 A new image in direct selling: Airtours-owned Direct Holidays facia and corporate design. (*Photographed by the author*)

It is significant that three major direct-sell operators are, in fact, divisions of three of the leading tour operators in Britain. Although agents might be thought to be concerned about the challenge of direct-sell operations, they have fought shy of any direct confrontation with these large operators, possibly out of fear that this could jeopardize their sales of the powerful mass-market holidays marketed by the companies. They also believed that the proportion of direct sales made in the UK had stabilized, although with the introduction of the Internet this is certain to be far from the truth. Early claims that direct sell would undercut the price of holidays sold through agents were shown to be inaccurate, as a close examination of the companies' pricing structure revealed that low prices were highly selective, rather than across-the-board. Whether this will remain the case as a greater proportion of holidays is booked through the Internet remains to be seen.

Agents today have much more to fear from advances in computerization, which are now beginning to lead to direct access to operators' CRSs by the travelling public. This has already occurred to a limited extent in the USA and France, and, as we have seen, it is already becoming a reality among business travellers. It is likely to be common for leisure travel bookings in the UK by the early years of the twenty-first century, an issue which will now be examined.

The impact of computer technology

As we have already noted at the end of Chapter 12, the industry has been profoundly affected by developments in technology, most notably computers, over the past decade. Since innovations in this field are constantly being launched or improved, information about this sphere of travel activity tends to date very quickly, so there will be little benefit to be gained from examining the detailed merits of any existing system in this text. Suffice to say that even the smallest travel agents can today benefit from computer technology to handle their back office and front office functions – in fact, many would argue that no agent can afford to be without back office computer aids, and in terms of making reservations, it is now mandatory to use computers rather than the telephone to make bookings with the leading companies. This final section will focus on the trends in information technology used in the industry and their impact on retailers.

The travel industry is ideally suited for computer technology. It offers products that cannot be inspected directly before purchase, but may be viewed with the use of brochures or screens; it requires some system for determining the availability of transport and accommodation, often at short notice, and the ability to make immediate reservations, amendments or cancellations; complex fares and conditions of travel must be accessed and quoted; documents such as tickets, invoices, vouchers and itineraries must be processed rapidly. The back office also needs to process an ever-increasing amount of accounting and management information quickly. All of these functions are available today to agents using computer technology.

Computer systems in travel agencies are designed to offer three distinct facilities:

1. front office 'client relations' systems enabling a counter clerk to access principals' CRSs, check availability and make reservations;
2. back office systems enabling documents such as invoices, vouchers, tickets and itineraries to be issued, and accounts to be processed with principals;

3. management systems, producing updated figures on the company's performance to assist managers in guiding and controlling operations.

Systems have now been developed which will provide all three facilities for even the smallest independent agent, at prices which continue to fall, or equipment can be leased to reduce capital investment and spread costs.

In considering systems which are designed to access travel principals' reservations systems, one can distinguish between those developed by carriers and those developed by tour operators. In Britain, because of the importance of 'interlining' (common ticket issuing and ability to transfer bookings between carriers), any system used must be capable of booking seats on a large number of different airlines. Agents currently achieve this principally by the use of one of the four major global distribution systems, those of Galileo, Amadeus, Sabre and Worldspan. Tour operators' reservations are likewise accessed live on the computer, generally 'hard-wired', allowing agents to enter the CRS without using their telephone line to dial up separately on each occasion. Similarly, back office systems offer not only faster means of carrying out accounting and documentation procedures, but also help to cut costs.

At the turn of the new century, technology appears to be moving in two distinct directions. First, while connections between suppliers and agents are being made simpler, agents are being forced to come to terms with constant advances in technology, providing a new learning curve to master. Many of those who have embraced the technology wholeheartedly have also recognized the advantage of becoming e-tailers, or electronic retailers (the term e-travel agent is beginning to be used to describe this function). Such agencies are adapting new technology to reach their clients online, through the web or even through interactive digital television (IDTV). Second, in parallel with the new intermediary online agencies that are being created, suppliers, notably the airlines, are creating their own web sites against which the e-tailers will have to compete. More widely, there is a rapid growth in business-to-consumer (b2c) sites which are designed to cut out the intermediaries and sell direct to the public.

An explosion of high-tech distributors is occurring, notably in the field of travel. Companies such as Expedia, lastminute.com and ebookers have established web sites (occasionally with the aid of considerable media hype) designed to sell, *inter alia*, discounted and late availability travel – mainly airline seats, hotel accommodation and car rental, rather than package holidays, the sale of which by Internet is still in its infancy. The advantage of these web sites to the consumer is that they are independent of the suppliers, and may be seen as unbiased in their range of products on offer, while airlines value these outlets as a means of unloading surplus stock without degrading the brand. The airlines' own web sites are focusing on selling tickets at published fares.

Many suppliers are also now establishing their own web sites, individually or in some cases in concert with their rivals. The airlines are leaders in this field. A number of these in the USA have linked to create a web site to sell their joint flights direct to the public, while BA and some other European airlines followed suit shortly afterwards. If these web sites can gain a significant share of the published fares market, they will threaten to undermine sales through agents and GDSs.

In tour operating, the success of the TV Travel

Figure 13.6 Galileo's computer reservation system in use. (*Courtesy Galileo International*)

Shop, established in 1998, surprised many in the trade. By the end of 1999, this new company had captured 4 per cent of the inclusive tour market, marketing via TV channels and taking bookings via a call centre. The company plans to develop a booking system which will interact with the web and IDTV. Already, rival companies are being attracted into this sphere of e-tailing, notably Travel Deals Direct, which has a close working relationship with Airtours.

As discussed in the previous chapter, the critical question is whether the high street agent can survive in the face of these new methods of distribution. There are claims that while the World Wide Web offers more options to the customer, it does not necessarily replace existing forms of distribution, since answers to specific questions will need to be raised with agents. The question remains as to how agents can avoid clients coming to them to pick their brains and then going home to book their holidays through the Internet.

Opinion is confused about whether the majority of agents, or only a handful of the most adaptable, can survive the Internet explosion. Those that survive will be the most adaptable, offering a more personal service which will include expert advice. The fact remains, however, that most agents have neither the knowledge nor the resources to undertake such change. Salaries are already low in the industry, and the level of expertise among agents questionable when confronted with an increasingly sophisticated and well-travelled clientele – yet the move to cutting commissions and, in the case of the airlines, withdrawing commission entirely, must encourage many agents to transfer to a fee-charging basis. If agents are to become professionals like solicitors, as many are arguing, how do they pay the salaries and obtain the staff with the qualifications that will be required to deliver this level of expertise?

The future of travel retailing

Not just the travel agent, but the entire travel industry faces greater uncertainty than ever before. The introduction of b2c in travel, with suppliers pro-viding the direct interface with their clients, threatens both agents and tour operators, since if a customer is encouraged to book flights and hotels direct at a lower cost than is possible through intermediaries, how long will it be before it becomes customary for that same customer to put together their own package?

New methods of retailing travel products are continually being launched, as we have seen. Outsiders such as banks, department stores and petrol stations can be tempted to re-examine the benefits of selling travel, if costs can be controlled. In an effort to achieve better profit margins in an increasingly competitive business environment, travel principals will be constantly evaluating new ways to distribute their products to the public. There may be further expansion of multiple or miniple agents buying tours from operators in bulk at net prices and selling these under their own brand names (Thomas Cook has already done so), and the squeeze on independents by the multiples is not expected to slow down. Common promotional tactics of the past few years, such as 5 per cent or no-deposit bookings, are likely to become typical rather than exceptional marketing ploys. Holidays at 30 per cent discount were on offer for summer 2001, so there is no apparent end in sight to deep discounting in the industry, a technique which favours the multiples and reduces agent profitability. Other agents may expand on the initiative taken by one agency, which recruits home-based sales staff to visit customers in their homes, taking bookings through customized laptop computers which are linked with the operators' reservations systems. A free-lance sales force such as this, available at short notice twenty-four hours a day, may offer another solution to ensuring that the travel agent has a future. It is certain that the traditional 'corner-shop' travel agent that we have known in the past is set to largely disappear. The agent of the future will be flexible, innovative, and willing to move with the times and make use of the new tools of marketing which technology has made available. They can no longer be expected to share the range of product knowledge required by an increasingly sophisticated travelling public, but must find the means to access and make this information available to their clients more effectively, and at a cost to the customer that offers value for money.

Meanwhile, a steadily increasing number of bookings will be made direct between principals and customers. In the USA in 1999, 29 per cent of all travel sales were achieved via the Internet. In Europe, some 64 million citizens were regular users of the Internet in the same year. In the UK alone, 30 per cent of the population were connected to the service as this book went to print, and 57 per cent of these used the system either to book or to research travel arrangements. Very shortly, digital TV will have hundreds of channels available for special-interest programmes, including travel, making it an ideal marketing medium; by 2010 at the latest, digital is to become the standard in Britain, replacing the analogue TV. At the same time, mobile phones will interact with the Internet and TV channels to enable travellers to call up information anywhere and at any time, check availability and make travel arrangements. The retail sector is the fastest moving sector of the industry, and is soon to be subject to the greatest changes of all.

Questions and discussion points

1. Why has Britain not adopted the US strategy of the 'Certified Travel Counsellor'? Could it do so?

2. Is travel retailing poorly paid only in Britain, or is this a symptom common to most countries of Europe? What is the image of the agent in France and in Germany? Compare educational backgrounds and average ages of counter staff in these three countries. What patterns are to be found, and how do you account for any differences?

3. Travel agency niche-marketing has largely been confined to the sale of up-market, tailor-made holidays or cruises. How well equipped are the staff of such agencies to sell these services, and how are suitable staff recruited and trained? How can technology help these staff in their product knowledge and marketing?

4. After the announcement by the DTI of the new rules governing the sale of package holidays by vertically integrated agents, many criticized the Minister responsible as not having understood the industry. What were the weaknesses in the ruling, and how do you believe it could have been improved to the benefit of consumers?

Assignment topics

1. Assume for the purposes of this assignment that you have been employed by a retail travel agency in your area (you may choose the company). You have been asked by your manager, in view of your studies, to undertake a study of the agency's brochure racking policy, to see whether it is adequate or could be improved. Undertake some field research in travel agencies in the area to estimate the typical number of spaces available for racking, and the various strategies adopted to categorize and display brochures. Taking into account present practice in your own agency, and the market which the agency draws, examine alternative solutions and produce a report for your manager which makes recommendations for changes. You should also consider the question of the 'marginal demand' brochures for which racking space cannot be found. Include a recommendation on tactics, such as whether a supply of brochures, or an individual brochure only, should be accommodated in each rack.

2. You are appointed as senior counter clerk in a small independent agency (three branches) in a large provincial town with a population of 350,000 people. The directors of the agency, aware of your educational background, have invited you to participate in discussions about the future of the agency. The Managing Director is keen to amend the company's policy by aiming at 'niche' markets, but is uncertain which market to try to attract. Write a brief report to her, making recommendations, following research and supported by the evidence of your research.

Your recommendations should be as detailed as possible, containing also an examination of the implications of the changes for brochure racking, layout and design of the agency etc.

Chapter 14   Ancillary tourism services

Objectives

After studying this chapter, you should be able to:

- understand the role of guides, couriers, insurance and financial services in meeting tourist demand;
- be aware of training and education available for those in the industry;
- understand the role and value of the trade press to the industry;
- identify the principal guides and timetables in use by travel agents, and their contents;
- be aware of marketing and consultancy services available to members of the industry.

Introduction

Attempts to analyse the tourism industry, as we have seen earlier, lead to the problem of defining the parameters of the industry. Some services depend largely or entirely upon the movement of tourists, but are seldom considered to be part of the industry itself. Customs services or visa issuing offices are cases in point. Other services which derive much of their revenue from tourism and yet are clearly not part of the industry include companies specializing in the design and construction of hotels, theatres, restaurants and other centres of entertainment.

However, there is a further category of miscellaneous tourism services which deserves to be examined more closely here. We will call these *ancillary*

services, and they are provided either to the tourist or to the suppliers of tourist services. Each will be dealt with in turn.

Services to the tourist

Guide/courier services

Unfortunately, there is as yet no term which will conveniently embrace all the mediators whose function it is to shepherd, guide, inform and interpret for groups of tourists. Nor can one conveniently link their functions to one particular sector of the industry. Some are employed by carriers and tour operators; others work independently, or provide their services freelance to companies in the industry.

In an industry which is becoming increasingly impersonal, as companies grow in size, and tourism products themselves become more homogeneous, the role of those who interface with the tourist becomes more and more important. Indeed, it may be the only feature of the package which distinguishes one product from another, yet curiously, it is a role which is becoming progressively downgraded by the larger companies, often as a means of cutting costs. The role of the resort representative has already been discussed in this context. Here we will examine two similar roles, those of the courier and the guide.

Couriers are employed by coach companies or tour operators to supervise and shepherd groups of tourists participating in tours (either on extended tours or day excursions). As well as couriers, they may be known as tour escorts, tour leaders, tour managers or tour directors (the latter terms imply greater levels of responsibility and status). One of their functions will be to offer a sightseeing commentary on the country or region through which they are travelling, and to act as a source of information.

Some companies dispense with the separate services of a courier in favour of a driver–courier, who takes on the responsibility of both driving the coach and looking after the passengers. These, however, may be inhibited in their information-giving roles by less general knowledge and training, and by their need to focus simultaneously on driving the coach. There is also a safety issue here, and some countries frown on coach drivers who give commentaries while their coach is in motion, or forbid the practice.

Courier work offers little opportunity for careers, tending by its nature to be seasonal, and consequently it depends upon recruiting high numbers of temporary workers, although many of these do choose to return to the job year after year. In some cases, such as in major cities where jobs are less seasonal, all-year-round work can be found, or couriers will be able to find alternative work during the off-season in winter sun or winter sports resorts.

Couriers are still employed largely on the strength of their prior experience. Qualifications applying to

this sector of the industry are being introduced, although they are not widely accepted in the UK yet. The role is attractive to graduates with relevant qualifications such as languages, but companies tend to recruit couriers largely on the strength of their personality, their ability to handle clients with sensitivity and tact, and their stamina, both physical and mental. Increasingly, employers are emphasizing sales ability, as couriers and resort representatives both play an important role in selling supplementary services such as optional excursions. Arguably, this is

Figure 14.1 A guide addresses tourists with the aid of a handheld microphone, Japan. (*Photographed by the author*)

changing the nature of the role, as commercial acumen replaces sociability.

Couriers differ from guides in the sense that the latter stress their information-giving role, even though they may perform shepherding functions in their job. Guides, or guide lecturers, are retained by operators for their expertise in general or specialist subjects. Their employment is again generally freelance and intermittent, off-season jobs being harder to come by outside the large cities. Guides take pride in their professionalism, and have well-established regional and national bodies to represent their interests. The largest of these is the London-based Guild of Guide Lecturers, which draws on a national membership. This body's efforts to establish agreed professional fees for members, however, ran counter to rulings by the Office of Fair Trading on price fixing in the industry, although the Guild continues to encourage the travel industry to employ professional guides with well-established training qualifications. These qualifications are achieved through formal courses of varying length, validated by the Regional Tourist Boards for guiding within the region. In other European countries, such a qualification is often seen as vital if a guide is to be given a licence to operate; in France, for example, a local guide must be employed to guide in Paris, having demonstrated local knowledge in formally approved qualifications (although such qualifications can also be obtained by other EU member countries' guides, of course).

Obtaining registered guide status does not, of course, guarantee job security, and many coach operators continue to employ non-registered guides who will accept lower fees for their services. The 'added value' of a qualified guide is still seen by many employers as a luxury they cannot afford in a climate where cutting costs to achieve sales is imperative.

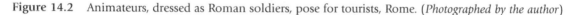

Figure 14.2 Animateurs, dressed as Roman soldiers, pose for tourists, Rome. (*Photographed by the author*)

The role of the animateur

The term 'animateur' is now becoming more widely known in the British tourism industry. It applies to those members of the industry who entertain tourists, either by acting out a role, or providing entertainment or instruction. The English term 'entertainer' is not strictly comparable, as this tends to be restricted to an acting role: the French term will also cover those whose task it is to interact with tourists to ensure that they enjoy themselves. They could be involved with instructing tourists in sports or hobbies, lecturing to cruise passengers or teaching them how to play bridge, or entertaining in the evening on stage at a European campsite. In Disney's theme parks there are a variety of animateur roles, the best known of which personify Mickey Mouse, but a host of other Disney characters are to be found on site, dressed as Alice in Wonderland, Snow White, and even the Chipmunks. These workers normally have no speaking role, and are there to make friends with younger visitors, posing for photographs etc. Others may take on a historical role at a heritage site; for example, at Williamsburg in Virginia, a number of staff are dressed in eighteenth-century costumes, and will maintain this role if questioned by visitors. The job might be thought of as fairly basic, in terms of skills, but Continental Europeans take a different view, and animation appears on the syllabus of French tourism and leisure qualifications, to cite just one example. This reflects the seriousness with which Continental tourism employees and employers view the role as one providing a professional service.

Financial services

This section will deal with financial services for the tourist – insurance, foreign exchange and credit.

Insurance

Insurance is an important, and in some cases obliga-tory, aspect of a tourist's travel arrangements, embracing coverage for one or more of the following contingencies:

- medical care and hospitalization (and, where necessary, repatriation, important where hospital services are of low standard);
- personal accident;
- cancellation or curtailment of holiday;
- delayed departure;
- baggage loss or delay;
- money loss;
- personal liability.

Some policies are now also including coverage for the collapse of the travel agent or tour operator through which the tour was purchased – an increasingly important option in view of the growing instability in the industry.

Tourists may purchase insurance either in the form of a selective policy, covering one or more of the above items, or, more commonly, in the form of a standard 'package' which will include all or most of the above. The latter policy, although inflexible in its coverage, invariably offers the best value if comprehensive coverage is sought. Although most tour operators encourage their clients to buy the operators' own comprehensive policies, these may be more expensive to purchase than a comprehensive policy offered by an independent insurance company. Travel agents may offer better-value insurance policies than those of the operator, but these too may be biased in favour of schemes paying the agent higher commissions. It is no longer legal to enforce the purchase of a particular policy, although operators can demand evidence that the customer is insured. Other retailers are now competing with travel agents to sell travel insurance, including companies such as Boots and Tesco, while cut-price annual policies are marketed direct by insurance agents, so travel agents are faced with a very competitive environment in selling this product, notwithstanding the attractive commissions paid.

Key issues in choosing a policy are to ensure that medical coverage is sufficient to meet the needs (in the USA, bills in excess of $1 million are not uncommon for serious illnesses), and that loss of any treasured individual items will be covered in full. The normal comprehensive coverage may limit compensation for total valuables to a figure which may not even cover the tourist's camera, so it is important for holiday-makers to consider covering such valuables within their house contents insurance.

Insurance remains a lucrative business for both operators and agents, although claims have been rising in recent years. Some reports estimate that 10 per cent of holiday-makers make claims, many fraudulent, against their policy, and this has led insurers to increase premiums to offset losses. Free insurance has consequently become an attractive incentive in marketing package tours.

Foreign transactions

Travellers today have an ever-widening choice of ways in which they can pay for services and goods while abroad. These include:

- taking sterling or foreign banknotes with them. This can lead to loss or theft, and certain foreign countries have restrictions on the import or export of their currencies;
- taking traveller's cheques, in sterling or foreign currency, or in euros;
- arranging for the advance transfer of funds to a specified foreign bank, or for an open credit to be made available, through their own bank, at a foreign bank;
- using National Girobank postcheques;
- taking Eurocheques;
- using travel vouchers;
- using credit cards or charge cards.

Eurocheques are being phased out as increasingly travellers abroad arrange to take small amounts of currency and settle bills through their credit or debit cards, drawing further local currency as needed using these cards. Credit cards such as those of Visa and Mastercard (Eurocard abroad) are very widely accepted throughout the world, but since transac-

tions can take some time to filter through to one's bank account, users take a chance on the fluctuations of exchange rates. Charge cards such as American Express or Diners Club provide similar advantages and drawbacks (charge cards differ from credit cards in that accounts are due for settlement in full after receipt of an invoice from the company. Credit is not extended. However, the limit on charge card transactions is generally much higher than on credit cards – indeed, the company may impose no ceiling on the amount the holder may charge to their account).

With the introduction of the euro as common currency in many EU countries (and perhaps in time in the UK), financial transactions for tourists visiting a number of European countries will be greatly eased, a fact which is likely to encourage travel to those countries using the euro. Many leading travel agency chains, including Lunn Poly, Going Places and Travel Choice, operate their own foreign exchange desks, and the post office in Britain has also introduced a foreign exchange desk.

Traveller's cheques are also still widely used, being readily acceptable throughout the world by banks and commercial institutions. They offer the holder guaranteed security with rapid compensation for theft or loss, an advantage which outweighs the standard premium charged of 1 per cent of face value. The value of the system for suppliers is that there is generally a considerable lapse of time between the tourist purchasing traveller's cheques and cashing them. The money invested in the interim at market rates of interest provides the supplier with substantial profits. Market leaders in traveller's cheque sales in the UK are Thomas Cook (whose 'circular note', the predecessor of the traveller's cheque, originated in 1873), and American Express, which first introduced the concept in 1891, but a growing proportion are being issued by the clearing house banks.

Travel vouchers such as Barclay's Visa and Citicorp provide for sterling prepayment for travel services like car hire and hotel accommodation. Although prepaid vouchers of this kind have been in existence in the travel industry for many years, the credit organizations have greatly boosted their use in recent years.

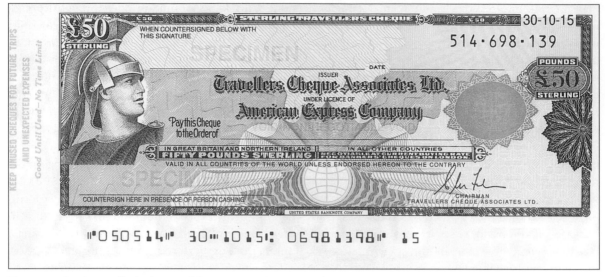

Figure 14.3 A traveller's cheque. (*Courtesy American Express*)

Apart from the popular Visa and Mastercard, there are a large number of other credit cards issued for the purchase of specific goods and services, such as car hire and hotels. Among these, mention should be made of the Universal Air Travel Plan (UATP) card, used for the purchase of IATA tickets throughout the world (although more commonly in use in North America than Europe). However, with the growth in popularity of the two leading credit card organizations, the use of other cards for international credit transactions is now limited. Since agents are required to pay a fee to the card companies when accepting credit cards in payment for travel, there has been some reluctance to accept them, but credit card sales are increasing at such a rate that no agent can afford to turn this form of business away. Payment by credit card offers the additional advantage to the traveller that funds are protected in the event of the collapse of the agent, operator or airline with which they are dealing.

The large number of foreign exchange facilities available provides the market with a very wide choice, but charges fluctuate considerably, and both rate of conversion and fixed charges need to be compared to judge what represents best value for money.

Work is under way to introduce smart cards which have a microchip built into the card storing credit. These have been use in France for some years, and have been tested in some supermarket outlets in the UK. It is likely that we shall see these in use for travel purchases before very long.

Incentive travel vouchers

Incentive travel has shown considerable growth over the past few years, with companies providing their employees or dealers with attractive travel packages as rewards for achievement. One option taken up by some companies is the travel voucher, issued in various denominations, which allows the recipient to choose their own travel arrangements. This is simply monetary reward for achievement in another form, but the appeal of travel has proved to be a stronger motivator than either cash or consumer durables, offers greater flexibility, and can be given in smaller denominations – to reward, for example, low absenteeism or the achievement of weekly targets. Some of these vouchers can only be exchanged against specific travel products, or through certain travel agents, while others can be used to pay for any holiday arrangements purchased through any agent.

Duty-free shopping

Under the category of services to tourists, mention should also be made of duty-free shopping facilities, although the subject has been discussed elsewhere in this text. The purchase of duty-free goods at airports, on board ships and aircraft, or at specially designated duty-free ports has exerted a strong attraction for tourists for a very long time. Introduced during the first half of the twentieth century, mainly to satisfy the demands of travellers on the great ocean liners, it was extended to aircraft in 1944. The first airside duty-free shopping arrived in 1947, when the Irish parliament passed the Custom-free Airport Act, giving Shannon the world's first duty-free shop. Since those days, duty-free purchases of spirits and tobacco in particular have been effectively marketed by airports and carriers alike, and the profits and sales of such items have always been substantial, accounting for large shares in the profits of many companies. Airports have achieved up to half their total operating profits through such sales, while ferry companies in Scandinavia have obtained up to 70 per cent of their income in this manner.

This has led in some quarters to criticisms of profiteering, but airports reply to such criticism by claiming that without these profits, they would be forced to increase their landing charges; this would have a knock-on effect on carriers, which would then be forced to raise their fares. Without the benefit of duty-free shopping, transport fares do tend to rise appreciably; estimates typically point to increases ranging from 10 per cent to as high as 30 per cent. BAA in fact reduced its estimate of increases in charges to airlines using its airports after expanding its retail shopping outlets and forecasting rapid increases in duty-paid sales (rising congestion at airports, requiring earlier check-in times, and flight delays all tend to enhance sales in airport shops).

Tax harmonization in the European Union led to the withdrawal of duty-free privileges for travel between Member States in July 1999. The impact of this regulation on travel industry sectors has still to be assessed, but it is evident that many companies were badly hit by the move; to take one example, Eurotunnel alone saw a 72 per cent fall in its retail revenues in the months following the ending of duty-free sales. As a result, fares on cross-Channel ferries and Eurotunnel services were raised sharply, and companies redirected their marketing efforts to selling duty-paid goods, often at French prices, which substantially undercut those in Britain. How this new regulation is affecting travel patterns between EU and other European countries is not yet clear, although some destination switching is certain to have occurred as passengers face higher fares on some routes while others can still attract the duty-free consumer. Countries such as Tunisia, Malta and Turkey are likely to have benefited from the change.

Services to the supplier

Education and training

The approach to training in the tourism industry has been historically a sectoral one. In the past, each sector of the industry was primarily concerned with training staff to become competent within its own sector, focusing on narrow job-specific abilities. In an industry comprising mainly small units with entrepreneurial styles of management, the benefits of formal education and training have seldom been acknowledged. Most employees of travel agencies, tour operators and hotels were trained on the job, often by observing supervisors at work, although a handful of companies, such as Thomas Cook, were notable for their early recognition of the need for more formal, although in-house, training.

With the growing institutionalization of sectors, greater emphasis is placed on professionalism, the introduction of national standards and more formal modes of training. The professional bodies within industry introduced their own programmes of training and vocational education leading to membership, often carried out through full-time or part-time courses at local colleges of further or higher education. Examples of these early developments included courses offered by the Hotel and Catering

International Management Association (HCIMA), the Chartered Institute of Transport (CIT) and the Institute of Travel and Tourism (ITT). However, with the rapid expansion of nationally validated travel and tourism courses in colleges of further and higher education which occurred from the 1970s onwards, there has been a move to recognize formal qualifications, especially those offered by such bodies as the City and Guilds of London Institute (CGLI).

In-service training for travel agents was formalized with the introduction of the Certificate of Travel Agency Competence (COTAC), nationally validated by the CGLI and supported by ABTA's National Training Board (now known as TTC Training). Since this date, formal training has had a bumpy ride, with frequent changes in qualification and supervisory body, and at the time of writing, the CGLI and TTC are working together to develop a structure and range of qualifications which will be acceptable to the majority of those in the industry, especially travel agencies and tour operating companies.

The industry is working towards the recognition of nationally agreed benchmarks for service excellence, based on standards established originally by the British Standards Institution (BSI). National standards under the ISO 9000 scheme have given way to the programmes 'Investors in People' (IIP) and, most recently, 'Hospitality Assured' as evidence of standards achieved.

The difficulty of organizing day release for employees of smaller travel companies encouraged the development of distance learning packages. British Airways fares and ticketing courses, for example, which are offered either full-time or through self-study packs, have found national acceptance as a standard for those seeking to work in travel agencies and airlines, while Lufthansa provides similar nationally accepted courses in Germany, and the World Tourism Organisation (WTO) and International Air Transport Association (IATA) have organized internationally recognized distance-learning packs for students of tourism throughout the world.

As we have seen earlier, courses for registered guides have been created in the UK and elsewhere, but these are validated individually in Britain by the Regional Tourist Boards and national standards have not yet been laid down for such courses. With vocational courses of this nature, the question of balance between job-specific skills and broader conceptual knowledge has long taxed employers and educationalists alike. Unlike most countries in Europe, Britain still does not hold formal qualifications in high respect, preferring to provide the job skills that are seen as essential to fulfil basic, sector-specific roles in the industry. However, public sector colleges have offered courses since the late 1960s which were designed to provide not just essential skills, but a broader knowledge of the industry and the world of business, and although these were slow to achieve credibility with employers, the eventual support given by ABTA to the national diplomas with tourism helped to establish credibility for formal education. In 1986 the first degrees in travel and tourism were introduced, to join the already well-established Higher National Diplomas (HNDs), postgraduate diplomas and masters' degrees in the subject, so that tourism can now be studied formally at all levels of post-school education. The popularity of degree-level tourism programmes led to a huge expansion of courses on offer in the new universities during the 1990s, with an output of qualified students far in excess of suitable posts available. Recent trends have led to the establishment of more specialized degrees, including the first MSc in e-tourism, for advanced students who want to take advantage of opportunities to work in positions relating to the increasing use of communications technology within the industry.

Within the school system itself, GCSEs at ordinary and advanced level specializing in travel and tourism have also been introduced, with the support of key members of the industry, in order to interest school leavers in a career in travel. Attitudes among careers counsellors in schools, however, are slow to change, and tourism continues to be seen by many as a career for the less academically able. Low salaries paid to those on the lower levels of employment tend to reinforce this attitude. The industry, especially the

Figure 14.4 The weekly trade papers. (*Permission of* Travel Weekly *and* Travel Trade Gazette)

Weekly provide an invaluable service to the industry, covering news of both social and commercial activities, as well as providing the heaviest concentration of advertisements for jobs in the industry.

In an industry as fast-moving as tourism, employees can only update their knowledge of travel products by regular reading of the trade press. The newspapers complement the work of the training bodies, while for untrained staff they may well act as the principal source of new information. The trade press depends largely upon advertising for its revenue, as the two weeklies are distributed free to members of industry; in return, they support the industry by sponsoring trade fairs, seminars and other events.

Within the general category of the press one must also include those who are responsible for the publication of travel guides and timetables. The major publications in the field are shown in Table 14.1, and are those most commonly used in travel agencies. The task of updating the information is obviously immense, especially in view of the worldwide scope of many of these publications. Since their production becomes more complex each year, this is also a field which lends itself to computerization. ABC Guides now provide access for agents to their air timetables and fares information electronically, and within a few years most of these travel resources can be expected to be retrieved electronically by the trade at least, and no doubt even by members of the general public.

retail travel sector, is now agonizing over how better qualified staff can be obtained to pay the salaries that must be expected in a professional organization where fees may now have to be charged in lieu of commissions.

The trade press

In addition to specialized academic journals, there is a large selection of weekly and monthly journals devoted to the travel and tourism industry. The weekly trade papers *Travel Trade Gazette* and *Travel*

Marketing services

A number of services exist either wholly or in part to provide marketing support to members of the travel industry. These include marketing consultants, representative agencies, advertising agencies, brochure design, printing and distribution services, suppliers of travel point-of-sale material, and research and public relations organizations. To this list must be added the organizations which provide the hardware and software for the travel industry's computer systems.

Table 14.1 Travel publications

Publication	Details
British publications	
ABC World Airways Guide (monthly)	Flight and fares information, car hire
ABC Rail Guide (monthly)	Timetables between London and all stations
ABC Shipping Guide (monthly)	Worldwide passenger and cargo-passenger services
ABC Guide to International Travel (quarterly)	Passport, visa, health, currency regulations, customs, climate etc
ABC Hotel and Travel Index (quarterly)	Hotel and trade information
Thomas Cook Continental Timetable (monthly)	Rail and passenger shipping services throughout Europe and the Mediterranean
Thomas Cook Overseas Timetable (bi-monthly)	Road, rail and local shipping in America, Africa, Asia, Australia
National Express Coach Guide (biannual)	Express coach services for British Isles
Travel Trade Directory	Directory of travel industry in UK/Eire
IATA Travel Agents' Directory of Europe (annual)	Agents, airlines, hotel groups, car hire, tourist offices
Britain: Hotels and Restaurants (annual)	BTA official guide
AA Guide to Hotels and Restaurants (annual)	Listing of 5,000 recommended establishments in the British Isles
A–Z Worldwide Hotel Guide (biannual)	Comprehensive listing of international hotels and reservations offices
Holiday Guide (annual summer and winter edition)	Identifies tour operators providing package holidays to specific hotels and resorts worldwide
Car Ferry Guide (annual)	Index of car ferry routes and operators
Cahners Hotel and Travel Index	Quarterly guide to hotels worldwide
ABTA Members' Handbook	Annual guide for agents, including country guide and full details of the Code of Conduct for agents and operators
Eurolines Directory	Annual guide to coach lines operating from the UK throughout Europe
International publications	
International Hotel guide (annual)	Worldwide guide published by International Hotel Association
Michelin Red Guides	French annual guides to Great Britain and Ireland, France, Benelux, Spain, Portugal, Italy and Germany
Europa Camping and Caravanning (annual)	Guide to campsites
Jaeger's Intertravel (annual)	Directory of world's travel agencies

Note: Many agents now buy their directories on CD-ROM or use the Internet to access directories instead of subscribing to hard-print manuals.

This book does not propose to discuss in depth the marketing of tourism. The subject is fully covered in a companion text (*Marketing for Tourism*, Holloway and Robinson, Longman, 1995). Other texts dealing with the topic can be found in the bibliography at the end of this book. The point to be made here is that both large and small companies in the industry can benefit by employing these specialist agencies, while the services of some are seen as indispensable.

General marketing consultants

Management and marketing consultants offer advice to companies in the organization and operation of their businesses. They bring to the task two valuable attributes, expertise and objectivity. Most tourism consultants have years of experience in the industry on which to draw, and have been successful in their own fields before turning to consultancy; but with the recession of the 1990s and the inevitable rise in the number of companies either failing or being taken over, the pool of those former managers in the industry turning to consultancy work has increased; the consultants group affiliated to the Tourism Society alone now includes over 200 individuals.

Consultants, not being directly involved in the day-to-day running of the companies they are employed to help, can approach their task without any preconceived ideas. They can therefore advise companies either on the general reorganization of the business or on some ad hoc issue such as undertaking a feasibility study or the introduction of a new computer system.

Representative agencies

For a retainer or payment of royalties on sales, these organizations act as general sales agents for a company within a defined territory. This is a valuable service for smaller companies seeking representation abroad, for example. In the travel industry it is most commonly found in the hotel sector, but carriers, excursion operators and public sector tourist offices all make use of the facility in marketing their services abroad.

Advertising and promotional agencies

Many large travel companies, and an increasing number of smaller ones, retain an advertising agent, a number of whom specialize in handling travel accounts. Advertising agents do much more than design advertisements and place them in the media. They should be closely involved in the entire marketing strategy of the company, and will be involved with the design and production of travel brochures. Many are equipped to carry out marketing research, the production of publicity material and merchandising or public relations activities. Some larger agencies also produce their own hotel/resort guides, using their own staff's extensive knowledge.

Travel companies may have their brochures designed by the design studio of their advertising agent, they may arrange for them to be produced by an independent design studio, or in some cases their printer's studio may undertake the work. However, a growing number of brochures are now put together in-house, with the aid of sophisticated computer software now available for desktop publishing. Advertising agents can also help and advise in the selection of a printer for the production of brochures or other publicity material.

One recent innovation in publicity material for the trade is the use of video cassettes to supplement, and perhaps in time even to replace, the travel brochure. They are designed to help customers reach a decision on holiday destinations and services, and are already being used by agents, who loan them out to their clients. The cost of the cassette production is borne by the principals whose services are being promoted in this way. A number of companies are now specializing in the production of these travel aids. However, with the growth of the Internet and digital TV channels, it is becoming more likely that brochures will eventually be replaced by computer-accessed text and illustrations which can be quickly updated and repriced.

Finally, in the area of marketing services mention should be made of direct mail and distribution services, some of which specialize in handling travel accounts. The companies design and organize direct mail promotional literature aimed at specific target markets, or at travel retailers. They can also undertake distribution of a company's brochures to travel agents in the UK.

Microprocessor organizations

The rapid spread of computer use within all sectors of the travel industry has led to the establishment of specialist computer experts, who concentrate on designing and implementing purpose-made systems for their travel industry clients. Such systems include not only travel information and reservations functions, but also accounting and management information. Other computer organizations have been set up to provide networks which allow agents to access principals' computer reservations systems.

Questions and discussion points

1. The traditional role of the sales representative calling on travel agents has diminished sharply in recent years, to be replaced by merchandisers or other more impersonal forms of communication, on the grounds of efficiency. Discuss the merits and disadvantages of these various approaches, from both the agents' and the principals' perspectives.

2. Evaluate the two weekly trade papers, *Travel Trade Gazette* and *Travel Weekly*. As manager of a small travel agency whose staff are always too busy to read both, which would you recommend they read regularly, and why?

3. Is it in the interests of the travel industry and their customers for Britain to adopt the euro as official currency? Are there logical, as opposed to emotional, reasons to retain the pound sterling to meet the expenses of foreign travel?

4. 'What value to the customer is an 18-year-old who hasn't travelled to any real degree and knows less about the product than the customer?' Kevin Abbey, MD, Bakers Dolphin Travel, referring to inexperienced young travel agents

Can inexperience be offset by good training and/or education? Would better training for those in the industry improve profitability and make the survival of travel agents in particular more probable? And how important is a good general education, compared with practical experience, in selling to travel customers?

Assignment topics

1. Mr H, a successful travel agency proprietor for nearly thirty years (in association with his father, now dead), has received an offer from a multiple for the purchase of his three agencies which he finds difficult to refuse, given the uncertainty of the retailing sector's future. However, it has been made clear that there would be no future for him in his former company, and he feels it is too early to retire (he is 53). He is thinking about setting up as a consultant to the travel industry.

   What advice would you give him, and what would he need apart from his existing experience to make a success of this new role?

2. The travel industry boasts two separate professional bodies, the Tourism Society (which draws its members particularly from the hotel, attractions, public sector, educational and consultancy sectors) and the Institute of Travel and Tourism (whose membership is largely composed of tour operators and travel agents). Should these two bodies unite to provide a single professional voice for the industry? What problems might this suggestion pose for the bodies themselves or their members, and how could these be resolved? What would be the principal benefits of a merger?

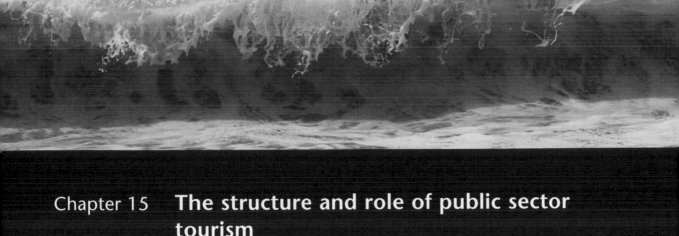

Chapter 15   The structure and role of public sector tourism

Objectives

After studying this chapter, you should be able to:

- understand the part played by local and central governments in the planning and promotion of tourism in a country;
- recognize why governments are becoming increasingly involved with all aspects of tourism in some countries;
- understand the meaning of the term 'social tourism' and its importance;
- show how governments and local authorities in Britain and elsewhere control and supervise tourism;
- explain how public sector tourism is organized in Britain.

Introduction

In the opening chapter of this text, tourism was revealed to play an important part in a nation's economy by providing opportunities for regional employment, by contributing to the balance of payments and by stimulating economic growth. On the other hand, countries that experience an influx of large numbers of tourists also suffer the environmental and social consequences of mass tourism, unless care is taken to plan for and control the flow of tourists. For both economic and social reasons, therefore, governments take a direct interest in the development of tourism within their countries, and

the more a nation becomes involved in tourism, whether domestic, inbound or outbound, the more likely it is that the government will play a role in the industry.

The nature of government involvement

The system of government of a country will of course be reflected in the mode and extent of government intervention. At one end of the scale, centrally planned economies may choose to exercise virtually complete control, from policy making and planning to the building and operating of tourist facilities, the organization of tourist movements and the promotion of tourism at home and abroad. Since the collapse of the Soviet empire, such central control is limited to very few countries, and even those nations still ostensibly operating centrally planned economies, such as China, Cuba and Vietnam, recognize and accept the importance of private enterprise, and the benefits of private investment, in their tourism plans. Thus China, for example, has cooperated with privately owned American hotel corporations to establish chains of tourist hotels in major centres of tourism within the country.

Most other nations have mixed economies in which public and private sectors coexist and collaborate in the development of tourism within their borders; only the balance of public versus private involvement will vary. Thus the United States, with its belief in a free enterprise system and a federal constitution, delegates much of the responsibility for overseas promotion of the nation either to individual states or even to private organizations created for the purpose. Central government intervention in that country is limited to measures designed to protect the health and safety of its citizens (such as aircraft safety and air traffic control). The US Travel and Tourism Administration closed its overseas offices, and overseas marketing is now undertaken by the privately sponsored Travel Industry Association of America (TIA) which markets the United States under a number of brands, including Visit USA, Discover USA and Discover America, and in some cases maintains its own offices abroad to serve trade (but not public) needs.

The *system* of government is not the only factor dictating the extent of state intervention. If a country is highly dependent upon tourism for its economic survival, its government is likely to become far more involved in the industry. Spain, for example, has a Ministry of Tourism, Transport and Communications, while in Kenya, the Ministry of Tourism and Wildlife takes on this responsibility. In these countries, tourism as an economic activity will feature prominently in policy making and planning

directives. Britain, where tourism is important but to a lesser extent than in the Mediterranean countries, has an under secretary with responsibility for tourism within the Department for Culture, Media and Sport – a government creation much criticized by the travel industry for its failure to include tourism in its title.

Countries where tourism has only relatively recently become a significant factor in the economy, and where this sudden growth has become problematic, are likely to exercise stronger control over tourism development than are those where tourism is either in its early stages of development or has developed slowly over a long period of time. Mauritius, for example, recognized that the sudden surge of interest it experienced in the early 1980s could lead to the country being swamped, destroying the very attractions that brought the visitor to the islands, unless the country took steps to control such key activities as hotel construction. Tunisia, too, learned the lesson and introduced control over hotel and other tourism construction early in the development of mass tourism to that destination. Unfortunately, however, the potential for quick riches can exercise a greater influence than the long-term interests of the country, and there are all too many examples of countries which have suffered from lack of sufficient control over building and development, leading eventually to a drop in visits as tourists turn to less exploited destinations. Overbuilding in Spain was held up as an example in the late 1960s, and could have influenced subsequent development in other Mediterranean countries to which tourists turned en masse somewhat later. Nevertheless, in the 1980s and 1990s we have seen in turn over-development in key regions of first Greece, then the Portuguese Algarve, and later (in spite of initial efforts to control hotel building) in Turkey. Corruption and nepotism – the significance of having influential 'connections' to overcome planning controls should never be underestimated – are very real enemies of sustainable tourism policies.

All countries, however, depend upon the provision of a sound infrastructure in order to encourage tourism in the first place, and this is a role which must be undertaken by government. Adequate public services, roads, railways and airports must all be in place before the private sector can become interested in investing in the equally necessary superstructure of hotels, restaurants, entertainment, attractions and other facilities which will bring in the tourists.

Less-developed nations may have a further incentive for government involvement; private developers will be reluctant to invest in speculative tourist ventures, preferring to concentrate their resources in countries where there is already proven demand. In this case, it may fall to the government either to aid private developers, in the form of grants or loans for hotel construction, or even to build and operate the hotels and other tourist amenities which will first attract the tourist. Where the private sector can be persuaded to invest, it is often companies from the generating countries that become involved, with the result that profits may be repatriated rather than benefiting the local economy. There is also the danger that private speculators will be overly concerned to achieve a quick return on their investment, rather than the slow but secure long-term development which will benefit the country most.

The state is called upon to play a coordinating role in planning the provision of tourist amenities and attractions. Supply should match demand as closely as possible, and the state can ensure that facilities are available when and where required, and that they are of the right standard.

As tourism grows in the economy, so its organization, if uncontrolled, can result in the domination of the market by a handful of large companies. Even in a capitalist system, the state has the duty to restrict the power of monopolies, to protect the consumer against malpractice such as unfair constraints on trade or exorbitant prices.

Apart from these economic reasons for which governments become involved in tourism, there are also social and political reasons. In many countries, especially in less-developed states, national airlines are state owned and operated. While of course the income accruing from the operation of the airline is important to the state, there is also the political prestige of operating an airline, even if the national flag-carrier is economically non-viable. In other situations, certain airline routes may be unprofitable, but since they may provide an important economic lifeline to the communities they serve, they will therefore be subsidized by the government.

Governments also have a duty to safeguard a nation's heritage. Buildings of historical or architectural interest, particularly those of international importance such as Stonehenge, must be protected and maintained, as must sites of exceptional landscape merit. Sometimes governments are caught up in a conflict between the needs for economic development and for protection of a cherished site, as in the case of Twyford Down, a cherished English beauty spot in Hampshire, which, in the face of an outcry from conservationists, was bisected in 1993 in order to build an extension to a motorway. The long search for a third London airport was extended by several years while the government weighed up the relative merits of the economic benefits of a particular site and the environmental damage which the development would cause. Still more recently, conflict between conservation and economic development is evident in the UK in the cases of the construction of a fifth terminal at London's Heathrow Airport (still unresolved at the time of writing) and the expansion of Manchester Airport. Needless to say, the power of political lobbying may be the critical factor in any decision taken by the public authorities, as was the case in London's third airport.

We can sum up by saying that a national government's role in tourism can be manifested in the following ways:

1. in the planning and facilitating of tourism, including the provision of financial and other aid;
2. in the supervision and control of the component sectors of the tourism industry;
3. in direct ownership and operation of components of the industry;
4. in the promotion of the nation and its tourist products to home and overseas markets.

These issues will be examined in the remainder of this chapter.

Planning and facilitating tourism

Any country in which tourism plays a prominent role in national income and employment can expect its government to devise policies and plans for the development of tourism. This will include generating guidelines and objectives for the growth and management of tourism, both in the short and the long term, and devising strategies designed to achieve these objectives.

British government policy on tourism has fluctuated considerably in recent years, wavering between the need to create employment, which favoured investment in tourism, and pressures on public spending, which inhibited it. The Conservative government's approach was initially to support tourism through grant aid and other strategies, but by the 1990s the government took the view that they had established the necessary 'pump priming', that the industry was now 'mature' and that further investment should be left to the private sector. It was also the government's intention to interfere as little as possible in tourism planning and development, which were to be overseen by the British Tourist Authority and the regional bodies. In practice, however, governments have been tempted time and again to 'recommend' approaches which were not necessarily those favoured by the tourist boards – the devolution of power from the English Tourist Board to the Regional Tourist Boards in the 1990s is a case in point.

The British Tourist Authority (BTA), as a quasi-autonomous national government organization with the responsibility to promote Britain abroad, had as its aims not just an increase in the total number of tourists to Britain but also a more even spread of visitors throughout the region and across the months, to avoid the congestion of demand in the south and during the summer months. In Spain, since demand had already been created by the private sector for the popular east-coast resorts and the Balearic Islands, national tourist office policy has focused on promoting the less familiar northwest coast and central regions of the country, while coastal development became subject to increasing control.

Tourism planning calls for research, first to assess the level of demand or potential demand to a particular region, second to estimate the resources required in order to cater for that demand, and finally to determine how these resources should best be distributed. As we have seen, demand is unlikely to be generated to any extent until an adequate infrastructure and superstructure are in place, but it is not sufficient simply to provide these amenities. Tourists also need staff to service the facilities – hotel workers, travel agents, guides – trained to an acceptable level of performance. Planning therefore implicitly includes ensuring the availability of a pool of labour, as well as the provision of training through hotel, catering and tourism schools, to provide the skills and knowledge the industry requires.

In some cases, providing the facilities which tourists want can actually have a negative impact on tourism to the region. To take one example, while the building of airports on some of the smaller islands in Greece opened up these islands to larger flows of tourists, it made the islands less attractive for the up-market high-spending tourist, who preferred the relative isolation achieved when accessibility was restricted to ferry operations.

Much earlier in the text, we examined the need for accessibility as a key factor in the development of tourism. This depends not only on adequate transport, but also the absence of any political barriers to travel. If visas are required for entry to a country, this will discourage incoming tourism. At the beginning of the 1990s, the UK imposed a visa requirement on citizens of Turkey seeking to enter Britain; the Turks retaliated by imposing in turn a visa requirement on British visitors to their country. However, the flow of tourists is almost entirely one way, and the Turks emerged as the clear losers, as the visa requirement dissuaded tourists from visiting their country. In 1988, the USA abandoned visas for many visitors from Western Europe (albeit with some limitations which continued to hinder the free flow of tourism), having recognized the barrier that this bureaucratic constraint exercised at a time when other factors, such as relative exchange rates, were favouring the rapid expansion of tourism to North America. Similarly, the ending of visa requirements for the Baltic States following the collapse of communism led to a substantial increase in tourist visits. Russia, by contrast, continues to insist on visas, at a cost of £30 at the time of writing (£40 through operators or agents). Only 55,000 tourists from Britain travelled to Russia in 1999 (although the perceived instability of the country will undoubtedly have also contributed to this low figure), and more people visited Estonia than Russia that year. Kenya, a country heavily dependent upon tourism, raised visa charges to £35 in 2001, in spite of having lost large numbers of visitors following a similar move in 1997, which it had reversed two years later. Maximizing revenue from inbound tourism flows is always a temptation among governments, but it is a practice which can backfire if visitors can simply switch to alternative destinations offering similar attractions – such as Botswana or Tanzania in this case. Arguably, long-haul travellers will be more willing to accept reasonably high visa costs when travelling extensively in a country, but such costs are offputting for short-break visits or calls by cruise liner – and Mombasa in Kenya is currently an important point of embarkation for cruises in the Indian Ocean.

Taxation can also hinder tourism flows within the European Union. In 1993, Greece increased its airport departure tax threefold, to 5,200 drachmas (roughly £15), sufficient to antagonize tour operators and to persuade the 'marginal' tourist to switch to other Mediterranean destinations. The British government's imposition in the 1993 budget of an airport departure tax of £5 in the European Union and £10 elsewhere was widely criticized in the press; the decision to double this rate from November 1997 provoked fury in the trade. When one sets such figures against the new low-cost fares offered within Europe by carriers such as easyJet, it is apparent that airport taxes can account for as much as 25 per cent of the air transport costs. Likewise, heavy airport tax burdens were introduced in 1997 both into and out of the state of Florida, which would result in a family of four flying to Disney World paying another £70 in taxation – a very considerable proportion of their flight costs. In 2000, Majorca proposed to introduce an 'eco-levy' tax of £10, to be collected either through airport or hotel accommodation taxation, a means of discouraging low-cost visitors and to enhance the infrastructure of the island to attract more up-market visitors. There was an immediate negative reaction from the trade, which feared falling load factors on aircraft and package tours. A decision on whether to go ahead is pending at the time of writing, but the aim is understandable, given the numbers travelling to the island – some 7 million a year, with a resident island population of only 600,000.

Another important factor determining tourism flow is the attitude of nationals of the host country towards visitors in general, and towards visitors from specific countries in particular. Many countries heavily dependent upon tourism have had to mount political campaigns aimed at their residents, to encourage them to show more friendliness towards foreign visitors. Those residents who most frequently come into contact with tourists, such as customs officers, immigration officials, shopkeepers, hotel staff and taxi drivers, must be trained to be polite and friendly; first impressions are important for long-term image-building of a country. The USA has introduced campaigns to improve the politeness and friendliness of officials dealing with incoming visitors, while countries of the Caribbean have been forced to mount campaigns to deal with growing xenophobia among the local population. The British tourism industry has also taken steps to improve its own handling of foreign tourists through training programmes such as Welcome Host, and encouragement has been given to learning foreign languages, a major weakness among personnel in the industry.

One difficulty which faces governments in the planning of tourism is the split between the responsibilities of central and local governments with respect to issues affecting tourism. In Britain, local authorities were given responsibility for developing tourism in their areas under the Local Government Act 1972. This included responsibility for planning and infrastructure, and encouraged tourism to be considered when drawing up local planning policies. In consequence, local authorities have direct responsibility for a number of issues which directly affect visiting tourists, including the provision of car and coach parking, litter control, maintenance of footpaths and promenades, public parks and gardens and, where appropriate, beach management and monitoring of seawater for bathing. These responsibilities are to some extent split between city and county councils, and conflicting views may appear between local authorities, as well as between local and central government. Local authorities are, of course, greatly influenced by the views of their ratepayers, who are often unsympathetic to the expansion of tourism in their area.

Although tourism in Britain comes within the area of responsibility of the Department for Culture, Media and Sport, no single government department is responsible for all facets of the industry. The Department of the Environment, Department of Transport, Local Government and the Regions and the Department for Environment, Food and Rural Affairs will also have some role to play in the development of tourism. In practice, coordination between these various departments is difficult to achieve, hindering the overall planning of tourism within the country.

Financial aid for tourism

Governments also contribute to tourism growth through financing development of new projects. On a massive scale, developments such as those of Cancun, Mexico or the regional development of the Languedoc-Roussillon area in the South of France demonstrate the effectiveness of massive private and public sector cooperation in developing entirely new tourism resorts, with the public sector providing the huge funds necessary for land acquisition and infrastructure (and in the case of Languedoc-Roussillon,

the substantial costs of mosquito eradication throughout the district). On a smaller scale, many governments aid the private sector by providing loans at preferential rates of interest, or outright grants, for schemes which are in keeping with government policy. One example of the way such schemes operate in less-developed countries is for loans to be made on which interest only is paid during the first three or four years, with repayment of capital postponed until the later years of the project, by which time it should have become self-financing. Other forms of government aid include subsidies such as tax rebates or tax relief on operating expenses.

Financial aid for tourism projects can also be provided internationally from a number of sources. Less-developed countries have received aid from the International Development Association, a subsidiary of the World Bank, which provides interest-free or low-rate loans, while another World Bank subsidiary, the International Bank for Reconstruction and Development, offers loans at commercial rates of interest to countries where alternate sources of funding may be difficult to find.

On a regional scale, within Europe the European Investment Bank (EIB) provides loans at commercial rates of interest to small companies (normally those employing fewer than 500 staff). These loans have been provided for up to 50 per cent of fixed asset costs, with repayment terms up to eight years. Interest rates may be slightly lower in areas designated 'Assisted Areas' within the EU.

The European Regional Development Fund offers financial assistance (usually up to 30 per cent of the capital costs) for tourism projects generated by public sector bodies within the Assisted Areas. This money can be used not only as pump priming for direct tourist attractions such as museums, but also for infrastructure development to support tourism, such as airports or car parking facilities. *Objective 1* status provides support for severely impoverished areas, which include Greece, southern Italy, parts of Spain, western Ireland and in the UK, Liverpool.

Objective 2 status defines support available for deep rural areas (which includes parts of Devon, for example) or depressed urban areas. Tourism projects in both the Irish Republic and Northern Ireland have greatly benefited under the terms of these funds, especially in small projects such as theatres, art galleries, waterways, parks and nature reserves, and the establishment of tourist offices and visitor centres.

European tourism may also benefit, under some circumstances, from the European Social Fund or the European Agricultural Guidance and Guarantee Fund. Financing available only within Great Britain will be dealt with a little later in this chapter.

Social tourism

Reference should also be made here to the government's role in encouraging *social tourism*. This has been defined as the 'furtherance of the economically weak or dependent classes of the population', and is designed to provide aid for low-income families, single-parent families, the elderly, handicapped and other deprived minorities within a population. Aid may be offered in the form of finance (grants, low-interest loans and the like) or in direct support through the provision of free coach trips or holiday accommodation. Under this generic term one might also include the public funding of health tourism, which it has been the practice of some countries' governments to subsidize as part of the general public health and well-being of the populations.

Social tourism is of course more likely to benefit from countries whose governments have planned economies. Holidays are seen by these countries as necessary to maintain the health and well-being of the working population. In mixed economies like those in Europe, several countries have been active in providing subsidized tourism for their deprived citizens, led by Belgium, France and the southern countries of the EU. The Brussels-based International Bureau of Social Tourism (BITS) has been active since 1963 as a base for the study and debate of social tourism issues, and maintains a databank, issues publications and conducts seminars on the subject. There are well-established programmes of aid on the Continent for holidays for the mentally, physically and socially handicapped, although financial pressures are reducing these opportunities. The French government, for example, terminated its programme of welfare-funded spa holidays in 1999, a severe blow to the spa tourism industry, which hosted over 600,000 French visitors who had been able to recover up to 70 per cent of their costs through the social security system in that country. However, its well-established VVF (*Village Vacance Famille*) programme of social tourism remains in place.

Comparatively little support of this kind is provided in Britain for the disadvantaged, although Britain has over 6 million registered disabled people. Responsibility for providing this service is delegated to local authorities (the Chronically Sick and Disabled Act 1970 imposed a statutory duty on local authorities to fund holidays for the disabled). Many authorities provided coach outings for the elderly and other disadvantaged groups, but in the closing years of the twentieth century cutbacks in local authority funding sharply reduced these services, and the number of those receiving financial help from local councils slumped. The result has been that social tourism has largely become the responsibility of the private sector. Sponsored by the English Tourist Board (now the ETC), and with the full support of the travel industry in the UK, the Holiday Care Service was set up in 1981, essentially to provide information about holiday opportunities for the disadvantaged. Later, this was expanded to include training programmes for members of the tourism industry. A number of specialist operators then turned to catering to the needs of these groups, or providing discounted holidays for those with limited means. Holidays are also organized by the trade unions in Britain, which have established holiday homes and subsidize holidays for their members; other bodies arranging holidays for the disadvantaged include Mencap, the Red Cross, the Multiple

Sclerosis Society and the Winged Fellowship Trust. Both SCOPE (the Spastics Society) and the Spina Bifida Association own holiday homes where holidays can be provided for those suffering from these illnesses.

Control and supervision in tourism

The state plays an important part in controlling and supervising tourism, as well as helping to facilitate it. This is necessary to restrain undesirable growth, to maintain quality standards, to match supply and demand, and to protect tourists against industrial malpractice or failure.

A government can act to restrain tourism in a number of ways, whether through central directives or through local authority control. Refusal of planning permission is an obvious example of the exercise of control over tourism development. However, this is seldom totally effective, since if an area is a major attraction for tourists, the authorities will be unlikely to dissuade them from visiting the district simply by, say, refusing planning permission for new hotels; the result may simply be that overnight visitors are replaced by excursionists, or that private bed and breakfast accommodation moves in to fill the gap left by the lack of hotel beds. Cornwall has had measures to control caravan sites since 1954, but the local authority has still found it difficult to prevent the growth of unlicensed sites.

The option of failing to expand the infrastructure is taken by some authorities. This can be partially effective, but unfortunately its effects are felt equally by local residents, whose frustrations with, say, inadequate road systems may lead to a political backlash. The price mechanism can also be used to control tourist traffic. Venice has a severe problem of overpopulation by tourists, and has become so choked by water-borne traffic that it has introduced a two-tier pricing structure, with visitors paying eight times as much for transport as locals. Similarly, in 2001 India raised entry prices to its principal attraction, the Taj Mahal, to $10 for foreign visitors as a measure

to control the numbers and reduce erosion of the building. Moves such as this have the added advantage of raising revenue for the government or local authority. For example, selective taxation on hotel accommodation or higher charges for parking can be imposed, but these moves are criticized on the grounds that they are regressive, affecting the less well off but having little effect on the wealthy.

Limiting access through some form of visa or licence is a practical alternative, or access can be denied to tourists arriving by private car, a measure now being employed in the Lake District. Ports can limit traffic very easily, by simply refusing permission for cruise ships to dock. Bermuda, a small but popular island destination, exercises close control over the number of visitors permitted to land. It has imposed a ceiling of 10,000 beds on the island (only 464 have been added to the bedstock in the past 25 years) and a maximum of 150,000 cruise ship passengers are permitted ashore each year. Florence, perhaps the most congested of Italian cities, limits permits to 500 coaches and 50,000 visitors a day. Remote areas impose even more stringent rulings: in Costa Rica, only 100 visitors are allowed at a time into the Monteverde Cloud Forest, while Bhutan limits tourists to a few thousand a year, each paying £65 a day for the privilege. Thus control by licence simultaneously restricts tourists and provides the government with useful revenue.

Perhaps a more acceptable form of control is exercised through effective marketing, concentrating publicity on less popular attractions or geographical regions, and promoting the off-season. Thus the BTA will stress the appeal of the northeast of England in its marketing abroad, making little reference to the southwest, which already attracts a high proportion of domestic tourists. However, attempts to do this may be frustrated by private sector promotion. Airlines, for example, will prefer to concentrate on promoting those destinations to which they already fly and which attract strong markets. There is always the danger, too, that if the public sector strategy is successful, the amenities and attractions at the more popular sites may well suffer a serious downturn in business. London has been the greatest attraction for the majority of overseas visitors to Britain, but on occasions it has experienced fall-offs in the number of visitors, which have seriously affected the theatres, taxis and other amenities that depend upon tourist support. Due to the cost of living in London, hotel accommodation has tended to move up-market, since the high costs of building and running a hotel can only be viable when high room charges are levied. The result has been a serious dearth of good quality, modern, budget-priced hotels for the price-conscious tourist – a problem which may lead to the overseas tourists switching their travel arrangements to Paris instead. Some tourism experts have called for a new government-sponsored initiative in the UK, similar to the 1969 Act discussed later in this chapter, to pump more public funds into the hotel industry, in effect subsidizing the capital costs in order to retain this important sector of the tourist market. However, the Labour government elected in 1997 has made it clear that, as with the preceding Conservative government, its support for tourism does not extend to increasing financial aid.

Up to a point, planning for the more extensive use of existing facilities can delay the need to de-market certain attractions or destinations, but it has to be recognized that some tourist destinations are the victims of their own success. An extreme form of control is to deny access to tourists. In areas of Britain where traffic has reached saturation, it is now common to find *park and ride* schemes, which require the visitors to leave their cars and proceed into the centre by public transport. In France, the prehistoric cave paintings at Lascaux have been so damaged by the effect of countless visitors' breath changing the climate in the caves that the French government has been obliged to introduce a total ban on entry to the site. However, an artificial replica has been built on an adjacent site, and continues to attract many visitors.

Britain has not yet followed the example of some of its other European neighbours in attempting to stagger holiday taking by legislation, although there have been moves towards a five-term school year,

Figure 15.1 Downturns in the tourism business can seriously affect London's theatres. (*Photographed by the author*)

and in 2000 the Local Government Association launched plans for a six-term year. Either of these schemes would greatly aid the tourism industry, and help to avoid the worst peaking problems of the summer months. Some experiments along these lines have already taken place within certain local authorities' regions. In Germany, the *Länder* (states) are required to take their holidays on a rota basis over an eleven-year cycle, thus avoiding the holiday rush which is common in Britain at the end of the school summer term. Factories, schools and businesses all plan their closures in keeping with the rota. France, too, divides the country into three zones, each of which takes the summer holiday at a different time. While this helps to avoid national peaking, it is not without drawbacks (for example, the mass exodus of German holiday-makers clogging the motorways from their particular *Land* when their turn arrives!).

Sometimes governments exercise control over tourism flows for economic reasons. As we saw earlier in this text, governments may attempt to protect their balance of payments by imposing currency restrictions or banning the export of foreign currency, in an attempt to reduce the numbers of its citizens travelling abroad. The last significant control of this kind in Britain occurred in 1966, when the government of the day imposed a £50 travel allowance, and France also imposed restrictions on the amount of currency that could be exported in the early 1980s. There is little evidence to suggest that these controls are particularly effective in preventing the outflow of foreign currency, and since the advent of the free movement of currency within the European Union, the right of its members to travel within the EU will no longer be restricted. The introduction of the euro, whether or not Britain decides to join at some point in the future, is likely to benefit all tourists, including the British, who will no longer be required to change currencies as they cross borders between the member countries.

Governments also exercise control over the various sectors of the tourism industry. As we have seen, the need to ensure passenger safety in transport leads to the licensing of transport companies, and tour operators are also subject to control through the imposition of Air Travel Organisers' Licences (ATOLs). The government's introduction of the Air Travel Reserve Fund (later becoming known as the Air Travel Trust Fund) between 1975 and 1977 was designed to protect consumers against possible collapse of package holiday companies, funds provided by ABTA being seen as insufficient for the purpose. In many countries (although not yet in the UK), travel agencies are required to have a government licence to operate, and, as we saw in Chapter 14, tour guides are licensed by the government in some countries. In France, those using motorboats are also required to be licensed, even if visiting from abroad, owing to an increase in accidents caused by poor navigation.

The British government will also intervene where it is thought that the takeover or merger of large companies could result in the emergence of a monopoly. The Competition Commission exists to investigate such situations, but in general it has taken a relaxed attitude towards horizontal integration on the grounds that tourists have not been disadvantaged by the moves. The European Union, however, has tended to take a stronger line on this issue.

Perhaps the most common form of government supervision of the tourism industry in all countries is to be found in the hotel sector. Apart from safety and hygiene requirements, many governments also require hotels to be compulsorily registered and graded, prices are required to be displayed, and the buildings are subject to regular inspection. Camping and caravan sites may also be subject to inspection to ensure consistent standards and acceptable operating conditions.

The organization of public sector tourism

For the most part, government policies and objectives for tourism are defined and implemented through national tourist boards (although in many cases other bodies directly concerned with recreation or environmental planning will also have a hand in the development of tourism). The functional responsibilities of a national board are likely to include all or most of the following:

Planning and control functions

- product research and planning for tourism plant and facilities;
- protection or restoration of tourism assets;
- human resources planning and training;
- licensing and supervision of sectors of the industry;
- implementation of pricing or other regulations affecting tourism.

Marketing functions

- representing the nation as a tourist destination;
- undertaking market research, forecasting trends and collecting and publishing relevant statistics;
- producing and distributing tourism literature;
- providing and staffing tourist information centres;
- advertising, sales promotion and public relations activities directed at home and overseas markets.

Financial functions

- advising industry on capital investment and development;
- directing, approving and controlling programmes of government aid for tourism projects.

Coordinating functions

- linking with trade and professional bodies, government and regional or local tourist organizations;
- undertaking coordinated marketing activities with private tourist enterprises;
- organizing 'workshops' or similar opportunities for buyers and sellers of travel and tourism to meet and do business.

In some countries, some of these activities may be delegated to regional tourist offices, with the national board coordinating or overseeing their implementation.

National tourist boards will generally establish offices overseas in those countries from which they can attract the most tourists, while their head office in the home country will be organized along functional lines. This is demonstrated in Figure 15.2, taking the example of the Netherlands Board of Tourism.

Figure 15.2 Organization chart, Netherlands Board of Tourism

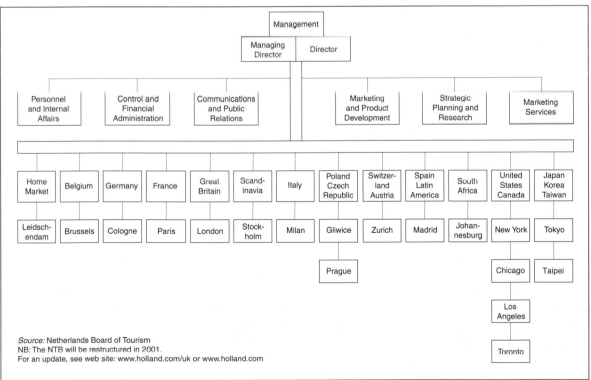

Source: Netherlands Board of Tourism
NB: The NTB will be restructured in 2001.
For an update, see web site: www.holland.com/uk or www.holland.com

Public sector tourism in Britain

Britain has long been at the forefront of international tourism, both as a destination and a generating country, though before 1969 tourism played little part in government policy making. Forty years earlier, the government of the day had provided the first finance for tourism marketing, by funding (to the tune of £5,000) the Travel Association of Great Britain and Northern Ireland, in order to encourage travel to Britain from overseas. During the inter-war years this evolved into the British Travel Association, which was given the additional task of promoting domestic holidays for British residents. No clear policies were laid down for its activities, however, and its powers were limited.

Voluntary tourist boards were established in Scotland in 1930, and in Wales in 1948, the same year in which a board was first established in Northern Ireland. It was to be more than twenty years, however, before a coordinated framework for public sector tourism was to be established in the United Kingdom as a whole.

The Development of Tourism Act

By the late 1960s, following the rapid growth in popularity of Britain as a tourist destination, it was clear that a new framework for tourism was needed in the country. This was manifested in the Development of Tourism Act 1969, the first statutory legislation in the country specifically concerned with tourism.

The Act, in three parts, dealt with the organization of public sector tourism, with the provision of financial assistance for much-needed hotel development, and also provided for a system of compulsory registration of tourist accommodation. The last part of the Act, which was designed to include rights of inspection by government officials, has never been fully implemented, although the compulsory display of prices was subsequently introduced. The accommodation sector preferred to follow a system of voluntary classification and grading of tourist accommodation, persuading the government not to enforce a compulsory system. The result was a mixed success, as the voluntary system fails to embrace a substantial amount of the stock of available accommodation in the UK; however, the implementation of the first two parts of the Act were to have far-reaching consequences for tourism in Britain.

That part of the Act dealing with financial assistance for the hotel industry was designed in the short term to improve the stock and quality of hotel bedrooms, in order to meet changing demand and overcome scarcity. Grants and loans, administered by the three new national tourist boards, were to be made available for hotel construction and improvement until 1973 (during which time some 55,000 bedrooms were added to the stock). Unfortunately, because the Act failed to specify the location in which new hotels were to be built, much of the increased stock was located in London, leading to temporary over-capacity in the city, while areas where hotel construction involved greater financial risk, such as Scotland and the North of England, did not benefit to anything like the extent needed.

The first part of the Act called for the establishment of four national boards to become responsible for tourism, and defined the structure and responsibilities of each of these. At the apex, the British Tourist Authority, to replace the old British Travel Association, was to be the sole body responsible overseas for the marketing of tourism to Britain, and would also advise ministers on tourism matters in general. Tourism issues that concerned Britain as a whole were to be dealt with by the BTA, while three further boards – the English Tourist Board, the Scottish Tourist Board and the Wales Tourist Board – became responsible for tourism development within their own territories, and for the marketing of their territories within the UK. Scotland was later given the freedom to undertake overseas marketing itself, under the terms of the Tourism (Overseas Promotion) (Scotland) Act, 1984, and Wales followed suit in 1992.

Northern Ireland was not affected by this Act, having established its own Tourist Board under the Development of Tourist Traffic Act (Northern Ireland) in 1948. Subsequent legislation, the Tourist Traffic (Northern Ireland) Order 1972, amended the Act to allow local authorities to provide or assist in the provision of tourist amenities. Similarly, the Isle of Man Tourist Board and the States of Jersey and Guernsey Tourist Committees operate independently outside the jurisdiction of the Act.

Initially, both the BTA and the English Tourist Board were responsible to the Board of Trade, while the Scottish and Wales Boards were responsible to their respective Secretaries of State. Later, responsibility of the BTA and ETB passed to, first the Department of Employment and subsequently, in 1992, to the newly created Department of National Heritage, which absorbed a number of other related interests, including the royal parks and palaces, arts and libraries, sport, broadcasting and the press as well as heritage sites. This Department became known as the Department for Culture, Media and Sport when the Labour government came to power in 1997. Following the devolution of power in Scotland and Wales, the Scottish Tourist Board became the responsibility of the Department of Enterprise and Life-Long Learning within the devolved Scottish Parliament, while the Wales Tourist Board in turn became the responsibility of the Economic Development Committee of the Welsh Assembly. The Scottish Tourist Board has now been rebranded as VisitScotland.

All four bodies were established by the Act as independent statutory bodies, and were to be financed by grants-in-aid from the central government. They were empowered in turn to provide financial assistance for tourism projects (the so-called 'Section 4' scheme within the Act), although this scheme has since been abandoned in favour of alternative forms of funding. In 1999, the English Tourist Board's title was changed to the English Tourism Council.

Regional Tourist Boards

The Act made no provision for a statutory regional public sector structure for tourism. Before the Act, some attempt had been made to establish regional tourist associations, these being more advanced in Scotland and Wales than in England. However, following the establishment of the three national boards, each set about creating its own regional tourism structure. The result was the establishment of twelve Regional Tourist Boards in England, to be funded jointly by the ETB, local authorities and contributions from local private sector tourism interests. This number was reduced to ten during the 1990s, as the ETB determined it could no longer afford to fund twelve boards; first by the financial collapse in 1992 of the Thames and Chilterns Tourist Board, whose territory was allocated to the adjoining regions, and in 1996, by the formation of the East of England Tourist Board, constructed from the former East Midlands and East Anglian Tourist Board regions, coupled with Lincolnshire.

The Wales Tourist Board established three Regional Offices in North, Mid and South Wales, which became responsible for the management of most of the Tourist Information Centres in Wales, in conjunction with local authorities. Three Tourism Councils were also created, one in each region, supported by the Regional Offices, and designed to advise the Board on a wide range of tourism-related issues. The Councils draw their membership from local authorities and the tourist industry.

In Scotland, the picture was more complicated. Before the Act, regional tourism promotion was in the hands of the eight regional councils, with a separate voluntary association (Dumfries and Galloway) and a statutory development board responsible for the Highlands and Islands. This board subsequently established fifteen Area Tourist Boards within its region. Under the terms of the Local Government and Planning (Scotland) Act 1982, the district councils in Scotland were empowered to set up area tourist boards which would become responsible for marketing tourism and running the tourist

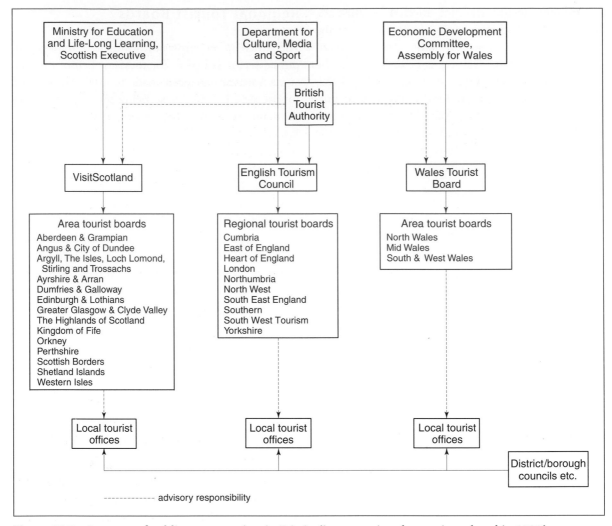

Figure 15.3 Structure of public sector tourism in Britain (incorporating changes introduced in 1999)

information centres in their region. The Highlands and Islands scheme was used as a model for the extension of the scheme throughout Scotland, and the new boards were established as a co-partnership between the Scottish Tourist Board, one or more district councils and the tourist trade, with finance provided by grant aid and private contributions. Thirty-two Area Tourist Boards were established, with a further four district councils deciding to retain their autonomy over tourism matters, while a further six districts failed to decide whether to participate in the scheme. The Highlands and Islands retained an interest in tourism within its territory, but changed its title to Highlands and Islands Enterprise. However, scarcely had this new structure been put into place before a further revision was introduced in legislation in 1993, replacing the thirty-two boards with fourteen new boards, all with greatly expanded territories. These were in place by 1996. Accompanying financial constraints led to the closure of a number of the tourist information centres in the country. Local enterprise companies were

Cumbria Tourist Board
Cumbria

East of England Tourist Board
Cambridgeshire, Essex, Hertfordshire, Bedfordshire, Norfolk, Suffolk, Lincolnshire

Heart of England Tourist Board
Gloucestershire, Hereford & Worcestershire, Shropshire, Staffordshire, Warwickshire and West Midlands, District of Cherwell and West Oxfordshire, Derbyshire, Leicestershire, Northamptonshire, Nottinghamshire and Rutland

London Tourist Board
Greater London

Northumbria Tourist Board
The Tees Valley, Durham, Northumberland, Tyne & Wear

North West Tourist Board
Cheshire, Greater Manchester, Lancashire, Merseyside, High Peak district of Derbyshire

South East England Tourist Board
East Sussex, West Sussex, Kent, Surrey

Southern Tourist Board
East and North Dorset, Hampshire, Isle of Wight, Berkshire, Buckinghamshire, Oxfordshire

South West Tourism
Bath, Bristol, Cornwall and the Isles of Scilly, Devon, West Dorset, Somerset, Wiltshire

Yorkshire Tourist Board
Yorkshire, North East Lincolnshire

Figure 15.4a   Regional tourist boards in England. (*Courtesy English Tourism Council*)

now given the role of operating the financial assistance programmes which were formerly the responsibility of the Scottish Tourist Board, while at the same time local authority tourism marketing was required to be channelled through the new statutory, but private-sector-dominated, boards.

Northern Ireland has also established five new regional tourist boards, entitled Causeway Coast and Glens, Kingdoms of Down, Fermanagh Lakeland Tourism, Belfast Visitor and Convention Bureau and Derry Visitor and Convention Bureau. The Northern Ireland Tourist Board is also cooperating with that of the Irish Republic to promote jointly the six counties of Ulster and the adjacent six Irish Republic counties.

The structure of public sector tourism appears in Figure 15.3, while the regional distribution of tourist boards for England, Wales and Scotland is illustrated in Figure 15.4 (a), (b), (c).

Government policy and tourism in the UK

The new structure of public sector tourism in Britain was to greatly improve the planning and coordination of tourism in the UK. Nevertheless, the diverse nature of tourism and its impact on so many different facets of British life make cohesive planning difficult. Quite apart from the fact that tourism issues cut across the interests of many different government departments, there are a number of public or quasi-public bodies whose roles also impinge in one way or another on tourism. The water authorities represent one obvious example, since water-based recreation plays such an important part in leisure and tourism planning. In this respect, it is interesting to note the extent to which tourism featured in the planning and development of the Kielder Reservoir in Northumbria, by comparison with earlier reservoir development. Local authorities, and the water

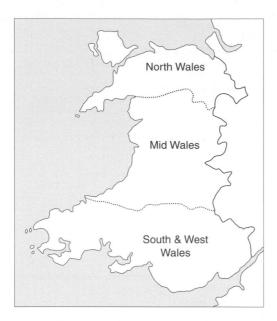

Figure 15.4b Regional tourism councils in Wales. (*Courtesy Wales Tourist Board*)

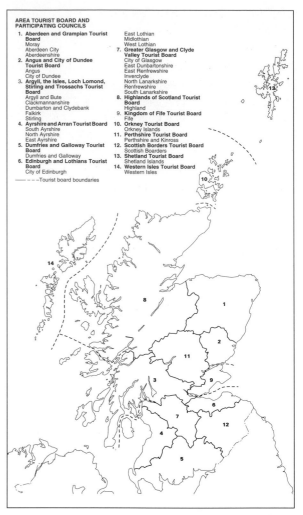

Figure 15.4c Area tourist boards in Scotland. (*Courtesy VisitScotland*)

authorities themselves, are now fully aware of the commercial leisure opportunities associated with large expanses of water.

Bodies such as the Countryside Agency, the Forestry Commission, the Nature Conservancy Council, the Arts and Sports Councils, the National Trust and the Council for the Preservation of Rural England, to take just a few examples, each have an interest in issues relating to tourism, yet there is no common coordinating body to bring these interests together.

Within the government, we have already seen how several departments may have responsibilities for some features of tourism, even though ostensibly this is the brief of the Department for Culture, Media and Sport. Again, coordination between the various interests at government level is not easy. An all-party Interdepartmental Tourism Coordinating Committee was established with the aim of facilitating this, but in practice this committee meets very seldom. However, when one thinks of some of the issues under discussion within the government which impact on tourism, the full extent of the prob-

lem will be apparent – issues such as the reform of alcoholic licensing, which extended drinking hours in public houses and had a huge impact on tourist spend, or legislation ending the long-standing ban on Sunday shopping, which also supported tourism. Efforts were made to bring Britain's clocks into line with the rest of Europe by changing to Central European Time; in the event, this motion was defeated, but the extra hour of daylight this would have given in the early evening would have also greatly benefited the tourism industry, which estimated that it would have enhanced spend by some £500 million per annum.

The Department of Transport, Local Government and the Regions, quite apart from its public transport responsibilities, exercises control over certain types of signposting, and the signposting of attractions is of immense importance to the success of tourism. In January 1996, the relaxation of control over brown and white directive road signs for tourism sites led to information about these sites becoming far more readily available to passing tourists, enhancing tourist spend.

Changing governments, changing policies

The period of Conservative government rule between 1979 and 1997 saw marked and frequent changes of direction in terms of tourism policy, with a noted failure to produce a clear and consistent policy. The early years of the Thatcher government were notable for outspoken support for the tourism industry, and recognition of the contribution which tourism makes to the British economy, following reviews of the industry in 1983, and promises were made to expand Section 4 grants nationwide. In 1985, the Young Report (*Pleasure, Leisure and Jobs: the Business of Tourism*, issued by the Cabinet Office Enterprise Unit) promised to 'remove unnecessary obstacles' in the path of tourism development, and emphasized the role which small firms and self-employment would continue to play in the industry. Importance was attached to encouraging young people to enter the industry, and to ensure they were well trained. In the same year, the House of Commons Trade and Industry Committee proposed a radical restructuring of public sector tourism in Britain, which although not adopted in its entirety, influenced government thinking in its later policies.

Towards the end of the 1980s, the commitment to tourism was wavering. Far from enhancing Section 4 grant aid, this was terminated in England during 1989–90. Although political considerations at the time ensured they remained in place in Scotland and

Wales, they have since been replaced by alternative strategies for aid in both countries. The Department of National Heritage review of tourism in 1992 made drastic cuts in the tourism budgets provided to the BTA and ETB, and in 1995 a total restructuring of the BTA and ETB took place which brought the two bodies closer together to avoid duplication and combine resources. Tourism, which had already moved from the Department of Trade and Industry to the Department of Employment, was transferred to the newly created Department of National Heritage. Ministers with tourism portfolios were changed with dramatic frequency, scarcely finding time to get to grips with the nature of the industry. Often, the post was given to members of the House of Lords, further sidelining the industry. With the change in government to a Labour administration in 1997, the Department of National Heritage was given a new name, and new priorities; in spite of pre-election rhetoric, the creation of a Department for Culture, Media and Sport not only failed to incorporate tourism into its title, but continued Conservative policy of reducing support for tourism, which became the responsibility of low-profile ministers whose role was also expected to encompass film and broadcasting. Funding was frozen at approximately £10 million per annum for the three years 1997–2000 for the ETC; this compares with £15.5 million in 1992 and more generous funding for the Scottish and Welsh boards in 1999 (£19.3 million and £11.75 million respectively). Of this £10 million, half has to be redirected to the Regional Tourist Boards, leading to huge cuts in staffing and activities within the ETC. The RTBs in England are now responsible for their own marketing, resulting in a lack of overall coordination of the marketing function in England.

The attitude of successive governments in recent years is clearly that tourism has reached a stage in which its future funding and promotion must be the responsibility of the private sector, in spite of the fact that 90 per cent of the industry is represented by small businesses. When the Regional Tourist Boards were established, it was the intention that these would be a means for collaboration between the private and public sectors, with a third of the income to come from the private sector. Yet, as Ken Robinson, former Chairman of the Tourism Society, pointed out, of the 226,000 businesses involved in tourism in the UK, only 16,000 actually became members of their RTBs. Is it likely that the Regional Tourist Boards, facing cuts in both central government funding and a lessening of support from cash-starved local authorities, can survive by moving towards privatization? The one board most heavily funded privately in the past, the Thames and Chilterns, was forced into bankruptcy. The belief that private enterprise money can replace public support is questionable, based on the record of the industry to date.

English boards have moved towards becoming more enterprising during the 1990s. In Northampton, to cite one example, the local Tourist Information Centre (TIC) established an ETB-backed travel agency in 1996 as a pilot project to sell domestic tourism products, and a similar move was taken by Chester TIC in 1997. However, direct intercession by the public sector into commercial activities is not necessarily the best way forward. Efforts by the Wales Tourist Board to establish commercial tour operations to support tourism into Wales have failed to generate the support of the retail trade, in spite of ensuring that a commissionable domestic product would be available for agents to sell. At the same time, it is proving difficult to change attitudes towards selling and stocking domestic products in the retail agencies; only a very small proportion of UK holidays are sold in this way.

The illogicality of government policy towards tourism over the past twenty years has been a noted feature; the promise of support, while funds were simultaneously cut, the lack of development grants for tourism in depressed regions while manufacturing could benefit, the withdrawal of grants in poor English regions such as Cornwall while grants were awarded in Wales and Scotland regardless of the state of local economies, the decline in support for the English Tourist Board/English Tourism Council in

particular vis-à-vis the other national boards, all suggest a failure on the part of successive governments to think through rational policies for tourism. Even the decline in seaside resorts is unlikely to be halted, given the costs involved to regenerate them, in spite of government advocacy for this policy in 2000. In short, pressures on government spending will make it unlikely that the policy of self-support will be reversed, notwithstanding a steady and substantial deficit in the balance of payments on the UK tourism account.

A new factor in the equation is the introduction of Regional Development Agencies (RDAs) to promote economic growth. As the brief for these agencies also encompasses tourism, the Regional Tourist Boards will find it necessary to work closely with the RDAs to achieve their aims.

It is also important to note that areas designated by the government as 'Assisted Areas' still qualify for economic aid, which can of course include aid for tourism projects. There are some 125 Intermediate and Development Areas in Britain, the latter qualifying for higher grants. Funding can be provided through two schemes:

1. Selective Assistance schemes, aimed at investment projects which create or safeguard jobs;
2. Regional Enterprise Grants, providing aid to small firms.

The expansion of the Assisted Areas in 1993 brought some of England's fading seaside resorts into the scheme, including Kent resorts such as Broadstairs, Margate and Ramsgate, which have benefited from funds.

Criticism has focused on the unfavourable rate of VAT in the UK compared to other countries, especially as it applies to hotel accommodation, on the imposition of passenger levies on air transport, which are now seen by governments as a comparatively painless means of raising extra revenue, and have already been doubled since their introduction, and on the continued failure to provide an integrated transport policy which would facilitate tourism.

Local authorities and tourism

At local authority level, the County Councils and District Councils have diverse statutory responsibilities and interests in the provision of tourist facilities, as we have noted earlier. The Local Government Act 1948 empowered local authorities to set up information and publicity services for tourism, and this was reinforced by the Local Government Act of 1972, giving local authorities the power to encourage visitors to their area and to provide suitable facilities for them.

The organization of tourism at local level is often curiously piecemeal. Counties and districts on the whole relegate responsibility for tourism to departments which are concerned with a range of other activities, with the result that it is seldom given the significance which its economic impact on the area merits. Evidence suggests that less than 50 per cent of local authorities in the past included any strategy relating to tourism in their planning, although Circular 13/79 urged them particularly to consider providing for tourism in local structure plans, and the ETB drew up guidelines which local authorities should follow, emphasizing the following key points:

- assess the number and distribution of tourists in the area;
- estimate future changes in tourism flow, and implications of this for land use;
- identify growth opportunities;
- assess the impact of tourism on employment and income in the area;
- assess the tourists' effect on traffic flows;
- assess the tourists' demand for leisure and recreation;
- identify the need for conservation and protection;
- evaluate the contribution tourism could make to development, especially in the use of derelict land and obsolete buildings.

Local plans, too, should take into account the impact of tourism, in terms of the provision of car and coach parks, toilets, information centres, tourist attractions and the demand for local accommodation. The inadequacy of parking and toilet facilities in resorts has been a frequent topic of criticism, and cutbacks in local funding have magnified the problem recently.

By the beginning of the 1980s, tourism needs were beginning to find their way into several Local Authority Structure Plans, and local authorities were coming to appreciate the economic contribution which tourism could make even in traditionally non-tourist areas. Training courses such as COTICC (Certificate of Tourist Information Centre Competence), and later NVQs (National Vocational Qualifications) were developed to cover the need for basic skills among TIC staff, and some local authorities were even starting actively to recruit staff with formal tourism education or experience.

The principal responsibilities of county and district authorities which bear on tourism are as follows:

1. Provision of leisure facilities for tourists (e.g. conference centres) and for residents (e.g. theatres, parks, sports centres, museums).
2. Planning (under town and country planning policies). Note that District Councils produce local plans to fit the broad strategy of the County Council Structure Plans. These plans are certified by the County Council.
3. Development control powers over land use.
4. Provision of visitor services (usually in conjunction with tourist bodies).
5. Parking for coaches and cars.
6. Provision of caravan sites (with licensing and management the responsibility of the District Councils).
7. Production of statistics on tourism, for use by the Regional Tourist Boards.
8. Marketing the area.
9. Upkeep of historic buildings.
10. Public health, including food hygiene, and safety issues. This is taken to include matters such as litter disposal and the provision of public toilet facilities.

Local authorities may also own and operate local airports. The provision of visitor services includes funding and managing the Tourist Information Centres in the UK, in cooperation with the Regional Tourist Boards, which set and monitor standards. Local authorities will also fund tourist information points, information boards found at lay-bys, car parks and city centres.

Local authorities which have set out actively to encourage tourism have a number of objectives, some of which may conflict, and each of which will compete for scarce resources. Local tourist officers will need to identify the resources they require to achieve their stated objectives, and to determine their priorities. Typical objectives might include:

- increasing visitor numbers;
- extending visitor stays;
- increasing visitor spend;
- increasing and upgrading local attractions;
- creating or improving the image of the area as a tourist destination;
- stimulating private sector involvement in tourism.

Local tourist officers act as catalysts between the public and private sectors and voluntary aided bodies. As a focus for tourism in the area or resort, they become a point of reference, advising on development and grant-aided opportunities. Officers will help the local authority to determine and establish the necessary infrastructure which will allow tourism to develop, and they will carry out research and planning activities themselves. In some areas, they may become involved in the provision and training of tourist guides. In addition, they will undertake a range of promotional and publicity functions, including the preparation of publications such as guides to the district, accommodation guides, information on current events and entertainment, and specialist brochures listing, for example, local walks or pubs. The cost of most of these publications will be met in part by contributions from the private sector, either through advertising or, as in the case of the accommodation brochures, through a charge for listing. Many resorts also now produce a trade manual, aimed at the travel trade and giving information on trade prices, conference facilities and coach parking. Tourist officers organize familiarization trips for the UK travel trade and press, and, if the resort shows sufficient potential, they may invite representatives of the overseas trade and press. They play a part in setting up and operating the local Tourist Information Centres, and may also offer a local bed booking service. Finally, on occasion they even take a part in actively packaging holidays for clients, such as activity weekends or special interest short breaks. It should be noted that all of these functions are frequently the responsibility of a very small team, on occasion no greater than a single tourist officer and a secretary.

Unlike the Regional Tourist Boards, whose aims are essentially promotional, the local authorities bear responsibilities for protecting the environment, and for tourism planning generally. They may consequently be as concerned to reduce or stabilize tourism as to develop it (particularly when, as is so often the case in the popular tourist resorts, local residents are opposed to increases in the numbers of tourists attracted). In providing for leisure, the authorities must be sensitive to local residents' needs as much as to those of incoming tourists. They must convince the residents of the merits of public sector funding for tourist projects. The development of conference centres in resorts such as Bournemouth and Harrogate was a controversial issue with local residents, since very few conference centres are viewed as viable investments for the private sector, and public sector funding of this kind will greatly increase the burden of debt on the council initially. It is hard to convince local residents of the wisdom of investments that do not appear to provide a direct profit; however, conferences do generate a healthy flow of indirect revenue through additional spend by delegates in local shops, hotels and restaurants, with the added bonus that much of this revenue will accrue outside the traditional holiday season.

The funding and staffing of local Tourist Information Centres is often the joint responsibility of local authorities and the Regional Tourist Boards, with material drawn from the regional and national boards. Many of these local TICs also provide a book-

Figure 15.5 Britain's national heritage: Bristol cathedral. (*Photographed by the author*)

Table 15.1 Listed sites in England of potential interest to tourists[a]

Listed buildings of architectural and historical merit	456,761[b]
Scheduled ancient monuments	18,275
Ecclesiastical buildings	c.17,000
Hotels of historical, literary or architectural merit	9,378[c]
Conservation areas of architectural or natural interest	8,889
Town trails	483
Historic battlefields	43

(a) Excluding around 1 million sites of archaeological interest.
(b) Of which 6,158 are listed Grade I.
(c) Including all forms of accommodation such as guesthouses, B&Bs, farmhouses etc.

Source: Heritage Monitor 2000, English Tourism Council.

ing service for tourists seeking accommodation in the area, and they also manage a scheme for booking accommodation from one TIC to another. This is known as the Book a bed ahead scheme (BABA). Local authorities contribute directly to RTB funds, and clearly will expect to play a role in the board's policy making. They will normally be represented on the board's committees or sub-committees dealing with tourism development in the area. However, since representatives of the private sector, such as local hoteliers, are also members of these committees, and the latter's interests and objectives may well differ from those of the local authority, this can lead to conflicts in policy making within the regional boards.

National heritage bodies

In Chapter 11 we examined the significance of the built environment for tourism. This plays a particularly important role in Britain, with its rich heritage of monuments, historic homes, cathedrals and similar attractions which go to make up our national heritage. While many of these attractions remain in private hands, or are the responsibility of bodies such as the Church Commissioners, a number of quasi-public or voluntary organizations exist to protect and enhance these heritage sites. These bodies therefore play their part in the tourism industry.

According to estimates made by the English Tourism Council, there are well over half a million sites of architectural or historical merit in England alone, broken down into categories (see Table 15.1).

One might be surprised by the very high number of valued buildings, but a walk through any country town in Britain will soon reveal a wealth of buildings worth more than a passing glance. While many are not open to the public, they are nevertheless attractive to view from the outside. Key sites such as Grade I listed buildings or internationally renowned sites

Figure 15.6 Stonehenge: one of English Heritage's responsibilities. (*Photographed by the author*)

such as Stonehenge will draw people from all over the world, and are carefully protected. Many of our great national monuments were originally under the control of the Department of the Environment, but growing concern about their protection and maintenance led to the establishment of the Historic Buildings and Monuments Commission in 1983, following the National Heritage Act in that year. This body, more familiarly known as 'English Heritage', which integrates the functions of the former Historic Buildings Council for England and the Ancient Monuments Board, has a dual conservation and promotion function. The organization is seeking to make the budget stretch further by raising financial support from industry and the public, either through sponsorship of individual buildings or subscriptions to a national membership scheme similar to that of the National Trust. There is an equivalent body, Cadw, in Wales, with similar responsibilities, while Historic Scotland is responsible for over 300 listed properties in its territory.

Apart from these key quasi-government bodies, the National Trust (and an equivalent body in Scotland) plays a vital role in protecting buildings of significant architectural or historic interest. Founded in 1895, the Trust cares for over 190 properties and a quarter of a million hectares of land, acquiring properties for the most part through inheritance. Its properties include villages, nature reserves and woodland, and it also operates a campaign, under the title Enterprise Neptune, to buy up and protect stretches of British coastline; to date, it has acquired over 500 miles of coast. Operational costs are met by subscriptions from the very large number of members in Britain, but the Trust also anticipates that properties left to them will be accompanied by sufficient money for their upkeep.

Apart from these key organizations, a great many smaller bodies exist to protect the British heritage. One of the earliest to be founded was the Society for the Protection of Ancient Buildings, dating back to 1877; other bodies include the Ancient Monuments Society, the Georgian Group, the Victorian Society, the National Piers Society and SAVE Britain's Heritage. Even modern buildings are now recognized as part of the national heritage, and the Twentieth Century Society exists to protect the best of these. To these bodies we must add a number of diverse trusts, all of which share an interest in the protection of sites of touristic appeal, including the Civic Trust, the Monument Trust, the Pilgrim Trust, the Landmark Trust and many others (over a thousand local amenity societies are known to exist in England alone). Some of these, such as the Landmark Trust and Pilgrim Trust, actually rent out their properties for holidays, so playing an active part in the tourist industry.

The new tourism

As we saw in Chapter 11, success in preserving our industrial heritage is evidenced in such sites as Ironbridge. Few would have believed, a few years ago, that vast numbers of tourists could be attracted to the former 'dark, Satanic mills' of eighteenth- and nineteenth-century Britain. The success of sites like Coalbrookdale and Blists Mill can be ascribed to a combination of nostalgia for a lost past with which many can still identify, and a growing awareness of our historical heritage in all its forms. It took the public sector to recognize the potential for tourism of this new kind which could be generated in Britain's decaying inner cities; the tourist boards, in partnership with local authorities and private enterprise, successfully established such unlikely places as Bradford ('A Surprising Place'), Glasgow ('The Friendly City') and Liverpool's Merseyside ('Full of Magic Memories') as worthy of a visit and, even better, an overnight stay. Wigan took advantage of an old music-hall joke (and the popularity of George Orwell's book *The Road to Wigan Pier*) to recreate a former coaling wharf as 'Wigan Pier', while the resurrection of Liverpool's Albert Dock has included a new wing of London's Tate Gallery to make it a place of pilgrimage for the culture-seeker. Living history museums have been created at Beamish in Northumbria and Quarry Bank Mill, a former cotton mill at Styal, Cheshire. Not only the inner cities, but

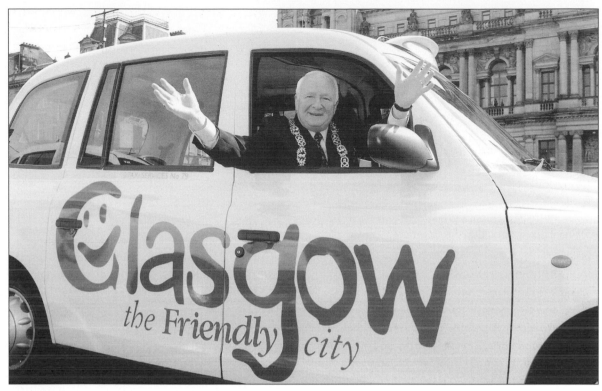

Figure 15.7 Glasgow's successful marketing strategy. (*Courtesy Glasgow City Council*)

derelict waterfront sites have also lent themselves to careful and tasteful restoration to create residential and leisure complexes which also attract tourism.

The way in which government policy has shifted from support for traditional tourism towards the encouragement of new forms of tourism in the economically depressed areas is among the most interesting fields of study for the tourism specialist, since it opens up the concept of what we understand tourism to be, and provides almost unlimited new opportunities to generate it.

The origins of this new policy can be traced to public sector policy to establish 'Tourism Growth Points' in the early 1970s, following a review of tourism policy. Areas like the Bude-Wadebridge area of Cornwall were identified as regions for planned tourism growth. While the Growth Points programme enjoyed mixed success, the development grants they attracted were later directed into Tourism

Development Action Plans (TDAPs), generally linked to inner cities; Bristol's floating harbour became the first of many such schemes to receive TDAP finance to help resurrect its decaying waterfront areas, before the programmes were brought to an abrupt end with the cuts in public sector funding, particularly the termination of Sector 4 grants in England. Nonetheless, the success of similar efforts at restoration in the United States, particularly in Baltimore, San Francisco and Boston, acted as a spur for similar programmes in Britain.

Tourism continues to benefit from the terms of Urban Regeneration Grants, designed to restore life to the decaying inner cities. Where the value of a completed project may be less than the initial cost of its development, government grants can be made available to bridge the gap, making the project possible where a feasibility study might indicate a purely private venture would be uneconomic.

Figure 15.8 Fisherman's Wharf, San Francisco: an area revitalized through redevelopment. (*Photographed by the author*)

Figure 15.9 Sellafield Visitor Centre – the Interatom. (*Reproduced with thanks to British Nuclear Fuels Ltd., Sellafield*)

New funding opportunities appeared on the scene in the late 1990s, with the introduction of first the National Lottery, for which funds were allocated for the development or enhancement of tourism attractions around the country, and, second, the allocation of funds from 1995 onwards to celebrate the millennium in the year 2000. Substantial sums of money were allocated by the government to support schemes which would enhance the celebrations, including sums approaching £1 billion for the ill-starred Millennium Dome at Greenwich. As we have seen in Chapter 11, not all of these schemes were successful, and there has been much criticism of the disproportionate amount of these funds finding their way to the London area, compared with the provinces.

We also noted in Chapter 11 how modern industry can also offer scope for tourist enterprise. The initiative owes much to British Nuclear Fuels, which opened its Sellafield (formerly Windscale) processing plant to visitors in order to assuage public concern about nuclear energy safety. The success of this venture (more than 100,000 were attracted in the first year) led to the government holding discussions with the CBI with a view to opening factories to tourists, to allow them to observe the processes of manufacture of British products. The public relations value of this exercise has appealed to many firms,

including Ford Motors which was the first to open its plant.

The Thames Barrier at Woolwich was recognized as having tourist potential even while under construction, and plans for tourist visits were incorporated into the operating programme. In Cheshire, the local authorities planned visits to such 'attractions' as power stations and fire stations, under the 'Insight into Industry' banner. Initiatives like these are expected to expand in future years.

Our recent history has also been successfully exploited for tourism, with the public opening in 1984 of Churchill's War Cabinet rooms below the streets of Whitehall, dating to World War II. Such schemes pay tribute to the astuteness of the public sector in recognizing and developing the tourism potential of sites in its charge.

Town twinning and tourism

No discussion of public sector tourism can be complete without exploring the role of town twinning, even though the impact of this relationship between towns is seldom considered as an element of the tourism business. The concept of town twinning emerged in the aftermath of World War II, as a means of forging greater understanding between communities in different countries. Usually, the selection of a twin town is based on some common characteristics such as population size, geographical features or commercial similarities. Local authorities and chambers of commerce arrange for the exchange of visits by residents of the twinned towns. Although conceived as a gesture of friendship and goodwill, the outcome has commercial implications for tourism, as visitor flows increase between the two twinned towns. While accommodation is normally provided in private homes, expenditure on transport, shopping and sightseeing can have a significant impact on the inflow of tourist revenue for the towns concerned – some of which have virtually no other form of tourist traffic. Friendships forming as a result of these links will also lead to subsequent travel demand. So far, no studies appear to have been made as to the financial contribution resulting from these links, but it is likely to be considerable.

Functions of the tourist boards

The British Tourist Authority

As we have seen, the Development of Tourism Act empowered the BTA to promote tourism to Britain in overseas countries. With the agreement of the respective territories, the Authority will also undertake foreign promotion on behalf of the tourist boards of Northern Ireland, the Isle of Man and the Channel Islands. With general responsibility for tourism throughout Great Britain, the Authority acts as adviser to the government on tourism issues, and is financed by an annual grant-in-aid from the Treasury, channelled through the Department for Culture, Media and Sport.

Stated objectives of BTA marketing policy have included extending the tourist season in Britain, promoting areas of high unemployment which can demonstrate tourist potential, and seeking to develop new markets and market segments for

tourism to Britain. Most recently this has included an emphasis on sport, youth and business tourists, with the particular aim of targeting 2 million youngsters between the ages of sixteen and twenty-five in 2000. With its depleted resources, the BTA is choosing to focus on twenty-seven key overseas markets. These will be adjusted according to circumstances such as changing exchange rates. It is interesting to note that in spite of paying lip service to quality improvements, the Authority's policy has been repeatedly to emphasize an increase in the numbers of tourists it wishes to attract to Britain; at no time has any finite limit been suggested to the number of visitors which Britain, or specific parts of the country, can absorb.

Apart from maintaining offices in more than twenty countries abroad, the BTA carries out research and liaises with the other national tourism bodies in the UK. The overseas offices help UK companies to reach foreign markets, by, for example, circulating details of inclusive packages to travel companies bringing tourists to Britain. The BTA also mounts workshops, either in Britain or in major centres of population in tourism-generating countries abroad, which are designed to bring together the buyers and sellers of travel services; for the smaller British company in the travel business, this may be the most effective way to reach the overseas market with a limited budget. Typical workshops include those for European coach and tour operators, special-interest travel or English language schools. Limitations on funding, particularly within recent times, mean that the Authority must necessarily restrict what it can do for travel companies, and this means that little help is available for the smaller independent companies. However, the Authority will provide certain services at commercial rates, such as distribution abroad of a company's brochures, or advising on overseas marketing.

Other functions include the publication of numerous sales and information guides and directories, and the magazines *In Britain* and *Hello Britain*. The Authority's Product Marketing Department has also initiated 'theme years' as an incentive to visit Britain in a particular year – a common promotional initiative used by national tourist boards around the world. Recent examples include 'Britain for all seasons' and 'Britain's Treasured Landscapes'. The Authority also sponsors an annual 'Come to Britain' trophy for top new tourist attractions or facilities.

The English Tourism Council, Wales Tourist Board and VisitScotland

Under the terms of the Development of Tourism Act, the functions of these national boards were established as:

- encouraging residents of the UK to travel within their own country;
- encouraging the provision and improvement of attractions and facilities for tourists in Britain;
- administering the Section 4 grants;
- advising the government on matters concerning tourism within their territory.

As we learned earlier, Section 4 grants are no longer available, and the ETC's role has increasingly had to become one of advice and encouragement rather than of dispensing financial assistance.

Like the BTA, the ETC is financed by a grant-in-aid from central government, administered by the Department for Culture, Media and Sport (in the case of Wales and Scotland, the regional governments are responsible for the distribution of these funds). Both the BTA and ETC report directly to the DCMS, from which they are in turn directly funded. While this funding is still discrete, recent policy has been, as we have discussed, to integrate wherever possible the offices and administration of the BTA and ETC.

The ETC's role, now greatly reduced, is to focus on

- research
- quality
- innovation
- data analysis
- sustainability.

Marketing has now become the responsibility of the regional boards. The Council supports the regenera-tion of the traditional seaside resorts and the development of niche markets, promoting particularly cultural, heritage and countryside attractions.

All of the boards cooperate in undertaking research and publishing a range of statistical data covering national as well as regional information, although the ETC's role in gathering data has also been affected by reduced funding. It has encouraged better standards by sponsoring an award, the England for Excellence scheme, and earlier played a major role in developing the short-break market with its 'Let's Go' promotion. The boards publish a variety of promotional literature, including guides on where to stay, short breaks and activity holidays. They also sponsor the British Travel Trade Fair, held annually in London and operated on their behalf by Reed Travel Exhibitions, with some 500 exhibitors attending.

The funding shortage has also meant that the boards are increasingly having to become more commercial in their approach. The Wales Tourist Board, to take one example, has farmed out some of its activities by establishing private limited companies to undertake some of its functions. One example of this is the establishment of Tourism Quality Services Ltd, which acts as the Wales Tourist Board's agents in carrying out inspection of holiday accommodation and attractions, and has widened the scope of its activities to carry out inspections outside of Wales, at commercial rates. The WTB has also attempted to promote holidays to Wales commercially, by the publication of a commissionable 'Holiday Wales' tour operating programme, for distribution through agents, but with only limited success.

Efforts to ensure cooperation and coordination at this level include the formation of a Tourism Forum, an advisory body linking the ETC, DCMS and members of the industry.

The Tourist Information Centres

TICs play a particularly important role in disseminating information about tourism, in the UK as elsewhere. There are well over 800 official Tourist Information Centres in Britain, with some 600 in

Figure 15.10 Tourist Information Centres can themselves attract the tourist: (a) TIC at Maine border, USA. (*Photographed by the author*)

(b) Gloucester TIC in a converted church. (*Photographed by the author*)

(c) A heritage building for a French TIC. (*Photographed by the author*)

(d) TIC at Gudhjem, Bornholm Island, Denmark. (*Photographed by the author*)

England alone. Funding comes now largely from the local authorities, assisted by the provision of support material and publications from the regional boards. The regional boards, acting on behalf of the national boards, also oversee the standards of each TIC and award them formal recognition. This has entailed, among other criteria, a requirement to employ salaried staff rather than relying upon voluntary labour, as had been the practice in some TICs. Improved access, especially for the disabled, and agreed minimum hours of opening have also become important benchmarks for recognition.

The TICs, like the boards, have been forced to become more commercial in the light of government policy, and with the decline in funding by cash-strapped local authorities, which do not, in fact, have a statutory duty to provide these services. Apart from the now well-established Book a bed ahead scheme, TICs are increasingly introducing commercial products for sale within their shops, while seeking ways of cutting costs to remain viable.

One means of providing information cheaply is through the Tourist Information Point (TIP), unattended stands providing information about local facilities. In some parts of the world, these will include sophisticated booking systems for local hotels, either using telephone connections or computer links.

A final point to make is the valuable contribution which TICs can make to tourism through the buildings they occupy. In many cases, TICs are housed in buildings of outstanding architectural or historic interest in a city, and their careful preservation and adaptation for this purpose has ensured that the buildings are not only put to good use, but provide an additional point of focus for the visiting tourist, who is able to see the interior of a building which might otherwise be restricted. Increasingly, local authorities have come to recognize the important role which the TIC can play in drawing attention to modern design as well, whether in the traditional style and materials of local building or in a more modern concept where the new building can itself become a stimulus for tourist interest. Examples of TICs based in buildings of local architectural or historical interest are illustrated in Figure 15.10.

Information technology initiatives in the public sector

The computer-linked accommodation reservation system is just one example of the important role which information technology is now coming to play in providing tourist services. Public sector tourism interests have not been slow to take advantage of the computerized information revolution, in offering both information and reservations facilities. Increasingly, these are becoming available via the web site.

The BTA devised its Visit Britain web site in 1997, which was being visited by over 300,000 monthly in 1999. It offers details of tourist attractions, events organizers, hotels and advertisements. A system developed jointly by the English national and regional boards goes further by providing a database of information which allows tourism staff to match accommodation to their clients' needs, indicate availability and print a confirmation for the client after the reservation is confirmed. The system will also build a database of names and addresses of those booking accommodation, allowing mailing lists to be developed which can be used in later campaigns. Information is also provided on local attractions and events. The ETC also announced in 2001 plans to establish a web site specifically to cover English resorts and accommodation, with a view to boosting tourist visits to the seaside resorts. An e-Tourism Advisory Group was set up in the same year to bring together public and private sector bodies in order to find new ways of using technology to promote tourism in the UK. Similarly, the Scottish Tourist Board developed its Ossian online booking system in 2000, in partnership with the private sector. On a smaller scale, the Star Collection of ten English tourist resorts uses RITA, an online reservations system, to allow travel agents to book rooms for their clients' domestic holidays.

Few can doubt that the web site will become the common means to access domestic hotel bookings within the space of the next few years. Other schemes proposed by some local authorities would allocate rooms within their districts to tour operators for package tour arrangements. Such a centrally controlled allocation of hotel rooms would enable hoteliers to reduce their individual commitments to tour operators, and therefore minimize wastage in the reservations process.

Perhaps one of the more noticeable features of the advance in information technology development within the public sector has been the emergence of Electronic Marketing Units (EMUs) at TICs. These are databases accessible to passers-by outside the TICs, and therefore their use is not limited to the opening times of the TICs themselves. Although the range of information available through these units is limited, it is expanding and already provides the basis for interactive communication between tourists and tourist facilities, which would allow visitors to make reservations for hotels, theatres and a host of other amenities.

Functions of the Regional Tourist Boards

While the example given here refers to the operation of the ten Regional Tourist Boards established in England, the Area Tourist Boards in Scotland and the three Tourism Councils in Wales operate in a similar fashion.

It was envisaged when the structure of the regional boards was set up that they would receive their financing through a mixture of national board, local authority and private sector funds, although private funding never achieved the levels anticipated. Additionally, the boards were to raise capital through commercial activities such as the sale of tourist products like maps and guides.

The objectives set for the Regional Tourist Boards when they were established were:

- to produce a coordinated strategy for tourism within their regions in association with the local authority;

- to represent the interests of the region at national level and the interests of the tourist industry within the region;
- to encourage the development of tourist amenities and facilities which meet the changing needs of the market;
- to market the region by providing reception and information services (in concert with the NTB), producing and supplying suitable literature and undertaking miscellaneous promotional activities.

Many RTBs also undertake the role of validating guiding courses for 'Blue Badge' guides within their regions.

Typically, an RTB will work with a very small staff of perhaps ten to fifteen members (although the London Tourist Board, due to its importance in the tourism economy, has a much larger number of employees). Coordination now has to be with a much wider range of bodies, including not only the local authorities and tourist trade, but also government offices for the regions and the Regional Development Agencies.

RTBs have a particularly difficult role in their relations with local authorities. They must work with these authorities and cooperate with them in tourism planning, but their aims may be in conflict with those of the local authority, which is often apathetic or negative towards the growth of tourism in its area. Moreover, local authorities are charged with certain functions which have a direct bearing on tourism, as we have seen. They can hinder the expansion of tourism by refusing planning permission, to take one example. However, they do also play an important role in safeguarding the countryside and coastal areas within their regions.

Geographically, RTB areas are often diverse and cannot logically be promoted as a single destination. Furthermore, political regions do not necessarily embrace what the tourist understands as a 'tourist region', and the RTB's role will include the promotion of a brand image for a region which may readily cross county borders. South West Tourism, to take one example, represents counties ranging from

Figure 15.11 National and Regional Tourist Boards promote their territories at international exhibitions: the World Travel Market in London. (*Photographed by the author*)

Cornwall at its western extremity to Bristol on its northern boundary, and parts of West Dorset on its eastern boundary. It is charged with the promotion of all these regions, although Bristol's Council makes no financial contribution to the Board's funds, while the promotion of Dorset would arguably be better handled as an integral destination. Producing a coordinated strategy for the promotion and development of tourism in the face of these diverse interests is no easy matter.

Cooperative marketing organizations

We have seen in this chapter how private and public sector interests can differ in tourism, the general lack of coordinated tourism policy, the severe and growing constraints being imposed by government upon tourism financing, and the areas of potential conflict which can arise in the public sector. As one means of overcoming some of these problems, several areas have opted for the formation of a tourism marketing board, made up of representatives from both the public and private sector interests. This could be seen as the first step in privatizing the public sector of tourism in the UK. Plymouth was the first city to launch a joint venture of this kind, in 1977. The city's marketing bureau draws its members from those nominated by the city council and others elected by

the private sector. The bureau is financed by a grant from the city council, by membership subscriptions and by commercial activities. Other cities have followed suit, and although not all have proved successful, this 'joint venture' approach appears to be an appropriate way forward, and has also been successfully introduced at national levels. The BTA, for example, cooperates in a great many joint marketing schemes abroad each year, in association with British and foreign interests in the private sector. The public sector also cooperates to undertake joint overseas promotion, as in the case of that between the BTA and regional tourist organizations. The British Travel Centre in Regent Street, London, is an example of joint funding between the BTA and the railway networks.

On a wider scale, we have seen in Chapter 6 how countries and regions of the globe come together in order to market their 'tourism region' more successfully, at the same time making more effective use of their limited budgets. In many cases these international consortia draw on private sector funding to support their aims, to the benefit of both sectors.

The role of the European Union

By contrast with some European Union nations, where tourism makes an equally important contribution to the economy, Britain has chosen largely to allow the free market economy to operate in the tourism field, with little attempt to centralize policy making. However, as Britain becomes more closely integrated with the EU, British travel and tourism interests have become subjected to EU legislation. Most importantly, since harmonization came into force at the beginning of 1993, any constraints of trade have been largely abolished, allowing travel firms to compete within the EU on an equal footing and without legal hindrance. So far, the evidence suggests that fellow Europeans are faster in taking advantage of the opportunities that this presents than is the UK, although British airlines have continued to expand into the Continent (see Chapter 7).

Within the European Commission, at least ten of

the twenty-three Directorates General (the Commission's departments) have some responsibilities that impact upon the tourism industry, although the Tourism Unit itself is located within DGXXIII, Enterprise Policy, Tourism and Social Economy. This is a relatively small unit, formed in 1989, before which date tourism was located within the Transport Directorate General. As with government departments in Britain, there is no system for coordinating tourism interests across the Directorates General. Unfortunately, the performance of the tourism unit was marred by corruption in the mid-1990s. The principal stated objectives of the EU as regards tourism include:

- the facilitation of tourist movements, through abolition of frontier controls, deregulation of transport, ease in transfer of foreign currencies, reciprocal health coverage and better information and protection for tourists themselves;
- more effective promotion, through state aid and other means;
- help in distributing the flow of tourists better, both geographically and seasonally, through emphasis on such features as rural tourism, and by staggering school holidays;
- other measures, to include better tourism training, easing taxation etc.

Many of these ambitions were already achieved to some extent before the introduction of harmonization; the scheduled airline industry, as we saw in Chapter 7, has been fully deregulated, and there have been no controls over charter flights within the EU. Shipping has also been largely deregulated. The free movement of capital and labour promises the possibility of huge changes in the way some sectors of industry, such as tour operating and travel agencies, are run, and we are already seeing the impact of this deregulation as companies merge across borders in these sectors. While the termination of duty-free facilities within the EU was damaging for the industry, the lifting of any ceiling on duty-paid goods stimulated sales to cross-border tourists. As we have noted earlier in the text, however, the most immediate impact has been the introduction of the Package Travel Directive, adopted after amendment in 1990, which was designed to provide tourists with better, more accurate information and greater protection. The additional burden placed on tour operators and travel agents has been problematic and costly for the industry, although the requirement for operators to bear the responsibility for virtually anything happening to their clients while abroad has undoubtedly marked a great advance in consumer protection for travellers within the EU.

Current EU policy at the time of writing favoured broad economic measures and more cross-border opportunities to stimulate tourism, rather than specific tourism-related measures of support.

Figure 15.12 A country's culture attracts the tourist: French food markets. (*Photographed by the author*)

Meanwhile, regulations will continue to emerge from Brussels which will impinge on the way the tourism industry is run, as well as affecting the decisions of the tourists themselves as to where they travel to, how they book and what they do while on holiday.

Questions and discussion points

1. Should Tourist Information Centres be service-oriented or profit-oriented? Can the two objectives co-exist? Pay a visit to your nearest TIC to see the extent to which it is commercially involved, then discuss the case for and against TICs becoming more commercial in their efforts to pay their way.

2. Have government changes to the ETC and English regional boards improved or weakened the effectiveness of these organizations? What further changes would you recommend to improve these bodies?

3. Are sources of financial aid for tourism in Britain adequate as they stand? What needs to be done to improve the situation, and how should more public sector funds be spent to benefit tourism? Why do you think it is that many developers appear reluctant to invest in leisure and tourism enterprises?

4. In a vote-catching exercise in 2000, the shadow Conservative government promised to introduce a grant of £15 million, to be matched by sponsorship from industry, in order to promote the UK abroad. Is such cooperative funding the best way forward, or should Britain be willing to fund all promotion via the public purse?

5. How can the current huge discrepancy in funding between England, Scotland and Wales be justified, given the statistics on visitor numbers from abroad to each of these regions (in 1999, per capita government spend on tourism in the UK was £8.45 for Northern Ireland, £3.76 for Scotland, £4.99 for Wales and 20p for England)?

Assignment topics

1. You have recently been appointed Assistant Tourism Officer in a south coast resort with a strong traditional market among the C2DE population. In taking stock of the present patterns in tourism, you are interested to find out whether social tourism plays a role in bringing tourism to your resort. As a first step, you need to discover what support social tourism currently has in towns where there are a significant number of underprivileged or disadvantaged people.

   Undertake some research within the local authority nearest you which has a significant number of deprived residents, and see what the authority's attitudes are towards social tourism. What funds are there available, and how are they spent? How has this funding changed over the past decade? What recommendations would you make on spending a limited amount of money, and how would you allocate this between the various deprived groups? Prepare a short report for your Tourist Officer with suggestions of how the resort should cater for these groups.

2. As Tourism Development Officer of a town of your own choice with tourism potential, draw up a tourism strategy for the town which:

   (a) reviews the existing provision by public and private sector;

   (b) identifies the potential for tourism in the town;

   (c) provides a basis for future action in collaboration with other bodies, by defining targets and priorities for action;

   (d) identifies how the plan will aid the town and its residents economically.

   Present your findings in a report to the Council.

Chapter 16   Tourism design and management

Objectives

After studying this chapter, you should be able to:

- define design and be aware of its role in the tourism business;
- appreciate the need for landscaping in the layout of sites;
- understand how the effective use of lighting can enhance a site;
- recognize the importance of good signposting within and outside tourist sites;
- be aware of the role of interpretation in tourism and how this is most effectively implemented;
- be aware of the chief principles of good site management and how these should be implemented.

Introduction

This chapter will introduce the reader to issues which are often ignored or overlooked in textbooks of tourism, although some will feature in complementary studies such as museum or attraction management. Others, such as architecture and landscaping issues, are more likely to be dealt with in studies in town and country planning. The purpose of introducing them here is to increase awareness among students of tourism of the cross-disciplinary nature and complexity of the tourism business, and to encourage both students and practitioners to think more broadly about what it is that actually appeals to tourists, encourages them to visit specific sites and

allows them to derive satisfaction from the experience. The discussion will necessarily have to be limited in a textbook of this nature, particularly in examining the role of features such as architecture and landscaping in tourism, but it is hoped that touching on these issues will whet the reader's appetite to learn more about them and will help to widen discussions on the nature of tourism generally.

The role of design in tourism

Architecture and design

Although all of us are affected by design, much of its effect on us is subconscious. Local architecture, the layout of our public parks, and the design of sign-posts are all features with which we have become familiar in our own home surroundings. As a result, we see these objects in a different light from the way visitors will see them. When we in turn visit other destinations, we will be aware of and critically examine things we tend to take for granted in our own environment. Yet everything we see is designed, from the buildings to the shopfronts, from roads to lamp posts, from street signs to ticket booths, and all these objects affect us and mould our attitude to our surroundings.

Design therefore represents a crucial element in tourism planning, whether we are designing a tourist attraction from scratch, such as Disneyland, or modifying the landscape to make it more attractive or suitable for tourist use, such as one of the principal approach roads by which tourists enter our town; or even arranging for a few cosmetic changes to the housing stock of the town, by encouraging residents to do a spot of painting (Paris underwent a frenzy of fascia-cleaning of buildings in the 1960s with the encouragement of President de Gaulle. As a result the city became vastly more attractive for tourism, and Parisians took a new pride in their city.)

Design has two roles. One is *functional*, in the sense that if something is well designed, it should do its job better; the other is *aesthetic*, meaning that it should look right, in itself and in its setting, and that it should have visual appeal.

However, when we refer to 'good' or 'bad' design, to some extent we are expressing subjective views. The controversy surrounding the rebuilding of Windsor Castle after the tragic fire of 1993 shows the depth of feeling about a heritage site which for some people is sacrosanct, and should be reconstructed exactly as it was (even though most architects agree that much of what was lost was no masterpiece, and the castle had in any case grown over the years into a mishmash of architectural styles). Others argued that the fire had produced an opportunity to add modern extensions reflecting the best of twentieth-century architecture. The fact that overseas tourists come to see our heritage does not rule out the potential that

modern buildings have to attract their own audience, and the best of these, too, will in time become part of the heritage.

Restoration, renewal and 'heritage'

In the matter of architectural design, the private and public sectors often have quite different objectives. The private sector developer is interested in good design only to the extent that it operates functionally, and that it satisfies the consumer and encourages them to return. The developer will generally try to produce the design which does these things at the lowest possible cost. The public sector can, if it chooses, exercise greater control, not just by insisting on sympathetic restoration instead of rebuilding, or by requiring buildings to make use of local building materials, but by rewarding and encouraging good design. Too often, however, local authorities take a short-sighted view of their role in promoting good design; in the 1960s, for example, the developers of the Seagram Building in New York were horrified to find they would be taxed far more heavily by the City because of the added value of their building which was quickly hailed as a masterpiece of twentieth-century architecture. This rapidly discouraged other developers from spending more than they needed on good design.

The extent to which a 'heritage building' should be restored also leads to considerable controversy. When reconstruction of the medieval Barley Hall in the centre of York was completed in 1992, architectural critics were enthusiastic about the care with which the work had been carried out, and the accuracy of the reconstruction; yet the Chairman of the Society for the Protection of Ancient Buildings quickly attacked the project for producing a replica of the original building and destroying many of the later additions which had made it organic. He dismissed the end result as 'another contribution to our Disneyland heritage'. Similar attacks have been launched on reconstructions of Roman fortifications along Hadrian's Wall, and of the Temple at Knossos in Crete (not only over-elaborate in its reconstruction; doubts have now been cast on the authenticity of the design, although many thousands of tourists were pleased to gain an insight into the way some of the world's oldest buildings may have actually looked in their heyday).

In Britain we are criticized for adopting a provincial attitude to new building which suggests that most of us are happier with the designs of the past. The result is that pastiche neo-Georgian or mock Tudor is more popular than the contemporary buildings that are springing up all over Europe. More legitimate criticism is that directed not at the form of the building, but at unsympathetic use of materials, such as raw concrete, or the fact that it is out of scale with other buildings in the area. Modern materials tend not to age attractively, while natural materials will become more attractive with the passing years.

Some of the issues surrounding the design of modern buildings have been examined in Chapter 11, where the potential of modern design to attract tourism was discussed. Certainly, issues of size and scale must be taken into consideration, as must the use of local materials in construction, which can be a major feature in attracting tourists. On the other

Figure 16.2 Modern office building, Bremen, Germany. (*Photographed by the author*)

Figure 16.1 Finlandia Hall, Helsinki. (*Photographed by the author*)

hand, given the right setting, and in the hands of a master architect, an uncompromisingly modern building can become the pride of its residents, and an international draw. Figure 16.1 is one such example, Eero Saarinen's Finlandia Hall in Helsinki, Finland, a country noted for the excellence of its design (which it promotes extensively to attract tourists to the country). The building succeeds in part because, set in its own landscaping and away from city centre buildings, it is not required to merge with the local traditional architecture. However, where this is required, modern adaptations of vernacular design can be undertaken and will merge sympathetically with their surroundings (see Figure 16.2).

From the point of view of the tourist, the significance of such design is not only that it reflects the

Figure 16.3   Modern public toilet in natural stone with slate roof, Ireland. (*Photographed by the author*)

due to shortages of money for maintenance and supervision. While Britain is not unique in facing this problem, it is interesting to note that in Japan, architectural competitions are promoted for public toilets, and the Chinese encourage architects to design toilets with the needs of American tourists in mind. The interest generated by the construction of the 'superloo' at Westbourne Grove in London, designed by architect Piers Gough in 1993 with an attached flower-shop, reveals just how important good toilet design can be for tourism. This particular example not only won design awards, but was featured in English Heritage's advertisements in

traditions of the local architecture and therefore merges effectively with the surrounding buildings, but it is also built on a human scale which does not dwarf the passer-by. Most visitors to a town will explore it on foot, and good street-level design is vital to maintain the visitor's satisfaction.

Local building materials are, unfortunately, often more expensive to use in construction, but the additional cost is well justified in the long run. In Britain, examples may be found in the use of Bath stone in Bath, Cotswold stone in the Cotswolds, black-and-white half-timbering in the border country, thatch in the West Country, and slate in the Lake District or Wales. Even for such mundane construction as public toilets, the use of local and natural building materials can greatly enhance the end result (see Figure 16.3) and is often insisted upon by local authority planning departments. The use of natural materials specific to the locality will help to reinforce the characteristics of the brand image which the attraction or tourist board is trying to create.

The importance of public toilets for tourists is an issue which is frequently overlooked, yet the subject of their inadequacies is regularly touched upon by those bodies like BITOA that are concerned with promoting tourism to the UK. Many tourist sites suffer from an inadequate supply of toilets, while others have had their toilets locked or shut down

Figure 16.4   Shopfront in Paris. (*Photographed by the author*)

Figure 16.5 Shopfront in London. (*Photographed by the author*)

1997. It should come as no surprise, therefore, that over eighty public toilets around Britain are actually listed buildings.

Shopping is a prime motive for tourism, and the design of shopfronts can do much to increase the pleasure of the tourist experience, particularly for window-shoppers. Figures 16.4, 16.5 and 16.6 illustrate three very contrasting ways of attracting the shopper. The first shop is an innovative and unashamedly modern design in Paris – controversial, given its siting between more traditional shopfronts, but guaranteed to rouse interest. The second, a design for David Mellor's store at Shad Thames in London's Docklands, is also simple and modern, but is designed principally to give a good view to the passing visitor of both the shop contents and the distant renovated warehouses across the water. The

third picture is of a much more traditional design, the carefully restored shopfront of a jewellers in Lillehammer, Norway, which retains the vernacular architecture of the area (even down to the rust-red colour of its paintwork).

In many cases, modern architecture may be actively disliked, but still provide a draw for tourism. The Pompidou centre in Paris is certainly not everybody's idea of a good modern building, but it is a major magnet for tourists. On a smaller scale, the highly controversial Cube Houses of Rotterdam, designed by Piet Blom, and their adjoining Potloodflat (pencil flat) building have become important features to attract tourists to Rotterdam, and are now featured extensively in tourist literature produced by the city. The Netherlands is a country which has experimented extensively in modern

Figure 16.6 Shopfront in Lillehammer, Norway. (*Photographed by the author*)

buildings throughout the twentieth century, and this is now paying off by attracting a growing number of tourists, whether out of architectural interest or for novelty. One private house, the Rietveld-Schröder house in Utrecht, designed by Gerrit Rietveld and recently restored as a museum, now brings students of architecture to visit from all over the world.

Landscape design

No building can be divorced from its setting, and just as thought must go into the design of the building itself, so the site must be landscaped attractively to maximize visitor appeal.

Part of the attraction of an English village is the way in which the houses lie in the landscape, blending as if they were made for the setting. Where a site for development is sloping, it becomes even more important to ensure that the buildings blend with the background, and if the buildings are to be exposed to view – for example, a group of self-catering chalets high in the Alps – great care has to be taken to integrate them into the landscape. Buildings should not stand out on the skyline, but if it is essential that they do, then their lines should be broken up with the use of trees and shrubs. On sloping sites, buildings can be 'stepped' or terraced up the hillside to keep their scale in harmony with the environment. Similarly, on watersite developments, build-

ings should be sited well clear of the waterfront itself, to allow for walkways along the banks that will attract both residents and visitors, and to ensure that those using the waterway are not intimidated by high buildings alongside.

The appeal of water is evident in the conversion of so many redundant harbours and waterways in Britain for leisure use. Here, the local authorities must determine whether the site is best retained as a dockland environment, or themed as an urban parkland. Enlightened authorities have come to recognize that retention of the traditional bollards, cranes and other paraphernalia of a dockside will provide a unique setting and a better lure for the visitor, with the addition of a modest number of trees or shrubs.

In the countryside of England, boundaries are a prominent feature which give the landscape much of its character. They range from the hedges of southern England (a significant proportion of which have sadly been lost since the end of World War II, as farmers tried to increase productivity on their land) to the dry-stone walls of the north which, using virtually no mortar, allow ferns and lichen to grow on their surfaces and soften their appearance. Fences also have characteristic local designs, complemented by the traditional five-barred gate; these designs can be incorporated into tourist settings, too. Public

Figure 16.7 Effective landscaping for a picnic site at a reservoir: Lake Clywedoc, Mid-Wales. (*Photographed by the author*)

Figure 16.8 The art of catching the visitor's attention: a car park at Bordeaux, France. (*Photographed by the author*)

sector grants have been made available to retain and restore dry-stone walling and hedging where these are characteristic of the local landscape.

Car parks are a particular problem for the tourism designer, since they occupy large areas of land and are visually intrusive. In the countryside, efforts are now made to ensure that the park appears as natural as possible; logs can be used to separate the bays, and substantial shrubbery planting will help to conceal the cars themselves. Good, but not intrusive, lighting is important, while the surface itself can be retained as a gravel site rather than asphalted. In some small parks, it may be possible to use honeycombed concrete blocks which allow the grass to grow through them, rendering the concrete surface almost invisible.

Car parks must, of course, be situated well away from any high-grade heritage sites, and this may mean that special provision must be made for the disabled. In cities, urban setting will mean the use of more man-made materials in car park construction, but this no longer means high-rise concrete. Designs have become more fanciful in recent years, including in one case a mock medieval fortification, while parks on open land have been attractively furnished with decorative modern lamps and plenty of trees to break up the land mass.

Telephone and public utility lines can disfigure even the most beautiful town or village. Fortunately, in Britain local authorities have generally taken an enlightened view on hiding these ugly necessities, but a visit to Spain or Greece will soon illustrate how much visual pollution is caused by overhead wires along streets and linking into houses. The cost of burying wires is much higher, but again in the long run it is worth the investment if it leaves the site appearing much more attractive to visitors.

Street furniture

Street furniture is something we all take for granted, yet it plays an important part in reflecting the national landscape, too. One has only to think of the classic red telephone kiosks or letter boxes in Britain, or the nineteenth-century 'pissoirs' (now sadly disappearing) and classic green boulevard chairs and tables still to be found on the streets of Paris, to realize that such items play a part in formulating our ideas about national characteristics. In Britain, a great deal of attention has been paid in recent years to designs of public seating and litter bins, but any item of street furniture, from post boxes to telephone kiosks, from litter bins to bus shelters, from public toilets to refreshment stalls, from lamp posts to railings, needs to be carefully designed to be in harmony with the surroundings and reflect the image of the area in which they are sited.

Local authorities must first determine whether to adopt a classic or modern design for their setting. Heritage sites such as York or Chester are more likely to opt for a traditional and classic design to blend with the architecture of the area. Unfortunately, this has led to the development of a ubiquitous design in cast iron with gold motifs, frequently bearing the crest of the city, which, while tasteful and elegant, does little to distinguish the city's streets from countless others in the country. However, these designs are to be welcomed over some of the products they replace, such as the plastic litter bin (all too often cracked or misshapen), in a choice of battleship grey or garish yellow. Litter bins in particular need to be

Figure 16.9 Different approaches to street furnishing: (a) a modern public toilet in Sweden. (*Photographed by the author*)

(b) A 'traditional' telephone kiosk in Stockholm. (*Photographed by the author*)

big enough to accommodate the huge amounts of litter created today by take-away shops, and the council must have a policy of emptying these frequently, or the benefits of good design will be lost, as rubbish piles up around the base of the bin.

Cities on the Continent, particularly those whose centres were substantially rebuilt after the war or which wish to promote a modern, dynamic image, will adopt more modern designs. These can work equally well in the appropriate setting. Figure 16.9 illustrates four different approaches to design in the street.

The green granite and metal modern toilet in Stockholm represents an expensive investment, but will clearly last, and be relatively easy to maintain. By contrast, in the *Gamla Stan* (old town) of the same city, the council has opted for a more traditional design for its telephone kiosks, a slightly whimsical reworking of the nineteenth-century design found in the area. A similar theme is evident in the design for a 'classic' letter box in Bremen, while Brussels chooses to project a more modern image with its contemporary bus shelters and litter bins. These well-designed features still manage to blend successfully with the more conservative buildings which surround them.

Providing seating in a town is a problem for the planners, as it tends to attract vagrants. However, the

(c) A 'classic' post box in Bremen. (*Photographed by the author*)

Figure 16.10   Polished marble 'rest areas' in downtown Toronto, Canada. Note the stainless steel litter bins. (*Photographed by the author*)

(d) A modern bus shelter and litter bin in Brussels. (*Photographed by the author*)

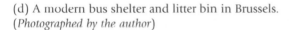

use of simple-to-maintain materials which will provide a brief respite for residents and tourists, but not a level of comfort encouraging longer stays, can be the answer to the problem, as demonstrated in Figure 16.10.

Pedestrianization

Many towns popular with tourists have pedestrianized some of their principal thoroughfares. The result can greatly enhance the atmosphere of a street and encourage visitors to come shopping. Some of Britain's most attractive town centres, such as those of York, Brighton, Bath and Chester, and many Continental towns, feature narrow pedestrian walkways which have never been wide enough to support motor vehicles. In these towns, the narrowness of the lanes is their very attraction. However, pedestrianizing will not in itself be enough to make the street a focal point for shoppers; the shops themselves must be appropriate for the setting, and the street must be enhanced by well-designed street furniture, tree planting and the display of flowers or shrubs in tubs or other containers. When this is done tastefully, the end result can transform a street. However, the fact

Figure 16.12 Three examples of pedestrianization. Note the substantial use of street furniture in the first example and the use of patterned brickwork to add interest in all three. (a) Gloucester. (*Photographed by the author*)

feature of their floral displays that they have become famous internationally; Bath's hanging basket displays are highly attractive features for the summer visitors, while the massed floral beds which highlight the seafronts of towns such as Eastbourne and Worthing are features which draw many older visitors to the resorts year after year. Aberdeen is noted

Figure 16.11 A pedestrian shopping lane in Bremen, Germany (the *Schnoor*). (*Photographed by the author*)

(b) St Helier, Jersey. (*Photographed by the author*)

that it will also attract much larger numbers of pedestrians can lead to congestion and to a litter problem which the council must be prepared to tackle.

Horticultural displays

The use of hanging baskets, floral beds in the centre of main access roads, extensive tree planting along the pavements and similar horticultural displays can make a pretty village outstanding, and an ugly town bearable. Some of Britain's towns have made such a

(c) Lillehammer, Norway (with Christmas decorations). (*Photographed by the author*)

for its display of formal rose beds along its main roads, while on the Continent, the flower-bedecked chalets of Switzerland and Austria are features that are automatically associated with these countries' villages, and highlighted in their tourist brochures.

The cost of transforming a town in this way is considerable, but any town seeking to attract the tourist can at very least consider investing funds to make the main approach roads more attractive, both those carrying visitor traffic to the centre and those which provide the principal access for pedestrians to the centre from bus or train terminals.

Art and tourism

There is a growing recognition today that art has a role to play in the tourist industry, not just through the museums, galleries and arts events organized to

Figure 16.13   Street sculpture drawing on Grimms' Fairy Tales, Bremen, Germany. (*Photographed by the author*)

attract the tourist, but in the everyday surroundings in which the visitors find themselves. Ostensibly, 'street art' is designed to heighten the visual appeal of a town for its residents, but once again, such embellishment will add to the attraction of the destination for the visitors, too, and if the work displayed is by artists of international reputation, this will widen the appeal of the destination to the international visitor. Sculptures by Henry Moore in Yorkshire or at the Serpentine in London attract a dedicated audience of overseas and domestic visitors. Cities in the United States enforce local regulations requiring a small percentage of the total cost of any new development to be spent on 'public art' at the site, and the prestigious offices of major corporations will also judge it appropriate to enhance their forecourts with sculptures by leading artists of the day. In London, prominent British artists such as Eduardo Paolozzi were recruited to design the wall tiling during the renovation of the Central London Underground railway stations.

Towns can reinforce their images by the imaginative use of sculpture or art. In Germany, for example, Hamelin will have its sculpture of the Pied Piper, while Bremen has greatly enhanced its pedestrian streets with scenes from Grimms' Fairy Tales (see Figure 16.13).

Britain is becoming more aware of the importance of art and the way in which it can serve the interests of the tourism industry. Notable features include two water fountain sculptures by William Pye, 'Slipstream' and 'Jetstream', commissioned by BAA at Gatwick Airport, a 130-foot long sculpture, 'Train' by David Mach, a monument to the record-breaking Mallard train and comprising 185,000 bricks, unveiled in Darlington in 1997 (to considerable local criticism but widespread national publicity), and the gigantic sculpture entitled 'The Angel of the North' by Anthony Gormley mounted on a hillside near Gateshead. This is clearly visible to hundreds of thousands of travellers and tourists using the nearby motorway each day, and has received enormous publicity. Perhaps surprisingly, it has captured the hearts and imagination of the local residents, and has attracted numerous tourists to visit.

Lighting

External street lighting can play an important role in enhancing a town, both with respect to the design of the lights themselves and to the effect they can create at night. Again, a choice must be made between traditional and modern lamps. Some towns have reinforced their quaintness by reverting to authentic gas lighting, which has great popular appeal for tourists. In Norwegian villages in the weeks leading up to Christmas, the shopping streets are illuminated with real flares, giving visitors an impression of warmth and cosiness at a time when the long periods of darkness could otherwise easily depress.

Floodlighting major attractions, long a recognized

Figure 16.14 Art and light combine to attract the evening visitor. Floodlit sculpture, Angers, France. (*Photographed by the author*)

THE ROLE OF DESIGN IN TOURISM

practice for the great monuments in leading cities, has become much more widespread, and its use can encourage tourists out on to the streets at night, thus extending the 'tourist day'. White lights are normally recommended; the use of coloured lights, apart from where a fairground atmosphere is appropriate, such as at the Blackpool illuminations, is best avoided. The use of coloured lights to floodlight Niagara Falls, many observers feel, turned a great spectacle into an example of down-market kitsch. Limited use of coloured lighting can be helpful in highlighting horticultural displays at night, however. Care must be taken not to overlight; strong lights are particularly inappropriate in a village setting, for example.

Signposting

All visitors look for signposts, so they become the most visible of all forms of street furniture. They serve three purposes: directional, informative and utility.

Directional

Traffic signs direct vehicles or pedestrians in particular directions, and to specific sights. They must therefore be clearly legible, especially from a distance, in the case of vehicle signs. They should be identified by use of a standard, immediately recognizable colour, and their size and shape should also be uniform. Generally, standards for road signs will be set by local authorities or government departments of transport.

Within towns, signposts directing tourists to specific attractions have received a lot of attention in Britain in recent years. Once again, a 'traditional' classic signpost has been devised, with modest variations in design, constructed of cast iron with white lettering (some towns have produced a variation on this; Bristol, for example, has introduced royal blue as the standard colour).

Informative

These are of two types. They may be used to alert tourists passing in vehicles to a particular attraction in the vicinity, and they will also be provided at a particular site, such as a viewpoint or monument, to give information about the site itself.

In the former case, following a long period where signposting was arbitrary and often banned from main roads in Britain, the Department of Transport introduced white-on-brown signs in 1986, with thirty-five different pictographs representing every conceivable variety of tourist attraction. Regulations on the use of these and other signs is complex and quite restrictive. The use of white-on-brown signs, for example, is dependent upon the numbers visiting the site (for example, historic houses must attract a minimum of 5,000 visitors a year for a road sign to be approved). This, of course, introduces a 'Catch-22' situation, where already well-established attractions are favoured over newly developed ones.

Signs outside a particular attraction will also be subject to local government regulations. For example, attractions in North America, which are generally very well signposted, often adopt a standard format for imparting information about national monuments (see a typical Canadian cast-iron-with-crest 'interpretation' plaque in Figure

Figure 16.15 Examples of signposts bearing different types of information. (a) Old City Hall, Toronto, Canada (a national monument with historical information). (*Photographed by the author*)

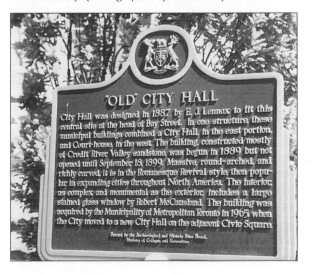

345

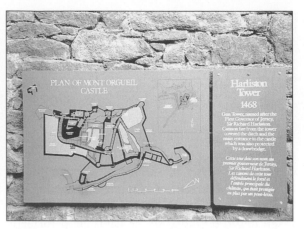

(c) Mont Orgueil Castle, Jersey (historical information coupled with a plan of the site). (*Photographed by the author*)

(b) Historic Mackenzie House, Toronto (an attractively displayed sign bearing information on opening hours and admission prices). (*Photographed by the author*)

16.15a). Visitors to such sights will also need to receive information about the layout of larger sites, together with details of opening hours and price of admission. Examples of signs bearing this information are given in Figures 16.15b and 16.15c. Such signs must still be clearly legible, but may have more character in their design.

Mention should be made of the traditional blue

plaques which are widely in use in Britain to advise the visitor of the fact that a property has been the home of some well-known person in the past. These are invariably of great interest to foreign visitors in particular, and the fact that they are often encountered by the tourist coincidentally in walking around the streets of a city gives them added appeal.

Utility

These signs are designed to direct visitors to public utilities such as toilets and telephone kiosks. They can be smaller in scale, and will often make use of symbols, as do the white-on-brown signs – a particular boon to foreign visitors. They may have their own design and colour, but are also often incorporated into information signs in popular tourist towns.

Within specific tourist attractions, imagination gives rein to a great variety of signs and symbols. In medieval times, as few people could read, this led to many shops hanging out symbols of their trade. These have been retained, and sometimes resurrected, by shops in tourist centres, and add visual appeal to the streets. The example shown (Figure 16.16) is one of a number of original street signs in the town of Ravensburg in southern Germany.

Figure 16.16 Attractive shop signs are a feature of Ravensburg, Germany. (*Photographed by the author*)

Figure 16.17 Poor maintenance of facilities discourages tourism. Parking lot and directional sign in Devon. (*Photographed by the author*)

The management of tourism sites

This textbook is not the place for a detailed examination of management techniques, but anyone studying tourism needs to be aware of some of the specific issues of management that are unique to tourism, and to recognize the problems that can arise. We will examine two issues here which are central to the study of tourism: those of interpretation and of visitor management.

Interpretation

The days when visitors expected no more than to stare passively at exhibited artefacts or buildings are now over. Today, visitors to tourist sites expect to be both educated and entertained, and the managers of tourist sites, especially those incorporating 'heritage' (however we interpret this term), must find ways of getting the visitor involved, and bringing the site 'alive' for them. This implies finding ways to impart information successfully, and is seen as giving added value to any tourist visit.

Interpretation has come a long way in the past few years, and whole courses of study are now devoted to understanding it. Thirty years ago, this would have involved nothing more than producing some attractive graphic design and handing out a few leaflets.

Today, attempts are made to transport the visitor into another age, through the use of costumed animateurs and the careful staging of settings to make them as realistic as possible. By way of example, barmaids in period costumes will pull pints of real ale in the pubs at the Ironbridge Gorge museum; and at Wigan Pier, an actor taking the role of a Victorian schoolmaster will invite the visitors to participate as pupils in a role play demonstrating school life of the period. At the Blaenavon Big Pit Mining Museum in Wales, visitors have to don mining helmets and lamps in order to accompany authentic ex-miners who guide them around the site; travel to the coal face is in an original mining cage, and the life and full horror of working underground are effectively communicated by the guides during the tour. At the Robin Hood

Figure 16.18 Small museums can be attractively presented. (a) The Leather Museum, Walsall, West Midlands. (*Photographed by the author*)

(b) Interior display and interpretative board, Walsall Leather Museum. (*Photographed by the author*)

Figure 16.19 The use of wax figures in historical settings to portray the period is increasing: Chinon Castle, France. (*Photographed by the author*)

Story exhibition in Nottingham, visitors have to find out the answers to a series of questions about Robin Hood, based on information contained in the interpretation plaques found throughout the exhibition, and those answering the questions correctly receive a 'good' certificate. A museum opened in Neasden, North London, in 1993, as a direct response to local demand, with an exhibition of 'Brent people'. Visitors are able to tap into audio history tapes by telephone, photos can be called up on screens by computer, and children are allowed to dress up in costumes of the 1920s, rather than observing them at a distance on dummies. Interactive communication of this kind is ideal as a means of involving children; however, such attractions all have to face one problem; is a single form of interpretation suited to every one of the variety of markets to which the attraction appeals? Plaques designed to be read by children will be dismissed by adults as patronizing, while too much information given to those seeking the detailed background to a site will put off those enjoying an entertaining day out. The answer is to provide a variety of different forms of communication, to cater successfully for each market segment served. Stately homes often meet the need for more detailed information by providing hand-held boards for use in each room with full particulars of the contents. These are sometimes offered in two or three foreign languages, also.

Managing visitor flows

Most attractions share a common problem in managing their visitors; that of uneven flows. Demand at a particular site will fluctuate, and cannot easily be spread over time. The result is that managers face problems of scheduling and queuing to which their own preferred solutions may not be those which most appeal to the customers themselves.

Popular attractions such as major exhibitions which are mounted for a limited period of time (e.g. Tutankhamun and the Treasures of Egypt at the British Museum, the Matisse Retrospective in Paris and London) or the key attractions at a Disney theme park, where demand will always outstrip supply, pose particular problems. One solution is to require advance reservations for entry, and to determine the maximum number to be admitted at any given time (admitting too many people to an exhibition of paintings will result in enormous disappointment if people are unable to see the paintings). Many attractions in London, including Madame Tussauds, Buckingham Palace and the London Eye, as well as special exhibitions in the national museums, arrange for timed entrances which guarantee the visitor entry to the attraction. The Millennium Dome attraction in London suffered not only from too few visitors during 2000, but too much demand for its key attraction, the Body Zone. The introduction of timed tickets in mid-season increased the through-flow from 1,500 to 2,300 an hour, with queues cut to a maximum of twenty minutes.

The Walt Disney attractions have years of experience in handling very large flows of tourists, and use timed entrances to handle peak demand. Their 'Fastpass' allows visitors to collect a ticket during their visit and return later in the day to join a shorter queue. They have also experimented with a 'single rider' line to top up the odd empty space on rides, but found that waiting families were angered by what they saw as 'queue-jumping' and abandoned the scheme.

Overpricing to manipulate or reduce demand is seen by many as an injustice, and is a solution seldom enforced. In 2000, the Alton Towers theme park in Staffordshire went so far as to introduce two-tier pricing for its attractions, with tickets designed to be purchased in advance on the Internet which allowed higher payers to jump queues. The so-called X-celerator, priced at more than three times the regular entry fee, allowed the first thirty buyers to travel on the busiest rides without waiting. There was a predictable backlash from the public, and the very high price charged (£65) meant that take-up was seldom 100 per cent. The scheme was abandoned.

At sites where advance bookings, for whatever reason, are less feasible, queues will have to be organized, and the tedium of waiting reduced as far as possible. Very long queues form for attractions like

Figure 16.20 Multiple ticket booths permit the smooth flow of a large number of visitors at the Ebbw Vale Garden Festival, Wales, 1993. (*Photographed by the author*)

Figure 16.21 Roofed waiting area at Baltimore Aquarium, USA. (*Photographed by the author*)

the Crown Jewels at the Tower of London, and the management of this site must find a means of getting the right balance between their own desire to move the crowds quickly past the display and the need to avoid antagonizing their customers, who will have waited a long time and expect to take their time seeing the attraction.

Large events designed to cater for many thousands of people every day must ensure that they have the means to admit them quickly. This means sufficient numbers of ticket booths to avoid long lines queuing to buy tickets (see Figure 16.20). Where queues are inevitable, such as on public holidays, a variety of techniques can be employed to reduce the tedium of waiting. At the aquarium at the Inner Harbour at Baltimore, an elaborate zig-zag 'maze' is devised to handle the queues. This has the result of making the queue appear shorter than it is, and to be contained under a relatively small roof area as shelter from intense heat, or rain. Queuers find themselves side by side, and can enter into conversation while they are waiting (see Figure 16.21).

Alton Towers management has had a great deal of experience in handling queues. A variety of different approaches are taken in trying to balance supply and demand – not always successfully, as we saw above. Well-established practices include queues which are

segmented to make them appear shorter, and the employment of buskers to entertain those waiting. Estimates of how long they can expect to wait are given to those in line, and barriers are in place to keep the crowd orderly. As with the Baltimore attraction, the snaked queues appear shorter and allow members of the public to engage in conversation while they wait.

In the case of certain forms of attraction, once the visitors are inside further problems of crowd control can arise. Many visitors prefer to tour sites in their own time, independently. This raises problems of managing the crowds (who will tend to take longer watching some displays than others) and of security – where exhibitions contain highly valuable artefacts, such as at stately homes, guides are normally assigned to accompany groups. However, at Aarhus's Gamle By, an original means of safeguarding treasures against theft or vandalism by independent visitors has been devised; rooms are 'sealed off' with the use of huge transparent plastic screens (see Figure 16.22). Similarly, glass partitions have been pressed into use to protect key rooms on show at the chateau at Fontainebleau, near Paris.

At sites such as Jorvik in York, Tralee in Ireland and the Robin Hood Story in Nottingham, where visitors are taken around in 'time carts' on a journey through

Figure 16.22 Room secured from the public by clear plastic screens, Gamle By, Aarhus. (*Photographed by the author*)

history, the carts control the flow of visitors, and determine the ceiling on the number of visitors who can be admitted. At stately homes, or sites like the Roman Baths at Bath, guides who accompany the visitors can delay or speed up the passage of visitors from one section of the building to another as the need arises. On occasions such as public holidays, greater numbers of visitors can be processed by the simple expedient of guides omitting some of the rooms usually visited on the tour, a common practice in sites that are small but very popular, such as

Elvis Presley's home Graceland. While this permits greater crowd control, it fails to overcome resistance that many tourists feel towards being herded. Tourists like to feel in control of their own movements, and if they are conscious of being unduly directed, their level of satisfaction will fall. They may also feel short-changed if rooms they were expecting to visit have clearly been omitted from their tour.

We have now seen some of the problems with which managers of tourist sites must contend. Solving these problems, and the day-to-day operational difficulties associated with running any form of attraction, while delivering satisfaction and maintaining the level of quality which the tourist has come to expect, is what tourist management is about. Recognition of the importance of this aspect has led both to a more professional approach within the local authorities towards managing their sites, and in an increasing number of cases to recruitment of professional teams who advise or manage the destination or site attraction on behalf of the owners or operators; so-called destination management organizations are taking on the responsibility for operating, controlling and marketing the destination product. This will include crisis management where severe disruption to tourism may have occurred, such as in the aftermath of an earthquake which may have devastated a particular region (such as Turkey), or sectarian strife (such as that in Fiji in the 1990s or Indonesia in the early 2000s). At the time of writing, rural tourism in Britain was facing a calamitous year following an outbreak of foot and mouth disease, which restricted access to many areas of the countryside, with catastrophic consequences for many small businesses dependent upon the summer tourist market. In cases such as these, the support of national and regional public bodies will be essential to overcome negative publicity and re-establish tourist flows when situations return to normal.

Let us complete this chapter with a look at one site owned and managed by a highly professional organization in the tourism business, Madame Tussauds, and highlight some of its practices designed to enhance the overall quality of the tourist experience.

The case of Warwick Castle

Warwick Castle is one of the leading tourist attractions in Britain, and is managed professionally by one of the country's leading tourism organizations, Madame Tussauds. The following are key elements in its strategy to attract and satisfy its large number of visitors.

Accessibility

The attraction is open every day from 10 a.m., apart from Christmas Day. This overcomes any uncertainty on the part of impromptu visitors about whether they will find the site open – a common problem with many heritage sites which have widely varying opening times. There are ample and clear road signs around the site, and adequate parking for cars and coaches on all but high peak days of the year. Car parks are hard surfaced and attractively landscaped.

Utilities

There are ample toilets for the numbers visiting, strategically placed at the entry to the site. Litter bins are positioned throughout the site. It is the policy of the organization to ensure that the site is kept clean at all times, and litter is picked up constantly. Particular attention is given to catering for the elderly, and for families with young children. Staff are trained in first aid emergency treatment.

Signposting and interpretation on site

All attractions are well signposted, and warning signs are posted outside the site if any facilities have to be closed for the day. A leaflet with comprehensive information about the site is given out with the tickets.

Crowd control

Visitors are directed, by additional signs, away from the most popular areas at times when queuing is likely to occur. Staff are on hand to supervise tourist flows, and queue warnings are given on peak days. Extra events, such as morris dancing, are mounted to entertain queues on these occasions.

Pricing

The policy is for an all-inclusive single payment for entry into every facility within the site. This has been found to achieve the highest level of satisfaction among visitors. The normal discounts are made available to those qualifying.

Questions and discussion points

1. Discuss the relative importance of design in each of the following tourism services: (a) a travel agency, (b) the public railway and (c) a local museum. Take into account both functional and aesthetic issues of design.

2. Taking as an example any popular event which you have recently attended (e.g. special exhibition, open-air pop festival, concert), describe how well crowds were handled, and look at ways in which crowd handling could have been improved.

3. How important is it to include foreign languages in messages directed at tourists in Britain? Identify the difficulties of doing so, and consider why more local authorities or private operators do not do so. Taking any three settings (e.g. directional signs, tourist attraction leaflets, information signposts etc.) discuss which languages would be most important, and how many languages should be used.

Assignment topics

1. Using as your model any tourist attraction (or local museum) in your area, undertake an analysis of its relative strengths and weaknesses, in terms of:

   (a) functional design;

   (b) aesthetic appeal;

   (c) information and interpretation for visitors;

   (d) management of visitor flows.

   Write a short report to the organization's executive in which you make recommendations for improving any of these, and determine the priority for action. Consider particularly any ways in which improved design could lead to increased revenue for the organization.

2. As an Assistant Tourist Officer for your local town, you have been asked to assess the quality of the environment for the visitor. Present a report to the Council which will include your evaluation of:

   (a) the street furniture;

   (b) facilities for seating;

   (c) lighting, including any floodlighting or other attempts to improve the cosmetic appeal of the town after dark;

   (d) any pedestrian walkways or other attempts to improve street materials (e.g. use of coloured bricks or patterns in the roads etc.); take into account the quality of the construction, too;

   (e) public toilets: number, positioning, attractiveness;

   (f) litter control.

   Your report should consider particularly the possibility of improvements to those routes used by actual or potential visitors on foot in the town. Make recommendations for action where urgent improvements are needed.

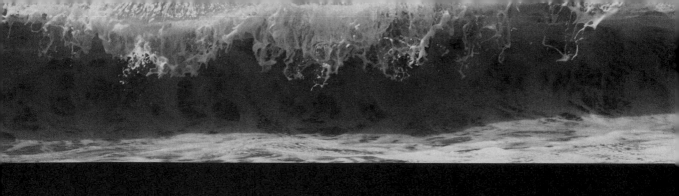

Chapter 17 The social and environmental impact of tourism

Objectives

After studying this chapter, you should be able to:

- understand the various ways in which tourism can impact on the environment;
- be aware of the socio-cultural effects of tourism on indigenous populations and on tourists;
- identify and evaluate different approaches to finding solutions to these problems;
- understand the concept, and the importance, of sustainable tourism;
- recognize the need for adequate planning, and for cooperation between the private and public sectors, as means of overcoming problems;
- be aware of future trends in tourism, and their likely impacts.

Introduction

In this closing chapter we will look at a different, and in many ways a darker, side of the tourism business – its impact on those who participate in tourism, on the residents of those countries subjected to tourist flows, and the effects of tourism on the destination itself.

Tourism, as we have seen, can be a potent force for economic and social good, creating employment and wealth, and widening our understanding of other societies. In this book, many illustrations have been given of the way in which tourism has benefited a particular place, building or cultural activity. In Britain, many great buildings, particularly those serv-ing the needs of eighteenth- and nineteenth-century industry, would have been lost had it not been poss-ible to convert these factories, mills and warehouses into living museums for the tourist. Whole inner cities and dockland areas have been restored and developed to make them attractive as tourist sites. Even a city like London would be a poorer place without the tourist; 40 per cent of West End theatre tickets are bought by tourists, and undoubtedly the wealth of theatres available to Londoners owes much to their patronage by visitors. In rural areas and small seaside resorts, many of the smaller shops could not be economically viable without the summer tourists, who also make it feasible to provide public transport such as rural bus services. The battle to save the

Settle–Carlisle branch line, one of Britain's most scenic railway routes, was won when British Rail recognized that the line could be profitable if based on the expectation of increasing tourist revenues. Country crafts, pubs, even the restoration of traditional pastimes such as morris dancing, all owe their survival to the presence of the tourist.

However, the rapid growth of tourism in the twentieth century produced problems, as well as opportunities, on a vast scale for both developed and developing countries. The governments of these countries have come to realize that unrestrained and unplanned tourist development can easily aggravate these problems to a point where tourists will no longer wish to visit the destination. In short, without adequate planning tourists may destroy what they have come to see. This problem is compounded, as long-haul travel to previously unaffected destinations increases. Now, such remote areas of the globe as the Antarctic continent are appearing on the tourist trail – a 100-bed hotel was recently opened in Antarctica by the Chilean armed forces to cater to tourists who are looking for diversions such as snow-mobile riding, and some 10,000 tourists are now visiting the continent each year, spurred on by the availability of cruises using Russian ice-breakers. One unexpected result of this influx has been that among the huge colonies of penguins inhabiting the area, a number are falling prey to chicken disease, thought to be the result of food carelessly discarded by tourists paying visits to the colonies. Ecologically sensitive regions such as the Galapagos Islands, Costa Rica and Belize are now controlling tourism development and introducing the concept of *sustainable tourism* to ensure that their environments are not destroyed by mass tourism. We will examine the environmental and social problems created by tourism in turn, and look at their possible solutions.

The environmental effects of tourism

Pollution

The technological complexity of contemporary living has led to various forms of pollution which are both initiated and compounded by tourism development, and by travel in particular. Large-scale tourist movement requires the use of mass transportation, and the fuel burn from aircraft adds to air pollution; civilian aircraft are said to account for the emission of 3 per cent of all carbon dioxide created by humans, and a similar amount of nitrous oxide (see L. Archer, *The Environmental Impact of Aircraft on the Atmosphere*, Oxford Institute for Energy Studies, 1994). The introduction of quieter, more fuel-efficient and cleaner jet engines unfortunately has the side effect of increasing the emission of nitrous oxide. On the 'polluter pays' principle, many environmentalists now argue that aviation fuel should no longer be tax-exempt – a proposal which has, of course, met fierce opposition from the airlines, and would lead to substantial increases in the price of air travel.

Emissions from the exhausts of cars and boats used in tourism compound the problem. Large cruise ships have been found guilty of disposing of waste or jettisoning oil in sensitive waterways of the world; Alaskans, once overjoyed at the arrival of tourist ships, are now angered by the rapidly increasing numbers of cruise ships visiting the state, fearing contamination of their waters, while the large number of vessels engaged in whale-watching is driving away these mammals from the Alaskan shores.

All three forms of transport can also contribute to unacceptable levels of noise, whether in rural surroundings or in residential areas, and noise, too, must be considered a form of pollution. Noise, and possible danger to life, has been a factor in attempts to reduce the use of water-bikes off-shore. Water-borne vessels, by dumping fuel or waste overboard, also contribute to water pollution, which in turn affects the wildlife on the rivers and in the sea.

Beaches give particular cause for concern, in that

polluted waters can lead to serious illness among bathers. Britain fares badly in the quality of its off-shore water, which is seriously affected in many regions by raw sewage and other pollutants. Beaches in Britain are monitored by three different agencies. The Tidy Britain group awards yellow-and-blue Seaside flags for beaches that meet their criteria, and the group also monitors beaches on behalf of the European Union, which awards Blue Flags for beaches meeting slightly more stringent criteria, as laid down in the Bathing Water Directive of 1976. Finally, the Marine Conservation Society also plays a role in monitoring beaches and bathing water. In 1999, 224 out of 535 beaches tested failed to meet the EU criteria, and 38 beaches failed even to meet the minimum standards laid down by the Tidy Britain group. Major tourist beaches such as those at Blackpool consistently fail these tests – perhaps it is as well that only some 7 per cent of those spending time on beaches in the UK actually indicate an intention to bathe!

Environmental 'pollution' is as much aesthetic as physical. An area of scenic beauty attracts greater numbers of tourists, so more and more of the natural landscape is lost to tourist development; the countryside retreats before the growth of hotels and other amenities which spring up to cater for the tourists' needs, with the eventual result that the site is no longer seen as 'scenic', and the tourist moves on to find somewhere more tranquil as well as beautiful. Similarly, without careful control, the stately home which tries to meet the needs of its visitors will provide an ever-expanding range of facilities such as larger car parks, cafes, shops, directional signposts and toilet facilities, all of which detract from the appeal of the main attraction. Extreme examples of despoliation of the scenery by signposting are readily found in the United States where, with fewer controls than are exercised in Britain, both countryside and towns can be destroyed by directional signs and advertising hoardings (however, some might argue that at night, the forest of illuminated signs in towns such as Reno or Las Vegas is very much part of the attraction of the resort). At the time of writing, con-

cern is being expressed that Britain is planning similarly to relax its rules on billboards sited in the countryside, and the fear is that this will lead to despoliation of the landscape.

Noise pollution is a problem of contemporary life, especially in towns, but tourism has also made a significant contribution to the problem. In the resorts of the Mediterranean, the peace of the night is destroyed by late-night disco bars catering to tourists. At the Treetops Hotel in Kenya's Masai Mara National Park, animals visiting the adjacent water-hole at night are driven from the site by the careless loud talk or laughter of a minority of the visitors waiting to see them. Noisy motorboats disturb the tranquillity of yachtspeople on the waterways, while aircraft taking off and landing at busy airports severely disturb local residents, especially if there are no restrictions on night flying.

Authorities have recognized the problem of air traffic noise, and some have taken action to reduce it. For example, aircraft are categorized under three classes, known as chapters, according to the noise levels they emit. Under government regulations, especially in the United States, the most recently introduced chapter 3 aircraft, such as the Airbus, are 85 per cent less noisy than were chapter 1 aircraft, and are consequently allowed greater freedom to operate. At a different level, Spanish police are now patrolling down-market resorts such as Magaluf and take action against pubs or nightclubs registering noise levels higher than 65 decibels.

Visual pollution can also be ascribed to insensitivity in the design of buildings for tourism. Lack of planning control is very often to blame, as developers prefer to build more cheaply, leading to high-rise concrete hotels lacking character and out of keeping with the surrounding architecture. British towns are also losing their local character, as builders choose to build in ubiquitous London brick rather than the materials available locally. In the seaside resorts around the world, the concrete skyscraper hotel has become the norm, and from Waikiki in Hawaii to Benidorm in Spain the tourist is confronted with a conformity of architecture which owes nothing to the culture or traditions of the country in which it is built. Some far-seeing authorities have recognized the damage potential, and brought in controls to limit it. In some cases this has led to insistence that hotels must be built in local materials, or conform to 'vernacular' styles of architecture; that is, those indigenous to the region. Others require buildings not to exceed a certain height – for example, Tunisia requires that new hotel developments in tourism resorts should be no higher than the normal height of the palm trees which will surround them. Mauritius has imposed constraints on both the architectural style and the materials employed in hotel building. While some critics have questioned the rather 'staged' results, with thatched cottages vaguely resembling African kraals, no one questions the appeal which these accommodation units have for tourists.

Such legislation clearly must apply to all buildings, not just those for tourism. On Lanzarote, in the Canary Islands, all housing, apartments and hotels are required to conform to rigorous building regulations imposed by the Department of Tourism on the island. These control not only the style of the buildings but the colours in which doors and windows may be painted; only white, blue and green paintwork is permitted. Sometimes, planning controls will have the effect of restricting innovation in architecture, leaving developers to play it safe by falling back on 'pastiche' or bland designs attractive only to the most conservative visitor. The attempt to protect local building styles and materials can sometimes have unexpected results, as in Ireland, where traditional corrugated roofs have now become such a familiar feature of the landscape that they have been designated 'vernacular' building material! (See Figure 17.1.)

Sometimes, the problem of scale can relate to far smaller buildings than hotels, but the significance of the problem is no less. During the early 1990s, two historic properties were both under threat due to plans either to build or to expand visitors' centres adjacent to the site. The Haworth Parsonage, home of the Brontë sisters in the Yorkshire Moors, was threatened with a massive expansion of the visitors' centre,

Figure 17.1 'Traditional' corrugated roofs on a restaurant in Ireland. (*Photographed by the author*)

which would have greatly exceeded the size of the original house; the project resulted in an outcry from the public, and a rethink of the plans. Similarly, trustees of the birthplace of Sir Edward Elgar, in the Malvern Hills, submitted plans for a new visitors' centre adjacent to, and much larger than, the composer's original cottage. This, too, led to a public outcry in the media, but construction went ahead, with a visitor centre resembling, according to one architectural critic, a Tesco supermarket. The problem of providing sufficient room to accommodate all the visitors, some 10,000 a year, at such a small site is a common one and offers no easy solution – or at least, no cheap solution. One plan proposed at Haworth was to conceal the new visitor centre underground, which although an ideal solution, proved to be too costly for the funds available.

Other common forms of visual pollution by tourists include littering, particularly in areas around picnic sites, and graffiti on buildings. It is a curious fact that even those tourists who come from large cities, where they are so used to seeing litter that they become unconscious of it, immediately become aware of the effects of litter in a tourist destination. Resorts which have made the effort to improve their image in recent years tend to start by undertaking a drive against both rubbish in the streets and graffiti on buildings. An important point here, discussed in

Chapter 16, is that litter bins should not only be readily available, but should also be attractively designed. Unfortunately, at many sites not only in Britain but also elsewhere, the fear of terrorist bombs or vandalism has caused rubbish bins to be sealed or removed, creating further difficulties in disposing of rubbish.

In very sensitive areas of the world, such as wilderness regions, littering becomes a major issue because these areas are too far from any public services which could resolve the problem. This is a very real issue in the Himalayas, as trekking becomes more popular in the region. Many trekkers and organized trekking parties are failing to carry out their litter, or to dig latrines to hide human waste, with the result that many valleys are now littered with unsightly rubbish, much of which fails to decompose at these altitudes. Environmentalists are encouraging visitors to ensure all rubbish is either burned or carried out (although local villagers can often make use of tins, bags or bottles), and to bury all human waste. The authorities are being encouraged to build more permanent composting toilets in frequented areas, using the 'twin vault' principle – each vault is used in alternative years, to allow waste to decompose. Nutrients from composted waste can then be used to encourage rapid growth in willow trees, to provide a much-needed timber source for local villagers.

Graffiti has become a common problem in the western world, with thoughtless tourists desecrating ancient monuments with spray-painted, or even chiselled, messages. This of course is no new development: the Romans were chiselling their names on Greek monuments two thousand years ago. But the sheer scale of modern tourism has forced authorities to take action. In extreme cases, this had led to denial of access, as in the case of Stonehenge, where visitors are no longer permitted to walk among the stones themselves, but must be content to view them from a distance.

Problems of congestion and erosion

Perhaps the most significant problem created by mass tourism is that of congestion. This is a complex problem, because it exists at both a *psychological* and a *physical* level.

The latter is more easily measured, in terms of the capacity of an area to absorb the tourist; car parks, streets, beaches, ski slopes, cathedrals and similar features all have a finite limit to the number of tourists which they can accommodate at any given time. However, it is also necessary to understand the psychological capacity of a site. This is the degree of congestion which the tourists will tolerate before the site starts to lose its appeal. Quantifying this is far more difficult, since the perception of capacity will differ, not only according to the nature of the site itself but also according to the market which is attracted to it. A beach in, say, Fiji will be judged overcrowded much more quickly than, say, Bournemouth, while in a resort such as Blackpool a much higher level of crowding may be tolerated, or even welcomed as part of the 'fun experience'. One attempt to measure the psychological capacity of a beach was carried out at Brittas Bay in Ireland in the early 1970s. Aerial photographs were made of the number of tourists on the beach on a crowded Sunday afternoon, and a questionnaire was circulated to those on the beach to receive their views about the congestion. It was found that most visitors would accept around 1,000 people per hectare (ten square metres per person) without feeling the beach was overcrowded.

In so-called *wilderness* areas, of course, the psychological capacity of the region may be very low, and areas sensitive to environmental damage may suffer physically from comparatively few visitors. In the United States, Yellowstone and the Everglades National Parks are both physically under severe threat from tourism, and psychologically they are so remote that any mass tourism will greatly reduce their attractiveness. In Britain, from the psychological viewpoint of the hiker, sites such as the Derbyshire Peak District should not support more than a handful of tourists per square kilometre, although the mass influx to its major centres such as Dovedale on an August Bank Holiday fails to act as a deterrent for the majority of day-trippers. Indeed, it

Table 17.1 Visitor capacity for selected sites

Site/activity	Visitors per day/hectare
Forest park	15
Suburban nature park	15–70
High-density picnicking	300–600
Low-density picnicking	60–200
Golf	10–15
Fishing/sailing	5–30
Speedboating	5–10
Waterskiing	5–15
Skiing	100 (per hectare of trails)
Nature trail hiking	40 (per kilometre)
Nature trail horseriding	25–80 (per kilometre)

Source: E Inskeep (1991).

has been demonstrated in the case of Cannock Chase, the beauty spot near Birmingham, that this area draws tourists from the Midlands as much for its role as a social meeting place as for its scenic beauty.

The behaviour of tourists at wilderness sites will be a factor in deciding their psychological capacity. Many trippers to an isolated area will tend to stay close to their cars, and hikers who are prepared to walk a mile or so away from the car park will readily find the solitude they seek. This is obviously a key for tourism planners, since by restricting car parking and access by vehicle to the more remote areas they can effectively restrict these areas to the serious hikers.

Some authorities have tried to set standards for particular types of tourist activity as a guide to planners. Table 17.1 offers one attempt, by the World Tourism Organisation (WTO), to lay down guidelines, in terms of visitors per day per hectare.

The ecological capacity to absorb tourists must also be taken into account. While too many tourists in a built-up area such as the narrow shopping lanes of York or Brighton can detract from tourism, the physical wear and tear on the environment is limited – at least, in the short term. However, too many tourists in a rural or otherwise fragile environment can destroy the balance of nature.

Some idea of the effect of erosion can be gained from a report in the *Guardian* (27 January 1990, 'Everyone a tourist now') which revealed that 400 tons of sand are removed from the beach of Benidorm each year on the soles of holiday-makers' feet!

Some sites are particularly fragile. Many sand dunes have been destroyed or seriously eroded in the United States by the use of beach buggies, and in the UK by motor cycle rallying, which can uproot the few clumps of dune grass on which the ecosystem depends. The UN Environment Programme has reported that three-quarters of all the sand dunes on the Mediterranean coastline between Spain and Sicily have disappeared as a direct result of tourism development. On the Great Barrier Reef off the coast of Queensland, Australia, and elsewhere in the Pacific and Indian Oceans, fragile coral reefs can be easily damaged by divers or snorkelers – even touching or standing on live coral can be sufficient to kill it, and some visitors go so far as to break off pieces for souvenirs. Coral can also be damaged by boats anchoring. However, the bigger companies taking tourists out to the reef by boat are taking on the responsibility to educate the visitors, and during the boat trip the tourists are given instructions on the fragility of the site and how it can be preserved by careful use.

Buildings which face very high levels of demand from tourism create an equally severe problem, with the only solution being strong measures to control access. This can of course lead to disappointment for the tourists. In recent years crowds visiting the Uffizi Gallery and Galleria dell'Accademia, the site of Michelangelo's David, in Florence during peak holiday periods have become so great that the local authorities have had to take the unusual step of temporarily closing the buildings. Florence and Venice face especially heavy demand from international tourists; the latter welcomes over 1.5 million tourists each year to the Doge's Palace and St Mark's Square alone, while on some days as many as 40,000 tourists have visited the Baptistry of San Giovanni and the adjoining Duomo in Florence. Such crowds produce high levels of condensation which affect the thirteenth- and fourteenth-century

Figure 17.2   Coral reef, Whitsunday Islands, Great Barrier Reef, Queensland, Australia. (*Courtesy Tourism Queensland*)

mosaics. The authorities have responded by reducing coaches to the city from 500 to 150 a day, coaches being charged high fees for the privilege and spot checks taking place on arterial roads out of the city to enforce compliance. Numbers admitted to the Baptistry are reduced to 150 at a time, and charges are now being applied for entry.

One particular destination, a UNESCO World Heritage site, became the focus of attention in 2000, when the Peruvian government announced its intention to build a cable car to carry tourists to the long-hidden Inca city of Machu Picchu, now the country's major tourist attraction. A public outcry from UNESCO and the environmental lobby forced a retraction of this plan, although the cable car would have eliminated growing concern about the environmental damage caused to the mountain on which the site is situated, as a result of buses climbing the present steep access road. Initially, the site could only be reached via the Inca Trail, a hazardous narrow footpath which placed a natural ceiling on visitor numbers. The arrival of a railway station near to the foot of the mountain, and now helicopter flights from Cuzco, have caused tourism flows to this popular attraction to rise to over 300,000 a year. The Inca Trail itself attracts some 60,000 trekkers each year, and has forced the Peruvian government to impose a daily limit of 500 trekkers to reduce erosion of the path.

Apart from the pollution caused by tourism, industrial pollution can also greatly reduce the attractiveness of a site to visitors. This can clearly be seen in the case of the Taj Mahal, India's premier tourist attraction, which is attacked by both tourism and industrial pollution. Its 10 million visitors a year are eroding the building, while the white marble exterior surface of the building is suffering the effects of marble cancer caused by pollution from nearby factory chimneys. Recognizing that if steps are not taken soon the building will be forced to close, the government is now controversially closing nearby factories and risking an economic downturn in the area in order to preserve tourism.

Congestion in Britain's National Parks

Many popular rural sites such as National Parks are at risk from the number of visitors they receive – and in the case of Britain, their proximity to centres of high population. Well over 100 million visitors visit the UK's National Parks each year, the Peak District being the most popular with over 22 million visitors – claimed to be the second most visited National Park in the world, after Mount Fuji in Japan. As a result, footpaths are overused, leading to soil becoming impacted, and grass and plants dying. Under some circumstances, the soil becomes loosened, and is then lost through wind erosion. One attempt was made in the early 1990s to counteract the effect on the footpath across the moors near Haworth; some 25,000 visitors had turned parts of the Brontë Way into a quagmire, necessitating flagstones being set into the track. Other running repairs have had to be made to long-distance footpaths such as those on the Pennine Way and Cleveland Way. Such artificial landscaping, of course, creates a very different visual landscape to the wild moorland it replaces, but it is a solution being used more widely, as such footpaths have to deal with greater numbers of visitors each year. In places, these popular paths in the National Parks have widened to 45 yards.

Climbers, too, will also damage the parks. With the increased interest in activity holidays, climbing is becoming a very popular pastime; some 250,000 people climb Mam Tor in Derbyshire every year, and this has so affected the mountain that the summit had to be restored with an importation of 300 tons of rock and soil.

The impact of winter sports tourism

One fragile ecosystem in Europe is under particular threat. This is the Alps, and because the system is spread across no fewer than seven countries, collaboration to prevent the worst of the environmental effects of tourism is more difficult. The Alps receive over 50 million international visitors a year, and some 7 million passenger vehicles cross them each year, as they lie at the heart of Europe. To accommodate the huge increase in winter sports tourism that has occurred since World War II, some 41,000 ski runs have been built, capable of handling 1.5 million skiers an hour.

The region suffers in a number of ways. The proliferation of ski-lifts, chalets and concrete villages above 6,000 feet, and the substantial deforestation required to make way for pistes, have led to soil erosion, while acid rain caused partly by high volumes of traffic crossing the Alps is having a serious impact on the remaining forests, 60 per cent of which are now affected. Artificial snow-making machines have smothered alpine plants, reducing the vegetation, while wildlife has also declined as the animals' territories are reduced. A new danger is posed by the introduction of roller skiing on grass and four-wheel drive car racing in summer. Potential damage, both ecological and economic, to the region is now so great that an organization, Alp Action, has been set up, with the support of the Aga Khan, to help preserve the Alps as a single ecosystem. It has to be added, however, that not all authorities welcome further control in this fashion; some Swiss cantons have expressed concern at the potential slowdown in the economic development of their region which results from this conservation movement.

Other authorities have already taken steps to control overuse. At Lech and Zuers in Austria, skiers are counted by computer through turnstiles which give them access to the pistes. Once 14,000, deemed capacity, have been admitted, tourists are diverted to other sites. Lillehammer in Norway, site of the 1994 Winter Olympic Games, took account of the problems already occurring in the Alps when designing its new facilities. Apart from efforts to minimize tree clearance, the authorities also took steps to avoid visual pollution in an area where comparatively few buildings exist; ski-jump runs were moulded into the mountainside to ensure they did not project above the tree line, and similar efforts were made to conceal bob and luge runs in the forests. The speed skating stadium was built twenty yards away from the water's edge to protect waterfowl, and leak-proof cooling systems were embedded underground in concrete containers. Private cars were excluded from the town during the period of the Games.

It is not only sports activities which can threaten a snowscape. Glaciers, whose ecosystems are invariably fragile, attract large numbers of sightseers when located in accessible regions. At the Columbia Icefield in Banff National Park, Canada, giant snowmobiles are employed to bring tourists on to the glacier (see Figure 17.3). The inevitable consequence of

too many vehicle trips will be damage to the surface of the site, unless careful control is exercised over the numbers carried.

Erosion of buildings by tourists on foot

Although constructed sites are less fragile, nonetheless they too can be affected by erosion in the long term. The Acropolis in Athens has had to be partially closed to tourists to avoid wear and tear on the floors of ancient buildings, while the wooden floors and staircases of popular attractions such as Shakespeare's birthplace in Stratford-upon-Avon or Beaulieu Palace in Hampshire also suffer from the countless footsteps to which they are subjected each year. Stratford, with a population of only 23,000, receives over 3.8 million visitors every year, a substantial proportion of whom will want to visit Shakespeare's birthplace or Anne Hathaway's cottage. These numbers led major attractions to construct artificial walkways above the level of the floor to preserve the original flooring. Nearly a million people visit Bath's Pump Room and Roman Baths complex each year, and inevitably there will be fears for the original stone flooring in the Baths; but it may put the problem into context when it is revealed that Roman visitors, wearing hob-nailed boots, did even more damage to the flooring than do contemporary visitors, though they were far fewer in number.

Figure 17.3 Snowmobiles at the Columbian Icefield, Alberta, Canada. (*Photographed by the author*)

The tourism danger to flora and fauna

Even souvenir-hunting can affect the ecological balance of a region. The removal of plants has long given cause for concern (the Swiss were expressing anxiety about the tourists' habit of picking gentians and other alpine flowers even before the start of the mass tourism movement), and in Arizona, visitors taking home cacti are affecting the ecology of the desert. The removal, either as souvenirs or for commercial sale by tourist enterprises, of coral and rare shells from regions in the Pacific is also giving cause for concern.

But perhaps of even greater concern is the threat to endangered animal species from tourism. There are many examples to cite. Animals hunted down by tourist safari vehicles in the African game reserves have declined due to lack of privacy to mate; logger-head turtles in Greece and Turkey are distracted from laying their eggs by the bright lights of tourist resorts and the use of searchlights to observe their coming ashore to lay their eggs on the beach. At Philip Island, near Melbourne in Australia, 500,000 people a year come to sit and watch the evening 'penguin parade' of fairy penguins coming ashore to their nests. This event has become highly commercialized, and the large crowds are proving hard to control, even though ropes are in place to prevent people getting too close to the penguins. Flash photography is forbidden, and wardens caution the audiences against noise or even standing up, all of which disturb and alarm the penguins; however, in practice the public frequently ignores these strictures.

Animal behaviour can change from prolonged exposure to tourists. In some countries, food lures are used to attract wildlife to a particular locality; for example, in Samburu National Park, Kenya, goats are slaughtered and hung up for crocodiles or leopards. This modifies hunting behaviour, and may encourage dependency upon human feeding. In some wildlife parks, hyenas are known to watch for assemblies of four-wheel drive vehicles in order to take the prey from cheetahs' hunts. 'Bearjams' are created in Yellowstone National Park, USA, as bears trade photo opportunities in exchange for offerings of food.

An excellent example of sustainable tourism at a wildlife park is demonstrated at Xigera Camp, in Botswana's Okavango Delta. A sandpit between the river and camp is raked clean each night, and the following morning the guide provides a short talk for the tourists by identifying the prints of nocturnal animals which have visited the site to drink.

The desire to bring back souvenirs of animals seen abroad poses another form of threat to endangered species. The Convention on International Trade in Endangered Species (CITES) imposes worldwide restrictions on the importation of certain animals and animal products from countries visited by tourists. Around 34,000 endangered species have been identified, and the importation of many of these or their by-products is banned, including ivory, sea turtle products, spotted cat furs, coral, reptile skins and sea shells, as well as certain rare plants. Concern is also expressed about the ill-treatment of animals which are kept in captivity for the amusement of tourists. Performing bears are still a common sight on the streets of some Eastern European countries, while even some EU countries tolerate the exploitation of chimpanzees or monkeys which are used for tourist photographs in Spain. A number of action groups in Britain have been set up to protect and free these animals.

Other environmental consequences of mass tourism

Many popular tourist towns have narrow roads, leading not only to problems of severe traffic congestion, but also to potential damage to buildings as coaches try to navigate through these streets. Increasingly, cars and particularly coaches are restricted from access to the centres of such towns, with park and ride schemes or other strategies employed to reduce traffic. However, impeding coaches from picking up and setting down passengers in the centre of towns like Bath or Oxford can make it very difficult for coach companies to operate, as many are on short stopover visits as part of a day trip.

Many developing countries face similar problems of congestion and erosion, as the popularity of long-haul travel expands. Goa in India was hailed by many operators as an 'unspoilt paradise', but its wide appeal since the 1990s has caused environmental lobbyists such as Tourism Concern to draw attention to the dangers the region faces. Water shortages in the area are aggravated by the tourist consumption (one five-star hotel uses as much water as five villages, and locals face water shortages while swimming pools are

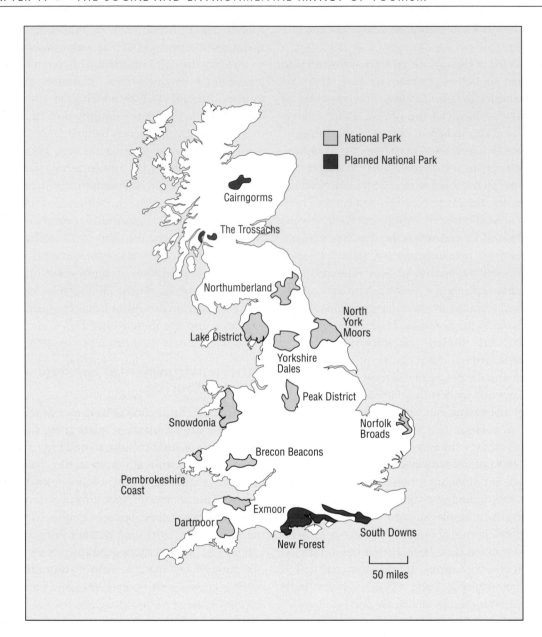

Figure 17.4 National Parks of England and Wales (including other parks of similar status)

filled), and sand dunes have been flattened. Apart from the environmental impact, there is also a social cost, with private beaches denying access to the locals, and a 'westernization' of the local carnival which dilutes the traditional identity and culture of the region. The problems of Goa have been well pub-

licized in recent years, but this has had little effect in reducing the number of visitors or ensuring that tourism in the area is sustainable.

Sometimes, well-meaning attempts by tourist officials to 'improve' an attraction can have the opposite effect. Historic rock carvings over 3,000 years old in

Scandinavia were painted to make them stand out for visitors. When the paint eventually flakes off, a process that has speeded up with the effect of acid rain, it takes part of the rock surface with it.

Any tourism development will invariably require the sacrifice of natural landscape to make way for tourist facilities. An extreme example of this is to be found in the demand for golf courses. Golf as a holiday activity, especially among Japanese tourists, has led to a huge increase in demand for courses in the Pacific region; for example, the island of Oahu in Hawaii, which had already constructed twenty-seven courses by 1985, received a further thirty applications after the Hawaii legislature agreed to allow them to be built on agricultural land. Apart from the loss of natural scenery, golf courses also require huge amounts of fresh water, which in some areas of low rainfall imposes a severe burden on local resources.

Planning for control and conservation

We have now seen many examples of the environmental impact of tourism, and a few illustrations of how the problems might be managed. Some argue that it is not enough for individual authorities to tackle the situation; that it should be tackled on a global scale. Unfortunately, governments so far have appeared unwilling to tackle the issue on this scale. International designation of an attraction as a World Heritage Site by UNESCO, the United Nations Educational, Scientific and Cultural Organisation, undoubtedly helps, but Stonehenge, arguably Britain's greatest heritage attraction, is so designated and yet the site has been called a 'national disgrace' by the Public Accounts Committee of the House of Commons, financial support from the Millennium fund was refused, and arguments continue about how best the site should be developed and protected.

In 1992 a UN Conference on Environment and Development, the so-called Earth Summit, was held at Rio de Janeiro. Although tourism did not appear as an issue on the agenda of this meeting, its development is influenced by some of the decisions taken at that conference, notably Agenda 21, a guide for local government action to reconcile development and sustainability of the environment. One promising development is that the United Nations has designated 2002 as the International Year of Ecotourism (IYE), and a world ecotourism summit is planned to be held in Canada that year, which will help to focus public interest on the issue. Elsewhere, leads have been given by the WTO and the World Travel and Tourism Council (WTTC), both of which support the concept of sustainable tourism which is designed to minimize damage to the environment, wildlife and local indigenous populations. They have particularly recommended the use of local building materials for tourist sites, the recycling of waste and water and the recruitment of locals for jobs within tourism. Together with the Earth Council, these two bodies published a report, *Agenda 21 for the Travel and Tourism Industry: Towards Environmentally Sustainable Development*, which encourages the industry to take the lead in preserving the environment in the areas they develop.

The European Union has taken an active role in recent years to attempt to control the worst effects of environmental pollution, with its Blue Flag scheme to identify beaches meeting agreed standards of cleanliness. Although Britain's record is not good in comparison with some other EU countries, not all countries carry out every required test at their beaches, so figures may not be comparable.

At a national level, the concept of managing and protecting tourism sites of scenic beauty is by no means a new one. As early as 1872, the United States established its first National Park at Yellowstone, while Europe's Abisco National Park in Sweden dates from 1909. The intention behind the creation of these parks was to ensure that visitors did not destroy the landscapes they had come to see. Sustainability may be a word of recent origin in tourism, but the concept is much older.

Protection in the UK

In Britain, growing concern over possible despoliation of the Lake District led to the formation of a Defence Society in 1883 to protect the region from commercial exploitation. The National Trust was created in 1894 to safeguard places of 'historic interest and natural beauty', and promptly bought four and a half acres of clifftop in Cardigan Bay.

The National Parks and Access to the Countryside Act 1949 led to the formation of ten National Parks in England and Wales, each administered by a National Park Authority. The Norfolk Broads achieved equivalent National Park status under the Norfolk and Suffolk Broads Act of 1988. The New Forest in Hampshire and the South Downs are planned to become new National Parks in England, the latter formed from two existing Areas of Outstanding Natural Beauty (see Figure 17.4), while in Scotland plans are under way to create the first designated national park, Loch Lomond and the Trossachs. The Cairngorms region is also to be considered as a further national park in Scotland.

The National Parks Act led to the designation of thirty-seven areas (nearly 8 per cent of the area of England and Wales) as Areas of Outstanding Natural Beauty meriting protection against exploitation; the first of these, the Quantock Hills in Somerset, was designated in 1957, and the last, the Tamar Valley in England's West Country, in 1995. Since this date, there have been numerous moves to protect features of historical or architectural interest, or areas of scenic beauty, from over-development, whether from tourism or other commercial interests. Notable among these are some 150 designated nature reserves and a large number of Sites of Special Scientific Interest (SSSI) which contain rare flora or fauna. An EU Wildlife and Habitats Directive gives stronger protection to some of the most notable SSSIs, which were decreed Special Areas of Conservation in 2000.

The UK government recognizes the growing threat posed by tourism, and more generally by leisure. The Government Task Force report, *Tourism and the Environment: Maintaining the Balance*, which is discussed later in this chapter, stressed the need for harmony between the visitor, the place and the host community, and a further report from the House of Commons Environment Committee, *The Environmental Impact of Leisure Activities*, appeared in 1995.

Managing sustainable tourism

Planning controls, whether executed centrally or regionally, are essential to avoid the inevitable conflicts of interest that arise between the public and private sectors. Private enterprise, unrestricted, will seek to maximize profits, often in the short term, and this can best be achieved by concentrating marketing effort on the most popular attractions and destinations, rather than seeking to develop new destinations. Airlines will find it more profitable to focus on the routes already producing the most traffic, while hotels in a boom resort will build large and relatively cheap properties, if this can be shown to produce the best level of profits. Of course, it would be wrong to suggest that this always occurs – other organizations will see the market gaps left for better quality development – but without some form of central control to ensure good design and careful restoration of old buildings, the original attraction of a traditional resort can be lost.

Local authorities can also be a partner to this despoliation, putting commercial advantage before aesthetic considerations. Spain experienced a sudden boom in tourism during the 1960s, but the resulting massive overdevelopment along its east coast and in the Balearic and Canary Islands nearly destroyed its success. Failure to maintain the quality of the environment in other directions can also lead to a massive loss of tourist business, as the popular Spanish resort of Salou found, following a drinking water scare in 1989. However, the widespread fall-off in visitors to Spain as a whole in the 1980s and 1990s caused a reversal of policy and much greater control over speculative tourism development. A good example of this can be found in the Balearics, whose parliament passed legislation in 1991 to nominate large tracts of land in Majorca, Ibiza and Formentera as restricted zones for further development. In Majorca, only four- and five-star hotels were permitted to be constructed, with a minimum of 120 square metres of land per bed, in an effort to drive tourism up-market; in order for planning permission to be granted for the construction of new hotels, developers have been required to purchase and knock down an existing and deteriorating hotel of inferior status. Badly run-down resorts like Magaluf were given an injection of capital to widen pavements, introduce traffic-free zones, plant trees and shrubs and install new litter bins and graffiti-free seating. In all, Spain spent over £300 million in the five years prior to 1993 in improving tourism facilities along its coasts. However, once a resort has gone down-market, the evidence suggests that it is very hard to bring back a higher quality of tourist, and there is a very real danger that new high-price hotels will still fail to attract a new market.

A general awareness of the problems which tourism creates led to a new movement to curtail its excesses. This movement called for a new tourism, variously described as 'sustainable tourism', 'eco-tourism', 'green tourism', 'soft tourism' or 'responsible tourism'. Proponents argued that tourism needed to be developed as part of a properly thought out management strategy, with collaboration between the private and public sectors, to prevent irreparable damage to the environment before it was too late.

This concern was first expressed when the WTO and the United Nations Environment Programme issued a joint declaration in 1982, calling for the rational management of tourism to protect, enhance and improve the environment. In the following year these bodies suggested employing zoning strategies to concentrate tourists in those regions which could absorb them and to disperse them where environments were too fragile to sustain mass tourism.

It is important to recognize that not all tourists are seeking the same forms of tourism, just as the terms used above to describe the new tourism are not necessarily synonymous. Eco-tourism has been

Figure 17.5 Sustainable tourism: signs can play a role in directing tourists towards good practice. (*Photographed by the author*)

described (by the environmentalist Hector Ceballos-Lascurain) as, 'travelling to relatively undisturbed or uncontaminated natural areas with the specific objective of studying, admiring and enjoying the scenery and its wild plants and animals, as well as any existing cultural manifestations ... found in these areas'. This is clearly not a description of the activities of the vast masses of tourists who go on holiday each year. However, it is appropriate to argue that all forms of tourism should be 'sustainable', and that they should not destroy the destination to which the tourist is attracted. The growth of tourism must be environmentally compatible, as the World Travel and Tourism Council proposed in its ten-point guideline (see Figure 17.6).

In Britain, a government Task Force issued a report in 1991 giving a British view on the problem. The report, *Tourism and the Environment: Maintaining the Balance*, offered similar homilies, but one fears that without sanctions, the degree of sensitivity to the environment exercised by tour operators or developers will be limited.

Where the public sector has introduced legislation prohibiting development, or controlling tourism, sustainable tourism shows promise of being achieved. There is also now a growing number of

1 Identify and minimize product and operational environmental problems, paying particular attention to new projects.

2 Pay due regard to environmental concerns in design, planning, construction and implementation.

3 Be sensitive to conservation of environmentally protected or threatened areas, species or scenic aesthetics, achieving landscape enhancement where possible.

4 Practise energy conservation, reduce and recycle waste, practise freshwater management and control sewage disposal.

5 Control and diminish air emissions and pollutants.

6 Monitor, control and reduce noise levels.

7 Control, reduce and eliminate environmentally unfriendly products, such as asbestos, CFCs, pesticides and toxic, corrosive, infectious, explosive or flammable material.

8 Respect and support historic or religious objects and sites.

9 Exercise due regard for the interests of local populations, including their history, traditions and culture and future development.

10 Consider environmental issues as a key factor in the overall development of travel and tourism destinations.

Figure 17.6   A guideline for sustainable tourism. (*Courtesy World Travel and Tourism Council*)

examples of private companies, as we shall see below, introducing their own initiatives to ensure tourism is sustainable. Actions undertaken by public or private bodies have included:

- closing sites, either permanently (in cases such as Stonehenge or Lascaux caves) or temporarily (as in the examples at Lech and Zuers given earlier);

- reducing publicity, e.g. by limiting road signs; local authorities have dropped reference to 'Constable Country' in their marketing of Dedham Vale (on the Essex–Suffolk border) due to congestion in the area caused by the popularity of visiting landscapes made famous by one of England's most renowned painters;

- requiring advance bookings, or admitting those with tickets bearing specific admission times;

- introducing campaigns, such as the 'Keep Britain Tidy' campaign, to create greater public awareness of the problem, or providing awards, such as the 'Tourism for Tomorrow' award, to reward organiz-

ations making the best efforts to market sustainable tourism products;

- pricing mechanisms to reduce or manage demand; road pricing has been proposed for the North York Moors, coupled with the banning of cars on peak days of the year. Highland councillors have proposed a £1 fee for ramblers climbing Ben Nevis, Britain's highest mountain, as a means of paying for toilet facilities, litter collection, car parks and repairs to the mountain paths damaged by thousands of walkers each year.

There are many examples of successful control drawing on variations of these techniques. Highly fragile destinations in the developing world such as the Galapagos Islands restrict the total numbers of tourists that will be admitted each year, as well as imposing a high-cost entry tax, receipts from which go towards the conservation of the territory; the islands are divided into three zones, of which only two are open to visitors. However, even here control has been inadequate; the original carrying capacity of the islands was judged to be 12,000, but increasing demand led this to be 're-interpreted' at 36,000. There is evidence that this figure is exceeded, especially taking into account the visits of private yachts, which are difficult to monitor. Some of these visiting yachts are known to have thrown refuse overboard, littering the shores. Nevertheless, the tight control over tourists visiting the island, all of whom must be accompanied by rangers, is an exemplary model for sustainable tourism: rules of conduct while ashore are given to each visitor (see Figure 17.7). Belize has also introduced very tight legislation drawing on a number of these techniques to avoid the destruction of its ecosystem, both in its rain forests and in the tropical waters of its shores.

Tourism, of course, can also be controlled simply by failing to provide the infrastructure it demands. Several of the most attractive Greek islands remain relatively unspoiled by tourism simply because they are accessible only by ferry or jetfoil craft; the failure to construct airports is a major factor in limiting tourism growth.

RULES TO BE OBSERVED WHILE IN
GALAPAGOS NATIONAL PARK

Galapagos is yours to enjoy. Will your grandchildren still have the chance to see it as you do? Your help is needed to protect it. Please help the National Park to conserve Galapagos by following and helping to enforce these rules:

1. NO PLANT, ANIMAL, OR REMAINS OF THEM (SHELLS, BONES, PIECES OF WOOD), OR OTHER NATURAL OBJECTS, SHOULD BE RE-MOVED OR DISTURBED.

   Actions such as these are illegal and cause serious harm to the island's ecological conditions.

2. BE CAREFUL NOT TO TRANSPORT ANY LIVE MATERIAL TO THE ISLANDS, OR FROM ISLAND TO ISLAND. Check your clothing before landing on any of the islands for seeds or insects and destroy them or keep them on your vessel for disposal later on. Check your boot or shoe soles for dried mud before you leave your boat. This material will frequently contain seed and spores of plants and animals. Inadvertent transport of these materials represents a special danger to Galapagos. Each island has its own unique fauna and flora, and introduced plants and animals can quickly destroy this uniqueness. These rules also apply to pets and other animals and plants. DO NOT BRING THEM TO THE ISLANDS. One of the most destructive forces in Galapagos are feral organisms (domesticated species gone wild) which have been brought to Galapagos by man.

3. For the same reasons expressed in No. 2 DO NOT TAKE ANY FOOD TO THE UNINHABITED ISLANDS. It is easy to introduce, together with the food, insects or other organisms which might be dangerous to the fragile island ecosystems. Fresh fruits and vegetables are especially dangerous. The orange seed that you drop may become a tree.

4. ANIMALS MAY NOT BE TOUCHED OR HAND-LED. All wild animals dislike this and will quickly lose their remarkable tameness if thus treated by human invaders.

5. ANIMALS MAY NOT BE FED. Not only can it be dangerous to your own person but in the long run it can destroy the animal's social structure and affect their reproduction. You came here to see a completely natural situation. Do not interfere with it.

Figure 17.7   Rules to be observed while in Galapagos National Park   *continued*

6. DO NOT STARTLE OR CHASE ANY ANIMAL FROM ITS RESTING OR NESTING SPOT. Exercise extreme care among the breeding colonies of sea birds. Be especially careful not to drive boobies, cormorants, gulls, or frigate birds from their nests. These birds will fly from their nests if startled, often knocking the egg or chick to the ground or leaving it exposed to the sun. (A recently hatched booby chick will die in 20 to 30 minutes if exposed to the sun; frigate birds will also eat any unguarded chick.)

7. DO NOT LEAVE THE AREAS WHICH ARE DESIGNATED AS VISITING SITES. In the more heavily used visitor sites there are trails or areas marked with wooden stakes within which the visitor should remain. The trails are designed to guide the visitor to all of the points of interest within a given visitor site, and at the same time to protect the resource.

8. LITTER OF ALL TYPES MUST BE KEPT OFF THE ISLANDS. DISPOSAL AT SEA MUST BE LIMITED TO CERTAIN TYPES OF GARBAGE, ONLY TO BE THROWN OVERBOARD IN SELECTED AREAS. Keep all rubbish (film wrappers, cigarette butts, chewing gum, tin cans, bottles, etc.) in a bag or pocket, to be disposed of on your boat. The crew of your vessel is responsible to the National Park for proper trash disposal. You should never throw anything overboard. A few examples of the damage that can be caused:
   – Sea lions will pick a tin off the bottom and play with it, cutting their highly sensitive muzzles.
   – Sea turtles will eat plastic thrown overboard and die, for it blocks their digestive tracts.
   – Rubbish thrown overboard near an island will usually be carried to shore where, as it accumulates, will convert a once beautiful area into a rubbish pile, in addition to causing problems for the native plants and animals.

9. DO NOT BUY SOUVENIRS OR OBJECTS MADE FROM PLANTS OR ANIMALS OF THE ISLANDS, with the exception of articles made from wood. The best way to discourage this trade is to simply not buy any of these articles. If anyone offers you any of these souvenirs, please advise the National Park.

10. CAMPING ANYWHERE IN GALAPAGOS WITHOUT A PERMIT IS AGAINST THE LAW.

Camping is permitted only in certain sites designated by the National Park. Consult with the central office of the National Park in Sta. Cruz for further information.

11. WHEN CAMPING, DO NOT BUILD CAMPFIRES. Use a gasoline or kerosene stove. Fire scars are ugly and the fire itself may easily cause a brushfire in this dry climate. Dead trees which one would use for fuel, play their own role in the island's ecosystem and are better left alone.

12. DO NOT PAINT NAMES OR GRAFFITI ON ROCKS. It is against the law and it is extremely ugly to look at. Immortality can't be more important than the Island's natural beauty.

13. ALL GROUPS WHICH VISIT THE NATIONAL PARK MUST BE ACCOMPANIED BY A QUALIFIED GUIDE APPROVED BY THE NATIONAL PARK. The visitor has the responsibility to follow the instructions of the guide of his group in any situation, since it is the guide who is responsible for assuring that the regulations of the National Park related to the conservation of the flora and fauna are complied with.

14. THE NATIONAL PARK IS DIVIDED INTO DIFFERENT ZONES TO FACILITATE ITS MANAGEMENT AND ADMINISTRATION. There are certain sites where tourist activities are permitted, and others where the public is restricted or prohibited. The boat captains and guides know which are the visitor sites and will be responsible for obtaining the proper permits. Nevertheless, the personnel in the office of the National Park are available to answer any questions you may have.

15. DO NOT HESITATE TO SHOW YOUR CONSERVATIONIST ATTITUDE. Explain these rules to others, and help to enforce them. Notify the National Park Service if you see any serious damage being done. You may be a decisive factor in the Island's preservation.

Always feel free to visit the National Park Service's offices and the Charles Darwin Research Station if you have any questions. Your understanding of the Islands is important to their conservation. Enjoy yourself fully, but never at the expense of what you came here to see.

GALAPAGOS NATIONAL PARK

Government policies to attract large numbers of tourists have given way to policies designed to attract particular tourist markets. While this has in most cases meant trying to attract wealthy, high-spend visitors, it has sometimes led to a move to encourage visits by those who will have the least impact on local populations, i.e. those who will integrate and accept local customs rather than seeking to impose their own standards on locals. In contrast, the local authority at Alassio, Italy, took rather extreme action in 1994, in an effort to discourage day-trippers and *sacopelisti* (sleeping-baggers), who slept on the beaches and brought little income into the town, by asking the railways to provide fewer trains to the resort on weekends. Tourists were also to be accosted and asked to show that they were carrying at least 50,000 lire as spending money.

One question which concerns governments is whether to opt for a policy of dispersing tourists, or concentrating them. Mass charter movements of tourists are naturally easier to contain in one area, while the independent tourist will be less satisfied to be accommodated in one area along with countless other tourists. The simple belief that the independent traveller is in some ways 'greener' than the mass tourist cannot necessarily be sustained, however. Certainly, in terms of energy consumption, a full charter aircraft of package tourists does less damage to the environment than the same number of independent travellers spread across several half-empty scheduled flights. Similarly, it can be argued that maintaining tourists in one area – the 'ghetto' principle of tourism planning – rather than dispersing them across the country has the effect of limiting the damage to one relatively small area, and avoids possible confrontations between hosts and tourists, although admittedly it reduces opportunities to 'meet the natives'. Public sector bodies have taken different directions on this issue, with Senegal and Indonesia attempting to disperse their tourists to avoid the development of tourism enclaves, in order to provide tourists with better contacts with the locals. Countries such as Tunisia, on the other hand, have developed resorts well away from populated areas to reduce the impact of tourism on the local population. Neither solution is the perfect answer. While the ghetto approach has advantages in conserving the environment away from the tourists, it alienates the tourist from the culture and life of the community and also impacts on the local economy, reducing the spend in local shops and enhancing it within the (often foreign-owned) hotels.

Industry's contribution to sustainable tourism

The public sector can impose controls, but without the cooperation of the tourism industry, sustainable tourism cannot be truly achieved. There is now evidence that many companies in Britain and elsewhere have come to understand the importance of sustainable tourism, not simply as a gimmick to attract public goodwill, but as a long-term strategy for survival and growth. In this, Britain's Green Flag International, a small lobby of concerned environmental interests, was influential in persuading travel companies during the 1990s to adopt a more responsible approach in their marketing and operations, awarding a Green Flag to those organizations it deemed to have reached an acceptable standard in this respect. Pointing to the huge wastage of travel brochures each year, it encouraged companies to recycle unused brochures. While a number of companies did switch to using recycled paper in their brochure production, few were willing to shoulder the cost burden of collecting and recycling brochures at the end of each year. In 1998, the World Travel and Tourism Council picked up this lead by introducing its Green Globe awards; certificates were given to companies from all sectors of the travel business which met agreed environmental standards. The Tourism Concern lobby in Britain exercises far more influence than could be expected from such an ill-funded organization in mounting campaigns for sustainable tourism. It has argued effectively against pollution of the Himalayas from climbing and trekking tourists, who leave litter on the mountainsides and use scarce wood resources for fires. It has also campaigned effectively against tourism to Burma, where it claims many of the population have been evacuated from their homes or pressed into labour to provide for the construction of tourist facilities. The Countryside Agency has also played a part, by introducing a Green Audit Kit which alerted companies as to how they could best 'green' their tourism businesses.

While the public sector has taken the lead in encouraging sustainable tourism, there have been numerous private sector initiatives also. The Association of Independent Tour Operators (AITO), which is composed of smaller companies, many carrying tourists to environmentally sensitive areas of the globe, encourages its members to adopt sustainable tourism policies. A Tour Operators' Initiative for sustainable tourism development was launched in 2000 with the cooperation of a number of international tour operators supported by the UN Environmental Programme, UNESCO and the WTO. The aim of this initiative is to get operators to share best practice in environmental management and auditing, to make more efficient use of energy and resources and to create tours with less environmental and social impact.

Individually, some companies, led by British Airways, have undertaken an 'environmental audit' of their operations. BA also plays a part in making annual awards to companies or destinations demonstrating good sustainable practice. The Intercontinental Hotels chain undertook its own worldwide environmental audit at the beginning of the 1990s, which led to a policy of recycling waste and introducing cruelty-free (not tested on animals) toiletries in the guest rooms. Some hotels in Hawaii have installed flow regulators on showers and taps to control water wastage. Other examples of hotel chains which have introduced environmental policies were examined in Chapter 10.

Walt Disney Enterprises recycle oils, paints and cleaning materials used on their sites. Thomson Holidays has shown a keen interest in sustainable tourism, and among other activities has sponsored new litter bins in resorts in the Mediterranean.

Center Parcs has made its resorts in the UK car-free zones, and offers visitors the use of bicycles during their stay. The specialist operator Turkish Delight Holidays, with the support of the environmentalist David Bellamy, launched a campaign to prevent further destruction by tourism of turtle nesting areas. The German airline Lufthansa introduced snacks at departure gates to avoid wastage resulting from serving in-flight meals (as well as being sustainable, this is also highly cost-efficient!).

There is still some scepticism as to the extent to which these activities are a genuine response to the threat to our environment, as opposed to a public relations exercise to win public favour. Nevertheless, what did start out for many companies as a marketing ploy has later turned to a genuine commitment to improve the environment. Perhaps the example of Cox and Kings, the oldest British tour operator, best demonstrates a commitment to sustainable tourism; the company promised that for every customer buying one of its 'environmental journey' holidays, it would buy one acre of rainforest in Belize, to be kept in its natural state in perpetuity. The relatively high cost of these package tours allows for some discretionary spending of this sort; the challenge will be to encourage down-market operators to increase their own prices to allow for a more sustainable product to be delivered. So far, however, the evidence in Britain suggests that while the public are keen on the concept, they are reluctant in practice to fund it through higher prices.

The socio-cultural effects of tourism

The cultural and social impact on a host country of large numbers of people, sharing different value systems and away from the constraints of their own environment, is a subject increasingly drawing the attention of social scientists and planners, especially those responsible for promoting tourism in the developing countries. The impact of mass tourism is most noticeable in less developed countries, but is by no means restricted to these; tourism has con-

Table 17.2 Adaptation of tourists to local norms

Type of tourist	Numbers of tourists	Adaptation to local norms
Explorer	Very limited	Adapts fully
Elite	Rarely seen	Adapts fully
Off-beat	Uncommon, but seen	Adapts well
Unusual	Occasional	Adapts somewhat
Incipient mass	Steady flow	Seeks western amenities
Mass	Continuous influx	Expects western amenities
Charter	Massive arrivals	Demands western amenities

Source: Reprinted from Valene Smith, *Hosts and Guests*, 1992, © Blackwell Publishers Ltd.

tributed to an increase in crime and other social problems in New York and London, in Hawaii and Miami, in Florence and Corfu.

Any influx of tourism, however small, will make some impact on a region, but the extent of the impact is dependent not just upon numbers but also on the kind of tourists which the region attracts. The mass tourist is less likely to adapt to the local cultures, and will seek amenities and standards found in the home country, while the independent traveller or backpacker will adapt more readily to an alien environment. This has been exemplified in a model devised by Valene Smith (see Table 17.2).

Explorers, or tourists whose main interest is to meet and understand people from different cultures and backgrounds, will fully accept and acclimatize to the foreign culture. These travellers will generally travel independently, and be as little visible as possible. However, as increasingly remote areas of the world are 'packaged' for wealthy tourists, and as ever larger numbers of tourists travel farther afield to find relaxation or adventure, these tourists bring with them their own value systems, either expecting or demanding the lifestyle and facilities to which they are accustomed in their own country.

At its simplest and most direct, this flow of comparatively wealthy tourists to a region will attract petty criminals, as evidenced by increases in thefts or muggings – a problem that has become serious in some areas of the Mediterranean, in Florida, Latin America, the Caribbean and Russia. As tourism expands in eastern Europe, taxi drivers in Poland, the Czech Republic and Hungary have been found to overcharge gullible tourists, in some cases by manipulating their meters. Tourists may also be seen as easy prey when making purchases in shops or from street vendors. This has become a noted problem in London, where street vendors overcharge tourists for ice-cream. Where gambling is a corner-stone of tourism growth, prostitution and organized crime often follow. Certain countries which have more relaxed laws on sexual behaviour than those in the west attract tourists for sexual encounters, and in some countries, notably Germany and Japan, tour operators organize package tours to destinations such as the Philippines and Thailand for this specific purpose. This public promotion of commercial sex, especially where it involves sex with minors, has come under increasing criticism in the western world from organizations like the World Council of Churches and Tourism Concern. Britain, following the example of other western countries, has passed legislation to enable paedophiles to be prosecuted in their home country for offences committed abroad.

There are a number of less direct, and perhaps less visible, effects on tourist localities, including the phenomenon known as 'relative deprivation'. The comparative wealth of tourists may be resented or envied by the locals, particularly where the influx is seen by the latter as a form of neo-colonialism, as in the Caribbean or some African countries. Locals come to experience dissatisfaction with their own standards of living or way of life, and seek to emulate that of the tourist. In some cases, the effect of this is marginal, as in the adoption of the tourists' dress or fashions, but in others the desire to emulate the tourist can threaten deep-seated traditions in the community, as well as leading to aspirations which are impossible to meet.

Job opportunities and the higher salaries paid to workers in the tourist industry will attract workers from agricultural and rural communities who, freed from the restrictions of their families and home environments, may abandon their traditional values. This can result in an increase in promiscuity, and the breakdown of marriages.

The problem of interaction between the host and tourist is that any relationships which develop are fleeting and superficial, and are often conducted for commercial ends. A report by UNESCO in 1976 identified four characteristics of host–guest relations in tourism:

1. relations are transitory and superficial;
2. they are undertaken under constraints of time and space, with visitors compacting sights into as limited amount of time as possible;
3. there is a lack of spontaneity in relations; meetings tend to be prearranged to fit tour schedules, and involve mainly financial transactions;
4. relations are unequal and imbalanced, due to disparities in wealth and status of the participants.

Most tourists visiting a new country for the first time, who may be spending no more than a week in that country and do not expect to return, will be eager to condense their experiences, to a point where each tends to be brief and superficial. Add to this an initial fear of contact with locals, and tourists' comparative isolation – hotels often being dispersed away from centres of local activity – and opportunities for any meaningful relationship become very limited. Few relationships are spontaneous; contact is generally with locals who work within the tourism industry, or else it is mediated by couriers. Language may form an impenetrable barrier to genuine local contact, and this limitation can lead to mutual misunderstanding. The relationship is further unbalanced by the status of the visitor, not only in terms of wealth but the fact

that the tourist is on holiday while the local is likely to be at work, often being paid to serve the needs of the tourist.

Sometimes, locals are exploited as 'tourist objects'. In British villages, local residents can be annoyed by coachloads of tourists emerging from their buses to peer through their windows. A more extreme example is to be found in Thailand, where on the border with Myanmar (Burma), Padaung tribeswomen from across the border have been forced into 'human zoos' as objects of curiosity for tourists; only outcries in the international press have helped to release some of these women from virtual slavery.

Exploitation of this kind can result in both sides seeing any contact in purely commercial terms. In Kenya's Masai Mara, the Maasai extract payment for photographs, of themselves or of a 'real' (but specially constructed) village. Charging for photographs has become a norm in many parts of the world. In exchange, feeling themselves exploited, tourists feel that it becomes acceptable to steal the towels from their hotel; the host–guest relationship has changed to one of supplier and customer.

In this situation, the role of the courier or representative as a 'culture broker' becomes vital. These members of the industry enjoy local knowledge (and are often from the local community), help to avoid misunderstandings, interpret the local culture for visitors and explain what is appropriate and inappropriate behaviour for the guests. Interpretation plays an important role in sustainable tourism, and the guide as interpreter of local customs provides one of the most effective means of communication.

The breakdown in host–guest relationships can be largely ascribed to the volume of visitors. Doxey (1975) developed an 'Irridex' model of the relationship between tourism growth and community stress (see Table 17.3). In the early stages of tourism development, the locals are euphoric, pleased to see investment and improved job prospects for local people. The comparatively small numbers, and the fact that most tourists will belong to the 'explorer' category and accept the norms and values of the

Table 17.3 Irridex model of stress relative to tourism development

Stages	Characteristics	Symptoms
Stage 1	Euphoria	Visitors welcomed, little formal development
Stage 2	Apathy	Visitors taken for granted, contacts become commercial
Stage 3	Irritation	Locals concerned about tourism, efforts made to improve infrastructure
Stage 4	Antagonism	Open hostility from locals, attempts to limit damage and tourism flows

Source: G. V. Doxey 'A causation theory of visitor–resident irritants', 1975.

hosts, mean that tourists are welcomed, and even cultivated as 'friends'. As locals become used to the benefits they receive from tourism, and become aware of the problems which tourism generates as it grows, so they come to accept it, and their meetings with tourists become more common and more commercial. Further growth leads to a general feeling among locals that tourists are an irritant rather than a benefit, as they note how tourism is changing their community and their cultural norms. In the final stages, locals show open antagonism towards the steady stream of visitors, many of whom will have the attitude that locals are there to meet the tourists' needs and will insist on western standards.

Naturally, this is a simplified model of the fairly complex relationships which actually develop between tourists and locals. Other factors that must be taken into account are the length of time a tourist stays in the community (longer-stay tourists will accommodate better and be seen as making a more effective contribution to the local economy), and the cultural gap between locals and tourists (domestic tourists sharing the values of the locals will be less resented).

Examples abound of the antagonism engendered between locals and tourists, even within Britain. An attitude change among locals can be detected by changes in the vocabulary of tourism – for example, in Cornwall, the term 'grockles' is used, and locals may carry bumper stickers on their cars saying 'I'm not a tourist: I live here'. More open hostility can be detected in Bath, where hoses have been turned on open-top touring coaches in which megaphones are used to provide a commentary. Breaking cultural

taboos can produce a backlash: Alassio banned bikinis in the streets, and in the Alto Adige region of the Italian Dolomites in 1993, a local movement erupted spontaneously to prevent the spread of topless bathing in the lakes – while other residents expressed their concern that the publicity accorded this might dissuade some tourists from visiting! In Greece, what has become known as the 'Shirley Valentine factor' – British women escaping a humdrum life at home to find romance in Greece – has led to a reaction from women in Corfu and Crete, who resent the attention paid to foreign females, and feel that Greek women are now undervalued. However, it is also true to say that some Greek women have welcomed the increasing liberation from male dominance which tourism has brought.

A lack of understanding of local cultural traditions is common where these traditions appear to be contrary to what we view as tasteful and appropriate. British tourists in Tokyo may be surprised to see signs outside some nightspots declaring 'Japanese only here', reflecting a nineteenth-century imperialist tradition which has long died out in the western world. Following the crash of a Pakistani Airlines plane over Nepal in 1992, it was reported that 'British Embassy officials were appalled by the public display of the bodies for relatives' of the English victims, which they described as a 'grotesque peepshow'. In Nepal, however, viewing the remains of the dead is an important part of the act of grieving, and the Nepalese were merely extending this courtesy to the foreign mourners.

While a considerable amount of research has now been undertaken into the effect of tourists on locals, rather less is available to tell us how locals in turn influence the tourists. We can undoubtedly ascribe our widening acceptance of foreign food and fashions in Britain to the influence, in part, of overseas travel, and the quality of foreign food, service, transport and hotel facilities have encouraged us to become more demanding in the provision of these in Britain. Research (Gullahorn and Gullahorn, 1963) also suggests that tourists go through three stages in adapting to the local culture of their holiday environment. In the first stage, the tourists are excited by the environment and the novelty of the situation; later, a second stage is reached in which the tourists become disillusioned, and more critical of the environment, as they become accustomed to the situation. Finally, in what may be a slow process, they learn to adapt to the new setting, and in doing so may experience 're-entry crisis', where it becomes difficult to readapt to their home environment when they return.

Other studies have examined the extent to which pre-travel attitudes affect adaptability, and whether travel broadens understanding or reinforces stereotypes (see, for example, Sutton 1967). The evidence suggests that the self-fulfilling prophecy is at work here; that if we travel with the expectation of positive experiences, we will experience them. However, much more work is needed to explore the relationship between the tourist and the host from the former's perspective.

Staged authenticity

Given the constraints of time and place, the tourist demands *instant culture*, an opportunity to sample, even if superficially, the 'foreignness' of the destination. This gives rise to what Dean MacCannell (1989) has referred to as *staged authenticity*, in which a search by tourists for authentic experiences of another culture leads to locals of that culture either providing those experiences, or staging them to appear as realistic as possible. Culture in this way is in danger of becoming commercialized and trivialized, as when 'authentic' folk dances are staged for

the package tourists as a form of cabaret in hotels, or traditional tribal dances are arranged, often in an artificially shortened form, as performances for groups of tourists. Such trivialization has been suggested in Britain, with a proposal that the traditional ceremony of Changing the Guard should be mounted more frequently each day, in order to give tourists more opportunity to view it. Similarly, it has been suggested that Stonehenge, which for reasons already discussed can no longer be viewed close up, should be replicated in fibreglass near the actual site, to give the tourist an 'authentic' experience of seeing the stones more closely.

Tourists will seek out local restaurants not frequented by other tourists in order to enjoy the 'authentic' cuisine and environment of the locals, but the very fact of their discovering such restaurants makes these tourist attractions in their turn, and ultimately the 'tourist traps' tourists sought to avoid. Meantime, the locals move on to find somewhere else to eat.

The downgrading of traditional hospitality towards the tourist in Hawaii is exemplified by the artificial welcome to which tourists are subjected on their arrival in the islands. Traditionally, welcoming natives would place a *lei* of flowers around the neck of each tourist, but the cost of this courtesy and the huge volume of tourists has now required the *lei* to be replaced by a plastic garland, which reinforces the commercial transaction which this has now become.

Tourists seek local artefacts as souvenirs or investments. In cases where genuine works are purchased, this can lead to loss of cultural treasures from a country, and many countries now impose strict bans on exports of such items. However, tourists are often satisfied to purchase what they believe to be an authentic example of local art; this has led to the mass production of poorly crafted works (sometimes referred to as *airport art*), common among African nations and the Pacific islands. Alternately, it encourages the freezing of art styles in pseudo-traditional form, as in the case of the apparently 'medieval' painted wooden religious statuary produced in Oberammergau and other villages of southern

Germany. In turn, artists and craftsmen are subtly encouraged to change their traditional styles, by making their works in the colours that are found to be most attractive to the tourists, or by reducing the size of their works to make them more readily transportable for tourists.

It is perhaps too easy to take a purist stance in criticizing these developments. One must point to the evident benefits which tourism has brought to the culture of many tourist destinations – indeed, in many cases it has helped to regenerate an awareness and pride in local culture and traditions. But for the advent of tourism, many of these traditions would have died out long ago. It is easy to ascribe cultural decline to the impact of tourism, whereas it is as likely to be the result of mass communication and technological development. Since western (and specifically American) culture is the dominant influence around the world, it will inevitably undermine other cultures, particularly those of the developing world. However, it is equally clear that tourism from the western nations has led to a revival of interest in tribal customs in other countries (and not just in developing countries; the revival of morris dancing in English communities is a direct result of the impact of tourism). Traditional local cuisines in Britain have been regenerated, with the support of the national tourist boards, in the 'taste of England', 'taste of Wales' and 'taste of Scotland' schemes. Dying local arts and crafts have been revived through cottage industries in rural areas which have benefited economically from the impact of tourism.

Figure 17.8 Traditional dance: Ramayana Ballet performance in Bali, Indonesia. (*Courtesy Garuda International*)

Managing the social impact of tourism

Sustainable tourism, in terms of the social impact of tourism on indigenous populations, needs to be managed in two ways. First, it is important that good relations are established between locals and guests, so that guests are welcomed to the region or country and social interaction benefits both parties. As we have seen earlier in this text, there are different approaches to ensuring this. The choice is between two diametrically opposed management methods. Responsible officials can attempt to integrate the guest into the local community, and to control the overall number of visitors so that the local population does not become swamped by tourists. This is really only practical where demand for the destination is limited to comparatively small numbers, and the market attracted shows empathy for, and sensitivity towards, local culture; specialist tourism will allow for this solution to be adopted, but mass tourism will not. Alternatively, officials can aim to concentrate the visitors in particular districts, sometimes referred to as tourist 'ghettos', often some distance away from residential neighbourhoods, so that any damage is limited to the few locals who will have contact with these guests, usually involving commercial transactions. In this way, most locals and visitors will not come into direct contact with each other, though this may also reduce the economic benefit of tourism to the local community. The integrated resort complex offering all-inclusive packages is becoming increasingly common at long-haul destinations, examples being found in Cancun, Mexico, Nusa Dua in Bali, Indonesia, Puerto Plata in the Dominican Republic and the Langkawi development in Malaysia.

The other issue is the need to ensure that locals benefit economically from incoming tourism, through the provision of employment at all levels, and through ownership of facilities. However, this requires a measure of sophistication among the local population, who need education and training, as well as assistance in raising finance for investment in local tourist businesses. The solution cannot be achieved merely by putting businesses into the hands of local residents. To illustrate this, the example can be given of a tour operating company in Arnhem Land, Australia, which was originally managed by foreign nationals, but was eventually handed over to local Aboriginal administration. While the new Aboriginal owners were fully capable of handling the operational aspects of the programme, they had little knowledge of, and no contacts with, the overseas markets they existed to serve, and in consequence they found it difficult to attract new business.

The future of tourism

We have seen in these chapters how tourism has developed to a point where it has become a major industry, a major force for social change and a major power for good, or if uncontrolled, for evil. We have also speculated upon the future of tourism, and the possible consequences of a five-fold or ten-fold increase in tourists in the early part of the twenty-first century. Some understanding of the magnitude of the problem can be seen in the rapid development of tourism to the former eastern European countries

following the collapse of the communist system in these countries. Soon after the fall of communism in Czechoslovakia, Prague was estimated to have been receiving some *83 million* visitors a year (admittedly, many of these were taking short trips across the border, and as few as 10 million were thought to be staying visitors). Similarly, huge numbers thronged to see the other new states, with their journeys made easy by the eradication of visa requirements. Tallinn, the attractive medieval capital city of Estonia, is a mere hour and forty minutes by boat from Helsinki, and it is common to see as many as eight giant ferries in harbour simultaneously, as Finns, Scandinavians and other westerners throng into this small town for bargain shopping. This sort of expansion, however, cannot be sustained on a worldwide scale, and global growth is unlikely ever again to reach the levels achieved during the 1950–1980 period.

Nevertheless, the world is in a period of rapid transition; the traditional tourist-generating countries are moving from an industrial stage to becoming post-industrial societies. With this change, lifestyles and values are also changing; the old desire to accumulate material possessions shows signs of abating. Leisure forecasters are now trying to determine whether this will result in a new desire, as prophesied by Alvin Toffler (1970), to accumulate experiences as avidly as we formerly collected possessions. The concern of the tourism industry will be to ascertain how this will affect the consumers' demand for travel.

Technical developments, although not advancing at the same speed as a few years ago, will still provide new opportunities for travel. Aviation experts agree that the development of jet aircraft has reached a plateau where productivity and efficiency are unlikely to be substantially improved, although prices may well fall further as larger aircraft, seating between 500 and 800 passengers, are introduced. With the crash of a Concorde airliner in mid-2000, the continuation of supersonic travel appeared initially to be in doubt – but in any case, this service was so costly that its scheduled transatlantic route attracted only the super-rich and the business traveller. Whether or not Concorde services are resumed, and this appeared likely at the time of writing – it seems impossible to believe that we have seen the end of supersonic flight development for all time, though such advances may not occur for another twenty years.

Curiously, there are forecasts for hypersonic flight to arrive much earlier. The WTO has estimated that sub-orbital flights into space might be available for tourists as early as 2005, at a cost of around $100,000, and at the time of writing an American has undergone training in Russia and has become the first commercial tourist into space (he is rumoured to have spent many millions of dollars for the privilege). Richard Branson is supporting a scheme to develop reusable eight-seat rockets which could provide trips into space for as little as £60,000, possibly by the end of the current decade, and both Japanese and American companies have plans to build and launch hotels in space; a realistic time scale for these to be in operation would be 2015–2025. Although the British government failed to support British Aerospace's own proposal to develop an experimental aircraft capable of leaving and re-entering the Earth's atmosphere (the so-called HOTOL concept), there is still some interest being expressed in this development in US aviation circles. This type of aircraft would carry its own supplies of liquid oxygen to burn when beyond Earth's atmosphere, but use oxygen from the air, as does a normal airliner, when flying within the atmosphere. Orbiting the globe up to 185 miles above the Earth's surface, the aircraft would be capable of flying between London and Sydney, Australia, in a little over one hour. However, most experts still believe that the development costs and uncertainties of such craft put their development well into the future, perhaps as far as thirty or more years from now. Meanwhile, NASA is known to be undertaking research work on a 'scramjet' engine, capable of thrusting aircraft at five times the speed of sound, and research is also under way on hyperSoar aircraft capable of achieving speeds of mach 10 (in excess of 7,200 mph). This would bring New York in

reach of Europe within an hour, a development of huge significance for leisure and business travellers alike.

Research continues in other areas of advanced transport, too. In shipping, work is continuing on designs for more fuel-efficient craft. Successful sea trials have taken place with vessels that complement the use of their engines with metal sails, increasing the overall speed while reducing costs – an important consideration at a time when fuel costs are rising sharply. The appeal of cruise ships that resemble floating hotels with a full range of leisure facilities is leading to the construction of ever larger vessels. Proposals have been advanced for much larger catamarans and trimarans (twin-hulled and triple-hulled vessels) capable of transporting large numbers of passengers at high speed and at far more comfort, without the customary problems of motion sickness experienced in single-hull ships. Such vessels might be constructed to cross the Atlantic in under 48 hours. An even more exciting venture was developed by the Russians beyond the prototype stage; a surface-skimming hydrobus known as the Ekranoplane. Developed by Soviet researchers as a form of military transport in the 1980s, it has the capacity to be developed as a civilian vessel capable of carrying 400 passengers at a cruising speed of over 300 mph, with a range of up to 10,000 miles. This would make possible transatlantic journeys overnight, and at comparatively cheap fares, reaching an entirely new market. German and American interests are still examining the feasibility of building such craft for commercial purposes. At the same time Japan is carrying out research on the use of electromagnetic thrusters for ships. Toshiba has designed a 150-ton vessel which is pushed through water by the effect of counteracting magnets. This could again lead to the development of vessels of much larger size. Sustainable transport development at sea is evident in the Solar Sailor ferry already in operation in Sydney, described in Chapter 8.

On land, as we have seen, railway development is making great strides. Japan's Linear Express, capable of cruising at speeds up to 300 mph, has already reached the prototype stage. This vehicle has the advantage of superspeed and super quietness; the track consists of a metal trough generating a magnetic field which repels magnets in the train, causing the vehicle to ride 10 cm above the track. There is therefore little wear and tear, and in consequence, much reduced maintenance cost. If the technology proves successful, rail services could certainly pose a major threat to air routes of distances over land up to 1,000 miles.

Some futurists have prophesied that there will be little need to travel away from home in the twenty-first century. Holographs are capable of reproducing any environment artificially, so that we will be able to recreate in the home any environment of our choosing to 'experience' foreign travel. This could include activity holidays such as simulating white water canoe and raft rides, winter sports or the piloting of an aircraft. BT announced in 1997 that it was working on the production of a machine which can reproduce some of the world's biggest attractions, not only on computer screens but also on wraparound screens or as holograms. Using the device, called 'Head', one can, in BT's words, 'visit Times Square or take a walk into a pyramid without leaving the room'. Whether this form of entertainment replaces travel, or only serves to whet the appetite of most of those viewing such destinations remains to be seen. What is certain is that those who cannot now travel – the very poor, the severely disabled – will for the first time be able to experience something akin to real world travel.

Other forecasters predict that underwater leisure cities will be built on the seabeds adjoining our coasts, where a controlled climate will make the annual exodus to the sun no longer necessary. Some of these predictions take us into the realms of science fiction. We can be safer in forecasting those short-term changes which expand on current trends, and which we can expect to take place within the next few years.

Holidays abroad have now become a habit for millions of people living in the developed countries. In spite of the economic set-back which southeast Asian nations experienced in 1997, by the turn of the century many of the so-called tiger economies were recovering rapidly and tourists from these countries were flocking back into the global travel market. The WTO forecasts 1.6 billion international tourists by 2020, spending over $2 trillion per annum. It sees China and Russia becoming major generators of tourists by that date, as their economies also thrive. Already there are large numbers of wealthy business people in Russia and the former satellite countries who are choosing to head for Mediterranean destinations in their millions with their families, anxious to experience the classic sun, sea, sand holidays which westerners have enjoyed since the 1960s. These new markets have already proved to be the saviour of some down-market Spanish resorts which had seen declining numbers of western tourists for several years.

For western Europeans, while the traditional sun, sea, sand holiday will remain a strong attraction, consumers will expect and demand more from it. The demand for activity and special-interest holidays is growing rapidly among all sectors of the travel market, and the passive beach holiday may become a thing of the past. This change may be hastened by the growth in skin cancer among North European nations resulting from exposure to the sun (heightened by the depletion of the ozone layer). In the short term, this fear is more likely to affect the older traveller than the young, who have so far shown little inclination to change their holiday habits; as with smoking, many youngsters feel that the risk is too remote for it to concern them. In the longer term, the message may get home, but reaction is more likely to be to cover up and to engage in different activities, rather than to shun the traditional sunshine holiday resorts of the Mediterranean or Caribbean.

Whether the more traditional British seaside resorts can survive in an age when so many Britons choose to holiday abroad at least once is debatable. Global warming may nudge up the average temperatures of our south coast resorts and improve their appeal, but in the short term only massive investment in facilities, particularly indoor entertainment, is likely to retain the domestic market. The success of Center Parcs' holiday centres in Britain has shown that if all-weather facilities are provided and the product offers value for money, the domestic market can still be attracted. The way forward may be epitomized in Japan's 'Seagaia Ocean Dome' on the island of Kyushu, which is based at the seaside but offers a covered beach with a volcano effect occurring every fifteen minutes, while wave machines create artificial *tsunami* wave effects to instil real excitement into the traditional pastime of sea bathing. This coupling of adventure and sea bathing has proved to be enormously popular with the Japanese domestic market. However, the British consumer continues to demonstrate a nostalgic commitment to tradition and the past, with respect to their choice of holidays as much as other products, and this has been to the benefit of heritage sites, steam railways and other attractions which emphasize their links with the past.

Changes in lifestyle will affect the traditional forms of holiday accommodation. The desire for greater flexibility, coupled with advances in 'convenience' food and more adventurous eating habits, suggest that the swing to self-catering, with more meals out for 'special occasions', will continue, and hotels and guesthouses will have to consider how they can adapt their product to win back this market.

The move up-market, evident in the 1990s, is also likely to continue. Value for money will play a more important role, counteracting the industry's own emphasis on low price. Long-haul holidays can be expected to continue to outpace short-haul in rate of growth. British tourists will take more frequent holidays and more short breaks, while many short breaks will be taken further afield.

The information revolution

Perhaps the biggest immediate advances are going to occur as a result of the impact of new technology. Significant changes have already been touched on in earlier chapters. The World Wide Web has created demand for up-to-date, relevant information, accessible instantaneously, and already available through laptop computers and mobile phones for those on the move. More and more tourism- and travel-related information is becoming available to the global traveller on business or on holiday, including rail, air, ferry and coach services listing all fares and timetables. Live webcam pictures of resorts can be conjured up, with up-to-the-minute weather reports on any destination. In Britain, a real-time National Rail Timetable will become available for railway staff in 2001, giving current information on timetables and fares for the entire rail network; this is likely to become available to the public, too, in due course. Inevitably, all transport networks will be linked by global positioning software to enable travellers to track the current location of any form of transport.

Battle has already been joined for supremacy in the race to provide a leisure global distribution system for all forms of travel, accessible by members of the public as well as the trade. Among other services to be available on such systems, the ability to display live pictures of destinations (and print out whatever is needed in hard format) – a facility which is already available on the web – would suggest the probable demise of the traditional hard-copy destination brochure.

Not only destinations and transportation can be currently called up on television screens; viewers are able to display and choose between a wide variety of different attractions and hotels. Specialist accommodation, such as villas with pools, is already available on-screen, and small companies are no longer limited in competing with larger organizations to market and distribute their products. However, some agreement will need to be reached shortly on the use of a global language for web sites; even in countries which are popular international tourist destinations, such as Denmark, much tourist information is often displayed only in the country's own language.

Individual holiday-makers in many parts of the world can already put together their own packages, book and pay for the booking by direct debit to their bank account, all without leaving their armchair. The ability to book from home would suggest a rise in impulse booking, and demand for even more 'late availability' products, coupled with a decline in traditional patterns of advanced booking. Indeed, if consumers can package their own holidays at home at the push of a button, conjuring up on their home TV screen all the images of the resorts they wish to choose from, the question must be asked – could this make the present tasks of operator and travel agent redundant? This is likely to be the case unless both can provide a level of service far exceeding what is offered at present. Agency counter staff in particular must be sufficiently skilled and knowledgeable to be able to offer a genuine counselling service, adding value to what is provided on-screen, but to date, there is little evidence to suggest that this will be practicable, or that the industry could pay the salaries that such skilled staff would demand. For students of the business of tourism, we live in interesting times!

Questions and discussion topics

1. Static caravan sites are frequently criticized for the 'visual pollution' they bring to a scenic region. Discuss current legislation to control this, and discuss what other steps could be taken to improve the situation. Can the design and management of these sites provide a more sustainable product?

2. Is there an inevitable conflict between conservation and tourism development? Examine examples of such conflict in any country of your choice, and discuss how harmony could be achieved.

3. Argue the case for a policy of concentrating tourists rather than dispersing them, using examples from both developing and developed countries.

4. How do you see your own holidays changing over the next few years? Discuss the factors that would account for these changes, such as age, family composition, income and changes within the tourism industry itself.

Assignment topics

1. You are a freelance journalist for one of the travel trade papers in Britain, and your editor has asked you to produce a short article for the paper which is designed to persuade tour operators to take a more responsible attitude to developing new destinations. Write an article, not to exceed six hundred words, with this objective.

2. Undertake an 'environmental audit' of any nearby town or destination which receives a significant number of tourists. Look at features such as litter, graffiti, visual pollution, parking etc. and produce a report (maximum 1,000 words) for the Director of Tourism for the location, identifying the major weaknesses you have found and making recommendations for action.

3. You have recently been appointed Resort Representative for a tour operating company which offers 'cheap and cheerful' package holidays in a down-market resort on the island of Corfu, Greece. There has been a good deal of friction lately between British tourists and Greek locals, and you have been asked by your company to try to help improve the relationship.

Prepare notes for a talk you will give your next group of incoming tourists, designed to effect this.

Bibliography

A note on this bibliography

The following is a selection of texts deemed of particular value to students following post-A level programmes of study in the field of tourism, whether as a core subject or as an option within wider fields of study, up to degree level. Books earlier than the 1980s are included only where they are seminal, or relevant for the study of the history of tourism. Publications other than books are largely excluded, again except where they are deemed vital to the contemporary study of the subject.

ABTA, *An Occupational Mapping of the Travel Services Industry*, ABTA 1991

Adamson S H, *Seaside Piers*, Batsford 1977

Addison W, *English Spas*, Batsford 1951

Aitchison C, Macleod N and Shaw S J, *Leisure and Tourism Landscapes*, Routledge 2000

Alderson F, *The Inland Resorts and Spas of Britain*, David and Charles 1973

Allcock J B, *Tourism in Centrally Planned Economies*, Pergamon 1990

Allcock J B, Bruner E M and Lanfant M-F (eds), *International Tourism: Identity and Change*, Sage 1993

Apostolopoulos Y, Leivadi S and Yiannakis A (eds), *The Sociology of Tourism*, Routledge 1996

Apostolopoulos Y, Leontidou L and Loukissas P (eds), *Mediterranean Tourism*, Routledge 2000

Aronsson L, *The Development of Sustainable Tourism*, Continuum 2000

Ashford N, Martin Stanton H P and Moore C A, *Airport Operations*, Pitman 1991

Ashworth G J, *Heritage Planning*, Geo Pers 1991

Ashworth G J and Dietvorst A G J, *Tourism and Spatial Transformations: Implications for Policy and Planning*, CAB International 1995

Ashworth G J and Goodall B, *Marketing Tourism Places*, Routledge 1990

Ashworth G J and Larkham P J, *Building a New Heritage: Tourism, Culture and Identity in the New Europe*, Routledge 1994

Ashworth G and Tunbridge J, *The Tourist-Historic City*, Belhaven Press 1990

Ashworth G J and Voogd H, *Selling the City: The Use of Publicity and Public Relations to Sell Cities and Regions*, Belhaven Press 1990

Audit Commission, *The Road to Wigan Pier? Managing Local Authority Museums and Art Galleries*, HMSO 1991

Bachmann P, *Tourism in Kenya: A Basic Need for Whom?* Peter Lang 1988

Badger A, *Trading Places: Tourism as Trade*, Tourism Concern 1996

Baldacchino G, *Global Tourism and Informal Labour Relations*, Mansell 1997

Barke M, Towner J and Newton M, *Tourism in Spain*, CAB International 1995

Barlay S, *Cleared for Take-off: Behind the Scenes of Air Travel*, Kyle Cathie 1994

Baud-Bovy M and Lawson F, *Tourism and Recreation Handbook of Planning and Design*, 2nd edn, Architectural Press 1998

Baum T (ed.), *Manpower in Tourism*, Butterworth Heinemann 1991

Baum T (ed.), *Human Resource Issues in International Tourism*, Butterworth Heinemann 1993

Baum T, *Managing Resources in the European Tourism and Hospitality Industry – A Strategic Approach*, Chapman & Hall 1995

Bell G, Bowen P and Fawcett P, *The Business of Transport*, M&E 1984

Bennett T, *The Birth of the Museum: History, Theory, Politics*, Routledge 1995

Benson D and Whitehead G, *Transport and Distribution*, Longman 1985

Binney M, *Our Vanishing Heritage*, Arlington 1985

Binney M and Hanna M, *Preservation Pays: Tourism and the Economic Benefits of Conserving Historic Buildings*, SAVE Britain's Heritage (n/d)

Blackshaw C, *Aviation Law and Regulation*, Pitman 1991

Boer A, Thomas R and Webster M, *Small Business Management: A Resource-based Approach for the Hospitality and Tourism Industries*, Cassell 1997

Boissevain J (ed.), *Revitalising European Rituals*, Routledge 1992

Boissevain J (ed.), *Coping with Tourists: European Reactions to Mass Tourism*, Berghan 1997

Boniface B and Cooper C, *Worldwide Destinations: The Geography of Travel and Tourism*, 3rd edn, Butterworth Heinemann 2001

Boniface P, *Dynamic Tourism: Journeying with Change*, Channel View 2001

Boniface P, *Managing Quality Cultural Tourism*, Routledge 1995

Boniface P and Fowler P, *Heritage and Tourism in the 'Global Village'*, Routledge 1993

Boo E, *Eco-Tourism: The Potentials and the Pitfalls*, World Wildlife Fund 1990

Boorstin D J, *The Image: A Guide to Pseudo-events in America*, Penguin 1962

Böröcz J, *Leisure Migration: A Sociological Study on Tourism*, Pergamon 1996

Bosselman F, Peterson C and McCarthy C, *Managing Tourism Growth: Issues and Applications*, Island Press 1999

Bottomley Renshaw M, *The Travel Agent*, 2nd edn, Business Education Publishers 1997

Bouquet M and Winter M, *Who from their Labours Rest? Conflict and Practice in Rural Tourism*, Avebury 1987

Bowdin G, Allen A, McDonnell I and O'Toole W, *Events Management*, Butterworth Heinemann 2001

Braggs S and Harris D, *Sun, Fun and Crowds: Seaside Holidays between the Wars*, Tempus 2000

Bramwell B and Lane B (eds), *Rural Tourism and Sustainable Rural Development*, Channel View 1993

Bramwell H, Henry I, Jackson G, Goytia Prat A, Richards G and van der Straaten J (eds), *Sustainable Tourism Management: Principles and Practice*, Tilburg University Press 1996

Bramwell B and Lane B (eds), *Tourism Collaboration and Partnership: Politics, Practice and Sustainability*, Channel View 2000

Bray R and Raitz V, *Flight to the Sun: The Story of the Holiday Revolution*, Continuum 2000

Brendon P, *Thomas Cook: 150 Years of Popular Tourism*, Secker 1991

Briggs S, *Successful Tourism Marketing: A Practical Handbook*, 2nd edn, Kogan Page 2001

Briguglio L, Archer B, Jafari J and Wall G (eds), *Sustainable Tourism in Islands and Small States: Issues and Policies*, Pinter 1996

Brotherton B (ed.), *The Handbook of Contemporary Hospitality Management Research*, Wiley 1999

Brown F, *Tourism Reassessed: Blight or Blessing?* Butterworth Heinemann 1998

Brown F and Hall D (eds), *Tourism in Peripheral Areas*, Channel View 2000

Brown M, *The Spiritual Tourist: A Personal Odyssey through the Outer Reaches of Belief*, Bloomsbury 1999

Brunt P, *Market Research in Travel and Tourism*, Butterworth Heinemann 1997

Buglear J, *Stats to Go: A Guide to Statistics for Hospitality, Leisure and Tourism Studies*, Butterworth Heinemann 2000

Bull A, *The Economics of Travel and Tourism*, 2nd edn, Longman 1995

Burkart A J and Medlik S, *Tourism: Past Present and Future*, Heinemann 1981

Burns P, *An Introduction to Tourism and Anthropology*, Routledge 1999

Burns P and Holden A, *Tourism: A New Perspective*, Prentice Hall 1995

Burton A and P, *The Green Bag Travellers: Britain's First Tourists*, Deutsch 1978

Burton J and L, *Interpersonal Skills for Travel and Tourism*, Longman 1994

Burton R, *Travel Geography*, 2nd edn, Pitman 1994

Butler R, Hall C M and Jenkins J, *Tourism and Recreation in Rural Areas*, Wiley 1998

Butler R W and Hinch T (eds), *Tourism and Indigenous Peoples*, International Thomson Business Press 1996

Butler R W and Pearce D (eds), *Change in Tourism: People, Places, Processes*, Routledge 1995

Button K (ed.), *Airline Deregulation*, David Fulton 1990

Buzzard J, *The Beaten Track: European Tourism, Literature and the Ways to Culture, 1800–1918*, Clarendon Press 1993

CAB International, *Fashionable Resort Regions: Their Evolution and Transformation*, CAB International 1993

CAB International, *Leisure Policies in Europe*, CAB International 1993

CAB International, *Tourism in Europe: Structures and Development*, CAB International 1993

Cabinet Office Enterprise Unit, *Pleasure, Leisure and Jobs: The Business of Tourism* (The Young Report), HMSO 1985

Callaghan P (ed.), *Travel and Tourism*, Business Education Publishers 1989

Carmouche R and Kelly N, *Behavioural Studies in Hospitality Management*, Chapman & Hall 1995

Carter J, Goodey B and Binks G (eds), *Heritage Interpretation Management: Audience Characteristics, Evaluation and Impact*, Wiley 1997

Cartwright R and Barid C, *The Development and Growth of the Cruise Industry*, Butterworth Heinemann 1999

Casson L, *Travel in the Ancient World*, George Allen and Unwin 1974

Cater E and Lowman G, *Ecotourism: A Sustainable Option?* Wiley 1994

Chaney E, *The Evolution of the Grand Tour*, Frank Cass 1998

Clark M, *Interpersonal Skills for Tourism and Hospitality Management*, Chapman & Hall 1995

Clarke J and Critcher C, *The Devil Makes Work – Leisure in Capitalist Britain*, Macmillan 1985

Clarke M, Riley M and Wood R C, *Research Methods in Hospitality and Tourism*, International Thomson Business Press 1997

Clift S and Carter S (eds), *Tourism and Sex: Culture, Commerce and Coercion*, Cassell 2000

Clift S and Grabowski P (eds), *Tourism and Health: Risks, Research and Responses*, Cassell 1997

Clift S and Page S, *Health and the International Tourist*, Routledge 1995

Committee of Inquiry into Civil Air Transport, *British Air Transport in the Seventies*, HMSO 1969

Conlin M V and Baum T, *Island Tourism: Management Principles and Practice*, Wiley 1995

Cooper C and Go F, *Tourism Education and Training*, Belhaven Press 1994

Cooper C and Wanhill S R, *Tourism Development: Environmental and Community Issues*, Wiley 1997

Cooper C, Shepherd R and Westlake J, *Tourism and Hospitality Education*, University of Surrey 1994

Cooper C, Fletcher J, Gilbert D and Wanhill S, *Tourism Principles and Practice*, 2nd edn, Pitman 1998

Coopers & Lybrand: Travel Agents' Benchmarking Survey 1997

Corbin A, *The Lure of the Sea: The Discovery of the Seaside in the Western World 1750–1840*, Polity Press 1994

Corke J, *Tourism Law*, 2nd edn, Elm Publications 1993

Cormack B, *A History of Holidays 1812–1990*, Routledge/Thoemmes Press 1998

Corner J and Harvey S, *Enterprise and Heritage: Cross-currents of National Culture*, Routledge 1991

Craig-Smith S and French C, *Learning to Live with Tourism*, Pitman 1994

Crick M, *Resplendent Sites, Discordant Voices: Sri Lankans and International Tourism*, Harwood Academic Publishers 1994

Croall J, *Preserve or Destroy: Tourism and the Environment*, Calouste Gulbenkian Foundation 1995

Crotts J and Ryan C (eds), *Marketing Issues in Pacific Area Tourism*, Haworth Press 1997

Crotts J and van Raaij W F (eds), *Economic Psychology of Travel and Tourism*, Haworth Press 1994

Crotts J, Buhalis D and March R (eds), *Global Alliances in Tourism and Hospitality Management*, Haworth 2000

Dandel S and Vialle G, *Yield Management: Applications to Air Transport and Other Service Industries*, Institute de Transport Aerien 1994

Dann G M S, *The Language of Tourism: A Sociolinguistic Perspective*, CAB International 1996

Davidoff D M, *Contact: Customer Service in the Hospitality and Tourism Industry*, Prentice Hall 1994

Davidson R, *Tourism*, 2nd edn, Pitman 1993

Davidson R, *Business Travel*, Pitman 1994

Davidson R, *Travel and Tourism in Europe*, 2nd edn, Longman 1998

Davidson R and Maitland R, *Tourism Destinations*, Hodder and Stoughton 1997

Deegan J and Dineen D, *Tourism Policy and Performance*, International Thomson Business Press 1997

Delgado A, *The Annual Outing and Other Excursions*, George Allen and Unwin 1977

Department for Culture, Media and Sport, *Tomorrow's Tourism: A Growth Industry for the New Millennium*, HMSO n/d (issued 1999)

Department of National Heritage, *Tourism: Competing with the Best*, HMSO 1995

Department of National Heritage, *Success through Partnership – A Strategy for Tourism: Competing with the Best*, HMSO 1997

Dickinson R H and Vladimir A N, *Selling the Sea: An Inside Look at the Cruise Industry*, Wiley 1997

Dieke P (ed.), *The Political Economy of Tourism in Africa*, Cognizant Communications 2000

Dobson A, *Flying in the Face of Competition*, Avebury Aviation/Ashgate Publishing 1994

Doganis R, *Flying off Course: The Economics of International Airlines*, 2nd edn, George Allen and Unwin 1991

Doganis R, *The Airport Business*, Routledge 1992

Doswell R, *Tourism: Understanding its Development and Management*, Butterworth Heinemann 1995

Doswell R, *Tourism: How Effective Management Makes the Difference*, Butterworth Heinemann 1997

Douglas N, *They Came for Savages: 100 Years of Tourism in Melanesia*, Southern Cross University Press 1996

Downes J and Paton T, *Travel Agency Law*, Pitman 1993

Doxey G V, 'A causation theory of visitor–resident irritants: methodology and research inferences', *Proceedings of the Travel Research Association Sixth Annual Conference*, San Diego 1975

Drower J, *Good Clean Fun: The Story of Britain's First Holiday Camp*, Arcadia 1982

Drummond S and Yeoman I, *Quality Issues in Heritage Visitor Attractions*, Butterworth Heinemann 2000

Dutton G, *Sun, Sea, Surf and Sand – The Myth of the Beach*, OUP 1985

Eaton A J, *The International Airline Business: Globalisation in Action*, Avebury Aviation/Ashgate Publishing 1995

Eaton B, *European Leisure Businesses: Strategies for the Future*, Elm Publications 1996

Eber S (ed.), *Beyond the Green Horizon: A Discussion Paper on Principles for Sustainable Tourism*, Tourism Concern/World Wildlife Fund 1992

Eco U, *Faith in Fakes*, Secker and Warburg 1986

Eco U, *Travels in Hyper-Reality*, Secker and Warburg 1987

Edensor T, *Tourists at the Taj: Performance and Meaning at a Symbolic Site*, Routledge 1998

Edgell D, *International Tourism Policy*, Van Nostrand Reinhold 1990

Edgell D, *Tourism Policy: The Next Millennium*, Sagamore 1999

Edgerton R, *Alone Together: Social Order on an Urban Beach*, University of California Press 1979

Edington J and M A, *Ecology, Recreation and Tourism*, CUP 1986

Elkington J and Hailes J, *Holidays that Don't Cost the Earth*, Gollancz 1992

Elliott J, *Tourism: Politics and Public Sector Management*, Routledge 1997

European Tourism Universities Partnership (ETUP), *European Resort Management: Case Studies and Learning Materials*, Continuum 2000

Evans N and Robinson M, *Issues in Travel and Tourism*, Vol. 1, Centre for Travel and Tourism/Business Education Publishers 1995

Farrell B (ed.) *Tourism and the Physical Environment*, Pergamon 1987

Faulkner B, Laws E and Moscardo G (eds), *Tourism in the 21st Century*, Continuum 2001

Fayos Sola E (ed.), *Human Capital in the Tourism Industry of the 21st Century*, WTO 1997

Feifer M, *Going Places: The Ways of the Tourist from Imperial Rome to the Present Day*, Macmillan 1985

Fennell D A, *Ecotourism: An Introduction*, Routledge 1999

Fjellman S, *Vinyl Leaves: Walt Disney World and America*, Westview Press 1992

Foley M, *Doing your Dissertation: A Guide for Students in Tourism, Leisure and Hospitality Management*, Chapman & Hall 1995

Foley M and Lennon J, *Dark Tourism*, Continuum 2000

Foley M, Lennon J and Maxwell G (eds), *Hospitality, Tourism and Leisure Management: Issues in Strategy and Culture*, Cassell 1997

Font X and Tribe J (eds), *Forest Tourism and Recreation: Case Studies in Environmental Management*, CAB International 1999

Forsyth T, *Sustainable Tourism: Moving from Theory to Practice*, Tourism Concern/Worldwide Fund for Nature 1996

Foster D, *The Business of Travel Agency Operations*, McGraw Hill 1991

Foster D, *First Class: An Introduction to Travel and Tourism*, 2nd edn, Macmillan/McGraw-Hill, 1994

Foster D, *Sales and Marketing for the Travel Professional*, McGraw-Hill 1991

Fowler P J, *The Past in Contemporary Society: Then, Now*, Routledge 1992

France L (ed.), *The Earthscan Reader in Sustainable Tourism*, Earthscan (Kogan Page) 1997

Frechtling D, *Forecasting Tourism Demand: Methods and Strategies*, Butterworth Heinemann 2001

French Y, *The Handbook of Public Relations for Museums, Galleries, Historic Houses, the Visual Arts and Heritage Attractions*, Museum Development Co 1991

Fridgen J D, *Dimensions of Tourism*, Educational Institute of the American Hotel and Motel Association, 1991

Gabler K, Maier G, Mazenac J and Wober K, *International City Tourism: Analysis and Strategy*, Pinter Cassell 1997

Gammon S and Jones I, *Sports Tourism: An Introduction*, Continuum 2001

Gayle D and Goodrich J (eds), *Tourism Marketing and Management in the Caribbean*, Routledge 1993

Gee C, Makens J and Choy D, *The Travel Industry*, 3rd edn, Wiley 1997

Gee G, *Calculations for the Leisure, Travel and Tourism Industries*, Hodder and Stoughton 1991

Getz D, *Festivals, Special Events and Tourism*, Van Nostrand Reinhold 1990

Getz D and Page S, *Business of Rural Tourism*, International Thomson Business Press 1997

Gialloreto L, *Strategic Airline Management: The Global War Begins*, Pitman 1988

Glasson J, Godfrey K and Goodey B, *Towards Visitor Management*, Anthony Rowe 1995

Go F and Jenkins C (eds), *Tourism and Economic Development in Asia and Australia*, Pinter 1998

Go F and Pine R, *Globalization Strategy in the Hotel Industry*, International Thomson Business Press 1995

Godde P M, Price M and Zimmermann F, *Tourism Development in Mountain Regions*, CAB International 2000

Godfrey K and Clarke J, *The Tourism Development Handbook: A Practical Approach to Planning and Marketing*, Cassell 2000

Goeldner J R, Brent Ritchie J R and McIntosh R W, *Tourism: Principles, Practices, Philosophies*, 8th edn, Wiley 2000

Gold J R and Ward S V (eds), *Place Promotion: The Use of Publicity and Marketing to Sell Towns and Regions*, Wiley 1994

Goldblatt J J, *Special Events: The Art and Science of Celebration*, Van Nostrand Reinhold 1990

Goodall B and Ashworth G, *Marketing in the Tourism Industry: The Promotion of Destination Regions*, Routledge 1987

Goodey B (ed.), *The Handbook of Interpretive Practice at Heritage Sites*, Wiley 1997

Gordon S, *Holidays*, Batsford 1972

Graburn N H H (ed.), *Ethnic and Tourist Arts: Cultural Expressions from the Fourth World*, University of California Press 1976

Graham A, *Managaing Airports: An International Perspective*, Butterworth Heinemann 2001

Graham B, *Geography and Air Transport*, Wiley 1995

Grant D and Mason S, *The EC Directive on Package Travel, Package Holidays and Package Tours*, University of Northumbria 1993

Gullahorn J E and Gullahorn J T, 'An extension of the U-curve hypothesis', *Journal of Social Sciences*, 19: 33–47 1963

Gunn C, *Tourism Planning: Basic Concepts and Cases*, 3rd edn, Taylor and Francis 1994

Gunn C, *Vacationscape: Designing Tourist Regions*, 4th edn, Van Nostrand Reinhold 1997

Hall C M, *Hallmark Tourist Events: Impacts, Management and Planning*, Wiley 1992

Hall C M, *Tourism and Politics: Policy, Power and Place*, Wiley 1994

Hall C M, *Tourism in the Pacific: Development, Impacts and Markets*, Pitman 1994

Hall C M (ed.), *Sustainable Tourism: A Geographical Perspective*, Longman 1998

Hall C M and Jenkins J M, *Tourism and Public Policy*, Routledge 1995

Hall C M and Johnston M, *Polar Tourism: Tourism in the Arctic and Antarctic Regions*, Wiley 1995

Hall C M and Page S J, *The Geography of Tourism and Recreation: Environment, Place and Space*, Routledge 1999

Hall C M and Page S J (eds), *Tourism in the Pacific: Issues and Challenges*, International Thomson Business Press 1996

Hanlon J P, *Global Airlines: Competition in a Transnational Industry*, 2nd edn, Butterworth Heinemann 1999

Harrington D and Lenehan T, *Managing Quality in Tourism: Theory and Practice*, Oak Tree Press 1998

Harris G and Katz K, *Promoting International Tourism to the Year 2000 and Beyond*, 2nd edn, The Americas Group 1996

Harris R, Griffin T, Williams, P, Heath E and Toepper L (eds), *Sustainable Tourism: A Global Perspective*, 2nd edn, Butterworth Heinemann 2001

Harrison D, *Tourism and the Less Developed Countries*, 2nd edn, Wiley 1995

Harrison L and Husbands W, *Practising Responsible Tourism: International Case Studies in Tourism Planning, Policy and Development*, Wiley 1996

Harrison R, *Manual of Heritage Management*, Butterworth Heinemann 1994 van Harssel J, *Tourism: An Exploration*, 3rd edn, Prentice Hall 1993

Havins P J N, *The Spas of England*, Robert Hale 1976

Hayles J et al., *Guide to Green Tourism*, Victor Gollancz 1991

Hayter R, *Careers in Training in Hotels, Catering and Tourism*, Butterworth Heinemann 1993

Heath E and Wall G, *Marketing Tourism Destinations: A Strategic Planning Approach*, Wiley 1992

Hembry P, *The English Spa 1560–1815: A Social History*, Athlone Press 1990

Henley Centre, *Inbound Tourism: A Packaged Future?* Tourism and Leisure Sector Group, NEDC 1993

Herbert D (ed.), *Heritage, Tourism and Society*, Mansell 1995

Hern A, *The Seaside Holiday – The History of the English Seaside Resort*, Cresset Press 1967

Hewison R, *The Heritage Industry: Britain in a Climate of Decline*, Methuen 1987

Hibbert C, *The Grand Tour*, Weidenfeld and Nicolson 1969

Hill J M M, *The Holiday*, Tavistock Institute of Human Relations 1965

Hindley G, *Tourists, Travellers and Pilgrims*, Hutchinson 1983

Hitchcock M, King V and Parnwell M, *Tourism in South East Asia*, Routledge 1992

Hodgson A (ed.), *The Travel and Tourism Industry: Strategies for the Future*, Pergamon Press 1987

Hodgson G, *A New Grand Tour*, Viking 1995

Holloway J C and Robinson C, *Marketing for Tourism*, 3rd edn, Longman 1995

Honey M, *Ecotourism and Sustainable Development: Who Owns Paradise?* Island Press 1999

Horne D, *The Great Museum: The Representation of History*, Pluto Press 1984

Horner P, *The Travel Industry in Britain*, Stanley Thornes 1991

Horner P, *Travel Geography for Tourism: Part 1 United Kingdom, Part 2 Worldwide*, Stanley Thornes 1993

Horner P, *Travel Agency Practice*, Longman 1996

Horner S and Swarbrooke J, *Marketing Tourism, Hospitality and Leisure in Europe*, International Thomson Business Press 1996

Howie F, *Managing the Tourist Destination: A Practical Interactive Guide*, Continuum 2001

Hudman L and Hawkins D, *Tourism in Contemporary Society: An Introductory Text*, Prentice Hall 1989

Hudson K, *Air Travel: A Social History*, Adams and Dart 1972

Hudson K, *A Social History of Museums*, Macmillan 1975

Hudson K and Pettifer J, *Diamonds in the Sky: A Social History of Air Travel*, BBC Publications 1979

Hudson S, *Snow Business: A Study of the International Ski Industry*, Cassell 1999

Hughes H, *Arts, Entertainment and Tourism*, Butterworth Heinemann 2000

Hunter C and Green H, *Tourism and the Environment: A Sustainable Relationship?* Routledge 1995

Ingold A, McMahon U and Yeoman I (eds), *Yield Management: Strategies for the Service Industries*, 2nd edn, Continuum 2000

Inkpen G, *Information Technology for Travel and Tourism*, 2nd edn, Pitman 1998

Inskeep E, *Tourism Planning: An Integrated and Sustainable Development*, Van Nostrand Reinhold 1991

Inskeep E, *National and Regional Tourism Planning: Methodologies and Case Studies*, Routledge 1994

Inskeep E and Kallenberger M, *An Integrated Approach to Resort Development: Six Case Studies*, World Tourism Organization 1992

Ioannides D, Apostolopoulos Y and Sonmez S (eds), *Mediterranean Islands and Sustainable Tourism Development: Practices, Management and Policies*, Continuum 2001

Ioannides D and Debbage K G (eds), *The Economic Geography of the Tourist Industry: A Supply-side Analysis*, Routledge 1998

Islam M S, *The Ethics of Travel, from Marco Polo to Kafka*, Manchester University Press 1996

Jackson I, *An Introduction to Tourism*, Hospitality Press 1994

Jafari J (ed.) *Encyclopedia of Tourism*, Routledge 2000

Jakle J A, *The Tourist: Travel in 20th Century North America*, University of Nebraska Press 1985

Jefferson A and Lickorish L J, *Marketing Tourism*, 2nd edn, Longman 1991

Jeffries D, *Governments and Tourism*, Butterworth Heinemann 2001

Johnson P and Thomas B (eds), *Choice and Demand in Tourism*, Mansell 1992

Johnson P and Thomas B (eds), *Perspectives on Tourism Policy*, Mansell 1992

Johnson P and Thomas B, *Tourism, Museums and the Local Economy*, Edward Elgar 1992

Judd D R and Fainstein S, *The Tourist City*, Yale University Press 1999

de Kadt E, *Tourism – Passport to Development?* OUP 1979

Kaiser C and Helber L E, *Tourism Planning and Development*, Heinemann 1978

Kärcher K, *Reinventing the Package Holiday Business*, Deutscher Universitäts Verlag 1997

Kearns G and Philo C, *Selling Places: The City as Cultural Capital, Past and Present*, Pergamon Press 1993

Khan M A, Olsen M and Var T, *VNR's Encyclopaedia of Hospitality and Tourism*, Van Nostrand Reinhold 1993

Khan M A, Minish R and Khan M M, *Hospitality and Tourism Management: The Profession of the 21st Century*, Wiley 1997

King B, *Creating Island Resorts*, Routledge 1997

King B and Hyde G, *Tourism Marketing in Australia*, Hospitality Press 1989

Kinnaird V H and Hall D, *Tourism Development: The Gender Dimension*, Wiley 1994

Klugman K, Kuenz J, Waldrep S and Willis S, *Inside the Mouse: Work and Play at Disneyworld*, Duke University Press 1995

Knowles T, Diamantis D and Bey El-Mourhabi J, *The Globalisation of Tourism and Hospitality: A Strategic Perspective*, Continuum 2001

Kockel U (ed.), *Culture, Tourism and Development: The Case of Ireland*, Liverpool University Press 1994

Kotler P, Bowen J and Makens J, *Marketing for Hospitality and Tourism*, 2nd edn, Prentice Hall 1999

Krippendorf J, *The Holiday Makers: Understanding the Impact of Leisure and Travel*, 2nd edn, Heinemann 1991

Ladkin A, Szivas E and Riley M, *Tourism Employment: Analysis and Planning*, Channel View 2002

Landry J L and Fesmire A H, *The World is Out There Waiting: An Introduction to Travel and Tourism*, Prentice Hall 1993

Lane B and Bramwell B, *Sustainable Tourism: Principles and Practice*, Wiley 1997

Lanfant M-F, Allcock J and Bruner E, *International Tourism: Identity and Change*, Sage 1995

Lavery P, *Travel and Tourism*, 3rd edn, Elm Publications 1996

Lavery P and Van Doren C, *Travel and Tourism: A North American–European Perspective*, Elm Publications 1990

Law, C M (ed.), *Tourism in Major Cities*, International Thomson Business Press 1996

Law C M, *Urban Tourism: The Visitor Economy of Major Cities*, 2nd edn, Continuum 2001

Laws E, *Tourism Marketing: Service and Quality Management Perspectives*, Stanley Thornes 1991

Laws E, *Tourism Destination Management: Issues, Analysis and Policies*, International Thomson Business Press 1995

Laws E, *Managing Packaged Tourism*, International Thomson Business Press 1997

Laws E and Buhalis D (eds), *Tourism Distribution Channels: Practices, Issues and Transformations*, Continuum 2001

Laws E, Faulkner B and Moscardo G (eds), *Embracing and Managing Change in Tourism: International Case Studies*, Routledge 1998

Lawson F, *Hotels and Resorts: Planning, Design and Refurbishment*, Butterworth Heinemann 1995

Lea J, *Tourism and Development in the Third World*, Routledge 1988

Leask A and Yeoman I (eds), *Heritage Visitor Attractions: An Operations Management Perspective*, Cassell 1999

Leed E J, *The Mind of the Traveller*, Basic Books 1991

Lencek L and Bosker G, *The Beach: The History of Paradise on Earth*, Secker and Warburg 1998

Lennon J (ed.), *Tourism Statistics: International Perspectives and Current Issues*, Continuum 2001

Leslie D and Muir F, *Local Agenda 21, Local Authorities and Tourism: A UK Perspective*, Glasgow Caledonian University 1997

Lewes F and Brady G, *Holidays in Britain*, Ginn and Co 1970

Lewis R and Wild M, *French Ski Resorts and UK Ski Tour Operators: An Industry Analysis*, Sheffield Hallam University 1995

Lickorish L J and Jenkins C, *An Introduction to Tourism*, Butterworth Heinemann 1995

Lickorish L J and Kershaw A G, *The Travel Trade*, Practical Press 1958

Lickorish L J, Bodlender J, Jefferson A and Jenkins C L, *Developing Tourism Destinations: Policies and Perspectives*, Longman 1991

Lino B (ed.), *Sustainable Tourism in Islands, Vol 1. Issues and Policies, Vol. 2 Case Studies*, Mansell 1996

Lockhart D and Smith D (eds), *Island Tourism: Trends and Prospects*, Cassell 1996

Lockwood A and Medlik S (eds), *Tourism and Hospitality in the 21st Century*, Butterworth Heinemann 2001

Lowenthal D, *The Past is a Foreign Country*, CUP 1985

Lowenthal D, *The Heritage Crusade and the Spoils of History*, Viking 1996

Lumley R (ed.), *The Museum Time Machine*, Routledge 1988

Lumsdon L, *Marketing for Tourism: Case Study Assignments*, Macmillan 1992

Lumsdon L, *Tourism Marketing*, International Thomson Business Press 1997

Lumsdon L and Swift J, *Tourism in Latin America*, Continuum 2001

Lundberg D and C, *International Travel and Tourism*, 2nd edn, Wiley 1993

Lundberg D, Stavenga M H and Krishnamoorthy M, *Tourism Economics*, Wiley 1995

MacCannell D, *The Tourist: A New Theory of the Leisure Class*, 2nd edn, Schocken (NY) 1989

MacCannell D, *Empty Meeting Grounds: The Tourist Papers*, Routledge 1992

Mancini M, *Selling Destinations: Geography for the Travel Professional*, South West Publishing 1992

Mason P, *Tourism: Environment and Development Perspectives*, World Wildlife Fund 1990

Mawson S, *The Fundamentals of Hospitality Marketing*, Continuum 2000

Mayo E J and Jarvis L P, *The Psychology of Leisure Travel: Effective Marketing and Selling of Travel Services*, CBI 1981

McNeill L, *Travel in the Digital Age*, Bowerdean 1997

Medlik S, *Managing Tourism*, Butterworth Heinemann 1995

Medlik S, *Dictionary of Travel, Tourism and Hospitality*, 2nd edn, Butterworth Heinemann 1996

Medlik S, *Understanding Tourism*, Butterworth Heinemann 1999

Medlik S, *The Business of Hotels*, 4th edn, Butterworth Heinemann 2000

Mele A, *Polluting for Pleasure*, W W Norton 1993

Middleton V, *New Visions for Independent Museums in the UK*, Association of Independent Museums, Andover 1990

Middleton V with Clarke J, *Marketing in Travel and Tourism*, 3rd edn, Butterworth Heinemann 2001

Middleton V with Hawkings R, *Sustainable Tourism: A Marketing Perspective*, Butterworth Heinemann 1998

Mill R C, *Tourism: The International Business*, Prentice Hall 1990

Mill R C and Morrison A, *The Tourism System: An Introductory Text*, 2nd edn, Prentice Hall 1992

Mills E, *Design for Holidays and Tourism*, Butterworth 1983

Mills P, *Quality in the Leisure Industry*, Longman 1992

Minhinnick R, *A Postcard Home: Tourism in the Mid-1990s*, Gower 1993

Moir E, *The Discovery of Britain: The English Tourists 1540–1840*, Routledge and Kegan Paul 1964

Montarani A and Williams A (eds), *European Tourism: Regions, Spaces and Restructuring*, Wiley 1995

Morgan N and Pritchard A, *Tourism Promotion and Power: Creating Images, Creating Identities*, Wiley 1998

Morgan N and Pritchard A, *Advertising in Tourism and Leisure*, Butterworth Heinemann 2000

Morgan N, Pritchard A and Pride R (eds), *Destination Branding: Developing a Destination Proposition*, Butterworth Heinemann 2001

Morinis E A (ed.), *Sacred Journeys: Anthropology of Pilgrimage*, Greenwood Press 1993

Morrison A, *Hospitality and Travel Marketing*, 2nd edn, Delmar 1996

Morrison A, Rummington M and Williams C, *Entrepreneurship in the Hospitality, Tourism and Leisure Industries*, Butterworth Heinemann 1999

Moutinho L (ed.) *Strategic Management in Tourism*, CAB International 2000

Moutinho L, Rita P and Curry B, *Expert Systems in Tourism Marketing*, Routledge 1996

Mowforth M and Munt I, *Tourism and Sustainability: New Tourism in the Third World*, Routledge 1998

Munday S and Doolan C, *Information Technology in Leisure and Tourism*, Cassell 1996

Murphy P E, *Tourism: A Community Approach*, Methuen 1985

Murphy P E, *Quality Management in Urban Tourism*, Wiley 1996

Nash D, *Anthropology of Tourism*, Pergamon 1996

Neale G (ed.), *The Green Travel Guide*, Kogan Page 1997

Nelson Jones J and Stewart P, *A Practical Guide to Package Holiday Law and Contracts*, 3rd edn, Tolley Publishing 1993

Newsome D, Moore S and Dowling R, *Natural Area Tourism: Ecology, Impacts and Management*, Channel View 2002

North R, *The Butlin Story*, Jarrolds 1962

Norval A J, *The Tourist Industry*, Pitman 1931

Oakes T, *Tourism and Modernity in China*, Routledge 1999

O'Connor P, *Electronic Information Distribution in Tourism and Hospitality*, CAB International 1999

Ogilvie F W, *The Tourist Movement*, Staples Press 1933

Oppermann M (ed.), *Pacific Rim Tourism*, CAB International 1998

Oppermann M and Chon K-S, *Tourism in Developing Countries*, International Thomson Business Press 1997

Orams M, *Marine Tourism: Development, Impacts and Management*, Routledge 1999

Ousby I, *The Englishman's England: Taste, Travel and the Rise of Tourism*, CUP 1990

Owen G, *Accounting for Hospitality, Tourism and Leisure*, Pitman 1994

Page S J, *Urban Tourism*, Routledge 1995

Page S J, *Transport and Tourism*, Longman 1999

Page S J and Getz D, *The Business of Rural Tourism: International Perspectives*, International Thomson Business Press 1997

Pape R, 'Touristry – a type of occupational mobility', *Social Problems* 2/4 Spring 1964

Pattullo P, *Last Resorts: The Cost of Tourism in the Caribbean*, Cassell 1996

Pearce D, *Tourist Development*, 2nd edn, Longman 1989

Pearce D, *Tourism Organisations*, Longman 1992

Pearce D, *Tourism Today: A Geographical Analysis*, 2nd edn, Longman 1995

Pearce D G and Butler R W (eds), *Contemporary Issues in Tourism Development*, Routledge 1999

Pearce D G and Butler R W (eds), *Tourism Research: Critiques and Challenges*, Routledge 1992

Pearce P L, *The Social Psychology of Tourist Behaviour*, Pergamon 1982

Pearce P L, Moscardo G M and Ross G F, *Tourism Community Relationships*, Elsevier Science 1997

Pender L, *Travel Trade and Transport: An Introduction*, Continuum 2001

Peters M, *International Tourism*, Hutchinson 1969

Phillips P A and Moutinho L, *Strategic Planning Systems in Hospitality and Tourism*, CAB International 1998

Phipps D, *The Management of Aviation Security*, Pitman 1991

Pimlott J A R, *The Englishman's Holiday*, Harvester Press 1976

Pizam A and Mansfield Y (eds), *Tourism, Crime and International Security Issues*, Wiley 1995

Pizam A and Mansfield Y (eds), *Consumer Behaviour in Travel and Tourism*, Haworth Press 1999

Plog S, *Leisure Travel: Making it a Growth Market Again!* Wiley 1991

Pompl W and Lavery P, *Tourism in Europe: Structures and Development*, CAB International 1993

Pond K L, *The Professional Guide: Dynamics of Tour Guiding*, Van Nostrand Reinhold 1993

Poon A, *Tourism, Technology and Competitive Strategies*, CAB International 1993

Poustie M, Ross J, Geddes N and Stewart W, *Hospitality and Tourism Law*, International Thomson Business Press 1999

Powers T, *Marketing Hospitality*, Wiley 1990

Poynter J, *Foreign Independent Tours: Planning, Pricing and Processing*, Delmar 1989

Poynter J, *Tour Design, Marketing and Management*, Prentice Hall 1993

Poynter J M, *How to Research and Write a Thesis in Hospitality and Tourism: A Step by Step Guide for College Students*, Wiley 1993

Prentice R, *Tourism and Heritage Attractions*, Routledge 1993

Price M (ed.), *People and Tourism in Fragile Environments*, Wiley 1996

Priestley G K, Edwards J A and Coccossis H (eds), *Sustainable Tourism? European Experiences*, CAB International 1996

Quest M, *Horwath Book of Tourism*, Horwath Consulting 1990

Rafferty M D, *A Geography of World Tourism*, Prentice Hall 1993

Rapoport R and R N, 'Four themes in the sociology of leisure', *British Journal of Sociology* XXV/2 June 1974

Reader I and Walter T (eds), *Pilgrimage in Popular Culture*, Macmillan 1993

Reason J, *Man in Motion: The Psychology of Travel*, George Weidenfeld and Nicolson 1974

Reily Collins V, *Becoming a Tour Guide: Principles of Guiding and Site Interpretation*, Continuum 2000

Rennie N, *Far Fetched Facts: The Literature of Travel and the Idea of the South Seas*, Clarendon Press 1995

Richards B, *How to Market Tourism Attractions, Festivals and Special Events*, Longman 1992

Richards G, *Case Studies in Tourism Management*, PNL Press 1991

Richards G, (ed.) *Cultural Tourism in Europe*, CAB International 1996

Richards G and Hall D (eds), *Tourism and Sustainable Community Development*, Routledge 2000

Ringer G (ed.), *Destinations: Cultural Landscapes of Tourism*, Routledge 1998

Ritchie J R Brent and Goeldner C (eds), *Travel, Tourism and Hospitality Research: A Handbook for Managers and Researchers*, 2nd edn, Wiley 1994

Robinson M and Andersen H-C (eds), *Tourism and Literature: Explorations of Tourism, Writers and Writings*, Continuum 2001

Robinson M and Boniface P (eds), *Tourism and Cultural Conflicts*, CAB International 1998

Robinson M, Evans N and Callaghan P (eds), *Culture as the Tourist Product*, Business Education Publishers 1996

Robinson M, Evans N and Callaghan P (eds), *Managing Cultural Resources for the Tourist*, Business Education Publishers 1996

Robinson M, Evans N and Callaghan P (eds), *Tourism and Culture: Image, Identity and Marketing*, Business Education Publishers 1996

Robinson T, Gammon S and Jones I, *Sports Tourism: An Introduction*, Continuum 2000

Rogers H A and Slinn J, *Tourism: Management of Facilities*, Pitman 1993

Rogers T, *Conferences – A Twenty-first Century Industry*, Addison Wesley Longman 1998

Rojek C, *Ways of Escape: Modern Transformations in Leisure and Travel*, Macmillan 1993

Rojek C, *Decentring Leisure: Rethinking Leisure Theory*, Sage 1995

Rojek C and Urry J, *Touring Cultures: Transformation of Travel and Theory*, Routledge 1997

Rosenow J and Pulsipher G L, *Tourism: The Good, the Bad and the Ugly*, Century Three Press 1979

Ross G F, *The Psychology of Tourism*, Australian Studies in Tourism No. 1, Hospitality Press 1994

Rutherford D, *Introduction to the Conventions, Expositions and Meetings Industry*, Van Nostrand Reinhold 1990

Ryan C, *Recreational Tourism: A Social Science Perspective*, Routledge 1991

Ryan C, *Tourism, Terrorism and Violence*, Research Institute for the Study of Conflict and Terrorism, London 1991

Ryan C, *Researching Tourist Satisfaction: Issues, Concepts, Problems*, Routledge 1995

Ryan C (ed.), *The Tourist Experience: A New Introduction*, Cassell 1997

Ryan C and Page S (eds), *Tourism Management: Towards the New Millennium*, Elsevier 2000

Sampson A, *Empires of the Sky: The Politics, Contests and Cartels of World Airlines*, Hodder and Stoughton 1984

Searle M, *Bathing Machines and Bloomers*, Midas 1977

Seaton A V and Bennett M, *Marketing Tourism Products: Concepts, Issues, Cases*, International Thomson Business Press 1996

Seaton A V, Jenkins C L, Wood R C, Dieke P U C, Bennett M M, MacLellan L R and Smith R (eds), *Tourism: The State of the Art*, Wiley 1994

Seddon S, *Travel*, Alan Sutton/Thomas Cook 1991

Selwyn T (ed.), *The Tourism Image: Myths and Myth Making in Tourism*, Wiley 1996

Shackley M, *Wildlife Tourism*, International Thomson Business Press 1996

Shackley M (ed.), *Visitor Management: Case Studies from World Heritage Sites*, Butterworth Heinemann 2000

Shackley M, *Managing Sacred Sites*, Continuum 2001

Sharpley R, *Tourism and Leisure in the Countryside*, 2nd edn, Elm Publications 1996

Sharpley R, *Tourism, Tourists and Society*, 2nd edn, Elm Publications 1999

Sharpley R and J, *Rural Tourism: An Introduction*, International Thomson Business Press 1997

Sharpley R and Telfer D, *Tourism and Development: Concepts and Issues*, Channel View 2002

Shaw C and Chase M (eds), *The Imagined Past: History and Nostalgia*, Manchester University Press 1989

Shaw G and Williams A M, *Critical Issues in Tourism: A Geographical Perspective*, Blackwell 1994

Shaw G and Williams A M (eds), *The Rise and Fall of British Coastal Tourism: Cultural and Economic Perspectives*, Mansell 1996

Shaw S, *Air Transport: A Marketing Perspective*, Pitman 1981

Shaw S, *Airline Marketing and Management*, 3rd edn, Pitman 1990

Sheldon P J, *Tourism Information Technology*, CAB International 1997

Shone A, *The Business of Conferences*, Butterworth Heinemann 1998

Shone A with Parry B, *Successful Event Management: A Practical Handbook*, Continuum 2001

Sigaux G, *History of Tourism*, Leisure Arts 1966

Sillitoe A, *Leading the Blind: A Century of Guide Book Travel 1815–1914*, Macmillan 1995

Sinclair M T (ed.), *Gender, Work and Tourism*, Routledge 1997

Sinclair M T and Stabler M (eds), *The Tourism Industry: An International Analysis*, CAB International 1991

Sinclair M T and Stabler M, *The Economics of Tourism*, Routledge 1997

Singh T V and Singh S (eds), *Tourism Development in Critical Environments*, Cognizant Communication 1999

Sixsmith M (ed.), *Touring Exhibitions: The Touring Exhibitions Group's Manual of Good Practice*, Butterworth Heinemann 1995

Smith P (ed.), *The History of Tourism: Thomas Cook and the Origins of Leisure Travel*, Routledge/Thoemmes Press 1998

Smith S L J, *Tourism Analysis: A Practical Handbook for Students*, 2nd edn, Longman 1995

Smith V (ed.), *Hosts and Guests: An Anthropology of Tourism*, Blackwell 1992

Smith V L and Eadington W R, *Tourism Alternatives: Potentials and Problems in the Development of Tourism*, Wiley 1994

Soane J V N, *Fashionable Resort Regions: Their Evolution and Transformation*, CAB International 1993

Somerville C, *Britain beside the Sea*, Grafton 1990

Song H and Witt S F, *Tourism Demand Modelling and Forecasting*, Pergamon 2000

Stabler M J (ed), *Tourism and Sustainability: Principles to Practice*, CAB International 1997

Stokes H G, *The Very First History of the English Seaside*, Sylvan Press 1947

Studd R G, *The Holiday Story*, Percival Marshall 1948

Stutts A, *The Travel Safety Handbook*, Van Nostrand Reinhold 1990

Sutton W A, 'Travel and understanding: notes on the

social structure of touring', *International Journal of Comparative Sociology* 8/2 1967

Swarbrooke J, *Sustainable Tourism Management*, CAB International 1999

Swarbrooke J, *The Development and Management of Visitor Attractions*, 2nd edn, Butterworth Heinemann 2001

Swarbrooke J and Horner S, *Consumer Behaviour in Tourism*, Butterworth Heinemann 1999

Swarbrooke J and Horner S, *Business Travel and Tourism*, Butterworth Heinemann 2001

Swarbrooke J, Beard C, Leckie S and Pomfret G, *Adventure Tourism: The New Frontier*, Butterworth Heinemann 2001

Swinglehurst E, *Cook's Tours: The Story of Popular Travel*, Blandford Press 1982

Swinglehurst E, *The Romantic Journey: The Story of Thomas Cook and Victorian Travel*, Pica 1974

Syme G J, *The Planning and Evaluation of Hallmark Events*, Gower 1989

Syratt G, *Manual of Travel Agency Practice*, 2nd edn, Butterworth Heinemann 1995

Taylor D, *Fortune, Fame and Folly: British Hotels and Catering from 1878 to 1978*, Caterer and Hotelkeeper 1977

Taylor J, *A Dream of England: Landscape Photography and the Tourist Imagination*, OUP 1994

Teare R and Ingram H, *Strategic Management: A Resource-based Approach for the Hospitality and Tourism Industries*, Cassell 1993

Teare R, Calver S and Costa J, *Hospitality and Tourism Marketing Management*, Cassell 1994

Teare R, Calver S, Mazanec J and Crawford Welch S, *Marketing in Hospitality and Tourism: A Consumer Focus*, Cassell 1994

Teare R, Canziani B and Brown G (eds), *Global Directions: New Strategies for Hospitality and Tourism*, Cassell 1997

Teare R, Bowen J and Hing N (eds), *New Directions in Hospitality and Tourism: A Worldwide Review*, Cassell 1998

Theobald W (ed.), *Global Tourism: The Next Decade*, 2nd edn, Butterworth Heinemann 1998

Thomas R (ed.), *The Hospitality Industry, Tourism and Europe: Perspectives on Policies*, Cassell 1996

Thomas R (ed.), *The Management of Small Tourism and Hospitality Firms*, Cassell 1998

Timothy D J and Wall G, *Tourism and Political Boundaries*, Routledge 2000

Toffler A, *Future Shock*, Bodley Head 1970

Tolley R S and Turton B J, *Transport Systems, Policy and Planning*, Longman 1995

Towner J, *An Historical Geography of Recreation and Tourism in the Western World 1540–1940*, Wiley 1996

Tribe J, *Corporate Strategy for Tourism*, International Thomson Business Press 1997

Tribe J, *The Economics of Leisure and Tourism*, 2nd edn, Butterworth Heinemann 1999

Tribe J, Font X, Griffiths N, Vickery R and Yale K, *Environmental Management for Rural Tourism and Recreation*, Continuum 2000

Tunbridge J E and Ashworth G, *Dissonant Heritage*, Wiley 1995

Turner L and Ash J, *The Golden Hordes: International Tourism and the Pleasure Periphery*, Constable 1975

Tyler D, Guerrier Y and Robertson M (eds), *Managing Tourism in Cities: Policy, Process and Practice*, Wiley 1998

Urry J, *The Tourist Gaze: Leisure and Travel in Contemporary Societies*, Sage 1990

Urry J, *Consuming Places*, Routledge 1995

Uysal M (ed.), *Global Tourist Behaviour*, International Business Press 1994

Uysal M and Fesenmaier D (eds), *Communication and Channel Systems in Tourism Marketing*, Haworth Press 1993

Uzzell D (ed.), *Heritage Interpretation: Vol 1 The Natural and Built Environment, Vol. 2 The Visitor Experience*, Belhaven Press 1989

Vallois F, *International Tourism: An Economic Perspective*, Macmillan 1995

Veal A J, *Research Methods for Leisure and Tourism*, Longman 1992

Vellas F and Bécherel L, *International Tourism*, Macmillan 1995

Vergo P (ed.), *The New Museology*, Reaktion Books 1989

Vladimir A, *The Complete Travel Marketing Handbook*, NTC Business Books 1988

Voase R, *Tourism: The Human Perspective*, Hodder and Stoughton 1995

Vukonic B, *Tourism and Religion*, Elsevier Science 1997

Wahab S and Pigram J (eds), *Tourism Development and Growth: The Challenge of Sustainability*, Routledge 1997

Waldren J, *Insiders and Outsiders: Paradise and Reality in Majorca*, Berghan 1997

Wall G and Mathieson A, *Tourism: Change, Impacts and Opportunities*, 2nd edn, Longman 1997

Walsh K, *The Representation of the Past: Museums and Heritage in the Post-Modern World*, Routledge 1992

Walsh-Heron J and Stevens T, *The Management of Visitor Attractions and Events*, National Publishers 1990

Walton J K, *The English Seaside Resort: A Social History 1750–1914*, University of Leicester Press 1983

Walton J K, *The British Seaside: Holidays and Resorts in the Twentieth Century*, Manchester University Press 2000

Walton J K and Walvin J, *Leisure in Britain 1780–1939*, Manchester University Press 1983

Walvin J, *Beside the Seaside: A Social History of the Popular Seaside Holiday*, Allen Lane 1978

Ward C and Hardy D, *Goodnight Campers! The History of the British Holiday Camps*, Mansell 1986

Ward S V, *Selling Places: The Marketing and Promotion of Towns and Cities 1850–2000*, E&F Spon 1998

Watt D, *Leisure and Tourism Event Management and Organisation Manual*, Longman 1992

Watt D, *Event Management in Leisure and Tourism*, Addison Wesley Longman 1998

Wearing S and Neil J, *Ecotourism: Impacts, Potentials and Possibilities*, Butterworth Heinemann 1999

Weaver D B, *Ecotourism in the Less Developed World*, CAB International 1998

Weiler B and Hall C M (eds), *Special Interest Tourism*, Belhaven Press 1992

Wells A T, *A Casebook for Air Transportation*, Wadsworth 1990

Wells A T, *Air Transportation: A Management Perspective*, 3rd edn, Wadsworth 1994

Weston S A, *Commercial Recreation and Tourism: An Introduction to Business Oriented Recreation*, Brown and Benchmark 1996

Wheatcroft S, *Aviation and Tourism Policies*, Routledge 1994

Williams A and Shaw G (eds), *Tourism and Economic Development: Western European Experiences*, 2nd edn, Wiley 1991

Williams G, *The Airline Industry and the Impact of Deregulation*, Avebury Aviation/Ashgate Publishing 1994

Williams S, *Tourism Geography*, Routledge 1998

Wilson A, *The Culture of Nature: North American Landscape from Disney to the Exxon Valdez*, Blackwell 1992

Witt S F, Brooke M Z and Buckley P J, *The Management of International Tourism*, 2nd edn, Unwin Hyman 1995

Witt S F and Moutinho L, *Tourism Marketing and Management Handbook*, 2nd edn, Prentice Hall 1994

Witt S F and Witt C A, *Modeling and Forecasting Demand in Tourism*, Academic Press 1992

Wood K and House S, *The Good Tourist*, Mandarin 1991

Woodside A, Crouch G, Mazanek J, Oppermann M and Sakai M (eds), *Consumer Psychology of Tourism, Hospitality and Leisure*, CAB International 1999

World Tourism Organisation, *Global Distribution Systems*, WTO 1996

World Tourism Organisation, *International Tourism: A Global Perspective*, WTO 1999

Wright P, *On Living in an Old Country: The National Past in Contemporary Britain*, Verso 1985

Yale P, *From Tourist Attractions to Heritage Tourism*, Elm Publications 1991

Yale P, *Tourism in the UK: A Basic Textbook*, Elm Publications 1991

Yale P, *The Business of Tour Operations*, Longman 1995

Yaqub Z and Bedford B (eds), *European Travel Law*, Wiley 1996

Youell R, *Tourism: An Introduction*, Addison Wesley Longman 1998

Young G, *Tourism: Blessing or Blight?* Pelican 1973

Zurick D, *Errant Journeys: Adventure Travel in a Modern Age*, University of Texas Press 1995

KEY TRADE, PROFESSIONAL AND ACADEMIC MAGAZINES AND JOURNALS OF RELEVANCE TO TRAVEL AND TOURISM

ABTA News	monthly
AIEST Tourist Review (*Revue de Tourisme*) (Switzerland)	quarterly
Airline World	weekly
Annals of Tourism Research (USA)	quarterly
ASTA Travel News (USA)	monthly
British Travel Brief (BTA)	quarterly
British Traveller	monthly
Buses	monthly
Business Traveller	10 p a
Business Travel World	monthly
Coaching Journal and Bus Review	monthly
Countryside Commission News	monthly
Current Issues in Tourism	bi-monthly
Executive Travel	monthly
Executive World (British Airways)	monthly
Flight International	weekly
Holiday Which? (Consumers Association)	quarterly
ICAO Bulletin	monthly
In Britain (BTA)	monthly
Insights (ETB)	monthly
International Tourism Quarterly (EIU)	quarterly
International Journal of Tourism Research	bi-monthly
International Journal of Tourism and Hospitality Research	quarterly
Journal of Air Transport Management	quarterly
Journal of Ecotourism	quarterly
Journal of the ITT	quarterly
Journal of Leisure Research	quarterly
Journal of Sustainable Tourism	bi-monthly
Journal of Tourism Studies (Australia)	biannual
Journal of Transport Economics and Policy	Jan/May/Sept
Journal of Travel Research (USA)	quarterly
Journal of Travel and Tourism Marketing	quarterly
Journal of Vacation Marketing	quarterly
Leisure, Recreation and Tourism Abstracts (CAB International)	quarterly
Leisure Studies (Leisure Studies Association)	quarterly
Motor Transport Weekly	weekly
Progress in Tourism and Hospitality Research	quarterly
Revue de l'Académie Internationale du Tourisme	3 per year
Service Industries Journal	Mar/Jul/Nov
Tourism (Bulletin of the Tourism Society)	quarterly

Tourism and Hospitality Research	quarterly
Tourism, Culture and Communication	quarterly
Tourism Enterprise (ETB)	monthly
Tourism Geographies	quarterly
Tourism Geography	quarterly
Tourism in Focus	quarterly
Tourism Intelligence Quarterly (BTA)	quarterly
Tourism Management	bi-monthly
Tourism Trendspotter	bi-monthly
Tourist Studies	3 per year
Transport (CIT)	bi-monthly
Transport Management	quarterly
Transport Reviews	quarterly
Travel Agency	bi-monthly
Travel and Tourism Analyst (EIU)	bi-monthly
Travel Business Analyst	10 p a
Travel GBI	monthly
Travel Industry Monitor (EIU)	quarterly
Travel Research Journal	quarterly
Travel Trade Gazette	weekly
Travel Trade Gazette Europa (Continental edition)	weekly
Travel Weekly	weekly
World Travel (*Tourisme Mondiale*) (WTO)	bi-monthly

TourCD (*Leisure, Recreation and Tourism Abstracts*) CD-ROM database CAB International

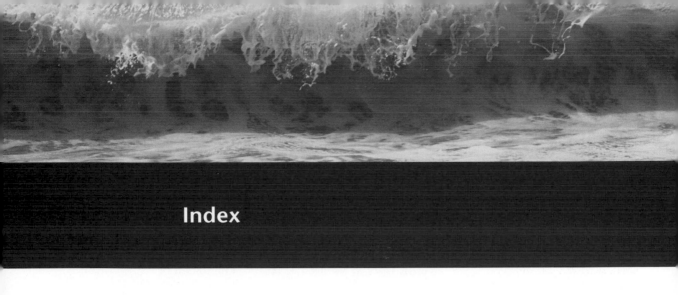

Index